...ersifying the Discourse:

The Florence Howe Award

for Outstanding Feminist

Scholarship, 1990–2004

Diversifying the Discourse: The Florence Howe Award for Outstanding Feminist Scholarship, 1990–2004

Edited by

MIHOKO SUZUKI

and

ROSEANNA DUFAULT

The Modern Language Association of America
~ New York 2006 ~

© 2006 by The Modern Language Association of America
All rights reserved. Printed in the United States of America

For information about obtaining permission to reprint material from MLA book publications, send your request by mail (see address below), e-mail (permissions@mla.org), or fax (646 458-0030).

Library of Congress Cataloging-in-Publication Data

Diversifing the discourse: the Florence Howe Award for Outstanding Feminist Scholarship, 1990-2004/edited by Mihoko Suzuki and Roseanna Dufault.
    p. cm.
        Includes bibiliographical references and index.
        ISBN-13: 978-0-87352-946-4 (alk. paper)
        ISBN-10: 0-87352-946-4 (alk. paper)
        ISBN-13: 978-0-87352-947-1 (pbk. : alk. paper)
        ISBN-10: 0-87352-947-2 (pbk. : alk. paper)
1. Feminist literary criticism. 2. Feminism and literature. 3. Women and literature. 4. Literature–Women authors–History and criticism. 5. Feminism. I. Suzuki, Mihoko, 1953-
II. Dufault, Roseanna Lewis, 1954-
        PN98. W64D58 2006
        809'.89287—dc22   2006015598

Published by The Modern Language Association of America
26 Broadway, New York, NY 10004-1789
www.mla.org

~ CONTENTS ~

~ ACKNOWLEDGMENTS ~

WE WOULD LIKE to thank first the authors of the essays for being wonderful collaborators in this common effort, especially in contributing their thoughtful afterwords to their essays. Thanks also to Florence Howe and Annette Kolodny for graciously agreeing to participate despite their large number of other commitments.

Joan Hartman and Frances Kavenik generously contributed their knowledge of the history of the Women's Caucus to fill the gaps in our initial list of the prizewinning essays. Jennifer Rodriguez helped in locating and assembling them. The editors would like to thank MLA's Publications Committee and the anonymous readers of both the proposal and final manuscript for their insightful suggestions. Frank Palmeri contributed to the project from its inception and throughout the process.

This collection would not have been possible without the hard work of the Florence Howe selection committees of the Women's Caucus for the Modern Languages as well as Joanne Glasgow and Angela Ingram, the editors of the first collection of essays, *Courage and Tools*. We hope this volume will serve as a record of the committee's work and of the contribution of the Women's Caucus to the profession and that future committees will carry on this important project.

Permissions

Jean Ferguson Carr, "The Polemics of Incomprehension: Mother and Daughter in *Pride and Prejudice*," in *Tradition and the Talents of Woman*, ed. Florence Howe (Urbana: University of Illinois Press, 1991), 68–86. © 1991 by the Board of Trustees of the University of Illinois. Reprinted with permission of the University of Illinois Press.

Stacy Carson Hubbard, "'A Splintery Box': Race and Gender in the Sonnets of Gwendolyn Brooks," *Genre* 25 (1992): 47–64. © 1992 by the University of Oklahoma. Reprinted with permission of the Regents of the University of Oklahoma.

Joyce Zonana, "The Sultan and the Slave: Feminist Orientalism and the Structure of *Jane Eyre*," *Signs* 18.3 (1993): 592–617. © 1993 by the University of Chicago. Reprinted with permission of the University of Chicago.

Susan Fraiman, "Geometries of Race and Gender: Eve Sedgwick, Spike Lee, Charlayne Hunter-Gault," *Feminist Studies* 20.1 (1994): 67–85. Reprinted with permission of the publisher, *Feminist Studies*.

Kristine Ibsen, "On Recipes, Reading, and Revolution: Postboom Parody in *Como agua para chocolate*," in *The Other Mirror: Women's Narrative in Mexico, 1980–1995*, ed. Kristine Ibsen (Westport, CT: Greenwood Publishing Group, 1997), 111–122. Reprinted with permission. Note: This is an expanded version of the prize-winning essay as it appeared in *Hispanic Review* 63.2 (1995): 133–46.

Carolyn Dever, "Obstructive Behavior: Dykes in the Mainstream of Feminist Theory," in *Cross-Purposes: Lesbians, Feminists, and the Limits of Alliance*, ed. Dana Hellern (Bloomington: Indiana University Press, 1997), 19–41. Reprinted with permission of the publisher.

Linda S. Bergmann, "Widows, Hacks, and Biographers: The Voice of Professionalism in Elizabeth Agassiz's *Louis Aggasiz: His Life and Correspondence*," *a/b: Auto/Biography Studies* 12.1 (1997): 1–21. Reprinted with permission of the publisher.

Mary Paniccia Carden, "'The Ears of the Palefaces Could Not Hear Me': Languages of Self-Representation in Zitkala-Ša's Autobiographical Essays," *Prose Studies* 20.1 (1997): 58–76. Reprinted with permission of Taylor and Francis Ltd. <http://www.tandfco.uk/journals>.

Sandra Zagarell, "Crosscurrents: Registers of Nordicism, Community, and Culture in Jewett's *Country of the Pointed Firs*," *Yale Journal of Criticism* 10.2 (1997): 355–72. © Yale University and The Johns Hopkins University Press. Reprinted with permission of the Johns Hopkins University Press.

Roberta Rubenstein, "Feminism, Eros, and the Coming of Age," *Frontiers: A Journal of Women's Studies* 22.2 (2001): 1–19. © 2002 by the Frontiers Editorial Collective. Reprinted with permission of the University of Nebraska Press.

Molly Hite, "Virginia Woolf's Two Bodies," *Genders* 31 (2000): 36 paragraphs.

Abby Lynn Coykendall, "Bodies Cinematic, Bodies Politic: The 'Male' Gaze and the 'Female' Gothic in De Palma's *Carrie*," *Journal of Narrative Theory* 30.3 (2000): 332–63. Reprinted with permission of the publisher.

Alison Rice, "The Improper Name: Ownership and Authorship in the Literary Production of Assia Djebar," in *Sonderdruck aus: Assia Djebar*, ed. Ernstpeter Ruhe (Würzburg: Verlag Könighausen & Neumann, 2001), 49–77.

Melissa Dinverno, "Gendered Geographies: Remapping the Space of the Woman Intellectual in Concha Méndez's *Memorias habladas, memorias armadas*," *Revista de estudios hispánicos* 37.1 (2003): 49–74. Reprinted with permission of the publisher.

Rachel Warburton, "Reading Rape in Chaucer; or Are Cecily, Lucretia, and Philomela *Good Women*?" *Henry Street* 10.1 (2003): 5–28. © Rachel Warburton. Reprinted with permission of the author.

Amal Amireh, "Between Complicity and Subversion: Body Politics in Palestinian National Narrative," *South Atlantic Quarterly* 102.4 (2003): 747–72. © 2003 Duke University Press. Reprinted with permission of Duke University Press.

Lisa Vollendorf, "Good Sex, Bad Sex: Women and Intimacy in Early Modern Spain," *Hispania* 87.1 (2004): 1–12. Reprinted with permission of the publisher.

~ FOREWORD ~

Florence Howe

Write, write or die.
—*HD*

First fight. Then fiddle.
—*Gwendolyn Brooks*

I WRITE THIS brief essay facing the deck of a beautiful East Hampton house in the woods. Birds flash around the feeder. My friend Joanne Markell trims bonsai trees. And I think of the thirty years that have flown by since the Women's Caucus named a literary prize after me in my forty-fifth year. This week, I have taken time out of my editing of the three forthcoming volumes in the Women Writing Africa series to reread *Courage and Tools* and to read the essays in *Diversifying the Discourse*.[1] The volumes honor me, and here I want to honor their richness. Together, the two volumes inscribe strands of the three and a half decades of women's studies and feminist literary criticism.

Inevitably for one of my generation, while the new volume offers the intrigues of the unfamiliar, the first affords the special pleasures of the familiar. Yes, of course, I remember that Phyllis Franklin wrote back in 1974, "We must not be afraid of heuristic studies" (16). The essays in both volumes and thousands of other books testify to the fearlessness of feminists. And yes, what a "classic" Annette Kolodny's "Dancing through the Minefields" has become, even to including her apology about the omission of women of color and lesbians from her essay. The minefields are still dangerous, and we are still dancing through them in this volume. On the other hand, the significance of Joanna Russ's sentence, "Culture is male" (28) in her essay "What Can a Heroine Do? Or, Why Women Can't Write" has changed for me since I first read it.

Once I saw it as a challenge, needing the following response: "we" will describe female culture—in literature and in life—and then the world will change. Fat chance, as my mother would say. Now I read it as the unremittingly exhausting and exhaustive work of a seemingly endless future—if we are lucky enough to have that future. I see superbly competent volumes of feminist scholarship contributing to that future, however far off that time may be.

In both volumes feminist critics dissect male chauvinist writers and, in the process, reveal aspects of female culture under patriarchy. In both volumes mothers and fathers are contested figures in the lives of writers and in the production of literature. The literature and film analyzed and evaluated in these essays begin in and speak to the powerful relationships at the center of individual lives. Thus in *Courage and Tools* an essay about *Middlemarch* and in *Diversifying the Discourse* another on *Pride and Prejudice* argue that the inequalities in male-female relationships destroy marriages and even motherhood. Further, in the first volume, award-winners map the father-centered worlds that control the literary production of Fanny Burney and Hannah More and a century later the struggles of Elizabeth Barrett Browning to overcome the same elements of patriarchy. And in this current volume, though fear of the father still reigns, essays describe an early-twentieth-century Native American, Zitkala-Ša, and a contemporary Algerian, Assia Djebar, who defiantly assume their own, not their fathers', names and then write themselves into history.

So why don't I feel more cheerful about Joanna Russ's challenge? Few of the essays in either volume offer representations of female culture as perceived by female writers. Essays on HD in the first volume Virginia Woolf in the second, deconstruct the writers' "visions" of themselves, but not of their worlds. While the most vivid portraits of women's culture appear in the discussion of two African American writers, Toni Morrison in the first volumes and Gwendolyn Brooks in the second, they cannot be seen except against shades of American racism, which is hardly fading away. In an important essay on lesbian culture, Caroline Dever worries about being caught between the allegedly inclusive early perspective of Adrienne Rich, in which all women-centered women are lesbians, and the disappearance of lesbians from view altogether in queer studies, once imagined also as inclusive. Roberta Rubenstein reviews women aging through two novels published in 1996 by Doris Lessing and Marilyn French and then through her personal sense of a world unfriendly to older women. It's hard for a woman of my generation to refrain from asking, Where are the free women we looked to in the 1960s?

Perhaps I am one of them, a survivor of the three decades of feminism behind us and a woman worried about the future for my granddaughters and grandson. Especially horrifying in the first volume was Linda Kauffman's dissection of Margaret Atwood's *The Handmaid's Tale*. Today it seems no longer only fantasy: in a totally male-controlled culture, a woman manages to produce a furtive (and dangerous) scribbling, retrieved in this fiction by a man in a future world even more male-controlled than the one in which she lived and died. Is it not shocking that right now, in the summer of 2004, two well-known American feminist writers have novels, which illuminate women's past and present culture and which have no publisher.[2]

Diversifying the Discourse, like the historical development of women's studies through the 1990s, is not for sissies. The portraits of sexism, broadened geographically, include canvases of war, of rape and other kinds of sexual battery, in fiction and in real life, as well as in film. Even allegedly cheerful writers like Geoffrey Chaucer and Stephen King—an odd pair, needless to say—appear in essays that illuminate the seemingly intractable male views of women's bodies as loci for rape or other forms of sexual abuse. The essay by Susan Fraiman, which describes an incident in Vietnam, reminds us of the daily newspaper's record of the raping of women in Sudan and elsewhere. In these and other essays, feminist critics reveal also the sexism of male literary historians, critics, and filmmakers.

I don't think the dark portrait of women's lives reported in the volume is an accident having to do with the selection of essays. Feminist critics have experienced the deepening resistance to the struggles they began in the optimistic 1970s. For many of us, equality, meaning the gaining of male privilege (by already privileged women), has become an empty slogan. We know now that more is at stake than privilege for women all over the world. And we also know that we have few allies among the powerful in politics, the media, and religion.

I was pleased to learn a great deal about the writers of these incisive essays through the inclusion of briefer essays called afterwords. Compelling reminders of the continuing high energy of women's studies, as it attempts to be inclusive, to reach all students, and to internationalize its horizons, these afterwords reveal writers who are vigorous and inventive, prolific and necessarily frugal about time. That many of the award-winning essays are parts of forthcoming books reminds me of a finding of my 1985 survey, in which ninety percent of women's studies faculty members across the United States reported that they were writing books. Not surprisingly, the afterwords also reveal networks of feminist friends who have been personal readers and critics.

Most interesting are the afterwords that describe as motivation teaching needs, a reminder of how women's studies began in the first place. Mary Paniccia Carden, writing about her essay on Zitkala-Ša's memoirs, describes the students her research has served: "Even students resolutely indifferent to the issues of gender and race . . . are moved and inspired by her [Zitkala-Ša] courage in resisting the definitions imposed on her." Still more personal is the account of Joyce Zonana, whose "impulse" to write her essay on *Jane Eyre* "grew out of [her] own experience as an 'oriental' woman living in the West." She writes, "The relation between Islam and the West remains one of the most pressing problems of our times. . . ." She adds, "The roots of feminist orientalism (let alone 'regular' orientalism) run deep," noting that they are "at work in contemporary efforts to justify the wars in Iraq and Afghanistan and even Palestine."

And so I find solace on this bright July day in the scrupulously careful scholarship of these prize-winning essays, in the openness of these critics to share news of their lives, their goals, even their errors. I conclude by invoking the two instructions that appear as epitaphs to this foreword. The first comes from Susan Stanford Friedman's early reclamation of HD's mythos of the mother/muse who urges her to "Write, write or die" (*Courage and Tools* 78). We all need that direction, both women of my generation and the younger women in this volume. If we are not to repeat the history that has trammeled us, we must know that history, even as some of the essays in this volume retrieve it. We must insist that women write their own histories in our time.

The other instruction, Gwendolyn Brooks's "First fight. Then fiddle," the opening line of a sonnet quoted in Stacy Carson Hubbard's essay in this volume, suggests what women of color know—that their battles, whether or not they are artists, are ongoing. The rest of us need to study that instruction, which, like HD's, might apply as well to the Africans I have been editing, whose female cultural history has been invisible for centuries to the wider world. These women have often fought real wars for nationhood, and then and now they have continued to "write" their female culture—using the orature of their tradition or the pens they can also wield as weapons. Perhaps when the next volume of these award-winning essays is readied for publication, some of these writers will find themselves on its pages.

July 2004
East Hampton, New York

NOTES

[1] One of these volumes has since been published: *Women Writing Africa: West Africa and the Sahel* (New York: Feminist Press, 2005).

[2] The Feminist Press has just published one of them, *In the Name of Friendship*, by Marilyn French.

~ INTRODUCTION ~

Mihoko Suzuki and Roseanna Dufault

Feminist Criticism and Theory since
Courage and Tools: 1990–2004

The year 2004 marks the thirtieth anniversary of the inception of the Florence Howe Award for Feminist Scholarship, administered by the Women's Caucus for the Modern Languages. Needless to say, feminist scholarship looks very different in 2004 from what it did in 1974; but even since 1990, when Joanne Glasgow and Angela Ingram edited and published the first fifteen award-winning essays in *Courage and Tools*, feminist criticism and theory in the United States have witnessed rapid and momentous change. As editors of the second set of essays, from 1990 to 2004, we chose *Diversifying the Discourse* as the title of our volume, because we were struck by the multiplicity of discourses that marked this set of essays. Susan Gubar in *Critical Condition: Feminism at the Turn of the Century* describes her initial dismay and frustration over what she perceived as the fracturing and divisiveness that renders a common feminist project no longer tenable; yet she also recounts how she came to see the internal critique and disagreements as positive indications of the vital energy and resilience of a still-developing practice.[1] In the introduction to *Feminist Consequences: Theory for the New Century*, Misha Kavka similarly emphasizes "the pluralized, diversified state of feminism at the turn of the new century." This state of affairs "has had the effect of splintering what had been a recognizable feminist project into unrecognizability, even into a paradoxical state of visible invisibility" (ix). Yet Kavka also discerns positive consequences of this development in the interdisciplinarity and interdiscursiveness that characterize present-day feminism (xviii). A new generation of theorists and critics has now achieved prominence, their influence not being limited to feminist criticism: for example, Eve Sedgwick's theory of homosociality (*Between Men*) and Judith Butler's theory of the performativity of gender (*Gender Trouble*) have entered the general lexicon of literary studies.[2] That both Butler and Sedgwick have identified their projects with feminist criticism and concerned themselves with sexuality indicates as well the importance of that topic in the conversation among critics today.

Among the essays included in this volume, two have formed part of recently published books that carry forward the ongoing conversation about the history and future of feminist theory and criticism: Carolyn Dever's *Skeptical Feminism: Activist Theory, Activist Practice* and Susan Fraiman's *Cool Men and the Second Sex*. Dever focuses on the relation between theory and practice: the ambivalence of feminists toward theory and the skepticism toward abstraction that has been vital to the development of feminism. She analyzes the history of the movement in its various manifestations—popular, activist, and academic, from the 1970s to the current engagement with queer studies—and explores debates over psycho-analysis, sexuality, and the preoccupation, both uneasy and utopian, with lesbian sexuality.[3] Addressing Gubar's question about the fracturing of feminism, Dever identifies the "double-bind of feminist theory: the effort to locate and valorize women's voices, subject positions, identities, experiences, and desires comes up against ethical resistance to the proposition that any one voice speak for the rest" (162). Yet Dever agrees with Bonnie Zimmerman in affirming "the competing, potentially incoherent, certainly uncomfortable abundance of 'multiple points of view'" (170). Fraiman concerns herself not with the much publicized conservative backlash against feminism (which is the subject of Rita Felski's *Literature after Feminism*) but with what she calls "a lingering, systemic masculinism" among progressive filmmakers and critics, many of whom explicitly ally themselves with women's concerns (xi). Combining analyses of filmmakers and critics, her work exemplifies a cultural studies approach. Interestingly, she includes in her critique female theorists such as Sedgwick, Butler, and Judith Halberstam, who affirm "a kind of dissident, hip masculinity," defined against a more "'conventional' femi-nine" (xii). Here Fraiman extends feminist criticism to gender studies, for she in-terrogates a kind of youth-identified masculinity that defines itself against the feminine, which is constructed as maternal; her work also recalls earlier feminists' critique of the Marxist focus on class at the expense of gender, since she identi-fies this type of "cutting-edge" academic discourse as left-leaning (xiii). On the one hand, Dever sees Nancy Chodorow's defamiliarization of the premise that "women mother" as paradigmatic of the kind of challenge that Butler poses to "the straitjacket of feminine convention," a critique that Dever sees as a consti-tutive goal of both feminist theory and praxis (78, 168). Fraiman, on the other hand, calls for a return to "our list of feminist demands back in the early 1980s: scholarly attention to women and gender; defense of practices and values marked as feminine, political outrage and agency for women" as a foundation for "rein-venting feminist critique for the twenty-first century" (159).[4]

Fraiman's book forms part of Columbia University Press's Gender and Culture series, edited by Carolyn G. Heilbrun and Nancy K. Miller, which has published thirty-four titles as of 2004. It includes many important and influential books, in-cluding Sedgwick's *Between Men*, Terry Castle's *The Apparitional Lesbian*, and Gu-bar's *Critical Condition*. While feminist scholarship now appears on every publish-er's list and in most scholarly journals, Columbia's and other series and journals focusing on women's writing or feminist criticism (e.g., *Tulsa Studies in Women's Literature*, *Women's Studies*, and *Feminist Studies*) continue to be important outlets for feminist criticism. Although most books and articles appear to focus on feminist scholarship on Anglo-American writers since the nineteenth century, the Gender and Culture series also published Joan DeJean's *Tender Geographies*, on women and the early French novel. Other important publications since 1990 on feminist scholarship of pre-nineteenth-century texts and culture include Carolyn Dinshaw on sexuality in Chaucer, Lynn Staley on the "dissenting fictions" of Margery Kempe, Maureen Quilligan on the "allegory of female authority" in Christine de Pizan, Margaret Ferguson on late medieval and early modern literacy and empire,

Ann Rosalind Jones on women's love lyric in early modern Europe, Kim Hall on early modern constructions of race, Valerie Traub on early modern lesbianism, Catherine Gallagher on women novelists in the eighteenth century, Laura Brown on race and imperialism in the eighteenth century, and Moira Ferguson on colonial slavery in the long eighteenth century.

The success of feminist theory and criticism has affected not only literary scholarship but also the curriculum studied in the university and secondary schools. A focus on gender and sexuality (as well as race, ethnicity, and class) has put pressure on the traditional canon at all levels of instruction. Many high school students arrive in our classrooms having read newly canonized authors such as Toni Morrison; they also appear familiar with some basic principles of feminist criticism. In fact, the MLA has found that feminist criticism has had more influence on the teaching of literature than any other school of criticism (Felski 5). Sandra Gilbert and Gubar's *Norton Anthology of Literature by Women*, now in its second edition, serves as a text for an increasing number of survey courses of women writers. Robyn Warhol and Diane Price-Herndl's *Feminisms: An Anthology of Literary Theory and Criticism*, first published in 1991, was revised in a second edition that appeared in 1997, indicating the continued vitality of the instruction of feminist theory in the classroom and the need to reflect changes in the field, specifically the shift from feminist studies "as a domain of white, middle-class, straight women who share much of the cultural privilege of their male counterparts" to one that "work[s] through the common assertion that race, sexual orientation, and class always inflect understandings of gender" (xi). While the first edition represented fifty-three critics, the new edition includes sixty-six, and the editors emphasize the "multiplicity of perspectives and approaches" and the "diversity of motivation, method, and experience among feminist academics," a diversity that "can be a model for cultural heterogeneity"(ix–x). True to this statement, the edition presents a variety of recent essays on race, ethnicity, and sexuality.[5] Although the scope of *Feminisms* is impressive in its own right, the "mainstreaming" of feminist theory and criticism can be witnessed in the inclusion of feminism and gender studies, gay and lesbian studies, and queer theory in anthologies such as Julie Rivkin and Michael Ryan's *Literary Theory: An Anthology*, first published in 1998. The 2004, second edition includes work that reflects the intersection of feminist criticism with cultural studies and transnational studies.

Despite the reported crisis in scholarly publishing, some university and other presses have made available a large number of primary texts that are suitable for use in the classroom. The MLA has published 17 titles in dual editions, in English translation and in the original language, including French, Spanish, Italian, German, and Russian: for example, works by Françoise de Graffigny, Emilia Pardo Bazán, Anna Banti, Eleonore Thon, and Sofya Kovalevskaya and the first novel by a woman of sub-Saharan francophone Africa, Thérèse Kuoh-Moukoury. Broadview Press has published a large number of eighteenth- and nineteenth-century works by women, many otherwise unavailable in modern editions; the University of Chicago series The Other Voice in Early Modern Europe, edited by Margaret King and Albert Rabil, Jr., has published over 30 texts translated from French and Italian (some not yet available in modern editions in their original languages) since its inception in 1996; the projected total is 120 titles. The University Press of Kentucky has published 13 titles in the series Eighteenth-Century Novels by Women, edited by Isobel Grundy. However, the still-difficult economics of publishing may have prevented the continuation of Oxford University Press's series Women Writers in English, 1350–1850, edited by Susanne Woods and Elizabeth Hageman, which published 15 titles between 1993 and 1999.

The media attention accorded Henry Louis Gates Jr.'s discovery of the first novel written by an African American woman, Hanna Craft, which he edited and published in 2002 as *The Bondwoman's Narrative*, indicates the continuing interest in uncovering works, especially by women writers who experienced slavery. Harriet Jacobs's *Incidents in the Life of a Slave Girl*, first brought to public attention in 1987 by Jean Fagan Yellin, is now available in multiple editions and has entered the canon of American literature. Yellin's recent publication of Jacobs's biography has also garnered general notice. As exemplified by these two works, the critical and scholarly interest in women writers, especially as they focus on race and ethnicity, has extended to the general reading public. Examples among contemporary writers include Morrison, Sandra Cisneros, and Maxine Hong Kingston. The Feminist Press, founded and for many years directed by Florence Howe, continues its project of making available to both an academic and general readership works not only by African American and ethnic American writers but also by contemporary writers from Africa, Asia, the Middle East, and Europe.[6]

Diversifying the Discourse: 1990–2004

As successor to *Courage and Tools*, *Diversifying the Discourse* provides an account of the history of feminist scholarship in the United States in the 1990s and the early years of the twenty-first century. The essays reflect the multiplicity and diversity of approaches that mark contemporary feminist criticism, including race and ethnicity studies, theories of sexuality and queer theory, discourses of aging, psychoanalysis and film theory, nationhood and nationalism, postmodernism, postcolonialism, and cultural studies. Subject matter ranges from British and American literature to African and Native American studies, Hispanic literature, francophone literature, Palestinian literature, and film. In preparing this volume, we were struck by how cogent each author was in deploying her theoretical approach and how successful in explicating texts and writers both canonical and less familiar; each author pursued an ambitious and wide-ranging argument with implications for feminist theory beyond the specific text(s) discussed. For this reason, the essays point the way toward further developments in the field.

Following the example of *Courage and Tools*, we asked the authors to write afterwords in which they reflect on their essays and their critical practice; many, as well, discuss the relation between pedagogy and scholarship and raise questions about the methodology of the essay. These reflections about the communication of feminist theory to students and about the ongoing process of scholarship and writing even beyond the completion and publication of the project would be especially useful in the classroom and as models for students writing their own essays or envisioning themselves as scholars and critics. We are also pleased to include a foreword to the collection by Florence Howe and an afterword by Annette Kolodny, author of the landmark "Dancing through the Minefield," an early recipient of the Florence Howe Award, published in *Courage and Tools*.[7]

Many of these essays were published in major feminist journals, including *Signs, Genders, Feminist Studies*, and *Frontiers*, as well as in journals such as *Genre, Prose Studies, alb:Auto/Biography Studies, Journal of Narrative Theory, Yale Journal of Criticism, South Atlantic Quarterly*, and *Hispanic Review*, indicating the interest and acknowledgment of feminist theory and scholarship by the mainstream. Some are less accessible, having been published in essay collections, and are now made available here to a wider public. The essays treat authors ranging from Jane Austen, Charlotte Brontë, Virginia Woolf, Gwendolyn Brooks, and Doris Lessing to less familiar authors such as Elizabeth Agassiz, the Native American writer Zitkala-Ša, the contemporary Mexican novelist Laura Esquivel, the Maghreb author Assia Djebar, the Spanish poet Concha Méndez, the Palestinian novelists Liana Badr and Sahar Khalifeh, and ordinary women whose voices are recorded in the archives of early modern Spain. In addition, the essays analyze male-authored texts ranging from Chaucer's *The Legend of Good Women* to the films of Spike Lee and Brian De Palma and take up cultural studies topics such as the Central Park jogger and the 1991 Gulf War. Some of the essays focus on the ideology of literary form such as the sonnet and autobiography and the ways women writers negotiate the gendered implications of these forms in their specific historical context. In fact, all the essays are meticulous and illuminating in situating their analysis among historical particulars: for example, the intellectual history of "feminist orientalism" from Mary Wollstonecraft to Charlotte Brontë, the implication of *Pride and Prejudice* in the nineteenth-century discourse of motherhood and the nation, the political use of the sonnet form by writers of the Harlem Renaissance, and the history of the vexed relationship between lesbians and mainstream feminists from the 1970s to the present. Finally, these essays are marked by their acknowledgment of and engagement with tensions, contradictions, resistances, and occlusions: for example, the deployment of the maternal figure as an object of ridicule and scapegoating; the displacement of Western patriarchy onto a stereotypical and demonized "orient" in order to critique it; the contradiction between the feminist discourse of women's community and the exclusionary discourse of nationalism and racial superiority; the tensions between feminist discourse and Palestinian nationalist and patriarchal ideology.

Jean Ferguson Carr's "The Polemics of Incomprehension: Mother and Daughter in *Pride and Prejudice*" takes a primarily psychoanalytic approach to investigate the figure of the mother in Austen's novel as one whose speech is marked by incomprehension and nonsense. Referring to Freud's theory of tendentious jokes, but also deploying Mikhail Bakhtin's theory of heteroglossia and dialogicality, as well as Pierre Macheray's theory of the paradoxical function of occlusions and silences in calling attention to gaps in ideology, Carr deftly situates Austen's strategic deployment of the maternal figure in the context of contemporary advice books that represented mothers as at once central and marginal to nineteenth-century culture and ideas of nationhood, and as responsible and blameworthy for the broad cultural changes that disrupted the family.

In "'A Splintery Box': Race and Gender in the Sonnets of Gwendolyn Brooks," Stacy Carson Hubbard focuses on Brooks's double (and ironic) revision of the sonnet from the perspectives of race and gender. Brooks, Hubbard argues, at once dramatizes the exclusion of the black female from hegemonic cultural forms and challenges the lyric tradition's figurations of authoritative subjectivity. Using parody and irony, as well as emphasizing "vitality, energy, excess," Brooks constructs a new representation of the sonnet lady and thereby redefines black women's relation to society and to a white and male tradition. She thus successfully challenges the sonnet form's figuration as an enclosure and burial ground that defines, immortalizes, and kills the female beloved.

Joyce Zonana investigates Charlotte Brontë's use of the trope of the harem (or seraglio) and a demonized Islam in "The Sultan and the Slave: Feminist Orientalism and the Structure of *Jane Eyre*." Basing her work on Edward Said's *Orientalism*, but also on feminist postcolonial theorists such as Gayatri Spivak, Leila Ahmed, and Chandra Mohanty, Zonana argues that Brontë neutralizes and makes more acceptable her critique of Western patriarchy by displacing it onto a stereotypical "orient." By figuring Rochester as a "Mahomettan" and a "sultan," the narrative moves to "convert" him from patriarchal tyranny by the ministrations of Jane, functioning in the role of the missionary. Zonana traces "feminist Orientalism" as a rhetorical strategy and mode of cultural analysis to Mary Wollstonecraft's *Vindication of the Rights of Woman* and charts its intellectual history through Mary Shelley, Anna Jameson, Elizabeth Barrett Browning, and Florence Nightingale.

In "Geometries of Race and Gender: Eve Sedgwick, Spike Lee, Charlayne Hunter-Gault," Susan Fraiman takes a cultural studies approach to critique and extend Sedgwick's influential theory concerning homosocial relations "between men." Arguing that Sedgwick has not paid sufficient attention to relations of dominance and submission between men because of her interest in erotic and affective relations and that she has ignored relations between men inflected by race, Fraiman examines various scenarios of rape from contemporary culture in which women's violated bodies are used to figure power relations between men of different races: the Central Park jogger, the 1991 Persian Gulf War, and the films of Brian De Palma and Spike Lee. Fraiman proposes an alternate "geometry," by examining Charlayne Hunter-Gault's interview of women in the military during the Gulf War, where the focus is on relations "between women" and women's complicity with racism and other exploitations.

Kristine Ibsen's "On Recipes, Reading, and Revolution: Postboom Parody in *Como agua para chocolate*" takes up Laura Esquivel's novel as an example of Linda Hutcheon's theory of postmodern parody. In addition to appropriating Gabriel García Marquez's magic realism, Esquivel ironically inverts high and low by incorporating popular and female traditions of the *calendarios por señoritas* (nineteenth-century women's magazines), *novella rosa*, *folletin*, and *telenovela*, as well as culinary discourses. She thereby undermines the binary opposition between the two types of discourse as well as overturns canonical hierarchy. She further reevaluates official history and discourse through her revision of the highly masculine tradition of the literature and cinema of the Mexican Revolution, by emphasizing a female point of view, as well as by questioning conventional roles between the sexes.

In "Obstructive Behavior: Dykes in the Mainstream of Feminist Theory," Caroline Dever posits lesbians as the limit case against which mainstream heterosexual feminists have defined themselves. Taking stock of the history of feminism and feminist scholarship since the 1970s, Dever charts the ambivalent and vexed relationship between feminists and dykes, whose connotations of obstruction and liminality she punningly emphasizes, thereby calling attention to the conflict between gender and sexuality that has marked the feminist movement. In her discussion of the late 1980s, Dever turns to critique Sedgwick (as did Fraiman), this time for the absence of lesbianism from her work, and challenges queer theory in general for focusing almost exclusively on male homosexuality; she thereby calls for an acknowledgment of and engagement with the specificity of lesbian discourses and desires as a historically complex cultural phenomenon in its own right.

Linda S. Bergmann raises the question of biographical "truth" in "Widows, Hacks, and Biographers: The Voice of Professionalism in Elizabeth Agassiz's *Louis Agassiz: His Life and Correspondence*." Bergmann identifies a unique case study—among predominantly male professional biographers—of Elizabeth Agassiz's meticulously documented biography of her husband, Louis Agassiz, that helped set a standard for future professional biographers. She demonstrates how the process of writing a careful, dispassionate, legitimate biography of her husband (departing from the prevalent celebrations of their husbands by widows) transformed Elizabeth Agassiz from a faculty wife and amanuensis to a scholar and public figure in her own right, the founder of Radcliffe and its first president. Acknowledging her own "longing" to reclaim the "true subjectivity" of Elizabeth Agassiz, Bergmann sheds light on the role of biographers as mediators and the professional and institutional situation of the biographer that shapes these investigations and discourses.

In "'The Ears of the Palefaces Could Not Hear Me': Languages of Self-Representation in Zitkala-Ša's Autobiographical Essays," Mary Paniccia Carden uses as paradigms feminist theories of autobiography, theories of race, and postcolonial theory to examine the significance of the choice by Zitkala-Ša (née Gertrude Simmons) to adopt English—the "master's" language—in order to intervene in American discourses on "race" and to critique the supposedly benevolent practices of the assimilation of Native Americans. This choice enables her to articulate her self-determination in the colonizer's language, effectively subverting notions of the silent "squaw" as well as the hegemony of the white speaker. Although Zitkala-Ša's autobiography represents her prolonged engagement with the coercive and often hidden powers of the colonizer's language, she nevertheless succeeds in firmly establishing a claim to her own identity, however ambiguous and liminal.

In "Crosscurrents: Registers of Nordicism, Community, and Culture in Jewett's *Country of the Pointed Firs*," Sandra A. Zagarell combines poststructuralist theory and a cultural studies approach, with an emphasis on postcolonial theory and discourses of race and nation, to propose a critical method for examining conflicting readings of a complex text that attends to the frameworks of gender, race, and historical context. Of particular concern to Zagarell is Jewett's evocation of an idealized, woman-centered community, which is explicitly positioned against the racist exclusiveness of nativist Anglo-Norman nationalism, whose narrative of progress contradicts the regionalist celebration of Maine's self-sufficient and traditional community. Challenging the desire for a "coherence effect" for multivocal texts, Zagarell proposes a more mobile, dynamic way of reading that incorporates registers and narratives marked by discontinuity and discordance, for such reading practices reflect more accurately the complex self-contradictions of their cultural contexts.

Roberta Rubenstein's "Feminism, Eros, and the Coming of Age," like Dever's essay, takes stock of the history of contemporary United States feminism; Rubenstein contrasts the second and third waves of feminism, noting that several prominent, controversial authors of the 1970s turned to writing their memoirs and contemplations on aging in the 1990s. She demonstrates that two novels portraying desiring older women, Doris Lessing's *Love Again: A Novel* and Marilyn French's *My Summer with George: A Novel of Love at a Certain Age*, illustrate ways in which internalized and social notions of aging hinder women from achieving true gender equity. Yet paradoxically, it is the "inappropriate" and socially transgressive desires of these female protagonists, who happen also to be writers, that form the bases of these novels.

In "Virginia Woolf's Two Bodies," Molly Hite sheds new light on Woolf's notorious aversion to physicality. In Hite's analysis, Woolf consistently depicted—and perhaps experienced—two kinds of woman's body: a social body for fulfilling prescribed roles and a "visionary" body, in which a passionate woman may experience sensuous delight without incurring adverse societal consequences. Woolf associates the weak and vulnerable social body with submissive mothers, such as her own, and with literary foremothers, such as George Sand. Woolf's notion of the visionary body offers a modernist woman writer the possibility of freely expressing desires—even toward women—without becoming embroiled in social consequences. Hite thereby emphasizes Woolf's strategy of safeguarding lesbian desires from the "social" by locating them in the "visionary" body and giving it pride of place.

Abby Lynn Coykendall, in "Bodies Cinematic, Bodies Politic: The 'Male' Gaze and the 'Female' Gothic in De Palma's *Carrie*," bases her argument on a wide range of male theorists of deconstruction, psychoanalysis, carnival, postmodernism, and postcolonialism, as well as on feminist theorists such as Laura Mulvey, Jacqueline Rose, Luce Irigaray, Kaja Silverman, Mary Russo, and Malek Alloula. Coykendall argues that De Palma deploys the voyeuristic gaze to deconstruct and undermine the psychopathology of the male gaze. He challenges the ideology of phallocentrism and the commodification and fetishization of women by means of ironic parody/pastiche and the use of embedded counternarratives. According to Coykendall, De Palma locates the "female gothic" as a site of subversion that lies outside the law and the dominant ideology, overturning the tradition of the fantastic as one that relies on sexist, racist, and classist constructions of the other for the reference points of its pleasure.

In "The Improper Name: Ownership and Authorship in the Literary Production of Assia Djebar," Alison Rice studies the work of Assia Djebar, a renowned Algerian novelist and filmmaker who writes in French and currently holds an appointment at New York University. Rice addresses the complexities of *métissage culturel*, or cultural blending, and authorial presence in hybrid, polyvocal texts, by examining the ways in which Djebar's identity as a writer and as a person have merged in her pseudonym to express a hybrid, "colonized" identity. To examine the meaning of "authorship" in the context of Djebar's semiautobiographical works, Rice evokes theorists such as Derrida, Foucault, and Barthes and concludes that Djebar gives voice to generations of nameless Algerian women without compromising her identity, which includes land, blood, and language as well as her own name and experiences.

Melissa Dinverno, in "Gendered Geographies," draws attention to the representations of space as articulations of female subjectivity and power in the memoirs of Concha Méndez, a female peer of the male-dominated Spanish Generation of 1927. Méndez formulated a critique of women's marginalization in literary and intellectual circles, launching her literary career by "crossing over" from forbidden, illicit spaces into the public forum and establishing connections with other literary women such as Consuelo Berges and Alfonsina Storni. Dinverno brings Méndez's extraordinary life into focus and illuminates her struggle for intellectual advancement by emphasizing the transgressive impact of Méndez's performative practices as well as the fragility of her oppositional, identity-building project.

Chaucer's *Legend of Good Women* is the locus of Rachel Warburton's discussion of the gendered ownership of interpretation, and of euphemism, ellipsis, and apostrophe as inherited models for reading and writing rape. Warburton examines the legends of Lucretia and Philomela, both based on Ovid, along with the historical record of Cecily Chaumpaigne's 1380 complaint against the poet, her legal guardian (a complaint that scholars have tended to explain away to exonerate Chaucer). In each case, the woman is rendered passive and silent, and men take center stage. By demonstrating that the prologue calls attention to and the legends enact the circulation of ancient stories about women among male readers and writers, Warburton reveals the troubling proximity of rape and male literary inheritance.

In "Between Complicity and Subversion: Body Politics in Palestinian National Narrative," Amal Amireh examines the intersection between gender and nationalism in Palestinian nationalist narratives and a discourse "that uses women as fictional constructs and ideological signs." She demonstrates ways in which contemporary women writers such as Liana Badr and Sahar Khalifeh subvert the erotically charged, masculine construct of Palestinian identity. In contrast to the dominant ideology, which portrays Palestine as a bride and the Palestinian fighter/martyr as her groom, novelists such as Badr, exemplifying Fredric Jameson's understanding of the Third World novel as nationalist allegory, seek to write women as mothers into the nationalist narrative as a source of hope and continuity. Yet, as Amireh acknowledges, such counterdiscourses nevertheless reveal the tensions between feminist and nationalist discourses and the limitations of feminist discourse circumscribed within nationalist and patriarchal ideology.

Lisa Vollendorf's "Good Sex, Bad Sex: Women and Intimacy in Early Modern Spain" extends Foucault's late work on the history of sexuality to sixteenth- and seventeenth-century Spain. By examining literature (fiction by María de Zayas and plays by Golden Age women), nonfiction (biography and autobiography), and archival documents (convent and Inquisition records), Vollendorf reveals that these texts contain surprisingly rich information about female friendship and desire. Glimpses into the everyday lives of women show that they routinely appropriated dominant beliefs about their gender and used them to legitimate themselves and gain authority. Vollendorf's analysis of women's voices that attends to the intersections among gender, social class, and minority status offers an important corrective to the history of women in early modern Spain that is still largely based on accounts by male politicians, authors, and clerics.

As we hope the foregoing account of the prize-winning essays from 1990 to 2004 demonstrates, feminist discourse has indeed become more expansive. Whereas in the introduction to *Courage and Tools*, Glasgow and Ingram deplore "the total absence of African Americans (until 1989), Native Americans, Chicanas, Asian Americans (except for 1984), and non-English-speaking women writers," as well as the lack of lesbian literary criticism (xxi), the essays included in the present volume demonstrate that many, if not all, of these absences have been addressed during the subsequent fifteen years. In addition, two of the more recent award-winning essays reflect the importance of feminist criticism to medieval and early modern studies, as well as the effective use of historical archives by feminist scholars of earlier periods. The great range in the chronology, race, class, sexuality, and nationality of the subjects addressed by the essays will interest anyone who seeks to gain a perspective on the diversity as well as the trajectory of feminist criticism in the past fifteen years. We hope the book will be especially useful for graduate students and advanced undergraduates seeking to build a grounding in the field, in providing an introduction to the diversity of approaches that characterizes the practice of feminist theory and criticism at the beginning of the new century.

Even so, the Florence Howe Awards selection committee has noticed that the dominance of English studies in the United States makes it difficult to recognize work in non-English and American literatures.[8] The Women's Caucus recently adopted the practice of making two awards, one in English and another in foreign languages, hoping to correct the Anglocentric focus, especially in an age when globalization has made a notable mark not only in our understanding of culture but also in literary scholarship in the form of transnational studies.[9] Thanks to the Internet, information about the award can now be disseminated through the WCML Web site and electronic discussion list, as well as the electronic discussion lists of the MLA-affiliated Feministas Unidas, Women in French, Women in German, the Gay and Lesbian Caucus, and the Graduate Student Caucus.

Although the publication of this volume certainly indicates that feminist scholarship has come of age, we have learned from contributors that the recognition represented by the award has continued to make a difference for their professional and academic careers, for example, in landing a tenure-track position, as well as earning tenure and promotion. It is our hope, then, that *Diversifying the Discourse* exemplifies the Women's Caucus's continuing project of recognizing outstanding feminist scholarship through the Florence Howe Award and reflects the remarkable development of concerns and approaches in feminist literary criticism of the last fifteen years.

NOTES

[1] Gubar's initially more pessimistic statement, "What Ails Feminist Criticism?," is included with a revised conclusion in *Critical Condition*, where she now sees "disputes" and "contentiousness" in a more positive light, as "generat[ing] the powerful modifications staged in feminism at the end of the twentieth century" (12).

[2] A number of the Florence Howe essays manifest the influence of (and in two instances a critique of) Sedgwick, who was one of the founders of the developing field of studies of sexuality and queer theory (see Barber and Clark). Her statement of the theory of male homosociality and its consequences—the commodification of women, on the one hand, and homophobia, on the other—has been widely influential. She has been criticized, however, by, for example, Terry Castle, for her attention to male homosexuality at the expense of lesbianism (not only in *Between Men* but also in *The Epistemology of the Closet*).

Since 1990, Butler has emerged as an important thinker and theorist, as indicated by the recent publication of *The Judith Butler Reader* (see also Breen and Blumenfeld). Her groundbreaking work on gender and performance, *Gender Trouble*, which first appeared in 1990, was reissued in 1999 in a tenth-anniversary edition. Her turn to politics, as seen in the collection of essays she coedited with Joan Scott, *Feminists Theorize the Political*, also marks her *Psychic Life of Power* and *Antigone's Claim*, both of which combine psychoanalysis and political thought. It is notable that both Sedgwick and Butler base their work on psychoanalysis, which was a major focus of feminist theory and criticism of the 1980s, but extend their insights into the social and the political registers.

Other feminist theorists who have been influential in the last decade include Gayatri Spivak (postcolonial studies), Susan Bordo (on the body and embodiment), and Donna Haraway (on cyborgs and primates).

[3] On this topic, see also Heller. Castle's recent anthology *The Literature of Lesbianism* seeks to historicize the debate concerning lesbianism by collecting texts, by both female and male authors, since the Renaissance.

[4] In a postscript (156–59), Fraiman offers as corrective examples of recent scholarship Ann McClintock's, on "race, gender, and sexuality in the colonial context"; Angela McRobbie's, on youth culture; Tania Modleski's recent collection of essays on contemporary culture; Deborah McDowell's race-gender metacriticism; Teresa de Lauretis's writings on lesbianism in feminist and queer theory alike; and Biddy Martin's work on sexual difference in queer theory.

[5] The authors of these essays include Gloria Anzaldúa, Cordelia Chávez Candelaria, Terry Castle, bell hooks, Shirley Geok-lin Lim, Deborah E. McDowell, Biddy Martin and Chandra Talpade Mohanty, Rosaura Sánchez, Barbara Smith, and Valerie Smith.

[6] The publishing program of the Feminist Press mirrors the "diversifying discourse" of feminist pedagogy and scholarship from the 1970s to the present: the press, under the directorship of Howe, began in the early 1970s by publishing works by United States women writers of the nineteenth and twentieth centuries (e.g., Rebecca Harding Davis, Charlotte Perkins Gilman); its list expanded to include more recent works by African American writers, other United States women writers of color, and lesbian writers (e.g., Paule Marshall, Shirley Geok-lin Lim, Valerie Miner). More recently, the press has published international writers (e.g., Dacia Maraini from Italy, Shahrnush Parsipur from Iran). Howe currently directs the series Women Writing Africa.

[7] This influential essay has been included in a number of anthologies of feminist criticism, including the second edition of Warhol and Price-Herndl's *Feminisms*.

[8] Warhol and Price-Herndl limit their selections in *Feminisms* to work on "British and North American literature of the nineteenth and twentieth centuries" (xv). Gilbert and Gubar's Norton anthology is also limited to "the tradition in English." The focus of the Howe essays approximates that of Felski's recent survey *Literature after Feminism*: "more on novels than poetry or drama, also more about twentieth century than about other periods" and "on feminist literary studies as it has developed in the United States" (21).

[9] The administration of the Howe award has evolved from the earlier years when MLA Regional Caucus representatives formed the selection committee; in recent years, that task has been assumed by members of the Women's Caucus Executive Committee—the president, first vice president, and second vice president, the last of whom is responsible for disseminating the information concerning the competition and receiving submissions. In recent years the calls for submissions have stipulated that qualifying essays treating a feminist topic or presenting a feminist perspective must have been published in a book or journal during the previous academic year. In earlier years, essays were not required to have been already published; the award in such cases facilitated publication.

WORKS CITED

Banti, Anna. *"The Signorina" and Other Stories*. Trans. Martha King and Carol Lazzaro-Weis. New York: MLA, 2002.

Barber, Stephen M., and David Clark, eds. *Regarding Sedgwick: Essays on Critical Theory and Queer Culture*. New York: Routledge, 2002.

Bordo, Susan. *Unbearable Weight: Feminism, Western Culture, and the Body*. Berkeley: U of California P, 1993.

Breen, Margaret Sonser, and Warren Blumenfeld, eds. *Butler Matters: Judith Butler's Impact on Feminist and Queer Studies*. Aldershot: Ashgate, 2005.

Bronfen, Elisabeth, and Misha Kavka, eds. *Feminist Consequences: Theory for the New Century*. New York: Columbia UP, 2001.

Brown, Laura. *Ends of Empire: Women and Ideology in Early Eighteenth-Century English Literature*. Ithaca: Cornell UP, 1993.

Butler, Judith, and Joan W. Scott, eds. *Feminists Theorize the Political*. New York: Routledge, 1992.

Butler, Judith. *Antigone's Claim: Kinship between Life and Death*. New York: Columbia UP, 2000.

———. *Gender Trouble: Feminism and the Subversion of Identity*. 1990. New York: Routledge, 1999.

———. *The Judith Butler Reader*. Ed. Sara Salih, with Butler. Maldon: Blackwell, 2004.

———. *Psychic Life of Power: Theories in Subjection*. Stanford: Stanford UP, 1997.

Castle, Terry. *The Apparitional Lesbian: Female Homosexuality and Modern Culture*. New York: Columbia UP, 1993.

———, ed. *The Literature of Lesbianism*. New York: Columbia UP, 2003.

DeJean, Joan. *Tender Geographies: Women and the Origins of the Novel in France*. New York: Columbia UP, 1991.

Dever, Carolyn. *Skeptical Feminism: Activist Theory, Activist Practice*. Minneapolis: U of Minnessota P, 2004.

Dinshaw, Carolyn. *Chaucer's Sexual Politics*. Madison: U of Wisconsin P, 1990.

Felski, Rita. *Literature after Feminism*. Chicago: U of Chicago P, 2003.

Ferguson, Margaret W. *Dido's Daughters: Literacy, Gender, and Empire in Early Modern England and France*. Chicago: U of Chicago P, 2003.

Ferguson, Moira. *Subject to Others: British Women Writers and Colonial Slavery, 1670-1834*. New York: Routledge, 1992.

Fraiman, Susan. *Cool Men and the Second Sex*. New York: Columbia UP, 2003.

Gallagher, Catherine. *Nobody's Story: The Vanishing Acts of Women Writers in the Marketplace, 1670–1820*. Berkeley: U of California P, 1994.

Gates, Henry Louis, Jr., ed. *Harriet Craft's* The Bondwoman's Narrative. New York: Warner, 2002.

Gilbert, Sandra, and Susan M. Gubar, eds. *The Norton Anthology of Literature by Women: The Tradition in English*. New York: Norton, 1985.

Glasgow, Joanne, and Angela Ingram, eds. *Courage and Tools: The Florence Howe Award for Feminist Scholarship, 1974–1989*. New York: MLA, 1990.

Graffigny, Françoise de. *Letters from a Peruvian Woman*. Trans. David Kornacker. New York: MLA, 1993.

Gubar, Susan. *Critical Condition: Feminism at the Turn of the Century*. New York: Columbia UP, 2000.

———. "What Ails Feminist Criticism?" *Critical Inquiry* 24 (1998): 878–902.

Hall, Kim. *Things of Darkness: Economies of Race and Gender in Early Modern England*. Ithaca: Cornell UP, 1996.

Haraway, Donna Jeanne. *Simians, Cyborgs, and Women: The Reinvention of Nature*. New York: Routledge, 1991.

Heller, Dana, ed. *Cross-Purposes: Lesbians, Feminists, and the Limits of Alliance*. Bloomington: Indiana UP, 1997.

Jones, Ann Rosalind. *The Currency of Eros: Women's Love Lyric in Europe, 1540–1620*. Bloomington: Indiana UP, 1996.

Kavka, Misha. Introduction. Bronfen and Kavka ix–xxvi.

Kovalevskaya, Sofya. *Nihilist Girl*. Trans. Natasha Kolchevska, with Mary Zirin. New York: MLA, 2002.

Kuoh-Moukoury, Thérèse. *Essential Encounters*. Trans. Cheryl Toman. New York: MLA, 2002.

Pardo Bazán, Emilia. *"Torn Lace" and Other Stories*. Trans. Maria Cristina Urruela. New York: MLA, 1997.

Quilligan, Maureen. *The Allegory of Female Authority: Christine de Pizan's* Cité des Dames. Ithaca: Cornell UP, 1991.

Rivkin, Julie, and Michael Ryan, eds. *Literary Theory: An Anthology*. 1998. 2nd ed. Maldon: Blackwell, 2004.

Sedgwick, Eve. *Between Men: English Literature and Male Homosocial Desire*. New York: Columbia UP, 1986.

———. *The Epistemology of the Closet*. Berkeley: U of California P, 1990.

Staley, Lynn. *Margery Kempe's Dissenting Fictions*. University Park: Pennsylvania State UP, 1994.

Spivak, Gayatri Chakravorty. *The Spivak Reader*. Ed. Donna Landry and Gerald Maclean. New York: Routledge, 1995.

Thon, Eleanore. *Adelheit von Rastenberg*. Trans. George F. Peters. New York: MLA, 1997.

Traub, Valerie. *The Renaissance of Lesbianism in Early Modern England*. Cambridge: Cambridge UP, 2002.

Warhol, Robyn, and Diane Price-Herndl, eds. *Feminisms: An Anthology of Literary Theory and Criticism*. 1991. 2nd ed. New Brunswick: Rutgers UP, 1997.

Yellin, Jean Fagan. *Harriet Jacobs: A Life*. New York: Basic, 2003.

———, ed. *Incidents in the Life of a Slave Girl, Written by Herself.* By Harriet Jacobs. Cambridge: Harvard UP, 2000.

~ 1990 ~

The Polemics of Incomprehension: Mother and Daughter in *Pride and Prejudice*

Jean Ferguson Carr

She was a woman of mean understanding, little information, and uncertain temper.
—Jane Austen, Pride and Prejudice

Stupidity (incomprehension) in the novel is always polemical: it interacts dialogically with an intelligence (a lofty pseudo intelligence) with which it polemicizes and whose mask it tears away. . . . at its heart always lies a polemical failure to understand someone else's discourse, someone else's pathos-charged lie that has appropriated the world and aspires to conceptualize it, a polemical failure to understand generally accepted, canonized, inveterately false languages with their lofty labels for things and events.
—Mikhail Bakhtin, "Discourse in the Novel"

MY FIRST EPIGRAPH depicts the fictional mother, Mrs. Bennet in Jane Austen's *Pride and Prejudice* (1813), who is identified by her exclusion from the realms of sense and power, and is contained within her comic role.[1] As such, she stands in uneasy relationship to her daughter, Elizabeth, who both shares her mother's exclusion and seeks to dissociate herself from her devalued position by being knowing and witty where her mother is merely foolish.

My second epigraph, from Bakhtin's *The Dialogic Imagination*, raises questions about the social functions and effects of what is perceived as knowing discourse and what is perceived as meaningless babble.[2] What is usually identified as intelligence is the force that constructs the social order, creates canons, names names, and decides what is acceptable. It is central, focal, organizing. This "authoritative word," what Bakhtin terms "the word of the fathers," "permits no play with the context framing it, no play with its borders, no gradual and flexible transitions, no spontaneously creative stylizing variants on it.... One cannot divide it up—agree with one part, accept but not completely another part, reject utterly a third part" (pp. 342–43). Stupidity appears as a weakness that has no place in this proper order, that does the wrong thing and uses the wrong words, is unacceptable or embarrassing. Judged by the unity of the father's word, it seems incoherent or unproductive. Yet such "stupidity (incomprehension) in the novel is always polemical" (p. 403), interacting dialogically with authoritative discourse to disrupt its proper names and categories.

Incomprehension exposes the father's words to play, to jokes. The prototypical literary character who deploys such incomprehension is the fool, whose nonsense reveals gaps in the seamless authority of the father's word, for "by his very uncomprehending presence he makes strange the world of social conventionality" (p. 404). Yet as Freud argues in *Jokes and Their Relation to the Unconscious*, the naïve's "effect" depends on our conviction that he is unaware of (in Freud's terms, "it is not present in him" or he "does not possess") the inhibitions that govern most social discourse, or else he will be judged "not naïve but impudent." If we are not so convinced, "we do not laugh at him but are indignant at him."[3] The fool is a professional who plays the part of a naïve. His power is instrumental, defined not in terms of what he can "possess" for himself but by the effect he has on those in power. Fools exemplify what Freud calls a *"misleading [misverständlich] naïveté,"* representing "themselves as naïve, so as to enjoy a liberty that they would not otherwise be granted" (*Jokes*, p. 184). As long as liberty is something that is "granted," as long as fools do not expect to be made kings, the power of the father remains fundamentally intact.

Yet there is a type of incomprehension whose polemical effects are not finally so easily contained. Its social and literary prototype is the figure of the mother, who shares her child's exclusion from the languages of adulthood and power, and who has an interest in exposing the restraints imposed by patriarchy. A mother like Mrs. Bennet of *Pride and Prejudice* is not in a position to understand the polemics of her incomprehension. In the patriarchal culture in which Austen wrote, such an exposure must be indirect and guarded, or even unaware of its own threat and seriousness. The mother cannot afford to get her own jokes, nor can others accept the implications of her comedy. Her comedy hovers uncomfortably between unawareness and impudence, between triviality and threat. Unlike the fool, her "stupidity (incomprehension)" may not be sanctioned by the novel's explicit directives. It is often understood as simply ridiculous, even by the novel's other outsiders.

It is a critical commonplace to laud a fool's ability to "teach" authoritative speakers to laugh at their rigidity or to expose the faults and follies of a society's discourse.[4] But Mrs. Bennet is primarily defined not in such a direct relationship with authoritative speakers, not as "wife" who challenges "husband," but in her displaced role of mother who guides and restrains her children according to conventions that she herself need not comprehend and has not authorized. Her comedy is constrained by this dual role, by the effect of her foolishness on the children who must grow up under patriarchy. Yet stupidity is *always* polemical even when it is not explicitly understood, even when it is not incorporated into the novel's thematic designs. It may function not as a local challenge to individual failures of perception but as a sign of a general ideological confusion. The mother's position can be neither dismissed nor acknowledged. She persists at the margins of the novel as an irritating, troublesome, and yet indispensable figure.

In *Pride and Prejudice*, as in many nineteenth-century novels, the mother's function is misleadingly represented. Mrs. Bennet *is* a "woman of mean understanding, little information, and uncertain temper," but this representation serves complex interests. To accept her as merely a figure of ridicule is to prevent any investigation of those interests, to ignore the ways in which this novel, in Pierre Macherey's words, is "haunted" by what it cannot say. We must, instead, conduct a double reading, attending not only to what Macherey describes as "that which is formally accounted for, expressed, and even concluded" but also to what is left unspoken or implicit.[5] We need to attend to the novel's resistances, to what is produced only to be quickly dismissed. We thus "make strange" not only the ideology figured in the novel's social world but the ideology guiding the author's representations of social relations and conventions. We thereby consider tensions that remain tacit, that are neither authorized nor expunged, but that make the novel's resolution of social conflicts unfinished or overdetermined. Such a double reading extends our literary interests outside of the novel's social world to the exchanges between the novel and its formative culture. By reading doubly we question the insistence with which cues are delivered and the ways in which constructions are buttressed. We consider what is at stake when certain details are treated as error or as slips of the pen.

Mrs. Bennet is denied the prerogatives of a comic literary tradition: she does not win pleasure for her comedic scenes, forgiveness for her foibles, or credit for her effect on the social world. With an energy that seems excessive, given her slight role in the narrative, she is ridiculed both by powerful characters and the narrator. She is harshly criticized for a role she does not fulfill, for serious effects she does not achieve. She marks a lack of adult feminine power in the culture, a lack felt strongly by the young women she is supposed to educate and protect, and she is blamed for the excesses of the patriarchal culture. This essay explores what unspoken interests produce such a contradictory role for Mrs. Bennet. What interests are served by novelistic insistence that this character does not matter, that she is one-dimensional, that she has no effect? And how does such insistence coexist with the nagging, unsettling effect of the "trivial" character, with the threat she seems to pose to the social world of the novel, to her husband and daughters, to the possibility of women's discourse? Why should Mrs. Bennet's outbursts be found intolerable rather than humorous or socially productive?

Adrienne Rich calls the relationship between mothers and daughters in nineteenth-century fiction "the great unwritten story."[6] Mothers are thoroughly erased from these novels—rejected by their daughters, who wish to distance themselves from the socially conforming and repressed circumstances of their mothers, and disposed of by authors, who write them out of the story by imagining them as dead, bedridden, or left behind while the daughter journeys to Bath. They are, all too often, dismissed or ignored by critics who accept their marginalized status. The few mothers who do appear vanish into narrow stereotypes, both social and fictional. They are either dutiful and selfless or silly and self-indulgent, more likely to humiliate their daughters than to become role models or friends. They are not even given the dubious recognition afforded in twentieth-century fiction of being powerful, damaging adversaries.[7] Mothers are treated as wayward children, likely to say embarrassing things in front of company, needing to be cajoled and pampered, but not a very serious force—for good or ill.

As Nina Auerbach has argued, most nineteenth-century heroines strive to escape the "community of women," which "may suggest less the honor of fellowship than an antisociety, an austere banishment from both social power and biological rewards" (p. 3). They reject the more confined social world their mothers occupy to challenge the expectations of their fathers, brothers, or lovers. The great plot concerns not mothers and daughters but courtship,[8] which leads the heroine away from her mother and ends, conveniently, before marriage or childbirth, before the heroine must find a way to reconcile herself to that woman's world she earlier rejected. Through the ritual of courtship the heroine demonstrates her difference from her parents, especially her mother, whose concern with social rules, respectability, or safety is challenged, if not rejected. Yet the liberation of young, unmarried heroines leaves other women subject to patriarchy. The heroine (or the woman writer) is understood as the one woman who can negotiate the perils of the patriarchal world.

In *The Madwoman in the Attic*, Gilbert and Gubar discuss the "absence of enlightened maternal affection" in Austen's novels, which produces mothers "who fail in their nurturing of daughters" and daughters who are "literally or figuratively motherless." The relationship of mother and daughter is defined by "matrophobia—fear of becoming one's mother" (pp. 125–26). As a result, a mythical "mother-goddess" replaces the problematic social mother and becomes the figure of a feminine tradition that has been "dismembered, dis-remembered, disintegrated" under patriarchy (p. 98).[9] To "remember" and "become a member" of this "shattered tradition that is her matrilineal heritage" (p. 98), the nineteenth-century woman writer/heroine must "kill" the images imposed by patriarchy, the social mothers whom the dutiful daughter is supposed to reflect and reproduce.[10]

One of the ways the daughter seeks to liberate herself is through sharing the male characters' perception of the mother as comic. The situation could have been presented as tragic or wasteful—for the mother, who has no relationship with those around her, and for the daughter, who suffers from the lack of a significant guide. Imagining the mother as a "joke" seems to mitigate this loss and allows the daughter to move beyond what her mother desired or imagined. Yet Freud warns that there is no such thing as an innocent joke, that all jokes are tendentious.[11] Certainly the representation of the mother as comic is tendentious, ultimately working against the daughter's own interests. However much she gains by differentiating herself from a ridiculous mother, she cannot afford to trivialize the position she herself may occupy. Her own possibilities are finally implicated in the mother's position.

Mrs. Bennet occupies just such an uncomfortable position in her culture and in relation to her daughter Elizabeth. She is repeatedly characterized as trivial, static, or uninfluential, the antithesis of Lizzie's complexity and change. Modern readers have willingly accepted such cues and seen her as a dehistoricized trope, as "simply unformed matter," "the embodiment of the unthinking life-force that works through women," or "a transparently scheming boor" who, "like the life force, will persist, as foolishly as ever."[12] Mrs. Bennet holds none of the valued positions of mothers in her culture: she has little influence over the domestic realm and is absent from her daughters' scenes of confession and self-discovery.

Elizabeth can "hardly help smiling" at Lady Catherine's concern that Mrs. Bennet has been "quite a slave to your education" (p. 199). Although Mrs. Bennet seems inescapable, constantly interrupting conversations and intruding where she is least wanted, she is ignored and countermanded by her husband and elder daughters. The narrator concludes the first chapter with an invitation to dismiss her as a static character of little interest. Having introduced Mr. Bennet as "so odd a mixture of quick parts, sarcastic humour, reserve, and caprice, that the experience of three and twenty years had been insufficient to make his wife understand his character," the narrator adds: "*Her* mind was less difficult to develope. She was a woman of mean understanding, little information, and uncertain temper. When she was discontented she fancied herself nervous. The business of her life was to get her daughters married; its solace was visiting and news" (p. 53). Although Mrs. Bennet is dismissed (p. 262) as a woman whose "weak understanding and illiberal mind" have lost her the "respect, esteem, and confidence" of her husband—and, by implication, of her daughter, the narrator, and readers—she is a constant enough force in the novel to evoke such strong criticism.[13] She is a serious handicap to her eldest daughters' romances and a serious instigator of her youngest daughters' folly.

Like Dickens's Mrs. Nickleby, who spoke "to nobody in particular . . . until her breath was exhausted,"[14] Mrs. Bennet's language reveals her self-absorbed inattention to her family's needs. She invariably misconstrues her effect on listeners, imagining specific insult from Darcy's general views about the country and city (p. 89) and missing the contempt with which the Netherfield ladies greet her comments (pp. 90, 144). She dwells in a land of "delightful persuasion" (p. 144), where she alone chooses how to interpret others' behavior. As when she bursts forth with her "exuberance" about Lydia's last-minute marriage, she cannot be shamed nor can her present feelings be disrupted with concern about the past or future.[15] Her well-rehearsed discourse on her "poor nerves" preempts her daughters' chances to complain or suffer publicly. After Lizzie rejects Mr. Collins, Mrs. Bennet recasts the entire episode as an attack on her. She does not imagine what the unpleasant scene may have cost Lizzie, nor does she consider how her daughter may have felt in rejecting a man her mother supports. Her complaints admit no cosufferers and need no audience: "nobody is on my side, nobody takes part with me, I am cruelly used, nobody feels for my poor nerves" (p. 153). Although she vows never to speak to her "undutiful children" again, she babbles on, lost in a self-contained grievance: "Not that I have much pleasure indeed in talking to any body. People who suffer as I do from nervous complaints can have no great inclination for talking. Nobody can tell what I suffer!—But it is always so. Those who do not complain are never pitied." Her complaints earn her no pity from her daughters, who "listened in silence to this effusion, sensible that any attempt to reason with or sooth her would only increase the irritation" (p. 154).

Although Lizzie is in some ways allied with her mother in a struggle with patriarchal powers, she does not willingly admit the allegiance. Embarrassed by her mother's failures and inadequacies, she can neither laugh her off as comic nor fully dissociate herself. Lizzie never speaks her criticism to her mother, treating her as someone beyond conversation or reform, beyond the improvement of sensibility evoked in the novel. Yet she clearly feels the burden of the association and struggles to convince others of their differences. Her mother has a surprising power to silence the heroine, who speaks out in every other situation. At Netherfield, in front of the critical audience of Darcy and Miss Bingley, Lizzie trembles "lest her mother should be exposing herself again. She longed to speak, but could think of nothing to say" (p. 90). She is all too aware of how powerful and final the response to such exposure can be; it is after such an outburst in front of the Netherfield set that "the mother was found to be intolerable" (p. 68). Physical distance does not shelter her from her identity as daughter of "such a mother" (p. 187),[16] and she suffers from the disturbing effects of Miss Bingley's reminders of their "dear friend's vulgar relations" (p. 83). It does not require her mother's presence, but only the "thought of her mother," to make her lose "confidence" in an argument with Darcy (p. 219). Lizzie's concern about exposure—her mother's and, more to the point, her own—shows her tenuous social position, her vulnerability to being judged by her rank or family rather than by her words, her fear that even her words will prove too daring, too revealing.

Lizzie's intense discomfort around her mother seems reciprocal: she is the "least dear" (p. 145) of Mrs. Bennet's children, the one chosen by Mr. Bennet to confound his opinion of women as "silly and ignorant" (p. 52). Such comments suggest that Lizzie has risen above the devalued position of her mother, both personally and socially. Yet Lizzie shares more with her mother, than her father or the narrator acknowledges or than she herself can recognize. Her disvalued fictional role allows Mrs. Bennet to voice more radical discontents than can the heroine of the novel. She is "beyond the reach of reason" in her diatribe against entailing an estate away from her daughters "in favour of a man whom nobody cared anything about" (pp. 106–7)—a complaint Elizabeth Bennet might well make if she were not too rational, too worldly wise. Lizzie shares her mother's shock at Charlotte's engagement to Mr. Collins, although she "recollected herself" (p. 165) in time to address her friend with guarded politeness. Like her mother, Lizzie allows herself "agreeable reflections" about what it would mean for Jane to marry Bingley, but whereas Lizzie keeps her dreams private, her mother speaks "freely, openly" (p. 140), causing her daughter to try "in vain . . . to check the rapidity of her mother's words, or persuade her to describe her felicity in a less audible whisper" (p. 141). Although Elizabeth has claimed she does not care what Darcy thinks of her, she "blushed and blushed again with shame and vexation" (p. 141) in watching his contempt for her mother's expressed social expectations. The aspiration of rising through marriage is thus displaced onto her mother's vulgarity, although Lizzie too has imagined Jane marrying into a fine house: "she saw her in idea settled in that very house in all the felicity which a marriage of true affection could bestow" (p. 140). Nor can Lizzie openly support her mother's eagerness to arrange for dinners or balls, contrivances necessary to promote the futures of five dependent girls. The calculation needed to achieve a secure marriage cannot be articulated except as comically disvalued speech.[17]

Mrs. Bennet, whose outbursts are a constant source of anxiety for her elder daughters, is regularly interrupted by her husband, her priorities ridiculed or diverted. Irked at her long tale about a ball and dancing partners, Mr. Bennet dismisses his wife's story and its mode of telling as designed only to irritate him (p. 60). That his daughters' futures depend on such slight details as who dances with whom and in what order, that they too must learn to read minute social signs, is of no concern to Mr. Bennet. As Nina Auerbach has argued, it is Mrs. Bennet who "forges her family's liaison with the outside world of marriage, morals, and money that eligible men embody. . . . While the mother builds connections, the father retreats from the business of marriage to his library" (p. 36).

Such nonchalance, such silence is the prerogative of the powerful, and in *Pride and Prejudice* it is permissible only for propertied men. Mr. Bennet regularly gains the upper hand by not answering his wife's addresses, and Darcy similarly maddens the importunate Miss Bingley. Mr. Bennet teases his family by postponing word that he has visited the new bachelors in town, and Darcy chooses when and how to impart the information he controls about Wickham and Georgiana. But when Jane or Lizzie is silent, the unusual behavior is noted and has serious consequences, causing Darcy, for one, to conclude that Jane is cold or Lizzie hostile. In her chapter on women's conversation in *The Women of England* (1838), Sarah Stickney Ellis codifies the "uses of being silent" for women, suggesting that a woman's silence and speech are alike secondary, functioning "rather to lead others out into animated and intelligent communications, than to be intent upon making communications from the resources of her own mind."[18] Woman's silence is thus very different from the silence of authority which, as the inverse of Bakhtin's "word of the fathers," need not be repeated to make itself felt. The women in *Pride and Prejudice* work to fill up silences, to repair the suggestion that they have no purpose, no presence. At Netherfield, the ladies, whose "powers of conversation were considerable" when the men were out of the room, are reduced to nervous stratagems to persuade the men to break the silence they instill (pp. 99–102). The struggle is described as a contest, and Miss Bingley's failure to "win" Darcy "to any conversation" shows the imbalance between men and women speakers. Lizzie comments on this contest, suggesting that "our surest way of disappointing him, will be to ask nothing about it." She thus appears to control the situation, to have seen through and assumed for herself the power of silence that Miss Bingley, described as "incapable of disappointing Mr Darcy in any thing," cannot manage.

But Lizzie's silence is only an imitation of Darcy's power to withhold his words, since she must explain that she is doing it and must perform the very role in the scene she hopes to evade, that of speaker who waits for Darcy's response. When Darcy is "surprise[d] at her silence," Lizzie tries to validate her silence as something she has determined to enact, not merely a product of her social position. She does so with a complicated speech that she expects will "affront him": "Oh! . . . I heard you before; but I could not immediately determine what to say in reply. You wanted me, I know, to say 'Yes,' that you might have the pleasure of despising my taste; but I always delight in overthrowing those kind of schemes, and cheating a person of their premeditated contempt. I have therefore made up my mind to tell you, that I do not want to dance a reel at all—and now despise me if you dare" (p. 96). Lizzie claims her silence as a powerful privilege, affording her time in which to *determine, know, delight,* and *make up her mind.* Yet she must speak to defend her silence, and her actions all respond to expectations that are beyond her control to change. She can refuse to dance, but she cannot alter the nature of dancing and conversing, nor can she alter her position as one who must first be invited, who can only startle "in reply." The social discourse is preconstituted.

The less powerful speakers in such scenes are regularly marked as "crying" out their speech, as breaking the decorum of a scene in which Darcy's words need only be "said" to have impact and to gain attention. Women are thus required to speak in excess if they are to be heard at all, but such excess marks their speech as negligible. Mrs. Bennet is described by the narrator as "sharp" in defense of her five daughters, as indulging in "raptures" and "exaggeration." Although her words are necessary to safeguard a minimal social and economic standard for the Bennet girls, she must "rail bitterly" to make her point. And Lizzie has constantly before her the warning of Lydia, whose energies to procure her own desires are described by the narrator as "put[ting] herself forward," as full of "high animal spirits, and a sort of natural self-consequence," full of "assurance" that makes her "insist" rather than "cry," and "very equal therefore to address Mr Bingley on the subject of the ball, and abruptly remind[ing] him of his promise" (p. 91).

Lizzie can only differentiate herself from these censured women by explaining at length how her words are to be taken. She does not have Darcy's luxury of silence or her father's indulgence of privacy. As she experiences in her painful encounters with Lady Catherine and Mr. Collins, she is drawn into public discourse despite every attempt at resistance. When Mr. Collins dismisses her careful rejection of his proposal as "merely words of course," the "usual practice of elegant females," Lizzie cannot extricate herself from the social construction he has imposed. "I know not how to express my refusal in such a way as may convince you of its being one," she says. "Can I speak plainer?" Her only recourse is to refer him to her father, "whose negative might be uttered in such a manner as must be decisive" (pp. 148–50). Similarly, although she struggles to mark off some prerogatives for herself in her conversations with Lady Catherine (telling her, "*You* may ask questions which *I* shall not choose to answer"), she cannot end the scene. She can deny that Lady Catherine is "entitled" to know her mind and can refuse to be "explicit," but she must continue to speak to reject further attacks. Even as she insists, "I have nothing farther to say," she is provoked into a string of defensive replies ("I will make no promise of the kind"; "I must beg, therefore, to be importuned no farther on the subject"; "I have said no such thing"). Her defeated reaction afterward—"to acknowledge the substance of their conversation was impossible"—reflects more than an unwillingness to confide in her mother; it also suggests how powerless she is to control the "substance" of conversations (pp. 364–68).

Lizzie has been warned about the limits on women's discourse by an offhanded remark of Miss Bingley's. When Lizzie recommends that they "punish" Darcy by teasing or laughing at him, Miss Bingley protests that laughter would only serve to "expose ourselves . . . by attempting to laugh without a subject" (pp. 101–2). Lizzie rejects such an "uncommon advantage" for her male peer, refusing to allow him to conceal himself from the considerable power of her laughter. Yet, although Lizzie "wins" this scene by appearing to reject the conventions of male–female difference, Miss Bingley's comment raises a disturbing problem about women's discourse in Austen's realm. Lizzie's power to laugh depends on having a "subject"; without it her humor will seem as absurd and self-absorbed as her mother's. Although she seems more in control than her mother, Lizzie can neither end nor begin a scene of her own volition. If Darcy does not raise objections for her to correct or mock, her laughter will be seen as having no substance, no social effect; it will emerge not as valiant independence but, like her mother's, as ignorant blindness of serious realities.

The treatment of her mother as comic allows Lizzie, and Austen, to displace the implicit challenge against social limitations with a parental battle that is simpler to fight. The daughter challenges restrictions voiced by a mother who has had no role in creating those rules. Her resentment toward her mother suggests an inability to confront her father's authority and responsibility, but it also gives her the chance to practice rebellion in a less threatening context.[19] Mrs. Bennet's embarrassing outbreaks concern Lizzie partially because they proclaim what she must conceal and partially because the reception of these remarks shows Lizzie the contradictory proscriptions for women. Her mother has warned Lizzie (with a "cry") to "remember where you are, and do not run on in the wild manner that you are suffered to do at home" (p. 88). But Lizzie is caught in a bind: she must be guarded in her words and tactful in her wit if she is to win Darcy (she must always remember she is not "at home"), yet she can win him only by seeming independent and daring (by not allowing him to determine where her home shall be). She vacillates between an astute political analysis and a repression of such insights. When, for example, Darcy confesses he has been attracted by the "liveliness" of her mind, she suggests it might more accurately be termed "impertinence" (p. 388). But she is careful to teach her prospective sister-in-law how "impertinence" gets translated into a permitted or even valued quality: "[Georgiana's] mind received knowledge which had never before fallen in her way. By Elizabeth's instructions she began to comprehend that a woman may take liberties with her husband, which a brother will not always allow in a sister more than ten years younger than himself" (p. 395). Lizzie instructs Georgiana in a mild, affectionate version of sexual politics, but even such casual reminders indicate how careful women must be in determining what is allowed and what will be censured. Lizzie does not presume that Darcy's fondness raises her to a permanent position of "liberty"; even after they have declared their love, she is guarded in her speech, "check[ing]" her "long[ing]" to tease him by remembering "that he had yet to learn to be laught at, and it was rather too early to begin" (p. 380).

Lizzie is also cautious about making explicit the power relations between men and women. She counters her sister Jane's belief that "women fancy admiration means more than it does" with a caustic "and men take care that they should." But when Jane pursues the issue of what is "designedly done," Lizzie demurs from the extremity of her views—"without scheming to do wrong, or to make others unhappy, there may be error, and there may be misery"—and finally offers to be silent before she offends by "saying what I think of persons you esteem. Stop me whilst you can" (pp. 174–75). In the very next chapter, however, she rearticulates the political awareness to her aunt Gardiner, who has attributed the failure of Jane's romance to "accident." "These things happen so often!" her aunt has concluded, and Lizzie sharply responds: "An excellent consolation in its way, but it will not do for *us*. We do not suffer by *accident*" (p. 178). She ultimately admits her father's complicity in Mrs. Bennet's ridiculed position, but even a private acknowledgment of this insight seems dangerous and must be carefully contained. Although she "had never been blind to the impropriety of her father's behavior as a husband" and "had always seen it with pain," she "endeavoured to forget what she could not overlook, and to banish [it] from her thoughts." It is only the public disaster of Lydia's seduction that allows her to blame her father as well as her mother for the "disadvantages which must attend the children of so unsuitable a marriage" (p. 262).

Lizzie is trapped between the equally unpleasant expectations of the "good" and "bad" daughter. The fall of Lydia, the bad daughter who is her mother's favorite, is instructive, since it reminds Lizzie of the danger of being judged as "fanciful" or "wayward." Mrs. Gardiner has warned Lizzie to be a good daughter, not of her mother but of her father: "you must not let your fancy run away with you. You have sense and we all expect you to use it. Your father would depend on *your* resolution and good conduct, I am sure. You must not disappoint your father" (p. 181). But Lizzie can see what society's "good sense" wins, what a good daughter can expect for herself. She is greatly unsettled by Charlotte's "sensible" marriage and has little sympathy with the "composure" with which both Jane and Charlotte repress their desires and observations. She also has the example of Miss Bingley, who has constructed herself as the perfect product of social rules, as exceedingly careful to do whatever it takes to win herself a powerful husband and house. In the fabulous world of *Pride and Prejudice*, it is Lizzie, the "bad" daughter, who succeeds and is allowed to laugh at her competitor and to outrank her sensible friend and sister. The happy ending rewrites the historically more likely outcome, the coopted marriage of Charlotte or the ridiculed position of her mother.[20] The heroine wins propriety and wealth through daring and rebellion made palatable to her world through her partial adherence to its rules. She succeeds by publicly being a "bad daughter" to her unworthy mother, but she also succeeds by evading the sense and directives of patriarchal culture.

Pride and Prejudice marks the beginning of a time, as Judith Lowder Newton has argued, of "general ideological crisis, a crisis of confidence over the status, the proper work, and the power of middle-class women" (p. 1). The ambivalent role of the mother, who in Austen's novel is both powerful and negligible, becomes a more conventional trope as it is codified and rationalized by a proliferation of advice books, novels about women's struggles, and treatises on the Woman Question. It is, therefore, productive to compare how the "foolish mother" is positioned in a novel in which the role is still implicit and how that position is solidified in a novel like Hardy's *Tess of the D'Urbervilles* (1891). By the end of the century, in *Tess*, Hardy presents a daughter passionately condemning her foolish mother, blaming the mother for the daughter's tragedy. Such a scene is unmentionable in Austen, and not only because of the differing conventions of polite discourse.

By 1891 it was relatively uncontroversial to represent the mother as scapegoat for cultural disorder. When Tess discovers that there is "danger in men-folk," it is her "poor foolish mother" she blames for not having warned her.[21] The mother's failure in the personal realm is given broad-ranging cultural implications. Tess's mother has seen their fall from "nobility" as merely a "passing accident" rather than the "haunting episode" that ruins her child's expectations (p. 162). Her foolishness thus becomes a historical emblem—of the peasantry's failure to understand the threat of the aristocracy and of the urban world, of the failure of the "past" to understand the demands of "the modern age," of the failure of seeing "accident" or "nature" as a sufficient cultural explanation. And it apparently makes sense to trace all these powerful failures to a mother who has not taken her responsibilities seriously enough: " 'O mother, my mother!' cried the agonized girl, turning passionately upon her parent as if her poor heart would break. 'How could I be expected to know? . . . Why didn't you warn me? Ladies know what to fend hands against, because they read novels that tell them of these tricks; but I never had the chance o' learning in that way, and you did not help me!' Her mother was subdued."

The implication is that ladies have an undue advantage over the daughter of a "poor foolish mother," an advantage which Tess sees as literary but which could more accurately be seen as the advantage of wealth and class. The mother's "simple vanity" becomes the focus for her daughter's anger, which cannot find its more appropriate targets, both individual and cultural. But when the novel has Tess blame her mother for not "telling" her of worldly dangers, and when such an accusation "subdues" the mother into a proper acceptance of guilt, there has been an important ideological manipulation of the role of mother. It is contradictory to locate the fault in not "telling"—in words—rather than in the "wrong doing" of men or the class inequities that make ladies better prepared to negotiate the perils of adult life. *Tess* thus provides a scapegoat for the powerful social transformations that affect the lives of women, for which daughters must be prepared. The mother, who is at best a commentator on the social realm, has taken the place of initiator, guardian, or betrayer.

Mid-nineteenth-century advice books, like the influential series by Mrs. Ellis—*Wives of England, Daughters of England,* and *Women of England*—similarly imply that mothers are the source of broad cultural changes that disrupt the family and the lives of their daughters. They charge women with the responsibility for correcting and upholding moral standards for man, who is "confused by the many voices, which in the mart, the exchange, or the public assembly, have addressed themselves to his inborn selfishness or his worldly pride [and . . .] stands corrected before the clear eye of woman, as it looked directly to the naked truth, and detected the lurking evil of the specious act he was about to commit" (*The Women of England,* p. 42). The blame for continued "selfishness" or confusion, for worldly pride or lurking evil, then rests not on the "confused" man but on the woman who fails to oppose him, to provide him with a "clear eye" in which to see his faults. In an 1832 essay on the "Education of Daughters," Lydia Maria Child cites as a "true, and therefore an old remark, that the situation and prospects of a country may be justly estimated by the character of its women" and stresses the important transmission of such influence from mother to daughter.[22] Such pronouncements suggest a cultural concern over what is perceived as women's and, more explicitly, mothers' responsibilities and failures. They also stress the narrow range of possibilities afforded mothers, in which the mother's behavior is always a failure, incapable of satisfying incommensurable demands. Deborah Gorham describes the mother-daughter relationships figured in Victorian literature and art as inevitably producing two outcomes: "one in which the mother fulfilled her maternal functions, and one in which she would not or could not do so" (p. 47). To be a "good" mother according to the culture's proscriptions was to be a failure in her daughter's eyes. But to be a "bad" mother was also to be a failure, to embarrass or commit her daughter to living outside the system of social rewards and approval only the father could bestow.

By working to institutionalize the "proper" discourses of women, to teach the emergent middle class how to be "good" mothers and "dutiful" daughters, nineteenth-century advice books suggest that the relationship between mother and daughter was not seen as "natural" or as the province of individuals, but as requiring considerable institutional support and guidance. The aim was not to create self-fulfilled individuals but to acquire facility in approved social functions. In *Women of England*, Mrs. Ellis warned against encouraging young women to be too "striking" or to stray from their proper "station" as "relative creatures": "If, therefore, they are endowed only with such faculties, as render them striking and distinguished in themselves, without the faculty of instrumentality, they are only as dead letters in the volume of human life, filling what would otherwise be a blank space, but doing nothing more" (p. 108). To be part of social discourse, to avoid the marginality of being a "dead letter," a "blank space" in the "volume of human life," young girls must learn to function in predetermined ways, to fulfill the "instrumentality" established as their role and use in culture. Like their mothers, like Freud's child, they must learn to accept what is "granted" to them by an authority they work to uphold. It would be difficult for a mother to speak from such a proscribed position, and it would be painful for a daughter to hear such words. Austen's Mrs. Bennet makes the position and its restrictions visible and laughable; she "fails" to become an appropriate function and thus remains outside approved social practices. Her daughter "succeeds," but she too is implicated in her mother's exclusion from the social world. The novel "forgets" the bleakness of women's prospects in its exuberant ending, but at the cost of banning the mother from its view and of suspending the objections she voiced.

NOTES

This essay is dedicated, with love and admiration, to my mother, Mary Anne Heyward Ferguson, who, unlike Mrs. Bennet, has been a wise comprehender and a supportive instigator of her daughters' efforts. An early version of this essay was presented at a Wellesley College symposium, "Mothers and Daughters in Literature," in February 1983.

[1] Jane Austen, *Pride and Prejudice*, 1813 (New York: Penguin, 1972), p. 53.

[2] Mikhail Bakhtin, *The Dialogic Imagination*, ed. Michael Holquist, trans. Caryl Emerson and Michael Holquist (Austin: University of Texas Press, 1981), p. 403.

[3] Sigmund Freud, *Jokes and Their Relation to the Unconscious*, 1905, ed. and trans. James Strachey (New York: W. W. Norton, 1963), p. 182. Freud wrote: "weil eine solche bei ihm nicht

vorhanden ist," "er besitze diese Hemmung nicht," and "lachen nicht über ihn, sondern sind über ihn entrüstet" (Sigmund Freud, *Der Witz und Seine Beziehung zum Unbewussten* [Leipzig and Vienna: Franz Deuticke, 1905], p. 156).

[4] Bakhtin locates the effect of incomprehension, not within the novel or in any specific character's ability to "teach" others, but in the novelist's awareness of multiple discourses: "A failure to understand languages that are otherwise generally accepted and that have the appearance of being universal teaches the novelist how to perceive them physically as *objects*, to see their relativity, to externalize them, to feel out their boundaries, that is, it teaches him how to expose and structure images of social languages" (*The Dialogic Imagination*, p. 404).

[5] Pierre Macherey, *A Theory of Literary Production*, trans. Geoffrey Wall (1966; London: Routledge and Kegan Paul, 1978), pp. 80, 83. Macherey argues that such a double reading seeks "the inscription of an *otherness* in the work, through which it maintains a relationship with that which it is not, that which happens at its margins" (p. 79).

[6] In *Of Woman Born: Motherhood as Experience and Institution* (New York: W. W. Norton, 1976), her influential analysis of American cultural attitudes toward motherhood, Rich claims: "This cathexis between mother and daughter—essential, distorted, misused—is the great unwritten story" (p. 225). See also Signe Hammer, *Daughters and Mothers: Mothers and Daughters* (New York: Quadrangle/New York Times Book Co., 1975); and Nancy Chodorow, *The Reproduction of Mothering: Psychoanalysis and the Sociology of Gender* (Berkeley: University of California Press, 1978). In her review essay on "Mothers and Daughters" (*Signs* 7 [1981], 200–222), Marianne Hirsch discusses the reasons for the historical "silence" and "the subsequent centrality of the mother–daughter relationship at this particular point in feminist scholarship" (p. 201). Her essay provides an extremely useful survey of recent studies that are "attempts to prove that the story of mother–daughter relationships has been written even if it has not been read, that it constitutes the hidden subtext of many texts" (p. 214). See also *The Lost Tradition: Mothers and Daughters in Literature*, ed. E. M. Broner and Cathy N. Davidson (New York: Frederick Ungar, 1980), a collection of essays on this issue. Studies that discuss the nineteenth-century scene in particular are: Patricia Meyer Spacks, *The Female Imagination* (New York: Avon Books, 1972); Françoise Basch, *Relative Creatures* (New York: Schocken Books, 1974); Ellen Moers, *Literary Women* (New York: Doubleday, 1976); Elaine Showalter, *A Literature of Their Own* (Princeton: Princeton University Press, 1977); Lynne Agress, *The Feminine Irony* (New York: University Press of America, 1978); Nina Auerbach, *Communities of Women* (Cambridge: Harvard University Press, 1978); Sandra M. Gilbert and Susan Gubar, *The Madwoman in the Attic: The Woman Writer and the Nineteenth-Century Literary Imagination* (New Haven: Yale University Press, 1979); Judith Lowder Newton, *Women, Power, and Subversion: Social Strategies in British Fiction* (Athens: University of Georgia Press, 1981; rpt. London: Methuen, 1986); and Deborah Gorham, *The Victorian Girl and the Feminine Ideal* (Bloomington: Indiana University Press, 1982).

[7] In "The Female World of Love and Ritual: Relations between Women in Nineteenth-Century America," *Signs* 1 (1975), 1–29, Carroll Smith-Rosenberg suggests that "taboos against female aggression and hostility" may have been "sufficiently strong to repress even that between mothers and their adolescent daughters" (p. 17). But she also challenges the modern assumption that hostility between generations, "today considered almost inevitable to an adolescent's struggle for autonomy and self-identity," is an essential ahistorical fact. Patricia Spacks explains the omission of mothers as a stylistic version of an unchanging resentment: "In nineteenth-century novels women express hostility toward their mothers by eliminating them from the narrative; twentieth-century fiction dramatizes the conflict" (*The Female Imagination*, p. 191).

[8] Ellen Moers calls courtship "a dreadful word" in Austen, "for it implies something a man does to a woman, and can include adultery." She prefers "marriageship," and argues Austen saw marriage as "the only act of choice in a woman's life" (*Literary Women*, p. 70). Gilbert and Gubar concur that marriage is "the only accessible form of self-definition for girls in [Austen's] society" (*Madwoman in the Attic*, p. 127).

[9] See Gilbert and Gubar, *Madwoman in the Attic*, pp. 97–104. Moers describes women writers as "an undercurrent" literary tradition (*Literary Women*, p. 42); Showalter discusses the "covert solidarity that sometimes amounted to a genteel conspiracy" between women novelists and readers in the nineteenth century (*A Literature of Their Own*, pp. 15–16).

[10] Showalter discusses the "remarkable frequency" with which nineteenth-century women writers identified with the father at the "loss of, or alienation from, the mother" (ibid., p. 61). "[M]ost mothers in middle-class families were more narrow-minded and conventional than the fathers, who had the advantages of education and mobility. . . . The daughter's nonconformity would increase the strains in her relationship with her mother and lead her to make greater demands upon her father for love and attention" (p. 62). Susan Peck MacDonald argues that the "absence of mothers" in Austen's novels derives "not from the impotence or unimportance of mothers, but from the almost excessive power of motherhood." The mother's power to "shield her daughter from the process of maturation" must be met by a "psychological rift" with the mother ("Jane Austen and the Tradition of the Absent Mother," in *The Lost Tradition*, ed. Broner and Davidson, pp. 58, 64). See also my discussion of Louisa Gradgrind's negotiation of her father's system and her mother's ineffectual resistance, in Jean Ferguson Carr, "Writing as a Woman: Dickens, *Hard Times*, and Feminine Discourses," *Dickens Studies Annual* 18 (1989), 159–76.

[11] "Jokes, even if the thought contained in them is non-tendentious and thus only serves theoretical intellectual interests, are in fact never non-tendentious. They pursue the second aim: to promote the thought by augmenting it and guarding it against criticism. Here they are once again expressing their original nature by setting themselves up against an inhibiting and restricting power—which is now the critical judgement" (Freud, *Jokes*, pp. 132–33). See also Sigmund Freud, *A General Introduction to Psychoanalysis*, 1924, trans. Joan Riviere (New York: Washington Square, 1952), in which he discusses slips of the tongue and other comical errors: "They are not accidents; they are serious mental acts; they have their meaning" (p. 48).

[12] The first two depictions are by Douglas Bush in his 1956 article "Mrs. Bennet and the Dark Gods: The Truth about Jane Austen," rpt. in *Twentieth-Century Interpretations of* Pride and Prejudice, ed. E. Rubenstein (Englewood Cliffs, N.J.: Prentice-Hall, 1969), p. 113, and the last two by Mark Schorer in his introduction to *Pride and Prejudice* (Cambridge: Houghton Mifflin, 1956), pp. xiii, xxi.

[13] Nina Auerbach argues for the "equivocal" nature of Austen's discussion of "direct female power" and cites Harriet Martineau's "oblique apology" in *Society and America* (1837) that English girls would obey such a "foolish mother" (*Communities of Women*, p. 50).

[14] Charles Dickens, *The Life and Adventures of Nicholas Nickleby* (London, 1838–39), ch. 11.

[15] On Lydia's return, Austen describes Mrs. Bennet as "disturbed by no fear for her felicity, nor humbled by any remembrance of her misconduct" (p. 320). Nina Auerbach discusses Mrs. Bennet as curiously vague about the details of domestic life, but sees Lizzie as "beyond a certain point devoid of memory": "if she shares nothing else with her mother, her faculty of nonremembrance confirms Mrs. Bennet's perception of the nonlife they have had together" (*Communities of Women*, p. 43).

[16] In her essay on Charlotte's prospects, "Why Marry Mr. Collins?" in *Sex, Class, and Culture* (1978; rpt. London: Metheun, 1986), Lillian Robinson discusses Lady Catherine's harsh reminder that although Lizzie's father is a gentleman she is not "the daughter of a gentlewoman as well" (p. 185).

[17] Judith Lowder Newton discusses *Pride and Prejudice*'s subversion of the issue of economic concerns by its association with Mrs. Bennet, "a woman whose worries we are not allowed to take seriously because they are continually undermined by their link with the comic and the absurd" (*Women, Power, and Subversion*, p. 70). See also Lillian Robinson's discussion of the economic difference the heroines would experience as daughters and as wives (*Sex, Class, and Culture*, p. 198).

[18] In *The Women of England, Their Social Duties, and Domestic Habits* (London, 1838; rpt. Philadelphia: Herman Hooker, 1841), Mrs. Ellis begins her chapter on "the uses of conversation" with what she admits is the "somewhat paradoxical" discussion of silence, the "peculiar province of a woman" which derives "from her position in society" (p. 101). In *The Wives of England: Their Relative Duties, Domestic Influence, and Social Obligations* (London, 1843; rpt. New York: D. Appleton, 1843), she provides a fitting example of the authority of men's silence and the contingency of women's speech. She advises men to leave the discipline of servants and children to their wives "because the master of a family with whom it rests to exercise real authority cannot so well unbend, and make himself familiar with the young people under his direction, the claims of

this part of the community are strong upon the wives of England" (p. 235). The husband retains "real" power by being silent but allows his wife to "unbend" in speech; her exercise of domestic power is granted on the condition that she make herself "familiar" to a "part of the community" that remains "under" the "master."

[19] A sociolinguistic study of mother–daughter relationships comments on the use of "indirection" by mothers to signal "to their children that a directive is meant more seriously than its surface structure suggests." They cite the view that "indirection occurs because mothers are less willing to demonstrate power openly than are fathers. They see in the mother's use of indirect means in controlling her children evidence of her discontent with the superordinate position of power which is available to her as a mother, but not elsewhere in her life." Their study suggests that such a doubled discourse both acknowledges and attempts to circumvent the disparity in social power of men and women, and its use arises from the mother's inexperience with power and her unwillingness to claim it openly. See Ruth Wodak and Muriel Schulz, *The Language of Love and Guilt: Mother–Daughter Relationships from a Cross-Cultural Perspective* (Amsterdam: John Benjamins, 1986), pp. 35–36. Wodak and Schulz discuss indirect means of control or instruction as a sign of the mother's need to domesticate her authority, to make it appear less intrusive or insistent, less like a usurpation of male prerogatives, but they also cite it as a manipulative practice which preserves the mother's power in a realm beyond critique, "because indirection denies the child a chance to respond" (p. 37). As is evident in the interviews, the mother's linguistic claim to power often arises from her borrowing of patriarchal languages. The signal to serious portent, or to powerful command, is achieved by moving outside the language used by mothers to children, by using those social discourses that remain the province of fathers—logic, proper language, or an approved state language. They provide many examples of such "metaphorical code switching (a switch from one register to another)": for example, American mothers' attempt to "convey seriousness by switching from a diminutive name to the child's full name" or Norwegian mothers' movement "from their local dialect into Standard Norwegian to emphasize a command" (p. 36).

[20] See Lillian Robinson's discussion of the ending as improbable, "outside the realm of [Lizzie's] own and Jane Austen's imaginings" (*Sex, Class, and Culture*, p. 188).

[21] Thomas Hardy, *Tess of the D'Urbervilles* (New York: W. W. Norton, 1979), pp. 69–70.

[22] Lydia Maria Child, "Hints to Persons of Moderate Fortune," in *The American Frugal Housewife: Dedicated to Those Who Are Not Ashamed of Economy* (Boston, 1832; rpt. Worthington, Ohio: Worthington Historical Society, 1965), p. 1.

AFTERWORD

I wrote the first version of this essay as a lecture, "Mothers and Daughters in Nineteenth-Century Fiction," given in 1983 at the Center for Research on Women at Wellesley College, in which I discussed two literary texts, Austen's *Pride and Prejudice* and Dickens's *Hard Times*. I was intrigued by how (and why) two such different writers exploited a tension between heroine-daughters and their ridiculously inarticulate mothers. I subsequently published the Dickens materials as "Writing as a Woman: *Dickens, Hard Times,* and Feminine Discourses" (*Dickens Studies Annual* 18 [1990]: 161–78).

These companion essays framed their discussions of characters' struggles with language in two ways: a retheorizing of issues of discourse and power and a historical contextualizing of issues of literacy and instruction, especially those designated for women. At that time the essays represented a turn in literary studies, from psychological or moral analysis of characters' virtues and foibles (and criticism or praise for the author of such denigrated or admirable models) to a historicized inquiry about the conditions under which characters (and writers) operate, conditions that constrain self-presentation, behavior, and value, conditions that might invite a powerful male writer like Dickens to experiment with women's discourses and positions.

Arguing for "writing as a woman" as a discursive rather than essential position, I investigated these authors' treatment of women's speech—both novels present older women who speak too loudly or with too little restraint, whose speech embarrasses or exposes their self-conscious daughters. I contended that such practices suggest a complex mixture of individual desire and community instruction, that rather than signal individual virtue or achievement per se, women's speech is constrained and marked by their social positions, education, and power. In both essays I looked beyond the more expected focus on the young heroines to the minor and less admirable older women, characters rendered as comic or trivial figures, whose attitudes and desires are treated as error, ignorance, or blindness. Both essays ask the questions, How are women taught to speak or write *as women*? What is the politics of devaluing, silencing, constraining, or ridiculing the mothers who so embarrass their daughters?

Since I wrote these paired essays, I have continued to write about the constraints on women's texts and speech, considering the effects, for example, of women's collaboration, of literacy instruction, or of prefaces that challenge masculinist literary culture. My central interests at the moment are in instruction—How do institutions and texts "oblige" (to use Roger Chartier's wonderful term) language users? How do they create the boundaries and expectations that shape discourse, speech, reading, writing, and behavior? In the Austen essay, I dipped my toe in such waters by working with advice books, with the writings of Mrs. Ellis on the "women of England." I have since then followed that interest, working on instructional materials—nineteenth-century reading books in the United States, periodical articles, and scenes of reading in fictions. I have juxtaposed the more insistently institutional texts (assigned textbooks like McGuffey's *Eclectic Readers* or Sigourney's *Girl's Reading Book*) with the diffused instruction found in fictions, periodicals, literary clubs, and literacy events.

"A Splintery Box": Race and Gender in the Sonnets of Gwendolyn Brooks

Stacy Carson Hubbard

GWENDOLYN BROOKS'S use of the sonnet form in her poetry of the 1940s and 50s signals her status as inheritor and critic of two Renaissance traditions, one originating in Europe during the fourteenth century and the other in Harlem around 1912. According to Henry Louis Gates, Jr., the texts of every Afro-American writer "occupy spaces in at least two traditions: a European or American literary tradition, and one of the several related but distinct black traditions. The 'heritage' of each black text written in a Western language is . . . a double heritage" (4). For Brooks, this doubleness in the text doubles yet again over the question of gender; the feminine voice in Brooks's poems, as in the lyric generally, is necessarily dislocated, occupying uneasy ground between the Western tradition's figurations of poetic authority and its representations of silent women. Brooks's ambivalent relation to literary tradition is dramatized in her revision of a single form from two separate traditions, one white, one black, and both predominantly male. In what follows, I want to explore Brooks's accommodation of this highly traditional form to a non-traditional voice, black and feminine, through her ironic reworkings of its conventions of speaker, structure, and self-reflexive troping. My intention is to demonstrate how a literary form redolent with connotations of privilege and power can be adapted to serve very different aesthetic and political ends, and to suggest through this one example something of the complexity of Afro-American women's appropriative literary practices.

The sonnet was a popular form in the Harlem Renaissance: *Caroling Dusk*, Countee Cullen's 1927 anthology of black poetry, contains sonnets by ten different poets, and both Cullen and Claude McKay wrote extensively in the sonnet form. Most of McKay's sonnets are protests, with titles such as "The Lynching," "In Bondage," "Outcast," and "Enslaved." One might ask how a form so strongly linked to European aristocratic social structures and cultural assumptions came

~

I would like to thank Gwendolyn Brooks for generously giving permission to quote from her poems.

to house the protests of black American poets in the early part of this century. And how does a form whose accumulated gender myths so strongly mark the speaker as male, and poetry as a male vocation, allow for the construction of a feminine voice?[1] I hope to show that for Brooks, the form's very associations with white cultural hegemony and male-dominated discourse make it an apt, if ironic, vehicle for protests against social injustice and the tyrannies of poetic tradition. The sonnet, highly conventional and conspicuously constrained, lends itself to reflections on poetic form. The choice of the sonnet form announces that form, its strictures and possibilities, its definition and power to define, is at issue. For the poet who is defined by her status outside a dominant cultural tradition, the sonnet's history as a compulsory test for major poets challenges the usurper to confront the tradition's upholders within the boundaries of its fourteen lines. Furthermore, the extreme conventionality of the sonnet's themes, figures, and modes of address serves to create formal expectations that render the form particularly vulnerable to the subversions of irony. In Brooks's troping of the gender conventions of the courtly love sonnet, and her revision of the political sonnets of the Harlem Renaissance, one perceives the sort of "technical assault against the styles which have gone before" which Ralph Ellison rightly recognized as a mode of formal ideological protest (137).

The adaptation of the courtly love sonnet to political themes is facilitated by the similar ways in which the complaint poem and the protest poem conceive of themselves in relation to their addressees and to action in the world. Both the love sonnet and the political sonnet—the one with its object of seduction and the other of persuasion—rely on conventions of address which assert the power of poetry to bring about action. Brooks uses these conventions to dismantle accepted distinctions between the political and the poetic, and hence to politicize form itself. Because of the sonnet's particular aptness for dramatizing the construction of the speaking subject, the form provides a powerful vehicle for the exploration of issues of racial and gender identity. Brooks challenges the traditional sonnet's representation of the subject by transforming its spoken woman into a speaking woman and by exploiting the form's restrictions in order to dramatize questions of inclusion and exclusion as they relate to race and gender. For Brooks, the sonnet's "scanty plot of ground" is embattled territory, a structure which no longer merely mimics the movement from seduction to surrender,[2] polemic to persuasion, but becomes itself the site of conflict and the prize fought for: the traditional seduction sonnet's petition for access to a female form gives way to the struggle for access to a poetic one, the sonnet itself.

The Italian sonnet, with its imploring or complaining courtly lover and its roots in troubadour poetry, lent itself neatly to English conventions for expressing emotion (Ferry 73–78). The Petrarchan sonnet offered English writers a new vehicle for the complaint, a tightly structured frame for the syllogisms of love, in which structure and logic could be coordinated. Courtly love, like the sonnet itself, is a game governed by strict rules, wherein emotion and its attendant gestures are conventional and ritualized, and the relations of lovers conceived of in antagonistic terms: love is a game of strategy, a war of wits, wills, and words.

The argumentative structure of the Elizabethan love sonnet, what has been called the "cut and thrust" of the Shakespearian form (Nye 30), or the more leisurely persuasion of the Petrarchan, provides a discursive parallel for the play of power—opposition, surrender, conquest—in the political and sexual realms. As a complaint, the courtly love sonnet claims a place in the realm of action—a directive, grievance, or demand, it calls for other than linguistic redress, and backs its demands with an armory of argument. The lover's complaint demands that the beloved respond, not with more words, but with her person; the addressee of the sonnet is defined by her status *outside* the realm of discourse, her ability to be constituted *by* the poem—and to respond *to* the poem—but not to find voice within it. The verbal coup of the sonnet stands in for a sexual coup, the argument won providing precedent for, perhaps promising, the woman won. In its mimicking of the action it calls for (both in terms of its rhetorical movement, and in its troping of its own movement as sexual release, receding tides, and so forth), the love sonnet can be seen to contain a polemical structure accommodating to political themes; that is, it plays at bridging the gap between discourse and action.

Early political sonnets, however, most often eulogize historical events, heroic figures, or beloved countries. That is, they align themselves with figures of power, as Milton does in his sonnets to Cromwell and Fairfax; they do not so much complain as idealize or woo with flattery. Because the political sonnet from the Renaissance through the nineteenth century speaks not so much against, as from within, reigning structures of privilege and power, the rhetoric of *protest* remains largely confined to the realm of the *love* sonnet. It is for this reason, I believe, that the adoption of the sonnet form by twentieth-century black poets owes more to the tradition of the courtly love sonnet than it does to the political sonnets of Milton and Wordsworth. The sonneteers of the Harlem Renaissance speak not from within the elite circle of a powerful class and culture like that which supported the poet-lovers of the English Renaissance, but from the alleys of dispossession, and in the voices of the colonized, whose exploitation made possible the modern American state, as well as the high-court culture of that earlier Renaissance.

Although the poetry of the Harlem sonneteers is a call for, rather than a consolidation of, political and cultural power, they were able to find precedents for the formal representation of discontent in the rhetoric of the wronged courtly lover. G. M. Matthews sees the Renaissance sonnet's dual structure and conjoined elements of passion and formal restriction as having offered poets an ideal vehicle for articulating the contradictions between the loveless, but sanctified, economic institution of Renaissance marriage, and the courtly virtues of unruly passion. He views the popularity of the sonnet form as a response to this "abnormally overt and rigid contradiction in contemporary society" (120). Any comparison between these restrictions and those of racist societies may appear incongruous; but Matthews's observation is useful here because it calls attention to the ways in which, paradoxically, a particularly restrictive poetic form can serve to articulate rebellion against restrictive social structures. The adoption of the sonnet by black poets such as Claude McKay, Countee Cullen, and Gwendolyn Brooks stems not so much from a desire to "pass" as from the need for a formal expression of the contradictions of the poet's own position and those of American culture. As C. W. E. Bigsby has said,

> The poet was not merely using the form, he was taking possession of it for his own cultural purposes. . . . The form is familiar; the assertion of cultural distinctiveness and even opacity contradicts the claims implied in that familiarity. (264)

One would want to note, however, that the sonnet's petition undergoes a radical change in the hands of a black and/or female speaker. While the love sonnet's traditional speaker plays at powerlessness, assigning the feminine addressee a fictional mastery which belies woman's social and physical subjection, the black or female sonnet speaker's rhetorical stance parallels his or her social and literary historical status. The speaker in the sonnets of Brooks or McKay is neither the Wordsworthian epic poet choosing temporary confinement within the sonnet as respite from the "weight of too much liberty," nor the eager victim of Donne's "Batter my heart, three-personed God," who invites thralldom and ravishment. Because the historical conditions of women and blacks have been those of restriction, thralldom, and sexual exploitation, as well as exclusion from hegemonic cultural forms, the mock power relations of the courtly love sonnet no longer appear to be fictional when the speaker is black and/or female. While the Harlem Renaissance poets do sometimes beseech their oppressors within the sonnet's argumentative structure (as in McKay's "To the White Fiends"), their imperatives are frequently redirected from the powerful addressee (i.e., white readers) to the speaker's comrades in dispossession,[3] thus circumventing the discomfiting literalization of the speaker's pose. Such is the case in McKay's call to violent self-defense in "If We Must Die" and in Brooks's "First fight. Then fiddle."

From the sixteenth-century lover's complaint through the twentieth-century sonnet of political petition or protest, a rhetorical pattern persists: The sonnet's debate mimics a non-discursive conflict, at once calling for and verbally performing an action and attempting to extend beyond its boundaries an imperative to change. In "First fight. Then fiddle," Brooks plays off poetic action against political action to ironic effect:

> First fight. Then fiddle. Ply the slipping string
> With feathery sorcery; muzzle the note
> With hurting love; the music that they wrote
> Bewitch, bewilder. Qualify to sing
> Threadwise. Devise no salt, no hempen thing
> For the dear instrument to bear. Devote
> The bow to silks and honey. Be remote
> A while from malice and from murdering.
> But first to arms, to armor. Carry hate
> In front of you and harmony behind.
> Be deaf to music and to beauty blind.
> Win war. Rise bloody, maybe not too late

> For having first to civilize a space
> Wherein to play your violin with grace. (*Annie Allen* 38)

"First fight. Then fiddle" is insistently imperative, calling for two sorts of action, one violently political, the other artistic. Its ambivalence concerning the relation between poetry and social change reflects Brooks's own position as a black poet writing between the years of the Harlem Renaissance and the emergence of the Black Arts Movement in the mid-1960s. Despite her fondness for traditional poetic forms, which has rendered her early work politically suspect in the eyes of many later black poets, Brooks's poetry never was solely for art's sake. Rather, her lyricism at once challenges the lyric tradition's figurations of authoritative subjectivity, its simultaneous exclusiveness and claims to universality, and those structures of cultural and political power which it articulates and parallels. Where the sonneteers of the Harlem Renaissance generally confined themselves to extending the sonnet's subject matter, while continuing to adhere to its conventions of syntax, diction, rhyme, and line structure, Brooks extends these revisionary strategies to the level of form: She fractures syntax, plays off line against sentence structure, and integrates the sound patterns of a latinate vocabulary with the embedded rhythms of black speech. Brooks's self-declared project has been to "polish [her] technique . . . that [it] may be more insinuating and, therefore, more overwhelming" (*Report* 149).

While "First fight. Then fiddle" appears to give precedence to the fight, the poem itself as a form of "fiddling" reverses the order of its dictates—it creates in order to say that creation must be postponed until after destruction. The poem attempts to segregate the realms of hate and harmony, advising that one not burden the song with "salt" or "hempen things," tears or lyncher's ropes, yet is itself burdened with its message of anger, its call "to arms and armor." Yet the very language of this call, in its echoing of the Renaissance sonnet's trope of love as a siege, works to resituate this battle on the ground of poetic tradition. The retrieval of the battle conceit from the love sonnet tradition, and its literalization in the context of racial struggle, itself constitutes an act of war on the discourse of the high literary tradition. The poem's structure reveals further the hypocrisy of its mandate—its octave instructs in the art of fiddling, advocating a subversive beauty which assaults tradition from within ("the music that they wrote / Bewitch, bewilder"), before the sonnet turns with "But first to arms" to re-establish the priority of violent protest in the sestet. The logical structure of "First fight" is neither that of deduction nor of confutation; rather, its progression is from a hierarchy of imperatives, through a seeming lapse or digression (on ways of fiddling) which threatens to reverse the called-for sequence, to a reassertion of the original hierarchy. The sestet attempts to recuperate the values undermined by the seemingly irresistible impulse of the digression on fiddling. The poem's concluding couplet introduces the possibility that the prescribed sequence of events may preclude the very activity one fights to make possible. "Maybe" one will not be "too late," having postponed aesthetic creation until after the revolution.[4] The shift from imperative to infinitive mood reflects the poem's subtle undermining of its own command, whereby the "first" of line 13 is undercut by its belated position in the poem. The poem calls for action to precede poetry, but cannot undo its own testimony to the primacy of poetic discourse, the power of "fiddling." The poem plays its confusion on what "they wrote," not with the insipid windings of romantic violins nor the obliviousness amid turmoil of Nero's fiddling,[5] but with an aggressive revisionary music which fights *by* fiddling. While attempting to assign to poetry the status of decorative latecomer, beneficiary of but not instigator of change, the poem succeeds in civilizing its own space; it calls into question the necessity of "war" as advance guard for beauty, while establishing in the realm of "silks and honey" a place for "malice" and for "murdering." The poem speaks of violent appropriation in the measures and with the tropes of love, and in so doing commits an appropriation of its own at the level of language. While ostensibly privileging non-verbal action, the poem covertly draws to itself the power to act and authorize, demonstrating the impossibility of poetry's existing above, outside, or after politics.

The wrestle for priority played out in this sonnet makes itself further felt in the push and pull of syntax and line. The rhyme's strict muzzling within Petrarchan structure is "bewildered" by the sliding beneath it of enjambed lines and by the mid-line cessation of sentences. The rebellion advocated in the sonnet's opening and closing permeates the poem's relation to its own structure. Like a jazz riff, it undoes and redoes its own chosen model, stopping short where the line extends, racing past where the rhyme calls halt, and plying the stiffness of iambic pentameter with syntactical interruptions and occasional dactylic and spondaic intrusions. The poem honors the Italian sonnet's distinctive turn at line 9—"But first to arms"—while simultaneously reaping the epigrammatic effect of the English form's concluding couplet. Ironically, only line 11—"Be deaf to music and to beauty blind"—perfectly trims sentence structure to the length of the line, and adopts the sedate antithetical structure and inverted syntax of a more traditional "pretty" sonnet. This line may be said to parody the kind of obedient beauty to which the protest poem must be blind if it does not wish to wait for that "space" which the couplet so tentatively anticipates. The typically illusory quality of the couplet's resolution serves to cast doubt on the confident imperatives of the sestet's first four lines. This counterpointing of the sonnet's formal devices works to ironize from within both the poem's relation to literary tradition and to non-discursive action.

In a sonnet such as "First fight. Then fiddle," Brooks extends and complicates what must be seen as the already ironic adaptations of the political sonnet by earlier black poets. However, unlike that of the Harlem Renaissance sonneteers, Brooks's conception of the political extends to a critical rewriting of the sonnet's construction of gender and its ideology of romance.

The love sonnet has frequently presented itself as an object of exchange—a sonnet for a kiss, or more—between an implied speaker and an implied listener, characters in a framing drama who are constituted by their positions in the exchange. It is in part this dramatic context which lures readers into the illusion of the sonnet speaker's reality, his or her presence as a speaking consciousness. The Petrarchan sonnet has been described as "a modified lyric, speaking with the simple lyric's immediacy and poignancy, yet so serious and premeditated that it would set forth a total attitude to life" (Lever 3). This model of immediacy and foregrounding of the speaking "I" continues throughout the tradition of sonnets in English, along with the quality of premeditation which links a particular logical organization to a particular rhyme scheme. Anthony Easthope, in his discussion of Shakespeare's "Sonnet 73," claims that the force of this implied speaker is to create the illusion of presence, de-emphasizing the poem as language, and that this positioning of the speaking voice as transcendental ego, "simply *there* rather than constructed" (italics added), works to disclaim the poem's status as ideology. However, it is precisely the deceptive "presence" of this voice—the effect of which is to appear at once natural and pointedly artificial—which makes possible the radically de-centering effect produced by an unconventional speaker.

This centrality of the personal lyric voice which plays at being present within an actual dramatic situation renders the sonnet ripe for the kind of "personal" politics which concern Gwendolyn Brooks. She exploits the sonnet's traditional preoccupation with defining self and other in order to explore the politics of race and gender, wherein identity is conceived in terms of participation in an oppositional relationship. The primacy of the speaking "I" makes possible the redefinition of black womanhood through expropriation of the poem's voice, whereby that which has been subject to definition takes on the power to define. The woman, long subject to the sonnet's coercion and frequently conflated with the poem as a work of art, speaks, and in so doing upsets the balance of power within the conventional address by asserting a new self-definition.[6] Similarly, Brooks foregrounds issues of racial identity by using the lyric voice to redefine the identity of the individual in relation to a society whose restrictive definitions have denied him or her a voice. However, as Paul Fussell notes, it is traditional to think of social commentary and representations of social and ethical action as belonging to blank verse or the epic, while in the lyric we expect reflection and celebration (110). That is, we look for politics in one form and emotion in another, with generic bars separating the personal from the political. However, it is precisely Brooks's purpose to upset these expectations, to make powerfully evident the inseparability of the personal from the political and the revolution's imperative to shake even the tranquil throne of the reflective lyric bard. In this context it is worth noting that Brooks's only "epic" poem, "The Anniad," addresses themes very similar to those of her sonnets and ballads, and in her "leaves from a loose-leaf war diary" she "invents" the sonnet-ballad in an attempt to bring together the "high" and "low" traditions of personal lyric and popular folk ballad.[7] In Brooks's poetry, generic boundaries, along with sexual and racial ones, are targeted for transgression.

The Renaissance sonnet, with its construction of the female addressee as cruel demon or pure goddess, relies heavily on the languages of romantic love and religious worship. The sonnet defines woman as the one who is addressed, implored, admonished, but who does not and cannot respond with words of her own: lover is defined as (male) speaker, beloved as silent (female or feminized) listener. A telling exception to this pattern, which illustrates as well the conflation of romantic and religious rhetoric, is the sonnet spoken by Romeo and Juliet at their first meeting, the dialogic structure of which permits a rare instance of female response. The dramatic context of this sonnet emphasizes the appropriateness of the sonnet's insertion into a physical exchange (and calls to mind the love poem's importance as an object of exchange in Renaissance courtly intrigues). Romeo and Juliet exchange lines as they exchange kisses, with similar insatiability, and similar artifice—"You kiss by the book" (I.v.112). The sonnet is instigated by Romeo's "profanation" of Juliet's hand ("this holy shrine") and is a petition for absolution (a kiss) from her lips. Significantly, the woman's power to respond within the poem is counterbalanced here by a loss of power and mobility in the physical realm—Juliet may not be silent, but she is immobile, playing the role of statue in their exchange, and remaining "unmoved" while Romeo "takes" his "prayer's effect." But while Juliet's voice may trespass on the sonnet's ground, the rules of the game undergo more drastic revision when the poet/speaker, or petitioner, is marked as female. In "A Lovely Love," which may allude to the *Romeo and Juliet* sonnet via its parodic revision in the embedded sonnet of Eliot's *Waste Land*, Brooks ironically reverses the gender of speaker and listener along with the values of sacred and profane by way of making room for the "definitionless" within the sonnet's "strict atmosphere."

"A Lovely Love," like "First fight. Then fiddle," addresses its listener with an imperative, this time an appeal for resignation or acceptance:

> Let it be alleys. Let it be a hall
> Whose janitor javelins epithet and thought
> To cheapen hyacinth darkness that we sought
> And played we found, rot, make the petals fall.
> Let it be stairways, and a splintery box
> Where you have thrown me, scraped me with your kiss,
> Have honed me, have released me after this
> Cavern kindness, smiled away our shocks. (*The Bean Eaters* 49)

With an abruptness uncharacteristic of the sonnet, this speaker neither pauses to name nor eulogize her addressee. Rather, she issues an unadorned call for acceptance—perhaps even defiant choosing—of the unromantic, of conditions whose cheapness belies the imagined trappings of a "lovely" romance—hyacinths and darkness. The call is for a place befitting their rough-edged, "shock[ing]" love and the woman's voice echoes along the sonnet's tradition of idealized women with a stark, pragmatic invitation to make love under fire. This is "trespass sweetly urged" not only because the poet trespasses on the traditional ground of the male speaker, but because she legitimizes trespass as the only avenue open to the dispossessed. The lovers will love on public ground, in the narrows of "alleys," "hall[s]," and "stairways," in lieu of a place of their own, just as the poem appropriates the genteel sonnet and makes of it a "splintery box" for its very ungenteel "scraping" and "honing." Love's holiness is discarded along with its reticence and romance:

> That is the birthright of our lovely love
> In swaddling clothes. Not like that Other one.
> Not lit by any fondling star above.
> Not found by any wise men, either. Run.

> People are coming. They must not catch us here
> Definitionless in this strict atmosphere.

The love conceived of as holy and conceiving holy issue is rejected with disdain—"Not like that Other one." If one hears in this a response to the Harlem poets' frequent characterization of the black man as Christ, via the analogy between cross and lynching tree, then the speaker here must be seen as rejecting not only the idealized status of saint or virgin accorded to the sonnet ladies of the English Renaissance, but also the identity of Black Madonna and her role in giving birth to the universal victim. It is "People," not "wise men," who are likely to discover these lovers; the poem's final imperative to "Run" clarifies the clandestine nature of their occupancy, their tenuous status "here" in the public halls, and the public tradition of love sonnets within whose "strict atmosphere" they are "definition-less" because unprecedented. They and their "play[ing]" cannot be defined by traditional notions of courtly love or reverential worship; rather, it is the janitor's "epithets" which, by naming them as trespassers, define them.[8] Thus the poem, in part through the unconventionality of its speaker, both calls for and enacts a trespass and a redefinition.

The introduction of a feminine speaker into the sonnet disrupts our expectations not only because we are accustomed to the woman portrayed and/or implored in the sonnet, but because "woman" is one of a number of common tropes for the sonnet itself, at once the thing the poem creates and a figure for the poem: winning at love is a metaphor for winning at poetry. In addition, the sonnet has frequently presented itself as a tombstone or memorial which would impart immortality to a mortal woman by standing, as tombstones do, in place of her and speaking for her.[9] As a memorial, the sonnet promises life to its addressee—she will live while the poem lives—while at the same time ominously hinting that the sonnet is a sort of female burial ground. The woman engraved on the sonnet's tablet is also entombed by it—silenced, immobilized, confined through definition and inscription. The woman's voice, when it finally appropriates the sonnet, is thus also a posthumous voice speaking after long burial, accusatorially haunting the sonnet's ground.

Whereas in "A Lovely Love" the woman's idealized status is undone by her self-articulated desire, in "the rites for Cousin Vit" Brooks presents a woman, dead and decorative, exploding from the confines of her coffin as she shatters the mold of the sonnet's still, silent lady.

> Carried her unprotesting out the door.
> Kicked back the casket-stand. But it can't hold her,
> That stuff and satin aiming to enfold her,
> The lid's contrition nor the bolts before.
> Oh oh. Too much. Too much. Even now, surmise,
> She rises in the sunshine. There she goes,
> Back to the bars she knew and the repose
> In love-rooms and the things in people's eyes.
> Too vital and too squeaking. Must emerge.
> Even now she does the snake-hips with a hiss,

> Slops the bad wine across her shantung, talks
> Of pregnancy, guitars and bridgework, walks
> In parks or alleys, comes haply on the verge
> Of happiness, haply hysterics. Is. (*Annie Allen* 45)

Like a number of Brooks's poems, this one begins in the middle of an action and proceeds with the rushing momentum produced by sentence fragments, omitted agents, and thick alliteration. The first line presents us with woman as object: acted upon, but "unprotesting," she is "carried . . . out the door." Yet Vit's lack of protest is no submission; she enacts, rather than articulates, her refusal of the death prepared for her, a process which seems to comment on the poem's own formal and linguistic enactment of a protest which it does not explicitly state. The poem's argument, like Vit's rising, is "a concealed assertion of identity," a covert yet "public gesture" (Bigsby 257), reconstructing the sonnet speaker's relation to the woman as object of contemplation and to the sonnet's implied audience. The poem's title, with its bringing together of a woman whose name signifies life ("Vit") and "rites," or rituals formal and artificial, supposedly "for" her, prepares us for the inevitable "but" of line 2. "But it can't hold her, / That stuff and satin aiming to enfold her / The lid's contrition nor the bolts before." Speaker and audience share in a revisioning of the woman posed within and imposed upon by the sonnet, a woman who is herself vitality, energy, excess: "Too much. Too much. / Too vital and too squeaking."

The poem's description is repeatedly fractured by referential markers— "Oh oh," "Too much," "Even now, surmise," "There she goes," "Even now" —which point to evidence just outside our range, conjuring up a dramatic context in which the poem's subject is felt to live.[10] To be moved by these effects to envision Vit as an actor in this drama is to participate in the fiction of the woman's escape from death, and hence to imagine as well a challenge to the deathliness of the feminine subject engraved in the sonnet tradition. The sonnet's coffin, its tradition of entombed women, proves too narrow to contain Vit's vitality—she refuses to be stilled by the sonnet's decorum. "Saints move not," but Vit certainly does, as the speaker's dramatic elegy moves us towards a new perception of the sonnet lady.

The bolts and satin of the box, the combined rigidity and fluidity of the sonnet's frame, seem not so much to "enfold" Vit as to be enfolded by her, wound round by the coils of this snakey dancer and the winding lines which chronicle her movements. Her proper place is not within the propriety and formality of the bolted box, but in the "bars," "parks," and "alleys," and in that other "repose / In love-rooms." She "rises," she "emerges," she dances "the snake-hips with a hiss," she "talks," "hysterics," and, finally, "Is." Coming "haply on the verge / Of happiness," she finds pleasure by chance or risk, her being defined by the link between energy, transgression, and femaleness: the "hiss" of line 10, calling up the extravagant insinuations of Eden's serpent, is echoed in the "hiss" of "hysteria" and the poem's conclusion on "Is"—she "is" feminine rebellion. The poem's project is the creation, or recreation, of the woman, her resurrection, like that of some parodic Christ more snakily subversive than holy, from confined and beatified object to the incarnation of being as energy: the poem's "surmise" is simply—boldly—that she "Is."

While "the rites for Cousin Vit" is predominantly dramatic rather than argumentative, what it asserts is a new definition of woman; one "surmises" that "She rises" because she "must," and that the poem is responsible for resurrecting her from her moribund state into the realm of "Is." The poem reverses the progress of seduction by dramatizing the woman's movement from passivity to self-assertion, her transcendence of those confining "rites" supposedly performed in her honor. Here, as elsewhere, Brooks uses the image of a box or coffin as a figure for the sonnet itself, calling attention to the power of poetic rites to define, legitimize, or exclude. In "Vit," as in "A Lovely Love," the sonnet-coffin is refigured as an alley, a narrow defile bursting with disorderly conduct, a place which bad women may call their own.

The sonnet's traditional figures for itself imply smallness, self-containment, tension, restriction, and permanence. Samuel Daniel saw the sonnet as an "ark" and a "trophy," a monument, as are many of Shakespeare's sonnets, to the beloved, which will enshrine her for posterity. For Shakespeare, the sonnet conceived of as progeny was also a stay against time, and for Dante Gabriel Rossetti it was a "moment's monument,— / Memorial from the Soul's eternity / To one dead deathless hour," or it was a coin to be paid to death (74). For Keats, the sonnet was Andromeda chained or "garland[ed]" (222–23). Brooks's revisionary project includes troping these traditional tropes for the sonnet, a refiguration which at once redefines the black woman's relation to society and the relation of her poetry to white and male traditions by focusing on the sonnet as an enclosure which can either imprison or shut out. Traditional tropes of confinement are revised by Brooks in order to dramatize the poet's choice between alternative forms of restriction. Getting *out* of the box marked "black"—as in her sonnet entitled "The white troops had their orders but the Negroes looked like men"—can mean getting *into* the box marked "tradition," or "sonnet," inclusion providing solace for the weight of too much exclusion. Elsewhere, Brooks variously figures the sonnet as "proper stone" to be graven, "little jars and cabinets of [the] will," a dead body's "prescribed pose," a "gorgeous Nothingness," a "narrow room,"[11] or a "splintery box." Through all of these figures runs the paradox of the confinement which frees, of the deathly form chosen in an act of self-assertion, as well as the recurring image of containers whose contents explode or simply slip away. Brooks manipulates the image of the sonnet as confined and structured so as to highlight the paradoxical nature of those forms and rituals (poetry, war, funerals) which both define, immortalize, and kill. Her sonnets depict an ongoing struggle between the shapeless vitality of (black) life and the desire for and fear of beautiful and lifeless forms. As is common in the literature of oppression, death itself acquires an ambiguous status in Brooks's poetry—it is both threat and laurel, a victory won in an uneven battle and an act of self-acknowledgment. Likewise, the boxing of vitality essential to the achievement of form is seen as both a sacrifice and a process of self-creation and self-definition.

In "What shall I give my children? Who are poor," a mother responds to her "unfinished," "contraband" children's plea for "a brisk contour" with a complaint which seems to conflate poetry with epitaph by identifying the poet with the stonecutter: "My hand is stuffed with mode, design, device. / But I lack access to my proper stone" (*Annie Allen* 36). Though the children are unfinished because "graven by a hand / Less than angelic, admirable or sure," the poem suggests that their inclusion within the brisk contours of poetry might be likely to "finish" them in both senses of the word. Likewise, the children of "When my dears die," whose "motion" and "repartee" are "enchanted" into "tightness" and "politeness" by their "crisp encounter" with death, seem almost to have been transformed into art through the rigors of poetic diction and form. Yet they are said to discover in the strange terrain of the sonnet-epitaph an all too familiar chill:

> I say they may, so granitely discreet,
> The little crooked questionings inbound,
> Concede themselves on most familiar ground,
> Cold an old predicament of the breath. (*Annie Allen* 39)

Hence, the sonnet as cold prison or tomb, or as knot of unanswerable questions, proves ironically suitable to these "contraband" occupants. Similarly, when in "the white troops had their orders" racial categories prove less than watertight, it is uncertain whether such a breakdown of boundaries represents a gain.

> Such as boxed
> Their feelings properly, complete to tags—
> A box for dark men and a box for Other—
> Would often find the contents had been scrambled.
> Or even switched. (*Street* 52)

What kinds of boxes are these, these containers so baffled by their contents? While it is, ostensibly, feelings which are "boxed," these lines powerfully suggest that it is the Negroes and their white comrades who, as corpses, are "boxed" in coffins, "tags" attached to their toes, the switching and commingling the result of the kind of grotesque bodily distortions and dismemberments which might allow for such confusion. If so, then the black soldiers' inclusion amounts to admission into a macabre fraternity of death (what Brooks elsewhere calls "the university of death" [*Annie Allen* 39]). In that case, the indifference of the cosmos ("Neither the earth nor heaven ever trembled. / And there was nothing startling in the weather") seems directed less at the violation of racial boundaries than at the leveling effects of war. A deadly irony therefore colors this image of breaking in, as it does similar images of switching and crossing in so many of Brooks's poems. Thus, in her association of the strictures of poetic form with death—of the sonnet with coffin or box—as well as with legitimating "contours" and insinuating chords, Brooks expresses simultaneously the attractions and the dangers of inclusion within a hostile poetic tradition.

In her revision of English Renaissance conventions, Brooks succeeds in making of the sonnet a vehicle for her own form of complaint, a poetry of power trespassing on the restricted ground of the traditionally male, and white, sonnet. In her extension of the Harlem Renaissance's political concerns to include the construction of gender and the politics of form, she insists on the ideological nature of both the subject and its language. While petitioning for power in the world, Brooks acts out this appropriation at the level of the poem. By forcing the sonnet's shackled and corseted form to embody questions of race and gender, she forces us to recognize the ideological power of form itself, as well as the subversions which that same power makes possible.

NOTES

[1]Although we tend to associate the Renaissance sonnet with its pre-eminent male practitioners (and Brooks certainly does), there were early women sonneteers as well: Mary Wroth, Catherine de Roches and Louise Labé to name a few. For a discussion of these and other Renaissance women poets, see Jones. Jones sees these women poets as engaged in "negotiation" of "dominant cultural forms," one aspect of which is the adoption of "an oppositional position from which the ideological message and force of the reigning code is rearticulated, that is, pulled out of its dominant frame of reference and subversively inserted into an 'alternative frame of reference'" such that "[t]he code is maintained but its benefits are reassigned to a nonhegemonic group" (5–6). This process of "negotiation" resembles what I am calling Brooks's "appropriative practice." For discussions of the sonnet's gender associations and two modern women poets' negotiations of them, see Fried and Mermin.

[2]On this kind of mimicry in the sonnet, see Fussell, 116.

[3]Locke notes this shift in address: "Where formerly they [Negro poets] spoke to others and tried to interpret, they now speak to their own and try to express" (48). Gates, however, emphasizes that black-authored texts always presuppose two audiences, a white and a black, regardless of the explicit addressee. This accounts for a quality of doubleness in the poetic address, and, of course, complicates the model of the complaint. Brooks's choice of the sonnet form, even when the implied addressee is black, may be seen as acknowledging the presence of an educated white audience; hence, the sonnets addressed to black auditors still function, at some level, within the paradigmatic power relations of the complaint.

[4]One could certainly read "First fight," written in 1946, with reference to World War II. However, this would not substantially alter the thrust of my reading. Treatment of the world wars within Afro-American literature in general, and Brooks's poetry in particular, works predominantly to highlight the hypocrisies of American democracy or, in Bigsby's words, "the disjunction between the ideals for which black men fought and the realities which had determined their lives" (274). Wartime disruptions of racial codes are frequently treated by black writers as harbingers of more violent domestic disruptions yet to come. Hence the "war" of "First fight," whether one sees its primary referent as international conflict or domestic riot, demands to be read in the context of racial struggle.

[5]I am indebted to Debra Fried for suggesting this image in connection with "First fight," as well as for numerous other suggestions in response to earlier versions of this essay.

[6]Brooks is not, of course, the first black woman to write sonnets, nor the first to address within the sonnet the subject of racial oppression. See in particular Henrietta Cordelia Ray's "To My Father" and "Robert G. Shaw" (1910), two anti-slavery protests in the form of sonnet elegies, and Frances E.W. Harper's "She's Free" (1854), which invites comparison with Brooks's "the rites for Cousin Vit." Rosalie Jones's "Brother Baptis' on Woman Suffrage" (1912) is notable not only for its explicit yoking of racial and sexual oppression, but for the way in which it both invokes and refuses the sonnet's form: the poem has fourteen lines, but is written in couplets and in distinctly non-iambic dialect. All of these poems can be found in Stetson, ed.

[7] Of the sonnet-ballad Brooks says, "Its one claim to fame is that I invented it" (*Report* 186).

[8] One is tempted to detect in this javelin-wielding janitor not only a resemblance to Cupid with his arrows, but also a sly allusion to those custodians of the sonnet tradition—Petrarch, Shakespeare, Donne, and co.

[9] On the eternizing conceit in the sonnet, see Lever (151, 155, 246–72) and John, 126–34.

[10] On the role of such deictics in the production of poetic persona in the lyric, see Culler, 164–70.

[11] Brooks's sonnet entitled "the birth in a narrow room" (*Annie Allen*) invites being read as a revision of Wordsworth's "Nuns Fret Not at Their Convent's Narrow Room" (199). The girl in Brooks's poem frets a good deal at her confinement.

WORKS CITED

Bigsby, C.W.E. "The Black Poet as Cultural Sign" in *The Second Black Renaissance: Essays in Black Literature*. London: Greenwood P, 1980.

Brooks, Gwendolyn. *Annie Allen*. New York: Harper & Brothers, 1949.

———. *The Bean Eaters*. New York: Harper & Brothers, 1950.

———. *Report From Part One*. Detroit: Broadside P, 1972.

———. *A Street in Bronzeville*. New York and London: Harper & Brothers, 1945.

Cullen, Countee, ed. *Caroling Dusk*. New York: Harper & Brothers, 1927.

Culler, Jonathan. *Structuralist Poetics: Structuralism, Linguistics, and the Study of Literature*. Ithaca: Cornell UP, 1975.

Daniel, Samuel. "Sonnet 46" from "Delia." *Delia*. 1592; Menston, Eng.: Scholar P, 1969.

Easthope, Antony. *Poetry as Discourse*. London: Methuen, 1983.

Ellison, Ralph. "The World and the Jug" in *Shadow and Act*. 1953; New York: Random House, 1964.

Ferry, Anne. *The "Inward" Language*. Chicago: U of Chicago P, 1983.

Fried, Debra. "Andromeda Unbound: Adroit Designs in Millay's Sonnets." *Twentieth Century Literature* 32.1 (1986).

Fussell, Paul. *Poetic Meter and Poetic Form*. New York: Random House, 1979.

Gates, Henry Louis, Jr. "Criticism in the Jungle" in *Black Literature and Literary Theory*. Ed. Henry Louis Gates, Jr. New York: Methuen, 1984.

John, Lisle Cecil. "The 'Eternalizing' Conceit" in *The Elizabethan Sonnet Sequences: Studies in Conventional Conceits*. New York: Columbia UP, 1938; New York: Russell and Russell, 1964.

Jones, Ann Rosalind. *The Currency of Eros: Women's Love Lyric in Europe, 1540–1620*. Bloomington: Indiana UP, 1990.

Keats, John. "On the Sonnet" in *The Poetical Works and Other Writings* 4. Ed. H. Buxton Forman. New York: Phaeton P, 1970.

Lever, J. W. *The Elizabethan Love Sonnet*. London: Methuen, 1974.

Locke, Alain Le Roy. "Negro Youth Speaks" in *The New Negro*. Ed. Alain Le Roy Locke. New York: Albert and Charles Boni, 1925.

Matthews, G. M. "Sex and the Sonnet." *Essays in Criticism* 2.2 (1952).

McKay, Claude. *Selected Poems*. Intro. John Dewey. Biographical note Max Eastman. New York: Bookman Associates, 1973.

Mermin, Dorothy. "The Female Poet and the Embarrassed Reader: Elizabeth Barrett Browning's *Sonnets From the Portuguese*." *ELH* 48.2 (1981): 351–67.

Nye, Robert. Intro. *A Book of Sonnets*. New York: Oxford UP, 1976.

Rossetti, D. G. "A Sonnet" from "The House of Life" in *The Works of Dante Gabriel Rossetti*. Ed., pref. and notes William M. Rossetti. London: Hazel Watson and Viney, 1911.

Shakespeare, William. *Romeo and Juliet. The Complete Signet Classic Shakespeare*. Ed. Sylvan Barnet. New York: Harcourt Brace Jovanovich, 1972.

Stetson, Erlene, ed. *Black Sister: Poetry by Black American Women, 1746–1980*. Bloomington: Indiana UP, 1981.
Wordsworth, William. *Poetical Works*. Ed. Thomas Hutchinson, rev. Ernest De Selincourt. 1904; London: Oxford UP, 1974.

AFTERWORD

"'A Splintery Box'" began as an essay for a graduate seminar on the forms of poetry taught by Debra Fried at Cornell and later evolved into a dissertation chapter. On rereading it, I can see just how much Fried's extraordinary work on women's sonnets (as well as that of Dorothy Mermin, another of my teachers) influenced my approach to Brooks. My interest in Brooks, and in African American poetry generally, was cultivated in relative isolation, however. At the time, no one was teaching African American literature courses at Cornell, and much of the groundbreaking work being published in the field focused on fiction rather than poetry. What criticism there was of Brooks's poetry tended to downplay gender issues in the interests of assessing her racial politics, particularly the influence on her post-1960 work of significant male figures from the Black Arts Movement. The critical consensus seemed to be that Brooks had written "white" before her involvement in the movement and "black" after. Yet that characterization of her career felt inadequate, in part because it was the earlier works (formal, allusive, aesthetically complex) that focused predominantly on black women's lives rather than on public events and male heroes of the black community. Moreover, the early works were stunning poetic performances— complex, rhetorically sophisticated, powerfully ironic in their adaptations of lyric conventions and modernist stylistic innovations. In researching and writing the essay, I hoped to find a better way to understand the poetry's interplay of race and rhetoric, form and politics, gender and aesthetics, and to propose Brooks's use of the sonnet as something more complex than mere imitation of a white form.

Of course, there were many African American feminist critics breaking open the field of black women's writing at the time that I began working on Brooks (around 1984), and I absorbed with great interest the work of Barbara Christian, Hortense Spillers, Toni Cade Bambara, Mary Helen Washington, and others. As I reread my essay now, I am struck by its intense formalism and its rootedness in English literary history. At a later moment in my career, I might have emphasized more Brooks's relation to the wide spectrum of African American writing in addition to European traditions. Though the influence of contemporary feminist and African American criticism is rather muted in the essay itself, it is obvious that without the work of the many critics who were, in the early 1980s, helping to move discussion of women's poetry beyond the personal and biographical onto rhetorical, formal, and historical ground and the exciting work emerging at the same time around African American writing generally, my essay would never have come together as it did.

The sonnets I discuss here are ones that I continue to teach frequently and read with great pleasure. They have the same electric effect on students that they had on me almost twenty years ago. "'A Splintery Box'" was a passionate project for me: it grew out of a long-standing love for Brooks's poetry (and a general fascination with sonnets) combined with indignation that Brooks was so little known among white readers and so undervalued among black critics. I'm happy to say that in the past twenty years, the attention to Brooks's work has grown immensely, and the approaches to it have multiplied fruitfully; Brooks is now widely acknowledged as a major American—and feminist—poet.

The Sultan and the Slave: Feminist Orientalism and the Structure of *Jane Eyre*

Joyce Zonana

I proposed to myself to display the folly of those who use authority to bring a woman to reason; and I chose for an example a sultan and his slave, as being two extremes of power and dependence.

—Jean François Marmontel

ON THE DAY following Jane Eyre's betrothal to her "master" Rochester, Jane finds herself "obliged" to go with him to a silk warehouse at Millcote, where she is "ordered to choose half a dozen dresses." Although she makes it clear that she "hated the business," Jane cannot free herself from it. All she can manage, "by dint of entreaties expressed in energetic whispers," is a reduction in the number of dresses, though "these . . . [Rochester] vowed he would select himself." Anxiously, Jane protests and "with infinite difficulty" secures Rochester's grudging acceptance of her choice: a "sober black satin and pearl-gray silk." The ordeal is not over; after the silk warehouse, Rochester takes Jane to a jeweller's, where "the more he bought me," she reports, "the more my cheek burned with a sense of annoyance and degradation" (Brontë [1847] 1985, 296–97).[1]

The shopping trip to Millcote gently figures Rochester as a domestic despot: he commands and Jane is "obliged" to obey, though she feels degraded by that obedience. At this point in the narrative, Jane is not yet aware that in planning to marry her Rochester is consciously choosing to become a bigamist. Yet the image she uses to portray her experience of his mastery as he tries to dress her "like a doll" (297) signals that not only despotism but bigamy and the oriental trade in women are on Jane's mind. Riding with Rochester back to Thornfield, she notes: "He smiled; and I thought his smile was such as a sultan might, in a blissful and fond moment, bestow on a slave his gold and gems had enriched" (297). The image is startling in its extremity: surely Jane seems to overreact to Rochester's desire to see his bride beautifully dressed.

Yet by calling Rochester a "sultan" and herself a "slave," Jane provides herself and the reader with a culturally acceptable simile by which to understand and combat the patriarchal "despotism" (302) central to Rochester's character. Part of a large system of what I term feminist orientalist discourse that permeates *Jane Eyre*, Charlotte Brontë's sultan/slave simile displaces the source of patriarchal oppression onto an "Oriental," "Mahometan" society, enabling British readers to contemplate local problems without questioning their own self-definition as Westerners and Christians.[2] As I will demonstrate, in developing her simile throughout her narrative, Jane does not so much criticize (in the words of Mary Ellis Gibson) "domestic arrangements and British Christianity from the point of view of the 'pagan' woman" (1987, 2) as define herself as a Western missionary seeking to redeem not the "enslaved" woman outside the fold of Christianity and Western ideology but the despotic man who has been led astray within it.[3]

Brontë's use of feminist orientalism is both embedded in and brings into focus a long tradition of Western feminist writing. Beginning early in the eighteenth century, when European travelers' tales about visits to the Middle East became a popular genre, images of despotic sultans and desperate slave girls became a central part of an emerging liberal feminist discourse about the condition of women not in the East but in the West. From Mary Wollstonecraft to Elizabeth Barrett Browning to Margaret Fuller and Florence Nightingale, one discovers writer after writer turning to images of oriental life—and specifically the "Mahometan" or "Arabian" harem—in order to articulate their critiques of the life of women in the West. Part of the larger orientalism that Edward Said has shown to inform Western self-representation, the function of these images is not primarily to secure Western domination over the East, though certainly they assume and enforce that domination.[4] Rather, by figuring objectionable aspects of life in the West as "Eastern," these Western feminist writers rhetorically define their project as the removal of Eastern elements from Western life.

Feminist orientalism is a special case of the literary strategy of using the Orient as a means for what one writer has called Western "self-redemption": "transforming the Orient and Oriental Muslims into a vehicle for . . . criticism of the West itself" (Al-Bazei 1983, 6).[5] Specifically, feminist orientalism is a rhetorical strategy (and a form of thought) by which a speaker or writer neutralizes the threat inherent in feminist demands and makes them palatable to an audience that wishes to affirm its occidental superiority. If the lives of women in England or France or the United States can be compared to the lives of women in "Arabia," then the Western feminist's desire to change the status quo can be represented not as a radical attempt to restructure the West but as a conservative effort to make the West more like itself. Orientalism—the belief that the East is inferior to the West, and the representation of the Orient by means of unexamined, stereotypical images—thus becomes a major premise in the formulation of numerous Western feminist arguments.

The conviction that the harem is an inherently oppressive institution functions as an a priori assumption in the writing I examine here. Even in the twentieth century, such an assumption continues to appear in Western feminist discourse, as Leila Ahmed (1982) and Chandra Mohanty (1988) demonstrate. Actual research on or observation of the conditions of the harem is rare, and what little that has been written tends toward either defensive celebration or violent condemnation. The defenses are written with an awareness of the condemnations: their authors must challenge the Western feminist imagination that unquestioningly perceives polygamy as sexual slavery and domestic confinement as imprisonment.[6] The attempt to introduce a genuinely alternate vision is fraught with the difficulties both of documenting the actualities of life in the harem and of achieving a transcultural perspective, though some writers have made the effort.[7]

This article does not claim to demonstrate any truth about the harem that would definitively contradict or even modify the Western views presented here, nor does it systematically engage in the effort to achieve an objective estimate of the harem; rather, it seeks only to show how assumptions about the East have been used to further the Western feminist project instead of either spurring research and theorizing about the actual conditions of harem life or establishing genuine alliances among women of different cultures. For what is most crucial about what I am calling feminist orientalism is that it is directed not toward the understanding or even the reform of the harem itself but toward transformation of Western society—even while preserving basic institutions and ideologies of the West. Coming to recognize the feminist orientalism in *Jane Eyre* and other formative Western feminist texts may help clear the way for a more self-critical, balanced analysis of the multiple forms both of patriarchy and of women's power, and it may also, indirectly, help free global feminism from the charge that it is a Western movement inapplicable to Eastern societies.[8]

That *Jane Eyre*, like so many nineteenth-century British texts, has a diffusely orientalist background has long been recognized and for the most part attributed to the influence of the *Arabian Nights*, a book known to have been a staple of the Brontës' childhood reading.[9] The first simile in the novel, in the fourth paragraph of the first chapter, places Jane, "cross-legged, like a Turk" (39) in the window seat of the Gateshead breakfast room. Not much later, Jane takes down a book of "Arabian tales" (70); she reveals that she is fascinated by "genii" (82); and eventually she makes it plain that the *Arabian Nights* was one of her three favorite childhood books (256). Other characters in the novel also display a loose familiarity and fascination with the Orient: the Dowager Lady Ingram dresses in a "crimson velvet robe, and a shawl turban" (201); her daughter Blanche admits that she "dote[s] on Corsairs" (208); Rochester worries when Jane assumes a "sphinx-like expression" (329).

The specifically feminist quality of *Jane Eyre's* orientalism, however, has not been recognized, perhaps because feminist orientalism has remained until recently an opaque, underexamined aspect of Western intellectual history. (Ahmed 1982, Spivak 1985, Mohanty 1988, and Perera 1991 are important exceptions.) The feminist orientalism of *Jane Eyre*, furthermore, is only made explicit in the sultan/ slave simile, and, although the chords struck in this passage resonate throughout the entire novel, they cannot properly be heard without an understanding of the full eighteenth- and nineteenth-century background that generates them. Before turning to that background, however, it may be helpful briefly to set in relief this key episode in which Jane not only compares Rochester to a sultan but engages with him in an extended discussion of women's rights and uses her comparison of him to a sultan as a means by which to secure more rights for herself.

Among the more interesting features of this passage is the fact that Jane does not tell Rochester that she is mentally comparing him to a sultan. She simply asks him to stop looking at her "in that way." Rochester is astute enough to understand Jane's unspoken reference, suggesting that feminist orientalist discourse is so pervasive as to be accessible to the very men it seeks to change: "'Oh, it is rich to see and hear her!' he exclaimed. 'Is she original? Is she piquant? I would not exchange this one little English girl for the Grand Turk's whole seraglio—gazelle-eyes, houri forms, and all!'"(297). Rochester suggests that he will take Jane instead of a harem, though Jane bristles at the "Eastern allusion": "'I'll not stand you an inch in the stead of a seraglio,' I said; 'so don't consider me an equivalent for one. If you have a fancy for anything in that line, away with you, sir, to the bazaars of Stamboul, without delay, and lay out in extensive slave-purchases some of that spare cash you seem at a loss to spend satisfactorily here'"(297).

When Rochester jokingly asks what Jane will do while he is "bargaining for so many tons of flesh and such an assortment of black eyes," Jane is ready with a playful but serious response: "I'll be preparing myself to go out as a missionary to preach liberty to them that are enslaved—your harem inmates among the rest. I'll get admitted there, and I'll stir up mutiny; and you, three-tailed bashaw as you are, sir, shall in a trice find yourself fettered amongst our hands: nor will I, for one, consent to cut your bonds till you have signed a charter, the most liberal that despot ever yet conferred!" (297–98). Although Jane promises Rochester that she will "go out as a missionary" to "Stamboul," the focus of her remarks is the reform of Rochester himself within England. Her concern is that she herself not be treated as a "harem inmate," and her action, immediately following this conversation, succeeds in accomplishing her goal.

It is precisely Jane's experience of degrading dependency, playfully figured here as the relation of rebellious harem slave to despotic Eastern sultan, that leads her to take the step that ultimately reveals Rochester as more like a sultan than Jane had imagined. For it is at this point that Jane makes and executes the decision to write to her Uncle John in Madeira, in the hope that he will settle some money on her. "If I had ever so small an independency," she reasons, "if I had but a prospect of one day bringing Mr. Rochester an accession of fortune, I could better endure to be kept by him now" (297). Jane's letter to John Eyre alerts Rochester's brother-in-law, Richard Mason, to Rochester's plans to become a bigamist, and Jane is freed from a marriage that would, in her own terms, have thoroughly enslaved her.

Jane's comparison of Rochester to a sultan proves to be no exaggeration. The narrative makes plain that it is because she sees him in this way that she later is able to free herself from a degrading relationship with a man who has bought women, is willing to become a bigamist, and acts like a despot. The plot thus validates the figurative language, making of it much more than a figure. This Western man is "Eastern" in his ways, and for Jane to be happy, he must be thoroughly Westernized. To the extent that Brontë has Jane Eyre present hers as a model life—"Reader, I married him"—she suggests that her female readers would also be well advised to identify and eliminate any such Eastern elements in their own spouses and suitors.

More than ten years ago, Peter A. Tasch observed that in having Jane call Rochester a "three-tailed bashaw," Brontë "was echoing the refrain in a song by George Colman the Younger for his extravaganza *Blue Beard.*" Tasch further notes that "the idea of an English girl in the 'grand Turk's' seraglio demanding liberty forms the theme of another stage comedy, [Isaac Bickerstaffe's] *The Sultan; or, A Peep into the Seraglio*" (1982, 232). Tasch may well be correct in identifying these specific sources for Brontë's allusions; yet the image of a harem inmate demanding liberty had by 1847 become so ingrained in Western feminist discourse that Brontë need not have had any specific text in mind; her audience, whether familiar with *Blue Beard* and *The Sultan* or not, would have had a full stock of harem images by which to understand and applaud Jane's sultan/slave simile.

The stage was set for the Western use of the harem as a metaphor for aspects of Western life as early as 1721, in Baron de Montesquieu's *Persian Letters*. The letters in Montesquieu's novel, written primarily by two "Persian" men traveling in Europe, offer dramatic images of both Eastern and Western ways of structuring domestic and political relations. Usbek and Rica, the travelers who report on the oddities of Western ways, are in constant contact with the women and eunuchs they have left behind in the harem. The Western reader moves between defamiliarized visions of Europe and "familiar" images of Persia, eventually coming to see, in the words of one modern commentator, that in the seraglio, constructed as the heart of oriental despotism, "It is myself, and our world, finally, that I rediscover" (Grosrichard 1979, 32–33, translation mine; for further commentary on the self-reflexive function of Western representations of the harem, see Richon 1984 and Alloula 1986).

Montesquieu's work focuses primarily on the nature of political despotism, using images of the Eastern and Western domestic enslavement of women as metaphors for the political enslavement of men. The condition of women is not Montesquieu's central concern, but because the harem is his functional model of despotism, the novel repeatedly returns to the question of "whether it is better to deprive women of their liberty or to leave them free" (Montesquieu [1721] 1923, 107) and draws recurrent analogies between the status of women in the East and the West. In its closing pages, *Persian Letters* portrays a full-scale rebellion in the seraglio: in the absence of their masters, the women have taken new lovers and sought to undo the system of surveillance that has kept them imprisoned.

As Katie Trumpener notes, "the last—and perhaps most powerful—voice in the book is Roxanna's" (1987, 185), the voice of a formerly enslaved harem inmate who willingly accepts her death as the price of her freedom: "How could you think that I was such a weakling as to imagine there was nothing for me in the world but to worship your caprices; that while you indulged all your desires, you should have the right to thwart me in all mine? No: I have lived in slavery, and yet always retained my freedom: I have remodeled your laws upon those of nature; and my mind has always maintained its independence" (350). Although Montesquieu may have had other applications in mind, the voice of his rebellious

Roxanna came to be the voice adopted by later writers seeking to expose the oppression of women.

Thus, as Pauline Kra has shown, after Montesquieu French literature of the
eighteenth century regularly used the "harem theme" to "demonstrate the subordinate status of women" in the West (1979, 274). Martha Conant notes that
Jean François Marmontel's 1761 popular Moral Tale, "Soliman II," features the
conquest of a sultan by a "pretty European slave, Roxalana," who appears to echo
Montesquieu's heroine. Roxalana's heart was "nourished in the bosom of liberty,"
and her expostulations "against the restraints of the seraglio" succeed in converting the sultan (1908, 205–7). In English literature as well the harem came to function as a metaphor for the Western oppression of women. Samuel Johnson's 1759
Rasselas includes an exposé of the oppressiveness of the harem and a defense of
women's rights to intellectual development;[10] the heroine of the 1775 play Tasch
identifies as a source of *Jane Eyre* (and which Conant traces to Marmontel) is
named "Roxalana"; and Defoe's feminist heroine of *The Fortunate Mistress* calls
herself "Roxanna" (Trumpener 1987, 187–88). The name of Montesquieu's rebellious harem inmate seems to have been so consistently associated with the demand
for female rights that when Mary Wollstonecraft has a character in *Maria or the
Wrongs of Woman* seek liberation from an oppressive husband, the man responds
by invoking her literary model: "Very pretty, upon my soul! very pretty, theatrical
flourishes! Pray, fair Roxana, stoop from your altitudes and remember that you
are acting a part in real life" ([1798] 1975, 116).

To the extent that Montesquieu demonstrates for Western readers that the oriental institution of the seraglio can shed light on Western practices, one can say
that his text inaugurates feminist orientalist discourse. But it is in Wollstonecraft's
1792 *Vindication of the Rights of Woman*, the founding text of Western liberal
feminism, that one finds the fullest explicit feminist orientalist perspective. Like
many of the enlightenment thinkers on whom she drew—including, of course,
Montesquieu—Wollstonecraft uncritically associates the East with despotism
and tyranny. Her text is replete with images that link any abuse of power with
"Eastern" ways: she is not above likening women who seek to dominate their
husbands with "Turkish bashaws" ([1792] 1982, 125). Yet she reserves her fullest
scorn for the gendered despotism that she sees as a defining feature of Eastern life
and a perverse corruption of Western values.

Any aspect of the European treatment of women that Wollstonecraft finds objectionable she labels as Eastern. Thus, she finds that European women's "limbs
and faculties" are "cramped with worse than Chinese bands" (Wollstonecraft
[1792] 1982, 128); Western women are educated in "worse than Egyptian bondage" (221); their masters are "worse than Egyptian task-masters" (319). Upper-
class women, "dissolved in luxury," have become weak and depraved "like the
Sybarites" (130); if women do not "grow more perfect when emancipated,"
Wollstonecraft advises that Europe should "open a fresh trade with Russia for
whips" (319).

Yet it is "Mahometanism"—and the "Mahometan" institution of the seraglio
or harem—that Wollstonecraft singles out as the grand type for all oppression of
women. Any Western writer who treats women "as a kind of subordinate beings,

and not as a part of the human species" is accused of writing "in the true style of Mahometanism" ([1792] 1982, 80). This is because what she believes about "Mahometanism" embodies for Wollstonecraft the antithesis of her own central claim: that women, like men, have souls. Although Ahmed asserts that she can find "no record . . . in the body of orthodox Muslim literature of the notion that women are animals or have no souls," she notes that views such as Wollstonecraft's are a staple of Western writing about Islam (1982, 526). Ahmed attributes the creation of this purported fact about Islamic culture to the same Western men who have insisted on the "inferiority of Western women" (523). Yet in *Vindication of the Rights of Woman*, a founder of modern feminism reproduces and intensifies the spurious "fact" about "Mahometanism," indeed, using it as a cornerstone of her argument for women's rights in the West.

A peculiarity of language may have led to or enforced Wollstonecraft's conviction that Muslims believe that women do not have souls. The *Oxford English Dictionary* (*OED*) notes that the Italian word *seraglio*, meaning "place of confinement," was used to render the Turkish *serai*, "lodging" or "palace." N. M. Penzer also observes that "the modern *seraglio* is directly derived from the Italian *serraglio*, 'a cage for wild animals,'" while the original Persian words, *sara* and *sarai*, meant simply "building" or "palace" (1936, 16). As late as the seventeenth century in England one finds *seraglio* used to refer to "a place where wild beasts are kept" *(OED)* as well as to the private apartments of women. Thus, when Wollstonecraft speaks of women being reduced to "mere animals" who are "only fit for a seraglio" (83), she invokes both meanings of *seraglio* and may have thought herself well justified in her view that "Mahometans" regarded women as animals.[11]

Wollstonecraft is so committed to her notion of Islamic culture that she goes so far as to accuse Milton, demonstrably a Christian thinker, of writing in the "true Mahometan strain" when he specifies the nature of Eve, "our first frail mother": "I cannot comprehend his meaning, unless, in the true Mahometan strain, he meant to deprive us of souls, and insinuate that we were beings only designed by sweet attractive grace, and docile blind obedience, to gratify the senses of man when he can no longer soar on the wing of contemplation" ([1792] 1982, 100–101).[12] Although Wollstonecraft here locates what she calls Mahometan belief at the center of Western Christian culture, she does not waver from her conviction that the West is fundamentally distinct from—and superior to—the East, claiming that the "despotism that kills virtue and genius in the bud" does not "hover over Europe with that destructive blast which desolates Turkey" (131).

Thus, for Wollstonecraft, the English husband "who lords it in his little harem" (167) is more guilty than his Eastern counterpart, for the despotism incarnate in the harem is not natural to Europe. Unlike the "Turk," the English husband goes against the grain of his race and culture, as does any Western woman who accepts such "Eastern" treatment of her. For example, Wollstonecraft responds to Rousseau's wish that "'a young Englishwoman cultivate her agreeable talents, in order to please her future husband, with as much care and assiduity as a young Circassian cultivates hers, to fit her for the harem of an Eastern bashaw'" (183) by criticizing the woman who could accept such a life: "In a seraglio, I grant, that all these arts are necessary; . . . but have women so little ambition as to be satisfied with such a condition? . . . Surely she has not an soul immortal who can loiter life away merely employed to adorn her person, that she may amuse the languid hours, and soften the cares of a fellow-creature" (112–13).

Though the Western emphasis on the marriageability of girls makes "mere animals" of them, "weak beings" who "are only fit for a seraglio" (Wollstonecraft [1792] 1982, 83), it is only "Mahometan" women who can accept such bondage: "If women are to be made virtuous by authority, which is a contradiction in terms, let them be immured in seraglios and watched with a jealous eye. Fear not that the iron will enter their souls—for the souls that can bear such treatment are made of yielding materials, just animated enough to give life to the body" (311).

If the seraglio exists unchallenged as an Eastern institution, Wollstonecraft implies, it is because "Mahometan" teachings are accurate in their representation of Eastern women: their souls are barely "animated." In the West, however, women are made of sterner stuff, and the seraglio—or anything that resembles it—has no place. The feminism of Wollstonecraft's *Vindication of the Rights of Woman* ultimately reduces itself to what would have been in her time a relatively noncontroversial plea: that the West rid itself of its oriental ways, becoming as a consequence more Western—that is, more rational, enlightened, reasonable.

Whether through direct influence or simply because the ideas on which she drew were circulating freely within the culture, the feminist orientalist strategy introduced by Wollstonecraft came to pervade nineteenth-century feminist discourse. Said has noted that orientalism characteristically emerges in Western writing as a "set of representative figures, or tropes," and he argues that to observe it "the things to look at are style, figures of speech, setting, narrative devices" (1979, 71, 21). In *Persian Letters* and *Vindication of the Rights of Woman*—as in *Jane Eyre*—the figures and tropes of the Orient are deeply woven into the fabric of the entire text. Other examples of feminist orientalist discourse are typically less elaborated and appear to be no more than random, casual allusions. Yet the very casualness of these allusions suggests that the writers are drawing upon a fully developed cultural code implicitly shared with their readers. There is no need to argue for or to prove any individual definition of Eastern ways nor any specific analogy between East and West, for the entire belief system that makes the individual references possible is taken for granted.

Among the elements that feminist writers return to again and again are three aspects of the Eastern treatment of women that Wollstonecraft had emphasized: (1) the central belief that women do not have souls, which justifies and explains the other practices; (2) the excessive sexuality of the harem, embodied partly in polygamy but also in luxury, indolence, and the trade in women; and (3) the enforced confinement, undereducation, and inactivity of women in the harem that reduces them to animals or children. A few more examples may help to establish the full context of the discourse that allowed Brontë to structure her novel as the drama of a Western woman oppressed by Eastern beliefs and practices.

One of the more extended instances of nineteenth-century feminist orientalism appears in the work of Wollstonecraft's daughter, Mary Shelley. Although it seems that Shelley did not fully share her mother's committed feminist activism, in her novel *Frankenstein* she nevertheless created a striking female character who insists on her existence as a soul.[13] This character, Safie, not only echoes the words and philosophy of Wollstonecraft but is also dramatically figured as a "lovely Arabian," a woman who barely escapes "being immured" within a harem:

> Safie related, that her mother was a Christian Arab, seized and made a slave by the Turks; recommended by her beauty, she had won the heart of the father of Safie, who married her. The young girl spoke in high and enthusiastic terms of her mother, who, born in freedom, spurned the bondage to which she was now reduced. She instructed her daughter in the tenets of the religion, and taught her to aspire to higher powers of intellect, and an independence of spirit, forbidden to the female followers of Mahomet. This lady died; but her lessons were indelibly impressed on the mind of Safie, who sickened at the prospect of again returning to Asia, and the being immured within the walls of a haram, allowed only to occupy herself with puerile amusements, ill-suited to the temper of her soul, now accustomed to grand ideas and a noble emulation for virtue. [Shelley (1818) 1974, 119]

"Let woman share the rights, and she will emulate the virtues of man," Wollstonecraft had written at the end of her *Vindication* ([1792] 1982, 319). Shelley echoes this sentiment in the person of her "lovely Arabian," inscribing it in the same orientalist frame as had her mother.

Feminist orientalism emerges again in the work of Anna Jameson, whose *Memoirs of the Loves of the Poets* is designed to show "the influence which the beauty and virtue of women have exercised over the characters and writings of men of genius" ([1824] 1890, vii). Hardly a feminist of the order of Wollstonecraft, Jameson is nevertheless deeply disturbed by the belief that women do not have souls, attributing it to the "Mahometan" East, where women are "held in seclusion, as mere soulless slaves of the passions and caprices of their masters" (25). Like Wollstonecraft, Jameson also discerns Eastern values operating in the West: she calls Lord Byron the "Grand Turk of amatory poetry," explaining that despite the beauty of his "female portraits," there is "something very Oriental in all his feelings and ideas about women; he seems to require nothing of us but beauty and submission" (507). One is reminded of Wollstonecraft's critique of Milton's "Mahometan" prescriptions for Eve: "sweet attractive grace, and docile blind obedience" (Wollstonecraft [1792] 1982, 100).

Jameson and Shelley echo one another when they repudiate the belief that women do not have souls. Yet they do not directly address the sexual practices that can be said to follow from this belief—polygamy and the buying and selling of women—though, as Alain Grosrichard has shown, polygamy tended to be a key feature of Western meditations upon the Orient (1979, 177–82). Later in the nineteenth century, however, while European male painters reveled in voyeuristic and vaguely pornographic representations of the multiplicity of female bodies available to masters of the harem, feminist writers learned to approach issues of sexuality by putting them in oriental terms. Prostitution, the marriage market, and the habit of keeping mistresses are all now figured as Eastern intrusions into a Western ideal of monogamous romantic love and marriage.

For example, when Jemima Bradshaw, a character in Elizabeth Gaskell's 1853 novel *Ruth*, contemplates the financial basis of her forthcoming marriage, she invokes a feminist orientalist image: "She felt as if she would rather be bought openly, like an Oriental daughter" ([1853] 1985, 240). In America, Margaret Fuller similarly compares the "selling" of English "daughters to the highest bidder" with "sending them to a Turkish slave-dealer." "You know how it was in the Oriental clime," she reminds her readers, though she defends the "Turkish" practice as less degrading than its Western counterpart, for "it is not done in defiance of an acknowledged law of right in the land and the age" ([1845] 1971, 139, 133, 139). What seems to be a healthy respect for difference is in fact a ratification of Western superiority. Like Wollstonecraft, Fuller accepts "Oriental" practices in the Orient—but not in the more temperate, enlightened West.

Likewise, when Elizabeth Barrett Browning justifies her discussion of prostitution in *Aurora Leigh*, she explains she is working to rid England of oriental prejudice: "I am deeply convinced that the corruption of our society requires not shut doors and windows, but light and air: and that is exactly because pure and prosperous women choose to *ignore* vice, that miserable women suffer wrong by it everywhere. Has paterfamilias, with his Oriental traditions and veiled female faces, very successfully dealt with a certain class of evil? What if materfamilias, with her quick sure instincts and honest innocent eyes, do more towards their expulsion by simply looking at them and calling them by their names?" (1897, 2:445). When Barrett Browning writes of "shut doors and windows" and "veiled female faces," she also indirectly hints at another central aspect of the life of Eastern women in the imaginations of Western feminists: the confinement of the harem. This is the aspect emphasized when Walter Besant, in 1897, comments on the "Oriental prejudice" that keeps British women out of certain professions and that earlier in the century resulted in their "seclusion . . . in the home, and their exclusion from active and practical life" ([1897] 1989, 2:1653, 2:1652).

And it is this aspect that emerges most tellingly in the writing of Florence Nightingale. "If heaven and hell exist on this earth, it is in the two worlds I saw that morning—the Dispensary and the Hareem," she writes at the conclusion of her 1849 tour of Egypt ([1849–50] 1988, 208). Nightingale's may be the most dramatic nineteenth-century feminist condemnation of the harem: it is for her literally hell on earth. What makes it so for Nightingale is not (at least not explicitly) its sensuality, nor its domination by a male despot, nor even the slavery of its women. Rather, what Nightingale finds horrifying about the harem are its all too familiar boredom and confinement: "A little more of such a place would have killed us . . . Oh, the *ennui* of that magnificent palace, it will stand in my memory as a circle of hell! Not one thing was there laying about, to be done or to be looked at" (208).

Although Nightingale is describing an actual visit to a harem, her description is conditioned both by her preexisting cultural images of the harem and the experience of her own life as a woman in England.[14] Her words echo those of Pekuah in Johnson's *Rasselas*, even as they anticipate her own analyses of family life in

England. Pekuah had noted of the harem that "the diversions of the women . . . were only childish play, by which the mind accustomed to stronger operations could not be kept busy. . . . They had no ideas but of the few things that were within their view, and had hardly names for anything but their clothes and their food" (Johnson [1759] 1977, 135). Nightingale herself writes: "The very windows into the garden were woodworked, so that you could not see out. The cold, the melancholy of that place! I felt inclined to cry" (Nightingale [1849–50] 1988, 208). In *Cassandra*, written a few years later, Nightingale condemns the "cold and oppressive conventional atmosphere" of women's family life, noting that women are forced to abandon "intellect as a vocation," taking it only "as we use the moon, by glimpses through . . . tight-closed window shutters" ([1852] 1980, 29, 37). Nightingale's description of domestic confinement, whether in Egypt or England, recalls one of Wollstonecraft's most chilling descriptions of women "immured in their families groping in the dark" ([1792] 1982, 87).

It is this image of domestic immurement that most obviously haunts *Jane Eyre* and shapes its very structure. Examining this narrative structure, one sees that each household in which Jane finds herself is constructed to resemble a harem; each of her oppressors is characterized as a Mahometan despot; and each of her rebellions or escapes bears the accents of Roxanna, the harem inmate declaring her existence as a free soul. At Gateshead, at Lowood, at Thornfield, and at Moor House, one discovers a series of communities of dependent women, all subject to the whim of a single master who rules in his absence as much as his presence and who subjects the imprisoned women to the searching power of his gaze.[15] In each of these households, Jane finds her own power of movement and of vision limited; even when she is most in love with Rochester at Thornfield, she recognizes that he stands in her way, "as an eclipse intervenes between man and the broad sun" (Brontë [1847] 1985, 302).

The pattern of home as harem is established at Gateshead, where the household consists of John Reed, Mrs. Reed, Eliza and Georgiana Reed, Jane, and the two female servants, Bessie and Abbott. There are also a male "butler and footman" (60), though these are shadowy presences, nameless men inconsequential in the dynamics and management of the household. The "master" is young John Reed, a boy of fourteen who demands that Jane call him "Master Reed" (41) and against whose arbitrary rule Jane has no appeal: "the servants did not like to offend their young master by taking my part against him, and Mrs. Reed was blind and deaf on the subject: she never saw him strike or heard him abuse me, though he did both now and then in her very presence" (42).

Like the sultans described by Montesquieu and the eighteenth-century travelers, John considers the privileges of seeing and knowing to be his. What enrages him in the novel's opening scene is that Jane is out of his sight. Hidden behind the curtain of the window seat, reading and looking out the window, she has usurped his role as the "Turk." "Where the dickens is she?" John asks his sisters, and when Eliza finds Jane for him, John castigates his cousin not only for "getting behind curtains" but also for reading: "You have no business to take our books" (42). In the course of his tirade, John calls Jane a "bad animal" (41) and a "rat" (42); later she will become a "wild cat" (59). John's descriptions of Jane as beast and his wish to keep her from educating herself through books may recall Wollstonecraft's definition of the "true style" of Mahometanism: the view of women as "domestic brutes" ([1792] 1982, 101), "not as a part of the human species" (80).

The sexuality of the harem is absent from the Reed home, but the indolent, pampered sensuality that so offends Wollstonecraft is not. In the opening scene, Mrs. Reed lies "reclined on a sofa by the fireside . . . with her darlings about her" (39). John is constantly plied with "cakes and sweetmeats," even though he "gorged himself habitually at table, which made him bilious, and gave him a dim and bleared eye with flabby cheeks" (41). John is the effete, attenuated tyrant made weak by his abuse of power, familiar from Wollstonecraft's characterizations of "bashaws." The Reed sisters are "universally indulged" (46) and "elaborately ring-leted" (60); their mother dresses regularly in silks. The luxury of Gateshead, asso-ciated as it is with the degeneracy and despotism of the harem, is something Jane learns to abhor, and this abhorrence informs her later attempts to resist Roches-ter's desire to see her "glittering like a parterre" (296).

Jane, not unlike Montesquieu's Roxanna, rebels against her imprisonment within Master Reed's "harem." Her physical violence is expressed against John, but she reserves her strongest words for Mrs. Reed, the adult who has enforced the "young master's" wishes: "If anyone asks me how I liked you, and how you treated me, I will say the very thought of you makes me sick, and that you treated me with miserable cruelty. . . . You think I have no feelings, and that I can do without one bit of love or kindness; but I cannot live so: and you have no pity" (68). Like Roxanna, Jane exposes the hypocrisy of her keeper, insisting on the freedom of her mind and on her desire for and right to genuine love.

Jane's outburst leads to her departure from Gateshead, though she soon finds herself in another institution that even more closely resembles the harem that haunts the Western feminist imagination. Lowood, "a large and irregular build-ing" through which on her arrival Jane is led "from compartment to compart-ment, from passage to passage" (76), perfectly embodies the confinement of the harem. The building is oppressive, dark, and gloomy, and the garden is no bet-ter: "a wide enclosure," it is "surrounded with walls so high as to exclude every glimpse of prospect" (80). These walls not only limit the vision of the institution's "inmates" but they are "spike-guarded" (107) to prohibit freedom of movement.

Within the confines of this dwelling, Jane discovers "a congregation of girls of every age. . . . Their number to me appeared countless" (76). Over this commu-nity of women rules the redoubtable Mr. Brocklehurst, "the black marble clergy-man" (98) whom Jane perceives as a "black column," a "piece of architecture" (94). Like John Reed, Brocklehurst's characteristic gesture is to gaze search-ingly upon his assembled dependents. When he makes his first appearance at Lo-wood, he "majestically surveyed the whole school" (95); a few moments later he "scrutinize[s]" the hair of the terrified girls. As with John Reed, Jane seeks to hide from this master's eyes: "I had sat well back on the form, and while seeming to be busy with my sum, had held my slate in such a manner as to conceal my face" (97). Jane does not escape Brocklehurst's look, however, and is forced to suffer the humiliation of his description of her as a liar. Jane is freed by the good offices of Miss Temple, and later, when the scandal of Brocklehurst's despotic rule is revealed (significantly, it takes the death of a number of the inmates to cause this revelation) he is stripped of some of his power. Lowood becomes a fairly happy home for Jane, though a "prison-ground" nonetheless (117).

It may be objected that the ascetic aspects of Lowood accord ill with the suggestion that it is figured as a harem. Certainly Lowood harbors neither the sensuality nor the overt sexuality associated with the harem. Yet its structure, with one man controlling an indefinite number of dependent women, mimics that of the seraglio. Further, Brocklehurst's wish to strip the girls of all adornment, of all possibilities of sensual gratification, has its parallel in the sultan's wish to keep the women of the harem restrained from any sexuality not under his control. That Brocklehurst is figured in plainly phallic terms only underscores his identification as a sultan whose perverse pleasure here consists in denying pleasure to the women he rules. For his wife and daughters, however—women over whom presumably he can exert even greater control—Brocklehurst allows a greater sensuality: these women are "splendidly attired in velvet, silk, and furs" (97).

When Jane leaves Lowood for her "new servitude" at Thornfield (117), she happily anticipates entering the domain of Mrs. Fairfax, an "elderly lady" (120) whom she believes to be the mistress of a "safe haven" (129), a "snug" and secure realm of feminine "domestic comfort" (127). To her initial dismay, Jane discovers that this new household of women also has a "master," the absent yet omnipotent Mr. Rochester. Jane first meets Rochester on the moonlit lane connecting Thornfield to the town of Hay, unaware he is her master. She perceives this stranger to have a "dark face, with stern features and a heavy brow" (145); later she will call his skin "swarthy," his features "Paynim" (212). The man has fallen from his horse, and Jane offers to assist him. Before accepting her help, however, he subjects her to intense "scrutiny" in order to determine her identity (146).

Jane reveals that she is the governess at Thornfield; Rochester offers no information about himself, except to say, when Jane fails in her effort to lead his horse to him: "I see . . . the mountain will never be brought to Mahomet, so all you can do is to aid Mahomet to go to the mountain" (146). Though uttered in jest, these words do not bode well for Jane's relationship with her master. Rochester gives himself the one name that, to a nineteenth-century audience, would unambiguously identify him as a polygamous, blasphemous despot—a sultan. After such an introduction, it comes as no surprise when Rochester chooses to dress "in shawls, with a turban on his head" for a game of charades, nor that Jane should see him as "the very model of an Eastern emir" (212).

The most striking identification of Rochester as an oriental despot—again a characterization that comes from his own lips—occurs when he begins to contemplate marriage with Jane. The intimacy between master and dependent has begun to develop and, in the course of guardedly discussing his past with the governess, Rochester admits that he "degenerated" when wronged by fate (167). As Jane and the reader will later learn, he is referring to his marriage with Bertha Mason, and his subsequent indulgence in "lust for a passion—vice for an occupation" (343). With no knowledge of the details of Rochester's "degeneration," Jane nevertheless encourages him to repent, though Rochester insists that only pleasure, "sweet, fresh pleasure" (167), can help him. Jane suggests that such pleasure "will taste bitter" (167) and warns Rochester against "error." Rochester, apparently referring to his wish to love Jane, replies that the "notion that flitted across my brain" is not error or temptation but "inspiration": "I am laying down good intentions, which I believe durable as flint. Certainly, my associates and pursuits shall be other than they have been. . . . You seem to doubt me; I don't doubt myself: I know what my aim is, what my motives are; and at this moment I pass a law, unalterable as that of the Medes and Persians, that both are right" (168–69).

Rochester's aim is to find happiness with Jane; his motives are to redeem himself from his association with Bertha; the unalterable law that he makes his own has its antecedent in the one decreed by King Ahasuerus—"written among the laws of the Persians and the Medes, that it not be altered"—when he banishes his Queen Vashti and vows to "give her royal estate unto another that is better than she" (Esther 1.19). Ahasuerus, to whom Jane will later compare Rochester (in the same chapter in which she compares him to a sultan [Brontë (1847) 1985, 290]), had been angered by Vashti's refusal to come at his command. His counselors point out that the queen's refusal to be commanded might "come abroad unto all women" (Esther 1.17), and the Persian king passes his law so that "every man should bear rule in his own house" (Esther 1.22). Rochester's decision to banish Bertha and marry Jane is dangerously like Ahasuerus's replacement of Vashti by Esther; Jane's resistance signals her engagement in both the reform of her master and the liberation of her people.

The conversation between Jane and Rochester about Rochester's "Persian" law offers readers clear signals about how they should perceive Rochester's relationship to Jane. Expressed as a conflict between Judeo-Christian law and Persian arrogance, the conflict can also be understood as Jane's struggle to retain possession of her soul, to claim her rights as a Western, Christian woman. Thus, when Rochester begins his actual proposal to her, Jane insists, "I have as much soul as you" (Brontë [1847] 1985, 281). Later, when she resists his wish to take her to a "white-washed villa on the shores of the Mediterranean," where, as his mistress, she would live a "guarded" life (331), she expresses her triumph in precisely the same terms: "I still possessed my soul" (344).[16]

It is at Thornfield, of course, that the confinement and sexuality of the seraglio/harem are most fully represented. Rochester has a wife whom he keeps literally caged in a "wild beast's den" (336), "a room without a window" (321). In her first explicit view of Bertha Mason, Jane depicts her in the ambiguous, non-human terms Wollstonecraft had applied to harem inmates: "What it was, whether beast or human being, one could not, at first sight tell: it grovelled, seemingly, on all fours; it snatched and growled like some strange wild animal: but it was covered with clothing, and a quantity of dark, grizzled hair, wild as a mane, hid its head and face" (321). Referred to by Jane as a "clothed hyena" (321), Bertha incarnates a brute sensuality that apparently justifies her imprisonment. Rochester calls her his "bad, mad, and embruted partner" (320), whom he married without being "sure of the existence of one virtue in her nature" (333).

When Rochester takes his first wife, he is himself acting purely on the basis of his own "excited" senses (332), not seeking a rational companion. He discovers in

Bertha a "nature wholly alien" to his own, a "cast of mind common, low, narrow, and singularly incapable of being led to anything higher, expanded to anything larger" (333). Bertha is characterized here as a woman without a soul. This Western man has married a figuratively Eastern woman, an "embruted" creature who, through the marriage bond, becomes a "part of" him (334). When Rochester, responding to the "sweet wind from Europe," decides to leave Jamaica and "go home to God" (335), his behavior continues to be governed by the "most gross, impure, depraved" nature that is permanently "associated" with his own (334). Instead of remaining faithful to his wife, he roams Europe seeking "a good and intelligent woman, whom I could love" (337). Of course he finds only the "unprincipled and violent," "mindless," and faithless mistresses his money buys him (338). Rochester knows that "hiring a mistress is the next worse thing to buying a slave" (339), yet he persists on this course—even with Jane—because, the narrative suggests, his association with Bertha has deformed him into a polygamous, sensual sultan.

Thus Brontë appears to displace the blame for Rochester's Eastern tendencies on the intrusion of this "Eastern" woman into his Western life. Though Jane protests in Bertha's behalf—"you are inexorable for that unfortunate lady" (328)—Rochester's account of his first marriage serves as the narrative explanation of his own oriental tendencies. The fact that he does not reform until Bertha dies suggests how powerful her oriental hold on him has been.[17]

Bertha, of course, is West Indian, not "Mahometan," and she scarcely resembles the conventional image of an alluring harem inmate—no "gazelle eyes" or "houri forms" here. Indeed, as Susan L. Meyer convincingly shows, she is consistently figured as a "nightmare" vision with "savage," "lurid," and "swelled" black features (1989, 253–54) and associated with the oppressed races subject to British colonialism. Yet, as Grosrichard points out, "The West Indies can end by rejoining, in the imagination, the East Indies" (1979, 32, translation mine). Bertha's characterization in other significant ways recalls the terms used by Wollstonecraft to depict the fate of "Mahometan" women: she is soulless, regarded as "not . . . a part of the human species," and her all-too-real imprisonment at Thornfield invokes the root meaning of *seraglio*: a place where wild beasts are kept. One might say that Bertha's characterization as a "clothed hyena" manifests the Western view of the underlying reality of the harem inmate, the philosophical view of women that underpins both their confinement within the harem and their more conventional adornment.[18]

Thus, to note Bertha's "blackness" and her birth in Jamaica need not preclude seeing that she is also, simultaneously, figured as an "Eastern" woman. Indeed, in Bertha's characterization a number of parallel discourses converge: she is the "black woman who signifies both the oppressed and the oppressor" (Meyer 1989, 266); she is Jane's "dark double" who enacts both Jane's and Brontë's repressed rage at patriarchal oppression (Gilbert and Gubar 1979, 360); she is the Indian woman consumed in sati (Perera 1991); she is Vashti, King Ahasuerus's uncontrollable queen; and she is a harem inmate whose purported soullessness justifies and enforces her own oppression. Bertha is overdetermined; as the "central locus of Brontë's anxieties about oppression" (Meyer 1989, 252) and as the spark for the redemptive fire that clears the way for Jane's fulfillment, she serves to focus a number of different systems of figuration that structure the novel.

Indeed, Brontë equivocates still further in her presentation of Bertha, never fully indicating whether she is inherently soulless or only made so by Rochester's treatment of her. In a few significant passages, Brontë allows her narrative to suggest that Bertha, like Jane, is consciously aware of and legitimately enraged by her enslavement. On the eve of the doomed wedding, Bertha enters Jane's room, not to harm her as Rochester fears but to rend the veil, which Rochester in his "princely extravagance" had insisted upon buying (Brontë [1847] 1985, 308). Jane sees in the veil an image of Rochester's "pride" (309). When Bertha rends it "in two parts" and "trample[s] on them" (311), her action may be explained as emanating from her resentment of and jealousy toward Jane. Or, it may be viewed as a warning to Jane about the "veiled" existence she would have to lead as Rochester's harem slave.

That Bertha kills herself in her attempt to burn down the house of her master can also be linked to Roxanna's ultimately self-destructive rebellion in *Persian Letters*. Defying the master who has enslaved her, she asserts her freedom only to find death as its inevitable price. As long as the despotic system is in place, no woman can truly be free, yet the suicide of a rebellious woman serves as a powerful condemnation—and potential transformation—of that system.[19] Thus it is no accident that Rochester is blinded in the conflagration caused by Bertha's rebellion. Stripped of his despotic privilege to see, he can no longer function as a sultan. Despite her earlier promises to "stir up mutiny" in the harem (298), Jane owes her freedom not to her own rebellion but to that of the actual "harem-inmate," the "dark double" who acts as her proxy.

After Bertha's death, Rochester is free to reform, and this reform is significantly figured as a conversion: "Jane! you think me, I dare say, an irreligious dog: but my heart swells with gratitude to the beneficent God of this earth just now. . . . I did wrong. . . . Of late, Jane—only—only of late—I began to see and acknowledge the hand of God in my doom. I began to experience remorse, repentance, the wish for reconcilement with my Maker. I began sometimes to pray" (471). The man who had passed a "Persian" law to justify his own behavior here acknowledges the authority of the Christian God who mandates monogamy and respect for the souls of women. Despite the many critiques of Christian ideology and practice that abound in *Jane Eyre*, Brontë's feminist orientalism here takes priority, as she obscures the patriarchal oppression that is also a part of Christianity.

And by ending her novel with the words of the Christian missionary St. John Rivers, himself one of the domestic despots Jane has had to defy, Brontë leaves the reader with an idealized vision of Christianity as the only satisfactory alternative to Eastern, "Mahometan"—and even Hindu—despotism. While this reversal in the characterization of St. John and the expressed attitude toward Christianity has struck many readers as a self-contradictory shift in Brontë's focus, it in fact confirms and seals the pattern begun with Jane's promise to "go out as a missionary to preach liberty to them that are enslaved" (297).

The novel's concluding paean to St. John and to Christian values takes place against the backdrop not of a vaguely conceived Middle East but of the Far East,

India. The groundwork establishing India as another locale for gendered oriental despotism had been laid early in the novel, in the same chapter that features the "sultan/slave" simile. Back at Thornfield after the trip to Millcote, Jane objects to a "pagan" tendency in Rochester (301). Her master has just sung a song to her in which a woman swears "to live—to die" with her beloved (301). Jane seizes on the seemingly innocent phrase and asserts that she "had no intention of dying" with Rochester: "I had as good a right to die when my time came as he had: but I should bide that time, and not be hurried away in a suttee" (301).

Though this identification of India as another Eastern site for the oppression of women is not in my view extensively developed throughout the text, it returns in the novel's conclusion, as well as in the penultimate section of the novel, when Jane faces the threat of being "grilled alive in Calcutta" (441) if she chooses to accompany St. John to India. For during her stay at Moor House, Jane once again encounters a man with a "despotic nature" (434) who rules over a household of dependent women and who threatens not only to immure but also to immolate her (430).

At first Jane finds Moor House less oppressive than her earlier homes. Yet when Jane consents to give up her study of German in order to help St. John learn Hindustani, she discovers another form of "servitude" (423) and she experiences the kiss that St. John gives her as a "seal affixed to my fetters" (424). Jane's subjection to St. John is in fact stronger than any she has felt before. "I could not resist him," she uncharacteristically admits (425). Part of Jane's difficulty in resisting St. John's wishes is that they come cloaked in Christian doctrine. Jane recognizes the despotism in St. John, knowing that to accede to his wishes would be "almost equivalent to committing suicide" (439). Yet because St. John is a "sincere Christian" (434), not an "irreligious dog," she has a harder time extricating herself from the seductions of his proposal that she marry him and accompany him to India: "Religion called—Angels beckoned—God commanded" (444).

Brontë here reveals the motive behind feminist orientalism as a mode of cultural analysis as well as a rhetorical strategy. Jane finds it possible to resist Rochester because he calls himself and acts in ways that clearly echo the Western conception of "Mahomet," not Christ. But a man who assumes the language and posture of Christ is harder to combat. Jane ultimately does find the strength to resist St. John, however, when he unwittingly sets her a challenge that obviously mimics the behavior of a Western feminist's notion of a sultan.

What St. John asks of Jane is that she abandon her already established love for Rochester. With this demand, he manifests what was, to Western feminists, perhaps the most threatening feature of "Mahometan" practice: interference with a woman's free choice of love object. Indeed, what had motivated Roxanna's rebellion in *Persian Letters* was not her desire to escape confinement nor her position as one of many wives. Rather, it was her desire to be free to love another man, coupled with her abhorrence of her sexual "master." In denying Jane her freedom to love (and in promising to impose the forms of sexual love upon her), St. John becomes the most brutal (and literal) of her harem masters and thus the one who evokes from her the greatest effort of rebellion.[20]

Yet in the concluding paragraphs of the novel, St. John—the archetypal Christian man—is redeemed from the flaw in his own nature. By her resistance to his desire to enslave her, Jane frees him from his own oriental tendencies. If she is not a slave, he cannot be a master. Brontë makes explicit the implication behind Wollstonecraft's assertion that the women of the harem have souls "just animated enough to give life to the body." A woman of soul, as Jane has by now firmly established herself to be, has the power not only to resist the harem but to transform it: as Jane had once promised Rochester, "you, three-tailed bashaw as you are, sir, shall in a trice find yourself fettered amongst our hands" (298).

St. John, like Rochester, becomes a true Christian after his encounter with Jane and thus is free to pursue her orientalist project. For St. John, as a Christian missionary in India, "labours for his race" with the same impulses as do Jane and her author: "Firm, faithful, and devoted, full of energy and zeal, and truth . . . he clears their painful way to improvement; he hews down like a giant the prejudices of creed and caste that encumber it" (477). Jane Eyre ends her story with St. John's words—"Amen; even so, come, Lord Jesus!" (477)—because they externalize and make global what has been her own internal and local project all along: the purging of oriental elements from her society, the replacement of "Mahometan" law by Christian doctrine. In voicing these words, St. John is recommitting himself to the specifically Christian project of combating alien religious forms. Thus, although the novel's primary focus is the occidentalization of the Occident, it ends with the vision of the occidentalization of the Orient that simultaneously underlies and expands that focus. Readers, both male and female, are encouraged to follow both St. John and Jane in the task of clearing the thicket of oriental "prejudices" abroad, at home, and within their own souls. It remains for readers in the twentieth century to clear yet another thicket, the tangle of feminist orientalist prejudice that continues to encumber Western feminist discourse.

NOTES

I am indebted to the anonymous readers for *Signs* who helped clarify and refine my argument. Nancy Easterlin, Jimmy Griffin, Cynthia Hogue, Peter Schock, and Les White provided valuable comments on early drafts, while Ruth Walker always listened and encouraged. Mark Kerr helped with the initial research; Maria McGarrity assisted in the final stages. For her excellent copyediting, I am grateful to Jeanne Barker-Nunn.

[1] Hereafter, unidentified page numbers in text refer to the Penguin edition of *Jane Eyre*.

[2] Although the feminist orientalism I discern in the novel is parallel to the "figurative use of blackness" earlier identified by Susan L. Meyer (1989, 250), it also has significant differences. Whereas Meyer focuses on the opposition "white/black," I examine the opposition "West/East." The two forms of opposition are related but not identical: the one privileges skin color or "race," and the other "culture," a phenomenon that may be associated with but that is not necessarily reducible to "race." Meyer's essay admirably demonstrates how *Jane Eyre* uses racial oppression as a metaphor for class and gender oppression. However, in systematically linking gender oppression to oriental despotism, *Jane Eyre* focuses on a form of oppression that is, from the first, conceived by Westerners in terms of gender.

[3] Gibson, one of the few critics to note how the sultan image pervades *Jane Eyre*, makes the sanguine assumption that Brontë's critique of Eastern despotism "extends to British imperialist

impulses themselves," leading Gibson, like many critics, to find the novel's conclusion "strange" (1987, 1, 7). As I shall show, however, Jane's concluding paean to her missionary cousin in India is thoroughly grounded in the novel's figurative structure. Gayatri Spivak, for her part, argues that Brontë's novel reproduces the "axiomatics of imperialism" (1985, 247) and that its "imperialist project" remains inaccessible to the "nascent 'feminist' scenario" (249). My argument emphasizes less the acts of political domination that constitute imperialism than how its ideology (and specifically its orientalism) infects the analysis of domestic relations "at home" and posits that orientalism is in fact put to the service of feminism. See also Suvendrini Perera's discussion of how "the vocabulary of oriental misogyny" became "an invisible component in feminist representations" in the nineteenth century (1991, 79). Perera's chapter on *Jane Eyre*, published after the research for this article had been completed, focuses on sati as the text's "central image" (93), while my reading emphasizes the use of the harem as the central image of gender oppression. Western feminist uses of both sati and the harem function equally, as Perera points out, to objectify the "colonized or imagined 'oriental' female subject" (82).

[4] See Said 1979 for the definitive exposition of orientalism as a "Western style for dominating, restructuring, and having authority over the Orient" (71).

[5] Al-Bazei's excellent study does not consider the specifically feminist adaptation of this strategy. Interestingly, however, Al-Bazei identifies Byron's Turkish Tales as a crucial locus for the development of "self-redemption" as the dominant mode of nineteenth-century literary orientalism. Byron's influence on Brontë has been well documented, and further study might establish a link between his Turkish Tales and Brontë's feminist orientalism.

[6] For a recent defense of polygamy in the context of Western Mormonism, see Joseph 1991. Earlier in this century, Demetra Vaka argued that women living in harems were "healthy and happy," possessing a "sublimity of soul . . . lacking in our European civilization" (1909, 29, 127–28). Ahmed 1982 argues that the harem can be construed as an inviolable and empowering "women's space" that enables Islamic women to have "frequent and easy access to other women in their community, vertically, across class lines, as well as horizontally" (524).

[7] See, e.g., Makhlouf-Obermeyer 1979; Gordon (1865) 1983; Delplato 1988; Croutier 1989; Gendron 1991; Leonowens (1872) 1991.

[8] See Ahmed 1982 for a pointed analysis of how fundamentalist Islamic movements "target" feminism as "'Western' and as particularly repugnant and evil" (533). Similarly, Hatem 1989 shows how in the late nineteenth and early twentieth centuries "European and Egyptian women were influenced by modern national ideologies and rivalries . . . prevent[ing] them from using each other's experience to push for a more radical critique of their own societies" (183).

[9] See, e.g., Conant 1908; Stedman 1965; Ali 1981; Caracciolo 1988; Workman 1988.

[10] Jane Eyre's friend Helen Burns reads *Rasselas* at Lowood; though Jane's "brief examination" of the book convinces her it is "dull" (Brontë [1847] 1985, 82), the text's presence within *Jane Eyre* signals Brontë's familiarity with—and interest in highlighting—a key source of feminist orientalism. Kringas 1992 points out that *Rasselas* not only exposes the oppressiveness of the harem but, by juxtaposing the experiences of Nekayah and Pekuah, specifically links the lives of women in the harem with the lives of uneducated, middle-class women outside the seraglio (33).

[11] In this context, it may also be worth noting that *harem*, derived from the Arabic *haram*, designates places that are "'holy,' 'protected,' 'sacred,' 'inviolate,' and lastly 'forbidden'" (Penzer 1936, 15). In Western usage, the holiness of *harem* is elided, and the caging aspect of *seraglio* is introduced.

[12] Samuel Johnson had levied a similar charge against Milton, claiming in his 1779 *Life* of Milton that "there appears in his books something like a Turkish contempt of females as subordinate and inferior beings. . . . He thought woman made only for obedience, and man only for rebellion" (85).

[13] See Zonana 1991 for an extended argument that Safie in fact articulates *Frankenstein*'s thematic center. For a more qualified view of Shelley's feminism, see Poovey 1984. See also Spivak 1985 for the view that *Frankenstein* resists its culture's pervasive orientalism.

[14] See Barrell 1991 for a provocative discussion of how tourists such as Nightingale brought their own fantasies and preoccupations to their descriptions of the sights in Egypt.

[15] Grosrichard convincingly demonstrates that, in the Western construction of the seraglio, "To be the master . . . is to see. In the despotic state, where one always obeys 'blindly,' the blind man is the emblematic figure of the subject" (73, translation mine). See also Bellis 1987 for an exploration of the politics of vision in *Jane Eyre*.

[16] The other Old Testament reference to a "law of the Medes and Persians, which altereth not" occurs in chap. 6 of the book of Daniel. Here the Persian king Darius orders that anyone who petitions "any God or Man" other than the king "shall be cast into the den of lions" (Dan. 6.7). Daniel prays to the God of the Hebrews; the king casts him in the lion's den; Daniel's miraculous deliverance converts Darius to an acknowledgment of the "living God" (Dan. 6.26). Jane Eyre names Daniel as one of her favorite books in the Bible early in the novel (Brontë [1847] 1985, 65); Daniel's ordeal, as well as Esther's, serves as a model for her own resistance to her master's desire to strip her of "soul." I am indebted to Jimmy Griffin for bringing to my attention the relevant biblical passages.

[17] See Meyer 1989 for fuller discussion of how contact with the Other serves to besmirch the Englishman in *Jane Eyre*.

[18] The reader may be reminded of Horace Walpole's comment that Mary Wollstonecraft was a "hyena in petticoats" (Wollstonecraft [1792] 1982, 17).

[19] See Donaldson 1988 for a similar argument about the self-assertion implicit in Bertha's suicide; Perera 1991, on the contrary, sees Bertha's death as a denial of her subjectivity.

[20] See Leonowens (1872) 1991 for a fuller elaboration of this idea: the greatest horror of the harem, for Leonowens, is not polygamy, not confinement, not enforced sexual submission, but denial of the freedom to love.

WORKS CITED

Ahmed, Leila. 1982. "Western Ethnocentrism and Perceptions of the Harem." *Feminist Studies* 8(3):521–34.

Al-Bazei, Saad Abdulrahman. 1983. "Literary Orientalism in Nineteenth-Century Anglo-American Literature: Its Formation and Continuity." Ph.D. dissertation, Purdue University.

Ali, Muhsin Jassim. 1981. *Scheherazade in England: A Study of Nineteenth-Century English Criticism of the "Arabian Nights."* Washington, D.C.: Three Continents.

Alloula, Malek. 1986. *The Colonial Harem*, trans. Myrna Godzich and Wlad Godzich. Theory and History of Literature, vol. 21. Minneapolis: University of Minnesota Press.

Barrell, John. 1991. "Death on the Nile: Fantasy and the Literature of Tourism, 1840–1860." *Essays in Criticism* 41(2):97–127.

Barrett Browning, Elizabeth. 1897. *The Letters of Elizabeth Barrett Browning*, ed. Frederic G. Kenyon. 2 vols. New York: Macmillan.

Bellis, Peter J. 1987. "In the Window-Seat: Vision and Power in *Jane Eyre*." *ELH* 54(3):639–52.

Besant, Walter. (1897) 1986. *The Queen's Reign*. In *Norton Anthology of English Literature*, ed. M. H. Abrams. 5th ed. New York: Norton.

Brontë, Charlotte. (1847) 1985. *Jane Eyre*. New York: Penguin.

Caracciolo, Peter L., ed. 1988. *"The Arabian Nights" in English Literature: Studies in the Reception of "The Thousand and One Nights" into British Culture*. New York: St. Martin's.

Conant, Martha Pike. 1908. *The Oriental Tale in England in the Eighteenth Century*. New York: Columbia University Press.

Croutier, Alev Lytle. 1989. *Harem: The World behind the Veil*. New York: Abbeville.

Delplato, Joan. 1988. "An English 'Feminist' in the Turkish Harem: A Portrait of Lady Mary Wortley Montagu." In *Eighteenth-Century Women and the Arts*, ed. Frederick M. Keener and Susan E. Lorsch. Westport, CT: Greenwood.

Donaldson, Laura E. 1988. "The Miranda Complex: Colonialism and the Question of Feminist Reading." *Diacritics* 18(3):65–77.

Fuller, Margaret. (1854) 1971. *Woman in the Nineteenth Century*. New York: Norton.

Gaskell, Elizabeth. (1853) 1985. *Ruth*. New York: Oxford.

Gendron, Charisse. 1991. "Images of Middle-Eastern Women in Victorian Travel Books." *Victorian Newsletter*, no. 79, 18–23.

Gibson, Mary Ellis. 1987. "The Seraglio or Suttee: Brontë's *Jane Eyre*." *Postscript* 4:1–8.

Gilbert, Sandra, and Susan Gubar. 1979. *The Madwoman in the Attic: The Woman Writer and the Nineteenth-Century Literary Imagination*. New Haven, Conn.: Yale University Press.

Gordon, Lucie Duff. (1865) 1983. *Letters from Egypt*. London: Virago.

Grosrichard, Alain. 1979. *Structure du Serail: La Fiction du Despotisme Asiatique dans L'Occident Classique*. Paris: Editions Seuil.

Hatem, Mervat. 1989. "Through Each Other's Eyes: Egyptian, Levantine-Egyptian, and European Women's Images of Themselves and of Each Other." *Women's Studies International Forum* 12(2):183–98.

Jameson, Anna. (1829) 1890. *Memoirs of the Loves of the Poets: Biographical Sketches of Women Celebrated in Ancient and Modern Poetry*. Boston and New York: Houghton Mifflin.

Johnson, Samuel. (1779) 1975. *Lives of the English Poets: A Selection*, ed. John Wain. London: Everyman.

———. (1759) 1977. *Rasselas*. In *Selected Poetry and Prose*, ed. Frank Brady and W. K. Wimsatt. Berkeley: University of California Press.

Joseph, Elizabeth. 1991. "My Husband's Nine Wives." *New York Times*, May 23.

Kra, Pauline. 1979. "The Role of the Harem in Imitations of Montesquieu's *Lettres Persanes*." *Studies on Voltaire and the Eighteenth Century* 182:273–283.

Kringas, Connie George. 1992. "The Women of *Rasselas*: A Journey of Education and Empowerment." M.A. thesis, University of New Orleans.

Leonowens, Anna. (1872) 1991. *The Romance of the Harem*, ed. Susan Morgan. Charlottesville: University Press of Virginia.

Makhlouf-Obermeyer, Carla. 1979. *Changing Veils: A Study of Women in South Arabia*. Austin: University of Texas Press.

Marmontel, Jean François. 1764. *Moral Tales by M. Marmontel Translated from the French*. 3 vols. London.

Meyer, Susan L. 1989. "Colonialism and the Figurative Strategy of *Jane Eyre*." *Victorian Studies* 33(2):247–68.

Mohanty, Chandra. 1988. "Under Western Eyes: Feminist Scholarship and Colonial Discourses." *Feminist Review* 30(Autumn):61–88.

Montesquieu, Charles de Secondat Baron de. (1721) 1923. *Persian Letters*, trans. John Davidson. London: Routledge.

Nightingale, Florence. (1852) 1980. *Cassandra*. New York: Feminist Press.

———. (1849–50) 1988. *Letters from Egypt: A Journey on the Nile, 1849–1850*. New York: Widenfeld & Nicolson.

Penzer, N. M. 1936. *The Harem: An Account of the Institution as It Existed in the Palace of the Turkish Sultans with a History of the Grand Seraglio from Its Foundation to Modern Times*. London: Spring Books.

Perera, Suvendrini. 1991. *Reaches of Empire: The English Novel from Edgeworth to Dickens*. New York: Columbia University Press.

Poovey, Mary. 1984. *The Proper Lady and the Woman Writer: Ideology as Style in the Works of Mary Wollstonecraft, Mary Shelley, and Jane Austen*. Chicago: University of Chicago Press.

Richon, Olivier. 1985. "Representation, the Despot and the Harem: Some Questions around an Academic Orientalist Painting by Lecomte-du-Nouy (1885)." In *Europe and Its Others*, ed. Francis Barker, Peter Hulme, Margaret Iverson, and Diana Loxley. Vol. 1. Colchester: University of Essex.

Said, Edward. 1979. *Orientalism*. New York: Vintage Books.

Shelley, Mary Wollstonecraft. (1818) 1974. *Frankenstein or the Modern Prometheus: The 1818 Text*, ed. James Rieger. New York: Bobbs-Merrill.

Spivak, Gayatri Chakravorty. 1985. "Three Women's Texts and a Critique of Imperialism." *Critical Inquiry* 12(1):243–61.

Stedman, Jane W. 1965. "The Genesis of the Genii." *Brontë Society Transactions* 14(5):16–19.

Tasch, Peter A. 1982. "Jane Eyre's 'Three-Tailed Bashaw.'" *Notes & Queries* 227(June):232.

Trumpener, Katie. 1987. "Rewriting Roxane: Orientalism and Intertextuality in Montesquieu's *Lettres Persanes* and Defoe's *The Fortunate Mistress.*" *Stanford French Review* 11(2): 177–91.

Vaka, Demetra (Mrs. Kenneth Brown). 1909. *Haremlik: Some Pages from the Life of Turkish Women.* Boston and New York: Houghton Mifflin.

Wollstonecraft, Mary. (1798) 1975. *Maria or the Wrongs of Woman.* New York: Norton.

———. (1792) 1982. *Vindication of the Rights of Woman.* London: Penguin.

Workman, Nancy V. 1988. "Scheherazade at Thornfield: Mythic Elements in *Jane Eyre.*" *Essays in Literature* 15(2):177–92.

Zonana, Joyce. 1991. " 'They Will Prove the Truth of My Tale': Safie's Letters as the Feminist Core of Mary Shelley's *Frankenstein.*" *Journal of Narrative Technique* 21(2):170–84.

AFTERWORD

I researched and wrote "The Sultan and the Slave: Feminist Orientalism and the Structure of *Jane Eyre*" in a frenzy of effort, stunned by the pattern of using "Eastern" oppression of women as a model for what was wrong with Western gender relations and driven by the conviction that such orientalism still marred Western feminist thought. I had perceived the pattern by chance while teaching a course on nineteenth-century British women's literature at the University of Oklahoma. We began with a close reading of Mary Wollstonecraft's *Vindication of the Rights of Woman*, where I was struck by Wollstonecraft's use of "Mahometan" thought and behavior as signifiers of patriarchy. The same topos marked her daughter Mary Shelley's *Frankenstein* and helped make sense of it for me. When I found Charlotte Brontë's Rochester referred to as a "sultan," I suspected something much bigger was at work here.

References proliferated as (with the help of two wonderful graduate assistants, Mark Kerr, at the University of Oklahoma, and Maria McGarrity, at the University of New Orleans) I pursued my hunch; *Jane Eyre* fell into place as a primal text that both reflected and projected the pattern. Never before or since have I felt so clearly onto something in my research, and never before or since have I written with such assurance. It has been simultaneously gratifying and humbling to find my work so abundantly cited and reprinted—gratifying because it is a pleasure to enter the mainstream of thought; humbling because, while the essay was certainly my idea, I could never have had or articulated such an idea without the theorizing of the postcolonial critics Edward Said and Gayatri Spivak. To the extent that what I argue is persuasive, it is because the evidence I cite speaks for itself.

Yet while I am convinced of the objective basis for my argument in "The Sultan and the Slave," I also want to acknowledge and celebrate the subjective, private function of this work for me, both in its sources and in its ultimate results. Oscar Wilde has asserted that "all criticism is autobiographical," and this, my most "objective" piece of scholarship, has taught me of the truth of his remark. For why was I so driven to do this work, why was I the one to set myself the task of uncovering Western feminist bias in this way? And what were the consequences for me of my project?

The impulse to write "The Sultan and the Slave" grew out of my own experience as an "oriental" woman living in the West. Born in Cairo in 1949, I emigrated to the United States with my parents when I was two years old. Although my family was markedly Middle Eastern in many of its values and customs, we set ourselves apart from Arabs and Muslims, identifying as European and Jewish. What was this East with which we were allied and yet from which we felt the need to distinguish ourselves? This question pervaded my childhood and early adulthood, even as I internalized my parents' pain about leaving Cairo and their fear of returning. Like them, I learned to repress and deny the East within me. I grew up to become a professor of English literature, working to master the discourse that had mastered us. What a surprise and opportunity then to discover, at the core of Western feminist literature, the very oppositions that had structured my experience. Writing "The Sultan and the Slave" became my chance to explore the sources of that experience.

The most profound result of my effort was its bringing me to a friendship with Mervat Hatem, a Muslim political scientist whose work on relationships between European and Egyptian feminists at the turn of the century I had cited. When Hatem came to New Orleans to speak about Arab feminism, I introduced myself. She had read my essay. "I always wondered how an American woman could write such a piece," she said. "I'm Egyptian," I said, "and Jewish." "Then you are my sister," she exclaimed.

Born in Cairo the same year as I was, Mervat became my bridge back to the culture my family had felt forced to abandon in 1951. As we delicately forged a friendship, renegotiating the divide between Arab and Jew, Eastern and Western, we found common ground in our feminism and commitment to respect for the other. It was Mervat who ultimately made possible my long-deferred return to Cairo and who assisted me in my effort to reintegrate and lay claim to the denied identity. Thus writing and finding an audience for my work brought me full circle, reconnecting me with my deepest core. It would take much more than my allotted space here to reflect fully on the implications of this interplay among literature, culture, experience, and scholarship—but it is part of what makes it a pleasure to live my life today as a feminist teacher, scholar, and writer.

The relation between Islam and the West remains one of the most pressing problems of our times. The roots of feminist orientalism (let alone "regular" orientalism) run deep. We see them at work in contemporary efforts to justify wars in Iraq and Afghanistan and even Palestine in terms of liberating women. Yet on a recent trip to Cairo, I was overwhelmed and unnerved by the increased presence of covered women. Some smiled at me, an obvious Westerner with my close-cropped hair and bare arms. Others eyed me suspiciously. Were they happy? Were they free? Was I? The lines of communication between us were down, cut once again by historical forces and by our own veiled presences to one another. Because I know that I myself have not undone my own orientalism and feminist orientalism, I know that I have much work to do, and I fear that many others of us—Eastern and Western, Muslim, Christian, Hindu, pagan, Jewish, and Buddhist—have similar work to do as well.

Geometries of Race and Gender: Eve Sedgwick, Spike Lee, Charlayne Hunter-Gault

Susan Fraiman

EVER SINCE EVE Sedgwick's *Between Men: English Literature and Male Homosocial Desire* (1985), the erotic triangle in which two men bond over the body of a woman has proved more compelling for literary and cultural critics, and certainly more demonstrable, than that mysteriously attractive triangle near Bermuda.[1] In Victorian novels and postmodern movies, the Sedgwickian triangle— the woman between men—seems to meet us at every turn. My article takes as its starting point the tremendous explanatory force of this three-sided figure. Proceeding through a series of triangulated scenarios drawn from American culture in recent memory, I would propose, however, a somewhat different typology—one that schematizes relations involving not only gender and sexuality but also race.

Sedgwick's work draws, of course, on Lévi-Strauss's famous reasoning about exogamous marriage—that male-headed groups exchange women in order to bind themselves to each other in relationships of reciprocity and kinship. Like money or words, brides are circulated for the purpose of organizing and extending masculine society. The result is what Gayle Rubin went on to call the "traffic in women," in which men are designated as givers, women as gifts. "It is the partners, not the presents," Rubin noted, "upon whom reciprocal exchange confers its quasi-mystical power of social linkage." Luce Irigaray, in "Commodities among Themselves," has also commented on the implications of this traffic for the commodity: "Woman exists only as an occasion for mediation, transaction, transition, transference, between man and his fellow man."[2] Although Rubin points out that gift exchange may involve male rivalries and disputes as well as diplomacy, the emphasis of all these analyses is on the role women play in fostering positive conjunctions between men—in bringing them together as affines, political allies, economic partners, and, in Sedgwick's formulation, as cohorts of a "potentially erotic" kind. This formulation suggests, briefly, that in a patriarchy such as ours—based on male ties but at the same time violently homophobic—men will be required to route their intimacy through women. Elaborating on René Girard's study of erotic triangles in European fiction, Sedgwick's important argument only makes explicit the assumption, intimated by precursor accounts, that what women mediate is basically men's desire for each other.

Sedgwick is particularly concerned to take up this triangular paradigm "not as an ahistorical, Platonic form, a deadly symmetry from which the historical accidents of gender, language, class, and power detract, but as a sensitive register precisely for delineating relationships of power and meaning." As evidence of the way racial ideologies, for example, can shape and splinter sexual meanings, she observes that *Gone with the Wind* (book and film) automatically construes the vaguest Black male–white female encounters as "rape," while refusing to perceive white-on-white sexual assault as anything but "blissful marriage."[3] And in numerous brilliant readings Sedgwick goes on to show how literary representations of male homosocial desire are variously inflected by shifting, historically specific constructions of class, male homosexuality, gender, and English imperialism. Yet in spite of this self-conscious and elucidating attention to the way erotic triangles get tossed on historical seas, there is still a sense in which their significance for Sedgwick remains the same: they are always finally about the forbidden embrace of men by men. What I wish to do in this article is to insist on some of the other meanings that may inform this configuration, meanings that in Sedgwick are perhaps too readily subsumed by the trope of love between men.

I would emphasize, first, that men's ties to each other are frequently characterized not simply by uneasy desire but also by political domination, on one side, and resistance to that domination, on the other—that race and racism, for example, cross and complicate relations between men so that the erotic, while undoubtedly present, may no longer be the predominant affect or agenda.[4] It is not that Sedgwick leaves conflict out of these relations but that in her account hostility and violence are essentially the signs of a highly charged but unrecognized intimacy. Thus, "the magnetism between the rivals in *Our Mutual Friend*, although intense, has to be inferred from the very violence of their hating intercourse."[5] In a homophobic society, the Freudian logic by which same-sex "rivalry" and "love" are complementary, even equivalent, intensities (and the privileged subtext is sexual) can clarify a good deal. Nor do I mean to deny that domination and desire are sometimes inseparable bedfellows. Yet it seems important to explore the way women also mediate rivalries between men that cannot be wholly assimilated to "love." In the American imagination today, women are often at the nexus of male struggles that, however eroticized, are more fully explained in terms of attempts both to enforce and to oppose white supremacy. My first four scenarios represent a set of interlocking variations on this theme. Each is centered on a woman's rape and emblematic, I think, of a story we tell ourselves about race relations in this culture. I have nevertheless tried to render them with some degree of subtlety and specificity, even while abstracting their triangular logics of race and/or gender so as to offer them as general types. In these abstracted terms, they delineate the following geometries: One, white men dominating men of color through a narrative involving a white woman's rape. Two, the same racial domination, only this time the pivotal rape involves a woman of color. Scenarios three and four, shifting from a white male to Black male subject position, are ostensibly parallel to the first two. In three, men of color resist the oppression of white men through a narrative involving the rape of a woman of color. And in four, resistance to racial domination turns on the rape of a white woman. In addition to glossing each of these four logics in some detail, I will also be remarking on the ways they fit together, on the cultural sum of their parts. Finally, in a fifth scenario, I attempt to move outside the Sedgwickian triangle altogether, hoping to suggest an alternative geometry.

Scenario One: The Central Park Jogger

I want to begin by returning, in effect, to Sedgwick's image of Scarlett O'Hara and the specter of the Black rapist. "The Central Park jogger" was the name given by the press to a woman raped, beaten, and left for dead in Central Park on April 19, 1989. The woman was young, white, and an investment banker at Salomon Brothers; those arrested and ultimately convicted for the crime were young, Black or Hispanic, and working-class. My concern here is not with the actual assault, whose brutality goes without saying and whose historical details remain, in any case, elusive. I am interested, rather, in the way this event was narrated by the white, male-dominated media, in the ideologies that were filtered through it, the allegorical meanings accruing to it over time. Lingering in the news for the next eighteen months (three of the defendants went on trial in the summer of 1990, two in the fall of 1990), the jogger became, among other things, a locus of white panic about crime in New York City. The woman's job, her use of leisure hours for aerobic exercise, and especially her young, blond femaleness combined to render her a symbol of privileged intactness suddenly violated. Beyond their horror at this particular rape, the class of New Yorkers accustomed to moving through the city sealed off from violence by whiteness and wealth were enraged by what they read as a general attack on their entitlement to be invulnerable. The racism under-lying their rage was barely disguised by the pseudosociological media inquiry into an alarming phenomenon known as "wilding." From what I can remember and imagine, the term originated something like this: a reporter from a white news-paper drove up to East 110th Street and quickly assembled around him a group of neighborhood kids eager to comment on the recent crime. One of them made what may in fact have been a reference to a popular song of the time, Tone-Loc's "Wild Thing." The newsman misheard and gravely reported that for young Black and Hispanic youths to go on a group spree of premeditated rape and maybe mur-der was a well-known practice referred to in street argot as "wilding." The effect of this widely publicized construct was implicitly to pathologize Black culture, to justify any irregularity in the obtaining of videotaped confessions from four of the accused, and to rationalize further Bernard Goetz-style preemptive strikes against groups of nonwhite male teens who ride the subways or use the parks.[6]

This logic—in which the myth of the Black rapist stalking white womanhood becomes a blanket excuse for the execution of Black men by white men—has, of course, a long and ugly history. As Hazel V. Carby, among others, has recently reminded us, the journalist Ida B. Wells exposed and condemned the racism of this logic in a series of pamphlets published between 1892 and 1900, a period during which the rate of lynchings had reached more than one hundred per year. Only about one-third of these involved accusations of rape or attempted rape, but all were at some irrational level justified to whites by the imagined Black threat to "their" women. The case of Emmett Till, a fourteen-year-old boy murdered in 1955 for whistling at a white woman, is only the most notorious example of subsequent lynchings thematized along these lines. And the pattern prevails not only in the backwoods of the unreconstructed South but also in the contemporary criminal justice system, which continues to punish Black-on-white rape more harshly than any other.[7] So I take the Central Park jogger case to stand for one paradigm of American racism, available during slavery but crystallized in the period following Reconstruction and still influential today, in which white men's control of Black men is mediated by the always-about-to-be-violated bodies of white women.

In this scenario, racism primarily (if not only) on the part of men and directed primarily at men operates alongside sexism in three respects. First, it makes white women coextensive with their sexuality, which is, moreover, taken to be tremblingly passive, never active and initiating. It assumes that no white woman would ever choose a Black (or any) lover, and it estimates women's value in terms of their newness or usedness as sexual goods, so that rape is less the violation of a female body than a trespass against male property. Above all, it perceives white women as frail, vulnerable, and wholly dependent for protection on chivalric white males.[8] Second, by fixing on the specter of the Black stranger-rapist, it obscures what is actually the far more habitual crime of white-on-white acquaintance rape. Current statistics suggest that the great majority of rapes are committed by men known to their victims and apt to belong to the same racial and class group.[9] And finally, by fetishizing the white woman as the quintessential victim of rape, it ignores the rape of Black women altogether, by white and Black men both. As the Black community was quick to point out, the most salient fact about the story of the Central Park jogger is that it became a story at all, when daily violence against Black women goes virtually unreported.[10] Angela Davis suggests further that, because "the mythical rapist implies the mythical whore," the jogger scenario may even encourage the rape of Black women, insofar as it supports the convenient view of Black people as naturally lascivious.[11]

Before moving on to my next scenario, I would like to point out that a similar logic—what we might call the white chivalric fallacy—is inevitably at work in imperialist U.S. wars waged against a racial Other. Here, too, white women back home are taken to represent decency and security, made to symbolize the intact national body, which must be shielded from penetration by dark, alien forces. Outright aggression is once more framed as "protection," the bombardment by white men of any enemy imagined as nonwhite and male, once again justified in the name of white women. Yet these women are, for the most part, not participants so much as symbolic currency in the exchange of fire power between men. Indeed, as Virginia Woolf argued in *Three Guineas* and as recent polls have seemed to confirm, women (like other disenfranchised groups) are apt to feel they have little to gain and much to lose from bids for national supremacy. The 1991 war in the Persian Gulf invoked the white chivalric fallacy on several mutually reinforcing levels. Certainly it generated televised images of a feminized home front—small Midwestern towns waving with yellow ribbons and corn-fed women trying to keep back the tears. Saddam Hussein was perfect as the swarthy psychopath, and to Americans raised on generic images of Arabs-as-terrorists, it hardly mattered in emotional terms what particular country he was from or that other Arab states were on our side.[12] Yet the difficulty in this case of making even Hussein's melodramatized villainy extend so far as our own backyards also required a clever recasting of the scene. As Susan Jeffords has demonstrated (following linguist George Lakoff), the helpless victim of this "rescue scenario" was less our own virgin land than Kuwait, an American satellite whose much-reiterated "rape" by Iraq cried out for our intervention. Jeffords derives this model not from that of lynching-for-rape but from an even older national story conjoining race and gender: the "captivity" narrative, popular in the late seventeenth and early eighteenth centuries, in which a Puritan woman must be rescued from her savage Indian captors by the heroic Puritan man.[13] There was one more, especially odd variation on this logic that emerged in relation to U.S. aggression in the Gulf. Appropriating "feminism" for jingoism, U.S. news reports cast at least some Islamic women in the role of wannabe Westerners. Subjected by Islamic men to a bizarre sexual confinement, such women cry out for salvation by a kinder and gentler American sexual politics. Underneath the chador, these stories implied, is an American soul struggling to free itself from the barbaric Arab male. This version of the rescue scenario with Western "feminism" in the white chivalric role, while enabled by an Orientalist strain of feminism (as well as Middle Eastern gender practices), was basically a disingenuous and opportunist act of impersonation by the mainstream media, serving at once further to justify our military invasion, and to project home team sexist guilt on to faraway lands.

Scenario Two: *Casualties of War*

I refer here to Brian De Palma's 1989 Vietnam movie (screenplay by David Rabe). Like the press coverage of the rape in Central Park, *Casualties of War* narrates a real atrocity, first reported in 1969 by Daniel Lang: the kidnapping, gang rape, and murder of a South Vietnamese woman, Phan Thi Mao, by four American soldiers, which took place in 1966.[14] Once again, however, I am less interested in the facts of the incident than in the way they have been mythologized by the dominant culture. In De Palma's myth, the story begins with the betrayal of Americans by innocent-seeming South Vietnamese villagers who turn out to be murderous Viet Cong. As a result of a surprise ambush, the squad's fearless and beloved Black sergeant, Brownie, is shot down just weeks before his tour is over. Brownie's mutilated body, anguished face, and pathetic bravado all serve to focus, for us and for his buddies, an image of the slant-eyed enemy as the incarnation of deceit and depravity. According to De Palma, the enemy's malignant and triumphant maleness is further indicated by his monopolizing of the Vietnamese whores on a night when the grieving Americans are desperate to get laid. The vicious attack on Phan follows soon thereafter. In this scenario, then, the body of the Asian female, site of the Viet Cong's imagined mastery, is quite naturally transformed into the site of the Americans' "revenge." As in the lynching model described earlier, white men's assault on darker men is staged not as aggression but as reasonable defense or retaliation, and once again this racial domination is achieved by means of the rapable female body. That rape is a weapon of war is hardly news. As Susan Brownmiller recounts in *Against Our Will: Men, Women, and Rape*, rape has been the victor's prerogative since *The Iliad* and has long been tolerated if not encouraged in spite of official prohibitions.[15] I take *Casualties of War*, therefore, to figure a racialized version of a military truism: that rape is an effective means of waging war and one of its oldest rewards. To summarize and schematize my argument so far, both triangulated scenarios one and two uphold white privilege and pivot on the objectified figure of a woman. From a white, male perspective, in the jogger scenario this woman is white, she is "ours," and "we" are protecting her from "them." This is what I have called the chivalric fallacy. In the De Palma scenario she is "yellow" (or at some other deviation from "white"), she is a condensation of our racial hatred, and we are raping her. This story-type is structured by what I call rape as a weapon of war.

The violence against women in the latter case is obvious, but *Casualties of War* adds an interesting twist to the role played by Phan Thi Mao. For De Palma's film dramatizes not only rationalized American violence against an Asian woman who stands for the Asian enemy (rationalized insofar as the rapists themselves are seen as "casualties" of war's moral chaos) but also American guilt about this violence. Perhaps De Palma—having butchered so many women of (techni)color in his earlier films—is working out some personal guilt as well. In any case, the protagonist of *Casualties of War* is a fifth soldier, Private First Class Eriksson played by Michael J. Fox, who witnesses the rapes and murder but refuses to participate in them. In fact he befriends Phan, tries to help her escape, and eventually succeeds in having her four assailants court-martialed. The result is that male America gets to see itself as the winsome hero of *Family Ties*, while Phan, in addition to being physically abused, is deprived even of the right to struggle and speak on her own behalf. De Palma portrays her as nothing but helpless terror—she's like a wounded child or animal—incapable of outrage and reliant on Eriksson even to prompt her escape. In a particularly implausible scene, she clings to him, refusing to flee unless he goes with her. Later, as she lies broken in a gully, he braves a hostile military hierarchy in order to win her justice. For this gallantry, the Asian woman (refigured as an Asian American student in the movie's frame) absolves America of guilt and reassures Eriksson that the "bad dream" of our violence against Vietnam is "over now." Any anger the Phan Thi Mao figure might have toward Americans in uniform is obscenely written over as gratitude. De Palma's feat is to enable this woman's brutalized and silenced body to mediate both American men's savagery toward the Vietnamese and their fantasy of being forgiven for it.

The incident on which *Casualties of War* is based occurred, we recall, in 1966: between the assassination of Malcolm X in 1965 and that of Martin Luther King, Jr., in 1968, between the Watts riots of 1965 and the Detroit riots of 1967, at a time when violent protests against racism exploded in more than a hundred urban neighborhoods. Scenes of Vietnamese huts and American inner cities aflame blur together in our national memory. More to the point, when *Casualties of War* was released in the summer of 1989, New York City was still at racial odds over the April jogger incident, and white fears ran high that the opening of Spike Lee's *Do the Right Thing*—in which a Black man is strangled by police and white property set afire—would make the summer very hot indeed. Given that America was and continues to be embattled over issues of race, and given the disproportionately large numbers of African Americans who saw combat in Vietnam, it seems inevitable that representations of Vietnam and wasted "gooks" would also bring up America's peculiar history of subordinating Blacks. I want to suggest that the oppression of African Americans, white investment in and guilt about this, is introduced as still another subtext of *Casualties of War*, by means of numerous implicit equations between the victimized Asian woman and the victimized Black man.[16]

First and most obviously, Brownie (his very name a crude marker for "coloredness") meets a gory fate that is an ante-type for the Vietnamese woman's; in the slasher-film idiom De Palma speaks so fluently, their murders are part of a single series. So although De Palma invents Brownie and his death largely as a rationale for the later rape and murder, the relation between these is one not only of cause and effect but also of structural equivalence. The deaths of Brownie and Phan mark the two points of greatest visual and emotional stress in the film, pairing these two figures as the most overt "casualties" of the war. Second, as frame opens on to inner story, the Asian American woman who prompts Eriksson's flashback gives way, in his mind, to shadowy figures patrolling a jungle; the first one to emerge into view is a Black commander we later meet as Lieutenant Riley, and he speaks the movie's first words. Riley's association with the woman is subtly reinforced by the fact that they (and no one else in the movie) both wear glasses. The effect of this conjunction is to hint that, at some deeper level, Eriksson's and De Palma's guilt-ridden dream is not about the Asian woman or Vietnam at all but about the Black man and race relations between men in America.

In his only extended scene, Riley responds to Eriksson's report of the Phan Thi Mao atrocity with a seemingly irrelevant story of his own about racism back home. Denied a bed in a white hospital, Riley's wife delivered their son on the reception room floor. Riley's righteous anger only got him locked up in the white man's jail, an experience which eventually taught him that "what happened is the way things are." "So why try to buck the system?" he concludes, finally addressing Eriksson's complaint by advising him just to "forget about it." What interests me here is that Riley's story actually, at this point, displaces Eriksson's about Phan. For De Palma chooses not to dramatize Eriksson's report to Riley, implying instead that it has already occurred when the film cuts to Riley's office. This scene opens with and indeed consists of nothing but Riley's narrative. Consequently, the crime *reported on screen* is not, in fact, the crime against Phan but the crime against Black Americans, who are represented by the Black husband and father. Stressing Riley's impotence and resignation before racial injustice, the movie once again stages the guiltiness of white masculinity only to reassert its superiority: it is in pointed contrast to both Riley and Phan that De Palma's Eriksson courageously pursues his court-martial, showing that he, if not they, has the balls to "buck the system." Thus, the white hero simultaneously redeems himself as a champion of the oppressed and reoppresses them by proving that he alone can speak on their behalf.

As for the relationship between the Asian female and African American male narratives, this returns us to my larger point, for in some sense the entire story of Phan's violated body operates as a cover for the antecedent story of white men's guilty but relentless domination of their Black brothers. The feminized Vietnam material mediates, as it were, an underlying drama of racial conflict between American males. Susan Jeffords stresses the appearance of cross-class and interracial fraternity as a key component of Vietnam narratives, heterogeneous men allying to exclude the feminine.[17] Yet I am arguing that one subtext of *Casualties of War* is the absence of interracial fraternity: a struggle to preserve racial hierarchies among men which does not exclude so much as rely upon the feminine as a switching point.

Scenario Three: *Do the Right Thing*

We move at this point to Black male subjectivity. Spike Lee's 1989 film is in many ways a compelling meditation on the complexities of racism—its smartest move being, in my opinion, Lee's controversial refusal either to condone or absolutely to rule out the use of violence in fighting the powers that be. Yet *Do the Right Thing* nevertheless shares with many other antiracist representations the assumption that racism, as well as the struggle against it, is something that happens exclusively between men.[18] There are no white women in this movie; the mother of Sal's sons is curiously absent from the Italian family romance and its racist ways. And the women who are present generally function as a kind of Greek chorus to the main action, chiding men to be responsible and keening in the aftermath of destruction men have wrought. The opening shots of Rosie Perez, in which she wears boxing gloves and does a pugilistic dance to Public Enemy's "Fight the Power," seem all the more merely decorative, given the fact that, in the ensuing drama, women never even enter the ring of racial combat. The relegation of women to the political sidelines is explicit in Lee's previous film, *School Daze*, where the battle over divestment at Mission College is waged between two male students—a Black nationalist (Dap) and a fraternity president (Julian)—while their female counterparts claw each other over men and hair. In *Do the Right Thing*, one of the women on the margins, Mookie's sister, Jade, is also in the middle of Mookie's racially vexed relation to his white employer, Sal.

The contradiction exemplified by Lee's film is, then, that it launches, on the one hand, a radical attack on the racism enforced by our first two scenarios while also apparently reproducing their placing of women between antagonistic males. It illustrates, we might say, another manifestation of the chivalric fallacy in which this time *Black* men rally to protect "our" women from "them." Thus we get Mookie's annoying paternalism toward Jade when he warns her to stay away from Sal because all Sal wants is sex. Although Jade protests, Mookie's view is glossed and legitimated by the graffiti on the wall behind them, which reads: "Tawana told the truth." Of course in one important sense Lee is right. Tawana Brawley—the Black teenager who accused several white men of raping and defacing her and whose story was later discredited—did tell the truth; for if the facts of her particular case have been hard to ascertain, we can nevertheless say with certainty that Brawley's story accurately represents the sordid and elided history of white men's sanctioned rape of Black women. To insist on this truth is a forceful and necessary counter to the use of rape as a weapon in the war against Black people. At the same time, however, another effect of this formulation—by Mookie/Lee or by Alton Maddox, Vernon Mason, and Al Sharpton—is to raise the violated Black female body as a kind of flag in the Black man's fight against racism. What seems like a campaign on the Black woman's behalf may assign her once again to silence and passivity, to a symbolically mediating and spoken-for position that works against her in several ways.[19] First, it imagines her (not unlike the Southern belle) as the helpless victim of male aggression, without desires and defiances of her own. Second, even as it articulates her racist and sexist abuse by white men, it obscures the extent to which Black men abuse her as well. We can see this, I think, in the Tawana Brawley case in which the Black male version of her narrative automatically discounts the theory that Brawley told her story in the first place because she was late coming home and wanted to avoid being beaten by her Black stepfather.

Scenario Four: *School Daze*

If the chivalric fallacy of scenario one is echoed by the paternalistic defense of Tawana Brawley or "Jade," so the use of rape as a weapon of war in scenario two is echoed by Lee's 1988 film about Black college life, *School Daze*. In an interview with Henry Louis Gates, Lee argued that to represent homophobia and sexism on screen is not necessarily to endorse them and may actually be, as Gates proposed, "an effective way of critiquing them."[20] I think that *School Daze* does attempt to critique the traffic in Black women among Black college men, distancing itself from the fraternity pledges with their chant of "pass the pussy." This argument culminates with Dap, the movie's moral authority, condemning his cousin Half Pint for accepting homecoming queen Jane as a sexual gift from her boyfriend Julian. Half Pint stands accused of proving his manhood by what amounts to a rape. More than this, I find *School Daze* quite knowing, in the Sedgwickian sense, about the way this kind of traffic articulates brotherly love. There is, for example, the humorous moment on a darkened dance floor when two men trade partners and, in the process, "mistakenly" embrace each other.

Yet if *School Daze* seems more or less aware that Black women may, to their disadvantage, mediate Black men's homosocial desires, it has far less critical distance on the strategic function of Jane's rape in the movie's war against racial injustice. For although Lee seems to lament her violation, the movie associates the light-skinned sorority girl with white domination and racial compromise to an extent that virtually requires her punishment and exile. Whereas Dap epitomizes racial integrity—"No white blood in me," he jokes in mock-African tones, "my stock one hundred percent pure"—Jane and her similarly complected clique are taken to embody not forced miscegenation but blamable wannabe-ism. And although Dap's friends tease him about his inflexible Africanism, the movie's call to "Wake Up" seems finally to validate notions of racial purity as well as pride. For what *School Daze* urges Blacks to wake up from is a messy history of complacency before and complicity with ruling-class whites, which is almost entirely projected on to women whose complexions are lighter and whose hair is straighter. I think this helps to explain why the depiction of Jane's extreme humiliation seems ultimately more punitive than sympathetic, and why (unlike her male counterpart, Julian) she is not included in, much less redeemed by, the film's closing utopian vision. While this last communal scene is bathed in the light of dawn, *School Daze* (like Julian) leaves Jane crumpled and alone in a dark room. To rape and reject the light-skinned woman is, the film finally implies, to strike a blow for racial freedom. Such logic is related, if not equivalent, to that of the young Eldridge Cleaver, for whom the white woman stood between Black men and their white masters as a kind of fatal attraction, making her rape "an insurrectionary act."[21] As in *Casualties of War*, the emotional reasoning of *School Daze* makes the torn body of the "other-ized" female a trophy, signaling victory over the enemy male.

In sum, then, scenarios three and four represent Black men resisting white male domination by invoking the vulnerability of Black women or the violability of light/white women taken to stand for white privilege. Even such powerfully antiracist polemics as Spike Lee's appear in this sense to rely on the same configuring of gender as scenarios one and two, the same relegation of objectified Black and white women to the no-man's land between men. In ideological terms they are riven by internal contradictions—oppositional in regard to race, conventional in regard to gender—making them continuous as well as discontinuous with the white, male texts considered above. For the Black chivalric fallacy would seem to map neatly on to the white version of this fallacy, as the use of rape as a weapon of war appears common to Black and white men alike. Nevertheless, and this cannot be overstressed, the structural similarities I have outlined do not mean that Black sexism can simply be conflated with white sexism. What I would emphasize, rather, is less the similarity than the interdependence of white and Black constructions of masculinity: for if white rapists logically produce Black chivalry, so white chivalry virtually invites a retaliatory use of rape as a weapon of racial self-defense. What appears at first glance to be a simple symmetry, parallel sexisms, is partly a case of cause and effect, in which the racial agendas of white masculinists generate a mirroring Black inverse. The relation of these white male to Black male texts is not, in truth, symmetrical so much as chiasmic—and the cross between them is burning.

Scenario Five: Charlayne Hunter-Gault

If there was ever a woman between men, it must be Charlayne Hunter-Gault of the *MacNeil/Lehrer Newshour*. There she is, night after night, between PBS anchors Robin MacNeil and Jim Lehrer. From about July 1990 through May 1991 she was, moreover, in an unusually tight spot between George Bush and Saddam Hussein.[22] Yet wartime has ironically proved, especially in this century, to be a time of increased opportunities for women, the positionings of female and male more unstable than ever. I would like to close by turning to a series of televised interviews from this recent period of war. Conducted by Hunter-Gault with three women in the U.S. Airforce—Susan Brown, Theresa Collier, and Prayon Meade—they have become in my mind an intriguing figure for geometries of race and gender beyond those examined thus far.[23]

The Hunter-Gault of these months, particularly in the unsure weeks before war actually broke out, before the total accession of aggressive virility, was on the move in the Middle East. I recall shots of her striding through a sandy landscape, seemingly at home amid professionals preparing for battle. Instead of still and studio-bound, her hair and casual clothing are in motion around her. Interviewing her subjects at a base in Dehran, Saudi Arabia, Hunter-Gault looks comfortable in pants, a sweater over her shoulders and sunglasses on her head. The servicewomen are wearing fatigues and combat boots, sitting or leaning on a military vehicle, with planes visible and audible in the background. Two of the women are white, two are Black. From the pale, red-headed Susan Brown to the blond Prayon Meade, honey-colored Charlayne Hunter-Gault, and dark-skinned Theresa Collier, they suggest a veritable rainbow coalition of womanhood.

What strikes me, of course, is that here are women in the news, on the screen, not between men but between other women. It feels unfamiliar, this conversation about war in which all of the voices are female. The usual furrow-browed face of PBS is nowhere to be seen. Inviting them to share their feelings about the uncertainties, stresses, and costs of violent conflict, Hunter-Gault is more group facilitator than grim war correspondent. "How about you, Prayon; what about that boy child of yours?" she asks (16 Jan. 1991). "You don't like war," she offers in response to Theresa's apprehensions (11 Feb. 1991). Calling them by their first names, Hunter-Gault develops with the women an apparently common language about children left behind, uncooperative husbands, dislike of violence, and the ambition to be fighter pilots. Even on the eve of the war—when male soldiers interviewed were hunkered down, intoning military mantras about "doing a job"—all the women speak openly about how scared they are. One of my favorite moments, because it occurs, poignantly, at the end of this particular interview, and because it would be inconceivable if even one of the group were male, is when Prayon signs off with "When we get back to the States, we'll do lunch" (16 Jan. 1991).

The final interview takes place on American soil, and at its conclusion the four women do, in fact, head off to share a meal. Yet we should have no illusion that what happens when women of diverse colors get together is simply "lunch," much less uncomplicated sisterhood. Indeed, they come together here as participants in an international racialized struggle, and their very Black and white Americanness cannot but refer (as in *Casualties of War*) to ongoing racial struggles at home. It is evident, for example, from Hunter-Gault's question about women in Saudi society that Arab women are wholly and mysteriously Other to the Americans (2 Oct. 1990). "I haven't seen one," Prayon says. "I don't know any," Theresa agrees.

Lacking any direct information, the servicewomen waver between glad-to-be-me-isms and a curious envy of the unencountered female. "I heard they have it real good over here, real good," Theresa comments. This is followed by an eager chorus: they have maids (Prayon); they have chauffeurs (Theresa); their husbands buy them expensive jewelry (Prayon); they're put on a pedestal (Theresa). Only Susan interjects, "They can't go to the gym." As earlier tones of superiority ("Over here, you're like, you don't see how a society has done it for so long") give way at this point to desire and resentment, the bewildering racial/cultural differences between American and Arab women seem suddenly to be rearticulated in terms of more familiar domestic differences of class and race. It is as if all the privileges associated with ruling-class white femininity in the States are projected wholesale on to the blankness of the Arab female, who is therefore looked up to wistfully even as she is scorned. A similar class/race rift between women is also invoked by the reference to "maids," who are not themselves regarded as Saudi women but only as part of the luxury surrounding those women whose femininity is recognized as such.[24]

Subtle divisions emerge, moreover, among the interviewees themselves. I notice, in particular, a tension between Prayon and Theresa over their relationship to America, beginning with the second interview (16 Jan. 1991). As U.S. planes prepare to bomb Baghdad, Prayon asserts that the United States is going to "kick butt," because "we've got an advantage like you would not believe." Prayon says she believes this "personally," and also "being American." Theresa responds with considerable irony: "Yeah, being American, apple pie, you know. I'm just as patriotic as the next person, but you know . . ." and she goes on to express doubts and fears about the war's outcome. A month into the war, Theresa is again more willing than her compatriot to be critical of the United States. She disagrees with Prayon's feeling that the conflict is "one man [Saddam Hussein] messing up the lives of millions." "I feel he's wrong," Theresa explains, "but it takes two to tango, you know" (11 Feb. 1991). And finally, in the postwar interview (15 May 1991) back home, at least one basis for Theresa's more examined and ambivalent citizenship becomes explicit. It is Theresa speaking:

> The first image that I saw after leaving Saudi Arabia was the police beating the hell out of Rodney King in L.A. and that really pissed me off. Excuse my French, but I couldn't believe it. I'm like, here I am, spent eight months over here to protect "my country" but yet people are getting beat, you know, people are getting beat for no apparent reason at home.

Without ever mentioning race, Theresa makes clear that she identifies less with those Americans kicking butt in Baghdad than with those getting beat in L.A., and she tells us she plans to leave the military. "I've gone to work for my country," she says. "Now let me stay home and work for my people." The gap opened up here between "my country" and "my people" is evidently not present for Prayon, whose first thought on her return is "What a great country!"

If Susan seems somewhat left out of all this, her relative obscurity in these interviews figures for me another line of fracture among women. As the only "single" woman, she is excluded from the extensive discussions of marriage and motherhood. She is eloquent, however (in the 11 Feb. 1991 interview), on why men resist the idea of women as fighter pilots:

> I think a lot of men out here still think they need to protect us, protect their mother or girlfriend or a woman. That feeling is still very much alive and that's going to take a long time to get rid of, but the women are ready. We're ready.

Given this clarity on the chivalric fallacy, no wonder, as we saw earlier, Susan seems to be on a different planet in the sequence about pampered Saudi wives. I choose to take Susan's investment, rather, in going "to the gym" as a sign of something else of—living and working (out) the female body against the grain of compulsory heterosexuality. In terms of sexuality, then, as well as race and class, it should be clear that domination in America, and opposition to it, is not a matter between men only, however much our most widely circulated cultural myths imagine it as such.

I began by asking how sustained attention to the U.S. racial imaginary might reinflect Sedgwick's powerful model. I hope my typology of scenarios evoking race and rape has shown that the traffic in women may involve male status as much as eros. But my goal in describing dominant gender mythologies, Black as well as white, is not only to demystify these but also, in the end, to contest their relegation of women to merely intermediary roles. I mean finally to urge so-called gender studies away from the alluring Sedgwickian triangle and back to women—to slighted representations of our bodies and ourselves, the geometries of our relations, however problematized and embattled "we" may be. I offer this last scenario, then, as a figure for women's particular complicity with racism and other exploitations, for the specificity of female domination and defiance, and for the elements of both power and desire that bind women in uneasy but undeniable relation to each other.

NOTES

I am grateful to Ralph Cohen and the Commonwealth Center for Literary and Cultural Change at the University of Virginia for inviting me to give the talk on which this essay is based. I would also like to thank the editors of *Feminist Studies*, and, for their various insights, Sara Blair, Saidiya Hartman, Deborah McDowell, Tania Modleski, Jahan Ramazani, Werner Sollors, and Kim Tso. Thanks, above all, to Eric Lott, whose views on race and popular culture have greatly influenced my work.

[1] Eve Kosofsky Sedgwick, *Between Men: English Literature and Male Homosocial Desire* (New York: Columbia University Press, 1985).

[2] Claude Lévi-Strauss, *The Elementary Structures of Kinship* (Boston: Beacon Press, 1969); Gayle Rubin, "The Traffic in Women: Notes on the 'Political Economy' of Sex," in *Toward an Anthropology of Women*, ed. Rayna [Rapp] Reiter (New York: Monthly Review Press, 1975), 174; Luce Irigaray, "Commodities among Themselves," in *This Sex Which Is Not One*, trans. Catherine Porter (Ithaca, N.Y.: Cornell University Press, 1985), 193.

[3] Sedgwick, 27, 9–10.

[4] Robyn Wiegman, in "Melville's Geography of Gender," *American Literary History* 1 (winter 1989): 735–53, makes a similar point about Robert Martin's and Joseph Boone's idealizing of

male bonding in Melville. According to Wiegman, the myth of male homosocial democracy not only suppresses the feminine but may also deny (and thereby help to maintain) racial and class inequities among men.

[5] Sedgwick, 181.

[6] For more on the popular narratives arising from this case, see Joan Didion, "New York: Sentimental Journeys," *The New York Review of Books*, 17 Jan. 1991, 45–56. While offering considerable insight into the way class (if not racial) ideologies circulated in relation to this case, Didion finally veers away from analyzing the struggle between New York's powerful and powerless into a decrial of Tammanyism seemingly removed from this struggle. See also Valerie Smith, "Split Affinities: The Case of Interracial Rape," in *Conflicts in Feminism*, ed. Marianne Hirsch and Evelyn Fox-Keller (New York: Routledge, 1990), 271–87.

[7] For references to studies suggesting racial bias in the prosecution of rape cases, see Susan Brownmiller *Against Our Will: Men, Women, and Rape* (Middlesex: Penguin, 1976), 215–16; Angela Y. Davis, "Rape, Racism, and the Myth of the Black Rapist," in her *Women, Race, and Class* (New York: Random House, 1983), 172; Jacqueline Dowd Hall, "'The Mind That Burns in Each Body': Women, Rape, and Racial Violence," in *Powers of Desire: The Politics of Sexuality*, ed. Ann Snitow, Christine Stansell, and Sharon Thompson (New York: Monthly Review Press, 1983), 349; and Susan Estrich, *Real Rape* (Cambridge: Harvard University Press, 1987), 107. For more on the history and politics of interracial rape, see also Ida B. Wells, *On Lynchings: Southern Horrors; A Red Record; Mob Rule in New Orleans* (New York: Arno Press, 1969); Hazel V. Carby, *Reconstructing Womanhood: The Emergence of the Afro-American Woman Novelist* (New York: Oxford University Press, 1987), 108–14; *Lynching and Rape: An Exchange of Views*, ed. Bettina Aptheker (San Jose: American Institute for Marxist Studies, 1977); Jacqueline Dowd Hall, *The Revolt against Chivalry: Jessie Daniel Ames and the Women's Campaign against Lynching* (New York: Columbia University Press, 1979); and Smith.

[8] See Hall's essay and book on Ames (founder of the Association of Southern Women for the Prevention of Lynching), who in 1930 first contested the logic of chivalry as a rationale for white vigilante violence. White women thus belatedly answered a long-standing appeal to join the Black women's antilynching movement, begun forty years earlier by Ida B. Wells (Davis, 195). On the earliest formulations of rape as "a property crime of man against man," see Brownmiller, 18.

[9] Estrich, 11–12.

[10] Even *The New York Times* picked up on this; see Don Terry's "A Week of Rapes: The Jogger and Twenty-eight Not in the News," 29 May 1989, 25. Most of the unremarked rape victims were Black or Hispanic.

[11] Davis, 191.

[12] On the "covering up" of complex and diverse Islamic histories and subjectivities by the Western media, see Edward W. Said, *Covering Islam: How the Media and the Experts Determine How We See the Rest of the World* (New York: Pantheon, 1981).

[13] Susan Jeffords, "Protection Racket," *The Women's Review of Books* 8 (July 1991): 10.

[14] Daniel Lang, *Casualties of War* (New York: McGraw-Hill, 1969). Brownmiller treats the incident in her section on Vietnam atrocities involving rape (pp. 101–3). On images of Vietnam, see also Susan Jeffords, *The Remasculinization of America: Gender and the Vietnam War* (Bloomington: Indiana University Press, 1989); and Linda Dittmar and Gene Michaud, eds., *From Hanoi to Hollywood: The Vietnam War in American Film* (New Brunswick, N.J.: Rutgers University Press, 1990).

[15] Brownmiller, 31–113.

[16] This article is principally concerned with mappings of Black-white relationships in America and does not attempt to describe the way different "people of color" are variously constructed. In this case, however, my point is that Blacks and Asians are, precisely, conflated in De Palma's white imaginary; if non-Anglo groups are distinguished and played off against each other, they are also, as here, collapsed into the general category of racial/ethnic Other, allowing the displacement of one by another.

[17] Jeffords, *Remasculinization of America*, 54–86.

[18] See Deborah E. McDowell, "Reading Family Matters," in *Changing Our Own Words: Essays on Critical Theory and Writing by Black Women*, ed. Cheryl A. Wall (New Brunswick, N.J.: Rutgers University Press, 1989), 83–84.

[19] See Patricia J. Williams, *The Alchemy of Race and Rights* (Cambridge: Harvard University Press, 1991), which argues that newspaper accounts of the case were not about Brawley at all—they increasingly denied the traumatized state in which she was found and preferred to play out a debate between "black manhood and white justice" (173). In the swirl of discourse, Brawley herself was virtually absent, "a shape, a hollow, an emptiness at the center" (175).

[20] Spike Lee, "Final Cut," interview with Henry Louis Gates, Jr., *Transition* 52 (1991): 182–83.

[21] Eldridge Cleaver, *Soul on Ice* (New York: Dell Press, 1970), 26. I want to differentiate as well as to associate the white woman and the light-skinned Black woman as tropes in the Black male imaginary—the latter having to do with *intra*racial attitudes. For this reason, Lee's *Jungle Fever* (1991), featuring the white woman as an emblem of racial temptation and fall, is a more exact recapitulation of Cleaver. Here the white heroine's ultimate rejection by the Black hero involves the punitive claim never to have loved her, in effect rewriting their sexual encounters as exploitive. Although not identical, she and the Jane-figure do, in this sense, occupy a comparable place—their sexual humiliations serving a comparable function—in scenarios of Black male revolt.

[22] For Hunter-Gault's account of the mediating role she played in the struggle to integrate the University of Georgia, see *In My Place* (New York: Farrar, Strauss, & Giroux, 1992).

[23] Susan Brown, Theresa Collier, and Prayon Meade, interview series with Charlayne Hunter-Gault, *MacNeil/Lehrer Newshour* (New York: PBS, 2 Oct. 1990, 16 Jan. 1991, 11 Feb. 1991, 15 May 1991).

[24] To be precise, the "maids" in Saudi Arabia are not, in fact, Saudi but foreign workers from such places as Sri Lanka and the Philippines. For more on the complex and hierarchical relations among women arising from the international traffic in domestic servants, see Cynthia Enloe, *Bananas, Beaches, and Bases: Making Feminist Sense of International Politics* (Berkeley: University of California Press, 1990), 177–94.

AFTERWORD

When I wrote this essay back in the early 1990s, it marked a rather dramatic shift in my work: from the study of women writers such as Frances Burney to a critique of contemporary forms ranging from Spike Lee movies to television coverage of the 1991 Persian Gulf war. In this turn—from literary to cultural studies, from women to intersecting ideas about race and gender—I was, relative to the profession at large, slightly behind the curve. In my department at the University of Virginia, however, I found myself ahead of it; film, not to mention the Central Park jogger, was hardly a suitable object (feminism was disconcerting enough), and the piece came very close to sinking my tenure. For this reason, receiving the Florence Howe award felt like a much-needed vindication, and I take this opportunity ten years later to express my gratitude.

Many of the matters I took up in 1993 look different a decade or so later. The MacNeil, Lehrer, and Hunter-Gault ménage has long since fallen apart, Jim Lehrer the sole survivor. In 2002, the defendants in the jogger case, no longer so youthful, were released from jail after being exonerated by new DNA evidence; the jogger for her part finally recovered enough to write a book about the ordeal. Naturally, the academic landscape has changed as well. If I were writing this piece now, I would be able to consult a body of queer scholarship elaborated in the 1990s that builds on Eve Sedgwick while delving into, as she does not, the permutations of queerness for women and nonwhites. Given, moreover, the significant developments in Asian American studies over the last ten years, writing today I would want to correct my relative inattention to the specific trope of Asianness as it figures in my discussion of *Casualties of War*. On a local note, happy to say, my department as it now stands would support and abet the tenor of these revisions.

Having said this, however, I am tempted to add that the more things change, the more there is still a Bush in office raining down destruction on the Persian Gulf. And likewise in academia, despite some crucial work to the contrary, there remains a tendency in queer theory to privilege relations between men (an issue I've gone on to explore in a recent book). Arguably, then, my call more than a decade ago for further scholarly investment in the ties and antagonisms binding women to one another has not yet outlived its usefulness.

~ 1994 ~

On Recipes, Reading, and Revolution: Postboom Parody in *Como agua para chocolate*

Kristine Ibsen

DESPITE ITS POPULARITY with the reading public, initial critical reaction to Laura Esquivel's *Como agua para chocolate* (1989, translated as *Like Water for Chocolate*, 1992) has frequently tended to dismiss the work as, at best, a poor imitation of the male canon. Typical of the often hostile reception within the Mexican cultural press, Antonio Marquet characterizes the novel as "simplistic . . . infantile . . . full of banal conventionalities, lacking any clearly defined stylistic intention and . . . whose only aspiration is to be trendy" (58, my translation); while Guillermo Fadanelli affirms: "The language is full of over-worked and facile phrases, weak colloquialism due more to the inability to create anything better than something done intentionally" (4, my translation). Closer to the mainstream of critical response, North American critic George McMurray considers the book "worthy of note," although, he contends, the episodes of magic realism "never would have been written without the precedent of *Cien años de soledad*" (1035–1036).[1] Undoubtedly, to read Esquivel's novel the critic must, to paraphrase Susan Leonardi, suspend his or her "academic skepticism" and admit the pleasure of the text (347). Nonetheless, I would like to take this reading one step further: A careful examination of the text reveals that Esquivel has neither *duplicated* the male canon nor popular "women's" literature. In fact, underlying the appearance of conventionality may be detected a playfully parodic appropriation[2] that serves not only to undermine the canon but, more importantly, to redirect its focus to an aesthetic project in which such binary oppositions as "high art" and "popular" literature are overturned.

Linda Hutcheon has observed that the transtextual parody of classics is one way of reformulating the tenets of male culture (*A Poetics of Postmodernism* 130). To assert an independent voice and at the same time facilitate communication, the author must effect a means of transtextual appropriation that at once inscribes and recontextualizes the parent text. Such parody, Hutcheon affirms, should be considered an ironic "inversion" or "transcontextualization," not necessarily at the expense of the parodied text (*A Theory of Parody* 6). By appropriating the resources of magic realism, Esquivel has consciously selected a mode that has become so much a part of the canon that it would be easily recognized by anyone even remotely familiar with contemporary Spanish American literature. Thus, although the hyperbolic episodes of magic realism that appear throughout *Como agua para chocolate* may indeed be indebted to *Cien años de soledad*, there is a marked difference in perspective between the two novels. While García Márquez's narrative centers on a re-examination of broad historical trends, Esquivel's work produces a meaning independent from the original text by concentrating on the individual experience in relation to history; rather than emphasizing issues of sexual domination and violence[3] upon which the Americas were founded, Esquivel "feminizes" her novel by presenting a community of women sustained through an activity—the preparation of food—that transcends social barriers of class, race, and generation (Leonardi 342).[4]

That Tita's personal record of her life is posited as an *alternate version* to the events recorded by canonized discourse is exemplified by the chapter in which her sister Gertrudis escapes with a revolutionary. In this episode, Pedro presents Tita with a bouquet of roses, which she holds so tightly to her chest that their petals mix with her blood. When she uses the bloodstained roses to prepare their meal, Gertrudis becomes so sexually aroused that her overheated body sets the shower on fire. Running nude through the fields, she is intercepted by a *villista* on horseback: "Without slowing his gallop, so as not to waste a moment, he leaned over, put his arm around her waist, and lifted her onto the horse in front of him, face to face, and carried her away" (55–56/60–61).[5] Endowed with incredible sexual prowess, the couple makes love in the saddle, as the horse continues to gallop. Later, in a parodic inversion of roles, Gertrudis finds that no one man can satisfy her and must spend time in a brothel on the border to placate her prodigious sexual appetite (133); subsequently she distinguishes herself on the battlefield and becomes a revolutionary general (180). This incident marks a turning point in the novel because it inspires Tita to begin to write *her* version of events. From Tita's perspective, the romantic encounter is more important than the events taking place on the battlefield, even though she is aware that official history will remember the incident differently (60). By recontextualizing such episodes from a female point of view, Esquivel effects a re-evaluation of official discourse, since the history that has been recorded does not always conform to the fantastic nature of perceived reality. At the same time, the parodic nature of the episode differentiates the novel from its literary precursors as well, as Esquivel plays not only with the supernatural sexual potency that García Márquez and others have imagined for their protagonists[6] but also the consecrated—and highly masculine—tradition of the literature (and cinema) of the Mexican Revolution.

As for Pedro and Tita's first sexual encounter, although the "explosiveness" of their passion lights the sky, the narrator does not pause for specific details: "Pedro . . . pulled her to a brass bed . . . and, throwing himself upon her, caused her to lose her virginity and learn of true love" (158/161). Although the violent prelude to this encounter is again reminiscent of similar scenes from the male canon,[7] the narrator's reticence to enumerate physical details, as well as other romanticized elements of their relation, would seem more typical of women's popular romances. This is consistent with the text's structure as a whole, which, as Carmen Ramos Escandón notes, is a conscious re-elaboration of the tradition of women's magazines that came into vogue during the mid-nineteenth century. These periodicals, sometimes called "*calendarios por señoritas*," included, like Esquivel's novel, recipes, home remedies, and, often, sentimental novels in monthly installments (45).

The appropriation of popular discourse, with its emphasis on such "feminine" values as nurturing and selflessness, is a means of undermining the patriarchal system (Showalter 131). Moreover, since both the *novela rosa* and related genres such as the *folletín* and the *telenovela* are forms of discourse often written *by* women and *for* a female public, Esquivel reinforces the idea of a community of women. Just as the rituals associated with cooking provide Tita with a sense of security (15), the fact that these popular genres often rely on formulae provides women with an order and a control that may not exist in their everyday world. Thus, the kitchen, from which men are traditionally excluded, is an area in which women may assert a small measure of control.[8] Furthermore, as with her appropriation of magic realism, Esquivel has chosen to use conventions from popular discourse that will be easily recognized by the reader: Tita, treated like a servant in her own home, is denied marriage to the man she loves due to the social sanctions represented by her mother; there is a growing tension between the lovers prior to the consummation of their relation; a series of impediments and tragedies including the death of Pedro's son and Tita's subsequent emotional crisis; Tita's rescue by a kindly older man (the fact that he is North American makes him particularly innocuous) whose selfless love cannot be reciprocated; the obligatory (false) pregnancy; and even a scene in which she swoons. In short, like the archetypal romantic heroine, Tita must go through difficult trials but is ultimately rewarded at the end as love triumphs. In addition, as is typical of serial discourse, there is a continual play in the novel of climax/anti-climax as each crisis is resolved and a new one takes its place, as well as a tendency to fall into melodramatic and overwrought prose: "Damn good manners! Damn Carreño's etiquette manual! Both were to blame that her body was hopelessly destined to wither away, little by little. . . . And damn Pedro, so decent, so proper, so manly, so . . . beloved!" (58/61–62; ellipsis in original, translation revised).

As Jean Franco points out, one of the common themes of the romance and the *telenovela* is that of a woman faced by "rules she has not made and over which she has no control" ("The Incorporation of Women" 123). Likewise, Tita, unable to marry the man she loves due to an outdated rule of conduct, battles throughout the novel with imposed conventions and her own desires: "[S]he couldn't resist the temptation to violate the oh-so-rigid rules her mother imposed in the kitchen . . . and in life" (198/199–200, ellipsis in original). Thus, although it relies on set formulae, the emphasis on individual desire over social propriety in such popular genres positions such discourse as a kind of alternate "formula" that lies outside the "recipes" dictated by society. Janice Radway has shown that popular romances share many characteristics with oral literature (25), which reinforces a connection to the orally transmitted traditions of cooking and household remedies that structure the novel. Similarly, both the *novela rosa* and the *telenovela* emphasize the notion of pleasure in storytelling, a pleasure that Radway considers utopian (207). Esquivel invites the reader to reassess conventional approaches to literature and to experience this pleasure, through flagrant sight-gags, such as when Tita drops the apricots on Pedro's head (38), and, especially, through the sensorial stimuli—the scents, tastes, colors, and textures—induced by food. Food functions as a narrative device in the novel: Like a cinematic montage, bridging both temporal and spatial displacements, it transports both the characters and the reader into a sensual dimension of reality. Obviously, the taste and scent of food as a device to stimulate memory is not unique. However, Esquivel again approaches the subject playfully, as Tita compares her emotional and physical state in terms of ludicrous culinary metaphors that question both the "seriousness" of canonized discourse and the time-worn metaphors of popular literature: "[I]t was then that she understood how dough feels when it is plunged into boiling oil" (16/21–22); "She felt so lost and lonely! One last chile in walnut sauce left on the platter after a fancy dinner couldn't feel any worse than she did" (57–58/61); "At thirty-nine she was still as sharp and fresh as a cucumber that had just been cut" (236/236). The narrator's means of expression is humorous but at the same time concrete; it transcends abstract notions of femininity and returns them to immediate experience.

Clearly, then, the novel's culinary metaphors suggest an approach to reality that emphasizes what is tangible over what is abstract and theoretical.[9] At the same time, however, the re-evaluation of *written texts* in the novel forces the reader to reconsider not only the previous texts but also the context in which they were written. Thus, the fact that Esquivel situates her novel at the time of the revolution suggests a specific historical moment in which the nineteenth-century values of the Porfiriato were overturned.[10] Indeed, although the women's magazines of this era represent, as Ramos Escandón asserts, an alternate space for female discourse,[11] they also fostered an attitude toward women that actually further circumscribed their role, since as Bridget Aldaraca notes: "Women were instructed in minute detail on how to be and act, what to do and think, and, especially, what they as superior beings might never aspire to. . . . The ideology of domesticity, which limited a woman's social existence to a sphere of activity within the family institution, gained in strength throughout the nineteenth century" (63). During this time, writers, both male and female, promulgated what Kathryn Rabuzzi calls the "sentimentalization of womanhood" (48). However, this notion of domesticity actually proved antithetical to the home: "Whether it is through false words, false behaviors, or false interiors . . . sentimental beliefs in Happily Ever After distort, trivialize, and artificially sweeten Home so that it loses its full meaning" (87). In *Como agua para chocolate*, the superficiality of this cult of domesticity is typified by Elena and Rosaura, who, although by all appearances conform to the marriage plot, become caricatures due to their blind acceptance of the imposed regulations on female behavior. Elena, who rules her home with an iron fist, is more concerned with the "proper" way of performing tasks than with the actual creativity involved in making the product (18–19). For her part, although she is genuinely upset when Pedro refuses to make love to her, Rosaura's primary concern is with the appearance of decency (215).

Significantly, as Marquet notes, both Rosaura and Elena's estrangement from their essential "female" nature is underscored by their inability to care for their own children and, especially, by their unnatural relations to food (60–62). Rosaura becomes a monstrous aberration who expands to enormous proportions after each child she bears, yet can neither nurse them nor care for them, and is ultimately forced to renounce her matrimonial responsibilities as well due to her huge size, halitosis, and flatulence, which in the end kill her. For her part, Elena's bitterness toward Tita leads her to taste poison in everything she eats; although she finally consents to let Tita prepare her meals, she secretly expels the food from her body with syrup of ipecac and eventually dies from vomiting (140). Tita, in contrast, is so closely attuned to her "feminine" nature that even though she is not yet sexually active, she is able to nurse her infant nephew (81). Clearly, the narration privileges the ancient oral tradition of female knowledge bequeathed to Tita by Nacha (53) over the artificial rules of conduct, upheld by Mamá Elena and reproduced by Rosaura.[12] That Tita feels circumscribed, precisely, by this textually mediated tradition, is indicated by her vehement rejection of Manuel Antonio Carreño's *Manual de urbanidad y buenas maneras*, a popular manual on etiquette that demarcates proper behaviors in every detail of human activity.[13] Although love triumphs at the end of the novel, by uniting the lovers in death, *Como agua para chocolate* further challenges the sentimental canon as it negates the formulaic "happy ending" —at least in a traditional sense.[14]

A close reading of Esquivel's text reveals that although the novel replicates popular forms on the surface, a deliberate inversion of roles has been effected that allows the author to appropriate this genre and challenge it at the same time. One obvious variation from the norm is that, unlike the characters in standard romance fiction, in which passivity is considered a virtue (Butler Flora 65–66),[15] in Esquivel's novel the female characters are stronger and more decisive than their male counterparts. The head of the family is a woman, one of the sisters becomes a general in the revolution, and it is Tita, not Pedro, who eventually dares to stand up to her mother and to Rosaura as well. Indeed, even before her rebellion, Tita wields an underground power through the strange effects produced by her cooking. In a subtle linguistic inversion, it is Tita who "penetrates" her beloved through the sensual power of her culinary creations: "It was as if a strange alchemical process had dissolved her entire being in the rose petal sauce, in the tender flesh of the quails, in the wine, and in each and every one of the meal's aromas. In this way she penetrated Pedro's body, hot, voluptuous, aromatic, totally sensuous" (52/57, translation revised).[16] Pedro, in contrast, is portrayed as weak and indecisive and, even as an adult, is subject to petty jealousies. Although he loves Tita, he does not challenge her mother's decision that Rosaura be his bride. As if there were any doubt that the facetious inversion of masculine and feminine characteristics is intentional, Pedro refuses to consummate his relation with Rosaura until months after their wedding, and when he finally relents, he recites: "Lord, this is not lust nor lewdness, but to make a child to serve you" (40/45). John also incarnates certain characteristics more generally associated with women: He is patient, nurturing and long-suffering. His intuition surprises Tita on more than one occasion (120, 222), and like the stereotypical self-sacrificing woman, he waits a lifetime for Tita only to ultimately give her up to Pedro. Even in the traditionally female domain of the kitchen, Esquivel questions the rigidity of conventional roles. Since recipes are a code to which only women normally have access, Ramos Escandón maintains that we may speak of a "female language" suggested by culinary discourse (45). Nonetheless, Esquivel is careful to note that such language is not biologically *determined* but *learned* through oral tradition. Thus, when Gertrudis attempts to read a recipe, although she is a woman she is unable to decipher its code: "Gertrudis read the recipe as if she were reading hieroglyphics" (192/194). Moreover, in a further inversion of anticipated gender roles, it is a man, Sargent Treviño, who manages to decode the words and successfully prepare the desired product (197–199).

As Marquet notes, the male characters in *Como agua para chocolate* are of such secondary importance that they are never described in physical detail, whereas the female body is frequently lauded (65–66). The fact that details of male anatomy are excluded from the narration is perhaps consistent with a more feminine vision of romance that conventionally has privileged idealistic or spiritual attraction over graphic explicitness (von Franz 179, 188). A careful reading of the text, moreover, reveals that every instance in which the female body is described in hyperbolic detail represents a moment in which the focalization of the episode has shifted to a male character. In such passages, Esquivel evokes the male gaze by which *a woman* is converted into *Woman*,[17] and her parody of the overwrought nineteenth-century prose is at its most exaggerated at these times. For example, it is through Juan's gaze that the nude Gertrudis is evoked as "an angel and devil in one woman" (55/59), and when Pedro inadvertently walks in on a bare-breasted Tita nursing his child, it is *his* vision that transforms her into "Ceres herself, goddess of plenty" (76/82). Aldaraca notes that one of the results of the sentimentalization of womanhood during the nineteenth century was, precisely, that women became "often perceived not as an individual but as a *genre*"(66). Hence, far from a "banal" imitation or of a female "egotism" that symbolically castrates the male characters—as Marquet suggests (66)—Esquivel has adroitly taken this tradition and used it to differentiate between the textually mediated archetypes of Woman and the real experiences of women. Each of the female characters has an individual identity that does not necessarily fit into the rigid dichotomies imposed by patriarchal thought. Furthermore, just as women are not Woman in Esquivel's novel, nor are men expected to represent Man, there are no superhuman qualities about them, and therefore no need to describe in detail their extraordinary sexual potencies. In short, *Como agua para chocolate* portrays women and men as individuals, not as allegorical Others. Real women, the novel shows us, may have "masculine" attributes such as strength and courage, just as real men may show "feminine," nurturing sides.

The use of traditional resources has the potential to become revolutionary when reorganized from the vantage point of women or any other marginalzed group. The fact that Esquivel has chosen discourses not just outside the canon but specifically associated with women's values and experiences allows her to set forth an alternative to the hegemonic standard, based upon real women's lives. As Teresa de Lauretis affirms, such an integration of everyday experiences into creative practice may serve to displace both aesthetic hierarchies and generic categories (10). In the canon, male voice and focalization are often privileged as the source of power. By humorously deconstructing this gaze and proclaiming women as a source of energy in their own right, the absolutes of the dominant order are undermined and an alternate order is posited. While reaffirming the traditional roles of women, Esquivel asserts their value with a project based on—*but not duplicating*—such roles. By dissolving the borders between canonized and popular literatures, between oral and written discourses, the hierarchy governing such distinctions is subverted as well.[18]

NOTES

[1] In McMurray's defense, his critique of the novel is limited to a brief book review; therefore, he does not examine this transtextual relation at length. Marquet's virulent denigration of the novel is a fascinating study in misreading, with examples too numerous to enumerate here. Essentially, for Marquet, the central themes of the novel are matricide and the sadistic annihilation of maternal figures; he further asserts that the novel's main purpose is to satisfy "feminine sexual fantasies" such as prostitution and exhibitionism (64–65). Fadanelli's analysis, while less sophisticated, surpasses that of Marquet in its misogynous undercurrent as he concludes: "Elena Poniatowska has celebrated the publication of *Como agua para chocolate* . . . [and] has promised . . . to run out to cook alongside Laura Esquivel. I hope, and have no doubt, that both of them will get indigestion from their cooking and from their literatures" (4, my translation).

[2] As Naomi Schor notes in her discussion of the female critic's relation to patriarchal theoretical discourse, it is important to recognize the *playful* nature of this appropriation. This process, which Schorr terms "patriody" and which may also be applied to narrative, refers to "a linguistic act of *repetition* and *difference* that hovers between *parody* and *parricide*" (xii, emphasis added). Similarly, as Beatriz González Stephan notes, Esquivel's appropriation of popular discourse *fluctuates* between parody of and homage to precursor texts (210). Kathleen Glenn also analyzes the novel as a parodic text.

[3] Significantly, this shift in focus is consistent with the differences that have been discerned between male and female humor. Gender-based studies on humor by Leigh Marlowe and Mary Crawford note that men's sexual humor typically "uses the symbolism of *domination* and *power*, not seduction and sensuality. *Exaggerations of male sexual prowess* and/or lack of same, abound, *with women almost invariably victims or butts of male sexuality*. The obvious conclusion is that sexual joking is a male privilege, emphasizing a sense of male community and male norms among the jokers" (Marlowe 149, emphasis added). Women's humor, Crawford suggests, "supports a goal of greater intimacy by being supportive and healing, while men's humor reinforces 'performance' goals of competition, the establishment of hierarchal relationships, and self-aggrandizement" (161).

[4] As Leonardi points out, the act of foodmaking as a collaborative activity implicates the reader as well since the nature of sharing recipes has "some interesting relationships to both reading and writing. . . . Even the root of *recipe*—the Latin *recipere*—implies an exchange, a giver and a receiver" (340). Indeed, as Leonardi observes, the receiver of the recipe is *encouraged* to reproduce it (344); thus, recipes by their very nature demand active readers.

[5] Unless otherwise noted, I use the translation of Carol and Thomas Christensen. The first set of page numbers in parenthesis corresponds to this translation; the second, to the original Spanish text.

[6] Examples of hyperbolic sexuality abound both in the "boom" novels and in postboom narrative as well. In *Cien años de soledad*, by Gabriel García Márquez, José Arcadio is so magnificently endowed that even Ursula becomes aroused at the sight of her son (36); in an episode reminiscent of D. H. Lawrence in Carlos Fuentes's *Gringo viejo*, Harriet Winslow marvels over

Tomás Arroyo's genitalia, which she describes in almost spiritual terms (120). García Márquez and Fuentes are, of course, playing with the institution of *machismo*; nonetheless such descriptions perpetuate certain stereotypes by retaining the use of the devotional female gaze to convey a masculine message. As a consequence of this male-centered consciousness and, in the case of García Márquez, by the categorization of female characters through archetypal conventions, the female experience is trivialized.

⁷ I am reminded of the scene in *Cien años de soledad* in which José Arcadio "draws and quarters" the virgin Rebeca (88).

⁸ This is true both in the preparation and the consumption of food, since the act of eating becomes, for many women, an act of will, as only she may decide when to deny or provide for herself. The connection between food and expression is underscored in the novel as Tita refuses to eat *and to speak* following her emotional breakdown.

⁹ As Deane Curtin observes, cooking is an activity in which practice is more important than theory, and this practice hinges on physical experience and contextual knowledge (10). Lisa Heldke calls this approach "bodily knowledge" because it is a kind of perception that transcends the subject/object dichotomy and admits an interrelationship between human subjects and food (218).

¹⁰ Although the names of North Americans in the novel (John and Mary Brown, for example) are contrived, the surnames of the principal characters, Tita de la Garza and Pedro Múzquiz, are likely borrowed from two historical figures from Coahuila, both associated with the revolution: Pablo de la Garza, attorney general under Venustiano Carranza and military commander of Nuevo León, and Rafael Múzquiz, one of Carranza's closest friends and a diplomat in the United States and Europe. Coincidentally, these names figure in a *female* version of the revolution, that of Leonor Villegas de Magnon. On the other hand, García Serrano's charge that Gertrudis's advancement to the rank of *generala* does not coincide with the real-life experiences of *soldaderas* in Villa's forces (200) fails to take into account the playful recontextualization of the stereotypes associated with literary and cinematic versions of the revolution. Indeed, readers familiar with Mexican literature and culture may detect in Gertrudis a rewriting of the disempowered mulata *coronela* in Francisco Rojas's *La negra angustias* (1944), made into a well-known film and reprinted in the widely distributed Colección Popular of the Fondo de Cultura Económica in 1984.

¹¹ In Mexico, literary production during the nineteenth century remained a predominantly male domain. Although, as Nora Pasternac has demonstrated, many contributors to these journals were female (399), Franco and Aldaraca's research suggests that both novels and journals designed for a female public were often published by men, thus permitting male ideals to control not only the public sphere but the private sphere as well (Franco, *Plotting Women* 82, 90–91; Aldaraca 75). Jane Herrick also finds that most women's magazines in Mexico during the nineteenth century were published by men and that, in fact, advice on etiquette and such matters as keeping one's hands white took precedence over sections on the more everyday aspects of domestic life as recipes (141). Moreover, in the journals Herrick examined, those that did include recipes emphasized a bland foreign cuisine dominated by puddings and such exotic advances as colored gelatin (142).

¹² A clear example in which orally transmitted knowledge is considered superior to textually mediated discourse is during the birth of Rosaura's first child. At a loss as to how to deliver a baby, Tita condemns her formal education as useless: "What good did it do her now to know the names of the planets and Carreño's manual from A to Z if her sister was practically dead and she couldn't help her" (71/78). Subsequently, however, she is able to revive the spirit of Nacha, whose *voice* successfully guides her through the process (79).

¹³ For a detailed discussion of Carreño's *Manual* in Esquivel's novel, see Salvador Oropesa.

¹⁴ Rachel Blau DuPlessis notes that in the nineteenth-century European novel death is the prescribed ending for characters with an "inappropriate relation to the 'social script' or plot designed to contain her legally, economically, and sexually" (15). In women's fiction of the twentieth century, however, death becomes more explicitly identified as "the vehicle for affirming the necessity for *critique of the conventions governing women and narrative structures*" (53, emphasis added). In the final chapter of her novel, which begins with the description of a wedding, Esquivel makes

clear that she is playing with popular formulae, since she leads the reader to believe, erroneously, that the novel will end with the marriage of the main characters.

[15] Butler further notes that not only is dependence conventionally seen as desirable in women (66) but the inability to take care of oneself is considered an "endearing feminine quality" (69).

[16] After completing the first version of this chapter I came across an interview with Esquivel that supported my intuition that this inversion is by no means gratuitous: "Writing this book taught me something: that cooking inverts the traditional sexual order. Man is the passive recipient, while woman is the active transmitter" ("El arte de la novela" 5, my translation).

[17] I am using the notion of the "gaze" as it is employed by Laura Mulvey, E. Ann Kaplan, and Teresa de Lauretis in their work on cinema. For more on the women/Woman distinction, see de Lauretis (*Alice Doesn't* 5).

[18] An earlier version of the essay presented in this chapter was read at the Kentucky Foreign Language Conference in April 1994 and subsequently published in *Hispanic Review* 63 (1995). I would like to thank the Women's Caucus for the Modern Languages and the Florence Howe award committed for their support.

WORKS CITED

Aldaraca, Bridget. "El ángel del hogar: The cult of domesticity in nineteenth-century Spain." *Theory and Practice of Feminist Literary Criticism.* Eds. Gabriela Mora and Karen S. Van Hooft. Ypsilanti, MI: Bilingual Press, 1977. 63–87.

Butler Flora, Cornelia. "The Passive Female and Social Change: A Cross-Cultural Comparison of Women's Magazine Fiction." *Female and Male in Latin America: Essays.* Ed. Ann Pescatello. Pittsburgh: U of Pittsburgh P, 1979. 59–86.

Carreño, Manuel Antonio. *Manual de urbanidad y buenas maneras, para uso de la juventud de ambos sexos; en el cual se encuentran las principales reglas de civilidad y etiqueta que deben observarse en las diversas situaciones sociales.* New York: Appleton, 1854.

Crawford, Mary. "Humor in Conversational Context: Beyond Biases in the Study of Gender and Humor." *Representations: Social Constructions of Gender.* Ed. Rhoda K. Unger. Amityville, NY: Baywood, 1989. 155–166.

Curtin, Deane W. "Food/Body/Person." *Cooking, Eating, Thinking: Transformative Philosophies of Food.* Eds. Deane W. Curtin and Lisa M. Heldke. Bloomington: Indiana UP, 1992.

De Lauretis, Teresa. *Alice Doesn't: Feminism, Semiotics, Cinema.* Bloomington: Indiana UP, 1983.

———. *Feminist Studies/Critical Studies.* Bloomington: Indiana UP, 1986.

DuPlessis, Rachel Blau. *Writing beyond the Ending: Narrative Strategies of Twentieth-Century Women Writers.* Bloomington: Indiana UP, 1985.

Esquivel, Laura. "El arte de la novela como una forma culinaria." With Alejandro Semo and Juan José Giovannini. *Excélsior* (8 abril 1990): 5.

———. *Como agua para chocolate: Novela de entregas mensuales con recetas, amores y remedios caseros.* Mexico: Planeta, 1989.

———. *Like Water for Chocolate: A Novel in Monthly Installments with Recipes, Romances and Home Remedies.* Trans. Carol and Thomas Christensen. New York: Doubleday, 1992.

Fadanelli, Guillermo. "La literatura a la que estamos condenados." *Uno más uno* (28 abril 1990): 4.

Franco, Jean. "The Incorporation of Women: A Comparison of North American and Mexican Popular Narrative." *Studies in Entertainment: Critical Approaches to Mass Culture.* Ed. Tania Modleski. Bloomington: Indiana UP, 1986. 119–138.

———. *Plotting Women: Gender and Representation in Mexico.* New York: Columbia UP, 1989.

Fuentes, Carlos. *Gringo viejo.* Mexico: Fondo de Cultura Económica, 1985.

García Márquez, Gabriel. *Cien años de soledad.* Buenos Aires: Sudamericana, 1981.

García Serrano, M. Victoria. "*Como agua para chocolate* de Laura Esquivel: Apuntes para un debate." *Indiana Journal of Hispanic Literature* 6–7 (1995): 185–206.

Glenn, Kathleen. "Postmodern Parody and Culinary-Narrative Art in Laura Esquivel's *Como agua para chocolate*." *Chasqui* 23.2 (1994): 39–47.

González Stephan, Beatriz. "Para comerte mejor: Cultura Calibanesca y formas literarias alternativas." *Nuevo Texto Crítico* V.9B10 (1993): 201–215.

Heldke, Lisa M. "Foodmaking as a Thoughtful Practice." *Cooking, Eating, Thinking: Transformative Philosophies of Food.* Eds. Deane W. Curtin and Lisa M. Heldke. Bloomington: Indiana UP, 1992.

Herrick, Jane. "Periodicals for Women in Mexico during the Nineteeth Century." *Americas* 14.2 (1957): 135–144.

Hutcheon, Linda. *A Poetics of Postmodernism: History, Theory, Fiction.* London: Routledge, 1988.

——. *A Theory of Parody.* New York: Methuen, 1985.

Kaplan, E. Ann. "Is the Gaze Male?" *Powers of Desire: The Politics of Sexuality.* Eds. Ann Snitow, et al. New York: Monthly Review, 1983. 309–327.

Leonardi, Susan J. "Recipes for Reading: Summer Pasta, Lobster à la Riseholme, and Key Lime Pie." *PMLA* 104.3 (1989): 340–347.

McMurray, George. "Two Mexican Feminist Writers." *Hispania* 73 (1990): 1035–1036.

Marlowe, Leigh. "A Sense of Humor." *Representations: Social Constructions of Gender.* Ed. Rhoda K. Unger. Amityville, NY: Baywood, 1989. 145–154.

Marquet, Antonio. "La receta de Laura Esquivel: ¿Cómo escribir un best-seller?" *Plural* 237 (1991): 58–67.

Mulvey, Laura. "Visual Pleasure and Narrative Cinema." *Visual and Other Pleasures.* Bloomington: Indiana UP, 1989. 14–28.

Oropesa, Salvador. "*Como agua para chocolate* de Laura Esquivel como lectura de *Manual de urbanidad y buenas costumbres* de Manuel Antonio Carreño." *Monographic Review/Revista Monográfica* 8 (1992): 252–260.

Pasternac, Nora. "El periodismo femenino en el siglo XIX: *Violetas de Anáhuac.*" *Las voces olvidadas: Antología crítica de narradoras mexicanas nacidas en el siglo XIX.* Eds. Ana Rosa Domatella y Nora Pasternac. Mexico: Colegio de México, 1991.

Rabuzzi, Kathryn Allen. *The Sacred and the Feminine: Toward a Theology of Housework.* New York: Seabury, 1982.

Radway, Janice. *Reading the Romance: Women, Patriarchy and Popular Literature.* Durham: U of North Carolina P, 1984.

Ramos Escandón, Carmen. "Receta y femineidad en *Como agua para chocolate.*" *Fem* 15.102 (1991): 45–48.

Schor, Naomi. *Breaking the Chain: Women, Theory, and French Realist Fiction.* New York: Columbia UP, 1985.

Showalter, Elaine. "Toward a Feminist Poetics." *The New Feminist Criticism: Essays on Women, Literature, and Theory.* New York: Pantheon, 1985. 125–143.

Villegas de Magnon, Leonor. *The Rebel.* Ed. Clara Lomas. Houston, TX: Arte Público, 1994.

Von Franz, M[arie]-L[ouise]. "The Process of Individuation." *Man and His Symbols.* Eds. Carl G. Jung and M. L. von Franz. London: Aldus, 1964. 158–229.

AFTERWORD

"On Recipes, Reading, and Revolution" was written during a polemical period in Mexican literary circles. The virulent response in the cultural press to Laura Esquivel's *Like Water for Chocolate* (sardonically dispatching even established women writers "back to the kitchen") and the no less disquieting snub by members of an exclusionist academy (most of whom had not actually read the novel) were what made me decide to write this essay, which endured a similarly winding path before finally being accepted for publication. "Our journal is dedicated to the study of *literature*," admonished one memorable reader report; another critic, ostensibly schooled in French feminism, took me to task for finding humor in a "novel about matricide." It is not my intention to exaggerate these circumstances or much less to mount a crusade in defense of Esquivel's work. My modest argument was that many academics were taking the novel too seriously, and, in the process, missing the point of its literary project. Why (I wondered) were so many scholars uncomfortable with a novel that played with supposedly female spaces and activities? How could it be (I asked myself, with a trace of discomfort of my own) that parody and the integration of popular culture celebrated in male-authored works were so often dismissed as second-rate imitation when penned by a woman? These were issues I hoped to address, if only implicitly, in my analysis.

My work would have not been possible were it not for a large and respected cadre of prominent female Hispanists (Debra Castillo, Jean Franco, Sylvia Molloy, and Mary Louise Pratt, to name just a few) who have informed my thinking on the reassessment of the codes and reading practices that create and perpetuate the parameters we use to assess literary value. Clearly, traditional critical resources may not always be effectively employed in the study of women's literature, since this kind of writing may be significant in ways other than those that typify and define the literary canon. At the same time, however, there is a danger in privileging discourse rooted in conventional definitions of femininity, as this may reinforce a view of women antithetical to social progress. *Like Water for Chocolate*, I suggest, attempts to negotiate this delicate balance in two important ways: first, by focusing on the everyday experiences of women, topics conventionally located outside serious literature; and second, by parodying both the national romance of the Mexican revolution and the equally consecrated (and profoundly masculine) canon of the new Latin American novel. That Esquivel addressed both these tasks with a gentle sense of ironic humor only further confounded academic readers, despite a number of precedents in Mexican literature, most notably, Rosario Castellanos's well-known short story "Cooking Lesson" (1971), although perhaps this text was more easily categorized within the lines of mainstream feminism.

Much has been accomplished in the decade since I wrote "On Recipes, Reading and Revolution," but much remains to be done. Although Esquivel's novel will probably never escape the stigma of its earlier best-seller status, it has been admitted into classrooms and the pages of scholarly journals (nearly seventy articles listed in the MLA bibliography at last count). Nonetheless, and although female authors are now regularly included in Spanish-language anthologies and the classroom, texts that engage women's experiences remain largely excluded from a narrowly defined notion of literary value still shaded with earlier preconceptions and practices. As valuable as such compensatory gestures have been, they are only the first step in opening the lines of mutual understanding. Some twenty-five years ago, Castellanos advocated laughter as "the first evidence of freedom." While the networks of privilege may remain intact, other voices are being heard, through laughter— and through tears.

Obstructive Behavior: Dykes in the Mainstream of Feminist Theory

Carolyn Dever

A Person or animal . . . that leaps over fences; . . . A transgressor of the laws of morality.
—Oxford English Dictionary[1]

THE "OBSTRUCTIVE BEHAVIOR" I hope to analyze in this chapter involves the consideration of "dykes," by which I mean obstructions that impede or redirect a current or flow. I want to argue that feminist theory has come into being in relation to a set of "dykes," through contact with critical obstructions that shape, divert, and otherwise help to define the mainstream. The function of these dykes is an ambiguous one; they are at once necessary and problematic, central yet diversionary. Dykes are not of the mainstream, but the mainstream necessarily shapes itself in response to the presence of dykes.

At its most literal level, my title should signify a concern with the tendentious shape-shifting that has characterized feminist theory, producing new and innovative theoretical concerns and applications. At another level, however, it should signify its concern with the discourse of "obstruction," with impudent behaviors and political impediments that have confronted, ideally to challenge and to change, academic feminism. At still another level, I am concerned with the discourses of sexuality in feminism, and the sense in which the issue of sexuality itself operates as a "dyke," as a shaping impediment. For colloquially, *dyke* itself signifies, sometimes rudely, sometimes not, a way of being named or self-identifying as lesbian.[2] And the question of lesbians in the mainstream of feminist criticism has been the single most powerful "dyke" in the evolution of this critical discourse.

The *Oxford English Dictionary* definition of *dyke* or *dike* (the latter is the "more conventional" spelling), depends on an interestingly redoubled sense of ambiguity. The *OED* traces the etymology of *dyke* through a series of exchanges of masculine and feminine cases, evolving, perhaps ironically, from versions of the word *dick* in the masculine to versions of the word *dyke* in the feminine, pausing only in Icelandic at the neuter. Its history of etymological indeterminacy notwithstanding, *dyke* consistently signifies a form of diversionary obstruction, whether ditch, trench, mound, embankment, or dam, though the obstruction is conceived alternately as *either* a trench or a wall: "The application thus varies between 'ditch, dug out place,' and 'mound formed by throwing up the earth,' and may include both." Under its first definition, a dyke is "an excavation narrow in proportion to its length, a long and narrow hollow dug out of the ground; a DITCH, trench, or fosse," "such a hollow dug out to hold or conduct water." Under its second, it is "an embankment, wall, causeway," and still more specifically, "'a bank formed by throwing the earth out of the ditch' (Bosworth)," or "a wall or fence. . . . The wall of a city, a fortification."

Dyke is a word that presupposes the complication, conflation, even the collapse of binary categories. Confounding notions of masculinity and femininity in the case of etymology, of structure in the architectural significance of a barrier, conflicting definitions of *dyke* exploit an ambiguity at the heart of the concept itself. In its first definition, a "narrow hollow dug out of the ground," the function of the dyke is to enable another activity, such as the holding or the conducting of water, but is essentially passive: it exists primarily not as a presence but as an absence, as negative space sculpted from the positive surface of the earth. Yet in its alternate definition, the dyke exceeds that positive surface, existing as the highly visible *surplus* of earth in fortifying relation to the populace whose existence it protects and enables; whether as a canal permitting transport from one place to another or as a protective wall impeding that transport, the well-being of its architects depends on the dyke's structural integrity. In either incarnation, the transformative capacity of the dyke remains its most powerful capital: articulating a space that is, by definition, both marginal and central, the dyke demarcates difference, transition, liminality, and vulnerability. That vulnerability inheres in the status of the dyke as a protective structure: without the need to guard against difference, against the threat of difference to destroy, the dyke would be completely unnecessary.

A slang definition, listed below and separated from the nearly three columns of dykes in the *OED*, reads as follows: "dike, dyke . . . [Of obscure origin.] A lesbian; a masculine woman."[3] Citing as its earliest usage a 1942 entry in the *American Thesaurus of Slang*, this dyke, of obscure origin, remains distinct from the *OED*'s other dykes, yet shares with them certain implications of liminality. Not only a lesbian but also a "masculine woman," the dyke, in this definition, blurs the borderline between masculinity and femininity. In her appearance, presumably in her affective alliances, she, like her fellow dykes, marks, embodies, and deconstructs that borderline by disrupting conventional practices of self-presentation and desire. Like the other dykes, this dyke offers a limit case and a liminal space, enabling definitions of inside and outside, enabling, through her location of and as a border, binary systems of logic which exploit fixed notions of identity and identifiability.

Mainstream feminism, I want to argue, has been defined by and against its relationship to dykes, depending precisely on the dyke's function as a borderline to mark the parameters of feminist theory and practice. For twenty-five years, feminists have displayed dramatic, symptomatic forms of ambivalence to lesbians in the mainstream. At once needing and abhorring the dykes that exist at and as the shaping margins of its discourse, feminist theory has struggled to accommodate competing desires for mainstream acceptance and individual sexual diversity.

Catalyzing questions about sex, sexuality, eroticism, pleasure, identity, politics, and power, the dyke in the mainstream has always been the site of contention, the source of troubling questions, both for and within feminism.

Feminist Theory in the 1970s

A ridge, embankment, long mound, or dam, thrown up to resist the encroachments of the sea, or to prevent low-lying lands from being flooded by seas, rivers, or streams.
—Oxford English Dictionary

From the vocabulary of lesbian separatism in the 1970s through queer theory today, feminists have always engaged questions of sexuality. But although the vantage point of history often associates the early women's movement with the political enthusiasms of the Sexual Revolution, in fact, the very personal politics of sexual difference have historically marked the most dramatic fault lines among feminists. As early as 1970, at the Second Congress to Unite Women, twenty women stormed the meeting's plenary session with the words "Lavender Menace" emblazoned on their chests. Prompted to act by Betty Friedan's notorious, and perhaps apocryphal, remark that lesbians in the women's movement were a "lavender menace" who would ultimately impede cultural acceptance of feminist sympathies, the women calling themselves the "Lavender Menace" challenged conference members to confront discrimination against lesbians in the women's movement. Later renaming themselves "Radicalesbians," this group soon produced an essay titled "The Woman-Identified Woman," which argued that all sexualities exist in the service of patriarchy and that a challenge to rigid notions of sexuality must accompany feminist critiques of patriarchy. Women who fail to consider the erotic potential of other women are trapped in a patriarchal web, living their lives, setting their expectations, only in terms of their relationships to men; thus feminists fail to confront their full investment in patriarchal power until they confront the personal politics of their bedrooms. "Real" women, "feminine" women, the Radicalesbians suggest,

are authentic, legitimate, real to the extent that we are the property of some man whose name we bear. To be a woman who belongs to no man is to be invisible, pathetic, inauthentic, unreal. He confirms his image of us—of what we have to be in order to be acceptable by him—but not our real selves; he confirms our womanhood—as he defines it, in relation to him—but cannot confirm our personhood, our own selves as absolutes. As long as we are dependent on the male culture for this definition, for this approval, we cannot be free.[4]

The Radicalesbians identify female homosexuality as a political choice. Lesbianism, within their rubric, is a political mandate more than an erotic one; the utopic vision of a lesbian-separatist community, often figured as the return of the Amazons, is frequently represented as the only plausible alternative within a radical and thoroughgoing critique of patriarchy. And indeed, this is a notion that looms large over the culture of feminist discourse to this day, for, as lesbian separatists throughout the early days of the Women's Movement insist, separatism remains a logical extreme of feminist critiques of patriarchy, a logical solution to often painfully paradoxical attempts to live a "feminist life." As Catharine MacKinnon writes, "Feminism is the epistemology of which lesbianism is an ontology."[5]

Lesbian separatism was one of the greatest challenges to and the greatest anxieties of early feminists. Ti-Grace Atkinson presents a summary of the theory informing political lesbianism in the collection *Amazon Odyssey*: "It is the commitment of individuals to common goals, and to the death if necessary, that determines the strength of the army. . . . Lesbianism is to feminism what the Communist Party was to the trade-union movement. Tactically, any feminist should fight to the death for lesbianism because of its strategic importance."[6] Invoking metaphors ranging from the martial to the economic, Atkinson emphasizes the importance of linking feminist theory and feminist practice: "I'm enormously less interested in whom you sleep with than I am in with whom you're prepared to die."[7] Atkinson interrogates the inherently "political" nature of lesbianism, suggesting that affectional and erotic object choices themselves do not necessarily make a politics, but that lesbianism has occupied a politically significant structural position within feminism.

> Because of their particularly unique attempt at revolt, the lesbian role within the male/female class system becomes critical. Lesbianism is the "criminal" zone, what I call the "buffer" zone, between the two major classes comprising the sex class system. The "buffer" has both a unique nature and function within the system. And it is crucial that both lesbians and feminists understand the strategical significance of lesbianism to feminism. (136–37)

In Atkinson's analysis, the liminal lesbian position, the "buffer," becomes strategic turf: it is the battlefield of actual feminist practice, the space intervening between "oppressor" and "oppressed," men and women. Semantically, however, within the discursive structure of Atkinson's vision, lesbians are not women, nor are they men, feminists, oppressors, or oppressed; they exist, as dykes so often have, as the means of defining the difference between feminists and their oppressors; significantly, though, lesbians themselves manage to elude definition, categorization, political importance, even inclusion in this framework. That both "lesbians" and "feminists" must understand the crucial significance of lesbianism to feminism sacrifices lesbian interests to a larger feminist cause; nowhere are lesbians supposed to consider the significance of feminists, they are simply assumed to be feminists. Despite Atkinson's comment that "feminists should fight to the death for lesbians," she more frequently assumes the opposite logic: she sees lesbians as the front lines of the feminist army. Mainstream feminism for Atkinson, regardless of its radical politics, is a heterosexual movement; dykes exist merely to facilitate, protect, and maintain that mainstream. Unlike the Radicalesbians, for whom lesbianism is feminist theory in its purest form, for Atkinson, lesbianism is a means to an end, a strategic position on a much larger battleground.

Atkinson's interest in the concept of lesbianism originates in the persistence of homophobic invective against feminists: "from the outset of the Movement, most men automatically called all feminists 'lesbians.' This connection was so widespread and consistent that I began to wonder myself if maybe men didn't perceive some connection the Movement was overlooking" (135–36). Atkinson, like the Radicalesbians, wonders why feminism engenders this response; "Generally speaking, the Movement has reacted defensively to the charge of lesbianism: 'No, I'm not!' 'Yes, you are!' 'No, I'm not!' 'Prove it.' For myself I was so puzzled about the connection that I became curious. . . . Whenever the enemy keeps lobbing bombs into some area you consider unrelated to your defense, it's always worth investigating."[8] As Miriam Schneir points out in a recent discussion of the Radicalesbians, "The lesbian issue continued to generate personal and ideological splits among feminists—including among radical feminists—that sisterhood could not always surmount. Lesbians and straights both played a part in this unfortunate turn of events: Some straight feminists were afraid of being labeled dykes and wished to dissociate both the movement and themselves from lesbianism, while some lesbians claimed that lesbianism was an example of feminism in action and preached that the only true feminists were those who renounced relations with the opposite sex entirely."[9] Rather than disavow the label "dyke," Atkinson attempts to appropriate it as "buffer": within her theoretical paradigm, lesbians exist on the front line of the gender wars. The logic here is that of a speech act: the men lobbing the explosive word *dyke* succeed in labeling all practicing feminists as dykes. Atkinson assumes that those who are called dykes necessarily become dykes, whether in theory or in practice. And within her vision of feminist activism, these dykes will be sacrificed, in theory or in practice, for a mainstream feminist utopic vision.

Feminist Theory in the Early 1980s

The application thus varies between 'ditch, dug out place,' and 'mound formed by throwing up the earth,' and may include both.
—Oxford English Dictionary

Split between defensive responses to internalized homophobia and the political logic of separatism, feminist definitions of *lesbian* during the early 1980s are marked by a noteworthy ambivalence toward questions of sexual practice and erotic pleasure: lesbianism, when it enters into definitions of *feminism* at all, enters almost exclusively as a political ideal, undistinguished by any real erotic significance. Adrienne Rich's landmark essay "Compulsory Heterosexuality and Lesbian Existence" appeared in *Signs* in 1980. Rich's articulation of a "lesbian continuum" indicates a significant development in popular feminist attempts at self-definition. Interrogating heterosexuality as a vestigial structure of patriarchal power, Rich argues in the tradition of early political lesbians that "the denial of reality and visibility to women's passion for women, women's choice of women as allies, life companions, and community, the forcing of such relationships into dissimulation and their disintegration under intense pressure have meant an incalculable loss to the power of all women *to change the social relations of the sexes, to liberate ourselves and each other.*"[10] In the terms of Rich's argument, feminists historically have been their own worst enemies, thwarting their own political agendas through their failure to truly challenge "the social relations of the sexes." Rich suggests that homophobia informs feminists' unwillingness to ally themselves fully—politically, personally, or intellectually—with lesbians, duplicating the oppression of women more generally under patriarchal power structures and undermining the viability of all feminist theory. Recalling the Radicalesbians' argument about the need to theorize heterosexuality rigorously, not as a "natural" category but as a complex and problematic construct, Rich modifies their concluding exhortation of lesbianism as the feminist political ideal through the development of two strategic arguments.

The first, which encompasses the mission statement of Rich's essay, calls for a more comprehensive and rigorous feminist theory that takes into consideration all forms of erotic, political, and intellectual individuality; extending a critique of Dorothy Dinnerstein to feminist theory as a whole, Rich writes: "[Dinnerstein] ignores, specifically, the history of women who—as witches, *femmes seules*, marriage resisters, spinsters, autonomous widows, and/or lesbians—have managed on various levels *not* to collaborate. It is this history, precisely, from which feminists have so much to learn and on which there is overall such blanketing silence" (230). Rich's form of feminist theory would have at its center the interrogation of "compulsory heterosexuality":

> The assumption that "most women are innately heterosexual" stands as a theoretical and political stumbling block for feminism. It remains a tenable assumption partly because lesbian existence has been written out of history or catalogued under disease, partly because it has been treated as exceptional rather than intrinsic, partly because to acknowledge that for women heterosexuality may not be a "preference" at all but something that has had to be imposed, managed, organized, propagandized, and maintained by force is an immense step to take if you consider yourself freely and "innately" heterosexual. Yet the failure to examine heterosexuality as an institution is like failing to admit that the economic system called capitalism or the caste system of racism is maintained by a variety of forces, including both physical violence and false consciousness. (238–39)

Calling for a rigorous analysis of the power dynamics at stake in "compulsory heterosexuality," Rich is sharply critical of feminist unwillingness to consider the full range of sexual diversity. Her suggestion that this analysis would be anxiety-producing because feminists themselves have something at stake in the institution of heterosexuality recalls the Radicalesbians' arguments about the political inconsistencies in most attempts to combine feminist theory with a bourgeois, heterosexual life. But Rich stops short of calling for political lesbianism, insisting instead on a feminist theoretical analysis of issues previously hidden by assumptions of normative heterosexuality.

In fact, Rich's second argument represents a neat appropriation of the anxieties that inevitably seem to accompany discussions of political lesbianism. She argues, through the radical expansion of the term *lesbian*, that all feminists, in fact, all women, are already lesbians; feminist thus becomes a subset of lesbian, rather than the other way around. She explains:

> I mean the term *lesbian continuum* to include a range—through each woman's life and throughout history—of woman-identified experience, not simply the fact that a woman has had or consciously desired genital sexual experience with another woman. If we expand it to embrace many more forms of primary intensity between and among women, including the sharing of a rich inner life, the bonding against male tyranny, the giving and receiving of practical and political support, if we can also hear it in such associations as *marriage resistance* and the "haggard," behavior identified by Mary Daly (obsolete meanings: "intractable," "willful," "wanton," and "unchaste," "a woman reluctant to yield to wooing"), we begin to grasp breadths of female history and psychology which have lain out of reach as a consequence of limited, mostly clinical, definitions of *lesbianism*.[11]

Rich's identification of the "lesbian continuum" is the logical yield of her interrogation of compulsory heterosexuality. She emphasizes that the deconstruction of the assumptions and dynamics informing compulsory heterosexuality will bring into view many forms of profound interconnections among women, connections that have always existed but have been obscured from view by assumptions of normative heterosexuality. In naming these relationships "lesbian," Rich accommodates and thus begins to value women's relationships with one another across a wide range of behaviors that presumably includes, but is not limited to, the erotic: "As the term lesbian has been held to limiting, clinical associations in its patriarchal definition, female friendship and comradeship have been set apart from the erotic, thus limiting the erotic itself" (240).

In addition to the notion of the "lesbian continuum" and the critique of compulsory heterosexuality, the other significant innovation of Rich's argument is its shift in the locus of activism. Identifying her task as a primarily critical one, Rich targets an audience composed principally of feminist academics. She identifies literary criticism, as well as related modes of historical and social scientific research, as central to feminist praxis and instrumental in the process of locating the lesbian continuum; literary critics and other academics possess the ability to produce a more accurate version of women's history. Significantly, however, even as Rich empowers academics within feminist activism, academics also occupy the center of her target of critique: she condemns "the virtual or total neglect of lesbian existence in a wide range of writings, including feminist scholarship" (229). By the early 1980s, literary criticism is at ground zero in what was previously a grassroots political movement, as academic work is increasingly valorized as a primary form of feminist activist intervention. Rich's focus on literary criticism constructs feminist politics as a battleground of metacriticism; the issues at stake concern not only the practicalities of feminist critique in the world at large, but also the novels of Colette, Charlotte Brontë, and Toni Morrison, and the theoretical paradigms of Mary Daly, Catharine MacKinnon, and Nancy Chodorow. Focusing on the historical period from which Rich's essay emerged, Jane Gallop, in *Around 1981: Academic Feminist Literary Theory*, argues that in the early 1980s, feminism "entered the heart of a contradiction": "It became secure and prospered in the academy while feminism as a social movement was encountering major setbacks in a climate of new conservatism. The Reagan-Bush years began; the ERA was defeated. In the American academy feminism gets more and more respect while in the larger society women cannot call themselves feminist."[12]

Underscoring Gallop's argument regarding the yawning divide between academic feminism and the lives of women "in the larger society," bell hooks, writing in 1984, sees academic discourse as part of the problem, alienating mainstream women from feminist activism. "The ability to 'translate' ideas to an audience that varies in age, sex, ethnicity, degree of literacy is a skill feminist educators need to develop. Concentration of feminist educators in universities encourages habitual use of an academic style that may make it impossible for teachers to communicate effectively with individuals who are not familiar with either academic style or jargon."[13] Hooks's critique of self-conscious academic language extends from the same metacritical impulse as Rich's critical rereading of feminist texts for their prescriptions of compulsory heterosexuality. But hooks's target audience is somewhat different from Rich's; hooks sees the exclusionary language of academic feminism as part of a problematic system of oppressive power relationships relating to race, class, and gender. Far from escaping the pernicious implications of these power relations, hooks argues that feminists consistently *duplicate* them in their blindness to and exclusion of women of color and poor women. While Rich's critique focuses on assumptions of normative heterosexuality, hooks's focuses on assumptions of normative white middle-class status:

> White women who dominate feminist discourse today rarely question whether or not their perspective on women's reality is true to the lived experiences of women as a collective group. Nor are they aware of the extent to which their perspectives reflect race and class biases, although there has been a greater awareness of biases in recent years. Racism abounds in the writings of white feminists, reinforcing white supremacy and negating the possibility that women will bond politically across ethnic and racial boundaries. Past feminist refusal to draw attention to and attack racial hierarchies suppressed the link between race and class. (3)

Given hooks's useful insistence on sex, race, and class discrimination as symptoms of larger systemic problems, it is noteworthy that discrimination based on sexuality drops out of her larger structure of critique. Hooks is deeply concerned that feminist theory address issues across lines of race and class, but to do so, she argues, feminism must begin to disassociate itself from its image as a movement consisting primarily of lesbians; she sees feminism as a movement dominated by dykes at the expense of diversity. Hooks is sharply critical of what she perceives as the facile equation in mainstream feminism of lesbian sexuality with political correctness: "women who are not lesbians, who may or may not be in relationships with men feel that they are not 'real' feminists. This is especially true of women who may support feminism but who do not publiclly [*sic*] support lesbian rights" (151).

Unwilling to apply the same critique to homophobia that she does to racism, hooks exhorts feminists to "diversify" the public face of feminism by making clear that feminists are not necessarily lesbians or man-haters. In hooks's view, the failure of feminism to become a truly massive social movement inheres in its anxiety-producing association with nonhetero sexualities:

My point is that feminism will never appeal to a mass-based group of women in our society who are heterosexual if they think that they will be looked down upon or seen as doing something wrong. . . . Just as feminist movement to end sexual oppression should create a social climate in which lesbians and gay men are no longer oppressed, a climate in which their sexual choices are affirmed, it should also create a climate in which heterosexual practice is freed from the constraints of heterosexism and can also be affirmed. One of the practical reasons for doing this is the recognition that the advancement of feminism as a political movement depends on the involvement of masses of women, a vast majority of whom are heterosexual. As long as feminist women (be they celibate, lesbian, heterosexual, etc.) condemn male sexuality, and by extension women who are involved sexually with men, feminist movement is undermined. (153)

The rhetoric of comprehensive, systemic analysis of power relations has shifted by this point to a more coercive rhetoric of marketing: "feminism will never appeal to a mass-based group of women in our society who are heterosexual *if* . . ." While hooks claims concern here for the discriminatory assumptions of heterosexism, nowhere else does she suggest that feminist theory pander to the comfort of the "vast majority" in exchange for a rigorous consideration of the rights and the existence of an endangered minority.

My critique of hooks's position is not a new one; in fact, the quote above is part of hooks's response to "lesbian feminist" Cheryl Clarke, who wrote an essay titled "The Failure to Transform: Homophobia in the Black Community," in which she remarks: "'Hooks delivers a backhanded slap at lesbian feminists, a considerable number of whom are black. Hooks would have done well to attack the institution of heterosexuality as it is a prime cause of black women's oppression in America.'"[14] Hooks replies, "Clearly Clarke misunderstands and misinterprets my point. I made no reference to heterosexism and it is the equation of heterosexual practice with heterosexism that makes it appear that Clarke is attacking the practice itself and not only heterosexism." Clarke's point, reminiscent of Rich, that hooks should examine "the institution of heterosexuality," is revealingly translated by hooks directly into "heterosexism": it is not Clarke but hooks who makes the equation of heterosexual practice and heterosexism.[15] The question of the problematic institutional dynamics of heterosexuality is neatly subsumed under this equation; hooks's discussion continues on into a critique of feminist heterophobic impulses, in defense of "the choice women make to be heterosexual" (154). Heterosexuality, not normally seen as an endangered category, makes a strange bedfellow with the other forms of oppression and exclusion hooks treats in this text, including racial and class prejudice. Hooks's heterosexuality is vulnerable, defensive, embattled, but ironically, her need to defend heterosexual practice duplicates a function of the dyke: she is eager to set up protective walls around heterosexuality, thus liberating women everywhere into the radical freedom of heterosexual object choice. In another twist of irony, hooks begins to set up dykes to defend against dykes.

Hooks's logic at this point is complicated, for several reasons. In her larger argument, her desire to ensure that feminists are consistent in their critique of *any* form of compulsory sexuality, whether gay or straight, is a direct extension of powerful early feminist critiques of limiting patriarchal roles for women. However, in a book critiquing feminist marginalizations of women of color, it is strange that hooks's analysis of phobic exclusionary practices should fail to extend to her discussion of sexuality. The apparent suggestion that feminists should disassociate themselves—at least publicly—from the issue of lesbian sexuality seems linked to another paradigm of the 1970s, the antifeminist rhetoric which labeled feminists, often arbitrarily, as dykes, intimidating through the invocation of internalized homophobia. Instead of reading "mass-based" anxiety about lesbianism as a need for "mass-based" education about forms of prejudice as pernicious in the case of sexuality as in the case of race, hooks seems to suggest that feminists need only change the window dressing in order to appeal to a wider range of women; her feminist paradigm seems to sacrifice sexual diversity in the cause of racial diversity, while she bars altogether the possibility that lesbians of color might exist. This platform clearly—and perhaps ironically—returns to the scene of the "lavender menace," and backlash against the suggestion that the marketing of the feminist movement must occur under the aegis of "normative" sexuality.

While Barbara Smith echoes hooks's sharp criticism of white, middle-class feminist narcissism, she does not see the interests of black women and lesbians as mutually exclusive or even in competition, insisting on the importance of a feminist discourse that considers race and sexuality together: "Long before I tried to write this I realized that I was attempting something unprecedented, something dangerous, merely by writing about Black women writers from a feminist perspective and about Black lesbian writers from any perspective at all. . . . All segments of the literary world—whether establishment, progressive, Black, female, or lesbian—do not know, or at least act as if they do not know, that Black women writers and Black lesbian writers exist."[16] Jane Gallop claims, in a discussion of *The New Feminist Criticism* (the anthology in which Smith's essay is reprinted), that feminist criticism of the early and mid-1980s struggled explicitly with problems of self-definition and with issues of inclusion and exclusion.[17] Judith Roof argues that "the myriad differences among women are often reduced to the formula 'black and lesbian.' . . . I suspect that this . . . critical reliance upon black and lesbian is symptomatic of some underlying critical difficulty with multiplicity."[18] I would concur that within the discourses of feminist theory and criticism of the mid-1980s, the categories "black" and "lesbian" demarcate similar modes of "difference," both existing, in most cases, as "other than" a norm. The white, middle-class, heterosexual assumptions of that norm are made visible only through the tension produced by the defining presence of the other.

Feminist Theory in the Late 1980s

A mass of mineral matter, usually igneous rock, filling up a fissure in the original strata, and sometimes rising from these like a mound or wall, when they have been worn down by denudation.

—Oxford English Dictionary

Feminist theorists became increasingly preoccupied with the discursive politics of "difference" in the years that followed these publications, to the extent that race and sexuality are equated less often. But the contentious and persistent question of dykes in the mainstream continued throughout this period to serve a uniquely definitional function for feminist theory. In the early 1980s, feminism was faced with a central division: some critics argued that feminism was all about, too much about, lesbianism and lesbian sexuality; others argued that the heterosexist bias in feminist discourse betrayed itself constantly in the marginalization and the silencing of lesbians and lesbian writers. This particular "dyke" shaped the peculiar path of feminist discourse in the second half of the 1980s.

Literary theory more generally was reinfused with the politics of activism in the mid-1980s; as the AIDS epidemic ravaged the gay male community, many critics turned to the complexities of male homoeroticism, discourses, and representation with a sense of political urgency unseen since the early days of the women's movement. Using the tools of feminist theory, literary theorists began to focus on homosexuality through the newly repoliticized discourses of masculinity. Interestingly and ironically, this development created yet another "dyke" in the world of literary criticism: while lesbians belonged to the gay rights movement and the feminist movement, suddenly they were *centrally* implicated in neither. Although questions of homosexuality were central to both feminist and gay male discourses, they were primarily about male homosexuality. Lesbians themselves existed at the discursive margins, in and as the space between these two newly prominent theoretical positions.

Through the middle years of the 1980s, the central terms of feminist literary theory underwent a significant paradigm shift, refocusing from a concern with the politics of female sex and sexuality to a theoretically broader concern with the notion of gender. As Elaine Showalter points out in the introduction to the anthology *Speaking of Gender*, which first appeared in 1989, "talking about gender means talking about both women and men." "The introduction of gender into the field of literary studies marks a new phase in feminist criticism, an investigation of the ways that all reading and writing, by men as well as by women, is marked by gender. Talking about gender, moreover, is a constant reminder of the other categories of difference, such as race and class, that structure our lives and texts, just as theorizing gender emphasizes the parallels between feminist criticism and other forms of minority discourse."[19] The rise of gender studies over the course of the 1980s served practical as well as theoretical functions. Among other things, it opened the doors of feminist theory unambiguously to male practitioners, and as Showalter points out, presented a much more sophisticated notion of the ways in which language and power converge to shape a speaking subject, whether "male" or "female." The focus on gender served to further dismantle monolithic notions of "maleness" and "femaleness" per se, in exchange for a theory of gender as cultural construct, symptomatically reflecting larger cultural investments.

Gender theory has proved both invigorating and problematic for more conventional feminist political concerns. As Showalter notes,

some readers . . . worry that "gender studies" could be a pallid assimilation
of feminist criticism into the mainstream (or male stream) of English studies,
a return to the old priorities and binary oppositions that will reinstate familiar
male canons while crowding hard-won courses on women writers out of the
curriculum. Others fear that talking about gender is a way for both male and
female critics to avoid the political commitment of feminism. Still others raise
the troubling possibility that gender will be isolated from issues of class and
race. (10)

Showalter suggests that many feminists were and remain concerned that to for-
sake the focus on "women" in favor of a broader focus on "gender" is to retrench
on feminist inroads in the academy; if there is no longer any basis for a practical
concern for and with women specifically, then what is the difference, they ask, between the academy now and the academy before early feminist pioneers appeared
on the horizon? The generalization outward of feminist political and theoretical
interests reflects more complex notions about the ways in which structures of gender and sexuality are supported; in a poststructuralist theoretical universe which
privileges indeterminacy, to talk about "women" alone is, in some sense, a return
to an artificial and potentially simplistic means of categorization. Yet this artifice
is belied by the materialist concerns of patriarchal class politics: the opening out
of feminist theory into gender theory certainly risks the reinstitutionalization of
male-centered concerns, a loss of ground in some sense, even as it represents an
enriched understanding of prevailing cultural constructs.

Feminist ventures in gender theory constantly engage this ambivalence. The important linkage of feminist and gay male theories of discourse and narrative was
facilitated by several prominent feminist critics, who are necessarily prompted at
every turn to theorize, even to justify, the gender politics of their methodologies.
For example, Eve Kosofsky Sedgwick, in the groundbreaking study *Between Men:
English Literature and Male Homosocial Desire*, both avows a feminist methodology and defends her exclusive focus on male subjectivity and male homosociality.
In her introduction, Sedgwick discusses "the isolation, not to mention the absolute subordination, of women, in the structural paradigm on which this study is
based." She writes: "The absence of lesbianism from the book was an early and,
I think, necessary decision, since my argument is structured around the distinctive relation of the male homosocial spectrum to the transmission of unequally
distributed power. Nevertheless, the exclusively heterosexual perspective of the
book's attention to women is seriously impoverishing in itself."[20] Profoundly feminist in its methodology, Sedgwick's rereading of Freud, Girard, and the structure
of triangulated desire does not offer a deeper understanding of the place of the
woman in that structure but instead demonstrates as central the vector connecting
its two male subjects in a rich analysis of the male homosocial relations previously
concealed by assumptions of normative heterosexuality. However, the single theoretical distinction Sedgwick makes between male and female homoeroticism is a
significant one; she justifies her focus on the distinction between homosociality
and homosexuality in men based on the fact that this is *more* of a distinction for
men than for women:

The diacritical opposition between the "homosocial" and the "homosexual" seems to be much less thorough and dichotomous for women, in our society, than for men. At this particular historical moment, an intelligible continuum of aims, emotions, and valuations links lesbianism with the other forms of women's attention to women: the bond of mother and daughter, for instance, the bond of sister and sister, women's friendship, "networking," and the active struggles of feminism. The continuum is crisscrossed with deep discontinuities—with much homophobia, with conflicts of race and class—but its intelligibility seems now a matter of simple common sense. (2)

Writing off the theoretical complexity, even the specific discernibility, of lesbian erotic desire as "simple common sense," Sedgwick inaugurates an era in which feminist practitioners fixate on male homoeroticism as an interesting problematic while dismissively relegating the "dyke" to the outer reaches of feminist discourse. Implicitly accepting Rich's notion of the "lesbian continuum" as theoretically exhaustive, Sedgwick ironically reinscribes the very problem Rich herself was hoping to dismantle. For Rich was concerned with precisely "how and why women's choice of women as passionate comrades, life partners, co-workers, lovers, community has been crushed, invalidated, forced into hiding and disguise; and . . . the virtual or total neglect of lesbian existence in a wide range of writings, including feminist scholarship." Rich concludes, in a startling prediction of a predicament redescribed a decade later: "I believe that much feminist theory and criticism is stranded on this shoal."[21]

In *The Apparitional Lesbian: Female Homosexuality and Modern Culture*, Terry Castle explores Sedgwick's resistance to or "blockage" against any form of rigorous consideration of female homosexuality:

Lesbians, defined . . . with telling vagueness only as "women who love women," are really no different, Sedgwick seems to imply, from "women promoting the interests of other women." Their way of bonding is so "congruent" with that of other women, it turns out, that one need no longer call it homosexual. "The adjective 'homosocial'; as applied to women's bonds," [Sedgwick] concludes, "*need not be pointedly dichotomized as against 'homosexual'; it can intelligibly denominate the entire continuum.*" By a disarming sleight of phrase, an entire category of women—lesbians—is lost to view.[22]

Castle's objection to Sedgwick's "uncharacteristically sentimental" (71) reliance on the "continuum" metaphor begins to indicate a major problem in conventional feminist analyses of homoeroticism. Castle's critique implicitly returns to and begins to trouble Adrienne Rich's notion of the "lesbian continuum," which pointedly desexualizes lesbianism in favor of a more pan-feminist vision of meaningful engagement among women. Castle's discomfort with the "lesbian continuum" betokens a new negotiation for feminist theory: a theoretical practice that interrogates the specificity of male homoerotic desire cannot rely complacently on a notion of lesbianism that is vague, deliberately broad, and explicitly detached from any form of eroticism or desire whatsoever. Rich's argument for the "lesbian continuum" was the product of a specific historical moment and served several important functions within the discourse of feminist theory, particularly in its defusing of the term *lesbian* and its situation of feminist methodology firmly in the center of literary critical practice. However, as Castle implies, Rich's project is not the lesbian equivalent to the carefully theorized analysis of male homosociality that Sedgwick conducts in *Between Men*. Indeed, Rich's essay announces as its goal the more rigorous *inclusion* of lesbians throughout the range of academic discourses; thus Sedgwick's appropriation of Rich, in order to justify the *exclusion* of lesbians, represents a perfect, if ironic, example of the phenomenon Rich had hoped to counteract.

Pursuing the implications of Castle's argument, I would agree that feminists, working from the heritage of such broad definitions as Rich's "lesbian continuum," are quick to assume that they already fully understand "lesbianism," most conventionally as something inherently "feminist" or as something having to do with (not necessarily sexual) "female bonding." Accompanying this model are assumptions suggesting that lesbianism is only occasionally or tangentially related to sex and sexual pleasure. These assumptions are engendered in part by the history, within feminism, of a political lesbianism which constructs lesbianism as a separatist opting out of patriarchy rather than as an erotic object choice. They are also facilitated by historical conventions of female friendship and Boston marriage, which again are perceived as related more to women's mutual empathy than to mutual erotic pleasure. These assumptions suggest a dramatic historical difference in cultural perceptions of female and male homosexuality. From Gay Liberation to queer theory, analyses of male homosexuality have rarely assumed that eroticism, sexual attraction, and sex acts, covert or explicit, are marginal or irrelevant issues. Following Sedgwick's lead, feminist- and queer-theoretical analyses of polymorphous sexualities ironically continue to fixate on problems of *male* homoeroticism because of the perception that these relations are somehow underexplored or more complex than female homoeroticism. In turn, lesbianism is too often dismissed as either coextensive with any sort of feminist practice or completely accessible within any conventional understanding of female friendship. "What may appear 'intelligible' or 'simple common sense' to a nonlesbian critic," writes Castle, "will hardly seem quite so simple to any female reader who has ever attempted to walk down a city street holding hands with, let alone kissing or embracing another woman." She continues:

> The homosexual panic elicited by women publicly signaling their sexual interest in one another continues, alas, even "at this particular historical moment," to be just as virulent as that inspired by male homosexuality, if not more so. To obscure the fact that lesbians are women who have sex with each other—and that this is not exactly the same, in the eyes of society, as voting for women or giving them jobs—is, in essence, not to acknowledge the separate peril and pleasure of lesbian existence. (71–72)

Explicitly detaching lesbianism from the broader concerns of feminism in general, Castle returns to Rich again, this time replacing the term that Sedgwick appropriates, "lesbian continuum," with the term that Rich uses in her title, the far more insistent and aggressive "lesbian existence." With this gesture, Castle begins to call for an analysis of female homosexuality, not homosociality, that accounts for the sexual pleasure and personal danger that accompany living as a lesbian. In response to Sedgwick's contention that male homosociality is the figure of patriarchal power, Castle suggests the insurgent potential of a theory of lesbian desire: "To theorize about female-female desire . . . is precisely to envision the taking apart of this supposedly intractable patriarchal structure. Female bonding, at least hypothetically, destabilizes the 'canonical' triangular arrangements of male desire, is an affront to it, and ultimately—in the radical form of lesbian bonding—displaces it entirely."[23]

Castle's discomfort with the feminist absorption of lesbian concerns is also reflected, somewhat differently, however, in the initial theoretical formulation of "queer theory," which occurred in a 1991 special issue of the journal *differences* dedicated to "Lesbian and Gay Sexualities." Again, the voice behind this formulation is that of a prominent feminist, Teresa de Lauretis. In her introduction to this issue, de Lauretis notes that while gay male and lesbian discourses have evolved along basically separate paths in the past, recent critical tendencies to see them as versions of one phenomenon, "lesbian and gay" (ladies first, of course), threaten to erase the specificity of that history. She writes, "our 'differences,' such as they may be, are less represented by the discursive coupling of those two terms in the politically correct phrase 'lesbian and gay,' than they are elided by most of the contexts in which the phrase is used; that is to say, differences are implied in it but then simply taken for granted or even covered over by the word 'and.'"[24] Thus occurs the birth of "queer theory," a metacritical praxis which is "intended to mark a certain critical distance" from the formulaic and reductive phrase "lesbian and gay." "Queer theory," writes de Lauretis, "conveys a double emphasis—on the conceptual and speculative work involved in discourse production, and on the necessary critical work of deconstructing our own discourses and their constructed silences" (iv). By definition a self-interrogating methodology, conditioned by a tradition of oppression, erasure, and silence to constantly examine its own "constructed silences," queer theory is, in theory, a school of thought that is always going back to school.

De Lauretis's logic is both provocative and problematic. To replace a phrase like "lesbian and gay" with a phrase like "queer theory" is quite literally to cover over any notion of lesbian and gay difference, to subsume male and female homosexuality within the single, potentially monolithic category "queer," to depend on the self-policing integrity of queer theorists themselves to "deconstruct . . . our own discourses and their constructed silences." In its ideal form, queer theory would be a constantly self-interrogating practice, and through that self-interrogation would succeed in retaining the specificity of lesbian and gay histories while also exploring the theoretical complexity of lesbian and gay difference. However, the replacement of a tripartite term—"lesbian and gay"—with a bipartite term—"queer theory"— appears to counteract de Lauretis's desire for increased specificity. And as queer theory begins to articulate itself as a practice distinct from feminist theory, the question of women, and particularly the question of lesbians, is persistently sidelined.

In the introduction to *Epistemology of the Closet*, Sedgwick addresses the question of a specifically lesbian-centered theoretical practice: "It seems inevitable to me that the work of defining the circumferential boundaries, vis-à-vis lesbian experience and identity, of any gay male-centered theoretical articulation can be done only from the point of view of an alternative, feminocentric theoretical space, not from the heart of the male-centered project itself."[25] Within the context of a book that is quite explicitly at "the heart of the male-centered project itself," Sedgwick's discussion of a lesbian implication to gay male theory demonstrates great ambivalence. While this introduction, like the introduction to *Between Men*, gives a nod to the urgent necessity for "feminocentric theoretical space," the place of lesbians in *Epistemology* is at best marginal. Acknowledging lesbian activists' work in the AIDS epidemic, Sedgwick writes, "The newly virulent homophobia of the 1980s, directed alike against women and men even though its medical pre-text ought, if anything, logically to give a relative exemptive privilege to lesbians, reminds urgently that it is more to friends than to enemies that gay women and gay men are perceptible as distinct groups." Noting that lesbians, too, are vulnerable to AIDS, Sedgwick sees gay and AIDS activism as deeply indebted to lesbian practitioners and feminist theories:

> The contributions of lesbians to current gay and AIDS activism are weighty, not despite, but because of the intervening lessons of feminism. Feminist perspectives on medicine and health-care issues, on civil disobedience, and on the politics of class and race as well as of sexuality have been centrally enabling for the recent waves of AIDS activism. What this activism returns to the lesbians involved in it may include a more richly pluralized range of imaginings of lines of gender and sexual identification. (38–39)

Sedgwick is significantly vague about the yield of lesbian investment; that activism "*may* include a more richly pluralized range of imaginings" seems tepid consolation within a context of "virulent homophobia." Sedgwick is cautionary about the tendency of gay male discourse to "subsume" lesbian "experience and definition":

> The 'gay theory' I have been comparing with feminist theory doesn't mean exclusively gay male theory, but for the purpose of this comparison it includes lesbian theory insofar as that (a) isn't simply coextensive with feminist theory (i.e., doesn't subsume sexuality fully under gender) and (b) doesn't a priori deny all theoretical continuity between male homosexuality and lesbianism. But, again, the extent, construction, and meaning, and especially the history of any such theoretical continuity—not to mention its consequences for practical politics— must be open to every interrogation. (39)

Sedgwick, like de Lauretis, is always careful to argue that male and female homosexuality are very different phenomena, a useful and critical point. In fact, in this passage, as she tries to articulate a sufficiently specific and differentiated theoretical agenda for her text, Sedgwick recurs to an implicit structure of triangulation: gay male theoretical concerns, lesbian theoretical concerns, and feminist theoretical concerns are all related yet distinct entities. Once again, the "dyke" operates as the border, the literal site of connection and distinction between feminist and "gay" concerns in general. But as with all triangulated structures, as Sedgwick has demonstrated, one term is inevitably subordinated in favor of a dynamic connection between the other two. In Sedgwick's *Epistemology*, as in *Between Men*, the coincidence of feminist methodology and gay male subject matter consistently produces lesbian concerns as that third term, emerging occasionally, marginally, and principally in introductory matter. This is one example of a larger critical phenomenon in which, once again, the dyke demarcates the border of internal and external, offering a frame of reference but not a *mise en abîme*.

At the risk of the inevitable pun, I would argue that while feminist theory engendered queer theory, the two remain distinct. By now the dualism that so profoundly shaped feminist discourse at the end of the 1970s and into the early 1980s is literalized in the separate entities of feminist and queer scholarship. But what has been factored out here, oddly enough, is the specificity of lesbian discourse: caught between the feminist and the queer, the lesbian, again, occupies the problematic third position in the triangular of contemporary critical discourse. And as with the triangular structure posited in Sedgwick's early analysis, the third term is not the one that counts; the animate connection here is the one between feminists and queers, while the third, the site of literal connection and disjunction, marks the space between without signifying itself. Lesbians occupy the subordinated place of the woman in the structure of triangular desire, in which the desiring relationship is constituted between feminists and queers.

Back in 1980, in "Compulsory Heterosexuality and Lesbian Existence," Rich produced what seems today a startlingly prescient commentary. She writes, "Lesbians have historically been deprived of a political existence through 'inclusion' as female versions of male homosexuality. To equate lesbian existence with male homosexuality because each is stigmatized is to erase female reality once again."[26] Equated not only with male homosexuals but with feminism in its most generalized form, lesbians remain consistently—and paradoxically—marginalized. And as a marginalized population, dykes serve a useful function within the context of feminist and queer theories alike, acting as the border against which the mainstream can define itself. The specific location of that margin, of that "dyke," is revealing of particular, often-shifting engagements within theoretical discourses as they struggle to define themselves, their constituencies, their politics, and their activism. The dyke in the mainstream marks the space of margin and connection, offering at once a point of view that is and is not of the central flow.

Within the metaphorical structure I have explored throughout this essay, I have argued that feminist theory has consistently seen the "dyke" as marginal, protective, and contingent, as facilitating the existence of a larger whole rather than independently significant. Yet the specificity of lesbian discourses and desires has independently significant value, not only as a metacritical instrument for the analysis of a broader feminist theory, but also as an historically complex cultural phenomenon in its own right. Behind the metaphorical, architectural dyke is another dyke, a figure too often marginalized, too frequently and too vaguely appropriated within larger theoretical paradigms of sexuality and politics. For let us recall that listed below and separated from the nearly three columns of *dykes* in the *OED* is the slang definition: "dike, dyke . . . *slang*. [Of obscure origin.] A lesbian; a masculine woman."

NOTES

With thanks to Kathryn Schwarz, Sarah Blake, David A. Hedrich Hirsch, and Marvin J. Taylor.

[1] "Dike, dyke," *Oxford English Dictionary*, 2d ed., vol. 4, 659–60. All epigraphs that follow are excerpted from *OED* definitions of *dyke*, as cited here.

[2] For a discussion of theoretical appropriations of such disparaging terms as *queer*, see Judith Butler, "Critically Queer," *Bodies That Matter*, esp. 226–30.

[3] *OED*, vol. 4, 660.

[4] Radicalesbians, "The Woman-Identified Woman" 166. Authorship of this essay has been attributed to Rita Mae Brown.

[5] Catharine A. MacKinnon, "Feminism, Marxism, Method, and the State" 247n46.

[6] Ti-Grace Atkinson, "Lesbianism and Feminism: Justice for Women as 'Unnatural,'" *Amazon Odyssey* 134, 132.

[7] Ti-Grace Atkinson, "Strategy and Tactics: A Presentation of Political Lesbianism," *Amazon Odyssey* 138.

[8] Atkinson, "Lesbianism and Feminism" 131.

[9] Miriam Schneir, Introduction to Radicalesbians, "The Woman-Identified Woman" 161.

[10] Adrienne Rich, "Compulsory Heterosexuality and Lesbian Existence" 244. Italics in original.

[11] Ibid. 239. Italics in original.

[12] Jane Gallop, *Around 1981* 10.

[13] bell hooks, *Feminist Theory from Margin to Center* 111.

[14] Quoted in hooks, *Feminist Theory* 153. Hooks responds again to the emotional, if not the intellectual, implications of this issue in the essay "Censorship from Left and Right," *Outlaw Culture* 71.

[15] Interestingly, hooks herself later criticizes Madonna's book *Sex* for *its* conflation of the heterosexual and the heterosexist: "Even in the realm of male homoeroticism/homosexuality, Madonna's image usurps, takes over, subordinates. Coded always in *Sex* as heterosexual, her image is the dominant expression of heterosexism. . . . In the context of *Sex*, gay culture remains irrevocably linked to a system of patriarchal control framed by a heterosexist pornographic gaze" ("Power to the Pussy," *Outlaw Culture* 16–17).

[16] Barbara Smith, "Toward a Black Feminist Criticism" 168.

[17] See esp. Gallop's chap. 2, "The Problem of Definition," *Around 1981*.

[18] Judith Roof, *A Lure of Knowledge* 217.

[19] Elaine Showalter, "Introduction: The Rise of Gender," in *Speaking of Gender* 2–3.

[20] Eve Kosofsky Sedgwick, *Between Men* 18.

[21] Rich, "Compulsory Heterosexuality" 229.

[22] Terry Castle, *The Apparitional Lesbian* 71. Italics in original.

[23] Ibid. 72. For an interesting revisionary reading of Sedgwick's paradigm of triangulated desire, see Castle's chap. 4, "Sylvia Townsend Warner and the Counterplot of Lesbian Fiction," ibid. 66–91.

[24] Teresa de Lauretis, "Queer Theory: Lesbian and Gay Sexualities, an Introduction" v–vi.

[25] Eve Kosofsky Sedgwick, *Epistemology of the Closet* 39.

[26] Rich, "Compulsory Heterosexuality" 239.

WORKS CITED

Atkinson, Ti-Grace. *Amazon Odyssey: The First Collection of Writings by the Political Pioneer of the Women's Movement*. New York: Links Books, 1974, 131–89.

Butler, Judith. *Bodies That Matter: On the Discursive Limits of "Sex."* New York: Routledge, 1993.

Castle, Terry. *The Apparitional Lesbian: Female Homosexuality and Modern Culture*. New York: Columbia University Press, 1993.

de Lauretis, Teresa. "Queer Theory: Lesbian and Gay Sexualities, an Introduction." *differences* 3.2 (Summer 1991).

Gallop, Jane. *Around 1981: Academic Feminist Literary Theory*. New York: Routledge, 1992.

hooks, bell. *Feminist Theory from Margin to Center*. Boston: South End Press, 1984.

———. *Outlaw Culture: Resisting Representations*. New York: Routledge, 1994.

MacKinnon, Catharine A. "Feminism, Marxism, Method, and the State: An Agenda for Theory." In *The Signs Reader: Women, Gender, and Scholarship*, ed. Elizabeth Abel and Emily K. Abel. Chicago: University of Chicago Press, 1983, 227–56.

Oxford English Dictionary, 2d ed. Oxford: Clarendon Press, 1989.

Radicalesbians. "The Woman-Identified Woman." In *Feminism in Our Time: The Essential Writings, World War II to the Present*, ed. Miriam Schneir. New York: Vintage, 1994, 162–67.

Rich, Adrienne. "Compulsory Heterosexuality and Lesbian Existence." In *The Lesbian and Gay Studies Reader*, ed. Henry Abelove, Michèle Aina Barale, and David M. Halperin. New York: Routledge, 1993, 227–54.

Roof, Judith. *A Lure of Knowledge: Lesbian Sexuality and Theory*. New York: Columbia University Press, 1991.

Schneir, Miriam. Introduction to Radicalesbians. "The Woman-Identified Woman." In *Feminism in Our Time* 160–62.

Sedgwick, Eve Kosofsky. *Between Men: English Literature and Male Homosocial Desire*. New York: Columbia University Press, 1985.

———. *Epistemology of the Closet*. Berkeley: University of California Press, 1990.

Showalter, Elaine. "Introduction: The Rise of Gender." In *Speaking of Gender*, ed. Elaine Showalter. New York: Routledge, 1989.

Smith, Barbara. "Toward a Black Feminist Criticism." In *New Feminist Criticism: Essays on Women, Literature, and Theory*, ed. Elaine Showalter. New York: Pantheon, 1985, 168–86.

AFTERWORD

"Obstructive Behavior: Dykes in the Mainstream of Feminist Theory" originated in the classroom. In the winter of 1994, I was teaching a graduate seminar in feminist theory at New York University to a marvelous and memorable group of English MA and PhD students: they were diverse, smart, contentious, and as committed to political engagement in their future academic careers as they were already in their private lives. The seminar happened to occur at a transitional moment for feminism and feminists. In United States colleges and universities, academic programs in women's studies were beginning to rename themselves gender studies or women's and gender studies, and the revolutionary imperatives of queer theory had begun to mature into what would surely be a lasting challenge to the contours, and the core assumptions, of feminism.

As each of these examples suggests, feminist theoretical paradigms were at this moment stretching to accommodate gender diversity; feminism was no longer about women exclusively but about "woman" as a category produced from within a broad and often unstable network of social relations. While this shift toward an analytics of gender was exciting—opening new interpretive and political doors every day—I was also concerned to understand it as a continuum of, rather than a departure from, the history of feminist practice in the United States. Other critics had taken note of the risks entailed in yielding forth "woman" as the privileged category of feminist analysis. For me one of those risks involved the persistent erasure or marginalization of lesbian sexuality from queer theory: wasn't it ironic that our shiny new analytical practice, focusing so incisively on same-sex eroticism, seemed almost exclusively invested in male sexuality?

Here was the problem, though: ironic though this omission may have been, such a writing out of lesbians was a pattern all too familiar within feminist discourses, as Adrienne Rich and others had observed of the women's liberation movement. "Obstructive Behavior" thus represents an early attempt to connect the dots among feminist theories, queer theories, and gender theories by addressing the rhetorical functions served by lesbian sexuality in each of these discourses. The essay also attempts to situate a particular moment, the already-long-ago-and-far-away mid-1990s, within the interpretive and political history of feminist discourses in the United States, in order to understand its consistencies rather than its anomalies.

The students in my seminar were an exacting bunch, always understanding that the drawing of new categories of distinction entails the circumscription or occlusion of others: new knowledge comes at a cost. The students' special brilliance, and the illuminating demand they made on me, involved their rigorous accounting of such costs for themselves as feminist academics and as feminist political agents. Queer, gender, and feminist theorists—and these are overlapping groups, to be sure—have indeed taken up complex questions of female same-sex eroticism in the decade that followed the particular transitional moment I have described here. Nonetheless, like lesbian, like dyke, categories of identity have always served, and will always serve, rhetorical ends. By tracing the problematic history of lesbian within feminist discourses, "Obstructive Behavior" attempts to show how feminists of many different stripes put to use a uniquely sensitive figure, sometimes knowingly, sometimes not, in service of larger political aims.

Widows, Hacks, and Biographers: The Voice of Professionalism in Elizabeth Agassiz's *Louis Agassiz: His Life and Correspondence*

LINDA S. BERGMANN

The Professionalization of Biography

The question of the "truth value" of nonfiction texts has caused critics considerable vexation in recent years. Indeed, a large portion of the 1992 edition of the MLA publication *Profession* was devoted to a presidential forum on "Discourses of Truth." It is hard not to have a certain sympathy with statements like the following by Nancy K. Miller: "The pull of autobiography as a cultural act for readers, I'm arguing, resides in the desire it figures to be read as autobiography, which we might also call autobiography's *truth effect*" (12). Although according to Miller we might find truth either in the acts described or in the consciousness of the describing autobiographer, we are looking for something like a "true story" when we read autobiography. Difficult as it may be to generate a firm and satisfying definition of truth, we expect at the very least to obtain a verifiably accurate rendition of the life from the autobiographical text.

I would like to suggest that if we are apt to read autobiography for its "truth effect," we are even more apt to read biography in this way. After all, in autobiography we may be as interested in the consciousness of the storyteller as in the actions of the subject being described. (These are, of course, the same person in different periods of the life, and much of the contemporary criticism of autobiography examines the relationship between these two aspects of the same person.) But in biography, we more often assume that we are not interested in the consciousness of the storyteller; instead, we expect that consciousness to be a transparent window into a clear and factual (dare I say "true"?) account of the subject's life. William Epstein observes that biography relies on denying the work of the text: "Hence a biographical 'fact' is usually treated as monumental or inflexible, as a cold, hard, silent thing. It does not hinge, fold, transform, or re-encode. It exists" (46). It is this assumption that, I think, explains why until recently much critical discussion of biography was dominated by biographers, who naturally tend to meld their descriptions of the nature of biography with prescriptions for doing biography and with explanations or justifications of their own practices as biographers. Twentieth-century biographers have tended to valorize accuracy, objectivity, and professionalism; they tend to represent biography as a genre of history and to conceive of history as the recovery, rather than the creation, of the past.[1] And until recently critics have followed their lead.

Only recently has biography come to be seen as a locus of the biographer's discourse as well as a more or less accurate version of the subject's life, and this recognition of and even acceptance of the mediation of the biographer proves troubling to critics who are also biographers because it violates their sense of professionalism.[2] The idea of the biographer as a mediator is particularly troubling to biographers because twentieth-century editorial and biographical practices actively disparage the kinds of selection and polishing of documents and life stories that were commonplace in the early nineteenth century. Contemporary biographical practice demands reproducing documents with all their flaws and exposing the secrets that biographical subjects and their intimates might have left discreetly hidden; in our time, biographers are expected to "discover" the "true" biographical story from these revelations rather than to document a story that is already known or to invent a story that is morally useful. We tend to smirk a bit at Jared Sparks' contention, concerning his editing of George Washington's letters, that "It would be an act of unpardonable injustice to any author, after his death, to bring forth compositions, and particularly letters, written with no design to their publication, and commit them to the press without previously subjecting them to a careful revision" (qtd. in Stevens 306). Only recently has a critic like Jerome McGann argued that all editors of letters and editions are engaging in collaborations, and that rather than being subverted by their editors, such collections are richer for this editorial presence (153–4).

The conventional twentieth-century sense of biography as objective, impartial, and essentially transparent has its roots in the historical period in which Elizabeth Agassiz was writing her biography of her husband, that is, in the last quarter of the nineteenth century. *Louis Agassiz: His Life and Correspondence* can be seen as a case study of the emergence of the standards of professional biography. Biographers of this period, like the Romantic biographers of the generations before them, for the most part sought to convey the lives of "great men," but they located that greatness less in the religious, patriotic, or moral example of the lives they were describing and more in the intellectual development and force of those lives. The development of the mind and the practice of a successful professional career constituted the significant life story (Epstein 140). William Epstein notes that James Anthony Froude claimed in his "Representative Men" of 1850 that biographies should offer "pattern great men" who illustrate the "ideal tendencies of the age" in the way that saints' lives did for earlier men and now-obsolete ideals (qtd. in Epstein 144); those ideal tendencies, Epstein observes, were in the Victorian era those appropriate to industrial capitalism and the new concept of professionalism to which it gave rise (144). These are the ideals that came of age in post-bellum America and particularly in the post-bellum American university.

But although biography was expected to be inspirational, it also had to be "true," and there was a growing consensus that it should be constructed from factual, documented, and unmodified sources.[3] An outgrowth of the focus on the mind was the growing expectation that the texts a writer produced, whether private letters or public documents, should not be violated in the editing process, although they could be judiciously selected and abridged to maintain the focus on the story that was supposed to be inherent in them.[4] Critics realized that these expectations could at times be incompatible. For example, in "The Ethics of Biography" (1883), M.O.W. Oliphant considers the question of what a biographer should do if he (sic) discovers "that the idea he has formed of the person whose good name is in his hands is an unfavorable one, and that all he can do by telling the story of his life is to lessen or destroy that good name—not indeed by revealing any system of hypocrisy or concealed vice, which it might be to the benefit of public morals to expose, but by an exhibition of personal idiosyncrasies repulsive to the ordinary mind and contradictory of the veneration with which the world has hitherto regarded a man of genius" (90). She suggests that the biographer faced with such a dilemma might well consider not writing the biography at all. In the same vein, she suggests that the biographer's pursuit of truth need not mean resurrecting "the old notions which a gossiping world once entertained of that well-known personage, and which we had put away, with all untimely smiles and nicknames, when he became a portion of the past" (93). Biographers were admonished not only to avoid idealizing the personage, but also to refrain from trivializing the life story by focusing on the intimacies of private life.[5]

Oliphant's title, "The Ethics of Biography," and her prescriptions for serious biographical discourse indicate the growing differentiation between those biographies that could be taken seriously and those that could not, that is between "professional biography" and the work of amateurs, since the formulation of an ethics and the establishment of conventions of professional discourse are crucial steps in the process of professionalization. Not only was the biography becoming the story of a professional life, but the biographer was coming to consider him or herself a professional writer producing a distinctly professional discourse. This articulation of biography as a professional genre, distinct from amateur forms of life writing, should, I think, be seen as a part of the widespread institution of professional standards and discourses that marked the last quarter of the nineteenth century. During this era, the professions in America were being molded into their modern form; intellectuals were staking claims to disciplinary respectability by carving out academic specialties and credentialing aspirants to them and by defining the standards of their discourses. As part of the process by which the "man of letters" was replaced by the English professor in the late nineteenth and early twentieth centuries,[6] biography, like other forms of literary discourse, was also professionalized by academic biographers and other credentialed and institutionally sanctioned professional intellectuals (Nadel, *Biography* 68).[7] These professional biographers carefully and sometimes aggressively distinguished their own practices—which they identified as being informed by science or craft or art or some combination thereof—from those of both popular biographies (written by "hacks") and the biographies written by family members (widows). For instance, in an article in *Blackwood's* entitled "Contemporary Literature" (1879), the professional biographer is contrasted to the "sorrowing widows and admiring intimates who seem to consider an elaborate memoir of the departed as much *de rigueur* as the tombstone that is to commemorate his gifts and virtues" (484). The professional biographers, according to Ira Bruce Nadel, aimed to record rather than to commemorate lives; their "professionalism was marked by their assiduous gathering of data, care in the composition of narrative, precision in the documentation of evidence and worry over the preservation of their material" (*Biography* 68). By the end of the century, theorists of biography like Edmund Gosse, Leslie Stephen, and Sidney Lee in England and William Roscoe Thayer in the United States could draw clear distinctions between what Gosse called "legitimate" biography and the mixed bag of life stories of various kinds, most of which they repudiated as biased, partisan, moralistic, or merely fallacious (Novarr 11–23). Gosse, for instance, roundly dismissed the work of "hacks and widows" (16), claming that biography should neither memorialize or expose a man nor use his life to make a historical, moral, or religious point; instead, it should reveal a great man's soul in all its individuality, a task that the professional biographer alone could undertake.[8]

One effect of this effort to define the genre of biography was to exclude much life writing by women from serious consideration. Biographies, particularly in the form of the "life and letters," before the triumph of professionalism were often written by the widow or other surviving female relative of a "great man." Since women seldom wrote autobiographies and seldom were, before Elizabeth Gaskell's *Charlotte Brontë* (1857), the subjects of biographies, this writing and editing offered women a voice in life writing that they might not otherwise have had. In the literature of professionalization, however, the woman biographer—and the "feminine" tropes of idealization and gossip—were contrasted with the accuracy, refinement, and significance of the public life story uncovered by the "professional" biographer. The woman biographers were dismissed as novices or amateurs (Ross 138–9), even though, since they had often served as their subject's secretary or amanuensis and as such were experienced at managing and orchestrating his correspondence, they were in a position to acquire both the skills and the knowledge necessary to compose a biography or to edit a collection. The whole question of whether they could be "objective" is, of course, a question of definition, much of it after the fact. Many of these works by women were subsequently dismissed as "hagiographies" by the professionalizing biographers and critics, who valorized their own purportedly objective stance as they promoted the professionalization of biography.[9] It was particularly important to map out the masculine terrain of biography as a public domain since, as Valerie Ross has shown, the men who dominated the emerging profession of literary criticism were tending to dismiss biography as private—and thus feminine—in comparison to the "manly" professional work of literary and philological analysis (Ross 154–7).[10]

The Professional Biography

Elizabeth Agassiz's biography of her husband, *Louis Agassiz: His Life and Correspondence* (1885), reflects an awareness of this emerging dichotomy between the widow's memoir and the "legitimate biography." I think that this awareness is a reflection of her own understanding of and involvement in related issues of professionalism and professional discourse, issues that were being debated and instituted at Harvard throughout her adult life. As a member of the Harvard community during the tenure of Charles W. Eliot (president of the University from 1869–1909), as the wife and amanuensis of the Harvard scientist Louis Agassiz, and as the founder and first president of Radcliffe College, she was aware of and involved in much of the intellectual and political turmoil that marked the transformation of Harvard into a modern university, a transformation that involved the emergence of both science and English studies from the activities of gentlemen into professional disciplines with departments, associations, and distinctively professional discourses (Bledstein 303–4). Louis Agassiz, who came to this country in 1846 and who was among the most well-known of nineteenth-century American scientists until his death in 1873, was known as a great popularizer of science to a mass audience in America. He also devoted considerable work to founding and maintaining institutions in which science could be taught and practiced as a profession.[11] As a founder of the American Association for the Advancement of Science (1848) and of the American Academy of Sciences (1864) and as one of the first systematic educators of graduate students at Harvard,[12] he had a strong conviction of his authority as a professional scientist, a conviction that led him into several serious public arguments with students and colleagues.[13]

Central to the professionalization of science was the distinction between the scientist and the non-scientist: the scientist thinks, the assistants (students, wives, technicians) assist, and the amateur appreciates. During his lifetime, working as her husband's amanuensis and editor, Elizabeth Agassiz carefully distinguished between his professional stature as a scientist and her own amateur efforts to assist him and extend his message by writing popularizations of natural science for adults and children. For example, in a letter to her sister in 1862, she expresses her doubts about her role in producing the series of articles for the *Atlantic Monthly* that were later published as *Methods of Study in Natural History*. She worries that what she identifies as her specifically female qualities will misrepresent his scientific thinking:

> About this May article I was especially anxious. You know the coral reefs are very attractive to me, and perhaps I have not understood any of his investigations better than those upon the Florida reefs; but I am conscious that what is beautiful and picturesque in his studies interests me more than what is purely scientific, and sometimes I am afraid that in my appreciation of that side of the subject I shall weaken his thought and give it a rather feminine character. (qtd. in Paton 67)

Thus, even though her husband's scientific career became for Elizabeth Agassiz something of a family enterprise, her deference to Louis Agassiz's role as the scientist attests to her conviction of the distinction between professional and amateur participation in science and between professional and popular scientific discourse. This is the distinction that Elizabeth Keeney traces in the field of botany between advancing and promoting science, a distinction that was increasingly apparent after the Civil War and that was institutionalized by the 1870s (130). The scientist investigates and understands; the amateur—and in particular the lady and the wife—responds to the "beautiful and picturesque."

Two decades later, in *Louis Agassiz: His Life and Correspondence*, Elizabeth Agassiz is still aware of the difference between a professional voice and the voice of the wife, although in this book she adopts the authoritative voice of the professional. She does not, to be sure, stake a claim to *scientific* authority; instead, she asserts for herself a *literary* authority, clearly situating the biography she was undertaking in the realm of "legitimate"—or professional—biography. Her awareness of the emerging divide between serious biography and the memoirs of widows and friends and her insistence that hers was going to be a "legitimate" biography are apparent in the preface—in which she distinguishes this text from "the fullness of personal narrative" as well as from "the closeness of scientific analysis" (iii). Writing to her publisher some six months before the date of the preface, she plans that her preface will "say that it is not a biography since it concerns only the intellectual life of Agassiz,"[14] but this assertion is dropped when she actually writes it. Although she uses the term "biography" here to indicate "personal narrative" rather than "intellectual career story," she clearly sees the distinction between these two types of life writing. My point here is that Elizabeth Agassiz quite consciously wrote an intellectual biography of her husband—not an intimate memoir of his life and friendships of the sort, for example, later produced by family members of Emerson and Longfellow, both of whom were friends of the Agassiz family. She applied to the work the linguistic and editorial skills of a scholar rather than the memories of a wife, and she aimed for an intellectual portrait of the man rather than an emotional response to him. For example, in a letter to her editor, Horace Scudder, as she was preparing the *Life and Correspondence* for publication, she says: "I have a dread of anything in the sentimental and of this I am perhaps not a good judge—I want it to be told simply and naturally,"[15] and she worries in a letter to her publisher that "my narrative errs on the side of meagerness."[16] Elizabeth Agassiz, however, did not dread the sentimental in general: she admired her sister Caroline Cary Curtis's sentimental novels (published under the name of Carroll Winchester), and she and her sister read and critiqued each other's manuscripts and proofs (Tharp 272).[17] It was not "anything" sentimental that she dreaded, but she did dread that this biography would appear to be a sentimental memoir rather than a professional and authoritative biography.

In editing the letters, she very literally turned herself from a wife into a scholar, expending nearly twelve years of regular, sustained effort, which included not only collecting, sorting, and glossing the letters, but also soliciting accounts of Louis Agassiz's earlier life from friends and family members in the United States and abroad. She translated many of the letters from the original French, in which she was fluent, and she took German lessons during these years so that she could translate or at least supervise the translation of the letters written in German.[18] Elizabeth Agassiz's correspondence with Horace Scudder shows her meticulous attention to the details of the manuscript down to the spelling of particular words and names. As she finished sections of the manuscript, she circulated them to a number of readers, including Louis Agassiz's cousin Auguste Mayor, the poet Henry Wadsworth Longfellow, and her sister Caroline. She was adamant that the biography be clear and accurate, and she took the pains necessary to produce that clarity and accuracy.

She founded that accuracy in documents, the letters she had so assiduously collected. She used her memories to shape the story and to situate and contextualize the letters, but what makes this a biography rather than a memoir is her care to see that it was primarily the documents—not her memories—that speak for Louis Agassiz. Her editor shared this concern. For instance, she wrote to Scudder while he was reading the proofs and editing them: "Then on p. 569 I have added something suggested by you in the last proof,—about the National Academy [of Sciences]—it was all I could find—but I well remember how often Agassiz used that argument in pleading for an intellectual institution."[19] Despite her confidence in her memory, the documentation is crucial, for such documentation is one of the significant differences between biography and memoir.

This self-transformation from wife to biographer was paralleled—and probably fed—by her concurrent transformation from faculty wife to the founder of the college for women at Harvard, eventually known as Radcliffe. During the same years in which she was writing the *Life and Correspondence* (1874–1885), she was also creating Radcliffe as an institution that would provide an intellectually rigorous education for women and give them the credentials to mark it. She was named Radcliffe College's first president in 1882,[20] three years before the publication of *The Life and Correspondence*. Elizabeth Agassiz's success at founding a college for women at Harvard was the result of decades of fundraising and of negotiations with Harvard President Charles William Eliot, who was during that time turning Harvard into a modern institution of graduate and professional education (Bledstein 130–1), and with the Harvard Corporation, which did not particularly want a women's college connected with the University (Tharp 256–61). She may have begun the college unassumingly, by inviting Harvard faculty members to supplement their rather meager incomes by repeating their College lectures to young ladies in private homes (Tharp 248–53). However, her success at building the institution and her adroit negotiations with Eliot and the Harvard Corporation indicate that she well understood the practical value of professional discourse and the importance of a diploma from Harvard as a credential for women.

The Life and Correspondence, I am arguing, worked to fix both her husband's memory and her own present and future place in the elite of merit that Eliot and his faculty were creating.[21] These were functions that a widow's memoir could not achieve; but a biography, recognized as such, could serve both as a monument to her husband's scientific mind and as an indicator of her own intellectual achievement. She tells a professional biographer's story—the story of her husband's *intellectual* life and development as a professional scientist—using the external evidence (as compared to personal knowledge) appropriate to legitimate biography. She finds in the letters the standard story of legitimate biography as it was emerging during this time: the story of the intellectual development of a strong individual mind, a story the significance of which was public rather than personal. The story, she writes in the preface, was not her invention; it was—as it should be—inherent in the letters. Echoing Benjamin Franklin, who claimed to have begun his autobiography by collecting reminiscences for his family and to have resumed it later with a consciousness of a larger public and didactic purpose, Elizabeth Agassiz describes in the Preface the development of her consciousness of audience and story as she worked with the letters:

> I thought little at first of the general public, when I began to weave together in narrative form the facts, letters, and journals contained in these volumes. My chief object was to prevent the dispersion and final loss of scattered papers which had an unquestionable family value. But, as my work grew upon my hands, I began to feel that the story of an intellectual life, which was marked by such rare coherence and unity of aim, might have a wider interest and usefulness; might, perhaps, serve as a stimulus and an encouragement to others. (ii–iv)

Her task as an editor was to compose that story so that it could be transmitted to a wider public, and her letters after publication reveal that she was relieved to know that her readers "got it." Her sense of the story and of her task she tells to William James in response to a letter praising the book:

> I feared the book, taken as a whole, might seem very inadequate; and yet I wanted the story to tell itself out of the materials which I held in trust, and to make upon others the impression it had made upon me, of unswerving steadfastness of purpose united by a rare enthusiasm.[22]

This is a biographer's story, even though it is told by a widow.

The Scientist as Professional

When *Louis Agassiz: His Life and Correspondence* is compared with Louis Agassiz's voluminous manuscript correspondence, we can see how Elizabeth Agassiz's selection process focuses our attention on the story of the emerging intellect of a deeply committed, highly professional natural scientist rather than on other aspects of his personal or professional life.[23] The emerging standards of professionalism were an overlay on the Romantic emulation of the "great man"—a union that had not yet become suspect. Like other Americans of her generation, Elizabeth Agassiz considered the realm of "science," like the realm of literature, to be above the realities of politics, money getting, and personalities; the parts of the correspondence that would reflect such inglorious activities are carefully excised and subordinated as irrelevant to the story. The professional scientist—much like the professional biographer—was supposed to be disinterested, apolitical, and impartial, and Elizabeth Agassiz constructed her husband's story to incorporate these essential qualities. Elizabeth Agassiz worked to reconcile the older, romantic image of the gentleman scientist driven by the love of his field with the newer ideal of the trained and credentialed academic scientist; the professional, although now distinguished from the amateur, was still a gentleman.[24] Science in Elizabeth Agassiz's book was the study of the beauty and intricacy of nature, conducted with that "enthusiasm controlled by patience and industry" that governed her portrait of Louis Agassiz (Paton 190). In *Louis Agassiz: His Life and Correspondence*, the enthusiasm of the gentleman amateur is controlled and enhanced by the patience and industry of the trained professional. The intellect of the professional scientist is above concerns of personalities, politics, or fundraising, and the great man's career is shaped by his genius, not by his manipulations, negotiations, or feelings.

To make Louis Agassiz seem disinterested, pursuing science for love of knowledge rather than for personal gain, required considerable contouring by Elizabeth Agassiz, for not only was he a very successful scientific entrepreneur, but he also tended to meld the boundaries between personal and professional finances as he did the boundaries between home and museum. The son of a Swiss minister, Louis Agassiz was not independently wealthy, and his scientific enterprises, his entourage of aides and assistants, his expeditions, and ultimately the Museum of Comparative Zoology, which he founded in 1859, necessitated continuous fundraising, at which he was highly successful. Elizabeth Agassiz could not leave out of her biography his youthful need for financial security or his relentless pursuit of monetary backing without falsifying the story she found in the letters. Instead, she inscribed Louis Agassiz's aggressive fund-raising, his scrounging of collections, and his prodigious abilities as a scientific entrepreneur as the manifestations of a kind of genteel fiscal innocence. In the *Life and Correspondence*, Louis Agassiz observes nature wisely and honestly, and so money drops into his lap—for the Thayer expedition to Brazil, for the Museum of Comparative Zoology, for the Anderson School (a summer school for high school teachers begun in the last year of his life). For example, when she writes of his collecting and fund-raising for his prospective museum in the years 1852–1855, in every sentence he is the object, not the agent, of financial concerns and pressures:

> The collections now in his possession included ample means for this kind of research [embryology], beside a fair representation of almost all classes of the animal kingdom. Packed together, however, in the narrowest quarters, they were hardly within his own reach, much less could they be made available for others. His own resources were strained to the utmost, merely to save these precious materials from destruction. It is true that in 1850 the sum of four hundred dollars, to be renewed annually, was allowed him by the University for their preservation, and a barrack-like wooden building on the college grounds, far preferable to the bath-house by the river, was provided for their storage. But the cost of keeping them was counted by thousands, not by hundreds, and the greater part of what Agassiz could make was swallowed up in this way. It was, perhaps, the knowledge of this which induced certain friends, interested in him and in science, to subscribe twelve thousand dollars for the purchase of his collections,

to be thus permanently secured to Cambridge. This gave him back, in part, the sum he had already spent upon them, and which he was more than ready to spend again in their maintenance and increase. (507–8)

Elizabeth Agassiz dealt with her husband's other income-producing projects in a similar way. Louis Agassiz continually supplemented his Harvard income with lectures, additional professorships, and other projects, but she never lets them seem to be undertaken out of mercenary motives. Elizabeth Agassiz renders these activities as opportunities eagerly seized to transmit the message of science, opportunities that often required such dire expenditure of energy that they threatened his health:

During the winters of 1847 and 1848 he lectured in all the large eastern cities, New York, Albany, Philadelphia, and Charleston, S.C. Everywhere he drew large crowds, and in those days his courses of lectures were rarely allowed to close without some public expression of gratitude from the listeners. . . . What he earned in this way enabled him to carry on his work and support his assistants. Still, the strain upon his strength, combined with all that he was doing beside in purely scientific work, was severe, and before the twelve-month was out he was seriously ill. (444)

The letters are so selected and framed that Louis Agassiz seems to be literally wearing himself out—indeed, perhaps killing himself—for science.

I suspect that the necessity to separate scientific goals from entrepreneurial or mercenary means was the reason Elizabeth Agassiz decided to leave out of the biography Louis Agassiz's correspondence from the Museum of Comparative Zoology, even though the museum was the major work and achievement of his career after 1859. She explains that "Such a correspondence is unfit for reproduction here, but its minuteness shows that almost the position of every specimen, and the daily, hourly work of every individual in the museum, were known to him" (681). Too much in these letters shows him as a manager, fundraiser, and entrepreneur to be appropriate for an *intellectual* biography, which was supposed to exemplify the progress of a scientific mind. Instead, she selects for the biography those letters that show him as being not of the world of money and management, even though he might find himself in it, and she positions his financial dealings so that he is never providing for himself, but always striving in the service of scientific progress and intellectual goals.

Similarly, Elizabeth Agassiz situates her husband above the world of politics, both academic and national. She carefully excises the manipulations and maneuvers that were a necessary means by which he founded his museum and forged his place in the forefront of American science. For example, she leaves out the draft of a letter to Abbot Lawrence in 1854, in which he uses his having been offered a professorship at the University of Zurich as leverage for generating the endowment for the museum at Harvard that he was planning to build:

You can certainly not find it impertinent if under the circumstances I take the liberty of recalling to your mind a vague plan of another building connected with the

Sc.[ience] School respecting which you once asked my opinion. To compete with similar institutions abroad the Lawrence Scientific School ought to be enlarged and endowed with a museum & other appliances. . . . All my sympathies are now with this country, my best affections are here; I have strength enough to fight my way through, but I am saddened by the thought that the means at my command do not allow me to make the best use of my opportunities and ability.[25]

In *The Life and Correspondence* she simply attributes his refusal of the post to his love for America and for his work here and to his hopes for founding his own museum (513–4), and she reproduces part of a letter to Oswald Heer in which he couches his decision in terms of his "duty toward science" (517). Similarly, she omits mention of the "Lazzaroni," the covert scientific brotherhood Louis Agassiz helped organize in 1853–1855, as she leaves out the maneuvers involved in the founding of the American Association for the Advancement of Science in 1847 and the National Academy of Sciences in 1863.

In *The Life and Correspondence*, Elizabeth Agassiz so shapes his activities to fit the professional ideal, that success merely comes to Louis Agassiz as the deserved reward of a life devoted to the study of nature. Edward Lurie notes in *Nature and the American Mind*:

Agassiz's ability to sharpen the sword of scientific politics to a fine edge to achieve his purposes, revealed in his letter to Anderson [concerning the founding of a new summer school at Penikese]—and many others like it—should underscore the fact that the new scientist had to excel in diplomatic, political, and social skills as well as intellectual brilliance in order to gain the opportunity to attempt cultural transformation. (62)

But this sword is barely visible in the *Life and Correspondence*; Elizabeth Agassiz cuts and edits out the letters in which it is wielded. Although according to Lurie the "new scientist" needed political expertise to function, he also notes that the values Louis Agassiz upheld were the romantic values of the old New England elite, "the good olden virtues of closeness to nature, sacredness of fact, and truth through beauty" (48). Such values served as a bulwark against both the vulgar rich and "the growing stench of political and economic fraud and corruption" (30–1). The problem Elizabeth Agassiz faced as editor was that although these "olden values" in which both she and her husband believed were supposed to be above politics, her husband was a highly political man; her solution is to maintain her focus on his sense of duty to science and on his thinking about nature and to ignore the web of alliances and plans that kept the scientific machine functioning.

Through similar positioning and sorting, Elizabeth Agassiz shaped her gregarious but contentious husband to fit the ideal of the impartial scientist. To render Louis Agassiz's impartial pursuit of scientific understanding, Elizabeth Agassiz emphasizes his role as a direct observer of natural phenomena, sorting out and highlighting the thread of science in the rich weave of scientific and personal relationships that is apparent in the unedited correspondence. For instance, his letters to James D. Dana, his friend and correspondent at Yale, were edited to remove most of the personal elements—such as remarks about their families, plans for family visits—and to highlight the exchange of observations and of information on their projects. The effect is to convey a sense of a scientific community that was cordial but purely scientific, a community held together by the pursuit of facts and the informed discussion of their significance, and to ignore the extent to which it was cemented by personal alliances and friendships. Furthermore, as friendships are subsumed by professional cordiality, personal antagonisms are muted into professional differences. Because she did not outline the personal relationship between Agassiz and Dana, she did not need to describe their bitter quarrel in 1864, a typical academic quarrel precipitated by the usual mix of personal and professional concerns (Lurie, *Agassiz* 342–4). She situates Louis Agassiz's biography in the realm of "impartial" science where personalities do not come into play, allowing only a few humanizing bits of "personal interest" to illustrate how much his students, friends, and colleagues loved him: a letter of "affectionate farewell" from Alexander von Humboldt, a description of a midnight serenade by his students for his fiftieth birthday, a birthday poem from Longfellow.[26]

Minimizing the personal not only allows her to transcend the concerns of the widow's memoir, but also to depict her husband's mind as developing independent of the complex web of personal relations in which he lived. The biography places him at the center of a scientific world in which savants (a favorite term of Louis Agassiz) seek truth, unaffected by the concerns of common life, although they might be occasionally called on for professional expertise that would affect that life.[27] Louis Agassiz, as the reviewers observed and everyone who came in contact with him knew, had a vibrant, charismatic personality, but in the *Life and Correspondence*, Elizabeth Agassiz adjusts the focus from his personal flamboyance to his intellectual force. She may have sensed that focusing on his personal style would detract from his professional weight; after all, P.T. Barnum, too, had been a popular lecturer with a museum of his own. Some close observers of Louis Agassiz like William James, who was for a time his student, and Thomas Cary, Elizabeth's brother and a museum trustee and administrator, reveal in their private letters that they saw him as both genius and "humbug,"[28] and she must have been aware of the danger that the "humbug" would predominate in his image. Elizabeth Agassiz disclosed a sense of this danger in her response to a later biography. When in 1896 Jules Marcou, an associate of Louis Agassiz, published his own version of Louis Agassiz's life and letters, she attacked it for portraying Louis Agassiz as theatrical, as a "poseur."[29] Her Louis Agassiz is a savant, not a showman, and the distinction became increasingly crucial as the standards of professional science were becoming more clearly defined. The professional man— the scientist as credentialed and institutionally sanctioned intellectual—was supposed to be profoundly aloof from bombast, scandal, and contention, and it is the professional Louis Agassiz—not her gregarious and contentious husband—that Elizabeth Agassiz shapes her story to illuminate. Neither his feelings nor his stratagems are opened to scrutiny. It is the mind of the man that is elucidated in this life and letters, and it is the mind—not the emotions and not the memories—of the woman that narrates and arranges that life. A great mind may stir the emotions of the public, but not of the professional biographer, particularly if that biographer is also his widow.

The Biographer as Professional

With the creation of this kind of text, Elizabeth Agassiz steps out of the space of "wife," transforming personal space into literary space and private life into professional biography. Elizabeth Agassiz situates herself as her husband's intellectual equal in this text, not as his helpmate, and she does this by writing the book like a scholar, not like a raconteur. At the same time as she edited and arranged his letters to represent him more as a disembodied intellect than the gregarious charmer his friends and associates knew him as,[30] she adopts for herself a narrative voice that is detached, disinterested, and professional. "Enthusiasm controlled by patience and industry" can as well be applied to her own voice in the life as to her husband's in the letters, as her voice becomes the voice of professional authority. This professional, public voice is a different voice than the one she used in her earlier volume, *A Journey in Brazil*, or in the popularizations of science she wrote with her husband and later with her stepson Alexander Agassiz. The voice in *A Journey in Brazil* is the voice of the scientist's wife and helpmate, chatting in public about their adventures on the Amazon. This voice offers the observations of an intelligent amateur who clearly subordinated her observations to the scientist's project.[31] She describes the expedition's work from her position near its center:

> And at this moment the laboratory rings with clink of hammer, and nails, and iron hoops. As usual, there are a number of uninvited spectators watching the breaking up of the scientific establishment, which has been, during the past month, a source of constant entertainment to the vagrant population of Teffe. In this country of open doors and windows one has not the same protection against intrusions as in a colder climate, and we have had a constant succession of curious visitors hanging about our premises. (242)

The voice in the *Life and Correspondence*, by way of contrast, nearly effaces any hint of Elizabeth Agassiz's personal self. Most tellingly, she describes her marriage as if it were someone else's:

> In the Spring of 1850 Agassiz married Elizabeth Cabot Cary, daughter of Thomas Graves Cary, of Boston. This marriage confirmed his resolve to remain, at least for the present, in the United States. It connected him by the closest ties with a large family circle, of which he was henceforth a beloved and honored member, and made him the brother-in-law of one of his most intimate friends, Professor C.C. Felton. (477)

This reads as though it were written by a stranger, as indeed it was intended to read.

Elizabeth Agassiz avoids both the sentimentality of a widow's memoir and the scandal-mongering of the popular biography,[32] leaving, as a reviewer in the *Atlantic Monthly* noted, the personal details of Louis Agassiz's life to be supplied by the minds of his friends who might read the volumes. Her dispassionate voice precludes intimacy—with her subject and with her reader—and leaves the impression of "meagerness" that she apprehended and that her reviewers lamented. The conversation between husband and wife is transmuted into a subdued dialogue between scholar and scientist. At the same time, however, the *Life and Correspondence* documents her own emergence as a public personage, a position she takes both by her representation of Louis Agassiz's voice and by the development of a new voice of her own with those same professionally desirable attributes of objectivity, impartiality, and disinterestedness. She has, in essence, taken on the professional biographers, played their game, and played it so well that her contemporary reviewers took her professionalism at face value. The Harvard botanist Asa Gray, for example, wrote that "the editorial work is so deftly and delicately done," that the story could "tell itself" (848–50).[33]

Producing a biography of her husband that was respected for its "truth value" and that cast her with the voice of a disinterested scholar did not only serve Elizabeth Agassiz as a way of putting her husband's life to rest and shaping the public memory of its significance. Writing a clearly "professional biography" of Louis Agassiz that showed him to be one of the "great minds" of her time also served as a way for the essentially uncredentialed Elizabeth Agassiz, who had had no formal education herself, to take up and use a power of her own in that intellectual community in which he had lived. The voice of the scholar was the voice of authority in the Cambridge that she shared with her husband and in the Harvard in which she was at that very time making an institutional space for women.

My point here is not that Elizabeth Agassiz distorted her husband's biography or miscast his role as a professional scientist. Indeed, her sense of her husband's life is quite similar to that of his contemporary biographer, Edward Lurie, whose biography of Louis Agassiz, first published in 1960 and reissued in 1988, was very well received by historians of science. Lurie included much of the academic politics and personal flamboyance and irksomeness that Elizabeth Agassiz left out, but his sense of the man and his significance is quite similar to hers. Instead of picking on particular biographers, my purpose is to problematize the idea of the objective, transparent biographer finding the "truth" or even "a truth" about the subject's life, an idea that is deeply ingrained in our literary culture, even though it has rejected the "truth value" of most other genres. This valorization of the objective and impartial biographer stands in sharp contrast to contemporary disregard for the "authority" of the author, a gap between biographical practice and critical theory that has been observed by critics such as James Clifford, Valerie Ross, and William Epstein. The "legitimate biography," I would argue, is no more transparent than the gossip of the hacks or the idealizations of the widows although its opacity is of a different and ostensibly more "respectable" sort. As James Anthony Froude noted in 1850, biographies tell life stories that constitute the "ideal pattern of the age," but it is the age in which they are written, not the age in which the personage lived, that sets the ideal. This is why we need and produce new biographies, and why when we read biographies from past eras our interest shifts from the life being described to the mind of the biographer. Thus, we read Henry James's *Nathaniel Hawthorne*, Elizabeth Gaskell's *Charlotte Brontë*, Ralph Waldo Emerson's *Representative Men,* and Thomas Carlyle's *Life of John Sterling*, for example, as much or more out of our interest in the biographer as out of interest in the subject. But although new eras need new stories to embody new ideals, it is a mistake to imagine that contemporary biography is or can be any more "true" than the biographies of the nineteenth century.

When biography is seen as a locus of the biographer's discourse more than as a rendering of the subject's life, our interest shifts from the quest for "objective truth" to the examination of the author's subjectivity (Atwood 6–7). If objectivity is simply not possible, our attention can shift to the dynamic relationship between biographer and subject—to the dialogue that may take place between them. Thus, for instance, Ira Nadel has argued that an element of autobiography is a necessary and even desirable aspect of biography, exposing "the essentially literary nature" of biography and providing a means of dealing with "the inadequacy of fact" ("Biographers" 24–31). Bringing the work of "widows and hacks" back into a larger fold of biography and reassessing the validity of the generic distinctions between "legitimate" biography and other kinds of life stories may allow us to understand the work of life writing in ways that have been obscured by the barriers erected in the name of professionalism. In particular, we can focus on how biography is situated in the life and culture of the biographer. This is interesting both in the case of nineteenth-century biographies by women and other marginalized groups, whose own life stories were often told by others and whose stories of other people's lives were dismissed, and also in the case of those "professional" biographers, who, as Leon Edel and others have suggested, become involved with the lives they are researching in ways that critics are only beginning to examine.

The longing for "truth value" in biography is, however, a persistent longing, and this very paper is an instance of that longing. However much I may examine the subjectivity that shaped Elizabeth Agassiz's story of Louis Agassiz's life and the institutional and professional circumstances in which that subjectivity operated, I write this paper as though I were reclaiming the true subjectivity of Elizabeth Agassiz. I draw upon previous biographies, collections of letters, and other sources as if they were true sources. And for the most part, I have maintained that professional voice, distant and urbane, that is the direct descendent of the critical voice developed with the professionalization of literary criticism during the last quarter of the nineteenth century. I leave out the elements of my own life story that led me to an interest in Elizabeth Agassiz as I leave out—with the exception of a few acknowledgements—the institutional situation in which my evidence was gathered and my own biographical writing has taken place. Although I query the distinction between the work of widows and hacks and the work of scholars—and in an earlier draft of this paper I blamed Elizabeth Agassiz for helping to erect that distinction—I make certain that I keep my work clearly in the camp of the professional scholars so that I am not mistaken for a widow or a hack.

NOTES

The research for this project was funded by a summer research grant from the Department of Humanities of the Illinois Institute of Technology and by a summer stipend from the National Endowment for the Humanities. The author owes debts of gratitude to John Root of the Illinois Institute of Technology for help in shaping this project into grant proposals that received funding, to Judith Yaross Lee of Ohio University, whose graduate seminar's response to an earlier draft provoked the conclusion of the paper, and to Lawrence Buell of Harvard University for help in maneuvering through the collections of Houghton Library.

[1] See, for example, Hayden White 82–3.

[2] Leon Edel, for instance, discusses the "transference" that often takes place between the biographer and the subject, observing that biographers tend to grow to either love or hate their subjects, and suggesting that they may be drawn to their subjects by various factors in their own personalities or life stories. This transference, Edel warns, may distort the biographer's perception of the subject or at least influence it in subtle ways:

> When a biographer identifies with the subject the emotions are bound to be more intense and the result is the blindness that results in idealization. We can discover that even when a subject is assigned to a biographer or undertaken as a chore for financial consideration, intrusive emotions may enter into the hackneyed job. Identifications and transferences occur whenever some inner chord of feeling is touched. ("Transference" 286)

See also "The Biographer and Psycho-Analysis" 228–31.

[3] Nadel shows this tension at work in John Forster's *Life of Dickens*:

> Altered texts, italicized passages, misdated letters, corrected originals—Forster committed all these misdeeds in an effort to maintain his conception of Dickens and their association, extending the continued dependence of the novelist on the advice of the friend. Such manipulation is indefensible on scholarly and factual grounds but is understandable if one is to absorb the powerful nature of Romantic biography as practiced in the Victorian period. Where allegiance to the portrait or vision of a subject takes precedence over fact the life must alter. . . . (*Biography* 91)

Nadel notes earlier that Forster was criticized for allowing himself too dominating a presence in the biography (87).

[4] See Skidelsky (2–4). Skidelsky dates the triumph of "truth telling biography"—by which he means essentially debunking biography—after World War Two, although "truth telling," redefined from "reflecting eternal verities" to "revealing faults or sins," was the object of considerable debate in the nineteenth century, following revelations in biographies about the personal lives of Percy Bysshe Shelley, George Eliot, Thomas Carlyle, and others.

[5] Mabel Dodge, for instance, identifies a profusion of personal detail in biography with feminine gossip and with political salesmanship (587–8).

[6] For a general account of this professionalization of literary studies, see Graff (59–64).

[7] Nadel notes that the professionalization of biography entailed obligations not just to "family, public or publisher," but to the genre itself (*Biography* 68).

[8] Here I am following Novarr's summary (15–8) of an article by Gosse published in the *Anglo-Saxon Review* in 1901.

[9] See for instance Novarr's account of Edward Gosse's dismissal of the works of "hacks and widows" (16).

[10] Ross notes that biographical criticism has not fared well with literary critics since their professionalization in the last quarter of the nineteenth century (152–3).

[11] The distinction between popular and professional science and scientific discourse was still emerging during Louis Agassiz's career, and his relationship to the issue is convoluted. A popular lecturer, noted teacher, and the founder of the Museum of Comparative Zoology at Harvard, which in its time seriously rivaled the Smithsonian Institution, he was the leading American scientist to oppose Darwin. Despite his active endeavors to mold American science into a professional activity, by the late 1850s, his work was becoming irrelevant to his contemporary scientists because of his opposition to the idea that all races of humankind are of the same species, and after Darwin's publication of *On the Origin of Species*, to the idea of evolution. His biographer Edward Lurie observes:

> But when the problem of defending his philosophy of nature came to be of increasing importance, his arguments were primarily addressed to laymen and not to his colleagues.

Only twice, for example, in the entire decade of his involvement on the question of the unity or plurality of mankind, did he advance his views in the professional forum. The result was that his interpretation of nature was accepted by non-scientists as the latest expression of scientific truth. But men like [Asa] Gray and [James Dwight] Dana, by 1857 avowed believers in the unity of mankind, were repelled by his public pronouncements. (Lurie, *Agassiz* 268)

[12] See Lurie, *Agassiz* (313–8) and Winsor (64).

[13] See Lurie, *Agassiz* (161, 312–7). See also Winsor (51–62 and elsewhere in Chapter 2, whose title, "I Have Been Disappointed in My Collaborators," is drawn from a quote from Louis Agassiz).

[14] Elizabeth Cary Agassiz to Messers. Houghton, Mifflin, & Co., 29 Dec. 1884, Houghton Library, Harvard University, bMS AM 1925 (21), by permission of the Houghton Library, Harvard University. This comment arose amid a discussion of the title of the book, which she originally proposed to call the *Scientific Life and Letters of Louis Agassiz*. Houghton stated, in proposing that she change the title to *Louis Agassiz: Life and Correspondence*:

To call the book explicitly the Scientific Life and Letters of Louis Agassiz would, I am quite sure, have the effect of warning off a large class of readers who really would find the book thoroughly enjoyable. While, as you say, the work is not strictly a biography, yet the personal element cannot be eliminated. It penetrates even the strictly scientific matter, and I think it would be unfair to create unnecessarily a prejudice in the minds of readers and compel more or less of a [protest?] or explanation in the notice of the book. (Letter from H. O. Houghton to Elizabeth Cary Agassiz, 31 Dec. 1884, H. O. Houghton Pressed Letter Book 9, Jan. 1884–16 July 1885, Houghton Library, Harvard University, MS AM 2030 (185), p. 563–564, by permission of the Houghton Library, Harvard University)

[15] Letter from Elizabeth Cary Agassiz to Horace Scudder, Monday [April?] 18th, Houghton Library, Harvard University, MS AM 801.4 (1), by permission of the Houghton Library, Harvard University.

[16] Letter from Elizabeth Cary Agassiz to Messers Houghton, Mifflin, & Co., 19 Dec. [1884], Houghton Library, Harvard University, bMS AM 1925 (21), by permission of the Houghton Library, Harvard University.

[17] Elizabeth Agassiz noted in her diary on Wed., 14 Jan. 1880: "Morning with Carrie [Curtis]—I wonder whether I [exaggerate?] the merit of her story [*From Madge to Margaret*]—it seems to me interesting—even very interesting," (Elizabeth Cary Agassiz Papers, Schlesinger Library, Harvard University, by permission of the Schlesinger Library).

[18] Elizabeth Agassiz kept diaries during these years, many of which are now in the Agassiz collection in the Schlesinger Library. These diaries record her mornings and afternoons at work, her German lessons, and some of her meetings and correspondence concerning the project. Family responsibilities—particularly the supervision of her three grandchildren, whose mother died several days after Louis Agassiz—often cut into the time available for her work and drew out the years necessary for its completion.

[19] Letter from Elizabeth Agassiz to Horace Scudder, 7 May [1885], Houghton Library, Harvard University. MS AM 801.4 (1), by permission of the Houghton Library, Harvard University.

[20] Radcliffe was begun by a committee of women in Cambridge in 1879. It was called "the Harvard Annex" until the name "Radcliffe College" was chosen in 1893, and it was chartered by the Massachusetts state legislature in 1894 (Tharp 248–52, 263–4).

[21] See Bledstein (323).

[22] Letter from Elizabeth Cary Agassiz to William James, 28 Oct. [1885?], Houghton Library, Harvard University, bMS AM 1092 (10), by permission of the Houghton Library, Harvard University.

[23] Her conception of his intellectual life as a strain distinctly separate from the personal can be seen in a letter to Cecile Mettenius in 1876: "I try to grasp the larger generalizations, the ideas underlying the whole, and to see when these thoughts first dawned upon him—how early in life the outline of his intellectual work was sketched out and how it was gradually filled in. This I

strive to do. He himself helped me to understand it—indeed he gave into my hand the key to his intellectual history" (qtd. in Paton 185).

[24] Kenneth Cmiel discusses the rift between the sense of intellectual work as general culture and the call for professional expertise, a rift that he notes was evident in science and engineering as well as in literature. He notes, however, that "if the term *professional* is set against *gentleman* it can mislead. The major philologists [although squarely on the professional expertise side of the rift] would have taken umbrage at the assertion that they were not gentlemen" (168). The scientists at Harvard and other universities would have taken similar umbrage.

[25] Draft of a Letter from Louis Agassiz to Abbot Lawrence, 20 May 1854, Houghton Library, Harvard University, bMS AM 419 (125), by permission of the Houghton Library, Harvard University.

[26] She discusses these inclusions with Scudder in a letter dated Monday 18 [April?] 1885. She says "In these personal passages I feel a little un[certain?],—at least not so good a judge as an outsider would be" (Houghton Library, Harvard University, MS AM 801.4(1), by permission of the Houghton Library, Harvard University).

[27] For example, Samuel Gridley Howe wrote to Louis Agassiz in August of 1863, requesting a scientific opinion on the future of the black race after slavery was abolished. Most of Louis Agassiz's reply is printed in the *Life and Correspondence* (590–617). In "Flaws in a Victorian Veil," Stephen Jay Gould has shown how Elizabeth Agassiz's editorial cuts softened the impact of Louis Agassiz's racism (169–76).

[28] William James wrote to his brother Henry early in the Brazil expedition, on which William James was a student assistant, the following description of "the Prof.": "Professor is a very interesting man. I don't yet understand him very well. There is more charlatanerie & humbug about him & more solid worth too than you meet with. His charlatanerie is almost as great as his solid worth; and it seems of an unconscious, childlike kind . . ." (William James to Henry James, Jr., 3 May 1865, Houghton Library, Harvard University, bMS AM 1092.9(2549), by permission of the Houghton Library, Harvard University and the James family).

[29] "Mr. Marcou represents Agassiz throughout the book as a 'poseur' and a clever actor and it really seems as if the whole [deathbed] scene with its theatrical 'le jeu est fini' were composed in order to keep up this idea to the end, for the very next line he says 'Life had been for him a long & successful play'" (Letter from Elizabeth Agassiz to Henry [?], 1895, Elizabeth Cary Agassiz Papers, Schlesinger Library, Harvard University, by permission of the Schlesinger Library).

[30] See, for instance, the biographical sketch by Edward Waldo Emerson in *The Early Years of the Saturday Club*, 1855–1870 (30–8).

[31] Despite this compliance, however, she does interpret what she sees in fundamentally different ways than her husband, which leads to implicit contradictions between her vision of Brazil and her husband's (Bergmann 85).

[32] She was well aware of how profoundly a biography could shape one's perception of the subject: She had radically revised her feelings about Charlotte Brontë after reading Elizabeth Gaskell's *Life and Letters* in 1868 (Elizabeth Cary Agassiz to Mary Ann Cushing Perkins Cary [her mother], 24 May 1868, Elizabeth Cary Agassiz Papers, Schlesinger Library, Harvard University). Furthermore, in 1885, as *Louis Agassiz: His Life and Correspondence* was undergoing its final editing, the literary public was reeling from the recent biography of George Eliot that made public her unconventional life. Such revelations were overshadowing the discussion of her literary achievements, as Elizabeth Porter Gould noted in "The Biography of the Future" (171).

[33] Like other reviewers, Gray noted the lack of "personal details."

WORKS CITED

Agassiz, Elizabeth Cary. *A Journey in Brazil*. Boston: Ticknor, 1868.

———. *Louis Agassiz: His Life and Correspondence*. 2 vols. Boston: Houghton, 1885.

Atwood, Margaret. "Biographobia: Some Personal Reflections on the Act of Biography." *Nineteenth-Century Lives: Essays Presented to Jerome Hamilton Buckley*. Ed. Lawrence S. Lockridge, John Maynard, and Donald D. Stone. Cambridge: Cambridge UP, 1989. 1–8.

Bergmann, Linda S. "A Troubled Marriage of Discourses: Science Writing and Travel Narrative in Louis and Elizabeth Agassiz's *A Journey in Brazil*." *Journal of American Culture* 18 (1995): 83–8.

Bledstein, Burton J. *The Culture of Professionalism: The Middle Class and the Development of Higher Education in America*. New York: Norton, 1978.

Cmiel, Kenneth. *Democratic Eloquence: The Fight over Popular Speech in Nineteenth-Century America*. Berkeley: U of California P, 1990.

"Contemporary Literature," 1879. *Victorian Biography: A Collection of Essays from the Period*. Ed. Ira Bruce Nadel. New York: Garland, 1986.

Dodge, Mabel. "The New School of Biography." *Atlantic Monthly* 14 (1864): 579–89.

Edel, Leon. "Transference: The Biographer's Dilemma." *Biography* 7 (Fall 1984): 283–91.

———. "The Biographer and Psycho-Analysis." 1960. *Biography as an Art: Selected Criticism 1560–1960*. Ed. James L. Clifford. New York: Oxford UP, 1962.

Emerson, Edward Waldo. *The Early Years of the Saturday Club, 1855–1870*. Boston: Houghton, 1918.

Epstein, William H. *Recognizing Biography*. Philadelphia: U of Pennsylvania P, 1987.

Froude, James Anthony. "Representative Men." *Short Studies on Great Subjects*. New York: Charles Scribner, 1850. 465–85.

Gosse, Edmund. "The Custom of Biography." *Anglo-Saxon Review* 8 (March 1901): 195–208.

Gould, Elizabeth Porter. "The Biography of the Future." *The Literary World* 16 (May 1885): 171.

Gould, Stephen Jay. "Flaws in a Victorian Veil." *The Panda's Thumb*. New York: Norton, 1989. 169–76.

Graff, Gerald. *Professing Literature: An Institutional History*. Chicago: U of Chicago P, 1987.

Gray, Asa. "Louis Agassiz." Rev. of *Louis Agassiz: His Life and Correspondence*, by Elizabeth Cary Agassiz. *Andover Review* 25 (1886): 38–45.

Keeney, Elizabeth B. *The Botanizers: Amateur Scientists in Nineteenth-Century America*. Chapel Hill: U of North Carolina P, 1992.

"Louis Agassiz." Rev. of *Louis Agassiz: His Life and Correspondence*, by Elizabeth Cary Agassiz. *Atlantic Monthly* 56 (1885): 848–50.

Lurie, Edward. *Louis Agassiz: A Life in Science*. 1960. Baltimore: Johns Hopkins UP, 1988.

———. *Nature and the American Mind: Louis Agassiz and the Culture of Science*. New York: Science History Publications, 1974.

McGann, Jerome. "The Case of *The Ambassadors* and the Textual Condition." *Palimpsest: Editorial Theory in the Humanities*. Ed. George Bornstein and Ralph G. Williams. Ann Arbor: U of Michigan P, 1993. 153–73.

Miller, Nancy K. "Facts, Pacts, Acts." *Profession* 92 (MLA): 12–8.

Nadel, Ira Bruce. "The Biographer's Secret." *Studies in Autobiography*. Ed. James Olney. New York: Oxford UP, 1988. 24–31.

———. *Biography: Fiction, Fact and Form*. New York: St. Martin's, 1984.

Novarr, David. *The Lines of Life: Theories of Biography, 1880–1970*. West Lafayette, IN: Purdue UP, 1986.

Oliphant, M.O.W. "The Ethics of Biography." 1883. *Victorian Biography: A Collection of Essays from the Period*. Ed. Ira Bruce Nadel. New York: Garland, 1986.

Paton, Lucy Allen. *Elizabeth Cary Agassiz: A Biography*. Boston: Houghton, 1919.

Ross, Valerie. "Too Close to Home: Repressing Biography, Instituting Authority." *Contesting the Subject: Essays in the Postmodern Theory and Practice of Biography and Biographical Criticism*. Ed. William H. Epstein. West Lafayette, IN: Purdue UP, 1991. 135–65.

Skidelsky, Robert. "Only Connect: Biography and Truth." *The Troubled Face of Biography*. Ed. Eric Homberger and John Charmley. London: Macmillan, 1988. 1–32.

Stevens, Michael E. "Jared Sparks." *American Historians: 1607–1865*. Ed. Clyde N. Wilson. *Dictionary of Literary Biography*, 30. Detroit: Gale Research, 1984. 298–310.

Tharp, Louisa Hall. *Adventurous Alliance: The Story of the Agassiz Family of Boston*. Boston: Little, Brown, 1959.

White, Hayden. "Historical Text as Literary Artifact." *Tropics of Discourse*. Baltimore: Johns Hopkins UP, 1985. 81–100.

Winsor, Mary P. *Reading the Shape of Nature: Comparative Zoology at the Agassiz Museum*. Chicago: U of Chicago P, 1991.

AFTERWORD

I wrote "Widows, Hacks, and Biographers" in the mid-1990s, by which time I had shifted my scholarship and professional identification from literary studies to rhetoric and composition. Although I had started to publish in composition studies, I knew that to earn tenure in the small, traditionally oriented humanities department in which I then worked, I had to produce publications recognizable as research to my senior colleagues—and that meant textual analyses. I happened across Louis and Elizabeth Agassiz while writing a paper on Charles Darwin and realized that they had authored a small trove of almost forgotten texts; these led me to the archival sources in the Harvard libraries on which I based much of my subsequent work. Since I had been a graduate student at the University of Chicago when its English department was dominated by neo-Aristotelians, it is hardly surprising that I examined Elizabeth Agassiz's biography of her husband by considering what she was trying to do and analyzing how she went about doing it. My interest in feminist theory inclined me to consider the implications of a man's life edited by a woman's hand and to celebrate the woman's emerging authority. I also drew on my ongoing interest in the emergence of professionalism in the last quarter of the nineteenth century and in professionalization in general.

Several years later, in "Women of Letters: Personal Narrative in Public and Private Voices," I examined my feelings about working with Elizabeth Agassiz's journal, letters, and diaries, and I reflected on how this work both derived from and contributed to my own growth as a woman and a scholar. In that article, I recognized that Elizabeth Agassiz's achieving self-definition and personal growth by turning personal experiences into public discourse resonated for me because I felt similarly situated:

> I see now that my interest in how Elizabeth Agassiz distinguished her own public voice from that of her scientist husband probably stemmed from *my* efforts to find a professional voice while subordinating my own career to my husband's career as a scientist. . . . Several conference papers and a journal article, in which I claimed that Elizabeth Agassiz used her letters as a means of finding a voice and establishing a presence in a world dominated by men, also served *me* as means of staking *my own* claim to a place in the academy and to a voice at home. Furthermore, my analyses of Elizabeth Agassiz's texts led to my imagining a personal relationship with her, even though she had died nearly half a century before I was born. (p. 96)

Today, however, I reread "Widows, Hacks, and Biographers" with considerable chagrin. It has become increasingly clear to me since reading Christoph Irmscher's *The Poetics of Natural History*, Cheryl Geisler's *Academic Literacy and the Nature of Expertise*, and Steven Katz's "Ethics of Expediency" that I failed to raise the question of value: whether writing a biography depicting her husband as the exemplary professional scientist was a *good* thing for Elizabeth Agassiz to have done. In focusing on how Elizabeth Agassiz built herself an intellectual life and significance, I overlooked the probability that her husband's very prominence and professional respectability muffled potential criticism of his racism, a racism rooted in his belief in the immutability of types. Having cited, in a footnote, Stephen Jay Gould's account of how she edited her husband's letters to mute his clear belief in the inferiority of African Americans, I relegated Louis Agassiz to the background and foregrounded the intellectual work of Elizabeth Agassiz as if it affected only her life—as if it were free of social, political, and moral implications and consequences. Moreover, I neglected to question the value of the professionalism she embraced, even though the culture of professionalism is at the very heart of my paper. I failed to ask whether it is a good thing that biography, science, and so much else in American culture have become professionalized, with the result that expertise has been separated from the personal sphere and that art, science, and technology can claim to be shielded from moral judgment. Indeed, my own expertise and my pleasure in synthesizing a cross-disciplinary array of theoretical and archival materials may have kept me from asking those very difficult questions. If I were to rewrite the article, these are the questions that would drive my work.

WORKS CITED

Bergmann, Linda. "Women of Letters: Personal Narrative in Public and Private Voices." *The Personal Narrative: Writing Ourselves as Teachers and Scholars.* Ed. Gil Haroian-Guerin. Portland: Calendar Island, 1999. 88–101.

Geisler, Cheryl. *Academic Literacy and the Nature of Expertise: Reading, Writing, and Knowing in Academic Philosophy.* Hillsdale: Erlbaum, 1994.

Irmscher, Christoph. *The Poetics of Natural History: From John Bartram to Henry James.* New Brunswick: Rutgers UP, 1999.

Katz, Steven B. "The Ethics of Expediency: Classical Rhetoric, Technology, and the Holocaust." *College English* 54 (1992): 255–75.

~ 1997 ~

"The Ears of the Palefaces Could Not Hear Me": Languages of Self-Representation in Zitkala-Ša's Autobiographical Essays

MARY PANICCIA CARDEN

The first turning away from the easy, natural flow of my life occurred in an early spring. It was in my eighth year. . . . At this age I knew but one language, and that was my mother's native tongue.

— *Zitkala-Ša*[1]

For the master's tools will never dismantle the master's house. They may allow us temporarily to beat him at his own game, but they will never enable us to bring about genuine change.

— *Audre Lorde*[2]

AUDRE LORDE'S OFT-QUOTED intervention into the politics of self-representation and the dynamics of oppression could conceivably have been addressed directly to the autobiographical practices of women and of colonized peoples. It speaks to the paradox lived and narrated by Zitkala-Ša, a Sioux woman of "mixed" parentage, whose autobiographical essays, *Impressions of an Indian Childhood, The School Days of an Indian Girl, An Indian Teacher Among the Indians*, and *Why I Am a Pagan* appeared in *Atlantic Monthly* in 1900 and 1902. Her essays record her attempt to intervene in American discourses on "race" through her mastery of English, "the magic design which promised [her] the white man's respect" (447).

Lorde conceptualizes "the master's house" as a prisonhouse for the woman of color who pursues self-definition in languages that have historically identified the valid speaking subject as white and male. What uses/abuses of language could enable the woman of color to represent a self that exceeds the parameters of race and gender created, disseminated, and maintained by the language that constructs her as "other"?[3] Must speaking "the master's" language result solely in reproduction of his symbolic order and thus reinforce his claim to the status of "dominating subject"? Or does entry into his signifying economy allow the (other) speaker to resist inscription as "dominated object"?[4] Highly charged elements of contemporary feminist, autobiographical, and post-colonial theories center on this issue in their investigations of the complex negotiations, subversions, and reformulations of language generated when a linguistic system owned and policed by representatives of the dominant race and gender is hijacked by women of color as a vehicle of self-identification.[5]

"To be a woman and to speak" is, in Bella Brodzki's words, "already to submit to the phallocentric order while gloriously contradicting it, to serve as the very sign of transgression itself."[6] To speak in the dominant language is to acknowledge its hegemony while recasting its terms and redirecting its meanings, wielding "the master's" discursive tools in order to project an identity that lies outside the mastery of his linguistic borders. Brodzki describes self-representation as the "effect of a constructed similarity or equivalence between identity and language, an attempt to cast in fixed terms the self-reflexive, discontinuous shifts in modality and perspective, temporal and spatial, that are inherent in human experience . . . and to ground them in a single subjectivity."[7] This essay takes up these vexed and vexing equivalencies, employing Lorde's interrogation of the efficacy of appropriating "the master's tools"[8] as the ground for an analysis of Zitkala-Ša's autobiographical project. As a woman and a colonized subject whose identity is both indeterminate and overdetermined, she finds the field of those equivalencies of identity and language uncertain, even treacherous. For her, both sides of this formula are unstable—identity is unfixed and language unequipped to construct a "self" that crosses linguistic boundaries.[9]

Zitkala-Ša was born Gertrude Simmons on the Yankton reservation in South Dakota in 1876.[10] Her father was a white man named Felker, her mother's third husband, who left the family before her birth. Ellen Simmons gave her daughter her second husband's name—Simmons. She was Gertrude Simmons until she argued with her sister-in-law over her participation in the white educational system. In a letter to a friend she explains that her sister-in-law suggested that since she had

> deserted home . . . I might give up my brother's name 'Simmons' too. Well, you can guess how queer I felt—away from my own people—homeless—penniless — and even without a name! Then I chose to make a name for myself—and I guess I have made 'Zitkala-Ša' known—for even Italy writes it in her language.[11]

Dexter Fisher remarks that "in creating her own name and essentially her own oral history," she asserts "at one and the same time her independence and her cultural ties. As Zitkala-Ša, she will try to recreate the spirit of her tribe in her collection of legends, though she is never able to return to Yankton permanently."[12] Fisher's explication of the doubleness underlying Zitkala-Ša's renaming suggests that her act mimics a self-birthing designed to take over and control representations of her identity in white and native discourses on racial and cultural subjectivities. With this expression of a new identity she erases an "English" name and replaces it with a name more readily identifiable as "Indian"; her construction of an Indian self—through her name and her autobiographical persona—veils her identity as a person of mixed blood. I read her non-attendance to her white father in her autobiographical writing in Teresa de Lauretis' terms, as a "political-personal strategy of survival and resistance that is also, at the same time, a critical practice *and* a mode of knowledge":[13] asserting her Indian identity, she maneuvers for self-determination in the colonizer's vocabulary.

Henry Louis Gates, Jr., has proposed that "race" is a trope, "a metaphor for something else and not an essence or a thing in itself, apart from its creation by an act of language."[14] Western writers, he argues, have

> tried to mystify these rhetorical figures of race, to make them natural, absolute, essential. In doing so, they have *inscribed* these differences as fixed and finite categories which they merely report or draw upon for authority. It takes little reflection, however, to recognize that these pseudoscientific categories are themselves figures. Who has seen a black or red person, a white, yellow, or brown? These terms are arbitrary constructs, not reports of reality. But language is not only the medium of this often insidious tendency; it is its *sign*. Current language use signifies the difference between cultures and their possession of power, spelling out the distance between subordinate and superordinate, between bondsman and lord in terms of their 'race.'[15]

Discursive demarcations of "race" as naturalized commonsensical markers signal claims to "essential" difference, but also indicate social and economic differences between cultures and perpetuate colonial relationships based in the hegemony of one privileged "race." However, as Zitkala-Ša's texts suggest, conflicted delineations of "race" disrupt (white) linguistic categories and binary oppositions coded to signify the desirable and deserved dominance enjoyed by the (white) speaker of the dominant language.

Moving into white America, she discovers literacy—defined narrowly as the ability to speak and write proper English—positioned as the means to civilization and full human-ness. But, having achieved this literacy, working "by daylight and lamplight . . . [spinning] with reeds and thistles, until [her] hands were tired from their weaving, the magic design which promised [her] the white man's respect" (447), she finds no empowering or respectful or even tolerable vocabulary with which to express her sense of identity there. Her autobiographical writing represents her prolonged engagement with the multiple, coercive, and often hidden powers of the colonizer's language. Encountering the matrix of labels, curses, and stereotypes applied to her—"squaw," "pagan," "primitive," "animalistic," "other"—she finds herself trapped by them at some moments, but at others manages to turn them around to signify back on white culture. Often, she empties them of their meaning and composes others; sometimes she simply contradicts them through anecdote, example, explanation. She uses the signs and symbols, syntax and semantics of "the white man's papers" (458) to write an identity that resists his names for her. What is most important, it seems to me, is not a quantitative measure of success or failure (if units of measure can be applied to such things), but rather a consideration of her own sense of turning "the magic design" to her own ends, her assertion that she can speak and write difference in a signifying economy that denies her that privilege, her record of loss and recovery of identity—of "spirit" (415)—through language.

As I have already suggested, one important but hidden way that she challenges the dominant culture can be discerned in her disregard for the language that establishes gradients of racially marked "blood." Because people of indeterminate "race" represent transgression of naturalized boundaries around identity, cultural battles of naming and defining take place over their bodies. Definitions of racial Indian-ness constituted a central component of the US government's continuing usurpation and "obliteration of the traditional relationships between native peoples and the lands they occupied."[16] Developing a vocabulary that enabled measurement of the degree of "race" inherent in colonized bodies, the American government compartmentalized indigenous peoples through "the so-called 'blood quantum' or 'degree of Indian blood' standard of American Indian identification which had been adopted by Congress in 1887 as part of the General Allotment Act."[17] This vocabulary did more than adjudicate Indian-ness for purposes of separating native peoples from lands promised them "as long as grass grows or water runs"[18]—it also "played a prominent role in bringing about [Indians'] generalized psychic disempowerment; if one is not allowed even to determine for one's self, or within one's peer group, the answer to the all-important question 'Who am I?,' what possible personal power can one feel s/he possesses?"[19] Hertha Dawn Wong points out that "in pre-reservation times it would have been unthinkable to question Indian identity—you were or were not Lakota or Hopi or Cherokee on the bases of tribe, band, clan, and family affiliations."[20] Indigenous peoples, Lenore Stiffarm observes, "defined themselves in terms of specific socio-cultural and political membership . . . rather than in terms of a racial category" and, given the frequency of "'intertribal' marriages . . . 'mixed bloodedness'—at least in traditional Indian terms—has always been normative."[21] However, as many commentators have noted, the language of blood quantum differentiation gradually interfered with long-standing cultural identifications and troubled interpersonal interactions.[22]

While Zitkala-Ša ignores ideologies on racial ambiguity by basing her autobiographical identity firmly in her Indian-ness, these discourses were certainly in the cultural air, and the slippery-yet-absolutely-defined difference between "white" and "Indian" is a locus of contention and resistance in her texts. The essays record her struggle to reconcile her positions in white and Sioux cultures by identifying herself as an intermediary between them. Her assumption of this role could be read as a kind of return of the repressed, as the rebounding of her mixed blood identity on her negation of it. But, more importantly, in her erasure of her white father she answers that "all-important question 'Who am I?'"—the self she considers genuine is a Sioux self. Quite possibly, she does not attend to the "ambiguity" of her "racial status" because for her it is simply not ambiguous. This formulation of selfhood resists the notion of an Indian-ness based in imposed "blood quantum" standards in favor of a definition of identity as a cultural phenomenon.

Because the "ears of the palefaces could not hear" (435) her Indian speech, she sets out to create a voice that would be intelligible in their culture. Zitkala-Ša embarks on this project at the turn of the century, a time when assimilationist policies in the United States sought to re-make Indians in the image of white culture, as dependent wards, as apprentice citizens. She, however, uses/abuses the "gifts" of the white educational system to challenge assimilation. Her essays trace the reductions she endures in return for "the white man's papers" and force her white reader to reconsider the so-called benevolent practices of Americanization through her eyes and her voice.

Impressions of an Indian Childhood represents the young Gertrude Simmons as the paradigmatic child of nature, "wild" and "free" (414–15), joyously "running loose in the open" and contentedly playing "in the lap of the prairie" (421).

> Loosely clad in a slip of brown buckskin, and light-footed with a pair of soft moccasins on my feet, I was as free as the wind that blew my hair, and no less spirited than a bounding deer. These were my mother's pride—my wild freedom and overflowing spirits. (414–15)

But this presentation of an idyllic Sioux childhood is ruptured by a gap between her grasp of cultural signifiers and that of her mother and of the older members of the tribe, a gap opened by white intervention. While the early episodes emphasize "the easy, natural flow" (429) of her Indian childhood, they simultaneously convey a sense of exclusion from Sioux discourses. For instance, she listens, but cannot hear the whistle of the "dead man's plum bush," which the "old folks" hear and have described to her (426), and is forbidden access to the meanings attached to "secret signs" (418) on the bodies of the tribe's elders. Listening to an "old warrior" recount the "old legends" (417) that she "love[s] best" (418), she is distracted by a mark on his forehead:

> I remember the glare of the fire shone upon a tattooed star on the brow of an old warrior who was telling a story. I watched him curiously as he made his unconscious gestures. The blue star upon his bronzed forehead was a puzzle to me. Looking about, I saw two parallel lines on the chin of one of the old women. The rest had none. I examined my mother's face, but found no sign there. (418)

The old woman, in lieu of an explanation of the tattooed symbols, tells a story of "a woman whose magic power lay hidden behind the marks upon her face" (419). But this woman's power is denied to Gertrude, who henceforth feels "suspicious of tattooed people," Indians who partake in a "secret" source of "terrible magic power" (419) connected to an unspeakable sign system. This story of the untranslatable signs and her exclusion from a powerful system of meaning within her culture makes an "acute" impression on her, which "remains vividly clear and pronounced" (419) as she writes. Possibly the meaning of these symbols would have come clear to her as she matured, but because she left Sioux society for the white educational system, her sense of an always-missing component of Sioux cultural knowledge haunts the adult writer's memories of her Sioux childhood and the ways she is able to represent it.[23]

This unspoken unknown of Sioux society, connected with the inscrutable symbolic system associated with the old people, disrupts her presentation of herself as a Sioux subject. The sense of outsiderness occasioned by the gap in her cultural understanding suggests that the Sioux society she knew as a child was always already something other than the culture the elders matured in and base their sense of Sioux-ness in. The young Gertrude Simmons lived in a society repressed by contact, held on reservations, and denied traditional lifestyles. Her mother tells her that the "paleface has stolen our lands and driven us hither" (415). They were forced to travel "not in the grand happy way that [they] moved camp when [she] was a little girl, but [they] were driven . . . like a herd of buffalo" (416). And even in "this western country" (416) they live with the danger that "the paleface" will "take away from [them] the river [they] drink" (415). Zitkala-Ša's experience of Sioux culture has never not been an experience of colonization. "Sioux-ness" thus becomes a signifier without a signified, a site of constant linguistic slippage and actual inaccessibility.

Edward Lazarus has investigated the consequences of "the nativist storm that swept the country"[24] in the late nineteenth century, when, following the massacre of almost 300 Sioux at Wounded Knee in 1890,

> America's policy, well articulated by Senator Dawes . . . remained unchanged: 'We may cry out against the violation of treaties, denounce flagrant disregard of inalienable rights and the inhumanity of our treatment of the defenseless . . . but the fact remains . . . Without doubt these Indians are somehow to be absorbed into and become a part of the 50,000,000 of our people. There does not seem to be any other way to deal with them.'[25]

This policy would prove difficult to enforce for several reasons—Indian resistance constituted one crucial hitch—but another sticking-point resided in the avowed purpose of the policy itself; assimilation could not work in Dawes' terms because most Indians did not share Anglo-American conceptualizations of "nation" and did not formulate group identity in the vocabulary of American "citizenship." Further, most Anglo-Americans were unlikely to consider Indians as "real" Americans. In the American imagination at the turn of the century, Indians appeared as both unpredictably bloodthirsty savages and children with potential for growth into civilized adulthood through the intervention of the US government. The defeated Indians were romanticized as the doomed remnant of the Noble Savage and condemned as lazy slackers exploiting welfare programs and perversely refusing to work for a living in the ways prescribed by white culture.[26] The American government insisted on absorbing Indians, while simultaneously separating them on the basis of their "otherness."

It is this process of absorption, a process rendered impossible from the outset by another kind of symbolic marking of bodies, by (linguistic) lines of race distinguishing an "Indian" from an "American," that Zitkala-Ša challenges in essays that rewrite narratives of assimilation. She frequently places her critique in her mother's voice, in Ellen Simmons' warnings of the threat posed to Sioux culture by continued white encroachment, her curses on "the paleface" who has displaced them, and her grief for her brother and daughter, victims of the forced march to the "western country" (415–16). Her mother's pain and rage politicize Zitkala-Ša's construction of an idyllic early childhood and echo through the later sketches.

Her mother stands in for Sioux culture, but Zitkala-Ša's re-creation of her childhood records her sense of exclusion from her mother's inner life. Ellen Simmons "seldom wept" in her daughter's presence, commanding that "'my little daughter must never talk about my tears'" (414). The grown writer attributes her dissociation from mother and culture to her sojourn in boarding school, which occurs when she "refuse[s] to harken to [her] mother's voice" (431), and chooses the "white men's lies" (430) over her mother's warnings. She represents this "choice" as a misguided one, prompted by duplicitous white missionaries and their promises of "nice red apples" and "a ride on the iron horse" (431). With the Christian symbol of the apple—the fruit that caused the fall—she recasts Christians, white missionaries, as devilish seducers and the Quaker boarding school as the hard, desolate world outside the gates of a Sioux Eden. *The School Days of an Indian Girl* contrasts her "eager[ness]" to "roam among" the "orchards of the East" (430) with the "iron routine" of the "civilizing machine" (442) which "tightly bound [her] individuality like a mummy for burial" (443).

Her mother warns: "'Don't believe a word they say! Their words are sweet, but, my child, their deeds are bitter'" (430). But even as she articulates the speciousness of white language, she admits that her daughter "'will need an education when she is grown, for then there will be fewer real Dakotas, and many more palefaces'" (431). Gertrude's ambivalent mother, who adopts "such of the white man's ways as pleased her" (454), suggests that Indians can use "the master's tools" to challenge his rule by creating his own economy as the battleground on which the Sioux will collect "'a large debt for stolen lands'" (431). But she also seems to suggest that white education is among the factors eroding the ground of "real Dakota" identity.

In the missionaries' custody Gertrude "no longer felt free to be [her]self, or to voice [her] own feelings" (432). On the "iron horse," she becomes the object of the colonizer's gaze, cognizant of her difference in white contexts, "kept . . . constantly on the verge of tears" (434) by the rudeness of white passengers who stare and point at "the children of absent mothers" (433). Separated from the love and support of her mother and from the communal politeness and hospitality of her mother culture, she becomes suddenly and starkly visible, situated as "other" by a foreign system of meaning, and her Indian body and appearance signify outside her control or understanding.

In white cultural space her "overflowing spirits" are forcibly subdued and her body becomes the unnatural locus of juridical attention. Her status in white culture becomes clear as she enters the school for the first time and is seized and thrown in the air by a white woman; she feels "both frightened and insulted by such trifling. . . . [Her] mother had never made a plaything out of her wee daughter" (435) but had "treated [her] as a dignified little individual" (420). Taken in hand as an object, she experiences the dissolution of the boundaries marking her sense of individuality. She loses control of the signifiers of identity inscribed on her body as she is surveyed, marked, and forced to comply with white cultural norms. "Stripped" of her blanket, she comments on the "immodesty" of the school's dress and "fe[els] like sinking to the floor" (436); forced to submit as her long hair is shorn, she exclaims "among our people, short hair was worn by mourners, and shingled hair by cowards" (437). As she suffers these and many other "indignities" she "[loses] [her] spirit" (437). She undergoes another kind of "tattooing"; the clothing and hair which represent her Sioux-ness are replaced with the school's standardized mold of Americanization and her body is policed for any sign of rebellious Indian-ness. Early in their boarding school experience, she and her playmates are punished for falling "lengthwise in the snow . . . to see [their] own impressions" (438); she is disciplined and restrained, forbidden any exercise of the "wild freedom and overflowing spirits" that seemed "easy" and "natural" on the prairie. White institutions efface the physical body that leaves its imprint in the snow in their mission to produce facsimiles of "American" subjects by erasing "Indian" bodies.

But even in the maw of the assimilationist machine Gertrude is not completely powerless. *The School Days of an Indian Girl* re-presents her dialogue with colonial institutions, casting her as an active agent signifying back on white discourses. As she begins to communicate in English, she is "possessed" by "a mischievous spirit of revenge" (439) that motivates her to resist the identity formulated for her by the school. When white authorities deploy the devil as a sign of the punishment that awaits disobedient girls, she uses a broken slate pencil to gouge "a ragged hole in the page where the picture of the devil had been" (441); making her mark in the text that justifies colonial law, she "beg[ins] by scratching out [the devil's] wicked eyes" (441), erasing his gaze, voiding his power to judge. Stressing her mischief and rebellion, she refuses to provide her white audience with the lens through which to read her as the subdued ground upon which assimilation takes place, but writes herself as a site of resistant individuality.

However, she does concede that she cannot avoid being written into the colonizer's "roll book" (442), marked by the "terrible power" of white language, classified and standardized through the relentless mechanism of the school's "iron routine" (442). Exposing the institutionalized action of assimilation as "the civilizing machine" that compels her to "trudg[e] in the day's harness heavy-footed, like a dumb sick brute" (442), she uses "the master's tools"—language—to critique his coercive system, while simultaneously acknowledging that she has been marked into the text of his dominance by the apparatus designed to produce compliant colonial subjects.

She is "neither a wild Indian nor a tame one" (444) and, suspended between identities, she "seemed to hang in the heart of chaos, beyond the touch or voice of human aid" (443). Returning home after three years at boarding school, she is "restless and unhappy" (444) with changing lifestyles on the reservation and with a mother not "capable of comforting her daughter who could read and write" (444). Her distance from her mother is the measure of her distance from her young Sioux self; her immersion in American culture estranges her from the Sioux culture embodied by her mother and evacuates mother-daughter communication. Zitkala-Ša recounts her mother's unsuccessful attempt to reach her by proffering "the white man's papers" and her rebuttal of her mother's offer of solace (445–6). Her "hot tears" (445) cause her mother's "helpless misery" (446); her "stony" (446) silence denies her mother access to her "suffering," reversing and repeating her mother's refusal to share her grief with her young daughter—in both instances, the "grief" that distances them from each other is caused by contact with whites. She cements her mother's helpless suffering when she "silence[s] her by deliberate disobedience" (447), going to college against her wishes. Her elision of her decision to attend college and her experiences there in the title of the segment describing this phase of her life—"Incurring my Mother's Displeasure"—suggests that she speaks and writes in white culture at the cost of her mother's acceptance; her voluntary and informed participation in the white educational system closes down access to her most powerful source of love and acceptance.

Renaming herself Zitkala-Ša, she attempts to relocate and reconstitute herself in both cultures. She erases the "Gertrude Simmons" marked into the book of the whites, and endeavors to create a way to re-mark the colonial narrative on "Indian" identity. In college, she becomes an orator—what better way to make your voice heard? But in the white man's public discursive space she encounters her Sioux self as it is written in the dominant narrative of Indian-ness. Appearing at a state oratorical contest, she watches as

> there, before that vast ocean of eyes, some college rowdies threw out a large white flag, with a drawing of a most forlorn Indian girl on it. Under this they had printed in bold black letters words that ridiculed the college which was represented by a 'squaw.' (448–9)

The signs on the flag reduce her to an abject Indian-female body, which can signify only its shameful Indian-femaleness. In this institution of white cultural literacy, "college rowdies" deploy the drawing and the word "squaw" to demarcate an identity for her in relation to American society—as an Indian woman she is not entitled to speak there. The banner, intended to render meaningless the speech that originates in an Indian woman's body, demonstrates that success wielding the white man's tools does not affect his formulation of her place in his culture. Her adoption of white language is rewarded to an extent—she wins a prize—but her racialized and gendered body remains the mark of her abject position in "the master's house." Zitkala-Ša finds herself in a double bind: only this speech can be heard in white culture, but she is denied the status of authorized speaker because her speech emanates from an "Indian" body.

Her discursive defeat of this attack on her right to speak for and to represent her college—to act as agent rather than object—does not satisfy her. She "laugh[s] no more in triumph" (449), but juxtaposes her brief and ambivalent victory with her displacement and with her mother's anger and alienation. Finding that her "little taste of victory" fails to "satisfy a hunger in [her] heart," she imagines her "mother far away on the Western plains . . . holding a charge against [her]" (449).

Although she remains an outsider, her intervention in the American literary tradition serves to subvert definitions of the Indian woman as a silent and abject "squaw." This Indian woman is not silent—she publishes her essays in *Atlantic Monthly*. She is not abject—she attacks American notions of the benefits of assimilation and challenges and manipulates stereotypes of Indian identity to re-present Indian-ness to a white audience. Zitkala-Ša coopts white discourses to reclaim her "overflowing spirits." Presenting herself as both resolutely indi-vidual (a quality often claimed as particularly "American") and innately "Indian" (through commonly held notions of Indians as essentially natural, free, wild), she yokes the qualities of independence likely to be appreciated by her audience with her Indian-ness.

Her renewed descriptions of her "overflowing spirits" and relation to the natu-ral world in the later sketches gestures toward an epistemology unavailable to readers caught up in the ways of knowing valorized by American society. As "the spirit swells [her] breast," she locates a more rewarding language in the "murmur-ing Missouri," in the "sweet, soft cadences of the river's song," and finds that the water, the sky, and the warmth of a summer day "bespeak with eloquence the loving Mystery round about us" (459). Away from white institutions, she re-formulates the "racial lines, which once were bitterly real" as forms simply "marking out a living mosaic of human beings" (461). Her formulation of this language of nature manipulates the primitivism ascribed to Indians living "in the state of nature" to construct a position from which she reflects on her experi-ences within the colonizing culture. Returning from her excursion in "natural gar-dens" (462), she "resum[es] the chair at [her] desk" feeling "in keen sympathy with [her] fellow creatures, for [she] seem[s] to see clearly again that all are akin" (461).

In this in-your-face final essay, *Why I Am a Pagan*, she talks back to the domi-nant discourse on Indian-ness by twisting the negative appellation "pagan" into a positive sign of personal independence and freedom from the restrictive doc-trines that structure white culture. With this last autobiographical piece, Zitkala-Ša takes over and re-works the colonial monologue on Indian identity by proudly characterizing herself as a "pagan," and by making "pagan" signify in opposition to the hypocrisy she sees in the Christianity underlying the assimilationist system. Following an encounter with a "converted Indian" (462) who threatens her with hell-fire, she remarks:

> [a] wee child toddling in a wonder world, I prefer to their dogma my excursions into the natural gardens where the voice of the Great Spirit is heard in the twit-tering of birds, the rippling of mighty waters, and the sweet breathing of flow-ers. If this is Paganism, then at present, at least, I am a Pagan. (462)

After her years of white education, Zitkala-Ša reclaims the "spirit" she exercised in "natural gardens," the "spirit" she enjoyed in her early childhood, as the tool—the alternate language—that enables her to resist the colonizer's institutions and discourses and to assert a resistant, "pagan," identity. Redefining pagan-ness, she redefines true knowledge and reconnects with the education begun in the "lap of the prairie."

Similarly, she struggles to resist totalizing linguistic systems and to assert her sense of self in other representations of alternate languages. In *An Indian Teacher Among the Indians*, she reports for work at the Carlisle school fully aware that her "car-smoked appearance had not concealed the lines of pain on [her] face," but does not exert herself to "make an improvement" (451). The lines on her face carry meaning outside spoken language, signifying the toll of dislocation. Here she manipulates her physical being to convey her own message; she refuses to alter her appearance in order to seem "improved" in the eyes of the school's "imposing" white director. Her employer is obviously "disappointed" with the discrepancy between "the little Indian girl who created the excitement among the college orators" of whom he has heard so much and the bedraggled person he encounters (451), but Zitkala-Ša retaliates for his be-"little"-ing evaluation and reductive gaze through her descriptions of him and of the system he represents. When he gives her instructions that reduce her to an animal ("'I am going to turn you loose to pasture'") she translates his speech for her reader ("he was sending me West to gather Indian pupils for the school, and this was his way of expressing it") (452), thereby placing him in the position of outsider-who-must-be-translated and appropriating his words for her purposes. Taking over and reversing the animalistic connotations of his use of "turn you out to pasture," she redeploys his language to convey her hunger for "nourishment" of "spirit," for relief from the grinding work of an Indian woman seeking both validation in the dominant culture and respite from its demands:

> I needed nourishment, but the midsummer's travel across the continent to search the hot prairies for overconfident parents who would intrust their children to strangers was a lean pasturage. However, I dwelt on the hope of seeing my mother. I tried to reason that a change was a rest. (452)

Taking the words out of her white employer's mouth—from the authority figure who controls language—she fills "turned out to pasture" with her meanings—her desire for the love and comfort of her mother and "rest" from white institutions—and empties the phrase of "the master's" degrading implications.

The sketch entitled "A Trip Westward" ostensibly records her trip recruiting Indian children for the Carlisle school, but her story seems more concerned with her equivocal feelings of homecoming and avoids attending to her ambivalent response to her role as agent of white education or to the tension generated between her nostalgia for a lost Sioux culture and her complicity in the colonizing machine.[27] It becomes apparent that within colonial institutions her desire to "spend [her] energies in a work for the Indian race" (450) will be channelled into subjecting others to the process that has caused her own alienation. *An Indian Teacher Among the Indians* ends with a reckoning of the price of her new identity in her enquiry "whether real life or long-lasting death lies beneath this semblance of civilization" (459). The final segments shift from her education in the "work" possible in the white educational system to her search for an alternate discursive structure.

While Zitkala-Ša gains access to the dominant language through her creation of herself as a writer, she is admitted and contained there as "other." Reporting critical reaction to Zitkala-Ša's essays and short stories, Fisher excerpts a *Harper's Bazaar* 1900 column entitled "Persons Who Interest Us":

> A young Indian girl, who is attracting much attention in Eastern cities on account of her beauty and many talents, is Zitkala-Ša. . . . [She] is of the Sioux

tribe of Dakota and until her ninth year was a veritable little savage, running wild over the prairie and speaking no language but her own. . . . She has also published lately a series of articles in a leading magazine . . . which display a rare command of English and much artistic feeling.[28]

As a writer, Zitkala-Ša challenges hegemonic notions of Indian-ness as well as the virtue and value of assimilation, but these resistant aspects of her texts can be at least partially neutralized when she is put in her place by the stereotypes used to classify Indians and thus reclaimed as a precocious but loveable younger sister, a good student with a commendable grasp of the (only important) language, an aesthetically pleasing performer on the colonial stage.

Fisher observes that in her "truly liminal position" she had "every right to feel nervous about her mission to become the literary counterpart of the oral story-tellers of her tribe because she felt compelled to live up to the critical expectations of her white audience."[29] Although she has become a skillful weaver of "the magic design which promised . . . the white man's respect" (447), she sees herself objectified through it, silenced in her middle place, unable to speak when her mother waits for her to comment on the "Great Father in Washington" and his treatment of the Sioux (455). Alone and "destitute" in her room, her "tomb" in the white school, she wishes her "heart's burdens would turn [her] to unfeeling stone"—she has become "like the petrified Indian woman of whom [her] mother used to tell [her]" (458). Playing by the colonizer's rules, she is silenced and incapacitated by the demands of competing cultures; her status remains liminal—it must be one or the other, and neither. She resides in a precarious middle space not validated by any culture. But her story does not end here. At the close of this sketch—"Retrospection"—which concludes *An Indian Teacher*, she announces that she has set out on a "new way of solving the problem of [her] inner self" (458). What her "new idea" (458) is, she does not say. By not explaining her new theory of "self," Zitkala-Ša withholds her plans and possibilities from her audience, turning away the colonial gaze.

Her dilemma exemplifies the paradox experienced by the colonized subject negotiating a satisfying and empowering sense of selfhood using "the master's tools": she risks incorporation into the civilizing machine in her attempts to derail it. William L. Andrews, in his introduction to his collection of her essays, proposes that Zitkala-Ša "is both converted and unconverted by her long encounter with white culture."[30] On the one hand, she acknowledges and even insists on the reductions of self occasioned by her foray into "the master's house":

> For the white man's papers I had given up my faith in the Great Spirit. For these same papers I had forgotten the healing in trees and brooks. . . . I made no friends among the race of people I loathed. Like a slender tree, I had been uprooted from my mother, nature, and God. I was shorn of my branches, which had waved in sympathy and love for home and friends. The natural coat of bark which had protected my oversensitive nature was scraped off to the very quick. (458)

On the other hand, she suggests that she has found room for play within the assimilationist system and that she might just locate a kind of empowerment in her seemingly impossible position. For although she compares herself to an uprooted tree, "a cold bare pole . . . planted in a strange earth," she "hop[es] a day would come when [her] mute aching head, reared upward to the sky, would flash a zigzag of lightning across the heavens" (458). And "this dream of vent for a long-pent consciousness" allows her the strength to overcome her petrification and silence, and to "wal[k] again amid the crowds" (458).

As in *Why I Am a Pagan*, there is a sense here that while she cannot replace what she has lost, she may be able to stake out her own claim to a space of respite. This vision of relief comes with her vision of an explosive new voice for herself, an alternate speech of "lightning," a language charged with light and power.[31] Although this new means of expression has not yet emerged from the morass of cultural identifications she contends with, it can be imagined; the tree stripped and uprooted has yet the potential to redeem its "muteness." The violent distinction between the electric language of lightning and the printed fixity of the language of "the white man's papers" suggests that the new expression she projects as powerful enough to explode the bonds of the dominant discourse must be of a radically different nature, perhaps more in line with her discontinued education on the prairie, maybe more like the language a "pagan" would speak. This gesture toward a new language together with her claim to pagan-ness—the closing scene situates her as a "pagan" at a desk—suggest that language remains the medium through which she works to gain control over representations of her Indian identity. *Why I Am a Pagan* is the last autobiographical piece she writes; her project ends with her defiant claim to a proudly resistant self-representation.

Until this powerful new language becomes manifest, her essays lay bare the process of cultural transformation enforced in colonial institutions, but also describe her rejection of the colonizer's authorizing mandate. They trace the painful process of assimilation and evaluate its consequences, engaging the complexities of deciphering and rewriting dominant notions of racial and gendered identity. Zitkala-Ša appropriates the master's tools—his language—to enter into dialogue with the discourses that adjudicate her oppression through their construction of the positions and possibilities of the Indian woman. With her marriage in 1902 to Raymond T. Bonnin, also a Sioux, she shifts to other forms of challenge to the colonizing mandate of Anglo-American culture. Following her marriage she taught and organized community activities, becoming a prominent activist for Indian rights.[32]

As Zitkala-Ša leaves the colonial stage and the assimilationist system, with its constricting formulation of Indian-ness and of valuable "work for the Indian race" (450), she discontinues her autobiographical record. Did she, as Andrews asks, "consider the four essays she published in the *Atlantic* sufficient to her purpose? Or were they just an opening address, a way of introducing herself and her project to a prospective American audience? We have no certain answer to these questions."[33] Possibly she found the "self" she was able to construct with "the master's tools" incommensurate to her desire for "nourishment" of "spirit." But it seems safe to speculate that whatever its deficiencies, writing—the act of self-representation—afforded her a sense of control over signifiers of her identity as well as the tools to chip away at dominant American discourses on difference.

This is not to denigrate Zitkala-Ša's autobiographical project as secondary to the "real" work of fighting oppression. In fact, I suggest that divisions between material intervention in the form of organized political action versus discursive intervention in representation of race and assimilation in the form of autobiographical writing obscures the "material oppression of individuals by discourses."[34] Zitkala-Ša encounters and addresses this oppression not only in her individual experience of colonization but also in her apprehension of colonization as a cultural experience. Her emphasis on language, on both repressive and liberatory potentials, illustrates that resistance of colonial institutions necessitates a challenge to the discourses that authorize and uphold those institutions and that frame and contain the "selves" possible in colonial economies.

Zitkala-Ša's interrogation of assimilation posits more complex ways of conceptualizing race and gender and of positioning self and other. And though she does not dismantle "the master's house"—his domination of culturally valid forms of identity—she uses his tools to pry open and denaturalize his exclusive ownership of speech and subjectivity in her bid for self-definition. Her autobiographical texts may not explode the bounds and bonds of "the master's" language but they do engage and undermine its authority on his own terms and turf; her use of his "tools" makes them visible *as* tools and refutes his claim to the universally normative status he has built with them. Interjecting a voice that is not subsumable into "the master's" categories for identity, the essays suggest alternate avenues of self-representation. Zitkala-Ša disputes and subverts dominant definitions of her identity, yet remains bound by them, a double bind shared by autobiographers writing both in and against ideologies deployed to represent colonized "others." She does not consider retreat from interrogation of this position as a solution. Silence turns the colonized woman to "stone," and muteness results in a helpless liminality. Speech, even flawed and incomplete, is her best, possibly her only, alternative—for the time being.

NOTES

My thanks to Sidonie Smith and to *Prose Studies'* anonymous reader. Their suggestions and observations improved this essay.

[1] Zitkala-Ša, *Impressions of an Indian Childhood. Classic American Autobiographies*, ed. William L. Andrews (New York: Mentor, 1992), 429. All references to the essays are from Andrews' collection (414–62), and will be indicated parenthetically.

[2] Audre Lorde, "The Master's Tools Will Never Dismantle the Master's House," in *This Bridge Called My Back*, ed. Cherríe Moraga and Gloria Anzaldúa (New York: Kitchen Table, 1981), 99.

[3] Theories of language as a phallocentric construct have been explored by critics of language, culture, and literature, and current theory acknowledges the racial bias of dominant languages (and theories). For examples of influential work in these areas see Judith Butler, *Gender Trouble* (New York: Routledge, 1990); Judith Butler, *Bodies That Matter* (New York: Routledge, 1993); Mae Gwendolyn Henderson, "Speaking in Tongues: Dialogics, Dialectics, and the Black Woman Writer's Literary Tradition," in *Feminists Theorize the Political*, ed. Judith Butler and John W. Scott (New York: Routledge, 1992); Luce Irigaray, *Speculum of the Other Woman*, trans. Gillian G. Gill (Ithaca: Cornell University Press, 1985); Elaine Marks and Isabelle de Courtivron, eds., *New French Feminisms* (New York: Schocken, 1981); Cherríe Moraga and Gloria Anzaldúa, eds.,

This Bridge Called My Back (New York: Kitchen Table, 1981); Trinh T. Minh-ha, *Woman, Native, Other* (Bloomington: Indiana University Press, 1989).

[4] These are Rey Chow's terms, See Rey Chow, "'It's you and not me': Domination and 'Othering' in Theorizing the Third World," in *Coming to Terms: Feminism, Theory, Politics*, ed. Elizabeth Weed (New York: Routledge, 1989), 157.

[5] For instance, the position of the oppressed and/or colonized woman who seeks self-expression in the dominant discourse is explored in Françoise Lionnet, *Autobiographical Voices: Race, Gender, Self-Portraiture* (Ithaca: Cornell University Press, 1989); and in Sidonie Smith and Julia Watson, eds., *De/Colonizing the Subject: The Politics of Gender in Women's Autobiography* (Minneapolis: University of Minnesota Press, 1992).

[6] Bella Brodzki, "Mothers, Displacement, and Language in the Autobiographies of Nathalie Sarrault and Christa Wolf," in *Life/Lines: Theorizing Women's Autobiography*, ed., Bella Brodzki and Celeste Schenck (Ithaca: Cornell University Press, 1988), 244.

[7] Brodzki, 244.

[8] My use of "the master" to reference colonial control is not meant to imply that women do not oppress or colonize other women or that women cannot occupy "the master's" position, as Lorde points out.

[9] Martha Cutter makes similar points in her argument that "it is only when we approach Zitkala-Ša's writing in terms of how it subverts traditional modes of autobiographical and linguistic self-authentication that we can come to see its full richness and complexity, and understand the unique problem of a 'canonical' search for language and identity in Native American writing" (31). Although we use many of the same examples, we differ in some significant aspects of analysis: my approach attempts to widen the applications of "linguistic self-authentication" and includes the fourth essay, *Why I Am a Pagan*, while Cutter acknowledges only three essays. It seems to me that even though *Why I am a Pagan* appeared in 1902 and the other essays in 1900, they should be considered together. They were published in the same venue and for the same audience, and they all concern Zitkala-Ša's use/abuse of the dominant language for resistant self-representation. To me, *Why I am a Pagan* seems to be an attempt to answer the questions raised at the end of *An Indian Teacher Among the Indians*. See Martha J. Cutter, "Zitkala-Ša's Autobiographical Writings: The Problems of a Canonical Search for Language and Identity," *MELUS* 19 (Spring 1994): 31–44.

[10] For biographical information on Zitkala-Ša, I rely on Dexter Fisher's research, which, at this writing, is the most in-depth and thoroughly supported I could find. Dexter Fisher, "Zitkala-Ša: The Evolution of a Writer," *American Indian Quarterly* 5.3 (1979): 229–38.

[11] Quoted in Fisher, 231. It is also interesting to note that, as Hertha Dawn Wong explains, it was common for nineteenth-century Sioux men to be given or to take for themselves "several names over a lifetime, revising their life narratives as they lived them. Generally, men acquired many more names than women, reflecting their personal secular and spiritual accomplishments. Women, however, sometimes took new names at transitional moments. . . . The idea is that altering one's name (one's fundamental self-representation) reshapes one's life." Hertha Dawn Wong, *Sending My Heart Back Across the Years: Tradition and Innovation in Native American Autobiography* (New York: Oxford University Press, 1992), 39–40.

[12] Fisher, 231-2.

[13] Teresa de Lauretis, "Issues, Terms, and Contexts," *Feminist Studies/Critical Studies* (Bloomington: Indiana University Press, 1986), 9. Lauretis writes that identity is not the "goal but rather the point of departure of the process of self-consciousness, a process by which one begins to know that and how the personal is political, that and how the subject is specifically and materially en-gendered in its social considerations and possibilities of existence."

[14] Henry Louis Gates, Jr., "Talkin' That Talk," in *Race, Writing, and Difference*, ed. Gates (Chicago: University of Chicago Press, 1985), 402.

[15] Henry Louis Gates, Jr., "Introduction: Writing 'Race' and the Difference it Makes," *Race, Writing, and Difference*, 5–6.

[16] Lenore A. Stiffarm with Phil Lane, Jr., "The Demography of Native North America. A Question of American Indian Survival," in M. Annette Jaimes, ed., *The State of Native America: Genocide, Colonization, and Resistance* (Boston: South End Press, 1992), 40.

[17] M. Annette Jaimes, "Federal Indian Identification Policy: A Usurpation of Indigenous Sovereignty in North America," in *The State of Native America*, 126.

[18] Howard Zinn, *A People's History of the United States* (New York: HarperCollins, 1980), 132.

[19] Jaimes, 136.

[20] Wong, 153.

[21] Stiffarm, 40.

[22] See *The State of Native America* for further analyses of the discourses and consequences of mixed bloodedness. See also Paula Gunn Allen's discussion of the "alienation" of the "breed" in *The Sacred Hoop: Recovering the Feminine in American Indian Traditions* (Boston: Beacon Press, 1986) and selected interviews in Joseph Bruchac, *Survival This Way: Interviews With American Indian Poets* (Tucson: Sun Tracks and University of Arizona Press, 1987).

[23] Sidonie Smith observes that "through her autobiographical sketches Zitkala-Ša remembers what has been forgotten in order for Americanization to take effect." She suggests that "Zitkala-Ša of the narrative is both/and—the national and the unnational subject. She unmakes herself as an American of conformity and docility, even as she can never entirely escape having been remade as American. . . . She critiques the civilizing mission from inside the effects of that mission." Sidonie Smith, "Cheesecake, Nymphs, and 'We the People': Un/National Subjects about 1900," *Prose Studies* 17.1 (1994), 135, 136.

[24] Edward Lazarus, *Black Hills/White Justice: The Sioux Nation Versus the United States 1775 to the Present* (New York: HarperCollins, 1991), 97. See Lazarus for a detailed account of the consequences of contact and colonization for the Sioux.

[25] Lazarus, 116.

[26] See Jaimes and Lazarus for detailed analyses of governmental relations with native peoples, and policies of civilization, Christianization, and citizenship, as well as for public perceptions of Indians. See also Francis Paul Prucha, *The Great Father: The United States Government and the American Indians* (Lincoln: University of Nebraska Press, 1984).

[27] Fisher reports that Zitkala-Ša taught at the Carlisle Indian School from 1898 to 1899. Here is Lazarus' account of the school's mission: "In 1879, Captain Richard Pratt arrived in Sioux country to enlist Sioux children for his Carlisle Indian Industrial School, the first and most famous of what would become a whole system of off-reservation boarding schools. . . . Neither parent nor pupil foresaw the short hair, the starched shirts and squeaky boots, the Christian names, or the other trappings of the assimilationist regimen to which Pratt harnessed his charges. When Spotted Tail witnessed firsthand the thorough anti-Indian indoctrination of Carlisle's operation, he withdrew his nine children in a rage. For several years after, most Sioux refused to trust their children to the 'kill the Indian, save the man' philosophy of off-reservation education. When enrollment . . . did pick up again in the mid-1880's, the schools at best achieved only qualified success. The complete severance from home and family succeeded in isolating the Indian students from their culture and instilling in them a heavy dose of white values, but it did not give them much of a future. As one Carlisle-educated Sioux leader observed, 'most girls [found] their life's work in city kitchens and most boys who [did] not drift back to the reservation lost their identity in a shop.' In any case, the reservation reclaimed most of its offspring, though few found themselves welcome" (101–2).

[28] Fisher, 229–30. Zitkala-Ša also wrote short stories and reproduced Sioux legends. Her work was collected in *Old Indian Legends* in 1901 and in *American Indian Stories* in 1921.

[29] Fisher, 233, 229.

[30] William L. Andrews, "Introduction," *Classic American Autobiographies*, ed. Andrews (New York: Penguin, 1992), 17.

[31] Conversely, Cutter views this coming "lightning" as "a form of action, of inscription, which goes beyond words" (41).

[32] Fisher reports that the Bonnins moved to Washington, DC in 1916 when she was "elected secretary of the Society of the American Indian" and that "under the auspices of SAI, Bonnin launched her life's work in Indian reform, lecturing and campaigning across the country for Indian citizenship, employment of Indians in the Bureau of Indian Affairs, equitable settlement of tribal land claims, and stabilization of laws relating to Indians. Her temporary post as editor

from 1918 to 1919 of the Society's publication, *The American Indian* magazine, gave her the opportunity to reach an even wider audience in print." In 1926 she founded "her own political organization, the National Council of American Indians, of which she was the single president until her death in 1936. The organization, as described in *Indian Truth*, was to 'create increased interest in behalf of the Indians, and secure for them added recognition of their personal and property rights.'" Fisher, 235.

[33] Andrews, 17.

[34] Monique Wittig, "The Straight Mind," *Feminist Issues* 1 (1980): 105–6. She argues that "when we use the overgeneralizing term 'ideology' to designate all the discourses of the dominating group, we relegate these discourses to the domain of Irreal Ideas, we forget the material (physical) violence that they directly do to the oppressed people, a violence produced by the abstract and 'scientific' discourses as well as by the discourses of the mass media. I would like to insist on the material oppression of individuals by discourses."

AFTERWORD

It seems fitting for "'The Ears of the Palefaces Could Not Hear Me': Languages of Self-Representation in Zitkala-Ša's Autobiographical Essays" to be collected in a volume entitled *Diversifying the Discourse*. Rereading the essay I wrote in 1996, I am struck by this theme's relevance to the life and work of Zitkala-Ša. I am also struck by how much she still has to offer readers a century later—feminists and equal rights activists, students, teachers, and scholars, Native Americans and every other kind of American.

Zitkala-Ša's narratives present a compelling picture of one woman's negotiation with dominant discourses that leave her with no comfortable place in America. Using the awkward tool of a language coded white and male, a language that had been used to keep her in her subordinate and silent place as an Indian woman, Zitkala-Ša raised the possibility of alternate ways to conceptualize and articulate gendered and raced identities. This reliance on the language that oppressed her seems risky, but at the same time necessary in order to reach people whose thinking about difference she wanted to alter. I think that my essay's emphasis on the partial, ambivalent outcomes of this negotiation points to a key element of her text and of the texts of other women fighting for change in contexts where they are denied voice, authority, individuality.

In the face of bitter criticism and reductive praise, Zitkala-Ša raised her voice in protest. Her courage in talking back to a nation that refused to recognize her humanity and in critiquing the assimilationist system that molded her reminds me that all of us—no matter how encumbered by our positions in entrenched systems of power—carry within us the potential to revise those systems. Her use of the flawed discourses available to her remind me that change is often barely perceptible and almost always a matter of degree. Such change is not to be dismissed lightly, as it begets more change, further revisions, and new uses of old languages.

I find evidence of the effectiveness of this kind of change in my students' reactions to Zitkala-Ša's work, and I often wonder what she would think about her impact on the twenty-first-century women and men who will play a part in directing America's future. Even students resolutely indifferent to the issues of gender and race I customarily raise in my classes are moved and inspired by her courage in resisting the definitions imposed on her. Even students certain of their own power to define themselves come to acknowledge the ways in which we are all constituted in language, by other people, our communities, and various institutions. Even students unaware of their own privilege in America see in her experience their occupation of a norm that excludes countless others. What these small changes mean for the long term I cannot say. But as I watch my students grappling with Zitkala-Ša's message, I have reason to hope for larger changes for women and people of color in an America developing alternative languages for difference.

Crosscurrents: Registers of Nordicism, Community, and Culture in Jewett's *Country of the Pointed Firs*

Sandra A. Zagarell

WHAT CRITICAL METHODS can literary critics and historians develop to further the rigorous scrutiny of ways in which foundational, historically shifting categories of socio-cultural organization—especially gender, class, race, nation—suffuse works of literature? How can we do justice to the power of each category in itself and as they interarticulate? How can we pursue this undertaking in ways which recognize them as discourses informed by and informing ideology while allowing for their particular connotations and the particular relationships among them in the work of different writers? How, further, do we engage in such enterprises in ways which preserve respect for the literary but do not sanctify individual texts as self-contained works of art?

As an Americanist committed to understanding the literary as it takes shape within identifiable historical forces such as race and gender but is not transparently and absolutely determined by them, I have a strong sense of urgency about such questions. I propose here one method for addressing them which I will develop using Sarah Orne Jewett's *Country of the Pointed Firs* (1896), a multifaceted text whose intricacies speak to the need for more mobile, dynamic ways of reading.[1] Having written about *Country* in essays which disagree about its representations of gender, I also have a personal stake in better coming to terms with its intricacies. My concern extends, moreover, to the large and disparate body of commentary on *Country*, which has been canonized and recanonized by successive waves of illuminating and persuasive scholarship. Many accounts of *Country* have been presented as "right"; by implication if not explicitly, they often cast other accounts as invalid, misguided or less complete. Such self-positioning, long a convention of critical discourse, reflects the commitment of established critical practices to render readings which are both coherent and whole. While these practices have served us well in many ways, they are ill-equipped either to engage with discontinuities and inconsistencies—which are arguably as constitutive of much literature as is coherence—or to open up ways of bringing apparently antagonistic readings to bear on one another.

Two strains of recent commentary on *Country* illustrate this situation.[2] Seeing it from a feminist vantage point, feminist critics over the past two decades have acclaimed it as a masterpiece of woman-centered literature. As feminist criticism has become increasingly concerned with issues of race and nationalism, however, some have taken *Country*'s representation of "woman" to task for its self-conscious and exclusive whiteness and participation in the nativist nationalism of its day. *Country* has also occupied a central role in some literary historians' recent reassessment of postbellum regionalist literature's implication in modernization. Richard Brodhead's important *Cultures of Letters*, for example, posits *Country* as an enthusiastic contributor to regionalism's work in consolidating postbellum literary capitalism, complementing the burgeoning tourist industry, and serving as a significant resource for the cultural self-identification of expanding urban elites.

The position (often only tacit) of each of these critical strains and of many of the commentators allied with them is that their readings of *Country* preclude others. My own work will serve as one example of feminist criticism. In an essay published in 1988 I assumed gender as the text's determinative element; in a later one I essentially repudiated the reliance of the first on gender as the self-contained source of *Country*'s language, structure, and values and identified whiteness and nationalism as factors which preconstitute its concepts of gender. For *Cultures of Letters*, by contrast, economic and cultural circumstances—class, the organization and appeal of postbellum capitalism—are formative in *Country*: race is at best a secondary concern and gender only incidental. *Cultures of Letters* opens up new and important ways of seeing *Country*. And while my own second essay is far more persuasive to me than the first, I now find myself unable to characterize it as "right" or to designate the first as unambiguously "wrong." Much of the other commentary on *Country* likewise seems illuminating to me, but also partial, despite its authors' tendency to assert its completeness. But how can this be? Are any readings whatsoever somewhat valid, partially illuminating? Are readings merely products of a potentially unlimited wealth of critical methods? Or do works of literature simply accommodate an indefinite number of interpretations?

The method I propose offers a way of engaging with textual discontinuities, and by extension for adjudicating among ways of reading, without embracing the relativism such questions imply. I suggest that we turn our attention to the identification of registers—distinct discourses with extra-textual coordinates—in multivocal texts such as *Country* and that we examine the interplay and tension among such registers. This proposal is grounded in the conviction that the specific historical and ideological climates in which texts come to life are constitutive, but not in ways that are fully predictable. It seeks to help us circumvent our still-prevalent preference for seeing texts as self-continuous and for prizing totalized readings, but rejects a pluralism which endorses all readings as equally valid. It also offers a means of exploring, in a given work of literature, the terms according to which elements like racial exclusiveness and woman-centeredness co-exist, mutually enable one another, and interact while at the same time focusing attention on textual expressions of their incompatibilities or of variations in the relations among them. Thus it can suggest a way not only of identifying constituent textual elements such as race and gender, but of approaching the relationship between them as a matter of inquiry, not a foregone conclusion.

My thinking is indebted to recent scholarship on Jewett and regionalism by Amy Kaplan, June Howard, and Susan Gillman, which works in various ways with textual-ideological discontinuities as well as coherences. Also indispensable has been work by poststructuralist theorist-critics which foregrounds race and gender without fully collapsing one into the other and takes particularities of individual authors and texts into account. My title's echo of Hortense J. Spillers' "Cross-currents, Discontinuities: Black Women's Fiction" reflects my debt to her discussion of the multiple crosscurrents which operate differentially in specific texts; my use of the linguistic concept of registers to characterize such currents is borrowed from Gayatri Chakravorty Spivak's "Three Women's Texts and Imperialism."[3] My discussion here is intended to be suggestive, not comprehensive. One important focus for further work is the material circumstances within which discursive registers took shape. With regard to *Country*, more sustained examination is needed of circumstances of the marketplace and cosmopolitanism and of the legal, economic, political and cultural constructions of race, gender, and nation which prevailed when Jewett was writing. My hope is that what I propose will be useful to others with concerns similar to mine, and that it will contribute to our productive engagement with the cultural politics which have long been a strong, if often unacknowledged, dimension of American literature and literary studies.

If divergent readings shed light on *Country*, the existence of several prominent registers within the text helps explain why. At least three primary registers inform Jewett's work of the 1880s and 1890s, particularly *Country*, the most complicated and sustained of these. One register is associated with a racialist, Nordicist version of Euro-American history which shades into racism, white supremacy and nativism; one with the celebration of a maternal-based community which is nurturant and inclusive; and one with the portrayal of a local, preindustrial Maine culture. These registers interconnect conceptually and ideologically; in some ways they are complementary, in other ways they conflict. Sometimes they appear contiguously, sometimes in sequence; sometimes two registers blend. The registers of maternal community and local culture predominate in *Country*, yet although they often intermingle, they are not fully translatable into one another and their relationships to the Nordicist register, which surfaces dramatically at several points, differ. Recognition of these registers works against reducing *Country* to a single coherent narrative. It also calls attention to the partial non-alignment in Jewett's work of categories which 1990s readers may be too ready to consolidate, including whiteness and women's culture, or, more generally, "race" and "gender." These registers, further, come into focus most clearly in the context of other writing by Jewett, which points to the importance of approaching a writer's work as a body of writing, not a set of singular works which speak for and in themselves.[4]

It is especially useful to keep this last point in mind when considering the Nordicist register, for familiarity with Jewett's work other than *Country* is helpful in bringing this register into view. Traces of a general narrative of history appear in much of Jewett's earlier writing, but *The Story of the Normans* (publ. 1886), a full-length history commissioned for Putnam's Story of the Nations series, seems to have prompted her to develop a fairly comprehensive historical narrative which connected northern Europe with the United States—or with New England, which, for Jewett, was the heart of the U.S. In this racial history, which traces the Normans from their Norse origins through the invasion of Normandy and the 1066 invasion of England, Jewett characterizes the Northman/Normans as the quintessentially Nordic race and praises this race's distinctly Aryan qualities: courage, adventurousness, strength, cleverness, discipline, literacy, as well as blue-eyed blondness.[5] For Jewett, the "progress of civilization" (or the rise of Europe) was made possible by Norman racial superiority, which included the drive for territorial expansion.[6] She praises the twelfth-century Normans' "crusader" spirit and celebrates the persistence of that spirit in England in such nineteenth-century undertakings as the Crimean War, Gordon's stand at Khartoum, Livingston's explorations in Africa (28). Indeed, Jewett attributes the best of England to its "Norman elements": "England the colonizer, England the country of intellectual and social progress, England the fosterer of ideas and chivalrous humanity" (356). And because she maintains that many Norman-descended English emigrants settled New England, her narrative of civilization's progress by means of Norman conquest and predominance places the United States in an implicitly internationalist position, poised at the brink of an unspecified but distinctly Atlanticist destiny. For she concludes *The Story of the Normans* by envisioning a northern Atlantic Nordicist alliance: "Today the Northman [Danes, Norwegians], the Norman, and the Englishman, and a young nation on this western shore of the Atlantic are all kindred who, possessing a rich inheritance, should own the closest of kindred ties" (366).[7]

In the 1895 story "A War Debt," Jewett returned to this racialized historical narrative to promote post–Civil War national reunion. The reinstitutionalization of racial feudalism in the American South and the reconstituting of a racially superior, English-descended, East-Coast elite are the necessary elements for reunion, this story asserts. Its New England Burtons and Virginia Bellamys share an Anglo-Norman racial heritage exemplified by the Bellamys' granddaughter, "the newer and finer Norman among Saxons. She [. . .] seemed to have that inheritance of swiftness of mind, of sureness of training. It was the highest type of English civilization refined still further by long growth in favoring soil."[8] The Burtons' and Bellamys' shared English stock and close antebellum ties cast the Civil War as the near-destruction of the race which constitutes America's natural aristocracy, for both families have been deeply damaged by the war. Of the Burtons, only youthful Tom and his elderly grandmother survive; of the Bellamys, only the elderly grandparents and one granddaughter. The symbolic act of Northern expiation on which the story hinges—Tom's pilgrimage to the South to return a family heirloom stolen when Union soldiers destroyed the Bellamy plantation—facilitates the merging of the two families, for Tom is clearly destined to marry the Bellamy granddaughter. Moreover, the long-term loan of his gun to old Colonel Bellamy not only assures Bellamy's resumption of hunting, but alludes approvingly to white supremacy, for in the 1890s Southern white armament, couched in the kind of chivalric language prominent in "A War Debt," evoked the violence of white supremacist groups.

The symbolic reunion of North and South, Northern and Southern elites, and the reestablishment of Southern feudalism promise to restore order to a nation threatened by economic burden and social menace resulting from the emancipation of African-American slaves. The railroad was critical in efforts to institutionalize Jim Crow as the law of the South which would culminate in the 1896 Supreme Court endorsement of racial apartheid in Plessy v. Ferguson, a case involving racial segregation on railroads; the railroad serves Jewett here as the resonant emblem of this political vision. On a train in Virginia Tom Burton sees a group of "negroes" who are "lawless, and unequal to holding their liberty with steady hands[;] [they] look poor and less respectable than in the old plantation days—it was as if the long discipline of their former state had counted for nothing" (71). Jewett continued to embellish her Nordicist narrative of Euro-American history, both in *Country*, as we shall see, and in the aftermath of the Spanish-American War. Her 1901 historical novel *The Tory Lover* applauds America's international presence and affirms its deep roots. Here, the War of 1812 prefigures America's later victory over an older nation—it attests to America's destiny to supersede England as the primary seapower of the Atlantic—and affords another opportunity for highlighting the true, Anglo-Norman character of the American nation. As in "A War Debt," Anglo-Normanism characterizes both Tidewater Virginia and coastal New England and provides the enduring historical and racial tie between the two regions.

In *Country*, Jewett's Nordicist idea of history surfaces mainly in the Bowden family reunion section, chapters 16 through 19. Here Jewett's Nordicist concept of the progress of civilization informs a combination of chauvinism, nativism, militarism, nationalism, and incipient internationalism. The narrator sees the Bowdens as Anglo-Norman and invokes Jewett's idea that it is "the Norman Englishman [. . .] who goes adventuring to a new world" as well as identifying the Bowdens' superior taste and civility as "Norman" traits.[9] *Country* also expresses the nativism related to Jewett's Nordicism. It celebrates the ancient and fundamental instincts of "patriotism [. . .] friendship [. . .] the ties of kindred" (96). Moreover, it endorses a racial exclusiveness consonant with Jewett's Nordicism. Mari' Harris, an unpopular Dunnet Landing resident who is not invited to the reunion, is denigrated through association with the only race legally banned from the United States in 1896, the Chinese. A reunion participant exclaims, "I always did think Mari' Harris resembled a Chinee" (103). In keeping with this nativism is the martial character of the reunion, which Elizabeth Ammons and Susan Gillman have recently discussed.[10] As war-obsessed, Anglo-Norman-descended Sant Bowden arranges the assembled Bowdens into military formation, military references like those which often accompanied the era's nativism and xenophobia abound: Sant "marshals" the assembled, who stand "speechless as a troop to await his orders"; there is talk of "canons," "tactics" and "the church military" (99, 102). A racist nationalism also emerges: the narrator aligns the Bowden reunion with Civil War commemorations, speculating that "it is the great national anniversaries which our country has lately kept, and the soldiers' meetings that take place everywhere, which have made reunions of every sort the fashion" (110). After the end of Reconstruction, "soldiers' meetings"—reunions of Northern and

Southern Civil War veterans—were a popular way of affirming that the United States was one nation. They repressed the subject of slavery and at least tacitly figured the nation as a white brotherhood: their participants were white only, and African-American veterans had to hold separate commemorations of the war and Emancipation.[11] All in all, identifying the context of the era's ideology and of the Anglo-Norman progress narrative to which Jewett returned over a fifteen-year period casts light not only on the Bowden Reunion chapters' Nordicist nativism and nationalism, but on their implicit positioning of "America" as the apex of civilization and thus a potential world power, the youngest and most vigorous descendent of the sea-going, civilizing Normans to whom Jewett attributed Europe's rise and England's empire.

Yet even in these chapters, *Country* tenders a vision of community and of a purely local culture which cannot be reduced to or fully aligned with nativist nationalism, and which attests to the text's complex self-discontinuousness. The discussion which follows of the register of maternal-based community relies on the extensive body of criticism on the prominence of women in *Country* and Dunnet's status as a woman-centered community, and will be brief. Two women form the emotional and spiritual center of Dunnet Landing, Mrs. Blackett and her daughter, Mrs. Todd. The Dunnet community, further, is animated by values that are maternal in ways which conflict conspicuously with the Norman "racial" traits of adventure, conquest and ongoing, restless progress. A sequence in which Mrs. Todd and the narrator visit Mrs. Blackett on Green Island (chapters 8 through 11) establishes the community's values as compassion, sensitivity, empathy, and a commitment to interdependence, all instrumental to Dunnet Landing's success in having maintained itself as a community. The values are summed up in the narrator's appreciation of Mrs. Blackett's "tact" and "sympathy" and of her spiritual graciousness (46). The unquestioned sharing of scarce resources (here, as often the case in regionalist literature, food) and other forms of hospitality are also fundamental to the communitarian ethos; the community's ready acceptance of the narrator underscores its inclusiveness.

The Bowden reunion chapters foreground these domestic, maternal-based qualities at least as much as they feature nativist nationalism, usually without subsuming one into the other. The reunion is a festival of maternal communitarianism which celebrates Mrs. Blackett as a "queen" and forms around the Bowden farmhouse, which looks like "a motherly brown hen" (97); the reunion chapters are filled with references to mothers and daughters. Moreover, the masculine-like martial procession is followed by a maternal feast which commemorates communal interdependence. The food is abundant because so many women contribute; its consumption is a ritual of reciprocity, with Mrs. Todd and the narrator sharing and eating the precepts decorating an "early apple pie" and the assembled company sharing a gingerbread replica of the ("motherly") Bowden homestead (108). Indeed, as exemplified by Mrs. Blackett, the maternal idea of community is explicitly positioned against the racial exclusiveness of the Nordicist ideal, for her humanitarianism extends to everyone, not just to Bowden kin. She parries exclusionary statements made by Mrs. Todd and her friend Mrs. Caplin and wants to "make the reunion pleasant" for "strangers" (91).

The third register involves Maine's preindustrial culture. Like most postbellum New England regionalist literature, *Country* portrays rural New England culture as appealingly self-sufficient and traditional. But Jewett is unusual in imagining an extensive history for her region, though it takes knowledge of her writing other than *Country* to recognize this history. She saw Maine's economy in its prime as having been essentially autonomous and local. Maine farmers produced what they needed and sent timber and extra produce downstream in Maine-built barges called gundalows, a local term derived from gondola. For Jewett, Maine's shipping industry was an extension of this local economy: ships made from Maine wood traded Maine farm-goods for goods such as china, textiles, and wallpaper. When the ships brought these items back to Maine, farmers bartered their goods for the merchandise. In the reminiscent "Looking Back on Girlhood" (1892), Jewett characterized this economy as "subsistence upon sea and forest bounties."[12]

In Jewett's eyes, Maine was fully cut off from the nation's postbellum development, brought to economic standstill by the demise of the shipping industry caused by the Embargo of 1807 and the War of 1812. Instead of undergoing urbanization and industrialization and shifting from an economy of production to one of consumption, coastal Maine, in her view, thus preserved its traditional economy and culture. It played no part in the nation's post-1812 progress towards empire. Further, although an embalmed premodern culture and economy are common in postbellum New England regionalist writing, Jewett's rural New England is vividly alive despite its stasis. Placing quotidian activities such as conversation and the "exchange of food, succor and information" in the foreground of *Country*, Jewett brings these activities to life as forms of cultural expression, suffused by Dunnet's basic cultural principles of negotiation and adaptability, and shows Dunnet's material culture to be suffused by these principles.[13] Attention to the way that culture exhibits the principle of adaptability will demonstrate what I see as a marked distinction between the internationalist, proto-imperialist Nordicist register of *Country* and the narrative's ethnographic strain—its representation of Dunnet's culture.

As Ammons emphasizes in "Material Culture, Empire and Jewett's *Country of the Pointed Firs*," Dunnet homes are filled with mementos of Maine's early nineteenth-century commerce. The home which elderly Elijah Tilley has preserved as it was when his much-loved wife died displays a set of dishes he purchased in Bordeaux when he was a sailor; among Mrs. Todd's prize possessions are a West Indian straw basket and a coral pin which her sea-going husband brought for his cousin Joanna Todd. Depending on one's definition of empire these objects may be the "traces" or "tiny trophies" of empire Ammons terms them ("Material Culture" 92), yet readers should also keep in mind that for Jewett they were the fruits of a pre-industrial trade network which had nothing to do with empire and simply extended a productive, historically circumscribed local economy. Contemporary readers can rightly observe that Jewett's writing erases the full character of that antebellum trade network, including the traffic in slaves, and may wish to pursue connections between antebellum shipping and commerce and America's postbellum economy and internationalist posture. Still, it is important to recognize that, for Jewett, coastal Maine's antebellum economy was local, and objects like the china and coral pin do not retain their foreignness or betoken international plunder or dominance. Rather, in keeping with the Dunnet principle of adaptability, such objects are accommodated to local taste and thoroughly recontextualized within Dunnet lives and ways. They exist only within a decidedly local aesthetic which affirms the primacy of Dunnet Landing. The houses of Dunnet, all designed in the same way, express this aesthetic. So do interior arrangements: all the parlors conform to the same pattern—decorated mantle, the display of prized items, the presence of a few chairs, a covering on the floor.[14] This aesthetic allows Dunnet to absorb goods brought by pre-Embargo trade into the local culture. The Tilleys' best room exemplifies the way this aesthetic adapts the foreign to the local taste and blends it with locally produced goods. In this room, purchased items are integrated with the home-made. The "glass vases on the mantlepiece" are filled with "bleached swamp grass and dusty marsh rosemary." The "best tea things" (the set of Bordeaux china) are no more valuable to Elijah Tilley than the "beautiful rugs" braided by his beloved wife (124). Like other Dunnet Landingers, moreover, Elijah Tilley values purchased goods because of their place in his history and his personal associations with them, not on account of their foreign provenance. The tea things express domesticity (he bought them "when we was first married") and have acquired further meaning because they precipitated his wife's single act of deceit—she could not bear to tell him when she broke a cup. Such associations equally characterize homemade things: the rugs recall comparisons Mrs. Tilley made between braided and hooked rugs and the Tilleys' loving jokes about the unfitness of Elijah's fisherman's legs to domestic floors. Adapted to the local aesthetic and intermingled with the home-made, foreign objects are in effect naturalized within *Country*'s resonant portrayal of a self-sufficient and eloquently local culture.

Each of these registers is associated with particular formal and stylistic elements, which interweave to produce the fabric of the text. The cultural register is conveyed by means of *Country*'s primary form, the ethnographic sketch. The sketch allows the foregrounding of microactivities such as conversation and the partaking of food, featuring them as complex processes. The capacity of the sketch to accommodate description and represent microdynamics as centers of narrative interest facilitates the portrayal of Dunnet's material life as cultural expression. While the maternal dimensions of *Country* complement the ethos of its culture and are brought to life in the sketches, they are also marked by a distinctly mythic aura imparted by the narrator's musings. Alluding to mother-daughter myths, particularly that of Persephone and Demeter, and emphasizing the motif of benign witchcraft, the narrator gives the female-maternal element a quasi-religious and fabulous dimension, associating it with a transcendent realm as well as with local Dunnet life.[15] A third mode, diachronic narrative—in which Jewett developed her Nordicism in *Story of the Normans*—is submerged in *Country*, but is referenced in the quest narrative on which Captain Littlepage relies to recount his adventures and those of an associate (chapters 5 through 8); it is also distantly evoked in the narrator's musings on the history of Anglo-Norman settlement of New England.

These registers are discontinuous in other ways as well. The adventuring and conquest impulse of the Nordicist narrative is incompatible with the generosity and inclusiveness of the maternal ethos; the Nordicist progress narrative is out of sync with *Country*'s commemoration of an enduring community. That one is masculine and active, the other feminine and domestic, suggests them to be complementary, even mutually constitutive. But these registers are also conspicuously at odds, and at several points their non-alignment becomes prominent. Engaging such discontinuities is not only important in exploring the work of this single author; it is compatible with contemporary efforts to come to terms with how, historically, expressions of expansionism, nativism and racism were in some cases not reconciled with or resolved into the expression of other values such as those of maternal-based community or local culture.

The sequence centering on Captain Littlepage's visit with the narrator is one instance in which these registers are complementary but at odds. It features the Captain's rather longwinded tale of a comrade's discovery and battle with "fog-shaped men" (25) near the North Pole and seems disproportionately long in this narrative informed by an aesthetic of economy—twenty-one pages in my one-hundred-and-thirty-three page edition. Scholars have sometimes strained to bring these chapters into line with otherwise coherent readings of *Country*; an approach which asks what elements are at play in them and what the dynamics between them are may shed new light on it. The different value-systems the Captain and the narrator embrace and the shifting relationship between them are prominent elements of the section. Littlepage's story is consonant with Jewett's narrative of Euro-American exploration and conquest, though not a part of that narrative. Like the Norsemen, Littlepage is a sailor of northern seas for adventure and gain and, indirectly, for conquest—he has sailed for the Hudson's Bay Company. His story is linked to canonical epic, often the medium of such narratives, and with heroic culture: he is steeped in the high British literary tradition typified by Milton and Shakespeare, whom he quotes enthusiastically, and he embellishes his account of battles with the ghost-like men with references to *Paradise Lost*. The narrator, by contrast, embraces the ethos of care and emotional sustenance of the community, into which its representative, Mrs. Todd has welcomed her.

At the inception of the visit the fit between these characters and the culture with which each identifies is somewhat precarious. Long retired from seafaring life, dissatisfied with the provincialism of Dunnet Landing, the Captain is an isolated old man. The narrator, having left a funeral to attend to some writing, is saddened at having "made myself and my friends remember that I did not really belong to Dunnet Landing" (15). Demonstrating the mutual reliance of the progress-through-conquest and maternal registers, the dynamics of their visit reaffirm the sense of cultural identity of each. The Captain, who is forgetful as well as lonely, needs the narrator's empathy and the assistance she gives him so he can preserve the flow of the tales which reinforce his sense of self. The narrator's embrace of the community ethos is confirmed by the support she gives him and the tact with which she conceals her boredom with his tales. (She is also thus explicitly distinguished from the reviled Mari' Harris: one reason Mrs. Todd condemns Mari' is that she refuses to "listen" to the Captain's "great stories" (103)). But a mutual repulsion between the registers, or at least their clear failure to speak to one another, also characterizes their conjunction. The section features the singlemindedness of the Captain's devotion to his story—he speaks at, not to, the narrator—and the fact that the narrator's deepfelt sympathy is for him but not the story that matters so much to him. It is compassion which moves her to provide him the audience he craves: "a sudden sense of his sufferings" makes her "[ask] to hear more with all the deference [for him, not the tale] I really felt" (18). Moreover, the nonconversation between the two evinces, with increasing clarity, the failure of the characters and the registers they embody to connect. As the Captain's enthusiasm for his story deepens he loses sight of his listener almost completely, at one point looking at her "blankly" when she asks a question. Similarly, the narrator's attention to his person overshadows her attention to what he says. Eventually they reach an impasse. The narrator's focus shifts decisively to the teller as she savors his "alert, determined look and the seafaring, ready aspect that had come to his face" (27). Without her assistance he becomes disoriented and "[forgets] his subject"; she then turns the conversation to a community ritual, the funeral (27–8). At this point the conversation drifts into pleasantries; then the narrator and the Captain part. Accentuating the distance between the two characters and registers, the sequence ends without closure.

The interplay and discord between these two registers is more complicated in the chapters depicting the Bowden Reunion, where one register takes the form of militaristically nationalist language and activities and the other is expressed in richly textured interactions with numerous participants. A shifting pattern of harmony and discord between the registers reflects the complementarity between nationalism (coded masculine) and community (coded maternal) at this juncture in American history; it also attests to the dilemma this complementarity presented for Jewett. Both registers have an unusually strong visual dimension here: each is blocked out in large-scale dramatic scenes. The parallelism of these scenes bespeaks their complementarity, yet it also captures their incompatibility. The Bowden family's militarist-nationalist procession is preceded and followed by scenes of visiting among family members whose fluidity of movement and expressions of personal attachment contrast sharply with the procession's orderly authoritarianism. Similarly, the narrator's reflections on each scene participate enthusiastically in its dominant register but jar with one another. The strident deliberations on Anglo-Normanism and national anniversaries discussed earlier are hers, but she celebrates the Bowdens' bonds of affection in an affective, communitarian key, characterizing the reunion as an expression of the "golden chain of love and dependence" which links this scattered family (90).

The registers of nativist nationalism and maternal community become sharply discordant in the segment following the description of Sant Bowden and his military exercises, suggesting that even as Jewett reproduced the complementarity of militarism and maternalism (which was often embraced by members of her own elite circles), she could or would not erase an uneasiness or tension about their conjunction. Sant's fixation with war prompts a set of exchanges which test the limits of the community's inclusiveness. These exchanges lay out connections between the two registers yet also cast that connection as troubling, even repugnant. The scene centers on four women associated with community, the narrator, Mrs. Todd,

Mrs. Caplin (called "Sister" Caplin here, a denomination which emphasizes her community membership), and Mrs. Blackett; their conversation involves the nature and composition of the Bowden community. Sister Caplin maintains that Sant is too eccentric for inclusion in the community; Mrs. Todd proclaims the importance of accepting "[s]trange folks" like him (103). Moving to the ostracized Mari' Harris, the conversation becomes a disagreement between the two community mainstays, Mrs. Todd and Mrs. Blackett, about how the community is defined. The women's enthusiastic participation in the procession has just demonstrated the implication of the maternal community in a nationalism of which, in the 1890s, bigotry was a major feature; Mrs. Todd endorses the bigotry which Sister Caplin expresses. Mrs. Blackett, however, embodies an ethic of connection which overrides nationalist exclusiveness; she continues to advocate openness. Immediately after Sister Caplin's comment that "I always did think Mari' Harris resembled a Chinee," Mrs. Blackett intervenes "in a pleasant voice" with the observation that "Mari' Harris was pretty as a child, I remember." Assuming a rare tone of truculence towards her mother, Mrs. Todd replies, "Yes, Mari' was one o' them pretty little lambs that makes dreadful homely old sheep" and embellishes this dismissal by classifying Mari' with "sordid creatur's." Mrs. Blackett then counters her daughter, urging "gently," "Live and let live" (103). Mrs. Blackett's maternal, inclusive rhetoric thus offsets Mrs. Todd's gruff exclusionary statements but, like the encounter between the narrator and Captain Littlepage, the disagreement between these two community pillars remains unresolved. Moreover, the compromised image of Mrs. Todd, who is usually generous and empathic, is not tempered. After Mrs. Blackett's second statement the conversation simply moves to other topics. Thus the scene not only dramatizes the incompatibility between racially inflected exclusion and communitarian inclusiveness, but plays out the possibility that the two may be profoundly—and disturbingly—connected. While several recent commentators, myself included, have called attention to the nativist racism of this exchange and of the Bowden Reunion, we must also recognize that this nativism, and the Nordicism which informs it, constitute *one* element of *Country*, even in this section. The text never repudiates or nullifies its racism and restrictiveness, although it does seek to counterpoint them with the maternal register. Moreover, by preserving both the connections and the contradictions between the values and tones of the two registers, it problematizes the simultaneous embrace of community and nationalism which was a commonplace of Jewett's era.

We cannot, in short, translate or fold one register of *Country* fully into another. It is useful and important to ask how the registers co-create, complement, enable and shade into one another; it is also useful and important to ask how and where they separate and where they may clash. Such work is essential if we are to engage the discursive complexity of *Country*, and of other texts—*Jane Eyre* and *Moby-Dick* are two which come to mind immediately. If we pursue the separate strands and discontinuities in texts like *Country* while at the same time reading for unity, we place ourselves in a strong position to ask what has made these texts seem coherent to so many readers. That question may be addressed in formal and aesthetic ways, for *Country*'s polish and style make it appear coherent, as do the continuity of the narrator's voice and her consistent appeals to readers' empathy and identification. But we also need to examine how critics and other readers have produced what might be called a "coherence effect" for *Country* and other multivocal texts. What strategies of reading, what understandings of history, of culture, of narrative, of text, have allowed readers to see, or seek, continuity in a narrative in which registers of racist nationalism, community, and a local culture coexist in shifting patterns of complementarity, separation, and discord? How, further, do we reconsider the coherence we have assumed for, or imposed on, other texts? And what literary and cultural histories emerge when we read for discontinuity as well as coherence? This discussion of Jewett and *Country* will not, I hope, simply enhance our understanding of the work of one writer, but suggest a means of approaching other writers who wrote within multiple sociocultural fields. Such a reading practice can cast in high relief the complex self-contradictions of our literature and our culture, and assist us in our efforts to come to terms with them in the present as well as the past.

NOTES

I want to thank Jan Cooper, June Howard, Patricia Mathews, and Laura Wexler for their challenging and useful comments on earlier drafts of this essay.

[1] As an individual and a writer, Jewett participated in several contexts which have been separated by many twentieth-century models of cultural and literary history. She was an enthusiast about and patriot of Maine, especially her own Piscataqua region, but also a cosmopolitan with lifelong urban, national and international ties. Well before she and Bostonite Annie Fields became companions she often spent many months away from Berwick annually, in Philadelphia, Cincinnati, the Boston area, New York and elsewhere. After she and Fields established a permanent relationship, she divided her time between South Berwick and Boston and also travelled widely as well as spending months each year in Fields' summer home in Manchester, Massachusetts. She celebrated local Maine culture and history, becoming a member of the Massachusetts Historical Association in 1903. She was a woman-centered woman who treasured bonds between women, domestic production and the domestic arts; a Swedenborgian much influenced by her mentor, the Reverend Theodophilus Parsons; a cultural internationalist who cherished the work of Arnold, Tennyson, Flaubert, Madame de Sévigné, the painters of the French Barbizon school. She belonged to a circle of women artists and writers, many of whom were dedicated to traditionally feminine or domestic arts (perhaps the best-known today is Celia Thaxter) and was a much-loved member of the circle of New England literati which included Horace Scudder, William Dean Howells, James Russell Lowell, John Greenleaf Whittier (her special friend), Thomas Bailey Aldrich and his wife Lillian, and others. Paula Blanchard, *Sarah Orne Jewett: Her World and Her Work*. Radcliffe Biography Series (Reading, MA: Addison-Wesley Publishing Co., 1994) is an outstanding source of information about Jewett and her circle.

[2] The critical reception of *Country* has a long history. It was long recognized by formalists as an aesthetic gem and by literary historians as the quintessential expression of postbellum regionalist literature's celebration of pre-modern rural life.

The aestheticist response, which began with the publication of *Country*, is evinced by Henry James's (qualified) praise of Jewett's "beautiful little quantum of achievement" in "Mr. and Mrs. James T. Fields" (quoted by Michael Bell, "Gender and American Realism in *Country of the Pointed Firs*," *New Essays on* The Country of the Pointed Firs, ed. June Howard (Cambridge: Cambridge University Press, 1994), 61). Werner Berthoff, "The Art of Jewett's *Pointed Firs*," *New England Quarterly* 342, no. 2 (March 1959): 31–53, is an outstanding reading of Dunnet Landing as a regional outpost. The 1980s and early 1990s saw an outpouring of many feminist readings of *Country* which moved in a different direction. Among those I have found particularly useful are Marcia McClintock Folsom, "'Tact is a Kind of Mind Reading': Empathic Style in Sarah Orne Jewett's *The Country of the Pointed Firs,*" *Colby Library Quarterly* 18, no. 1 (1982): 66–78; Josephine Donovan, *New England Local Color Literature: A Women's Tradition* (New York: Frederick Ungar, 1983); Elizabeth Ammons, "Going in Circles: The Female Geography of Sarah Orne Jewett's *The Country of the Pointed Firs,*" *Studies in the Literary Imagination* 16, no. 2 (Fall, 1983), revised and reprinted in Elizabeth Ammons, *Conflicting Stories: American Women Writers at the Turn into the Twentieth Century* (New York: Oxford University Press, 1991), 83–92; Sarah Way Sherman, *Sarah Orne Jewett, an American Persephone* (Hanover, NH: University Press of New England for the University Press of New Hampshire, 1989), Marilyn Sanders Mobley, *Folk Roots and Mythic Wings in Sarah Orne Jewett and Toni Morrison* (Baton Rouge and London: Louisiana State University Press, 1991); and much work by Judith Fetterley and Marjorie Pryse including their *American Women Regionalists, 1850–1919: A Norton Anthology* (New York: W. W. Norton, 1992). See also Sandra A. Zagarell, "Narrative of Community: The Identification of a Genre," *Signs: Journal of Women in Culture and Society* 13, no. 31 (Spring, 1988): 498–527. Feminist work that has located Jewett's representations of gender within the context of race includes Elizabeth Ammons, "Material Culture, Empire, and Jewett's *Country of the Pointed Firs*" and Sandra A. Zagarell, "*Country*'s Portrayal of Community and the Exclusion of Difference," both in *New Essays on* The Country of the Pointed Firs. Richard Brodhead's *Cultures of Letters: Scenes of Reading and Writing in Nineteenth-Century America* (Chicago, University of Chicago Press, 1993) pioneers recent revisionary work on postbellum regionalism. Stephanie Foote's recent "'I Feared To Find Myself a Foreigner': Revisiting Regionalism in Jewett's *Country*" (in *Arizona Quarterly* 52, no. 2 [Summer 1966]: 37–61) is an excellent study of intersections among discourses of regionalism, race, nation in *Country*.

[3] See Amy Kaplan, "Nation, Region, Empire," *Columbia Literary History of the American Novel*, ed. Emory Elliott (New York: Columbia University Press, 1991), 240–66; June Howard, "Introduction: Sarah Orne Jewett and the Traffic in Words" and Susan Gillman, "Regionalism and Nationalism in *The Country of the Pointed Firs*" in *New Essays on* The Country of the Pointed Firs, and June Howard, "Unraveling Regions, Unsettling Periods: Sarah Orne Jewett and American Literary History," *American Literature* 68, no. 2 (June 1996): 365–84. See as well Hortense J. Spillers, "Afterword. Cross-currents, Discontinuities: Black Women's Fiction" in *Conjuring: Black Women, Fiction, and Literary Tradition*, ed. Marjorie Pryse and Hortense J. Spillers (Bloomington: Indiana University Press, 1985), 249–61; and Gayatri Chakravorty Spivak, "Three Women's Texts and a Critique of Imperialism," *Critical Inquiry* 12, no. 1 (Autumn, 1985): 243–61. Jacques Derrida's "La loi du genre/The Law of Genre" in *Glyph: Textual Studies 7* (Baltimore: Johns Hopkins University Press, 1980) has also been invaluable to my efforts to conceptualize the non-coherence of literary works. Also important has been Mikhail Bakhtin's work on dialogics and multivocality, although Carla Kaplan's recent observation that while Bakhtin's work on "conflicting discourses" was "principally descriptive it has often been taken as programmatic" is well worth heeding (*The Erotics of Talk: Women's Writing and Feminist Paradigms* [Oxford: Oxford University Press, 1996], 11). Kaplan's proposition that the hard but urgent questions we need to pursue require us to ask how "conflicting agendas are negotiated and 'footings' are rearranged" in "concrete instances of dialogic exchange" encapsulates many of the concerns which underwrite this essay.

[4] I address discontinuities in Jewett's first full-length book and in regionalism from a somewhat different vantage point in a forthcoming essay in *American Literary History* tentatively entitled "Troubling Regionalism: Rural Life and the Cosmopolitan Eye in Jewett's *Deephaven.*"

[5] See my "*Country*'s Portrayal of Community" for a discussion of the hegemony of racialist discourse in Jewett's era and of the particular political connotations of that discourse in Jewett's circles.

[6] Sarah Orne Jewett, *The Story of the Normans. Told Chiefly in Relation to Their Conquest of England* (New York and London: G.P. Putnam's Sons, 1887), 24.

[7] This idea of history also informs some of Jewett's New England regional writing other than *Country*, including the Piscataqua sketch "The White Rose Road" (1889).

[8] Sarah Orne Jewett, "A War Debt." Reprinted in *The Life of Nancy* (Boston and New York: Houghton Mifflin and Co., 1896), 73.

[9] Sarah Orne Jewett, *The Country of the Pointed Firs and Other Stories*, ed. Marjorie Pryse (New York: W. W. Norton, 1981), 102, 104.

[10] Ammons, "Material Culture" and Gillman, op. cit.

[11] See Michael Kammen, *Mystic Chords of Memory: The Transformation of Tradition in American Culture* (New York: Vintage, 1993), esp. chapter 4.

[12] Sarah Orne Jewett, "Looking Back on Girlhood," reprinted in *Sarah Orne Jewett: Novels and Stories* (New York: Library of America, 1994), 756.

[13] Zagarell, "*Country*'s Portrayal of Community," 48. I discuss the principle of negotiation in this essay.

[14] Elements within interiors differ—Mrs. Blackett's and the Tilleys' "best rooms" mingle the purchased with the home-made, while the main room of Joanna Todd's house has only what she has made or found. But the pattern remains constant. In "Material Culture" Ammons discusses the aesthetic expressed by Dunnet's material culture, citing the architecture and interior design in ways I have found helpful, though her discussion of this aesthetic is quite different from mine.

[15] Classical references are also mobilized in the reunion sequence, where they enhance assertions about the racially originary Americanism of the Anglo-Norman Bowdens. The presence of aspects of one register in another reminds us that registers are never fully free-standing.

AFTERWORD

"Crosscurrents" is part of my ongoing reflection on women writers' participation in their culture and society, reflection much indebted to feminist literary recovery, to critiques of second-wave feminism that began to emerge several decades ago, and to deepening analyses of the pervasiveness and intricacy of ideology. I wanted to develop an approach to literary texts that could be attentive to writers' structural positions and individuality, their texts' political implications, and the multiplicity of literary writing—and that would work against wholesale veneration and endorsement on the one hand or wholesale dismissal on the other.

One presumption of "Crosscurrents" is that women are (of course) not exempt from the ideologies and practices of their era or their own circumstances—of class, race, sexuality, privilege or exploitation—and that these inform their writing. A complementary presumption is that aligning women's writing, or beliefs, or politics with fairly monolithic notions about a writer's position or ascribing monolithic beliefs to their writing leads to dead ends like unnuanced dismissal or unnuanced awe. These presumptions are linked to my recognition of the importance of conceptual and political categories and my concerns about their application. During the past three and a half decades, feminist criticism has developed categories essential to the recovery, theorizing, and critique of women writers, but we must be careful to avoid allowing them to obscure the existence of human agency or vitiate the unpredictable— and the unclassifiable—dimensions of literature. The reductiveness and determinism implicit in approaches to literature or culture—or to individuals' ethics or imagination— that regard these as the uninflected expression of foundational elements trouble me. They foreclose on the possibility of significant differences among similarly situated people and on possibilities for modification of individuals or groups. They also deflect from the way literature and the imagination can be unruly, sometimes frustratingly so, marked by variety and contradiction and fostering possibility.

While I resist the shopworn notion that literature is transcendent, I do think its status in many cultures has tended to encourage individuals' creativity and powers of exploration, to foster writers' imaginative, ethical, even spiritual capacities. "Crosscurrents" is an effort to grapple with these sometimes irreducible intricacies—with the co-existence of some elements whose coordinates are, say, racist or progressive and other elements that contradict them and with the predominance of certain values in some works by a given writer but not in others. Likewise, it cautions against assuming that the interplay of a text's elements is constant and proposes a way to be receptive to variability in that interplay. Further, it reflects both my embrace of historicizing and my sense that historicizing is intensely demanding. I was after a way of reading that combines particularized knowledge about a body of work and, when possible, its author with textured knowledge of larger-scale literary, social, and political history; such knowledge seems a prerequisite for identifying a text's registers.

Country appealed to me as a case study partly because feminist Americanists have returned to it repeatedly. Initially its woman-centeredness, its empathy, its representation of community, its beauty were celebrated; later its ethnic-racial exclusiveness, nationalism, and class-tinged nostalgia came into sharp focus. Jewett's fiction has long been central to my work, and I can almost chart changes in my thinking as a feminist/scholar by changes in my writing about it. What has been particularly challenging for me is that even as I have come to recognize problematic and distasteful aspects of *Country*, it has continued to speak to me aesthetically and emotionally. The intricacy of my responses has contributed to my wish to engage with literature's capacity for multifariousness.

I am still troubled by certain pitfalls of which I was aware as I wrote "Crosscurrents." I was, and remain, concerned that despite my efforts my thinking is too categorical. I remain concerned about the specter of tautology—registers discerned may too easily be those imposed by readers. I worry that focus on registers and their interplay can reinforce narrow ideas about "the literary" that deflect from consideration of the cultural-political implications of a text or can encourage a historicism that refuses to take the measure of texts', and writers', strongest political and ideological alliances. I try to remain mindful of these concerns in my work, and I welcome the occasion to express them. I recognize, of course, that categories are essential to thought and communication and that new categories—notably those feminists have developed—allow new ways of thinking and living. Finally, I recognize that without the categories feminist scholars initially had the courage and imagination to conceive, then the integrity and dedication to rethink, we could less readily continue the process of re-thinking, let alone reflect on the uncategorizable interplay of these and other categories or on expressions of the imagination for which categories cannot account.

~ 1999 ~

Feminism, Eros, and the Coming of Age

Roberta Rubenstein

NEARLY A HALF century ago, Simone de Beauvoir observed that the interval between "maturity" and "old age" is an especially problematic time for women. In her view, women who have outgrown their once clearly delimited social and biological functions as mates and mothers find no clear cultural scripts to guide them during the years and decades that succeed procreation and maternity. As she phrased it:

> From the day a woman consents to growing old, her situation changes. Up to that time she was still a young woman, intent on struggling against a misfortune that was mysteriously disfiguring and deforming her; now she becomes a different being, unsexed but complete: an old woman. It may be considered that the crisis of her "dangerous age" has been passed. But it should not be supposed that henceforth her life will be an easy one. When she has given up the struggle against the fatality of time, another combat begins: she must maintain a place on earth.[1]

Although one would like to declare de Beauvoir's statement "dated" by citing the many advances women have achieved in the decades since she published her groundbreaking analysis of the "second sex" (and, later, of "the coming of age"[2]), the fact is that midlife and the years that follow it still remain problematic for many women and disproportionately so for those who are not white, educated, or middle class.[3] Despite the profound social transformation generated (if not secured) by feminist activism over the past three decades, one may legitimately ask: Has the women's movement that empowered an entire generation remained a movement for young(er) women? Have the changes that feminism catalyzed in the public sphere, notably matters of economic and social equity, bypassed more intimate personal matters, notably aging, sexuality, and what might be termed *erotic equity*, particularly in the years of midlife and beyond?

As the cohort of feminists whose political activism catalyzed the women's movement of the 1970s reaches midlife and beyond at the beginning of the twenty-first century, and as the focused energy of "second-wave" feminism has given way to the less-focused goals of "third-wave" feminism, these questions remain far from closed.[4] The definition of *midlife* (the term that has replaced *middle age*) has itself advanced chronologically in tandem with gains in life expectancy during the past several decades. However, it seems to have expanded in the other direction as well. One scholar of aging states that in contemporary American and European cultures the designation *midlife* encompasses "roughly ages 30–70."[5] According to another scholar on the subject of aging, the answer to the question, "When do the middle years *begin?*" is *"When the culture gets you to say they do."*[6]

Certain elements of that impossibly broad category of midlife have recently been subjected to special scrutiny by feminists. Now that the cohort of women whose pioneering work defined the second wave of the women's movement has reached the life-stage of the women they once regarded as invisible or irrelevant, they have begun to address the challenges of aging from the perspective of their own experience as older women. Among others, Betty Friedan has bemoaned the outworn script underscored by de Beauvoir's assumptions about women and aging. Upon entering her sixties, Friedan began research for the book eventually published in 1993 as *The Fountain of Age*. Acknowledging her peers'—and her own—resistance to the subject, she wrote, "Why did we all seem to feel the need to distance ourselves from age, the closer we got to it?" Proposing the idea of an "age mystique" comparable to the paradigm-shifting "feminine mystique" she named and diagnosed in the sixties, she asserted, "If age itself is defined as 'problem,' then those over sixty-five who can no longer 'pass' as young are its carriers and must be quarantined lest they contaminate, in mind or body, the rest of society."[7]

A number of other feminist activists and novelists who came of age politically during the second wave have in recent years turned from the larger subject of feminism to their private histories, feminist and otherwise. For example, several novelists whose "mad housewife" fiction defined critical issues for women during the 1970s shifted to nonfiction in the form of personal memoir during the 1990s. Alix Kates Shulman, author of one of the classic novels of the second wave, *Memoirs of an Ex-Prom Queen* (1972), recently published *A Good Enough Daughter: A Memoir* (1999). During the same year, Anne Richardson Roiphe, author of *Up the Sandbox!* (1970), another early and influential second-wave novel, published *1185 Park Avenue: A Memoir* (1999). Two decades after writing the exuberant and taboo-shattering *Fear of Flying* (1973), Erica Jong articulated anxieties of another kind in the *Fear of Fifty* (1994), while in *Getting Over Getting Older: An Intimate Journey* (1996), activist Letty Cottin Pogrebin, author of *How to Make It in a Man's World* (1970), wrote a different kind of guide, using her own aging as the map. Similarly, academic feminist Carolyn Heilbrun, author of *Reinventing Womanhood* (1979), recently published *The Last Gift of Time: Life Beyond Sixty* (1997).[8]

Female aging in patriarchy may be understood as a time-advanced version of what Friedan termed "the problem that has no name." It is not yet clear whether contemporary feminist authors of fiction and theory have "named" the problem in ways that might enable women to imagine alternatives to culturally embedded negative scripts and to redirect our lives affirmatively during and beyond midlife. Pogrebin admits her wish that the words "older woman" might "evoke an image of a strong, wise, self-confident female, not a hag or a nobody. . . . It may not yet be possible in this society for a woman to *have* an ideal old age, but it is possible to imagine one."[9] Recognizing the difficulty in that very act of imagination, Heilbrun laments the paucity of emotional scripts available to independent women beyond midlife:

> If we could discover a word that meant "adventure" and did not mean "romance," we in our late decades would be able to free ourselves from the compulsion always to connect yearning and sex. If an ancient (by American standards) woman finds herself longing for something new, something as yet not found, must that something always be sex or till-death-do-us-part romance? The reason for the predominance of sexual aspiration, I have decided, is that no other adventure has quite the symbolic force, not to mention the force of the entire culture, behind it.[10]

The ideas of "adventure" and "romance" come to us through a variety of cultural expressions, including imaginative literature. There is a tradition of literature by and about women and aging that predates and overlaps with the period on which I focus here, including novels by (among others who might be mentioned) Margaret Laurence, May Sarton, Paule Marshall, Doris Lessing, and Anne Tyler.[11] If it is through the imaginative vision that many (then-younger) female readers discovered some of the issues concerning women's personal and political circumstances during the second wave, I would like to consider here two post-second-wave fictional "case studies" that extend comparable insights to women's later years. Both Doris Lessing and Marilyn French address in fictional form some of the questions that circulate between notions of eros and aging for women. Like many of the second-wave writers I have mentioned, Lessing and French reached ideological maturity in the shadow of de Beauvoir's pioneering words and moved beyond midlife as the century turned (Lessing and French were born in 1919 and 1929, respectively). I focus on two of their recent narratives not only because of the considerable influence of their fiction during the second wave but because, as they themselves have grown older, they have continued to write about matters of concern to women in later life-stages. From their positions as authors of galvanizing, era-defining narratives of young women's politically and erotically complex lives—Lessing's *The Golden Notebook* (1962) and French's *The Women's Room* (1977)—both Lessing and French have turned to matters of aging and loss but have maintained their attention to eros.[12]

In a rather remarkable coincidence of timing, two novels published the same year in the United States—Lessing's *Love, Again: A Novel* (1996) and French's *My Summer with George: A Novel of Love at a Certain Age* (1996)—revisit the subject of eros, this time focusing on mature, self-realized women who unexpectedly find themselves struggling to reconcile their self-sufficiency with the long-forgotten, overpowering pull of emotional intimacy and sexual desire.[13] Both authors focus on female characters who wrestle with the disturbing disjunctions between hard-won positions of autonomy in the public arena and the more intimate and problematic realm of eros for older women; both authors dare to imagine their female protagonists as independent, older, *desiring* women as they anatomize the longings and losses that accompany even highly successful women's later years. Through the prism of aging, both authors propose that matters of the heart—what might be called struggles with erotic equity—continue to challenge even emotionally self-sufficient women well beyond midlife.

Despite their compelling resemblances, however, Lessing's and French's novels map different trajectories of late-midlife female self-discovery, demonstrating and drawing different conclusions from the powerful socially constructed script of the female life span. As Margaret Gullette observes in her analysis of the ideology of aging, contemporary culture offers two sharply contrasting cultural scripts of midlife development: "progress" and "decline." Literary narratives that focus on midlife protagonists—usually female—typically reflect one or the other of these cultural scripts. In narratives of progress, "Recalling being younger is a way of expressing gratitude for having moved on in the life course. . . . The 'progress' such novels convincingly model is that it feels better to be older than younger." Among the functions of such narratives of progress is that of "redefin[ing] heroism at midlife to include self-rescue."[14]

However, not all novels about midlife articulate an affirmative process of "ripening" into age.[15] Rather, narratives of decline focus on a trajectory of renunciation, loss, and a kind of "identity-stripping" that "requires the self to reject or consider inconsequential all the counternarratives that emphasize aging into wisdom or maturity or any valued progress."[16] Of the two cultural scripts, the default narrative—the one that is far more pervasive and influential in its pessimistic charting of physical and mental deterioration over time—is the latter: "Our culture provides subjects with a master narrative of aging—something like the master narrative of gender or race: popularly disseminated, semi-conscious, so familiar and acceptable that it can be told automatically. The plot of this one is peak, entry, and decline, with acceleration on the downslope."[17] Moreover, although other cultural labels and sites of interpretation such as ethnicity or class may influence the cultural scripting of the body's progress or decline, gender is "probably the most important determinant of the details that give plausibility to the master narrative."[18]

Lessing's and French's novels may be instructively read in light of this "master narrative" of aging as they expose assumptions about the female body, erotic desire, and the enduring traces of earlier experiences that continue to influence inner growth beyond maturity. In fact, Lessing explicitly introduces a version of the master narrative early in *Love, Again*, as Sarah Durham is drawn to the memoir of an unnamed "society woman once known for her beauty" (4), published when its author was nearly a hundred years old. This extended cited passage encodes the script of aging as decline:

> Growing old gracefully . . . the way has been signposted. One might say the instructions are in an invisible script which becomes slowly legible as life exposes it. Then the appropriate words only have to be spoken. . . . The young do not know—it is hidden from them—that the flesh withers around an unchanged core. The old share with each other ironies appropriate to ghosts at a feast, seen by each other but not by the guests whose antics and posturings they watch, smiling, remembering. (Lessing 3–4)

Over the course of both Lessing's and French's novels, the central characters—women in late midlife—confront the dark underside of the erotic yearnings that enmesh them: the realities of "longing and loss and the terrible knowledge of the impossibility of satisfaction" (French 242). While the reawakening of desire catalyzes for each woman a serious reflection on her past and obliges her (and the reader) to consider the relationships among aging, gender, desire, and loss, Lessing's narrative traces a darker and more convoluted path than French's. *My Summer with George* is, according to the author, "a satirical novel about an aging woman's ludicrous love affair," written as an antidote to her experience of nearly fatal illness.[19]

The protagonists of both novels are attractive, successful women in their mid-sixties: Lessing's Sarah Durham, a scriptwriter and partner in a small London theatrical agency, and French's Hermione Beldame, "Queen of Hearts," the prolific best-selling author of romance novels. Each has been married and widowed at least once; both have grown children who are absent from the narratives, although Sarah is occasionally sought out by an emotionally troubled niece for whom she has for years been the "effective parent" (Lessing 13). Though Sarah has not been in the arms of a man since her husband's death twenty years earlier, she finds herself suddenly catapulted into a state that mimics adolescent longing for such an experience. French's Hermione finds herself in a similar state, attracted to a man who makes her feel desirable for the first time since her fourth husband died ten years before. As she phrases it, "I missed feeling desirable, but even more, I missed feeling desire" (French 66).

In the process of charting the vagaries of eros, Lessing invokes the "great cartographers" (Lessing, frontispiece) of the territory of love, ranging from Shakespeare and Stendhal to D. H. Lawrence and T. S. Eliot. Ironically, Eliot, a poet known more for his evocations of loss than of love, is one of the novel's presiding literary spirits. Whatever Sarah may think she is asserting about the progress of love, shadows of *The Waste Land* and of the loveless, emotionally stranded J. Alfred Prufrock insinuate a narrative of physical deterioration and decline. Through Sarah, Lessing laments the emotional sterility, the "desert of deprivation" (Lessing 141), that looms as unattached women (in particular) advance in age. Glossing from *The Waste Land*, Lessing transposes Eliot's image of Phlebas, the drowned sailor, into a woman who reprises "the stages of her age and youth, entering the whirlpool" (Lessing 164).[20] Similarly, French's Hermione Beldame is characterized as struggling against an undertow, "like a drowning person trying to keep her head above the waterline" (French 198). In both Lessing's and French's narratives, images of whirlpool and undertow come to stand for the contrary—and uncontrollable —pulls of desire and aging.

Further, Sarah, pondering her close friend Stephen Ellington-Smith's pathological romantic attachment to a long-dead woman, cites Eliot's Prufrock, whose acute emotional isolation is voiced in his lament, "'I have heard the mermaids singing, each to each. I do not think that they will sing to me'" (Lessing 154).[21] Interestingly, the ghost of J. Alfred appears in French's narrative as well. At the party where Hermione first meets George, she finds herself recalling—in a phrase whose irony is only later understood—"'Time for you and time for me / And time yet for a hundred indecisions . . .'" (French 21). Much later in the novel, after she has acknowledged the insubstantiality of her relationship with George, Hermione admits, in language that invokes another modernist poet's—Yeats's—famous words on the subject of aging:

> I do not know how to think about the fact that I may reach some great age, my face skeletal beneath the wrinkled folds of flesh pulled away from the bone, my eyes sunken into dark pockets of pain, my walk tottery and unsure, my body a tattered coat upon a stick, and still be on the lookout, have an eye out for, be seeking always and ever, a certain voice and eye, a certain look, a hand reached out, breath swiftly drawn, a catch in the voice, an invitation to the waltz. . . . It is humiliating. . . . My spirit is still a girl's, trapped inside a deteriorating container. (French 242–43)

One can legitimately wonder why, for both Lessing and French, the cultural reference points of aging are still framed in terms of images drawn from iconic male modernists who wrote during an era when women lacked even the right to vote. [22] These allusions may reflect an ironic form of gender equity: Although it may be perceived differently according to cultural attitudes toward the two sexes in senescence, in absolute terms the "deteriorating container" of the body does not discriminate on the basis of gender.

Through their female protagonists' efforts to reach beyond culturally mandated scripts of youth and romance, Lessing and French explore elements that exist in a different realm from the material one: the indelible emotional traces that endure, like a fossil record in the strata of the psyche, in the history of one's affectionate relationships. Lessing pointedly situates her inquiry within a theatrical setting, a location that exemplifies an underlying psychological premise of the narrative: Over time, the roles one plays, the masks one assumes, drive the authentic self into ever deeper and more hidden regions, until the task of recovering that self becomes so urgent that it ultimately displaces all others. Images of the ancient paired theatrical masks of tragedy and comedy recur throughout *Love, Again*, underscoring the contradictory nature of love as "sweet poison" and "cold fever" (Lessing 116). Indeed, depending on the reader's predilection, the novel may be read through the comic or the tragic mask.[23] However, as the master narrative of decline would have it, what lies beneath Eros's—and youth's—comic grin is Thanatos's grimace.

The catalyst for Lessing's anatomy of the collision between Eros and Thanatos is her central character's involvement as scriptwriter in the production of an opera. The story, based on the tragic life of a beautiful, talented woman who suffers—and loses—three lovers of different social ranks and ultimately ends her life by suicide, offers a perfect subject for operatic treatment. Virtually every participant in the production of the opera *Julie Vairon* is affected by the romantic story on which they collaborate. The melodramatic narrative of hearts broken and loves lost thus provides a text for Lessing's exploration of other kinds of scripts, namely the competing narratives of romance and aging. As the heightened intimacy and unreality of the production situation spill directly over into the group's personal lives and associations, Sarah Durham finds herself erotically reawakened and uncontrollably attracted to several men in the company, virtually all of whom are young enough to be her sons. In turn, several men, though not the same ones, are attracted to her. At times the story suggests the dreamy ambience as well as the irrational, mismatched lovers of *A Midsummer Night's Dream*, in this instance rescripted to highlight the more problematic misalignments between age and youth.

At other times, the narrative suggests a kind of ghost story, for each character in *Love, Again* brings to the experience of love a whole cast of phantoms of earlier attachments. Initially, Sarah observes these phantoms in other members of the company; soon, however, she is prompted by the seductive power of the collective theatrical experience to confront her own phantoms. Drawn involuntarily into the whirlpool, she struggles against the cultural master narrative of decline, which judges harshly an older woman's denial of bodily disintegration. Concurrently, she engages in a struggle with love as a primitive and entirely irrational force: an elixir closer to poison, infection, affliction, and madness than the scripts of romance would have us believe.

For French's Hermione, the season of romance is initiated by an encounter with a man a decade younger than she, a journalist to whom she is drawn at a friend's party. Infatuated with George, she fantasizes about a long-term relationship based on a comically minimal amount of time actually spent with him. To each of her friends, she repeats the magical mantra-like phrase, "I've met a man." Their respective responses provide a cross section of women's tenacious romantic expectations—feminist politics notwithstanding—regarding intimate relationships and the potentiality for genuine mutuality at various phases of the life cycle. As Hermione expresses it to her friends, "I thought I had a happy life until I met him. . . . Meeting him triggered something. You know—the happily-ever-after button? And what is so upsetting is discovering how powerful it is" (French 77).

What gives particular poignancy to both of these narratives of erotic intoxication and romantic fantasy is the authors' unsentimental attention to their characters' postmenopausal circumstances, registered in the women's "reading" of their bodies and physical appearance through—or against—the cultural script of aging. As Gullette characterizes this influential cultural narrative:

> Even our feelings [about aging] are learned, starting with anticipatory fear of midlife aging, including envy of or anger at the currently young, nostalgic reminiscence that amounts to envying oneself when young, sorrow or even shame about "losses," and premature fear of dying. Middle-ageism is a set of stereotypical meanings pumped out over the age class. Hyping special clothes, foods, interests, exercises, attitudes to sex, children, and death, in thousands of ways both superficially and deeply it governs the "experience" of approaching the mid-life or living it. The ideology wizens the middle years.[24]

French's Hermione agonizes far less about her physical aging than does Lessing's Sarah; indeed, she claims that her body is "still firm and fit, despite [her] years" (French 132). Moreover, while she is drawn to a man only moderately younger than herself, Sarah is attracted to far younger men, as Lessing acerbically illuminates the reality of a double standard that obtains far beyond youth: While it is easy and socially acceptable for older men to form relationships with young women, the reverse remains both unconventional and suspect.[25]

During the course of Lessing's narrative, Sarah frequently examines her "double"—her reflection in the mirror—as she attempts to reconcile her still-youthful inner image with her outward appearance. Interestingly, de Beauvoir anticipated this preoccupation of aging women with the discrepancies between inner self-image and mirror reflection:

> [W]hen one feels oneself a conscious, active, free being, the passive object on which the fatality [of aging or death] is operating seems necessarily as if it were another: . . . this cannot be *I*, this old woman reflected in the mirror! . . . The woman puts her trust in what is clear to her inner eye rather than in that strange world where time flows backward, where her double no longer resembles her, where the outcome has betrayed her.[26]

More recently, Pogrebin has echoed this process of reflection (in both senses) regarding the aging female body, noting:

> I am standing now in front of a full-length mirror ready to document my deterioration item by item from the top down. I don't love what I see; the discrepancy between my inner spirit (still thirty-six) and this outer body is hard to reconcile, but . . . the exercise of cataloguing my own physical collapse is the best way I know to redefine the 'flaws' of aging as the norm of aging.[27]

Pertinently, Kathleen M. Woodward has theorized a "mirror stage" of old age, "the inverse of the mirror stage of infancy" proposed by Lacan, wherein "what is whole is felt to reside *within*, not *without*, the subject. The image in the mirror is understood as uncannily prefiguring the disintegration and nursling dependence of advanced age."[28] In other words, the mirror image of the fully realized self of midlife (or even before and certainly thereafter), far from providing an "accurate" reflection of the self, mocks the achieved spirit with cruel reminders of the visibly deteriorating flesh. The discrepancy between inner and outer realities is what Thomas R. Cole calls the fundamental paradox of aging—"the tragic and ineradicable conflict between spirit and body."[29]

It is precisely those absolute and irreducible discrepancies—between outward appearance and inward self, between negating cultural script and inner self-regard, between corporeal and spiritual dimensions of being—that animate Lessing's and French's narrative explorations of the problematic negotiation, for self-realized women in particular, between eros and aging. Lessing's Sarah "makes herself return to the glass, again, again, because the person who is doing the looking feels herself to be exactly the same . . . as she was at twenty, thirty, forty" (Lessing 245). In a variant of the truism that youth is wasted on the young, Sarah acknowledges that youth is a "privileged class sexually" that one takes for granted at the time, only to relinquish it involuntarily as the peak of eroticism and physical attractiveness give way, inevitably and regretfully, to a "desert of deprivation"

(Lessing 141). Or, as French's Hermione phrases it, "It wasn't that twenty-odd-year-old boys no longer appealed to me (although, in truth, they no longer did). But mainly I dreaded being perceived as acting flirtatious or seductive toward anyone who might find my no longer young person repulsive" (French 65). The observation is a telling reiteration of the power of the cultural narrative of diminished expectations.

Lessing's and French's protagonists lament not so much the physical changes that their mirrors unsparingly register as the social and psychological consequences. Despite the inner strength, self-esteem, and worldly success that a mature woman may have acquired, she may still find herself vulnerable to the culturally inflected negative meanings that affix themselves, with her unwilling collaboration, to her aging body. Gullette uses the term "masochistic nostalgia" to describe the psychic residue of the influential cultural narrative of aging: "Every woman I know goes through some version of this age-graded dissatisfaction, learning the life-weariness of nostalgia as she goes. Accepting the formulas of nostalgia means learning that you are not beautiful or not sexy or not something, any more."[30]

In these fictional representations of the trajectory of aging, each woman's reading of her body's decline is also powerfully influenced by the unfinished business of past attachments. Phantoms of emotional history dating back to core experiences of childhood and even infancy increasingly break through both women's previously "solid and equable" positions as emotionally self-sufficient women (Lessing 113). Sarah, prompted by the gap the mocking mirror exposes between her chronological age and her attraction to young men, concludes that old age is "a secret hell, populated with the ghosts of lost loves, former personalities" (Lessing 177). During her state of infatuation with first one and then another younger man, she is haunted by "apparitions" (Lessing 265); one night, "ghostly lips kissed hers. A ghost's arms held her" (Lessing 253). Again, de Beauvoir presciently describes the specters that haunt Sarah, observing that the aging woman's dreams are "peopled with erotic phantoms . . .; she falls secretly in love with one young man after another."[31]

With amusement, Lessing's Sarah recalls her "first love," when she was only six and the object of her affections was a year younger. Although the scene that she had "put into a frame long ago" (Lessing 109) bears comic qualities, what she retrieves from the memory this time is its darker emotional residue, that of loss. At various points, she fleetingly connects the image of the "plump little boy" who first broke her heart with that of her younger brother, Hal, now a corpulent, insensitive doctor for whom she feels more contempt than affection. Yet that plump child was once loved—"God, how I did love you, my little brother, how I did love you" (Lessing 285)—a feeling Sarah recovers, in astonishment, through her attraction to one of the company members, Henry, whose name even echoes her younger brother's.[32] As a child, she had also hated that baby with equal intensity, an emotional truth that she recuperates through a recalled image of herself as a child "stabbing [a] doll" (Lessing 208).

Although Sarah concludes that her destructive behavior was an expression of sibling rivalry, a deeper psychoanalytic explanation is that she was acting out rage not toward her baby brother but toward her mother—anger that, as a young child, she could neither acknowledge nor express. From birth, her brother was "her mother's favourite. . . . He was the much wanted and loved boy, and she had taken second place from the moment he was born" (Lessing 86–87).[33] To acknowledge her younger brother's preeminence in her mother's affections and to recall so distinctly her own sense of inadequacy is to confront the profound effect that such emotional deprivations and losses may impose on later relationships. The narcissistic wound, experienced so early and so damagingly, may never entirely heal but may continue to bleed into and sabotage subsequent attachments, unless it is confronted and integrated into conscious awareness.[34]

Eventually Sarah reaches back to "that region where the baby in her lived" (Lessing 16). Once, she awakens from a dream in which she has occupied a "phantom body," a baby body filled with "a longing so violent the pain of it fed back into her own body" (Lessing 163). Beneath the masks of her adult life she discerns

the faces she had had as a young woman, as a girl, and as a baby. . . .

She was dissolved in longing. She could not remember ever feeling the rage of want that possessed her now. Surely never in her times of being in love had she felt this absolute, this peremptory need, an emptiness that hollowed out her body, as if life itself was being withheld from her.

Who is it that feels this degree of need, of dependence, and who has to lie helpless waiting for the warm arms and the moment of being lifted up into love? (Lessing 164–65)

On another occasion, she yearns to hold a baby against the "hollow of her left shoulder," only to admit that she longs to occupy that space herself: "an infinite vulnerability lay there: Sarah herself, who was both infant and what sheltered the infant" (Lessing 307).

French's Hermione also reflects, though less deeply, on the formative circumstances of her life. She reviews her personal history in an effort to recover her bearings and to reconcile her current life of success, wealth, and independence with an unhappy childhood, an unfortunate early marriage, and a legacy of emotional needs that illuminates her vulnerability to the myth of romantic love. The youngest of five children of a mother widowed when Hermione was only two, she has no memory of her father and recalls her mother as a self-sacrificing martyr. Family life was "bleak with depression, which hung over us all like a black umbrella" (French 33). Hermione's optimism at breaking away from her dreary family life to attend college was quickly crushed when her sole adolescent sexual experience led to pregnancy, quickly followed by marriage to a boy she didn't love, because, at the age of twenty in the 1950s, she could not envision either seeking an illegal abortion or bearing an illegitimate child. Several decades and several marriages later, her attraction to George catalyzes the feeling of being "sexually reborn" (French 66), although it also leads her to feel literally sick with longing for intimacy.

Though both French's and Lessing's female protagonists regard their condition as a kind of illness, Lessing goes further to establish links between what are ostensibly two different kinds of sensual longing. In *Love, Again*, the "again" is significant: the affections of adulthood are inevitably mapped onto submerged but still influential emotional patterns of attachment and affection (or their absence) experienced literally from the cradle. Sarah, aroused at one point by a young male company member's physical presence, feels her body reacting sensually, "alive and vibrant, but also painful. Her breasts burned, and the lower part of her abdomen ached. Her mouth threatened to seek kisses—like a baby's mouth turning and turning to find the nipple" (Lessing 186). Reflecting a similar but developmentally later phase of arousal, Hermione, stimulated by her fantasies of George, feels like "a horny adolescent": "My skin throbbed and my breasts ached" (French 98). Even the vocabulary of passion reflects the ambivalence of such erotic feelings: the expression "raging with desire" (Lessing 120) captures the sense that a reserve of (infantile) rage may lie just beneath Eros's mask.

Sarah's further descent into the vortex is analogous to a kind of psychological regression: "Forgotten selves kept appearing like bubbles in boiling liquid. . . . She was obviously dissolving into some kind of boiling soup, but presumably would reshape at some point" (Lessing 212).[35] Through feelings and sensations awakened from a long dormancy, she experiences nostalgia for the idealized bliss of infancy, colored by the inevitability of loss: "Perhaps the paradise we dream of when in love is the one we were ejected from, where all embraces are innocent" (Lessing 187). French's Hermione similarly recognizes the ever-beckoning fantasy of Eden, in the form of a person whose intimate presence might finally fill "that hurt empty spot that never goes away, that has been hurting since you were born, it seems. It would be wonderful. Paradise. I'd be happy for the rest of my life" (French 150). Hermione acknowledges that her unexpected yearning for emotional and erotic intimacy is beyond her control precisely because she has so successfully insulated herself from such feelings, only to discover that "maybe the punishment for that is being thrust back into adolescence, forced into the humiliating experience of love and longing, here on the edge of the grave" (French 236). While French traces the sources of Hermione's intoxicated longings only as far back as adolescence, Lessing locates Sarah's in the very earliest stage of emotional attachment, approaching the "desolation of being excluded from happiness" (Lessing 197) that dates from her earliest years of childhood.

Significantly, virtually all of what occurs in the passionate dramas of the narratives takes place only within the women's own imaginations: Scarcely a single embrace or kiss is actually exchanged between Sarah and the young men whom she privately desires, apart from a single fraternal kiss on the cheek from Henry. Acutely aware of the age gap between herself and the objects of her longing, she feels prohibited from acting on her desires, a fact that only intensifies her emotional distress as she retreats from impossible erotic liaisons. Similarly, Hermione kisses George once on the lips in an unreciprocated gesture that she promptly realizes is "a terrible, maybe fatal mistake" (French 200). Lessing engages more pessimistically than does French with the narrative of decline, interrogating the relations among desire, aging, and loss that, while initially seeming unrelated, are ultimately revealed to be inextricably entangled. First, Sarah questions Nature's obscure purpose in drawing an older person of either sex into intoxicated longing for a younger one. Later, the question assumes another form as she is consumed by grief not only for her friend Stephen, a casualty of unrequited (and unrequiteable) love, but for all of her own past loves and past selves. She wonders, "Why grief at all? What is it for?" (Lessing 327).

The relationship between grief and growth is central to understanding both Lessing's and French's narratives of late midlife erotic reawakening. The process of emotional review that both protagonists undertake parallels the "life review" that many psychologists and gerontologists, such as Robert N. Butler, regard as a fundamental task of aging:

> a naturally occurring universal mental process characterized by the progressive return to consciousness of past experiences and, particularly, the resurgence of unresolved conflicts; simultaneously, and normally, these experiences and conflicts can be surveyed and reintegrated. Presumably the process is prompted by the realization of approaching dissolution and death, and the inability to maintain one's sense of personal invulnerability. It is further shaped by contemporaneous experiences and its nature and outcome are affected by the life-long unfolding of character.[36]

However, the resolution of this life review is not inevitably positive, according to Peter G. Coleman: "The individual may remain obsessed with events and actions he [*sic*] regrets, find no solution and no peace, and develop chronic feelings of guilt and depression."[37]

Accordingly, following an interval of several months after the conclusion of her involvement with the production of *Julie Vairon*, Lessing's Sarah examines her image in a mirror again. She appears to have "aged by ten years. . . . Her hair, which for so long remained like a smooth dulled metal, now has grey bands across the front. She has acquired that slow cautious look of the elderly, as if afraid of what they will see around the next corner" (Lessing 349).[38] Indeed, she has surrendered, although not altogether willingly, to the narrative of decline: Relinquishing Eros, she acquiesces to old age. By contrast, French's *My Summer with George* concludes somewhat more sanguinely. Hermione, relinquishing her imaginary "relationship" with George, concedes that she has projected onto an unsuitable man amorous fantasies not too far removed from those that constitute her own formulaic romance fictions. Painfully wrenching herself away from those scripts, she likens herself to "an animal caught in a trap I could escape from only by tearing off my leg or arm" (French 215).

Ultimately, French permits her protagonist a somewhat more affirmative resolution than Lessing does hers. As French has acknowledged, the novel intentionally foregrounds "not intellectual argument but mocking glances at serious ideas; not profound emotional conflict but absurd emotions couched in everyday language."[39] Accordingly, Hermione finds in her disillusionment the inspiration for a new novel based on her extravagant erotic fantasies, wherein "the heroine and her lover are drunk with desire" and make passionate love in a number of romantic settings: "What would make it unusual is that at the very end, the reader discovers that the entire affair has taken place only in the heroine's imagination, that nothing actually happened with the man, that he rejected her early on, and that throughout the virtual time of the novel, she is wandering listlessly around, helpless with desire, dreaming it all up . . ." (French 219). However, Hermione acknowledges that, even as an author, she (like French herself) cannot invent a "happy ending" for her story without trivializing the experiences that constituted it. Nonetheless, the first-person narrator voices an affirmative female identity even in late midlife. Hermione, having struggled in the seductive vortex of romantic fantasy that disguises a destructive undertow, validates what she has discovered in that experience: "the sorry fact, or is it triumphant?" that "the unending drive, the geyser spurt of desire that is life, goes on and on, will not be stilled, in body or spirit. Till death do us part" (French 243).

For a female/feminist reader, the degree of ideological (if not aesthetic) satisfaction with *Love, Again* and *My Summer with George* may be equivocal. Given the novels' quite different conclusions, one may legitimately ask: As feminism settles in to the new millennium, and as the American population increasingly faces "the coming of age," which text provides a more honest imaginative map for guidance at the crossroads of female aging and desire? While the resolution of French's narrative, inflected by romantic fantasy, may be more comforting to readers wrestling with the disjunctions between eros and aging, Lessing's novel exposes the darker subtext in which these matters are embedded. *My Summer with George*, with its lighter—even self-mocking—tone, is defiant in its accommodations with aging. By contrast, the cost of Sarah's descent into the whirlpool is the defeat of her resistance to the master narrative of decline. In place of the self-renewing energy of eros is a much more muted process: the resolution of mourning for her lost younger selves, marked by her acceptance of the older woman she has become.

Just behind Sarah Durham and Hermione Beldame stand Doris Lessing and Marilyn French, wrestling equally—along with other women of their generation—with the unappeased phantoms of early life and the not-entirely-appeasable demons of advancing age.[40] Intrepid pathfinders in the less willingly traversed terrains of what Lessing terms "love's country," both authors dare to chart the hazards they discover in the landscape—or what Colette V. Browne terms the "agescape."[41] Through their imaginative explorations of deeply imbedded, and conflicting, cultural scripts associated with desire and decline, both authors enable us to imagine women's capacity for emotional renewal and growth during and beyond midlife. In illuminating the midlife version of "the problem that has no name," they demonstrate the power of forces, both internal and external, that hinder women's progress towards true erotic equity.

NOTES

[1] Simone de Beauvoir, *The Second Sex*, trans. H. M. Parshley (1952; reprint, New York: Knopf, 1993), 649.

[2] See Simone de Beauvoir, *The Coming of Age*, trans. Patrick O'Brian (New York: Putnam, 1972).

[3] As did feminism, the study of age and aging has begun to evolve from generalizations based on white, middle-class experience to an acknowledgement of differences based on race, class,

ethnicity, and nationality. See, for example, essays in *Welcome to Middle Age! (and Other Cultural Fictions)*, ed. Richard A. Shweder (Chicago: University of Chicago Press, 1998).

[4] Naomi Wolf, a "third-wave" feminist, observes that "even as more and more of feminism's ideals cross over into mainstream culture, more and more women distance themselves from the word 'feminist'" (*Fire with Fire: The New Female Power and How It Will Change the 21ˢᵗ Century* [New York: Random House, 1993], 57). A number of books published in the last decade illustrate the preoccupation within feminism with "generations." Devoney Looser and E. Ann Kaplan, co-editors of a collection of essays titled *Generations: Academic Feminists in Dialogue* (Minneapolis: University of Minnesota Press, 1997), observe that "divisions among feminist 'waves' or genera-tions are named only to be broken down. . . . Despite all of the difficulties involved in defining the beliefs (or even the members) of any given generation, we need more conversations about how we have come to perceive each other as feminists according to 'age'" (35). They conclude that "most feminists use *third wave* to refer to the 'new' feminisms and feminists emerging in the late 1980s and 1990s, many of whom purport to interrogate race, nation, and sexuality more thoroughly than did the second wave, and many of whom are skeptical about the unity of the category 'women'" (38).

[5] Shweder, *Welcome to Middle Age!*, vii.

[6] Margaret Morganroth Gullette, *Declining to Decline: Cultural Combat and the Politics of the Midlife* (Charlottesville: University Press of Virginia, 1997), 159, emphasis in the original. Gul-lette also notes that the significant changes in life expectancy during the twentieth century have oc-curred not during the later years but in the first five years of life (*Declining to Decline*, 254 n.1).

[7] Historian Lois W. Banner speculates that because feminist scholars of the second wave were, like herself, typically "young women, working out the dynamics of their own lives in their stud-ies" that "aging remained obscure to us partly because we were in rebellion against older genera-tions perceived as antifeminist. Moreover, reflecting traditional attitudes, we chose to look on old women as invisible and on our own youth as the real reality" (*In Full Flower: Aging Women, Power, and Sexuality* [New York: Knopf, 1992], 6). Betty Friedan, *The Fountain of Age* (New York: Simon and Schuster, 1993), 21, 60, 50. Despite Friedan's sustained and impassioned analysis of the sub-ject of aging, her book did not catalyze a cultural paradigm shif tivist groups had already staked out some of the same terrain that Friedan addresses in her argument for positive constructions of aging. Organizations such as Gray Panthers and, of course, the American Association of Retired Persons (AARP) actively lobby politically on behalf of various "age classes" as they pass through and beyond midlife. Margaret Gullette uses the term "age class" to identify "a culturally constructed unit" based solely on age: "Discourse about an age class takes for granted, as well as often explic-itly asserting, a commonality that is supposed to override gender, class, race, sexual orientation, national origin, personal psychology, politics, and so on" ("Midlife Discourses in the Twentieth-Century United States: An Essay on the Sexuality, Ideology, and Politics of 'Middle-Ageism,'" in Shweder, *Welcome to Middle Age!*, 3). However, within an "age class," there are indeed differences among people of different genders, races, and other aspects of socially labeled identity.

[8] Alix Kates Shulman, *Memoirs of an Ex-Prom Queen* (New York: Knopf, 1972) and *A Good Enough Daughter: A Memoir* (New York Schocken, 1999); Anne Richardson Roiphe, *Up the Sandbox!* (New York: Simon and Schuster, 1970) and *1185 Park Avenue: A Memoir* (New York: The Free Press, 1999); Erica Jong, *Fear of Flying* (New York: Holt, Rinehart and Winston, 1973) and *Fear of Fifty* (New York: HarperCollins, 1994); Letty Cottin Pogrebin, *How to Make It in a Man's World* (Garden City, N.Y.: Doubleday, 1970) and *Getting Over Getting Older: An Intimate Journey* (Boston: Little, Brown, 1996); and Carolyn G. Heilbrun, *Reinventing Womanhood* (New York: Norton, 1979), and *The Last Gift of Time: Life Beyond Sixty* (New York: Dial, 1997).

[9] Pogrebin, *Getting Over Getting Older*, 308, 310, emphasis in original.

[10] Heilbrun, *The Last Gift of Time*, 103.

[11] See Margaret Laurence, *The Stone Angel* (New York: Knopf, 1964); May Sarton, *As We Are Now* (New York: Norton, 1973); Paule Marshall, *Praisesong for the Widow* (New York: Putnam 1983); Doris Lessing, *The Summer Before the Dark* (New York: Knopf, 1973); and Anne Tyler, *Breathing Lessons* (New York: Knopf, 1988).

[12] Doris Lessing, *The Golden Notebook* (New York: Simon and Schuster, 1962). Three of Lessing's earlier novels—*The Summer Before the Dark*, *The Diaries of Jane Somers* (New York: Knopf, 1983–84), and *If the Old Could . . .* (reprinted in *The Diaries of Jane Somers*, 1984), the

latter two under the pseudonym Jane Somers—also reflect the author's interest in the female experience of aging. French's three novels published between *The Women's Room* (New York: Summit Books, 1977) and *My Summer with George: A Novel of Love at a Certain Age* (New York: Knopf, 1996) include *The Bleeding Heart* (New York: Summit Books, 1980), *Her Mother's Daughter: A Novel* (New York: Summit Books, 1987), and *Our Father: A Novel* (Boston: Little, Brown, 1994). Though the first focuses on romantic matters and the latter two involve family relationships, none of them focus on matters of female aging.

[13] Doris Lessing, *Love, Again: A Novel* (New York: HarperCollins, 1996); and French, *My Summer with George*. (Further references to these works are cited parenthetically in the text.)

[14] Gullette, *Declining to Decline*, 86, 82.

[15] Barbara Frey Waxman has coined the term *Reifungsroman*, the novel of ripening, to describe literary narratives that complement the traditional *Bildungsroman* in which a character matures from adolescence into adulthood (*From the Hearth to the Open Road: A Feminist Study of Aging in Contemporary Literature* [New York: Greenwood Press, 1990]).

[16] Gullette, *Declining to Decline*, 197.

[17] Gullette, *Declining to Decline*, 161.

[18] Gullette, *Declining to Decline*, 161.

[19] Marilyn French, *A Season in Hell: A Memoir* (New York: Knopf, 1998), 186.

[20] T. S. Eliot, *The Waste Land and Other Poems* (New York Harcourt, Brace, 1934), 41.

[21] The allusion invites recall of the preceding lines in the ironically titled "Love Song," in which Prufrock frets, "I grow old . . . I grow old / I shall wear the bottoms of my trousers rolled." Arnold H. Modell suggests that Eliot, who wrote "The Love Song of J. Alfred Prufrock" when he was in his late twenties, was "preternaturally middle-aged" ("Object Relations Theory: Psychic Aliveness in the Middle Years," in *The Middle Years: New Psychoanalytic Perspectives*, ed. John M. Oldham and Robert S. Liebert [New Haven, Conn.: Yale University Press, 1989], 17).

[22] Interestingly, Eliot's importance for Lessing dates back to the beginning of her career: The title of her first novel, *The Grass Is Singing* (London: Michael Joseph, 1950), echoes another phrase from *The Waste Land*.

[23] In a reading of *Love, Again* that emphasizes the narrative's comic and satiric dimensions, Veronica Geng draws conclusions opposite from those I develop in this essay. She regards Lessing as a "comic dramatist" who develops various scenes as a "revue of psychological satires" with connections to popular love songs ("There's No People Like Show People," review of *Love, Again*, in *The New York Times Book Review*, 21 [April 1996], 13).

[24] Gullette, *Declining to Decline*, 6.

[25] Lois Banner challenges this negative view of "age-disparate" relationships between older women and younger men, arguing that myth and history provide notable examples of independent older women—from Greek goddesses to Chaucer's Alison of Bath—whose relationships with younger men are regarded as socially acceptable. Although "the European tradition did not accord women high regard in their waning years, once they had become postmenopausal . . . there was an alternative point of view, one under which they could be, like Alison's crone, people of wisdom, spirit, and, ultimately, desire." However, "the emergence of romantic love as a major factor in marital choice . . . played a part in the decline in cross-age relationships between aging women and younger men" since the "youthful ideal" of physical and sexual attractiveness gained primacy as the essential matrix of romantic passion (*In Full Flower*, 185, 244).

[26] de Beauvoir, *The Second Sex*, 645.

[27] Pogrebin, *Getting Over Getting Older*, 127.

[28] Kathleen M. Woodward, *Aging and Its Discontents: Freud and Other Fictions* (Bloomington: Indiana University Press, 1991), 67, emphasis in the original.

[29] Thomas R. Cole, *The Journey of Life: A Cultural History of Aging in America* (New York: Cambridge University Press, 1992), 239.

[30] Gullette, *Declining to Decline*, 58.

[31] de Beauvoir, *The Second Sex*, 644.

[32] The names of both Henry and Hal—Sarah's younger brother's name—echo the name of Lessing's actual younger brother, Harry.

[33] The emotional pattern closely parallels events in Lessing's own childhood, as she has revealed in more than one autobiographical account. Describing her early relationship with her mother, she reveals that her mother wished for a son when Doris was born and felt no compunction about letting her daughter know

> that I was not wanted in the first place; that to have a girl was a disappointment that nearly did her in altogether. . . ; that she had no milk for me and I had to be bottle-fed from the start and I was half-starved for the first year. . . ; that I was an impossibly difficult baby and then a tiresome child, quite unlike my little brother Harry who was always so good. . . . My memories of her are all of antagonism, and fighting, and feeling shut out; of pain because the baby born two-and-a-half-years after me was so much loved when I was not (Doris Lessing, "Impertinent Daughters," *Granta* 14 (1984): 52–68).

[34] Milton H. Horowitz describes a psychoanalytic case study that bears startling parallels with Lessing's narrative: A woman in midlife,

> fearful of her loss of sexual attractiveness, agitated by her scanty menstrual periods and approaching menopause, frightened of death[,] had a passionate interest in much younger men. She gave the highly plausible explanation that younger men were more sexually vigorous, had better bodies, made her feel more youthful, and put her in touch with younger people. . . . Behind the seemingly realistic story was a lifelong fantasy of being a boy like her adored younger brother who had always claimed her mother's love. This fantasy had been expressed in a variety of vastly different forms throughout life. A wishful self-image had been transformed into an object-choice ("The Developmental and Structural Viewpoints: On the Fate of Unconscious Fantasies in Middle Life," in Oldham and Liebert, *The Middle Years*, 14–15).

[35] Sarah's "descent" into the whirlpool, during which she confronts painful and long-forgotten emotional experiences, recalls several of Lessing's earlier novels, including *The Golden Notebook*, which records Anna Wulf's disintegration into several different "selves." The opening passage of *Briefing for a Descent into Hell* (New York: Knopf, 1971) describes the lost Charles Watkins going "around and around and around in the whirlpool-like currents of the Sargasso Sea" (26).

[36] Robert N. Butler, "The Life Review: An Interpretation of Reminiscence in the Aged," *Psychiatry* 26 (February 1963): 66, quoted in *Yearning for Yesterday: A Sociology of Nostalgia*, Fred Davis (New York: The Free Press, 1979), 69.

[37] Peter G. Coleman, *Aging and Reminiscence Processes* (New York: John Wiley, 1986), 12.

[38] The image recalls Kate Brown of Lessing's *The Summer Before the Dark*, who, after having an affair of the heart with a younger man, returns home to declare her acceptance of middle age by permitting her dyed hair to grow back in its natural gray.

[39] French, *A Season in Hell*, 219.

[40] The observation acquires additional poignancy in the light of French's agonizing struggle against esophageal cancer, diagnosed in 1992. She began to write *My Summer with George* during her recovery from multiple and nearly fatal complications precipitated by aggressive treatment for the disease (*A Season in Hell*, especially 187, 218–19).

[41] Collette V. Browne, *Women, Feminism, and Aging* (New York: Springer, 1998), 258.

AFTERWORD

"Feminism, Eros, and the Coming of Age" was prompted by the coincidence of publication during the same year (1996) of two novels by major writers of interest to feminists—Doris Lessing and Marilyn French—each featuring a self-sufficient female protagonist of late middle age who, despite her resistance, finds herself infatuated with a younger man or men. Lessing's *Love, Again: A Novel* and French's *My Summer with George: A Novel of Love at a Certain Age* led me to ponder both the rarity and the meaning of such narratives, in which independent, successful older women "fall in love," with all its physical and psychological consequences. What struck me as I wrote at the very cusp of the twenty-first century—from which pivotal moment it was irresistible to look both forward and backward—was how, on the one hand, the subject of women and age seemed to be of relatively little interest to both writers and feminists and how, on the other, three decades earlier in *The Coming of Age*, our essential foremother, Simone de Beauvoir, had presciently articulated critical dimensions of the subject that were still cogent.

With the exception of de Beauvoir, who was forty-one when *The Second Sex* was published in French and sixty-two when *The Coming of Age* appeared, the women who pioneered the discourses of the second wave of feminism during the 1970s were typically in their early professional years and were thus oriented toward issues pertinent to that stage of life: sexuality and reproductive rights, motherhood, economic and professional equity, equity in relationships. The subject of age and aging was, with a few exceptions, both invisible and taboo—our generation's version of Betty Friedan's "problem that has no name." Aging—to say nothing of midlife and the years beyond—was associated not with our experience but with that of our mothers who, living traditional lives, were models from whom we vowed to diverge radically in our own lives.

Following the galvanizing decade of the 1970s, the women's movement—having discarded the politically charged term "liberation," somewhere along the way—became less white/middle-class in its ideological and critical focus. During the 1980s and 1990s, scholarly inquiry evolved to encompass the heterogeneity of female experience, based on increased awareness that race, class, ethnicity, and sexual preference necessarily altered earlier totalizing assumptions about women. However, the category of age was the last to be included in this expanded analysis. Even now, as feminists who reached adulthood during the peak years of the second wave inevitably have reached later chronological milestones, there are still few alternative scripts to guide women through those "invisible" years and decades.

If our readings of literature are really opportunities to read ourselves, I should note that by the time I wrote this essay I had myself reached midlife and had begun to reflect on subjects that were invisible or inconsequential to me when I was younger. Concurrent with the essay included in this volume, I was working on a book—since published as *Home Matters: Longing and Belonging, Nostalgia and Mourning in Women's Fiction*—in which I explored representations of home and loss in contemporary fiction by women. In that book, I also considered whether the meaning of nostalgia was influenced by changes in women's opportunities and life experiences, including—for characters in novels by Paule Marshall (*Praisesong for the Widow*, 1983), Toni Morrison (*Jazz*, 1993), and Anne Tyler (*Ladder of Years*, 1995)—those that come with age. Though my Florence Howe award-winning essay is not part of the book, I was interested in common concerns in Lessing's and French's novels, including their characters' nostalgia and longing for youthful versions of themselves. Yet the authors' focus on white, professionally successful women who, despite their resistance, succumb to the pull of infatuation and desire for younger men only partly challenges the traditional social scripts for women during midlife and beyond.

Nearly a decade since Lessing and French published their novels (and since I wrote the essay), it seems as if not much has changed. It is true that marketers, television commercials, and popular magazines, attentive to the demographics of an aging population, now address beauty and health issues for older women, that the pharmaceutical industry earnestly pitches products toward older women's health concerns, and that Botox has become almost a household word. Nonetheless, it remains the case that women's aging seems to be resistant to literary representation. Serious literary treatment of the lives and concerns of women in midlife and beyond ("old age" and "elderly" are taboo terms; "senior" is hardly ever used in a favorable or empowering sense) remains a rarity. Inevitably, the second wave lapsed into a trough, to be replaced by the energetic third wave of feminists of our daughters' generation: young women who, understandably, are motivated by concerns appropriate to their different chronological position in our shared historical moment. Affirmative—rather than infirm—older women are still virtually invisible as protagonists in fiction written by women (Fay Weldon's *Rhode Island Blues* is an exception; see Rubenstein, "'Mirror'") or, for that matter, by men. Perhaps the dialogue between feminism, *eros*, and "the coming of age" remains minimal because there is one script from whose ending none of us—regardless of ideology, gender, race, class, ethnicity, or sexual preference—can be liberated. Like Doris Lessing's Sarah Durham and Marilyn French's Hermione Beldame, Weldon's eighty-three-year-old, life-affirming Felicity regards her image in the mirror on multiple occasions. Late in the narrative, considering whether or not to marry a man a decade her junior, she deciphers its truest message: "Time's short. Don't waste what's left" (293).

WORKS CITED

Beauvoir, Simone de. *The Coming of Age.* Trans. Patrick O'Brian. New York: Putnam, 1972.

———. *The Second Sex.* Trans. H. M. Parshley, 1952. New York: Knopf, 1993.

French, Marilyn. *My Summer with George: A Novel of Love at a Certain Age.* New York: Knopf, 1996.

Friedan, Betty. *The Feminine Mystique.* New York: Norton, 1963.

Lessing, Doris. *Love, Again: A Novel.* New York: HarperCollins, 1996.

Rubenstein, Roberta. *Home Matters: Longing and Belonging, Nostalgia and Mourning in Women's Fiction.* New York: Palgrave/St. Martin's, 2001.

———"'Mirror, Mirror on the Wall': Fay Weldon's Fairy Tale of Late Romance." *Adventures of the Spirit: The Older Woman in the Works of Doris Lessing, Margaret Atwood, and Other Contemporary Women Writers.* Ed. Phyllis Perrakis. Columbus: Ohio State UP, forthcoming.

Weldon, Fay. *Rhode Island Blues.* New York: Atlantic Monthly, 2000.

~ 2000 ~

Virginia Woolf's Two Bodies

Molly Hite

IN A FAMOUS PASSAGE in her unfinished autobiography "A Sketch of the Past," Virginia Woolf described her revulsion at seeing herself in a looking glass, and went on to contrast this experience with the hedonic sensuousness of some of her earliest childhood moments. While this passage has attracted attention as a description of a traumatic symptom, her ensuing comment tends to pass as a truism and furthermore as evidence of her notorious shrinking from physicality. In this comment Woolf wrote, "I could feel ecstasies and raptures spontaneously and intensely and without any shame or the least sense of guilt, so long as they were disconnected with my own body."[1]

I want to suggest that this formulation is strikingly odd. After all, where else would one feel "ecstasies and raptures" if not in one's own body? Of the possible answers, "the intellect" seems simply wrong and "the soul" anachronistic except as a metaphor for the more rarefied sorts of bodily sensations. Furthermore, such philosophically idealist accounts are alien to the precise renderings of physical sensation that Woolf offered in her work. As Lily Briscoe reflects in *To the Lighthouse*, "It was one's body feeling, not one's mind,"[2] and the fiction, essays and personal writings that Woolf produced during her lifetime present a spectrum of sentient and sensuous bodies. I want to suggest further, however, that in these writings, the bodies allowed the most unrestricted experience of ecstasies and raptures (as well as of loss and horror) are bodies of a different order than those seen in the mirror: that is, than the bodies consolidated by and for the gaze of others. In essence, Woolf represented and perhaps experienced two kinds of body. One kind was the body for others, the body cast in social roles and bound by the laws of social interaction. The other, however, was fundamentally new to modernist representation although arguably always an element of experience. One of Woolf's signal contributions to a distinctively female modernism was this female modernist body.

In effect this body was a second physical presence in fundamental respects different from the gendered body constituted by the dominant social order. This "visionary" body, a term I adopt following Woolf's own distinction between novels "of fact" and "of vision" was especially the subject of Woolf's most experimental modernist fiction.[3] In the first part of this essay I consider how this visionary body enabled Woolf to create passionate and sensuous female characters without embroiling them in the societal consequences of female eroticism that had shaped the romance plot.

On the other hand, the visionary body also added to the ambivalence Woolf seems to have felt toward her most successful foremothers, who for her were literary and corporeal progenitors—precedents both for female writing and for public presentation as a female body. In the second part of this essay I discuss how the visionary body could exacerbate as well as allay the tension between two important aspects of Woolf's early and middle-period writing—feminist literary politics and the call for a disinterested and impersonal modernist aesthetics. A number of studies have proposed that for Woolf, the feminist attempt to think "back through our mothers" called for in *A Room of One's Own* can be viewed as a supplement to her modernist attempt to think forward, *against* the Edwardian fathers singled out in such manifestoes as "Modern Fiction" and "Mr Bennett and Mrs Brown." One desirable result would be a female and feminist modernism, fueled equally by a political commitment to dismantling masculinist traditions and an emotional commitment to a sort of generalized pre-Oedipal mother and a maternal legacy of linguistic *jouissance* licensing avant-garde play with the material dimensions of language.[4] In presenting the visionary body as a tactic for writing female subjects into modernism, a modernism that in Woolf's most important theoretical formulations was not disembodied but rather predicated on the primacy of acute—and often covertly sexual—physical sensations, I too find affinities between Woolf's feminist and modernist projects. But feminist and modernist strains did not merge unproblematically in Woolf's writing, and in particular the figure of the mother was a site more of conflict than of reconciliation. In thinking "through" literary foremothers, Woolf was inevitably confronted with the vulnerability and complicity of the female body in society. Her ambivalence about traditions of women's writing derived at least in part from her awareness that a woman in public and on view is a woman available for denigration and exploitation. As her story of mute, inglorious Judith Shakespeare attests, literary history is a narrative about social, not visionary bodies.

The visionary body was clearly a means to evade a maternal precedent in which female sexuality was identified with Victorian and Edwardian plots—both literary and social—of heterosexual appropriation. In the third part of this essay, however, I suggest that the visionary body could be a desiring body only in a very restricted and metaphorical sense. Woolf explored the limits of this ostensibly extra-social body in the novel that marks both the high point and the end of her "visionary" experimental period. *The Waves* examines the tragedy inherent in the understanding that no desire can be recognized or sustained wholly outside the realm of the social. Even the visionary body is not just limited, but in the final analysis constituted, by requirements of social coherence and intelligibility.

The Visionary Body

We see one of the clearest distinctions between the visionary body and the female body in society near the close of Woolf's second novel, *Night and Day*, when Katharine Hilbery experiences herself as curiously, if exhilaratingly, divided:

> If Denham could have seen how visible books of algebraic symbols, pages all speckled with dots and dashes and twisted bars, came before her eyes as they trod the Embankment, his secret joy in her attention might have been dispersed. She went on, saying, 'Yes, I see. . . . but how would that help you? . . . Your brother has passed his examinations?' so sensibly, that he had constantly to keep his brain in check; and all the time she was in fancy looking through a telescope at white shadow-clefts which were other worlds, until she felt herself possessed of two bodies, one walking by the river with Denham, the other concentrated in a silver globe aloft in the fine blue space above the scum of vapours that was covering the visible world.[5]

The division here—between attentiveness to the conversation of Ralph Denham and yearning to pursue mathematics—is not figured as a division within Katharine's mind, vacillating between the mundane marital concerns of the romance plot and the allure of an exalted intellectual calling. Nor is the division figured as between Katharine's body, treading the Embankment beside an ardent suitor, *and* Katharine's mind, abstracted to the ideal status of a concentrated silver globe and adrift in a Platonic empyrean lit by algebraic symbols. Instead of availing herself of the conventions of two long philosophic traditions, Woolf had her narrator present the experience in different terms: "she felt herself possessed of two bodies. . . ." Woolf thus ascribed to a particular corporeal experience what the most familiar tradition of representation ascribes to mind or spirit: transcendence of the quotidian, access to "other worlds," and ability to "see" a realm of reality otherwise obscured by "the scum of vapours that was covering the visible world." Because Katharine's object of desire is pure mathematics, the Pythagorean ground of Platonism, we may be likely to read this passage in the classical terms of mind-body dualism. But the conceit of the two bodies is not accidental, nor is it particular to this example. Woolf did sustain a dualism through her writings, critical and autobiographical as well as fictional. But in her most interesting formulations of this dualism, both alternatives are embodied, although in very different kinds of body.

I have called the two kinds of body social and visionary. The social body walks Katharine Hilbery through the comic version of the romance plot with its sanctioned euphoric conclusion. The visionary body is the site of her most acute sensations (p. 116). Katharine views these sensations as explicitly opposed to poetry, the domain of her eminent (and Stephen-like) family and ancestors, and thus of social obligation. But the narrator of *Night and Day* intimates that her longings also reach for another kind of representation, one opposing Victorian aesthetics with "vision" and "aloofness," qualities that in the 1929 essay "Women and Fiction" Woolf urged for female literary production. In this essay, an alternate version of *A Room of One's Own*, she posited a literary future in which women would produce work that is not only "genuine" and "interesting" but possesses the hallmarks of her own modernist practice: "The woman writer will be able to concentrate upon her vision without distraction from outside. The aloofness that was once within the reach of genius and originality is only now coming within the reach of ordinary women."[6]

Such newly impersonal representation attempts to render what in the memoir "A Sketch of the Past" Woolf called "some real thing behind appearances," the visionary apprehension of "being" as opposed to the quotidian norm of "non-being," which she elaborated as "a kind of nondescript cotton wool" ("Sketch," pp. 70, 72). At one climax of Katharine and Ralph's lovemaking in *Night and Day*, mere romance yields to the apprehension of such a reality, in which stock nineteenth-century figures like "the flower of youth" are wittily literalized and abstracted into an up-to-date rendering of vegetable love. Ralph and Katharine conjoin their powers in a discussion of botany:

> Circumstances had long forced her, as they forced most women in the flower of youth, to consider painfully and infinitely all the part of life which is so conspicuously without order; she had had to consider moods, and wishes, degrees of liking or disliking, and their effect upon the destiny of people dear to her; she had been forced to deny herself any contemplation of that other part of life where thought constructs a destiny which is independent of human being. As Denham spoke, she followed his words and considered their bearing with an easy vigour which spoke of a capacity long hoarded and unspent. The very trees and the green merging into the blue distance became symbols of the vast external world which recks so little of the happiness, of the marriages or deaths of individuals. (pp. 281–82)

Here, science rather than mathematics stands in for a disinterested modernist aesthetics, in pointed contrast to the disorderly realm of female domestic obligation. The "vast external world" is not the most conventional "outside" of subjective consciousness, the world of human communities, but instead a vital, fundamentally other realm, the object of scientific and also artistic apprehension. This world, "which recks so little of the happiness, of the marriages or deaths of individuals" has affinities with the experience of that far from ordinary faculty "an ordinary mind on an ordinary day," which Woolf invokes in her modernist manifesto "Modern Fiction," published the same year as *Night and Day*. Although the mention of a mind most often connotes disembodiment, the Democritean language of this essay, equating "a myriad impressions—trivial, fantastic, evanescent, or engraved with the sharpness of steel" with "an incessant shower of innumerable atoms," on the contrary insists on the material nature of sensation, the inescapable organicism of this "mind"—*especially* in its visionary contacts with the "real" or "being."[7]

The difference between a "modern fiction" representing this kind of palpable experience and the "materialist" novels of the Edwardians that Woolf denounced in "Modern Fiction" has less to do with mind-body dualism than with the emphasis and values of Edwardian naturalism. The body represented in the "materialist" novels is embedded in social life. All its experiences have social consequences. By contrast, that sensitive organism the "ordinary mind on an ordinary day" is alone, absorbing and contemplating its "myriad impressions" without thereby either contracting to be married or being "ruined"—the two eminently social conclusions for the female body as the subject of nineteenth-century realist representation.[8] The visionary body is the body that experiences without social implications.

As I noted, Lily Briscoe makes the point directly: "It was one's body feeling, not one's mind." But the body that undergoes rapture or, as in Lily's case, intense sensations of loss is almost by definition out of social contact with other bodies. Having rid herself of the importunities of Mr. Ramsay, Lily at this point experiences her grief alone, except for her hypothetical empathy—unintrusive *because* hypothetical—with the drowsing and wholly silent Mr. Carmichael. A more dramatic case in point is Clarissa Dalloway's orgasmic meditation on the "sudden revelation, a tinge like a blush which one tried to check and then, as it spread, one yielded to its expansion, and rushed to the farthest verge and there quivered and felt the world come closer, swollen with some astonishing significance, some pressure of rapture, which split its thin skin and gushed and poured with an extraordinary alleviation over the cracks and sores!" The subject of this virtuoso enactment is the recollection of "yielding to the charm of a woman." The passage thus establishes both the sensuality and the lesbianism of Clarissa. Both qualities could make her vulnerable to social repercussions, aligning her with the abject Miss Kilman or the homoerotically bereaved and traumatized Septimus Smith. The text, however, insists on inviolability as Clarissa's defining feature, and this passage guarantees inviolability by triply framing the erotic experience. First of all, it is a recollection rather than a present event. Second, it is a recollection of a verbal rather than an explicitly sexual incident ("a woman confessing, as to her they often did, some scrape, some folly"). Finally, the sexuality of the narration is a by-product of metaphor and the phonic materiality of the language employed. As the narrator reports, Clarissa did "undoubtedly then feel what men felt," but on the level of plot the experience is unshared and unwitnessed, safely sealed within her physical body.[9]

A strikingly similar effect occurs in *To the Lighthouse* as Mrs. Ramsay watches the third stroke—the word is freighted—of the Lighthouse and is in turn stroked by the Lighthouse into an arousal and release that the syntax enacts as a series of phrases and clauses deferring and increasing pressure on the key verb "felt":

> but for all that she thought watching it with fascination, hypnotised, as if it were stroking with its silver fingers some sealed vessel in her brain whose bursting would flood her with delight, she had known happiness, exquisite happiness, intense happiness, and it silvered the rough waves a little more brightly, as daylight faded, and the blue went out of the sea and it rolled in waves of pure lemon which curved and swelled and broke upon the beach and the ecstasy burst in her eyes and waves of pure delight raced over the floor of her mind and she felt, It is enough! It is enough! (*Lighthouse*, pp. 64–65)

Here again, the excitement of the swelling and bursting "vessel" occurs in privacy. Mrs. Ramsay does have a witness, but the extent of Mr. Ramsay's misunderstanding— "She was aloof from him now in her beauty and sadness" (p. 65)—affirms that her ecstasy is solitary and invisible. Mrs. Ramsay is indeed aloof from her husband's concerns, but her apparent unhappiness shields an erotically charged abandon quite separate from the emotions of her marriage. Indeed, this scene stands in pointed contrast to the earlier moment in *To the Lighthouse* when, in a role-reversed parody of heterosexual intercourse, Mrs. Ramsay "poured erect into the air a rain of energy, a column of spray," fertilizing "the fatal sterility of the male" while at the same time depleting herself (p. 37)—a depletion, according to the logic of the text, that has something to do with her abrupt, parenthetical death in the next section. The two moments in "The Window" invite us to compare two distinct modes of sexuality. In the passage dealing with the strokes of the Light-house we see a metaphorized, linguistically incarnated sexuality that is hermeti-cally contained within the body. In the description of Mrs. Ramsay's "spraying" Mr. Ramsay, we observe a linguistically incarnated sexual performance that, in being shared, spends itself. The visionary body experiences rapture. The social body undergoes evacuation and, eventually, death.

It is of course no accident that the bodies in all these examples are women's bodies. In all the novels I have mentioned Woolf emphasizes the demands made on Victorian and Edwardian women by a society that regards their embodiment as license to exploit and exhaust. The social female body is a body at risk. Far more than her predecessors, Woolf seems to have developed conventions of rep-resentation for avoiding that risk. The visionary body of these two novels is an inspired solution to the problem of women's culturally sanctioned vulnerability. It is the body sealed off from social consequences, secure from interruption or invasion: a corporeal correlative of the room of one's own.

On Not Thinking Back through Our Mothers

These considerations on the construction of the visionary body suggest some rea-sons for Woolf's ambivalent attitude toward female literary antecedents, espe-cially antecedents of the immediately preceding, maternal generation.[10] Despite her culturally productive observation that "we think back through our mothers if we are women," Woolf repeatedly depicted women's writing as at a more rudi-mentary stage of development than men's writing. In "Women and Fiction," for instance, she dismissed women's writing of "the past" as at best characterized by "divine spontaneity," and more often "chattering and garrulous—mere talk, spilt over paper and left to dry in pools and blots" (p. 199). This image of previous female literary production as both social ("mere talk") and domestically incom-petent ("spilt," "left to dry in pools and blots") recalls the messy realm of female responsibility that Katharine Hilbery longs to escape, "the part of life which is so conspicuously without order." As an avatar of both modernity and modern-ism, Katharine seeks detachment and impersonality, "that other part of life where thought constructs a destiny which is independent of human being." In "Women and Fiction" that other part of life is the realm of art. Woolf predicted, "In fu-ture, granted time and books and a little space in the house for herself, literature will become for women, as for men, an art to be studied. Women's gift will be trained and strengthened. The novel will cease to be the dumping ground for the personal emotions" (p. 199). The mess, the disorder, the pools and blots, even the "divine spontaneity" are hallmarks of the female sphere of interrelationships, the drawing room where ladies poured tea, made conversation, and by definition did nothing that could not be interrupted.[11] In this populous room, associated always with women, art was precarious if not impossible. In Woolf's account, the writing coming out of such conditions was likely to be spontaneous self-expression, most often "a dumping ground for the personal emotions."

The arguments of both "Women and Fiction" and *A Room of One's Own* are materialist and evolutionary. In both, Woolf maintained that because historically women's lives have been severely constrained, women's writing has progressed gradually, keeping pace with gains in education and economic independence. In a 1920 exchange of letters with Desmond MacCarthy in the *New Statesman*, in which she contested the premise that women are intellectually inferior to men, Woolf pointed to

> the fact which stares me, and I should have thought any other impartial observer, in the face, that the seventeenth century produced more remarkable women than the sixteenth, the eighteenth than the seventeenth, and the nineteenth than all three together. When I compare the Duchess of Newcastle with Jane Austen, the matchless Orinda and Emily Brontë, Mrs Heywood with George Eliot, Aphra Behn with Charlotte Brontë, Jane Grey with Jane Harrison, the advance in intellectual power seems to me not only sensible but immense. . . .[12]

One underlying assumption of such a progress narrative, however, is that women's literary productions, if not women's intrinsic abilities, have been inferior to those of men.

"Women and Fiction," like *A Room of One's Own*, explicitly points toward the future, when a woman finally endowed with an income and a room of her own will climb out of the primal ooze of self-expression and onto the solid ground of artistry. This unnamed woman (who inevitably resembles Virginia Woolf) is represented as newly embodied, indeed as reincarnated. In *Room* she is a successful manifestation of Judith Shakespeare, the Renaissance woman of genius who was betrayed into exploitation, dishonor and suicide by her social female body: "who shall measure the heat and violence of the poet's heart when caught and tangled in a woman's body?" (*Room*, p. 50). Having died in the conflict between heart and body—that is, between two versions of the body, one enclosed and propitious to poetry, one exposed and available for exploitation—Judith Shakespeare becomes the revenant of *A Room of One's Own*. As the specter of a female genius who, in Woolf's ironic appropriation of contemporary geneticist arguments, cannot be "born" because material circumstances allow her no opportunity to develop her abilities, she haunts Woolf's literary history, in abeyance until that moment when she "will put on the body which she has so often laid down" (p. 118).

Given the association of deficient or unwritten literature with the vulnerability of the female body, it is not surprising that Woolf in her most negative criticism of previous and contemporary women writers laid special stress on physical appearance. In a draft of *A Room of One's Own* she cautioned, "I am not asking you simply to write 'the book of the year' & have your photograph in the evening paper. I am not asking you to cut a dash & figure in the papers as the well known Mrs. Smith whose latest book entirely eclipses everything she has ever written" (*Women and Fiction*, p. 172). The "well known Mrs. Smith" was by this time a stock figure of modernist representation, the woman writer whose popularity was a self-evident indicator of her mediocrity. Woolf's emphasis here, however, fell on the photograph in the paper and the correlative requirement to "cut a dash"—to assume the glamour and perhaps notoriety of that equivocal figure the public woman. When Woolf went on in this draft to try to specify what she was asking the aspiring female writer to do, she fumbled, finally abandoning this part of the discussion entirely: "No: I [literature in my] view [is no] does not [consist of a] I am asking you to undertake a far more difficult and [yet] I think [more] important enterprise" (*Women and Fiction*, p. 172).[13] The vehemence of the preceding negations suggests that she was far more confident about what literature is not and what the young woman desiring to be a writer should not do. Both are somehow wound up with not being in papers, not being photographed, not cutting a dash—in short, not being publicly available as a physical presence that could be the object of speculation and ridicule.

Critical tradition had already established that speculation and ridicule could link the physical female body to a body of work. Woolf observed of George Eliot, "Her big nose, her little eyes, her heavy, horsey head loom from behind the printed page and make a critic of the other sex uneasy." The postulated uneasiness of "the other sex"—quite possibly of her father, Sir Leslie Stephen, who had written a major biography of Eliot—clearly made Woolf uneasy as well, insinuating as it did that an unpleasing or threatening countenance could "loom from behind the printed page" to contaminate a male reader's apprehension of a female writer's work. Woolf herself was not immune to such effects. She described one writer of the maternal generation, the celebrated poet and journalist Alice Meynell as having "a face like that of a transfixed hare," an appearance that "somehow made one dislike the notion of women who write."[14]

When the physical body was conflated with a body of writing, one consequence was to guarantee without further evidence that a novel written by a woman was a "dumping-ground for the personal emotions." In her discussion of Charlotte Brontë in *A Room of One's Own*, Woolf took this consequence for granted, quoting Jane Eyre's "'Anybody may blame me who likes'" and then asking, "What were they blaming Charlotte Brontë for, I wondered"(*Room*, p. 71). The unexplained leap from character to author was one of the legacies of Brontë criticism, practiced with perhaps most persuasive authority by none other than Leslie Stephen, who maintained that Charlotte Brontë never wrote about anything *but* herself: "In no books is the author more completely incarnated. She is the heroine of her two most powerful novels. . . . Her experience, we might say, has been scarcely transformed in passing through her mind." By a neat twist of tautology in Stephen's account, the presumption that the experience of the writer had to be the untransformed substance of her novels became the primary ground for relegating her to the rank of minor writer. Woolf took over the presumption, albeit with more sympathy, in *A Room of One's Own*, where her identification of an "awkward break" in *Jane Eyre* became the founding moment for reading Brontë's narrative inventiveness as evidence of flawed technique. Woolf discerned this "break" in the passage where "Grace Poole's laugh" interrupts Jane Eyre's denunciation of contemporary gender norms: "Anyone may blame me who likes" (*Room*, p. 71). Of course, the laugh comes not from the servant Grace Poole but from the imprisoned "mad" wife of Mr. Rochester. It rips through the fabric of Jane's rebellious meditation as a minatory foreshadowing of how society construes—and deals with—female insubordination.[15] Woolf's decontextualized reading isolated the passage, presupposed its inadvertent and anomalous character, and then used it to inaugurate a series of analogical displacements. Through these displacements, the narrating character's meditation became Charlotte Brontë's own anger bursting through narratorial conventions ("She will write of herself when she should write of her characters"); authorial anger became a metonymy for grotesquely defective writing ("Her books will be deformed and twisted"); and the mutilation of writing became equivalent to mutilation of the physical body, so that in effect Brontë was killed by her own prose ("How could she help but die young, cramped and thwarted?") (*Room*, pp. 72–73).

Woolf's representation of her foremothers entirely as social bodies seems associated with an unease about mothers in general. In "A Sketch of the Past" she described the body of her own mother, Julia Jackson Stephen, as a source of both ecstasy and trauma. Julia's physical presence provoked in the infant Virginia a euphoria simultaneously sensuous and ego-less: "I am hardly aware of myself but only of the sensation. I am only the container of the feeling of ecstasy, of the feeling of rapture" (p. 67). But precisely in her role as superabundant maternal presence, Julia Stephen also created an atmosphere of feminine deference and sacrifice that implicitly authorized masculine dominance. "She was a hero worshipper, simple, uncritical, enthusiastic," Woolf reported of her antifeminist mother (p. 9), and indeed her mother was one prototype of the Angel in the House, whom Woolf, in the 1931 essay "Professions for Women," represented as counseling "Be sympathetic; be tender; flatter; deceive; use all the arts and wiles of our sex. Never let anybody guess you have a mind of your own. Above all, be pure." Woolf went on in this speech to relate her own purported response: "I turned upon her and caught her by the throat. . . . Had I not killed her she would have killed me. She would have plucked the heart out of my writing." During Virginia's own adolescence and young womanhood, however, the influence of the Angel prevailed, and if she did not pluck the heart out of her daughter's writing she was instrumental in abstracting one sort of body from it, in that her precepts and example fostered compliance with the emotional demands of an overbearing father and the sexual demands of two predatory half-brothers.[16]

These humiliations and violations to the body of the female writer, equivocally endorsed by the ghost of her mother, suggest what grounds Woolf perceived for a wariness about the influence of female precursors. This wariness complicated both her defense of women writers in *A Room of One's Own* and her attack on the male Edwardians in "Modern Fiction" and "Mr Bennett and Mrs Brown." In an impassioned passage in *A Room of One's Own* she urged, "It is fatal for a woman to lay the least stress on any grievance; to plead even with justice any cause; in any way to speak consciously as a woman" (p. 108). She used similarly charged rhetoric in "Mr. Bennett and Mrs. Brown" when she wrote as a modernist of the characteristic devices of Bennett, Wells and Galsworthy: "For us those conventions are ruin, those tools are death" (*Essays v. 3*, pp. 430–31). Such injunctions poised the emergent female modernist between fatalities, prohibiting her from the political discourse of "grievance" and "cause" as well as from the representational strategies and social themes of Edwardian naturalism. Woolf seemed to enjoin aspiring women writers both to make it new and to be wholly unself-conscious about the project. The kinds of "smashing and . . . crashing" that in "Mr Bennett and Mrs Brown" she associated with Joyce and Eliot (p. 433) were off-limits to Mary Carmichael, who was urged with another set of metaphors for physical exertion: "it was her trial to take her fence without looking to right or left. If you stop to curse you are lost, I said to her; equally, if you stop to laugh. Hesitate or fumble and you are done for" (*Room*, p. 97). The incipient female modernist had to achieve a concentration amounting to tunnel vision, ignoring both her position as a woman in society and her status as a challenger to past literary traditions.

Such extreme restrictions seem aimed at giving the writer herself a sort of visionary body, a public persona not subject to the ridicule aimed at women writers of "the past." The bargain here appears to entail achieving moments of being by eschewing moments of polemic and satire. Yet Woolf herself never followed these rules. The brilliance of her middle-period novels stems from her ability to merge the visionary apprehension of "things in themselves" with biting social commentary, particularly commentary about women's contradictory social identities. Her creation of the visionary body seems less a means to supplant curses and laughter with high-minded approaches to metaphysical reality than a strategy to embed feminist critique in a much broader critique of the dominant social—and in the most conventional literary sense, "realist"—presuppositions about reality. By giving female characters this visionary body, Woolf actively distanced herself from her foremothers' domain, the combination of Victorian public and private spheres that defined the fictional universe of the realist novel.

Bodies, Passions and So On

In the allegory of the creative imagination presented in a 1931 speech that became the essay "Professions for Women," Woolf offered a striking depiction of the sexual female body. Connected to the decorously dressed female novelist by a fishing line identified as "a thread of reason," the imagination is a naked young woman who swims into "the world that lies submerged in our unconscious being" in order to "feed unfettered upon every crumb of [the writer's] experience." This libidinal nymph has appetites frequently at odds with the counsels of buttoned-up reason, and Woolf figured their clashes with hilariously erotic metaphors suggesting that social mores produce something like sexual frustration in the woman writer trying to use the full extent of her powers. In the first story of these two female figures, the imagination suffers a full-body detumescence because the novelist has given her too little experience to work with, floating "limply and dully and lifelessly upon the surface" and responding "rather tartly and disagreeably" to the novelist's questions while "pulling on its stockings." In the second story, reason restrains the imagination from darting "heaven knows where—into what dark pool of extraordinary experience," and on pulling the naked diver to the surface expostulates, "My dear you were going altogether too far. Men would be shocked," while the imagination "sits panting on the bank—panting with rage and disappointment." The novelist goes on,

> We have only got to wait fifty years or so. In fifty years I shall be able to use all this very queer knowledge that you are ready to bring me. But not now. You see I go on, trying to calm her, I cannot make use of what you tell me—about womens bodies for instance—their passions—and so on, because the conventions are still very strong. If I were to overcome the conventions I should need the courage of a hero, and I am not a hero.[17]

In this account, sexual desire is central to the female artist's work, and frustration of this desire is frustration *of* creativity. Yet "all this very queer knowledge . . . about womens bodies for instance—their passions—and so on" (at least some of it knowledge *of* queer passion, as the lesbian desires of a large number of "visionary" protagonists indicate) is off-limits as a subject of direct representation. Invoking once again the Charlotte Brontë principle whereby the discourse of "grievance"and "cause" maims the body of the writer, Woolf's speaker threatens the imagination with grotesque impotence. Noting that even a man like D. H. Lawrence injures his imagination by trying consciously to oppose the conventions, she maintains, "She becomes shrivelled and distorted; and you would not like to become shrivelled and distorted, would you?" The lesson is clear in Woolf's own case. Inasmuch as women's bodies and passions inform the novels "of vision," they do so in the absence of contact with other passionate bodies.

One of the most playful evocations of this principle occurs in *Orlando*, with the chapter chronicling the advent of that Bloomsbury bogey the Victorian era. Previously licensed by her publicly undecidable gender to enjoy some masculine privileges even when endowed with "female" biological characteristics, Orlando is for the first time seized by shame and, apparently as a concomitant effect of this shame, by an arousal befitting the age:

> she became conscious, as she stood at the window, of an extraordinary tingling and vibration all over her, as if she were made of a thousand wires upon which some breeze or errant fingers were playing scales. Now her toes tingled; now her marrow. She had the queerest sensation about the thigh bones. Her hairs seemed to erect themselves. Her arms sang and twanged as the telegraph wires would be singing and twanging in twenty years or so. But all this agitation seemed at length to concentrate in her hands; and then in one hand, and then in one finger of that hand, and then finally to contract itself so that it made a ring of quivering sensibility about the second finger of the left hand.[18]

In this parody of orthodox sexual maturation, Orlando seems to proceed from a state of unfocused bodily excitement to an increasingly localized, "genital" eroticism, except that her clitoral/phallic organ of desire is the ring finger, now experienced as acutely in want of a wedding ring. The bisexual or, perhaps more accurately, omnisexual protagonist is reined in by monogamous heterosexuality, which is defined as both culturally constructed ("they were somehow stuck together, couple after couple, but who had made it, and when, she could not guess. It did not seem to be Nature" [p. 242]), and specific to a particular historical period in which society mandated both reproductive and literary fecundity (pp. 229–30).

Yet the narrative of her relations with her adroitly acquired husband is as chaste as the tendentious and sentimental poetry that pours unbidden from her pen as if in illustration of how not only the novel can be a "dumping ground for the personal emotions." It is Orlando's life, rather than writing, that becomes a Charlotte Brontë novel, complete with the conveniently *Villette*-like dénouement of a husband who goes off to sea, thus allowing the heroine the maximum flexibility possible within Victorian requirements of femininity, by enabling her to occupy simultaneously the roles of single and married woman. This witty manipulating of wish-fulfillment within the confines of sanctioned heterosexual romance suggests that for Woolf, the visionary body of her modernist experiments offered a way not only around "the conventions" of decorous representation, but also around nineteenth-century narrative conventions that ruthlessly channeled female desire into the marriage plot.

Some of her most famous calls for a new kind of novel indicate that she found this enforced narrowing of female desire especially irritating, and that the visionary or impersonal alternative paradoxically allowed desire to multiply its objects. In the 1931 essay "The Narrow Bridge of Art," for instance, where she made essentially the same distinction between novels of vision and of fact as in her later comments on *The Waves* and *The Pargiters*, she called for a novel portraying "some more impersonal relationship" that fulfills the reader's longing "for ideas, for dreams, for imaginations, for poetry": qualities that seem at an opposite extreme from representations of women's bodies and passions. Her description in this essay of what such a novel should *not* be, however, is subtly but unmistakably gendered: "The psychological novelist has been too prone to limit psychology to the psychology of personal intercourse; we long sometimes to escape from the incessant, the remorseless analysis of falling into love and falling out of love, of what Tom feels for Judith and Judith does or does not altogether feel for Tom."[19] In terms of this rhetoric, not only "we" as readers but also "we" as writers are sick of the romance plot, which not only limits the female protagonist to the conventional goal of marriage, but traps her within the power imbalance of normative wooing and winning.

Woolf worked with this plot and its attendant power imbalance in her own first two novels. Confronted with what Terence Hewit feels for her, and aided by an aunt who acts as her surrogate mother, Rachel Vinrace in *The Voyage Out* enters into a system that translates her inchoate emotions into socially sanctioned desires. Like the simultaneously monstrous and miraculous undersea creatures with whom she is aligned as she begins her voyage into public identity, she cannot survive the pressure of being brought "out" and seems uncannily to die of the process of individuation necessary to establish her in Terence's gaze as "a body with the angles and hollows of a young woman's body not yet developed, but in no way distorted, and thus interesting and even lovable" (p. 227). In *Night and Day*, the attempt of Katharine Hilbery to discern what she does or does not altogether feel for Ralph Denham is bound up with her struggle to avoid an extension of conventional daughterhood into conventional wifehood. It is her mother who finally persuades the couple to become engaged, in a social milieu in which "engaged" is the only respectable name for the situation of a young woman who has passed her previous fiancé to a cousin and is contemplating a life devoted to mathematics. The happy ending (which most critics have found unsatisfactory) derives from the premise that Katharine can enter into a marriage without being translated back into the feminine realm of mess and servitude—that is, that she can sustain the division into "two bodies" indefinitely, never allowing the social to overcome the visionary.[20]

In these two stories of daughters who are to a greater or lesser extent, respectively, done in by a marriage plot that a mother figure implements, Woolf seems not only to have exhausted the potential of heterosexual romance for her fiction, but also to have written into this fiction her suspicion of mothers, both literary and literal. In *The Waves*, the novel that apotheosizes her "visionary" period, her six characters are presented in a vacuum of family and wholly in relation to each other, even in their early youth. For the most part, they are also presented in a vacuum of contact, their inviolability guaranteed by a mode of first-person, present-tense narration that shows them not acting and interacting, but instead providing ongoing accounts of their actions and interactions: "I stand with my back to you fidgeting," "I pad about the house all day long in apron and slippers, like my mother who died of cancer."[21] Far from being disembodied, however, these "speeches" are preoccupied with visceral sensation, from the synesthetic rendering of Jinny's first sip of wine—"Scent and flowers, radiance and heat, are distilled here to a fiery, to a yellow liquid" (p. 103)—to Bernard's account of individuation as the "bright arrows of sensation" produced by a wet bath sponge squeezed over a young body (pp. 26, 157, 239). But the sensations are confined to the individual bodies. The moments of heightened intensity set no romance plots in motion, and the spectacle that confounded Orlando, of heterosexual couples stuck permanently together, is banished to an altogether different kind of novel.[22]

Given the apparent security afforded to characters by this "visionary" mode of narration, we should not be surprised that in *The Waves* Woolf wrote her most nearly direct representation of female sexual arousal. In this account, the adolescent Rhoda reads a poem that provokes a longing at first pressing to the point of pain, then released in a (by now familiar) burst of liquidity:

> I will pick flowers; I will bind flowers in one garland and clasp them and present them—Oh! To whom? There is some check in the flow of my being; a deep stream presses on some obstacle; it jerks, it tugs, some knot in the center resists. Oh, this is pain, this is anguish! I faint, I fail. Now my body thaws; I am unsealed, I am incandescent. Now the stream pours in a deep tide fertilising, opening the shut, forcing the tight-folded, flooding free. To whom shall I give all that now flows through me, from my warm, my porous body? I will gather my flowers and present them—Oh! To whom? (p. 57)

The most obvious difference between this rendering of the visionary body and the descriptions in *Mrs. Dalloway* and *To the Lighthouse* is that the orgasmic cry expresses not fulfillment ("gushed and poured with an extraordinary alleviation over the cracks and sores!" "It is enough!") but desire in search of an object. Rhoda finds in Shelley's poem "The Question" her own cry of longing, "Oh! To whom?" This cry suggests that her object of desire is as yet undiscovered and, in context, that she is attracted primarily to women. These longings not only dare not speak their name but are culturally unintelligible in the fictional universe Rhoda inhabits. In the world of *The Waves*, gender dichotomies are far more rigid and defining than in any other of Woolf's novels. For example, all the male speakers have public lives—and all are writers. In contrast, not one of the female speakers tries to occupy a place in the public sphere or to be any sort of artist. Rather, each to some extent embodies a stereotype of conventional femininity: Susan as earth mother, Jinny as seductress, Rhoda as neurotic. And whereas Neville's homosexuality can claim an honorable classical tradition at Cambridge, Rhoda lives in a world where female homosexuality is unnamed and apparently unrecognized.

Passionately attracted to her headmistress (p. 45) and, in the drafts, to various other girls, Rhoda is, in terms Judith Butler has posed, precariously situated in a world where an assumption of normative heterosexuality undergirds gender polarities.[23] Unlike Clarissa Dalloway, Rhoda cannot reconcile her homoeroticism with an adjustment to conventional notions of femininity. Her love is never defined and never requited. She does not know "to whom" she wants to give herself because her desires are not representable in the aggressively heteronormative culture of the fictional universe. One radical corollary is that she has in the strict sense no "end in view," no teleology to draw succeeding moments into a chain of means and ends, wish and fulfillment:

> Because you have an end in view—one person, is it, to sit beside, an idea is it, your beauty is it? I do not know—your days and hours pass like the boughs of forest trees and the smooth green of forest rides to a hound running on the scent. But there is no single scent, no single body for me to follow. And I have no face. (p. 130)

Under the gaze of others she does not manifest a consolidated identity, a face to meet the faces that she meets. Rather, as if anticipating the thesis of *Gender Trouble*, she sees gendered identity in terms of distinct performances. She mimics Jinny and Susan as they dress (p. 43) and reads stability and coherence as a particular set of discursive actions and interactions: "They say, Yes; they say, No; they bring their fists down with a bang on the table" (p. 106).

At least partly because Rhoda lacks a recognizable object of desire, she does not experience time as continuous: as a passage through futurity guided by consciousness seeking its posited fulfillment. Instead, she is subjected to the "shock of sensation" in discrete, apocalyptic moments: "One moment does not lead to another. The door opens and the tiger leaps" (p. 130). Unlike Woolf herself, who wrote memorably that each disruptive "shock" of her most profound experiences was both "a token of some real thing behind appearances" and also (somewhat paradoxically) a thing she made real "by putting it into words," Rhoda produces no art that such painful illuminations might foster ("Sketch," pp. 71–72). Her long-ings lead to neither erotic nor aesthetic goals. In certain respects her terror is a privileged mode of apprehension because it lays bare a contingent reality beneath the reassuring succession imposed by individual human wants and plans. Further, it reveals that the coherent self is only an illusion produced by repeated perfor-mances. But the already-conceptualized, already-gendered fictional universe she inhabits has no room for such radical truths, at least not when voiced by a female misfit. In the social world of the novel, her unintelligible desires manifest a failure to achieve identity—although her own formulation, "Identity failed me" (p. 64), suggests the insufficiency of the category as well, an insufficiency consonant with Woolf's own frequently voiced discomfort with and aesthetic dislike of "ego" or the "self" (*Diary*, *v.* 2, p. 14). As a result, Rhoda functions in terms of the subnormal or even the subhuman: as maladjusted, inadequate, and thus "lacking a sense of proportion"—to invoke the terminology Woolf lampooned bitterly in *Mrs. Dallo-way*. Her vatic function is both recognized and read as symptomatic—for example, in Neville's question (which celebrates his own adjustment to the conditions of every-day social reality), "Why ask, like Louis, for a reason, or fly like Rhoda to some far grove and part the leaves of the laurels and look for statues?" (pp. 197–98).

When she can, Rhoda holds time together by dreaming of a world devoid of people. She turns to her imaginary landscapes especially when pressed by the het-erosexual social obligations attendant on her status as a middle-class woman: "I must take his hand; I must answer. But what answer shall I give? I am thrust back to stand burning in this clumsy, this ill-fitting body, to receive the shafts of his in-difference and his scorn, I who longed for marble columns and pools on the other side of the world where the swallow dips her wings" (p. 105). Her terror at the gendered requirements of an evening party, and particularly her discomfort with her "clumsy" and "ill-fitting" body, emphasize that her private erotic yearnings have social consequences. Unlike Clarissa Dalloway's metaphorized and memori-alized relationships, and unlike Mrs. Ramsay's intimacy with the inanimate "third stroke" of the Lighthouse, her ardent and anguished cry, "Oh, to whom?" reaches out for present intimacy with another body. While her lack of an "end in view" guarantees her fragmentary and unstable identity, her fear and loathing of exist-ing social arrangements— "Life, how I have dreaded you . . . oh, human beings, how I have hated you!" (p. 203)—lead to her suicide.

For Woolf, then, when scenes involving the visionary body moved too close to direct representation of "womens bodies . . . their passions—and so on," society reappeared to claim women for its own purposes—or to reject them as maladapted to its definitions of desire and identity. Rhoda goes beyond the accommodations of her lesbian-inflected predecessors in directing her desires outward rather than transforming them into the experiences of a second, visionary body. As a casu-alty of her social universe, she is only indirectly redeemed by the suggestion that her own life is part of a larger character in which all six speakers participate: one petal of Bernard's seven-sided flower; one self of Woolf's "autobiography" (*Waves*, p. 127; *Diary*, v. 3, p. 229). The overt representation of female sexuality in Woolf's most visionary novel returns the female body to social discipline.

In this respect *The Waves* anticipates the turn to "fact" that Woolf theorized when she began writing *The Pargiters*, the novel-essay in which she dealt most directly with bodies, passions and their less pleasant consequences. In *The Pargiters* a ten-year-old girl sees a man exposing himself and prompts the authorial narrator to write not only about the "curiosity and physical fear" the sight arouses, but also about "the instinct to turn away and hide the physical experience" in both little girl and grown novelist—an "instinct" unnervingly "supported by law, which forbids, whether rightly or wrongly, any plain description of the sight that Rose, in common with many other little girls, saw . . ." (pp. 50, 51). In *The Pargiters*, too, Woolf explicitly satirized Victorian (and later) conditioning of girls' sexual desire into "a furtive, ill-grown, secret, subterranean vice, to be concealed in shame, until by some fortunate chance, a man gave the girl a chance, by putting a wedding ring on her finger, to canalise all her passion solely upon him" (p. 110). The format of the novel-essay enabled her to focus on "the conventions" that were "too strong" for the buttoned-up writer depicted in the draft of "Professions for Woman." But in explaining how the social female body was constrained, maimed and thwarted of its desires, she turned away from her original strategy for representing arousal, yearning and fulfillment. The social body could experience only culturally-constructed longings.

In the last novels she treated these longings with sympathy as well as wit, but the point of view is external and the ecstasies and raptures are gingerly postulated rather than evoked in ecstatic, rapturous language. Delia Pargiter, who in *The Years* dreams of assignations with the Irish nationalist leader Parnell, and Isa Oliver, who in *Between the Acts* has vague sexual fantasies about a gentleman farmer in her neighborhood, are in this respect latter-day Emma Bovaries, who crave the idealized heterosexual romance common in the sort of fiction written by "the well known Mrs. Smith." The satirical edge is sharper in these late novels, in keeping with a national and even global range of political engagement. There is commensurately less of the oscillation of reader identification and disidentification that constitutes the empathetic-ironic tone of the middle-period novels. The logic of the novel "of vision," as it played out in *The Waves*, apparently brought Woolf back to the situation of the female body in society at a time when she had a strong interest in that body and in the society that shaped its possibilities. As Carolyn Heilbrun has observed, in beginning *The Pargiters* Woolf made a conscious decision not only to explore and express her political commitments, particularly her feminist commitments, but also to cross her self-drawn line between art and "propaganda."[24] In *The Pargiters*, *The Years* and *Between the Acts*, she dealt directly with the societal manufacture of desire and with social implications of adultery, homosexuality and various forms of voluntary and involuntary celibacy. This focus on "fact" mandated a different tone and a different narratorial position with regard to characters. It offered little occasion for evoking the felt experience of a body isolated and safe in its sensuous responses.

But the explicit political emphasis of these novels "of fact" retrospectively clarifies aspects of the novels "of vision," revealing how the visionary body was a political as well as an aesthetic strategy of representation, another means of circumventing conventions of decorum for female behavior and characterization. At the beginning of this essay I dissociated Woolf's two modes of experience from the familiar Western construct of mind-body dualism. The concept of a person with two bodies has its own tradition in European culture, however: a tradition more political than metaphysical. Like the public and private bodies of the King in the medieval doctrine of the King's Two Bodies, the notion of two female bodies was a strategy addressing problems of political order and continuity. But whereas the King's public body was decreed by law to survive disidentifying crises, from deposing to beheading ("the King is dead; long live the King!"), Woolf's visionary body was designed to help evade the snares that identity set for the middle-class English woman, offering an inviolable place for momentary but definitive experience. And whereas the King's public body was invented to maintain an established order in the face of change, Woolf's visionary body undermined this order, asserting its own desires in the interstices of official doctrines of ancillary femininity and heterosexuality.[25]

In proposing that Woolf wrote—and perhaps experienced—two kinds of body, I enter a long-standing and sometimes virulent controversy about Woolf's attitudes toward sexuality and toward physical experience generally. A number of critics, from Woolf's contemporaries to the present day, have regarded the prose and to some degree the woman as "disembodied"—that is, as preoccupied with transcendent and unworldly things and correspondingly alienated from or overtly hostile to everyday social life, especially the sloppy region of sensual and sexual experience.[26] In maintaining that the novel "of vision" was not for Woolf a realm of incorporeality but, on the contrary, a mode of representing female eroticism and other sensations without social consequences, I suggest a way to acknowledge the libidinal effects and contents of her middle-period fiction without denying the power of what in "A Sketch of the Past" she called "reality," the momentarily experienced "other orders" beyond the sanctioned and the habitual.

NOTES

I am grateful for suggestions by Talia Schaffer, Marianne DeKoven, Susan Stanford Friedman, Christine Froula and Ann Kibbey, all of which vastly improved this essay.

[1] "A Sketch of the Past," *Moments of Being: Unpublished Autobiographical Writings*, ed. Jeanne Schuylkind (New York and London: Harcourt Brace Jovanovich, 1976), p. 68. Further references to this work will be included parenthetically in the text.

[2] *To the Lighthouse* (New York: Harcourt Brace & Co., 1978), p. 178. Further page citations will refer to this edition and will appear within parentheses in the body of the essay.

[3] *The Diary of Virginia Woolf, v. 4: 1931–1935*, ed. Anne Olivier Bell with Andrew McNeillie (San Diego: Harcourt Brace Jovanovich, 1980), p. 151. Although Woolf had opposed fact to vision in other contexts, she only began using the term to distinguish between two modes of her own writing when she was in the process of composing *The Pargiters*, the innovative novel-essay that ultimately became two distinct works, the novel *The Years* and the essay *Three Guineas*. While in the above diary entry she wrote that *The Pargiters* was supposed to "combine them both," she went on to specify in the First Essay of *The Pargiters*, "'The Pargiters,' moreover, is not a novel of vision, but a novel of fact." See *The Pargiters: The Novel-Essay Portion of The Years*, ed. Mitchell A. Leaska (New York: New York Public Library and Readex Books, 1977), p. 9. In the April 1933 diary entry she made her most recently completed novel, *The Waves*, emblematic

of the novel of vision. Most critics have followed her implicit lead in regarding the famous, characteristically modernist novels, most of those of her middle period, as novels "of vision": *Jacob's Room, Mrs. Dalloway, To the Lighthouse* and *The Waves. Orlando* seems to fall outside both categories. See especially Alice Van Buren Kelley, *The Novels of Virginia Woolf: Fact and Vision* (Chicago: U of Chicago P, 1973).

⁴For feminist modernism, see especially Sandra Gilbert and Susan Gubar, *No Man's Land, v. 1: The War of the Words* (New Haven: Yale UP, 1988), Jane Marcus, *Virginia Woolf and the Languages of Patriarchy* (Bloomington: Indiana UP, 1987) and Bonnie Kime Scott, *Refiguring Modernism, v. 2: Postmodern Feminist Readings of Woolf, West and Barnes* (Bloomington: Indiana UP, 1995). For psychoanalytic feminist readings see especially Makiko Minow-Pinkney, *Virginia Woolf and the Problem of the Subject: Feminine Writing in the Major Novels* (New Brunswick: Rutgers UP, 1987) and Margaret Homans, *Bearing the Word: Language and Female Experience in Nineteenth-Century Women's Writing* (Chicago: U of Chicago P, 1986). The most important theoretical grounding for such readings is Julia Kristeva, *Revolution in Poetic Language*, trans. Leon S. Roudiez (New York: Columbia UP, 1984) and "Motherhood According to Bellini" in Kristeva, *Desire in Language: A Semiotic Approach to Literature and Art*, trans. Thomas Gora, Alice Jardine and Leon S. Roudier (New York: Columbia UP, 1980). For criticism of ways Freudian and Kristevan premises are used in reading Woolf, see Mary Jacobus, "'The Third Stroke': Reading Woolf With Freud," *Virginia Woolf*, ed. Rachel Bowlby (London: Longmans, 1992), pp. 102–120, and Lyndsey Stonebridge, *The Destructive Element: British Psychoanalysis and Modernism* (London: Routledge, 1998), pp. 79–107. The central study of Woolf's historical relation to psychoanalysis is Elizabeth Abel, *Virginia Woolf and the Fictions of Psychoanalysis* (Chicago: U of Chicago P, 1989).

⁵*Night and Day*, ed Julia Briggs (London: Penguin, 1992), p. 254. Further references to this work will be included parenthetically in the text.

⁶"Women and Fiction" was first published in *The Forum*, March 1929; rpt. in *Women and Fiction: The Manuscript Versions of 'A Room of One's Own'*, ed. S. P. Rosenbaum (Cambridge: Shakespeare Head/Blackwell, 1992), p. 48. On the Stephen family, see S.P. Rosenbaum, *Victorian Bloomsbury* (New York: St. Martin's, 1986) and Hermione Lee, *Virginia Woolf* (New York: Alfred A. Knopf, 1997).

⁷I take the quotation from the *Common Reader* revision, published as "Modern Novels" in *The Essays of Virginia Woolf, v. 4: 1925–1928*, ed. Andrew McNeillie (London: Hogarth, 1987), p. 160.

⁸For the (heterosexual) romance plot see Nancy Miller, *The Heroine's Text: Reading the French and English Novel, 1772–1782* (New York: Columbia UP, 1980), and Rachel Blau DuPlessis, *Writing Beyond the Ending: Narrative Strategies of Twentieth-Century Women Writers* (Bloomington: Indiana UP, 1985).

⁹*Mrs. Dalloway* (New York: Harcourt Brace & Co., 1990), p. 32. Further references to this work will be included parenthetically in the text. Septimus is also an example of a male body menaced through its incommensurate relation to social norms of gender and identity. His precariously middle-class status, one step from his working-class origins, makes him particularly vulnerable to social repercussions. But in his roles as seer and satirist ("They hunt in packs," [p. 89]) as well as his suggested homosexuality, he looks forward to Rhoda in *The Waves*.

¹⁰For the positive side of Woolf's relation to maternal figures see Jane Marcus's groundbreaking essay "Thinking Back through Our Mothers" in *Art and Anger: Reading Like a Woman* (Columbus: Ohio State UP, 1988), pp. 73–100. For an overview of the negative aspects see especially Sandra Gilbert and Susan Gubar, *No Man's Land, Volume 1: The War of the Words* (New Haven: Yale UP, 1988), pp. 165–224.

¹¹"A Sketch of the Past," pp. 129–30; *A Room of One's Own* (New York: Harcourt, Brace, Jovanovich, 1979), pp. 69–71.

¹²"The Intellectual Status of Women," *Virginia Woolf: Women and Writing*, ed. Michèle Barrett (New York: Harcourt Brace Jovanovich, 1979), pp. 55–56.

¹³In this respect, as in others, Woolf participated in the dominant high modernist tendency to feminize popular culture. See especially Andreas Huyssen, "Mass Culture as Woman: 'Modern-

ism's Other,'" *After the Great Divide: Modernism, Mass Culture, Postmodernism* (Bloomington: Indiana UP, 1986), pp. 44–62. For a contemporaneous feminist assessment of the "public woman," see Anonymous (Elizabeth Robins), *Ancilla's Share: An Indictment of Sex Antagonism* (Westport: Hyperion Press, 1976), p. 76. In the quotation from the draft of *A Room of One's Own*, I have put within brackets those passages that were crossed out in the manuscript.

14 Talia Schaffer first pointed out the Meynell reference to me in *A Passionate Apprentice: The Early Journals: 1897–1909*, ed. Mitchell A. Leaska (New York: Harcourt Brace Jovanovich, 1990), p. 398. Woolf's comment on George Eliot is from *The Essays of Virginia Woolf, v. 3*, p. 460. Sir Leslie Stephen, *George Eliot* (London: MacMillan, 1902). See also Elizabeth Robins's contemporary evaluation of this biography in *Way Stations* (New York: Dodd, Mead and Co., 1913) and Alison Booth, *Greatness Engendered: George Eliot and Virginia Woolf* (Ithaca: Cornell UP, 1992).

15 Sir Leslie Stephen, "Charlotte Brontë," *Hours in a Library, v. 3* (London: Smith, Elder and Co., 1892), p. 7. The classic reading of *Jane Eyre's* madwoman is Sandra Gilbert and Susan Gubar, *The Madwoman in the Attic: The Woman Writer and the Nineteenth-Century Literary Imagination* (New Haven: Yale UP, 1987), pp. 336–371.

16 "Professions for Women," *Women and Writing*, p. 103. "Sketch," pp. 68–69, 129, 125; "22 Hyde Park Gate" in *Moments of Being*, p. 155.

17 Essay 1, *The Pargiters*, pp. xxxviii–xxxix.

18 Virginia Woolf, *Orlando* (San Diego: Harcourt Brace Jovanovich, 1982), pp. 239–40. Further references to this work will be included parenthetically in the text.

19 *Collected Essays by Virginia Woolf, v. 2* (London: Hogarth, 1966), p. 225.

20 *The Voyage Out* (New York: Penguin, 1991), p. 16. Further references to this work will be included parenthetically in the text. See also Christine Froula, "Out of the Chrysalis: Female Initiation and Female Authority in Virginia Woolf's *The Voyage Out*," *Virginia Woolf: A Collection of Critical Essays*, ed. Margaret Homans (Englewood Cliffs: Prentice-Hall, 1993), pp. 138–61, and Patricia Ondek Laurence, *The Reading of Silence: Virginia Woolf in the English Tradition* (Stanford: Stanford UP, 1991), pp. 144–69. When she was beginning to compose *The Pargiters*, Woolf described *Night and Day* as her last novel "of fact": "What has happened of course is that after abstaining from the novel of fact all these years—since 1919—& N. & D. Indeed, I find myself infinitely delighting in facts for a change. . . ." *Diary v. 4*, p.129.

21 *The Waves* (New York: Harcourt Brace & Co., 1978), pp. 88, 172. Further references to this work will be included parenthetically in the text.

22 For two of the three female characters, this narrative structure forestalls the kinds of outcomes that conventionally follow from female desire. Jinny, who bears Woolf's own childhood nickname (*Diary, v. 4*, p. 79), is the clearest example. Glorying in her physicality ("Everything in my body seems thinned out with running and triumph" [46]) and sexuality ("My body instantly of its own accord puts forth a frill under his gaze" [63]), Jinny continues to "live in the body," like a siren sending out "the rough black 'No,' the golden 'Come' in rapid running arrows of sensation" (176) without ever being punished or betrayed. Susan, too, is extravagantly incarnate, her character intertwined with her physical characteristics ("I am squat . . . I am short, I have eyes that look close to the ground and see insects in the grass" [15]), her terse Catullan "I love and I hate" (15) of a piece with her passions for rural life ("I think I am the field, I am the barn, I am the trees" [97]) and motherhood ("I . . . am all spun to a fine thread round the cradle, wrapping in a cocoon made of my own blood the delicate limbs of my baby" [171]). While both speakers are in touch with the social limits of their embodiment and its apparent requirements—Jinny in the process of aging out of desirability, Susan in a surfeit of the satisfactions provided by maternity and prosperity—both continue to be bodies immersed in physical sensation.

23 For Rhoda's lesbian crushes see *The Waves: The Two Holograph Drafts*, ed. J. W. Graham (Toronto: U of Toronto P, 1976), pp. 122–23. For Butler's analysis see especially *Gender Trouble: Feminism and the Subversion of Identity* (New York: Routledge, 1990), pp. 16–17, and "Phantasmatic Identification and the Assumption of Sex" in *Bodies That Matter: On the Discursive Limits of 'Sex' (*New York: Routledge, 1993), p. 108. Jodie Medd suggests that "the lesbian" was an identity under construction during this interwar period. See "Re-Inverting Stephen Gordon: Rhoda Talks Back to Radclyffe Hall," *Virginia Woolf and Her Influences: Selected Papers from*

the Seventh Annual Conference on Virginia Woolf, ed. Laura Davis and Jeannette McVicker (New York: Pace UP, 1998). See also Annette Oxindine, "Rhoda Submerged: Lesbian Suicide in *The Waves*," *Virginia Woolf: Lesbian Readings*, ed. Eileen Barrett and Patricia Cramer (New York: New York UP, 1997), pp. 203–221.

[24] Carolyn G. Heilbrun, "Virginia Woolf in Her Fifties," *Virginia Woolf: A Feminist Slant*, ed. Jane Marcus (Lincoln: U of Nebraska P, 1984), pp. 236–53.

[25] Ernst H. Kantorowicz, *The King's Two Bodies: A Study in Mediaeval Political Theology* (Princeton: Princeton UP, 1957).

[26] Although the idea that Woolf feared and despised the corporeal was part of the early attacks on her class (and gender) standing as a "lady" mounted by F. R. and Q. D. Leavis and by Wyndham Lewis, the most influential statements of this position are in Quentin Bell's 1972 biography. Bell pronounced his aunt "sexually frigid" and hypothesized that her lesbian relationships were unconsummated "affair(s) of the heart." See F. R. Leavis, "Keynes, Lawrence and Cambridge," *The Common Pursuit* (London: Chatto and Windus, 1952), p. 257; Q. D. Leavis, "Caterpillars of the Commonwealth Unite!" *The Importance of "Scrutiny,"* ed. Eric Bentley (New York: New York UP, 1964), pp. 382-91; and Wyndham Lewis, *Men Without Art* (London: Cassell and Co., 1934). Much of the sense of Woolf as shrinkingly anti-corporeal also came from her comments that James Joyce's *Ulysses* was "indecent" (e.g. "Modern Fiction," p. 162). The most memorable feminist version of this attack came from Elaine Showalter, who wrote, "Woolf's vision of womanhood is as deadly as it is disembodied. The ultimate room of one's own is the grave." *A Literature of Their Own: British Women Novelists from Brontë to Lessing* (Princeton: Princeton UP, 1977), p. 297. Critics who challenged the notion that Woolf's writing was alienated from the world of bodies emphasized the politics of this writing, its immersion in the everyday and its concern with multiple sexualities. See especially Alex Zwerdling, *Virginia Woolf and the Real World* (Berkeley: U of California P, 1986), Jane Marcus, *Virginia Woolf and the Languages of Patriarchy*, Rachel Bowlby, *Feminist Destinations and Further Essays on Virginia Woolf* (Edinburgh: Edinburgh UP, 1997), Gillian Beer, *Virginia Woolf: The Common Ground* (Ann Arbor: U of Michigan P, 1996) and Joseph Allen Boone, "Virginia Woolf, *Mrs. Dalloway*: Representing 'The Unseen Part of Us Which Spreads Wide,'" *Libidinal Currents: Sexuality and the Shaping of Modernism* (Chicago: U of Chicago P, 1998), pp. 172–203.

AFTERWORD

"Virginia Woolf's Two Bodies" was the first part of a project I am still calling *Weird Woolf*. I meant (and mean) by that title not that Woolf as a person was strange, awkward, odd, abnormal (although it's arguable that she was all these things) but that her writing is not at all what we expect or what we've always thought—although Woolf has become so popular that it's often easy to assume that she simply articulates the opinions we think she should have.

In my essay, I see her coming out of a very strong and, to her, very daunting tradition of activist feminist writers—and in many respects opposing that tradition. In another piece, I've suggested there is an important historical sense in which we could call her postfeminist—not antifeminist, but both building on and criticizing a set of theories and practices of the maternal generation. Certainly the scandals raised by feminist Edwardian novelists, who chose to write about passionate, sexual women in social contexts that allowed neither their passion nor their sexuality, frightened and repelled Woolf, who did not wish to identify publicly with affronts to public sexual mores. Her "two bodies," I suggest, are a way to present female eroticism without forcing either characters or author to suffer social consequences.

I worked on this piece for years. I gave versions of it as talks at conferences and at various universities in the United States and Europe. After these talks, I constantly found myself facing hard questions that sent me back to recast my argument. Most of the questions came from the group of eminent feminist critics I think of as the Women Who Run with the Woolfs, people like Marianne deKoven, Christine Froula, Bonnie Kime Scott, Sydney Janet Kaplan, Lyndsey Stonebridge, and Vara Neverow. They were the gauntlet I ran in my initiation into Woolf studies. I am grateful to all of them.

~ 2 0 0 1 ~

Bodies Cinematic, Bodies Politic: The "Male" Gaze and the "Female" Gothic in De Palma's *Carrie*[1]

ABBY LYNN COYKENDALL

Technology changes things. Not art. Software. Birth control pills. Television. Those are the things that change the world.
—Brian De Palma, qtd. in Double De Palma *(163)*

We must insist upon the idea of culture-in-action, of culture growing within us as a new organ.
—*Antonin Artaud*, The Theatre and Its Double *(8)*

At first, the unconscious is manifested to us as something that holds itself in suspense in the area, I would say, of the unborn. That repression should discharge something into this area is not surprising. It is the abortionist's relation to limbo.
—*Jacques Lacan*, The Four Fundamental Concepts of Psychoanalysis *(23)*

PERHAPS MORE THAN any other American director, Brian De Palma provided Hollywood cinema with the increasingly codified structure of the "point of view" shot, a technique that simultaneously evokes, captures, and suspends what generations of feminists have infamously deemed the "male gaze." Yet in his early films, whether *Sisters* (1973), *Blow Out* (1981), or, more extensively, *Body Double* (1984), De Palma systematically doubles and decenters this gaze through an "interior" diegesis—the "film within the film"—that is overtly, but usually problematically, pornographic in content and that antagonistically rivals the meanings unfolding in the larger "primary" film. Like Paul de Man, De Palma gave precedence to the "self-conscious" over the "spontaneous, non-critical" viewers while nonetheless acknowledging that, however critical, the audience is invariably "bound to forget the mediations separating the text from the particular meaning that now captivates [its] attention" (de Man viii). In fact, more than de Man, De Palma was intent on catching his audience in this very lure. The directors whom De Palma inspired would imitate his suspense sequence over and over—a man watching a woman assaulted by another man, the woman's open mouth, the point-of-view shot, the penetration of her body by a large object—but few (perhaps with Quentin Tarantino as the most notable exception) would rely so heavily on the inherent deconstruction of the gaze that the embedded diegesis of the interior film inevitably provokes.

As a result, critiquing De Palma's phallocentricism is a far more difficult endeavor than it would otherwise seem, for in a number of ways, he has himself already performed his own manipulation of the scopic drive via a distinctly self-referential hermeneutics of desire. Both *Sisters* and *Blow Out* open by immediately confronting the viewer with an elaborate, protracted, yet ironic display of the male gaze, the obscenely voyeuristic leer. The initial sequence of *Sisters*, in which an African-American man (Lisle Wilson) stares at the blind Margot Kidder undressing, is only belatedly shown to be an episode of a television game show—"Peeping Tom"—that provides the film with its first apparent title. The game-show contestants, presumably like De Palma's own audience, misread Wilson's look, wrongly assuming that he will maintain his perverse, clandestine watch rather than chivalrously avert his gaze. Thus, from the outset of this film and his overall career, De Palma successfully turns away from the individual psychopathology of the gaze so predominant in Alfred Hitchcock to beckon instead—and thereby undermine—the larger structural sociopathology that triggers this voyeurism.

Indeed, the scopophilia that the opening sequence of *Sisters* elicits is guided less by *desire* than by the *desire to desire* entrenched and invested within the obscene, "pornographic" spectacle of commodity culture as a whole. Like Guy Debord, De Palma exposes how spectacle is

> not something *added* to the real world—not a decorative element, so to speak. On the contrary, it is the very heart of society's real unreality. In all its specific manifestations—news or propaganda, advertising or the actual consumption of entertainment—the spectacle epitomizes the prevailing model of social life. It is the omnipresent celebration of a choice *already made* in the sphere of production, and the consummate result of that choice. In form as in content the spectacle serves as total justification for the conditions and aims of the existing system. (13, original emphasis)

In *Sisters*, middle-America's sterile, laugh-track-guided consumption, commodification, and fetishization of the sexually and racially marked other(s) provide a "total justification for the conditions and aims of the existing system" in an extremely literal fashion, for both Margot Kidder and Lisle Wilson become violently entrapped in the "castrated" performances they had initially only been acting for the television audience. Wilson succeeds in "luring" Kidder to the complimentary dinner provided by the game show at "The African Room"—a restaurant that has an exotic décor complete with every fetish object the fanciful, primitive, but entirely eurocentric imagination can fathom—only to be stabbed to death by the "domestic" cutlery turned "phallic" objects of Kidder's repressed sexuality—the very commodities, feigning as "gifts," with which Kidder herself was provided.

In *Blow Out*, the fictitious visual security of the pornographic look is even further destabilized by an elaborate hermeneutics of sound. Following in the wake of such films as *The Texas Chainsaw Massacre* (1974), *Halloween* (1978), and

Friday the Thirteenth (1980), the opening sequence of *Blow Out* makes overt the sadistic voyeurism that such stalker films had, however emphatically, only latently solicited under the cover of the traditional man/animal-"hunts"-female/victim(s) horror plot. After a prolonged exhibition of the obviously espied, recorded, undressed, and seemingly rapturous community of college women at odds with their studious-minded peers, the interior film abruptly halts. In lieu of the climatic, *Psycho*-esque murder in the shower, we receive a prolonged exhibition of the masked murderer himself, one replete with the disjunctive, exaggerated sounds of his heavy breathing and one that ultimately marks this predator as far more categorically abject than the traditional horror director dares make his sadistic "hero." Likewise, *Blow Out*'s "signature" opening (a duplicitous, *auteur* entitlement for which De Palma is notorious) arises from aural rather than visual effects: Nancy Allen's scream—the same scream that, at the end of the film, she emits during her murder by the *Peeping Tom*-like sadist and that the sound man, John Travolta, uses to complete the snuff film "within" the film ("Co-Ed Frenzy")—also appears quite conspicuously via a studio-induced, post-production dub in conjunction with Allen's name in the opening credits. Thus, however circuitously, De Palma does indeed attempt to give "voice" to the constrained, "castrated" role that women—whether stars or even, in this case, wives—frequently play in films of any genre but especially the horror genre: namely, to display the audience's own disavowed fears and helpless, paranoid reactions.

That the gaze which De Palma stimulates and interrogates in his films is nonetheless intended to be the voyeuristic, masculine gaze that feminists have persistently, and rightly, criticized throughout his career is indisputable. If nothing else, De Palma's strenuous attempts to ensure that the shots in *Body Double* were *subjective* shots, i.e., those corresponding to the precise angle of his male protagonist's perspective, make this intention manifest.[2] De Palma may ambivalently double the camera, and even entirely spin it in a 360° circle, yet he also inevitably, and protectively, attempts to situate its gaze within the single economy, body, or "home" of a masculine and heterosexual desire. Nevertheless, De Palma's intention is far from relevant when addressing the fundamentally *multivalent* desires that his films evoke. Intentionality—and the "agency" that it presumes—have always been fraught with ambiguity whether in the literary, aesthetic, or filmic genres. Indeed, the very structure of cinema and the scopic drive by which it is constituted put the "intentionality" of the filmic "object" into a particularly vexed epistemological arena, for it is film's excessive epistemological indeterminacy that ultimately provides for its suspense and "agency."[3] De Palma's early film, *Carrie* (1976), makes this problem especially manifest; not only does *Carrie* put into radical question what Laura Mulvey refers to as the visual pleasure "split between active/male and passive/female," but it also represents a subject—telepathy—that provides no convenient border between such positions (62).[4] Carrie's telepathy, her ability to transform simple wish fulfillments into far-too-real and thereby disowned material events, ultimately mimics the most vulnerable "spot" of the cinematic apparatus itself: the inevitable transitivism and transvestitism, the interchangeability and vexed intersubjectivity, of these obsessively partitioned yet monstrously embodied subject/object, passive/aggressive dyads.

I.

The common assumption that the sadistic, cinematic gaze is necessarily a "male" gaze therefore deserves further interrogation, particularly with a film like *Carrie* where women are the primary recipients of as well as the primary bearers of the sadistic aggressivity unleashed by that gaze. Both the film *Carrie* and the Stephen King novel from which De Palma adapted it are filled with gender reversals at every level. Unlike Sigmund Freud's *Fragment of an Analysis of a Case of Hysteria*, a.k.a. "Dora," *Carrie's* action centers on the sexual exchange of a man between two women: Sue Snell's barter of her prom date and Carrie's half-complicit acquiescence. Moreover, the roles of both the Frau K. and maternal figures are far more pronounced: the gym teacher—"Miss Collins" or "Miss Desjardin"—dispenses sexual knowledge to other women largely without masculine intervention, and, of course, more notably, Carrie's mother is the one who administers the patriarchal renunciation of feminine sexuality through her St. Augustine-like religious mania. If Carrie is a "hysteric" in line with the (re)imagined Dora of Hélène Cixous and Catherine Clément's *La Jeune Née*, then her history is less silenced or repressed than bombastically displayed. Thus, when in 1976 Jacqueline Rose turned to Hitchcock's *The Birds*—a film "in which the woman is both cause and object of the aggressivity which drives the narrative"—to interrogate the propensity of psychoanalytically-laden film criticism of systematizing even further the "integration into the Symbolic through a successful [and implicitly masculine] Oedipal trajectory," she may well have examined the production of Hitchcock's devoted disciple of the same year ("Paranoia" 57).[5] On every level, *Carrie* invokes an environment in which the symbolic is a scene of, by, for, and between women.[6]

It is undoubtedly true that the "betweenness" and "inbetweenness" of the women in *Carrie* may be an elaborate façade. As Nancy K. Miller illustrates so well in "'I's in Drag: The Sex of Recollection," the pornographic tradition since *Memoirs of a Woman of Pleasure*—a.k.a. "Fanny Hill"—along with that of the most sacrosanct of British novelists—Defoe, Richardson, Fielding, et al.—has crucially depended on the transvestitism of the male author's "female" persona to sustain the ruse of a "phallic" guarantee of value.[7] Lacan's oft-quoted assertion about the essential masquerade of femininity—"The fact that femininity takes refuge in this mask, because of the *Verdrägung* [repression] inherent to the phallic mark of desire, has the strange consequence that virile display itself appears as feminine"—rings strangely true in terms of the *masculine* masquerade of femininity entangled within the history of authorship (*Fem. Sexuality* 85). Nonetheless, even such a refined theorist and advocate of feminine masquerade as Mary Russo opens her "Female Grotesques: Carnival and Theory" article by invoking the harsh "matronizing" tenor of the disciplining yet disembodied mother:

> There is a phrase that still resonates from childhood. Who says it? The mother's voice—not my own mother's, perhaps, but the voice of an aunt, an older sister, or the mother of a friend. *It is a harsh, matronizing phrase, and it is directed toward the behavior of other women: "'She' [the other woman] is making a spectacle out of herself."* Making a spectacle out of oneself seemed a specifically

feminine danger. The danger was of an exposure. (213; original notation, emphasis added)

If the suspense genre was inaugurated with Hitchcock's *Psycho*, it was also inaugurated with Mrs. Bates' execution of (and Norman Bates' subsequent travesty of) the panopticon-like power of the maternal gaze and voice. Although de Man is rightly suspicious of those symbols that betray "the nostalgia and the desire to coincide," Kaja Silverman's hypothesis of an earlier, maternal, and acoustic "mirror stage" does provide a salient allegory for the "distance in relation to its own origin" by which the ego, or "it," "establishes its language in the void of [its] temporal distance" (de Man 207).[8] That the aggressive maternal can be as horrifyingly evocative, if not more evocative, than the pre-supposed aggressive paternal is made quite clear by the enormous commercial success of *Carrie*, a film that first launched the careers of both King and De Palma. However much each may now disown *Carrie*'s seminal position in relation to their subsequent and apparently more significant *oeuvre*, this teenage girl's abjected, vengeful, and destructive rite-of-passage certainly hit a nerve.

In the end, feminism, the more "canonical" Hitchcock-inspired horror films, and psychoanalysis all put into radical question the inevitable masculinity of the gaze as well as the subjectivity that it constitutes. Stalker films may typically rely upon female "objects" to elicit the terrorizing effects of the gaze, but Lacan himself invariably uses masculine subjects to invoke what he refers to as its "capturing"—and thereby "taming"—effects (*Four Fund,* 107, 116). Most importantly, Lacan often portrays women as the *source* of that gaze as well as its commensurate hostility, particularly in "Aggressivity in Psychoanalysis" where a cannibalistic, "raving" mother ends up epitomizing his analysis of paranoia:

> we constantly observe [the aggressive drive] in the formative action of an individual on those dependent on him; intended aggressivity gnaws away, undermines, disintegrates; it castrates; it leads to death: "And I thought you were impotent!" growled the mother, suddenly transformed into a tigress, to her son, who, with great difficulty, had admitted to her his homosexual tendencies. And one could see that her permanent aggressivity as a virile woman had had its effect; I have always found it impossible, in such cases, to divert the blows away from the analytic experience. (*Écrits* 10–11)

Transference and *méconnaissance* embed Lacan's description at every level, for here even psychoanalysis itself seems a second, gentler mother supplementing that lost object of nostalgic origin. As if the palpable certainty of this mother's "intended" and "permanent" aggressivity could defray the subject's grandiose delusional "fixity" during the mirror stage, Lacan here extenuates the very irreparable dislocation that he elsewhere so resolutely seeks to underscore and problematize.[9] The primary tension that he identifies is, however, as old as Freud's "The 'Uncanny'":

> One of the most uncanny and wide-spread forms of superstitions is the dread of the evil eye . . . There never seems to have been any doubt about the source

of this dread. Whoever possesses something that is at once valuable and fragile is afraid of other people's envy, in so far as he projects on to them the envy he would have felt in their place . . . What is feared is thus a certain intention of doing harm, and certain signs are taken to mean that that intention has the necessary power at its command. (17: 240)

When Freud claims that there "never seems to have been any doubt about the source of this dread," he also means quite the reverse, for both the (penis) "envy" and the (inside/outside) "source" of that envy have the ambiguous, yet certain, structure of fetishistic disavowal, of simultaneously "knowing and not knowing." It is ultimately the very fear that something might be taken away that perpetuates the semblance of non-fragile, transportable, and thereby absolute value in the first place; however, in order to safeguard this illusory value, one must exasperate that fear even further and identify with two entirely incommensurate, but precariously interchangeable, subjective positions—that of the vulnerable yet precious victim and that of the ominous, malevolent interloper.

Like Freud's "penis" envy and like Lacan's phallic mother, the camera evokes an aggressive vacillation between projection and incorporation, for more than any other "object" in a film, and especially in the horror film, the camera is the last to be embodied but the first to betray harmful intentions. Yet, however terrifying that projection and however paranoid that incorporation, there is, in the end, no actual embodied threat: no phallus on, within, or without the defenseless subject; nor one on, within, or without the father, mother, stalker, or stalkerette who may appear to be lopping it off. There is no phallus "within" or "without" the subject just as there is no *single* camera embedded "within" or even "without" the remanufactured sequences of the film. When in "Art in the Age of Mechanical Reproduction," Walter Benjamin compares first the cameraman, next the editor, and at last the camera, audience, and critic to the experimental surgeon (whose "bold," conniving "penetrations" into the human body constitute the "first art form" in which "matter plays tricks on man"), he not only evokes the acute disembodiment that cinema engenders but also the absolute uncertainty as to the agent of that dislocation:

Guided by the cameraman, the camera continually changes its position with respect to the performance. The sequence of positional views which the editor composes from the material supplied him constitutes the completed film. It comprises certain factors of movement which are in reality those of the camera . . . Hence, the performance of the actor is subjected to a series of optical tests . . . This permits the audience to take the position of a critic, without experiencing any personal contact with the actor. The audience's identification with the actor is really an identification with the camera . . . its approach is that of testing. (249–250n, 228–29, 233–34)

In short, the camera is not only *phallic* but *cannibalistic*, for en route to opening the world up for analysis and dissection, the camera entangles the seen with the seer, its hallucinatory, anestheticized magic simultaneously engendering and consuming—transporting and transfixing—the viewer without itself offering a source to "cite" the origin of that embodiment or consumption. As a result, whether they be cinematic or pathological, obsessive fears of "castration"—here once more in line with what Lacan designates the "*imagoes* of the fragmented body"—have always already been about telepathy, the "evil eye," and the inevitably prosthetic transitivism of identification (*Écrits* 11).[10]

The "dread" of women, particularly "virile" women, coincides precisely with the moment when they, like Carrie's mother or like those depicted by Lacan and Russo, threaten to undermine the precarious facade of substance constituted both *within* and *against* a distinctively maternal register; in other words, when they, like Medusa's notorious head, return that "apparition of an image," that "object of anxiety *par excellence*," that "something faced with which all words cease and categories fail [*sic*]" once housing the reflected but fictitious subject itself (Lacan, *The Ego* 164). This dread becomes especially pronounced when women, such as the grotesque, menstruating Carrie, embody and reenact the monstrous antipode to the misrecognized unified *imago*. Echoing Mikhail Bakhtin, Russo describes the carnivalesque body as the "open, protruding, extended, secreting body, the body of becoming, process, and change," a description that certainly pertains to belatedly pubescent Carrie (218). In mimicking Bakhtin's argument, however, Russo makes the additional point that women were often, like Jews and other minorities, the preferred targets of abuse during Bakhtin's exalted and (re)imagined carnival festivities. Russo thus rightly insists that "women and their bodies, certain bodies, in certain public framings, in certain public spaces, are always already transgressive—dangerous, and in danger" (217).

Following the 1960s, the body became the première site through which to (re)negotiate one's identity and potential empowerment. Laura Badley argues that the horror film of the 1970s and 1980s "announced the crisis" of this readjustment "through its images—its bodies in pieces and organic machines, its sexual mutations and re-generations"—images which together "provided the crisis with an iconography, a fantastic body language for re-imagining the self" (21). It surely cannot be incidental that during the mid-1970s, when women's bodies were entering the traditionally homosocial workplace in large numbers and when the premenstrual "syndrome" first became massively (mis)diagnosed in order to prevent that influx, King and De Palma centered their artistic energies on the all-powerful, enraged, and menstruating Carrie White. Nor can it be a surprise that during the mid-1960s, an era when women were first coming to demand unprecedented access to contraception and abortion, Lacan would critique the metaphysics of men's reproduction of the "self" in the symbolic—including that endemic to the parthenogenetic "self-birthing" of Artaud's utopian, revolutionary subject—by deploying the "abortionist" as a metaphor for repression and castration. In short, it should not be a surprise that following the collapse of the masculine, modern aesthetic of epic sublimation, De Palma should dismiss the revolutionary value of his own artistic efforts in relation to the "software" of birth-control pills and television. If *Carrie* depicts the symbolic as a scene of, by, for, and between women, so too did the wide-scale fantasies and paranoias of the 1970s cultural imagination.

II.

Of all kinds of secretions, that of menstruation—that evoking the possibility of women bleeding in public—is certainly one of the most taboo, for however ambivalently, women have been the traditional guardians of the fabulously naturalistic, nostalgically maternal, yet somehow inviolable body. Journalists' reactions to Uta Pippig, who in 1996 won the Boston Marathon with menstrual blood at points dripping down her legs, illustrates this fact quite clearly. Even though Pippig's aim was to outrun the typically so constricting functions of the human body and even though, as a byproduct of that effort, Pippig experienced diarrhea along with other (usually unmentioned) embarrassments, the journalists fixated on this one particular "dysfunction" of menstruation to mark her victory as a feat of grotesque abjection rather than heroic sublimation. According to Eileen McNamara, "The talk radio was misogynistic and disgusting . . . When Pippig grabbed that water bottle to clean her legs, there were all of our private female moments made starkly public. That time you picked the wrong day to wear a white skirt. That time you had to back out of a dining room . . . Her victory was sweet as it was messy. Many men just saw the mess . . . They like their women athletes pretty, perky and photogenic. Uta Pippig has always been that. On Monday, though, those men had to confront the fact that this extraordinary athlete is no Marathon Barbie; she's a real flesh and blood woman" (qtd. in Conway 30–31).

William Paul, in *Laughing Screaming: Modern Hollywood Horror and Comedy*, describes the opening sequence of *Carrie* as a similar transformation from the picturesque to the horrific, but he, like the sportscasters above, concentrates most fully on the "pretty, perky, and photogenic" appearance of the women and avoids confronting the necessary *instability* and *constructedness* of that appearance. Paul skips the initial shot, in which we peer ominously above the athletic sportsmanship of a group of women, in order to crane quickly into the erotic display of their bodies in the shower:

> The scene immediately following the volleyball game is built on a contrast in its differing views of a woman's body, moving from a lyricism that prettifies to the horror of bloody excretion . . . the cause for lyricism lies in how the girls present themselves to the camera. While it might be more accurate to see the scene as a male fantasy of a girls' locker room, the audience, both male and female, is being set up to appreciate something here that will be destroyed. Indirectly, we come to regard this retrospectively as Carrie's first act of destruction. When the camera singles out Carrie, [f]ar from presenting her body as a gross object in itself, the camera beautifies it, anatomizing it to let different parts of the body dominate the image. (357)

Whether watched by a male or female viewer, the aesthetisized movement of the group of nude women in De Palma's soft-focused shower scene does indeed invoke a "male" fantasy—a fantastic dimension that any women would recognize at once and that the women within the scene, so noticeably "present[ing] themselves to the camera," must also have recognized in advance."[11] It would therefore be more accurate to say that both we and the women are being "set up" *not* in the visual pleasure that we are ultimately denied, but in the visual pleasure that we are in fact throughout so openly and forcibly permitted. What we see is what the camera sees and what the camera sees is not Carrie's "retrospective" destruction; we can no more reconstruct the fragmented, "anatomized" parts of Carrie's masturbating body into a nostalgic lyricism than we can reconstruct Carrie herself as the agent of the camera's own predatory intention to "single her out."

Even though discussing De Palma's film, Paul follows Stephen King in diverting the look away from the women's athletic activity rather than De Palma who focuses extensively on a volleyball game that is, according to Bruce Babington, "shockingly" competitive compared to how "girls are usually typed as less aggressive" (5).[12] King describes the volleyball game only in terms of the seductive, metonymic *objet petit a* which that activity left on the women's bodies: "The girls had been playing volleyball in Period One, and their morning sweat was light and eager" (4).[13] That King avoids depicting the game itself due to an extreme ambivalence about feminine strength is quite evident from how he portrays Miss Desjardin: "their slim, nonbreasted gym teacher," who like a camera, "stepped in, craned her neck around," wearing "shorts blinding white, her legs not too curved but striking in their unobtrusive muscularity" (5). Miss Desjardin's "striking," "blinding white" shorts mark her as directly, yet inversely, equated with the threatening yet awkward and unmuscular Carrie White; moreover, her supervisory power over both the game and the subsequent display in the shower liken her to the panopticon-like gaze of the camera. Although the "unobtrusive" muscularity and the "nonbreasted" masculinity of her body certainly indicate a desire to keep the omniscient, omnipowerful gaze a less threatening "male" gaze, her transvestitism nonetheless betrays how the phallus must inevitably assume a "monstrous," crossgendered, or, in some way, "inbetween" and duplicitous subjectivity in order to be represented.[14]

Of course, as Luce Irigaray has made clear, the image of women alone, absorbed in their own pleasure, has been an ambivalently pleasurable yet extremely threatening one long before cinema reified and thereby domesticated it. That Paul had to revert to King's *Carrie* in order to reinscribe the non-ambivalent pleasure of De Palma's shower sequence indicates how thoroughly De Palma had set out to sabotage the transparency of this exoticism and thereby return the predatory, diagnostic, exorbitant gaze back upon its owner. Like *Sisters* and *Blow Out*, *Carrie* opens by immediately confronting the viewer with an elaborate, protracted, yet ironic display of the "male" gaze, the obscenely voyeuristic leer. However, like *Sisters* and *Blow Out*, this confrontation is both a tease and a trap. As much as Lisle Wilson may have wanted to look at the disrobed Margot Kidder, *he* did not, but both *we* and the television audience have; likewise, as much as John Travolta may have sought to record and memorialize Nancy Allen's erotically-charged penultimate scream, it is we, the viewers of both *Blow Out* and "Co-Ed Frenzy," to whom he catered that violent climax.

Thus, no matter how much we may wish to become enmeshed in the fictitious unified *jouissance* of Carrie's autoerotic display in the shower, we simply cannot because De Palma inevitably revokes the very pleasure that he aims to solicit within us. Carrie's autoerotic gestures in fact contain a duplicity, a pop-cultural intertexuality, a "film within the film," that was obvious to the reviewers of *Carrie* from the outset. De Palma did not conceive of these "anatomized" camera tricks out of the clear blue sky; he, like Hitchcock himself, acquired them directly from postmodern consumer culture, from the episodic, day-time "soap operas" of the "Ivory," "Dial," or "Irish Springs" advertisements. De Palma's caricature of the soap ads corresponds to what Fredric Jameson terms the "pastiche" of post-modernity: "Pastiche is, like parody, the imitation of a peculiar or unique style, the wearing of a stylistic mask, speech in a dead language: but it is a neutral practice of such mimicry, without parody's ulterior motive, without the satirical impulse, without laughter, without that still latent feeling that there exists something *normal* compared to which what is being imitated is rather comic. Pastiche is blank parody, parody that has lost its sense of humor" (114).[15]

Although De Palma's reference to consumer culture may be read as either parody or pastiche, it is far more common to read this scene as evincing the ulterior motive of parody. Even De Palma's harshest critic (Serafina Bathrick, who laments his derivativeness in assembling the close-ups of Carrie's body and in "reveal[ing] all the self-touching gestures soap ads use") nevertheless assigns De Palma an ulterior motive—that of derogatory and satirical voyeurism (9). David Pirie, in contrast, reads De Palma's motive as precisely the opposite:

> It lends a Freudian and feminist aspect to what follows. If the blood is Carrie's ruthlessly repressed sexuality erupting at the appropriate moment of relaxation, it is also what singles her out [as] the only non-colonised woman in the film . . . mock[ing] the possibility of her development into a woman in any real sense. (23)

Paul overlooks both trends in the criticism, acknowledging the scene's oft-noted commercial source only to once again aesthetisize this "accuracy" after the fact: "with the same erotic lyricism these commercials grant to the act of washing," De Palma "enhance[s] the sensual beauty of the image and alludes to a real pleasure in cleanliness . . . The connection of washing to eros is given a purgative psychological dimension" (357). We must ask, however, of *what* are we being purged. That is, we must interrogate why the viewers need to be "cleansed" before Carrie bleeds, why the viewer's own psychological release tends to correspond with Carrie's autoeroticism, with, in other words, the very moment when Carrie *is* being "singled out" by the camera as the only "colonised" woman of the film, and, ultimately, why De Palma nullifies the catharsis of both Carrie and the viewer by so profoundly disturbing this image with her menstrual blood and with the violent reactions of the surrounding women.[16]

De Palma's redoubled opening sequence is unsettling largely because he un-domesticates this overdetermined and overinvested image of female autoeroticism via sound effects that abruptly switch from complete saturation to utter silence and once again to complete saturation. During the volleyball scene, the soundtrack provides what Slavoj Žižek, following Michel Chion, would call *rendu*: a "way of rendering reality in cinema" that "enabl[es] us to orient ourselves in the diegetic space" by "giv[ing] us the basic perspective, the 'map' of the situation" via the interpolation of "audible details that would be missed if we were to find ourselves in the 'reality' recorded by the film" (40).[17] Even before the visual sequences of the film commence, we hear the chaotic medley of sounds that so often hover around sporting events—the hit of the ball, the impatient commands of fellow team members, the movement of the women's tennis shoes across the concrete, and so on. After we see the events to which these sounds correspond, we primarily hear the disembodied voice and persistent whistle of Miss Collins, who directs and coordinates the ebb and flow of the action. However, once Carrie misses the ball (and thereafter receives an exaggeratedly loud hit on the head combined with a shrill chorus of insults), the scene unexpectedly shifts to the slow-motion, soft-focused images of the disrobing women within the locker room and the slow, subtle movements of Pino Domaggio's music score. With that shift, the camera position alters from its static station of vertical omniscience to a prolonged, horizontal dolly movement across the shower-room floor, catching alternating images of expansive, foggy space in which groups of women frolic and images of the black, obstructed space of the industrial lockers upon which the credits appear. The shower scene is thus not an isolated, lyric totality, what Žižek terms "floating islands of the signifier" in the "universal medium of the sound aquarium," but rather a haven, a reprieve, a noticeably constructed sanctuary away from the conflict and commotion of the scene before (40).

Because the shower sequence prohibits montage, it elicits an impression of prolonged, uninterrupted motion that noticeably lacks the reality effects of the previous scene. When the camera once again focuses on Carrie, the music slightly alters as if designed specifically for her pleasure; when she drops the soap, the lack of a corresponding sound becomes especially pronounced. In the very moment that she bleeds, the music halts and Carrie turns to look at the crowd beyond her; her delayed actions are met with a wall of silence, silence at last broken by the grounding yet confused clamor of the surrounding women. The juxtaposition of this noise with the former wall of silence makes it impossible to view these opening scenes together without becoming acutely aware of being forcibly put there, taken away, and once again returned; it also makes it impossible to view these scenes without likewise recognizing that the illusion of one's presence or absence crucially depends upon the fractured collage of images or the disjunctive assortment of sounds. As Silverman would say, De Palma refuses to mourn the "identification at the center of the cinematic experience," for rather than employing identification "as a vehicle for taking the spectator somewhere he or she has never been before" only to prohibit "the return journey," he makes "manifest the gap separating the gift of ideality from its recipient" and *"bring[s] us to a knowledge of our own productivity with respect to that ideality"* (102–3, emphasis added). For as in Michael Powell's *Peeping Tom* (where the sadist's camera is itself the weapon of choice), visual pleasure and aggressive intention are here two sides of the same coin: it is we ourselves who transport or, at least, wish to transport and "carry" our elect and insatiable weapons.

Such a redoubled self-consciousness is not to be found in the King novel, where, if anything, we encounter a redoubled self-denial. The very first lines of King's narrative, like William Paul's portrayal of Carrie's body, elicit a distinctly fetishistic and retrospective disavowal that constructs Miss Desjardin as the primary—literally "striking"—agent of the upcoming violence as well as the "blinding white" recipient of its ensuing effects:

> Nobody was really surprised when it happened, not really, not at the subconscious level where savage things grow. On the surface, all the girls in the shower room were shocked, thrilled, ashamed, or simply glad that the White bitch had taken it in the mouth again. Some of them might also have claimed surprise but of course their claim was untrue. (3)

The "it" here—that horrible event which is "known and not known"—is quite distinct from the event for which *Carrie* is notorious. "It" is not a group of women throwing tampons at the vulnerable, naked Carrie; "it" is Miss Desjardin slapping Carrie "smartly across the face," using the "standard tactic for hysterics" (11). Since Miss Desjardin hits Carrie only *after* the other women have bombarded her with tampons, their supposed claim of surprise would "of course" be untrue because they have displaced the recognition of the hostile actions of their own into a blinded, condensed recognition of only Miss Desjardin's authoritative yet arbitrarily punitive slap. In doing so, they not only transpose the culpability of their own actions into the culpability of that "it," that "miss of the garden" (*des jardin*) where "savage things grow," they also use their own tendentious and entirely fictitious telepathy—the guilty conceiving, watching, wishing, or, like us, reading and viewing the event—as a means to represent, project, manifest, and yet *negate* their own earlier, quite active participation in what they witness.

It is therefore neither Carrie nor even her double Miss Desjardin who possess the apparently phallic, telepathic evil eye. It is instead these women—as well as the readers and voyeurs, the authors, directors, and subsequent critics—who each in their own way fulfill their antagonistic, ostensibly animistic wishes first by assuming a front-row seat at the spectacle and participating by proxy in the abject humiliation of Carrie White and then by retroactively becoming *forgiven* through their (mis)identification with the phallic Miss Desjardin or *revenged* through their (mis)identification with Carrie White. That is, whether we vicariously identify with the all-powerful and in-advance justified agent of the destruction or whether we directly identify with the mortified but soon-to-be excessively revenged victim of that destruction is a moot point: in either case, we are able to identify unabashedly with the voracious but prosthetic evil eye.[18]

III.

Malek Alloula's analysis of the postcards of disrobed Algerian women in *The Colonial Harem* provides a further hint as to what this shower scene—a scene that King describes as exotic, "subterranean," and "Egyptian" and that De Palma magnifies into an even more grandiose, haremesque lesbian erotics—might represent:

> Incapable of representing the real feast, the postcard . . . will be content to evoke it by means of the impoverished signs that constitute its "aesthetics" of justification. The dancers that it pins are akin to the butterflies and insects that

museums of natural history and taxidermists exhibit in their glass display cases. Beyond the ethnographic alibi (folklore), we have a *vivisector's gaze . . .* It is the very gaze of colonization that defines, through the exclusion of the other (the colonized) a *naturalness* (the native) that is first circumscribed by the gaze . . . The postcard seeks to anticipate the desire of its user and fasten itself to this desire. It never transcends it; it lives in, and from, an osmosis that is its defining characteristic. (King 4; Alloula 92–96, original emphasis)

For if the kind of parody that the opening sequence of *Carrie* elicits is anything like De Palma's earlier film *Sisters*, then, in putting on what Jameson calls the "stylistic mask" of commercialized spectacle, we are also putting on—and be-ing trapped in—a mask that is pervaded with both sexual and racial ideologies.[19] Indeed, as Anne McClintock illustrates in *Imperial Leather: Race, Gender and Sexuality in the Colonial Context*, the "story of soap" is a far from innocent one:

Soap did not flourish when imperial ebullience was at its peak. It emerged com-mercially during an era of impending crisis and social calamity, serving to pre-serve, through fetish ritual, the uncertain boundaries of class, gender and race identity in a social order felt to be threatened by the fetid effluvia of the slums, the belching smoke of industry, social agitation, economic upheaval and anti-colonial resistance. Soap offered the promise of spiritual salvation and regenera-tion through commodity consumption, a regime of domestic hygiene that could restore the threatened potency of the imperial body politic and the race. (211)

While the Victorian soap ads that McClintock examines provide a "reformation allegory whereby the purification of the domestic body becomes a metaphor for the regeneration of the body politic," De Palma's and King's juxtapositions of soap and menstruation do the reverse, marking the *degeneration* of the body poli-tic through the *impurity* of the domestic and, implicitly, maternal body (214).

The connotations of racial, evolutionary determinism are overt in the novel from the first chapter: after being hit by the tampons, Carrie "slumped over, breasts pointing at the floor, her arms dangling limply. She looked like an ape. Her eyes were shiny and blank" (11). And even the reviewers of the film could readily read Carrie's traumatic experience as a "primitive" regression from human ascendance to animal-like submission: "She deals with the taunts of her peers by cowering in the corner of the shower like a wounded animal" (Citron 10). King's choice of Carrie White's name, his pun "in a dead language" on the "White House" in which she lives, his allusion to the "glass house" of Miss Desjardin's unwittingly violent participation in her mortification, along with his conjuring of the "Egyptian bathhouse" where her traumatic experience takes place are by no means accidents (25, 20, 4). Through Carrie's body, King is mourning the loss of the masculine, white, and western ethos: one that, after World War II, may have "rescued" and partly assimilated the Jewish émigrés of Europe, but only too late and only to find yet another group of refugees in the dissident PLO "terrorists" of the Middle East. Following the abortive World-War-II reveries in the fields of Vietnam, we could no longer assume the appearance of "pure," "legitimate" conquest; nor, following the massive dissemination of holocaust footage in the mid-1970s, could we wear the white robe of medical scientificism without also being uncomfortably reminded of what actually happens after the victim is handed a bar of soap in front of the gas showers. The fact that, in executing her vengeance, Carrie exceeds the eye-for-an-eye ethics and continues to destroy the entirety of the body politic indicates that the violence of the initial shower scene contains a kernel of a far more expansive sociopolitical violence.

Thus, if in the beginning Carrie's humiliation marks the violence of sexual repression as well as the violent reception of the sexual "revolution," by the end her abjected, repressed, feminine traits begin to mark instead the imagined traits of those disenfranchised from a larger nationalistic forum. Reflecting on the climatic prom scene, a female spectator employs two racial caricatures to evoke Carrie's image, caricatures which each underscore the incriminating gaze that Carrie returns back upon the viewer. The first, like that in De Palma's shower scene, derives from the "dead" yet nevertheless "motivated" language of American popular culture—a culture that extracted Joel Chandler Harris' "Uncle Remus" stories from the African-American literary tradition and, in doing so, supplanted Harris' own rendition of Southern oral traditions with those of Disney's quite distorted yet massively disseminated "storybook" illustrations:

> When I was a little girl I had a Walt Disney storybook called *Song of the South*, and it had that Uncle Remus story about the tarbaby in it. There was a picture of the tarbaby sitting in the middle of the road, looking like one of those old-time Negro minstrels with the blackface and great big white eyes. When Carrie opened her eyes it was like that. They were the only part of her that wasn't completely red. (King 167–68)

Whereas the first image depicts Carrie's body as hidden under a mask of "black" and thereby in-advance victimized, or "red," skin, the second image depicts Carrie as embedded within the red skin of a militant and soon-to-victimize terrorist: "I saw Carrie looking in, her face all smeared, like an Indian with war paint on" (170). Carrie's body ultimately represents what Homi Bhabha would call the "barred Nation It/Self," and her gaze becomes the emblem of the "tense locations of cultural difference" that disrupt the "power of the eye to naturalize the rhetoric of national affiliation and its forms of collective expression" (148).[20]

As with De Palma's use of the soap ads, however, King's intertextual references to American popular culture, to the unheroic seriality of television, of the Western, of what Bhabha calls the repeated yet ambivalent rituals that comprise the "rhetoric of national affiliation" are less an assertion of the gaze than an elegy for its decayed power, an elegy for the *lost* "power of the eye," the *lost* ability to naturalize or embody the "forms of collective expression." Even before Carrie's body is drenched in pigs' blood and the prom begins to turn into a drama of fetishized, ritualistic violence, that event and the whole psychological landscape of the American pastoral that the prom seems inevitably to emblematize was doomed from the start: "There was a gaining student move afoot to do away with the King and Queen business all together—some of the girls claimed that it was sexist, the boys thought it was just plain stupid and a little embarrassing. Chances were good that this was the last year the dance would be so formal or traditional" (108). The election for the "King" and "Queen"—a teenage equivalent for the larger national election—was in advance rigged on two counts. The men, no matter how athletic, no matter how gentile or "New England," had to rely on women to win, but the women themselves either refused to fade politely into the background of docile reproductive machinery or were unable to refuse in the first place because disqualified from emblematizing the "purity" that the New England helpmeet need appear to represent:

> GEORGE AND FRIEDA. No way. Frieda was a Jew.
>
> PETER AND MYRA. No way here, either. Myra was one of the female clique dedicated to erasing the whole horse race. She wouldn't serve even if elected. Besides she was about as goodlooking as the ass-end of old drayhorse Ethel.
>
> FRANK AND JESSICA. Quite possible. Frank Grier had made the All New England football team this year, but Jessica was another little sparrowfart with more pimples than brains.
>
> DON AND HELEN. Forget it. Helen couldn't get elected dog catcher.
>
> And the last pairing: Tommy and Sue. Only Sue, of course, had been crossed out, and Carrie's name had been written in. (108–9)

The exchangeability of Sue's and Carrie's names only once more betrays the blank that the other women filled—or were unwilling or unable to fill—in the symbolic replication of the patrilineal *nom du pere* from the beginning; likewise, the blood that Carrie ends up wearing instead of the light-pink bridal gown only once more betrays what was expected of the Queen in advance: to memorialize the soon-to-be-eradicated bloodline heroics of the "whole horse race."

As a result, the transformation of the shower scene into mass genocide—the dramatic climax in which concentration-camp-like electrical showers destroy nearly all the young, heterosexual, and reproductive for which the high-school graduating class stands as representative—is more a sterile redundancy than an actual return of the repressed. The world that Carrie destroyed was *already* profoundly destroyed by an underlying thematics of cultural genocide, the fascism inherent in everyday American life. Sue Snell's offer of her prom date to Carrie was less a "sacrifice" than a renunciation of what being a "Queen" would represent:

> [birth control] pills in circular yellow cases without number to insure against having to move out of the misses' sizes before it became absolutely necessary . . . against the intrusion of repulsive little strangers who shat in their pants and screamed for help at two in the morning; of fighting with desperate decorum to keep the niggers out of Kleen Korners, standing shoulder to shoulder with Teri Smith (Miss Potato Blossom of 1975) and Vicki Jones (Vice President of the Women's League) armed with signs and petitions. (46)

The "strangers" whom Sue might reproduce are as strange as those strange women who hold the purity of their strange race in hand. Thus, when Bhabha notes the centricity of the fetish in the structure of colonial discourse in "The Other Question," we must recollect that the sexual and racial fetishes are not equivalencies, but instead mutually determined and perhaps mutually destructive axes that each rest on the fundamental fetish of the maternal imago:

> Fixity, as the sign of cultural/historical/racial difference in the discourse of colonialism, is a paradoxical mode of representation: it connotes rigidity and an unchanging order as well as disorder, degeneracy and demonic repetition. Likewise the stereotype, which is its major discursive strategy, is a form of knowledge and identification that vacillates between what is always "in place," already known, and something that must be anxiously repeated . . . It is this process of *ambivalence*, central to the stereotype, that . . . gives the colonial stereotype its currency: ensures its repeatability in changing historical and discursive conjectures; informs its strategies of individuation and marginalization; produces that effect of probabilistic truth and predictability which, for the stereotype, must always be in *excess* of what can be empirically proved or logically construed. (66)

For, at least in *Carrie*, both the stereotyping and the demonic embodiment of the stereotyped are constructed as distinctly feminine endeavors. The prom committee is a female "Gestapo," headed by "Miss Moustache," and the traumatic destruction of the pastoral town, or "Maine holocaust," is facilitated by the "outlaw" telekinetic gene that "produces female Typhoid Marys capable of destroying almost at will" (101–3, 134). King employs the historical phenomenon of the holocaust as an allegory to critique American forms of societal alienation and violence, but, in doing so, he feminizes both the victim and the victimizer.

In the cultural field, the constructions of reproduction and, through reproduction, the constructions of femininity mark an extreme battle over the modes of intergenerational recognition. More than anything else, reproduction marks humanity's very problematic and often powerless relation to temporality. As Walter Benjamin remarks in *One Way Street*,

> The mastery of nature, so imperialists teach, is the purpose of all technology. But who would trust the cane wielder who proclaimed the mastery of children to be the purpose of education? Is not education above all the indispensable ordering of the relationship between generations and therefore mastery, if we are to use that term, of that relationship and not of children? And likewise technology is not the mastery of nature but of the relation of nature and man. (93)

Because the subject of mastery, that upon which it works, is the recognition (or the non-recognition) of the irreparably entangled, and mutually constituting, relation between both "man" and "nature," pedagogy's site of control and co-ordination, that upon which its ideological power is exerted, is not that which it ostensibly addresses—children—but instead generational recognition itself—the continuity and contiguity of what is recognized as "man." The drive to "order," whether it be via the technologies of reproduction, education, hygiene, or even war, is a drive both to map a field of recognition and to mask the interlocked relations of these multifarious natures. Paradoxically, or perhaps not too surprisingly, this supposed mastery steps in most violently at the precise moment when these relations are beyond a controllable field of recognition: via maternity, it steps in at the brink of its own history (the "ideal ego") and via pedagogy, it steps in at the brink of its own future (the "ego ideal"). At the "origin" of both drives, is the misrecognized maternal imago.

The excessive aggression deployed by the female spectators in the shower room masks a violence endemic to a colonizing and paranoid voyeurism that is not only repudiation of menstruation and reproductivity, but a repudiation of the indiscriminate miscegenation of the multifarious natures recognized as the "human" as well. The economy of fetishism, an economy integral to sexual, racial, and class distinctions, needs to be re-examined. The traditional scene of castration has notoriously been read from the wrong point of view. To reverse this point of view, to re-read the scene with the mother's eyes— or with the eyes of those other "others" disenfranchised from and thereby presumed to be "envious" of political, economic, or racial privileges—does little, for there is no *one* point of view corresponding to that gaze, nor is there *one* kind of body which that gaze captures. It is not that the subject, invariably male, encounters the "lack" of his mother's genitals, but instead that the subject (mis)identifies with her supposed "wholeness" and dexterity, thereby disavowing his or her own difference from that wholeness in a fetishistic glorification of the unity of the mother and, through the mother, the subject's own unity. This misperceived maternal imago can translate into fantasies of individual wholeness or it can translate into fantasies of national wholeness, but in either case, the structure of that subjectivity is the same: namely, paranoia. When one's sense of self-completeness or one's sense of national completeness is so invested in projected images of wholeness from the outside world, the aggression intrinsic to that fabulously aggrandized yet utterly divided subjective position is inevitable.

Thus, we could, like Rosemary Jackson, read the so-called "female gothic" as a site of subversion, as that which "points to or suggests the basis upon which cultural order rests . . . that which lies outside the law, that which is outside dominant value systems . . . that which has been silenced, made invisible, covered over and made 'absent'" (4). But, in doing so, we would have to acknowledge that the tradition of the fantastic is also the tradition of pornography and violence—the tradition of Matthew Lewis or the Marquis de Sade appropriating the works of Ann Radcliffe and the tradition still epitomized by the renegade John-Wayne reincarnated in Arnold Schwarzenegger or Mel Gibson. Moreover, whether manifested within sheer pornography or sublimated into epic violence, the gothic is inevitably a tradition that, more than any other, relies on sexist, racist, and classist constructions of the "other" for the reference points of its own transgressions and vicarious *jouissance*. Renaming the more "masculine," sexualized, or aggressive genre "horror," as some have done for the literary gothic tradition, does little to help this paradox, for the gothic, whether in cinema or literature, is by its very nature "uncanny"—that which returns from fantasy into the real and that which returns from the real into fantasy.

NOTES

[1] An earlier version of this essay was presented online for the "Symposium in Rhetoric: Emerging Rhetorics" conference hosted by the Texas Woman's University in April of 1999.

[2] "Many directors will do a point-of-view tracking shot by laying the track a few feet to the side of the moving character and running the camera along to the rear of him, the better to obscure the dolly track. This was not strictly the exact point of view of the character, but rather three-quarters of the point of view. Brian De Palma insisted on the exact article. His dolly was laid directly behind the moving character; the track up ahead was masked with sand, and as the dolly moved and the track was no longer in danger of entering the shot, the sand was swept away" (Dworkin 111).

[3] De Palma's career-long entanglement with Women Against Pornography illustrates how this ambiguity can ultimately turn into paranoia and aggression quite well. See Badley's excellent analysis of this interaction in *Film, Horror, and the Body Fantastic*, Contributions to the Study of Popular Culture No. 48 (London: Greenwood Press, 1995) 109–111.

[4] In her first sentence, Mulvey depicts the film spectator as masculine— "This paper intends to use psychoanalysis to discover where and how the fascination of film is reinforced by pre-existing patterns of fascination already at work within the individual subject and the social formations that have molded *him*" (57, emphasis added)—a slip that Mulvey remedies by examining the perspectives of the female spectator in "Afterthoughts on 'Visual Pleasure and Narrative Cinema'" (69–79).

[5] Rose did briefly address *Carrie* a year later, arguing that along with two other 1978 films, *Coma* and *Fedora*, *Carrie* "produces a self-consciousness of cinema, a kind of commentary on the very apparatus of the film, but then this very self-consciousness is reduced to the question of the body of the woman, of what is at stake in constituting her as the object (and subject) of the look" (*Sexuality* 220).

[6] If Katt Shea's *The Rage: Carrie 2* (1999) modernizes De Palma's *Carrie* through a more feminist perspective, it does so only by reversal, for in it, the sexual exchange is a highly stereotypical exploitation of women—"the game"—by a group of aggressive football players, the main female character has an abusive family with both paternal and maternal figures, and the director herself resubsumes the Carrie figure into the patriarchal Old-Testament tradition by renaming her "Rachel." The women in *The Rage* are not much different from the women in King's or De Palma's *Carrie*—preoccupied with the sex appeal that commodity culture offers—and the only non-white high-school students are the African-American athletes who, servant-like, assist the white football players in lifting weights. Moreover, by moving the violent finale of the prom to an upscale private party, Shea cuts off even the vicarious participation of those not already safely enclosed within an affluent white jet set appropriating the lingo, music, and style of the African-American cultural tradition. The original title for the film—*Carrie: Say You're Sorry*—indicates how reductive the intentions were in readapting De Palma's *Carrie*.

[7] See *Eighteenth Century: Theory and Interpretation* 22.1 (Winter 1981): 47–57.

[8] See Kaja Silverman's *The Acoustic Mirror: The Female Voice in Psychoanalysis and Cinema* (Bloomington: Indiana UP, 1988). The distinction that De Man here proposes discordantly resonates with the metaphysical economy of pity that Jacques Derrida traces in the works of Jean-Jacques Rousseau. Derrida shows that for Rousseau, the "natural" pity supposedly preceding "reflective" pity is that of the maternal voice, a voice which "takes the place of the law" when that law is lacking in nature. As a result, "natural," non-reflective pity is aligned with femininity, inanimateness, materiality, and death and thereby marked as amoral, atemporal, and ahistorical. In contrast to "natural" pity, the identification that is operative in "reflective" pity is one of distance and differentiation: the person who pities identifies the suffering of the other only as a suffering *outside* his or her "self." For Rousseau, this reflective distance inaugurates not only reason, but also the hierarchical positions that are linked to, and dependent upon, such distance (Derrida 173–4). Silverman's postulation of the "acoustic mirror" allows for the possibility that the maternal voice does not "take the place of the law," or symbolic, but that this voice itself institutes the distance and differentiation necessary for self-(mis)recognition and becoming. Rousseau's

"maternal voice" and those far more abrasive voices re-enacted by Norman Bates or Margaret White show how uncanny anything presumed so natural, so intimately familiar, can become. Yet De Palma's use of Nancy Allen's scream in *Blow Out* indicates that he was attempting to (re)induce both an absorptive and reflexive affinity with the so readily marked yet so eerily distant, non-sympathetic voice of the suffering other typically found in horror films.

[9] "The fact is that the total form of the body by which the subject anticipates in a mirage the maturation of his power is given to him only as *Gestalt*, that is to say, in an exteriority in which this form is certainly more constituent than constituted, but in which it appears to him above all in a contrasting size (*un relief de stature*) that fixes it and in a symmetry that inverts it, in contrast with the turbulent movements that the subject feels are animating him" (Lacan, *Écrits* 2).

[10] In "Vampires, Breast-Feeding, and Anxiety," Joan Copjec makes a similar argument: "Anxiety—again, like respect and terror—is not only not caused by any loss/lack of object . . . Rather than an object or its lack, anxiety signals a lack of a lack, a failure of the symbolic reality wherein all alienable objects, objects which can be given or taken away, lost and refound, are constituted and circulate . . . The danger that anxiety signals is the overproximity of th[e] object a, the object so *unalienable* that like Dracula and all other vampires of Gothic and Romantic fiction it cannot even be cast as a shadow or reflected as a mirror image" (26–27).

[11] The constructedness of the scene is quite apparent from Nancy Allen's comments about the context in which it was filmed: "The shooting was very difficult, especially for the shower scene because we all had to be naked. We even had to sign some releases because some of the girls didn't want to do it and the producer was afraid they might walk off the set" (qtd. in Bouzereau 43).

[12] Babington slightly exaggerates this aggressivity in an attempt to defend De Palma against the claims of the British Film Institute and feminists that *Carrie* remains within the exclusive discursive register of uncomplicated misogyny. Of the opening volleyball sequence, the BFI argue that the "elaborate crane shot draws attention to itself and shows the girls as an almost abstract pattern of color and movement—a 'stylistic' credit in addition to the authorial title" (qtd. in Babington 5). As Babington points out, this reading is wonderfully elaborate for a film supposedly so superficial. *Carrie*'s faux signature piece, like that of *Blow Out*, is an indirect acknowledgement of the restrictive visual role that both the actresses and women have, a role De Palma does not merely exploit, but thematizes in the remainder of the film. In fact, the incoherence for which the BFI indict De Palma is far more pronounced in the King novel that he was adapting. King, as Badley notes, "brought a cinematic perspective to the naturalistic novel," and he thus throughout employs conflicting and disjunctive points of view, eschewing the realist novelist's "objective" third-person perspective in favor of the gothic novelist's assembled pastiche of narratives from various cultural sources: scientific journals, legal transcripts, interviews, personal diaries, medical records, newspaper articles, and even Bob Dylan lyrics (8). De Palma's film is far more coherent, so coherent that had the BFI read the novel, they would have likely accused King of careless misogyny rather than De Palma. King's *Carrie* is particularly fractured in this opening section, and De Palma's camera maneuvers, however characteristically flamboyant, actually make the diegesis far less ambiguous and confusing.

[13] The awkward punning of "Period One," a pun quite pronounced throughout the opening section of *Carrie*, invokes an atmosphere in which even the symbolic spheres of timing, order, and chronology have been usurped by the chaotic and unlawful rhythms of women's bodily functions.

[14] De Palma's gym teacher, "Miss Collins" (Betty Buckley), is, in contrast, simultaneously buxom and muscular. Her white shorts take center stage during the first twenty minutes of the film, and her punishment of the women through a severe exercise regimen is the focus of at least half of the storyline. The shocking stain of Carrie's menstrual blood that is so pronounced on Miss Desjardin's white shorts in the King novel is, however, expunged from the film even though the other characters, notably the intimidated high-school principal, react to her shorts as if they do, in fact, betray the traumatic horror of the shower scene. The abrupt end of the film, when Carrie rises out of the grave with a desperate hand forward, repeats her initial bloody grab at Miss Collins' pristine white shorts in the shower.

[15] That "parody" may also have an ulterior motive, but one with a very distinct kind of laughter—one, moreover, which does not reinscribe the boundaries of the "normal"—witness Russo's

conclusion to "Female Grotesques": "For now, right now, as I acknowledge the work of feminists in reconstituting knowledge, I imagine us going forward, growing old (I hope), or being grotesque in other ways. I see us viewed by ourselves and others, in our bodies and in our work, in ways that are continuously shifting the terms of viewing, so that looking at us, there will be a new question, the question that never occurred to Bakhtin in front of the Kerch terracotta figurines—Why are those old hags laughing?" (226-7).

[16] King, in contrast, increases the "release" for the viewer after the shower scene, when Carrie masturbates more privately at home. During the shower scene, King describes Carrie's body in excessively demeaning terms but, during the masturbation scene, her body becomes beautified, piece-by-piece, as she "discovers" her own sexuality in front of the implicitly peeping-tom reader.

[17] See Michel Chion, "Revolution douce," *La toile trouée* (Paris: Cahiers du Cinema, 1988).

[18] In a similar fashion, René Girard describes the amorphous but ubiquitous function of the scapegoat as follows: "The scapegoat released to us by the text is a scapegoat both *in* and *for* the text. The scapegoat that we must disengage from the text for ourselves is the scapegoat *of* the text. He cannot appear in the text though he controls all its themes; he is never mentioned as such. He cannot become the theme of that he *shapes*. This is not a theme but a mechanism for giving *structure*" (118, original emphasis). Thus, as Girard says of Salome's dance, we may say of Carrie's autoeroticism: "The guests are all under Salome's spell . . . They were possessed by something that chained them and the dance frees them. The dancer can make the lame dance because her dance exorcises the demon that possesses them. She enables them to exchange all that wearies and torments them for the head of John the Baptist. She not only reveals the demon that possesses them but she also carries out the act of vengeance of which they dream . . . Everyone shares the same frenzy towards the model obstacle, and they all willingly mistake the object because the proposed object feeds their appetite for violence" (135).

[19] This "mask" is especially predominant in *Body Double*, wherein the satiric scene of fantasy-turned-murder alters in that the predator of the "film within the film" becomes a much more significant part of the action. The obsessively voyeuristic protagonist (Craig Wasson) witnesses the nightly erotic dancing of a woman via a telescope, scenes that culminate in what he presumes to be her death-by-drill from an Anglo-American man (Gregg Henry) in the guise of a large Native American. The mask that Henry puts on to delude Wasson took *five* hours for the makeup artists to construct every time it was used in a shot—an effort that bears witness not only to the main character's hyperbolic (mis)perception of the animalesque monster, but also to the audience's own complicity in the fantastic construction of racial otherness. De Palma likewise coerced the allegedly murdered female lead, the ex-Miss America Deborah Shelton, to perform rigorous exercise "drills" to shrink her already immaculate figure into the requisite but fantastic feminine shape. (Dworkin 126-27, 100)

[20] The "fairy tale"-gone-awry interpretation of both King's and De Palma's *Carrie* may have its first impulse with this storybook Uncle-Remus figure taking real-life revenge on those who misread (and film) him. That Joel Chandler Harris might have posed a "film within the film"-esque double for King, who has also aspired to be the folklorist of contemporary American traditions, seems possible from his reaction to De Palma's film: "The first time I saw *Carrie* with an audience was at a preview a week and a half before Halloween. The audience was full of black people. I thought: they are going to rate the hell out of this picture. What are they going to think about a skinny little white girl with her menstrual problems? And that's the way it started, and then, little by little, they got on her side, you know, and when she started doing her shtick, I mean, they're going, tear it up!—Go for it!—and all this other stuff. I knew it was going to be a hit!" (qtd. in Bouzereau 45). King's impersonation of the African-American audience's reaction inversely echoes the women in the shower scene who chant "Plug It Up! Plug It Up!" while Carrie bleeds (6-8). A notable contrast to King's minstrel-mask image, which aesthetisizes and thereby alienates the reader's potential identification with Carrie, is that in the primal scene of Kathryn Bigelow's *Strange Days*, where a man forces a women to experience her own rape and death through a virtual-reality device to which she, the rapist, and the audience itself are attached. Bigelow's redoubled diegesis forces the audience to identify with the woman, "Iris," rather than the rapist or camera during the violence, and as a result, the rapist's framing of her "huge white eyes"—the

turning of them into a picture with his gloved hands—forces the audience to confront their own aesthetization of the sexualized violence retroactively.

WORKS CITED

Alloula, Malak. *The Colonial Harem*. Intro. Barbara Harlow. Trans. Myrna Wlad Godzich. Theory and History of Literature 21. Minneapolis: University of Minnesota Press, 1986.

Artaud, Antonin. *The Theatre and Its Double*. Trans. Mary Caroline Richards. New York: Grove Press, 1958.

Babington, Bruce. "Twice a Victim: Carrie Meets the BFI." *Screen* 24.3 (1983): 4–18.

Badley, Linda. *Film, Horror, and the Body Fantastic*. Contributions to the Study of Popular Culture No. 48. London: Greenwood Press, 1995.

Bathrick, Serafina. "Carrie: Ragtime—the Horror of Growing Up Female." *Jump Cut* 14 (1976): 9–10.

Benjamin, Walter. "One Way Street." *Reflections: Essays, Aphorisms, Autobiographical Writings*. Ed. and Intro. Peter Demetz. Trans. Edmund Jephcott. New York: Schocken Books, 1986.

———. "Work of Art in the Age of Mechanical Reproduction." *Illuminations*. Ed. and Intro. Hannah Arendt. Trans. Harry Zohn. New York: Schocken Books, 1968.

Bhabha, Homi. *The Location of Culture*. New York: Routledge, 1994.

Blow Out. Dir. Brian De Palma. Cinema 77, 1981.

Body Double. Dir. Brian De Palma. Columbia, 1984.

Bouzereau, Laurent. *The De Palma Cut: The Films of America's Most Controversial Director*. New York: Dembner Books, 1988.

Carrie. Dir. Brian De Palma. Redbank Films, 1976.

Citron, Michelle. "*Carrie* Meets *Marathon Man*." *Jump Cut* 14 (1976): 10–12.

Conway, Lorie. "It's Time to Tell the Bloody Truth." *Nieman Reports* 50.2 (Summer 1996): 30–31.

Copjec, Joan. "Vampires, Breast-Feeding, and Anxiety." *October* 58 (Fall 1991): 25–43.

de Man, Paul. *Blindness and Insight: Essays in the Rhetoric of Contemporary Criticism*. Intro. Wlad Godzich. Theory and History of Literature 7. Minneapolis: University of Minnesota Press, 1983.

Debord, Guy. *Society of the Spectacle*. Trans. Donald Nicholson-Smith. New York: Zone Books, 1994.

Derrida, Jacques. *Of Grammatology*. Trans. Gayatri Chakravorty Spivak. Corrected ed. Baltimore: Johns Hopkins University Press, 1998.

Dworkin, Susan. *Double De Palma*. New York: Newmarket Press, 1984.

Freud, Sigmund. *The Standard Edition of the Complete Psychological Works of Sigmund Freud*. Trans. James Strachey. London: Hogarth Press, 1953–1974.

Girard, René. *The Scapegoat*. Trans. Yvonne Freccero. Baltimore: Johns Hopkins UP, 1986.

Halloween. Dir. John Carpenter. Falcon Films, 1978.

Jackson, Rosemary. *Fantasy: The Literature of Subversion*. London: Methuen, 1981.

Jameson, Fredric. "Postmodernism and Consumer Society." *Anti-Aesthetic: Essays on Postmodern Culture*. Ed. Hal Foster. Port Townsend: Bay Press, 1983.

King, Stephen. *Carrie*. New York: Signet, 1975.

Lacan, Jacques. *Écrits: A Selection*. Trans. Alan Sheridan. New York: Norton, 1977.

———. *The Ego in Freud's Theory and in the Technique of Psychoanalysis 1954–1955*. Ed. Jacques-Alain Miller. Trans. Sylvana Tomaselli. New York: Norton, 1988.

———. *Feminine Sexuality: Jacques Lacan and the "Ecole Freudian."* Ed. Juliet Mitchell and Jacqueline Rose. Trans. Jacqueline Rose. New York: Norton, 1982.

———. *The Four Fundamental Concepts of Psychoanalysis*. Ed. Jacques-Alain Miller. Trans. Alan Sheridan. New York: Norton, 1978.

McClintock, Anne. "Soft-Soaping Empire: Commodity Racism and Imperial Advertising." *Imperial Leather: Race, Gender and Sexuality in the Colonial Context*. New York: Routledge, 1995.

Mulvey, Laura. "Visual Pleasure and Narrative Cinema" and "Afterthoughts on 'Visual Pleasure and Narrative Cinema.'" *Feminism and Film Theory*. Ed. Constance Penley. New York: Routledge, 1988.

Paul, William. "Menstruation, Monstrosity, and Mothers." *Laughing Screaming: Modern Hollywood Horror and Comedy*. New York: Columbia UP, 1994.

Peeping Tom. Dir. Michael Powell. Rialto Pictures, 1960.

Pirie, David. "American Cinema in the '70s: *Carrie*." *Movie* 25: 20–24.

The Rage: Carrie 2. Dir. Katt Shea. United Artists, 1999.

Rose, Jacqueline. "Paranoia and the Film System." *Feminism and Film Theory*. Ed. Constance Penley. New York: Routledge, 1988.

———. *Sexuality in the Field of Vision*. London: Verso, 1986.

Russo, Mary. "Female Grotesques: Carnival and Theory." *Feminist Studies/Critical Studies*. Ed. Teresa de Lauretis. Theories of Contemporary Culture 8. Bloomington: Indiana UP, 1986.

Silverman, Kaja. *The Threshold of the Visible World*. New York: Routledge, 1996.

Sisters. Dir. Brian De Palma. AI Pictures, 1973.

Strange Days. Dir. Kathryn Bigelow. Lightstorm Ent., 1995.

The Texas Chain Saw Massacre. Dir. Tobe Hooper. Vortex, 1974.

Žižek, Slavoj. *Looking Awry: An Introduction to Jacques Lacan Through Popular Culture*. Cambridge: MIT Press, 1992.

AFTERWORD

The foregoing essay arose directly from an experience teaching—or, to be more honest, from an all-too-common experience of vexation while teaching. Each new generation of students served for me as a vital, though admittedly defective, yardstick for the potential of humankind as a whole. Yet each year, my students seemed to profess ever-increasing apathy toward the unenviable, and certainly unjustifiable, affliction of those residing outside their predominately middle-class purview. Inasmuch as I could, I resisted the impulse to construe this apathy as signaling an escalation of malice or insensitivity in the world as such, conjecturing instead that it was only a symptom of the rather intractable penchant for ideological stupor, or obliviousness to the obvious, which, unfortunately, we are all (and are all always) far too complaisant about and far too efficient in adopting. I thus sought, both in this essay and the classroom itself, to demystify the political and public investments in what we believe to be, and do in fact experience as, private fantasy.

To confront this manufactured consent most effectively, I decided to investigate texts that were mass produced, mass consumed, and hence known and appreciated on the widest scale possible. For inasmuch as I could approximate, these texts would speak the same language as my students—as well as my friends, family, and colleagues—facilitating an identification with and approach to the complexities of race, class, and gender (not to mention that most touchy of topics, sexuality) in a fashion most amenable to their being openly acknowledged and honestly addressed. Not surprisingly, the novel that I eventually selected was Stephen King's *Carrie*, coupled with Brian De Palma's filmic adaptation. Each reflects these concerns in form—telepathic identification or projection—as well as content: social alienation. Indeed, as I soon discovered, popular fiction is popular for a reason, hardly pulp at all; my students, without exception, related to this text, and I, without exception, related wholeheartedly to them. Teaching *Carrie* accordingly turned out to be a fortunate experience for both me and my students, to whom I am indebted for many of the ideas and much of the inspiration that I put into this article. Once everyone was on the same page, as it were, everything else of importance seemed to soon follow, even that which is most conventionally understood to compose a liberal education: humanistic self-examination, critical thinking with regard to self and society, and thence civic and cultural engagement at large.

In this case, the novel, and especially the popular novel, is the genre of choice. For more than anything else, the novel is a means of transport: it can be a vehicle for identification with others, differentiation from others, or even a way to escape the demands of human interaction altogether. Most important, the novel is a prime example of what Mary Louise Pratt terms a "contact zone," offering not only an ideal forum for staging encounters across cultures but also, at its best, an excellent medium for inducing what are truly multicultural points of view, free of insularity, cognizant of diversity, and receptive to the manifold ways of being and thinking practiced throughout the world. In fact, the novel is such an effectual means of identification that, at least temporarily, the mind of the reader, the mind of the narrator, and the minds of the assorted characters can blend together, thereby encouraging us to surmount otherwise intractable barriers of nationality, sexuality, ethnicity, or economic status, no matter how deeply entrenched those barriers may be in actuality.

In this vein, and in a manner that I hope will operate more as an incentive to begin (again) than as a means of closure, I would like to dedicate this essay to J. Douglas Canfield, formerly Regents Professor of English Literature at the University of Arizona, lately deceased, whose last request to his students—"keep fighting"—I cannot help repeat here. In a time when the humanities are undergoing so many profound changes and triggering such deep contention and introspection about their very function, it is important to remind ourselves why we study and teach literature, or even simply why we read it in the first place: to commune not only with a book, a character, or an author but also with unfamiliar aspects of ourselves, hitherto unmet or unacknowledged others, and of course that broader public which "we" and "they" together constitute. And it is for this reason, if not for any other, that novelists like Toni Morrison and Stephen King continue to receive National Book Awards and related honors despite the predictably contemptuous objections of "great books" advocates, who still act as if we ought to curb rather than commend the enjoyment of literature and to value only those works that attract the fewest enthusiasts.

The Improper Name: Ownership and Authorship in the Literary Production of Assia Djebar

Alison Rice

Ce qu'on appelle 'nom propre' est donc toujours déjà impropre, et l'acte de nomination qu'on voudrait comme origine et prototype du langage suppose l'écriture au sens élargi donné à ce mot par Derrida. (Bennington 102)[1]

ASSIA DJEBAR IS a renowned writer whose work is receiving increasing attention worldwide. She has recently been awarded a number of prestigious literary prizes in various countries, culminating in this year's esteemed "Friedenspreis des Deutschen Buchhandels" in Germany.[2] But the name under which these awards are listed is not the name this Algerian woman went by as a child; Assia Djebar is a pseudonym the author adopted upon the publication of her first novel, *La soif* (1957), when she was a university student of twenty. The choice of this pen name has not yet been fully explored, whether in Djebar's writings or in critical examinations of her work. But this action of "adopting a name," of "naming herself" and thereby "making a name for herself," merits close examination because of what it reveals about the proper name, autobiography, literature, and particularly ownership and authorship in Assia Djebar's writing. I will argue that her apparently hasty choice of a pseudonym involved much more than a cover under which to publish a clandestine novel. Djebar's experience presents an unusual case in which the pseudonym has become a proper name. Assia Djebar has completely "adopted" her *nom de plume*, "taking on" this name to the extent that it has become *her own*; her identity as a writer has inexorably merged with her identity as a person.

Critics of Assia Djebar's work have not entirely overlooked her pseudonym.[3] But it is surprising how briefly they have made mention of it and moved on;[4] their references are quick, fleeting, anecdotal at best, and there even seems to be some confusion as to the meaning of the pen name and the reasons behind its adoption.[5] Clarisse Zimra, in her afterword to the English translation of *Femmes d'Alger dans leur appartement*, provides the most complete version of how Assia

Djebar came upon her name. The young, soon-to-be-famous writer's book was going to print, and she needed to find a pen name quickly. Naturally, she didn't want her family to attribute the forthcoming novel to her, and her most pressing concern was to cover up her identity in the photos and accompanying bio sheet due to appear in the women's monthly *Elle*. To this end, she sought the help of her fiancé as their "taxi hurtled through the streets of Paris," asking him "to recite the ninety-nine ritual modes of address to Allah in the hope of finding herself a *nom de plume*. She selected djebbar, the phrase that praises 'Allah the intransigent,' but in her haste spelled it 'djébar,' unwittingly transforming the classical Arabic into the vernacular term for 'healer'" (160). It seems peculiar that this writer who treats names with such great care in her novels should hastily choose a name for herself and then erroneously transcribe it. But this is the way the story reads, and this anecdote has served as the basis for critical readings of Djebar's texts.[6]

When asked about the choice of her first name, "Assia," the writer said in an unpublished interview that "it was just a family first name that everybody liked" (160), but Zimra highlights the significance of this name just the same, insisting that "it has far-reaching symbolic resonances. In standard Arabic, it designates Asia and the mysterious Orient, thus 'orientalizing' its bearer" (160).[7] Whatever the meaning of "Assia Djebar" in the writer's native Arabic, it is important to note that its significance is not apparent in the French language in which she writes. The francophone reader does not perceive the intricacies of meaning inherent in the author's name, but one thing does stand out: the name is "other." Even to a reader ignorant of Arabic tradition and culture, the name "Assia Djebar" belongs to an Algerian woman. Unlike the famous *noms de plume* "George Sand" and "George Eliot," this pen name does not hide the sexual identity of its bearer. Nor does it dissimulate her origin; it is clear that the name is Arabic.

Since she does not try to mask her gender or her place of origin, the choice of a pen name for Fatima-Zohra Imalayène begs the question, "why?" An effort to hide her writing from her family seems a dubious answer because, according to Zimra's account, Djebar's act of defiance was discovered only a few weeks later when her mother was browsing through a magazine rack. If Djebar needed to hide her writing at all cost, she wouldn't have agreed to pose for *Elle*. The presence of the father seems to hang over the transgressive act of writing, even though he is the one who took her to school so that she could learn French in the first place. The complexity of this relationship between the young writer and her father certainly should not be dismissed, and Jeanne-Marie Clerc pertinently acknowledges the ambiguities of a situation in which the girl must hide the fact that she writes from the very man without whom writing would have been impossible:

> Ainsi, grâce [aux pères], les femmes algériennes ont reconquis le pouvoir [. . .] d'écrire. Pourtant, c'est pour que son père n'apprenne pas qu'elle écrivait, qu'Assia Djebar raconte avoir pris ce pseudonyme lors de la parution de son premier roman. Etrange ambiguïté d'une relation fondamentale qui reste empreinte du 'métissage' culturel problématique dont ces pères ont été les médiateurs. (67)[8]

The ambiguous situation in which the young writer finds herself with respect to her father comes to a head when her first book is to be published, and it is at this crucial point that she must reach a decision. Knowing that her father was opposed to her correspondence in French several years earlier, she fears that the scandalous act of writing, compounded by the publishing, the making public, of that writing, will once again come under his censorship, under "le diktat paternel." In her first openly autobiographical novel, *L'amour, la fantasia*, Djebar addresses the paternal presence that affected her as a teenager:

> Chaque lettre, même la plus innocente, supposerait l'oeil constant du père, avant de me parvenir. Mon écriture, en entretenant ce dialogue sous influence, devenait en moi tentative—ou tentation—de délimiter mon propre silence . . . (75)[9]

The significant gesture of taking a pseudonym marks the first, irreversible step in breaking with the paternal censor(ship) that haunted the young girl. In a sense, she is no longer accountable to him because she has claimed ownership, not only of her work, but of herself. It is an act of appropriating that which, for a woman in general and especially for a woman in a traditional Algerian family, is seldom "proper": the name.

French feminist critics have long understood and underlined the importance of the proper name and the woman's lack thereof.[10] Luce Irigaray makes the flat assertion that woman "has no 'proper' name," that the name does not belong to her.[11] Passed from father to husband, the typical woman has no name that she can call her own. Her last name, forever subject to change, is merely a label that is applied to her to reveal her affiliation; it is never something that reveals *her*. And her given name is "assigned" as well, applied to her from birth in an arbitrary manner.[12] In her feminist manifesto "Le Rire de la Méduse," Hélène Cixous maintains that women have learned to adapt to this unsteady relation to their name:

> Je dis qu'elle bouleverse le 'personnel': comme on lui a, par lois, mensonges, chantages, mariage, toujours extorqué son droit à elle-même en même temps que son nom, elle a dans le mouvement même de l'aliénation mortelle pu voir de plus près l'inanité du 'propre', la mesquinerie réductrice de l'économie subjective masculine-conjugale, à laquelle elle résiste doublement. (50)[13]

In Cixous's view, one of the ways women have learned to resist the "masculine-conjugal subjective economy" is to see themselves as individuals with "integrity," regardless of their changing name and status: "On the one hand she has constituted herself necessarily as that 'person' capable of losing a part of herself without losing her integrity" (357).

In taking the initiative and choosing her own name, Assia Djebar has upheld her integrity by removing herself completely from the "masculine-conjugal" economy. She has provided herself with a stable, unchanging title that is not dependent on her marital status. She and her first husband divorced and she married a second time, but these changes went unreflected in her name; "Assia Djebar" did not waver, despite the instability in her personal life.[14] The "coming to writing" ("*la venue à l'écriture*") to which Cixous incites women coincides in this case with the choice of the name. The writer adopts a new identity, in a way, which becomes at once synonymous with and distinct from her writing. It is an identity separate from family ties, demarcated by a name unique to her.

This act of naming herself, of choosing a pseudonym by which she has become known throughout the world in both public and private affairs, is fundamentally subversive. As if writing as an Algerian woman were not daring enough, naming herself is a deliberate action that undermines authority in a patriarchal society. Jacques Derrida's reflection on the biblical story of the Tower of Babel is helpful in understanding the rebellion inherent in Djebar's act of giving herself a name. Derrida notes that the "patronym" is essential to comprehension in the world (since we need different proper names in order to distinguish among people), but that the control of names is a powerful thing and therefore must be contained, according to the biblical account: "En donnant son nom, un nom de son choix, en donnant tous les noms, le père serait à l'origine du langage et ce pouvoir appartiendrait de droit à Dieu le père" (211).[15] In choosing her own name, Assia Djebar is assuming a divine rite; she is usurping authority that is not rightly hers. Derrida contends that the people building the Tower of Babel may have been repudiated for trying to build as high as the heavens, but the real reason for their punishment was "incontestablement d'avoir voulu *se faire un nom*, se donner à eux-mêmes le nom, se construire eux-mêmes leur propre nom, s'y rassembler ('que nous ne soyons plus dispersés') comme dans l'unité d'un lieu qui est à la fois une langue et une tour, l'une comme l'autre" (213).[16] The act of giving oneself a name in this instance is punishable, according to Derrida, because it demonstrates a desire to assure oneself "une généalogie unique et universelle" (213). In a similar way, Assia Djebar's efforts to "make a name for herself" through writing and filmmaking represent an attempt to assure her genealogy, but not on her father's side. It is her genealogy on her mother's side, the nameless side, that she seeks to vindicate through her work.

Djebar is deeply aware of the difference between the two sides of her family tree, as we discover in the love story that occupies the opening section of *Vaste est la prison*:

> Vous savez bien, la branche paternelle compte pour l'héritage, et donc pour les mariages d'intérêts, tandis que la lignée maternelle, par contre, est celle de la tendresse, des sentiments. (41)

The heritage Djebar investigates and embraces throughout her work has nothing to do with her paternal "inheritance," but is instead closely tied to the maternal heritage whose roots take hold much deeper in her consciousness. I will return to this idea of heritage and Djebar's maternal inheritance after an exploration of the proper name and its importance to the writing and publishing processes.

The proper name fulfills a specific function in the world, that of assuring the individuality of its bearer. In theory, it unambiguously designates a specific person, and reference to this individual is clear whenever the name is used. In *Jacques Derrida*, by Geoffrey Bennington and Jacques Derrida, this is how the proper name is meant to be understood:

Le nom propre devrait assurer un certain passage entre langage et monde, dans cette mesure où il devrait indiquer un individu concret, sans ambiguïté, sans avoir besoin de passer par les circuits de la signification. Même si on accepte que le système de la langue est constitué de différences et donc de traces, il semblerait que le nom propre, qui fait partie du langage, pointe directement vers l'individu qu'il nomme. (100–101)[17]

But the proper name, like the larger linguistic system in which it functions, fails to work as a transparent indicator of equivalence. It serves instead merely to differentiate among individuals:

Mais il n'y a pas de nom propre. Ce qu'on appelle du nom commun générique 'nom propre' doit bien fonctionner, lui aussi, dans un système de différences: tel ou tel nom propre plutôt qu'un autre désigne tel ou tel individu plutôt qu'un autre. (101)[18]

This ability to differentiate among people loses some of its efficacy when it comes to names from other places, originating in other languages. It is significant that Derrida addresses the proper name in an essay on translation, for a proper name is that which cannot be translated, as it is specific to a particular language system.[19] A proper name retains its form (or the closest possible equivalent) in translation, but as such it often confuses the reader unfamiliar with such names. The problems resulting from such mistakes are legion. Such African writers as Laye Camara and Ousmane Sembène have suffered from ignorance with respect to their family names. In scholarly articles and reviews of both writers' work, they have been repeatedly referred to by their first names rather than their surnames.[20] In the case of the transliteration of Arabic names into French form, something is inevitably lost in the transition. The meaning present in the Arabic disappears irrevocably from the French version of the name, as we have already seen in the case of Assia Djebar.[21]

The type of confusion caused by a lack of familiarity with a foreign name goes against the very conception of the name in Western tradition as that which distinguishes an individual, as the defining feature that sets someone apart from the anonymous crowd, as something which acquires nearly sacred significance. When it comes to publishing, the name is the most important, but definitely not the only, form of identification and authorization of a written work, as Christopher Miller points out in *Theories of Africans*:

An author's name [. . .] must be different from all other names in some way; the author must be an individual. If name alone does not eliminate confusion, then in the libraries of the West we attach birth dates and other identifying marks. The legal status of copyright depends on a legal notion of individual identity, backed up by the techniques of literate culture: birth certificates, identity cards, signatures. (115)

The repetition of the word "legal" in this passage underlines the close connection between the name and the law; one's name is official and great pains are taken to assure its proper documentation. Miller sets up this Western notion of the individuality of a name in contrast to the "fragmented authorship" found in oral traditions that don't possess this plethora of textual proofs of individuality:

> The name of a single author, legally responsible for the text that follows, belongs to the domain of written literature; the fragmented authorship and deferred authority of an oral text, inherited and modified, belongs to a different notion of originality and creation. (114)

In the domain of written literature, the name "must bear a considerable legal and philosophical burden" (115).[22] It carries tremendous weight because of the "responsibility" individual writers take upon themselves for the texts published in their name.[23]

In choosing a distinctively "Arabic" name as a pseudonym for a French-speaking readership, Assia Djebar takes a risk. She risks falling under a stereotypical categorization that would define her as an "Algerian woman" without acknowledging her individuality. She risks losing ownership of her work and the privileges of authorship by falling prey to the erasure of difference that occurs when writers from a foreign background are lumped together under a non-discriminating system of classification. In her insightful study on the prevalence of the "stereotype" in French culture, Mireille Rosello outlines how this powerful process works:

> Stereotyping reflexes turn the names of ethnic groups into undecidable units that share some of the characteristics of both proper names and common nouns. When a proper name is narrowly associated with someone's race, religion, or ethnicity, its functions are blurred and adulterated. The proper name loses its power of differentiation and is no longer capable of endowing one individual with a uniqueness irreducible to any form of regrouping. The mystery of otherness is lost and replaced by the dull but also pacifying comfort of generalizations. (141)

I would like to suggest that this risk, that of being confused with a larger number of people, that of slipping into anonymity as a representative of a group of women from her geographical region, is not as frightening for Assia Djebar as one might think. Certainly she has been influenced by a Western education and Western ideals of individuality and originality, but Djebar has not been untouched by her "feminine genealogy" in which her identity is not dependent upon her ability to distinguish herself above and beyond others. To the contrary, she seeks to give voice to other women, often illiterate women, in her texts and films, in an effort to let others "speak" through her media. This conception of authorship differs widely from the individualistic goals of most writers who want to "make a name for themselves" completely on their own. In contrast to them, Assia Djebar is happy to have her name associated with a multitude of nameless women, without whom her work wouldn't be possible.

Assia Djebar is perhaps best known for her autobiographical novels, beginning with the publication of *L'amour, la fantasia* in 1985.[24] This, the first book published after a significant period of silence,[25] followed the production of two films for which Djebar received considerable critical acclaim.[26] Her experience as a filmmaker in her Algerian homeland, capturing the images and sounds of women from her "tribe," inspired her to turn inward and examine her own relationship to the body and language, and ultimately to write (of) herself. She doesn't claim to be the first Algerian woman to write her story. Djebar is aware of her "filiation," of the women who have written their life stories before her. She acknowledges *Histoire de ma vie* by Fadhma Aït Mansour-Amrouche as the "première auto-biographie écrite par une Algérienne en langue française" (*Ces voix* 118).[27] This text, finally published in 1967, was begun two decades earlier and intended only for Fadhma's son.[28] But its itinerary is an interesting one, as it was saved by a daughter who added her voice to her mother's in a hybrid text that finally reached a wide audience; the work was published with a preface penned by well-known Algerian writer Kateb Yacine. Djebar, in her analysis of this unusual autobiography, pays close attention to the language in which Fadhma composes this account of her life. Like Djebar, this predecessor peppers her French with the sounds of her native Berber and Arabic tongues. Like Djebar, she takes ahold of her life, reappropriates it, in a sense, through the act of writing: "Fadhma reprend possession de sa vie, en l'écrivant à soixante-quatre ans" (*Ces voix* 123).[29] And, like Djebar, she pays little attention to establishing an "autobiographical pact" with the reader:

> Décidément, le 'pacte autobiographique' cher à Philippe Lejeune n'est pas prévu aussi variable, aussi aléatoire quand il s'agit ainsi d'une écriture, pour ainsi dire, couplée: mère et fille, la première écrivant, la seconde la suivant, la première continuant. . . (123)[30]

The flexible, seemingly random composition of both Fadhma's and Assia Djebar's autobiographical works seems to defy any attempt to theorize autobiography. In the case of Djebar, the question of the proper name brings to the forefront the inherently problematic categorization of any work as "autobiographical."

In his seminal study on the genre, Philippe Lejeune puts forth a rather rigid definition of autobiography that centers on a specific conception of identity. He asserts that an autobiographical work must contain an "*identity of name* between author, narrator, and protagonist" (14). While it is necessary to posit some criteria in order to classify a work as autobiographical, this narrow comprehension of the genre seems to revolve around a highly explicit treatment of the text as entirely dependent on the proper name. For him, "the deep subject of autobiography is the proper name" (20). In his assessment,

> C'est donc par rapport au *nom propre* que l'on doit situer les problèmes de l'autobiographie. . . Mais la place assignée à ce nom est capitale: elle est liée, par une convention sociale, à l'engagement de responsabilité d'une *personne ré-elle*. (22–23)[31]

This equivalence between a real person and the name on the cover of a book is essential to Lejeune's understanding of the "pact" or "contract" that must exist between the writer and reader of an autobiography. Without a proper name, there can be no autobiography; for Lejeune, there is no such thing as an anonymous autobiographical text.

Lejeune does not ignore the challenge that the widespread use of pseudonyms poses to this definition of the "autobiographical pact."[32] In fact, he handily fits an exploration of the pseudonymous text into his argument, maintaining that the pen name is perfectly valid as the name of the *author*:

> Les pseudonymes littéraires ne sont en général ni des mystères, ni des mystifica-tions; le second nom est aussi authentique que le premier, il signale simplement cette seconde naissance qu'est l'écriture publiée. Ecrivant son autobiographie, l'auteur à pseudonyme en donnera lui-même l'origine: ainsi, Raymond Abellio explique qu'il s'appelle Georges Soulès, et pourquoi il a choisi son pseudonyme. Le pseudonyme est simplement une différenciation, un dédoublement du nom, qui ne change rien à l'identité. (24)[33]

Lejeune's rapid dismissal of the pseudonym[34] as merely an equivalent of the au-thor's name may seem to gain even greater conviction in Assia Djebar's case, since her pseudonym has in essence become synonymous with her person. She does not maintain a distinction between her given name and her pen name; her chosen *nom de plume* has become the appellation by which she goes in both her professional and personal life. But I maintain that this apparent equivalence does not render "the autobiographical pact" any easier. To the contrary, it complicates matters.

As if the fact that she publishes under a pseudonym weren't enough to render the autobiographical project complex, Assia Djebar "plays" with the genre even further by exploring various possibilities within the text(s). In his essay on the complexity of categorizing Djebar's work, critic Ernstpeter Ruhe makes mention of the "double" characters in her autobiographical books:

> 'Vraiment, l'autobiographie?' Voilà la question fondamentale qu'Assia Djebar se pose et nous pose avec ces mots qu'elle a inscrits en dédicace dans un exem-plaire de *Vaste est la prison*. La complexité de ses textes rend la réponse dif-ficile. Un doublement les traverse dès leurs pages de titre, qui nous invitent à entrer dans la vie d'un personnage à pseudonyme. Le vrai nom de Fatima Zohra Imalayène n'apparaît jamais. Et lorsque nous ouvrons *Ombre Sultane*, le jeu des doubles (Isma, Hajila) redouble. L'entreprise autobiographique—si c'en est une—s'entoure de protections. Les noms propres multipliés font écran et voilent celle qui s'avance et se souvient. (161)

In his insightful analysis of the ways in which Djebar transforms (and "dis-seminates") herself within her texts, Ruhe demonstrates that we are so far from Lejeune's strict definition of the genre that even the "entreprise autobiographique" is called into question. Djebar herself highlights the indefinable nature of the genre when she poses a seemingly rhetorical query at the beginning of what she has called her "most autobiographical work" to date (*Ces voix* 207); this brief in-terrogation of the book's categorization is meant to provoke the reader to reflect on the complexity of autobiography. By refusing to use her name in a manner that would imply continuity with her real-life persona, she puts into question Lejeune's entire system of classification. Her refusal to establish any nominal connection between protagonist and writer dismantles a system that seems antiquated at any rate given the reflections of literary theorists such as Michel Foucault and Roland Barthes on the author.

Michel Foucault delivered a lecture before the Collège de France in 1969 and the words he pronounced there were to resonate in intellectual circles for years to come. His speech's title was a question: "What is an Author?" He proved that the answer was not obvious by tracing the history of the term and elaborating his conception of the "author-function."[35] He defended the assertion that the "name of an author is not precisely a proper name among others" (122), that it serves a specific purpose apart from identifying an individual, since the "single name implies that relationships of homogeneity, filiation, reciprocal explanation, authentification, or of common utilization were established among" texts attributed to one author. His conclusion that "the author's name characterizes a particular manner of existence of discourse" (123) draws upon one of his fundamental concepts for understanding the way language works in power relations. The possibility for a new "discourse" that arises from a new author revealed a particular conception of the possibility of authorship.

Foucault effectively pointed out that the way we perceive authorship has changed since the Middle Ages. Although "in our day, literary works are totally dominated by the sovereignty of the author" (126), this has not always been the case: "there was a time when those texts which we now call 'literary' (stories, folk tales, epics, and tragedies) were accepted, circulated, and valorized without any question about the identity of their author" (125). These texts that were once accepted without an established author are the texts that Djebar has recuperated in her work. She writes in a manner that reaffirms the authenticity and underscores the validity of these texts that "now" require the name of an author to be considered valid.[36] She recounts the stories of her Algerian women compatriots in her text, giving voice to their experience in her written work, and signing it all in her name: "Assia Djebar". But she doesn't claim "authorship" in the traditional sense of the word. Rather, she embraces a new way of writing which takes into account "the death of the author" to which Roland Barthes attests in his famous essay.

First published in 1968, "La mort de l'Auteur" divides literature into a "before and after" in which the age of the author gives way to the age of the text. Barthes asserts that the understood "removal of the Author [. . .] transforms the modern text" by changing its temporality. According to his analysis,

> L'Auteur, lorsqu'on y croit, est toujours conçu comme le passé de son propre livre [. . .]. Tout au contraire, le scripteur moderne naît en même temps que son texte ; il n'est d'aucune façon pourvu d'un être qui précèderait ou excèderait son écriture [. . .] il n'y a d'autre temps que celui de l'énonciation et tout texte est écrit éternellement *ici* et *maintenant*. (14–15)[37]

It is interesting to note that Lejeune makes passing reference to the erasure of the author, but maintains that the theory has not been "pursued": "The Tel Quel group, by calling into question the notion of the author (replacing it by that of 'scripteur'), heads in the same direction but does not pursue the thing any further" (20).

Djebar takes it further. She picks up the term "scripteur," transforms it into the feminine, and demonstrates that it is not enough to describe her project: "Je ne m'avance ni en diseuse, ni en scripteuse. Sur l'aire de la dépossession, je voudrais pouvoir en chanter" (*L'amour* 161).[38] This powerful statement comes in the midst of a poetic metanarrative on the process of translating a countrywoman's voice at once into written form and into a foreign tongue. The sound of Chérifa's words reminds Djebar of her paradoxical situation: "Mots torches qui éclairent mes compagnes, mes complices; d'elles, définitivement, ils me séparent" (*L'amour* 161).[39] The necessity and impossibility of translation present themselves unequivocally here, in the "here and now" of the writing process.

This "here and now" of the writing process, emphasized by Barthes in "The Death of the Author," closely resembles the Derridean conception of the *signature*. Derrida specifies the meaning of this term by contrasting it with the proper name.[40] By definition, the proper name has the capacity to function alone, in the absence of its bearer:

> Mon nom propre me survit. Après ma mort, on pourra encore me nommer et parler de moi. Comme tout signe, 'je' inclus, le nom propre comporte la possibilité nécessaire de pouvoir fonctionner en mon absence, de se détacher de son porteur. (140)[41]

If the proper name therefore does not *belong* to its bearer, since it can be *dissociated* from the person in question, the signature represents an attempt to *reappropriate* the property that should be inherent in the name:

> On dira donc que, même de mon vivant, mon nom marque ma mort. . . . La marque qui m'identifie, qui me fait moi plutôt qu'un autre, me désapproprie aussitôt en annonçant ma mort, et en se séparant *a priori* du même moi qu'elle constitue ou assure. . . . La signature, et c'est justement ce qui la distingue du nom propre en général, essaie de rattraper le propre qu'on a vu se déproprier aussitôt dans le nom. (140)[42]

At the end of Djebar's texts, there is a predictable notation of the place and date, usually in italics, always justified to the right margin. These "locators" constitute a signature according to Derridean definition:

> L'acte de signer, qui ne se réduit pas à la simple inscription de son nom propre, s'efforce, par un tour supplémentaire, de réapproprier la propriété toujours déjà perdue dans le nom lui-même. Ce qui implique que la signature, pour marquer un ici-maintenant, est toujours *en droit* accompagnée de la marque d'un lieu et d'une date. (142)[43]

If Assia Djebar does not hold tightly to her proper name, this does not mean she doesn't sign her works. The sense of ownership is present in the inclusion of the date and place that mark the *present* of the writing and thus highlight the specificity of the *moment* rather than the identity of the author.

In the significant quotation above on pseudonyms taken from *The Autobiographical Pact*, Lejeune suggests that the pen name will inevitably figure into the autobiographical work, that its origin and its history will play a significant role in the text(s). This allows him to conclude that the pseudonym functions like an author's real name on the cover of the book. But his assumption does not hold true in the autobiographical work of Djebar. Not only does she fail to address the adoption of her *nom de plume*, she fails to insert either her given name or her adopted name in any of her texts. She does not mention her name, not even once. She does not draw attention to her originality by addressing her birth and her "rebirth" through an exploration of her name.[44] In an *oeuvre* that pays close attention to names, in which they are documented with an historian's precision, the writer's name is missing. So, too, are the names of those closest to her. Their titles are present, their connection to the narrator is clear, but their names are strikingly absent.[45] It is as if what they are called is insignificant; what matters is their relationship.

I am not indicating that Djebar is unaware of the power of names. To the contrary, she demonstrates an acute awareness of their significance throughout her work, from various anecdotes to parenthetical asides. When in *Vaste est la prison* she tells with aching overtones the story of her love for a younger man, she relates a moment of extreme tension, marked by the articulation of her first name:

> J'avais dû tourner le dos, m'apprêtant à partir. C'est alors que je l'entendis m'appeler assez bas par mon prénom. Il me hélait. Pour la première fois, ainsi. Il fit un pas. Je me retournai, la voix chaleureuse:
> —Enfin, je ne suis plus 'madame'! [. . .]
> Il redit mon prénom tout bas. Distinctement. Je crois que je m'emplis d'une lampée de joie étourdissante; je m'illuminai. . . (70)

The deep emotion the narrator feels when she hears her name on the lips of her beloved is revealed by metaphors of warmth and light. Her name is so meaningful that its simple utterance brings her obvious joy. The question of which name he said—Fatima or Assia—is not addressed. What counts is that she was addressed, that he spoke directly to her, abandoning polite, anonymous forms of speech. The mention of her name marks the significance of this intimate moment; a different, deeper level of communication is characterized by the pronunciation of the first name.

This reference to the deep meaning of the first name is reminiscent of a passage in *L'amour, la fantasia* in which the narrator describes her parents' relationship. As her mother learns the French language, she is progressively liberated from the traditional formulaic ways of addressing people in her native Arabic tongue. She gradually ceases to refer to her husband in the third person and begins to speak of him by employing his name: "elle l'appelait, audacieuse nouveauté, par son prénom!" (47).[46] This process of "naming" serves to distinguish her father from the anonymous crowd of men in Algerian society:

> Ces oncles, cousins, parents par alliance se retrouvaient confondus dans l'anonymat du genre masculin, neutralité réductrice que leur réservait le parler allusif des épouses. (47)[47]

In response to her mother's familiar mode of evoking him, her father pulls an unprecedented move by daring to address a postcard to his wife, in her *name*:

> La révolution était manifeste: mon père, de sa propre écriture, et sur une carte qui allait voyager de ville en ville, qui allait passer sous tant et tant de regards masculins [. . .] mon père donc avait osé écrire le nom de sa femme. (48)[48]

These acts of naming, in her mother's conversations and in her father's writing, acquire profound significance in the eyes of the narrator: "L'un et l'autre [. . .] se nommaient réciproquement, autant dire s'aimaient ouvertement" (49).[49] The use of someone's name is never taken lightly in Algerian society. In the case of her parents, the narrator notes that this subversive act of naming is a sign of deep commitment and lasting love.

In *Vaste est la prison*, an exclamation in parentheses demonstrates the evocative power of a homonym which reminds the narrator of a dear relative:

> ô M'hamed, avec ce doux prénom si cher à ma tribu, le même que celui de mon oncle maternel assassiné juste avant 62, et dont la tendresse de coeur nous resta proverbiale! (333)

Names have significance, not simply because of the person they represent, but because of the connections and deeper meanings they evoke. Even the choice of a name for the narrator is not without forethought, as this reflexive question shows: "Appellerai-je à nouveau la narratrice Isma? 'Isma': 'le nom'" (331). But, despite these revealing tributes to the power of names, Assia Djebar knows well that names do not always do their bearers justice, that they are often inextricably linked to stereotypical, prejudicial labels that fail to represent people as individuals by hastily lumping them in an indistinguishable group.

In *Vaste est la prison*, the narrator tells the story of her mother's visit to her son in prison. After a tremendous ordeal, the woman finally arrives at the place where her boy is incarcerated. Once she reaches this destination, she is received with respect. Even if she can't quite pass for a Frenchwoman, she has certainly "Frenchified" herself in an admirable way:

> Elle parlait maintenant sans accent; ses cheveux châtain clair, sa toilette de la boutique la plus élégante d'Alger la faisaient prendre (quarante ans, elle en paraissait dix de moins, un peu raidie dans son air "chic") pas tellement pour une Française, plutôt pour une bourgeoise d'Italie du Nord, ou pour une Espagnole qui serait francisée. . . (188–189)

When the mother states her name and requests to see her son, the guard is taken aback. He is incredulous when he learns the identity of her offspring: "Un peu désarçonné par le nom arabe, ayant reconnu là un des noms des 'agitateurs'; il ne comprenait pas: cette dame avait si bon genre!" (189). The Arabic name seems to contradict her sophisticated appearance, her elegant mannerisms, and her command of the French language. She defies the stereotype that accompanies her name and throws into turmoil the Frenchman's presuppositions about women of Arabic origin. As Rosello points out in her study of the stereotype,

> In French, layers upon layers of cultural assumptions are implicitly revealed by a slight asymmetry between what would be called 'un nom arabe' (an Arab name) and 'un nom bien français' (an all-French name). (141)

Djebar, as a writer, turns her back on these "cultural assumptions" by refusing to place too much stock in her name. She knows that identity is much more than, and often has little or nothing to do with, one's name.

This awareness of the difference between identity and name is reminiscent of Friedrich Nietzsche's self-conscious highlighting of their lack of equivalence. In his analysis of Nietzsche's oeuvre, Derrida explores the relationship between identity and name, emphasizing the discrepancy between them. He argues in *Otobiographies* that Nietzsche purposely employs "masks"[50] which put his identity into question because his true person is so distant from the idea his contemporaries associate with his name.[51] Djebar's use of doubles in her autobiographical writing, most notably in *Ombre Sultane*, but in *L'amour, la fantasia* and *Vaste est la prison* as well (from shifting pronouns to the narrator's name), mirrors Nietzsche's effort to problematize the traditional Western conception of identity as stable, continuous, and self-same, and the idea of a single author responsible for the text and the life represented in it. This disruptive project reflects an understanding of identity as separate from the name. As Derrida explains,

> Sa propre identité, celle qu'il entend déclarer et qui n'a rien à voir, tant elle leur est disproportionnée, avec ce que les contemporains connaissent sous ce nom, sous son nom ou plutôt son homonyme, Friedrich Nietzsche, cette identité qu'il revendique, il ne la tient pas d'un contrat avec ces contemporains. Il la reçoit du contrat inouï qu'il a passé avec lui-même. (47)[52]

This notion of a different contract ("*contrat inouï*"), separate from a legal document with his contemporaries, marks a sharp diversion from the contract of the infamous "autobiographical pact."

In *Autobiographics*, Leigh Gilmore presents a feminist critique of Lejeune's definition of autobiography. Her criticism of his "contractual" model targets precisely this very narrow, patriarchal view of the name as that which guarantees textual identity and reaffirms "one's self as property based on models of patrimony and paternity" (77), a concept which poses an obvious problem for women writers. Gilmore insists that "to read beyond the name is already to subject the contract to review," and this is precisely what Djebar does by placing her work under a pseudonym. In so doing, she draws up a Nietzschean "contrat inouï" with herself and her readers, a contract based on a much more fluid conception of identity.

When she embarked on her first film project, Djebar gained entrance into places off-limits to all outsiders. She was permitted to focus her camera on sites and faces previously unrecorded; she was able to capture sounds and voices in a new way, but this unique privilege did not come from her name. As she explains, it was because she was her mother's daughter, and not because she was "Assia Djebar," that she was allowed to pursue this project:

> Au départ, j'avais décidé de faire un film qui se passerait dans les montagnes de mon enfance, où je n'étais pas retournée. . . Donc, c'est bien que je savais aussi que j'aurais un rapport de familiarité avec beaucoup de femmes non pas parce que j'étais romancière, non pas parce que je suis venue avec des techniciens [. . .] mais du fait que j'étais la fille de ma mère, que j'étais de telle tribu [. . .]. Donc, parce que j'étais la fille de Bahia et pas du tout Assia Djebar ou je ne sais pas quoi, j'ai pu entrer. . .[53]

In her homeland, her fame is not the ticket to entering hard-to-reach places; it is her feminine genealogy that gains her entrance. Her name serves only as a heading under which to reveal this maternal inheritance, this unique heritage she (re)claims through the stories of her women ancestors and friends.

Djebar's autobiographical texts include portions of personal exploration couched within larger themes including the history of her country, focusing most notably the experiences of other Algerian women. These women are closely related to Djebar, sometimes because of blood relation and other times simply due to similar geography and traditions. Djebar especially seeks the stories of older generations who have lived and seen things that predate her; she listens to their version of the events that figure differently in official accounts and transcribes their perspectives, thus altering the univocal view of the history of her country and people. This unusual structure fulfills Gilmore's description of the phenomenon of "metonymy" in women's autobiography: "some feminist critics find female self-representation to be figured metonymically in autobiography where women represent the self in relation to others" (77). Djebar undeniably presents her "self" in relation to others in her text, but not in a traditional sense. Her focus is as much on the others as it is on herself, and the inclusion of others in the text is not meant merely to highlight their relation to the autobiographical subject. The heritage Djebar vindicates throughout her work is not an individual inheritance, but a shared genealogy and tradition that gains value in its belonging to a collectivity. The group is more powerful than the individual.

In her texts, Djebar alternates between uplifting this maternal heritage and lamenting the fact that it escapes her, that she cannot truly claim ownership of it.[54] She indicates in *Vaste est la prison* that the richness of the maternal heritage is something she has lost: "Ayant perdu . . . ma richesse du départ, dans mon cas, celle de l'héritage maternel, et ayant gagné quoi, sinon la simple mobilité du corps dénudé, sinon la liberté" (172). But what exactly is this heritage she has given up for this corporeal freedom? The answer is based in language, as revealed in this phrase from *L'amour, la fantasia*: "je cherche, comme un lait dont on m'aurait autrefois écartée, la pléthore amoureuse de la langue de ma mère" (76).[55] There is nothing simple, however, about the "mother tongue," as Mireille Calle-Gruber points out:

> car la langue maternelle, elle-même bifide, est perte d'origine (perte de l'origine, perte à l'origine). . . C'est de ce legs ancestral [. . .] que l'écrivain Assia Djebar fait son véritable héritage, c'est-à-dire son départ d'écriture. (78)[56]

The loss of origin becomes the place of departure, the starting point for the writing project, which is forever in search of the "lost" maternal tongue(s).[57] This is clear in *L'amour, la fantasia*, when the narrator explains that writing brought her back to her "only" origin: "écrire m'a ramenée aux cris des femmes sourdement révoltées de mon enfance, à ma seule origine" (229).[58] The result of this quest to regain her lost origin is a unique literature that gives voice to the sounds of the languages of Algeria, of the Berber and dialectical Arabic that make up the speech of her fellow countrywomen. Even though her writing is limited to French, the rhythms and accents of other tongues penetrate the text, creating a literary oeuvre that is anything but ordinary: "Ainsi ma parole, pouvant être double, et peut-être même triple, participe de plusieurs cultures, alors que je n'ai qu'une seule écriture: la française" (*Ces voix* 42).[59]

It is not surprising that Djebar's comments on her maternal heritage should focus on the question of language.[60] She understands that "identity" is a broad term that must take a number of factors into account. As a writer whose identity is inextricably bound to her work, she refuses to limit her conception of "identity" to land and blood, but extends the idea of "belonging" to include language:

> Je suis femme algérienne, mais je devrais faire référence plutôt qu'à la terre natale, du moins à la langue des aïeux et des aïeules: 'je suis femme arabo-berbère', et en sus 'd'écriture française'. . . Parce que l'identité n'est pas que de papier, que de sang, mais aussi *de langue.* (*Ces voix* 42)[61]

Her reflections on writing reveal the extent to which the act of creating a novel is an "*aventure*" which brings about change in the writer: "Pourtant, trente ans après, je le constate, je me présente en premier comme écrivain, comme romancière, comme si l'acte d'écrire, quand il est quotidien, solitaire jusqu'à l'ascèse, venait modifier le poids de l'appartenance" (*Ces voix* 42).[62] In this passage, Djebar acknowledges the extent to which writing changes "belonging" and forms "identity." Djebar's comments on being a novelist and the undeniable importance of language in her work resonate with Calle-Gruber's assessment of the "place" of literature:

> La littérature est lieu de l'être: point de quête d'identité qui n'en passe par ses fabulations, qui n'oeuvre, immanquablement, dans l'écriture. C'est-à-dire dans les langues. Dualité. Pluralité. (". . . Et la voix s'écri(e)ra" 276)

Literature as the location *par excellence* of a plurality of languages is the place Djebar inhabits. The result of her embrace of a multiplicity of tongues is a polyphonic literary *oeuvre* signed in a particular, elusive name.

The sign of great literary production is often found in the unique writing style that characterizes the texts bearing their author's name. Writers seek to develop an inimitable style to distinguish themselves from the anonymous crowd of scribblers. Notable twentieth-century authors such as James Joyce and Franz Kafka have established their names by creating unusual works that unmistakably carry their "signature." Jacques Derrida refers to this type of literary specificity as "idiomatic":

> La littérature aspire à l'idiomatique. . . . Ecrivain, je veux écrire comme nul autre, et ainsi imposer mon nom propre ou plutôt ma signature (car une écriture qui me serait absolument propre et idiomatique devrait être considérée comme une signature). (Bennington 168–169)[63]

This aspiration to establish an idiomatic form of expression may require a certain self-conscious effort for most writers, but for Assia Djebar, the task is facilitated, in a sense, by other concerns that outweigh the necessity to "find a niche" and create an innovative writing style. Her different focus stems, in part, from her indifference to the concern of "imposing" her name upon her reader.

> Pour faire passer l'idiome de mon nom propre, pour imposer ma loi en clamant mon nom, je dois ainsi ruser avec la langue qui ne m'est justement pas propre (que je reçois comme la loi, disait Saussure—mais j'ai reçu également mon nom propre, je ne me baptise pas), je dois essayer de marquer cette langue subrepticement, faire avaler mon nom à un lecteur qui croit simplement lire de la littérature. (Bennington 169–170)[64]

Djebar's particular situation as an Algerian woman composing her work in French entails a relationship to writing that transcends an egotistical obsession with her name. She certainly does succeed in "surreptitiously marking" the French language, but not with the purpose of forcing the reader to unwittingly "swallow her name." It is important to note that the creation of her own name in some ways invalidates the assertion within parentheses in the above quotation; Assia Djebar did not receive her second, adopted "proper name," and she has, in a very real sense, "baptized herself" in this name. The name accompanies the text, for it is boldly printed on its cover.[65] But it is not even subtly introduced in its pages in an effort to "sign" the text with the inclusion of the proper name.[66] Her concerns are other, they are wrapped up in "others," and the establishment of her personal renown, the security and inimitability of her own name, is not the priority that it might be for male writers. Cixous articulates this absence of fear when faced with the prospect of anonymity, a boldness that she ascribes to "woman":

> A la différence de l'homme qui tellement tient à son titre et ses titres, bourses de valeurs, tête, couronne et tout ce qui est de son chef, la femme se moque bien de la peur de la décapitation (ou castration), s'aventurant sans le masculin tremblement dans l'anonymat, auquel elle sait se fondre sans s'anéantir: parce qu'elle est *donneuse*. (50)[67]

Djebar is not threatened by the possibility of sinking into anonymity, and this lack of fear with respect to her name permits her to focus on other things in her writing.

I do not want to dismiss the idea of authorship as "style," because I think it is very useful to an understanding of the particular form of authorship present in Djebar's literary production.[68] What I want to emphasize, however, is that Djebar's unique writing style is not the result of a deliberate quest to create an idiosyncratic, "idiomatic" *oeuvre*, but rather a natural result of her specific situation and her desire to communicate a rich heritage in a special way. Djebar associates her name with a number of individuals whose names she retains and gives credit to in her work. The inclusion of the stories of other women in her text gives evidence to her understanding that no great name can be completely "proper" and that openness to ideas and influences will only improve her writing, and thus her name. As Jane Gallop remarks, this openness is the condition of great names throughout history:

> If the thought were literally 'proper' to him, belonging to him alone, it would have no effect. If he is a historic thinker, then his work must be widely shared. The great names in the history of ideas are also tokens, markers of the nameless who shared their ideas, both those influenced by and those influencing the 'name.' (1049)

By opening herself up to the influence of many "nameless" Algerian women who share their experiences with her, Djebar is capable of filling an "author-function" and creating a new "discourse," in the Foucaldian sense.[69] In *L'amour, la fantasia*, Djebar's narrative voice enters into dialogue with voices from the past, engaging in conversation with written accounts of various historical events in her Algerian homeland; more important, her personal story is placed in conversation with stories from other women. The resulting hybrid, polyvocal text is richer because of this complex interaction between past and present, it is better because of this interweaving of sources that provide a multifaceted perspective. The narrator's voice intermingles with other voices, without claiming to possess the definitive version. The end result is a literary gem that is strengthened, not weakened, by the fact that its author does not claim to be "the" authority.

Since Djebar opens up her text to the voices of numerous women from her homeland, Derrida's words in *Circonfession* could easily be applied to her autobiographical project: "[. . .] je ne me confesse pas, je confesse plutôt les autres pour les impondérables et donc si lourds secrets dont j'hérite à mon insu [. . .]" (Bennington 175).[70] A number of critics have honed in on Djebar's willingness and ability to represent the experience of so many Algerian women, but Calle-Gruber's study of Djebar's work focuses on a special aspect of this inclusion of other women in her corpus: the birthing process. In a recent article that situates Djebar within a larger context of globalization, Calle-Gruber touches upon this analogy between writing and giving birth:

Car l'écriture littéraire d'Assia Djebar se construit, non moins, au titre des femmes: écrire, alors, c'est faire un travail qui donne vie, donne naissance. En particulier, à toutes les soeurs de gynécée, analphabètes, dont l'écrivain se fait non pas le porte-parole mais, humblement, le porte-voix. ("Pour une analytique" 216)[71]

In her writing, Djebar treats of childbirth on a very literal level, relating in another woman's voice this meaningful process as a moment of female solidarity:

Et chaque fois, c'est ainsi: je quitte cette ville, je vais chez les miens; je parle à peine là-bas, mais ma voix revient comme un filet, un tout petit filet. Surtout, j'accouche parmi mes soeurs, ma mère et ma tante à mon chevet. 'Le septième jour, après avoir enfin présenté le petit au jour et lui avoir donné un prénom, nous dansons toute la nuit, sous les palmiers, près de l'oued! Je revis! Et le bébé est alors si beau, plein de vigueur. Je reviens confiante. Je chante chaque matin. . .' (*Vaste est la prison* 312)

In this anecdotal passage, men are absent from the birthing scene. And it is, notably, a woman who gives the child a name. The power of naming has been removed, in this tradition, from the father and given over to the mother. The occasion of the newborn baby gives rise to dancing and celebration among the women present. Djebar relates their happiness just prior to revealing her own sterility and her resulting incapacity to share in the joys and pains of childbirth.[72] If she cannot engage in reproduction in a biological sense, she can certainly engage in production in a creative sense, and the result is a large *oeuvre* with far-reaching significance.

Assia Djebar, in giving herself a name that she has embraced and chosen as a lifelong appellation, has participated in a significant act of self-creation. This act has not gone unnoticed, as the following affirmation reveals:

Assia Djebar artiste prend modèle sur ce premier artiste du monde naissant, et en profitant de la forme équivoque de son nom francisé, elle se substitue à lui et le change en femme: Prométhée n'est plus Prometheus, mais Promethea. D'ailleurs, soit dit en passant—l'auteur était depuis longtemps présent dans ce mythe, vérité mise à jour paradoxalement par le masque du pseudonyme: La femme qu'aime Prométhée dans les textes anciens s'appelle—Asia. (Ruhe 168)[73]

In this comparison to the mythological character Prometheus, Djebar is seen to have taken a pseudonym with even greater significance than previously acknowledged. Her first name implies a connection to a legendary character known for his creative powers. I would argue that her power is even greater than his, for she has taken the liberty of "birthing" herself. Not only does Djebar take the subversive step of naming (like the woman in the anecdote in her autobiographical novel), but she gives *herself* a name; she conceives (of) her very existence and then assumes it. This self-given identity coincides and merges with her *oeuvre*; her *corps* emerges hand-in-hand with her *corpus*. This momentous act depends on something deceptively complicated, a name.

In the choice of her pseudonym, Djebar demonstrates a knowledge of the way names function in culture and language. She realizes that "personal names are a reflection of cultural politics, bearing the mark of Christianity, Islam, and local cultures" (Miller 116). She also realizes that "le nom propre *appartient sans appartenir* à la langue" (Bennington 160),[74] that names carry meaning which always eludes translation. She is aware, also, that names do not reveal their bearers, that there is no such thing as "référence absolue" (160). This is why, according to Zimra's report of the anecdote, Djebar finds the source for her surname in Islam, but copies it down wrong. The strict meaning of "djebbar" is disrupted in its faulty transcription as "djébar," and the eventual dropping of the accent further demonstrates the difficulty of pinning down the significance of this appellation. (As for "Assia," this common first name is open to even greater speculation as to its precise meaning.) Assia Djebar knows that names carry cultural and religious baggage, and by refusing to elaborate on her name, by neglecting to insert it into her autobiographical texts, she underlines its inherently elusive, untranslatable nature.

Hyperaware of the importance of names, the absence of commentary on her own name speaks volumes. It seems that her silence represents an attempt to sidestep the "*blessure du nom propre*" theorized by Abdelkebir Khatibi. The "injury" of naming and the "injury" of the name is what she seeks to circumvent by avoiding explanation. In *Ombre sultane*, the second wife carries a name with this very meaning:

> Derra en langue arabe, la nouvelle épousée, rivale d'une première femme d'un même homme, se désigne de ce mot, qui signifie "blessure": celle qui fait mal, qui ouvre les chairs, ou celle qui a mal, c'est pareil! (100)[75]

By unveiling the "wounds" of many Algerian women through her written accounts of their suffering, Djebar exposes the injustices against women in her homeland. By revealing the wrongs carried out in the name of "colonization" and "religion," Djebar demonstrates the misogynist, prejudicial practices under which her compatriots suffer. Her writing arises from this purpose, from the goal of denouncing these practices that bring such pain. Her writing also arises from her own suffering, from the difficulty of writing in a language inseparable from the violent history of the conquest of her country. According to Calle-Gruber, "c'est de la blessure, de la coupure à l'origine, du 'son coupé' des séquestrées analphabètes, que sourd la phrase en vérité" (216).[76] In order to nurse her own wounds, Djebar exposes those of the illiterate women who have suffered at the hand of brutal colonizers and inconsiderate men. The movement between "intransigent" and "healer" in her surname demonstrates the dilemma with which Djebar intentionally means to play, in the hope that the "intransigent" nature of established practices will give way to the "healing" she seeks to bring about through the written word.

Assia Djebar is an improper name. Like any name, it is insufficient to express its bearer; it does not fully resemble the person it seeks to represent. And, like any name, it is *not hers*, because the proper name belongs to the public domain, even though it is *distinctly hers*, since it is a name of her choosing. When Assia Djebar selected the name with which to sign her first novel, she may not have known that this pseudonym would become the *nom de plume* for a whole slew of texts, that it was to be the heading for an *oeuvre*. At the time, she may simply have been choosing an alternative appellation to accompany the publication of her first book. The complete adoption of this name and the assumption of a career united with it made of this act of naming much more than a whimsical moment, however. It marked the beginning of a unique literary project in which a pseudonym, often understood to be the false name of a person wishing to *dissimulate* their true identity, served paradoxically as a cover under which to *reveal* a true identity. Djebar's understanding that a name is not necessarily synonymous with the person to whom it refers has allowed her to distance herself from her background just enough to embrace it wholeheartedly in her literary and cinematic production. As a result, she has given birth to something that may not necessarily carry her name, but unquestionably bears her signature.

NOTES

[1] "That which we call 'proper name' is thus always already improper, and the act of nomination that we would like to consider as origin and prototype of language presupposes writing in the large sense given this word by Derrida."

[2] Assia Djebar was the recipient of the Prix Maurice-Maeterlinck (Brussels) in 1995, the International Literary Neustadt Prize (United States) in 1996, and the International Prize of Palma (Italy) in 1998.

[3] Mireille Calle-Gruber makes brief reference to the origin of the pseudonym in an article on globalization and "littératures de l'altérité" without elaborating on the meaning she attributes to this name: "L'écriture djebarienne est ainsi exercice d'intransigeance obstinée (Djebar, pseudonyme, est l'un des 99 noms du Prophète et signifie 'L'Intransigeant'). Seule la pesée des mots et du phrasé justifie l'oeuvre" ["Djebar's writing is thus an exercise in obstinate intransigence (Djebar, a pseudonym, is one of the 99 names of the Prophet and means "The Intransigent"). The weight of words and phrasing alone justifies the work"] (216).

[4] Jeanne-Marie Clerc addresses the adoption of the pseudonym in a paragraph addressing Djebar's four early novels, making only passing reference to the necessity for the *nom de plume*: "Le pseudonyme d'Assia Djebar, adopté pour dissimuler à son père son expérience littéraire, confirme qu'il ne s'agissait pour elle que d'une expérience accessoire qui n'était pas destinée à trahir la 'pudeur' propre à la femme de la tribu, et apte à la confiner dans la réserve ancestrale" (12).

[5] Unlike most articles, a recent introduction to an interview in a German periodical deems necessary an explanation of Assia Djebar's chosen name that goes beyond a simple reference to her given name. Schimmel's introduction reads as follows: "Die algerische Schriftstellerin Assia Djebar kam 1936 unter dem Namen Fatima-Zohra Imalayène in Cherchell, einer kleinen Küstenstadt bei Algier, zur Welt. 1954 wurde sie als erste Algerierin an der Ecole Normale Supérieure, einer Eliteschule in Paris, zugelassen. Da sie sich 1956 an einem Streik algerischer Studenten für den Unabhängigkeitskampf ihres Landes beteiligte, durfte sie an den Abschlussprüfungen nicht teilnehmen. Sie zog sich auf ihr Zimmer zurück und schrieb ihren ersten Roman, 'La Soif' (1957, dt. 'Die Zweifelnden' 1993). Für die Veröffentlichung wählte sie aus Rücksicht auf ihre Familie ein Pseudonym: 'djebbar'—'unversöhnlich'. Ein Schreibfehler machte daraus 'djebar', das arabische Wort für 'Heiler'. Assia wiederum, ein geläufiger Mädchenvorname, lässt die Bedeutung Asien, Orient mitklingen" [The Algerian writer came into the world under the name Fatima-Zohra Imalayène in 1936 in Cherchell, a small town near Algiers. In 1954 she became the first Algerian to attend the Ecole Normale Supérieure, an elite school in Paris] (Schimmel, 41).

[6] Katherine Gracki bases her analysis of Djebar's role as a "healer" on the account of the misspelling of the word "djebbar" in Zimra's account: "In an instinctive gesture, Djebar reached back into Arabic, part of her oral heritage, in order to select a sort of veil, a pen name, which would protect her family from the scandalous act of an Arab woman writing an erotic story. When Djebar hastily transcribed this oral Arabic recited by her fiancé into French script, however, she inadvertently changed the word and its meaning in the process of translation: djebbar became djébar, which means 'healer' in vernacular Arabic according to Zimra. Hence Assia Djebar's complex relationship to different languages and cultures enables her to (re)invent herself as a healer. This identity construction as healer of past, present, collective, and individual wounds ultimately foretells Djebar's journey into the subterranean realms of both a buried collective history and a buried story of the self" (835).

[7] Zimra goes on to elaborate other meanings of "Assia": "It also happens to be the name of the Egyptian princess who rescued Moses and is so honored in Algerian lore as a holy woman and called 'Pharaoh's sister.' In the vernacular, it designates the flower variously known as the immortelle or the edelweiss" (160).

[8] "Thus, thanks [to fathers], Algerian women re-gained the power . . . to write. And yet, it is to keep her father from learning that she has written that Assia Djebar recalls having taken this pseudonym on the occasion of the publication of her first novel. Strange ambiguity of the fundamental relationship that remains imprinted with the problematic cultural 'métissage' of which these fathers were the mediators."

[9] "Every expression of love that would ever be addressed to me would have to meet my father's approval. I could assume that he had his watchful eye on every letter, even the most innocent, before it reached me. By keeping up a dialogue with this presence that haunted me, my writing became an attempt—or a temptation—to set the limits on my own silence. . ." (*Fantasia* 61).

[10] The word "proper" (*propre*) is important to this discussion because of its multiple meanings. As in English, "propre" can carry the connotation of being right, proper, appropriate. It can also, and more importantly, indicate ownership. But even the term "nom propre" is ambiguous; it can refer to a "proper noun" as well as a "proper name." According to Jane Gallop's analysis of Hélène Cixous's "Le Rire de la Méduse": "The word *proper* (*propre*) set off in quotes has a sense of propriety (the sexual insubordination of 'Laugh'), a sense of property (the attack on masculine thrift), and, in resonance with patriarchal 'extortion' of woman's name, a sense of *nom propre*, the proper noun" (1048).

[11] In *Ce Sexe qui n'en est pas un*, Irigaray makes this statement about the lack of a proper name in the context of the "indefinability" of woman: "D'où ce mystère qu'elle représente dans une culture qui prétend tout énumérer, tout chiffrer par unités, tout inventorier par individualités. Elle n'est ni une ni deux. On ne peut, en toute rigueur, la déterminer comme une personne, pas davantage comme deux. Elle résiste à toute définition adéquate. Elle n'a d'ailleurs pas de nom 'propre'" ["Hence this mystery that she represents in a culture that claims to enumerate everything, to count all by units, to take inventory through individualities. She is neither one nor two. One cannot determine her as one person, nor as two. She resists every adequate definition. Besides, she does not have a 'proper' name"] (26).

[12] The first name is nonetheless more "personal" and, of course, lasting. Perhaps this is why women display a tendency to "go" by their first names in an informal way, in contrast to their male counterparts. This tendency came to the forefront in a pivotal issue of the French publication *L'Arc*. The 1975 issue in question focused on Simone de Beauvoir; in a series on famous people, this was the first devoted to a woman. In their comments on the inclusion of both her first and last name with respect to this publication, Catherine Clément and Bernard Pingaud "describe how Beauvoir's contradictory status centers on the question of proper name. . . In contrast to Sartre, she has a prénom; in contrast to the women, she has a name" (Gallop, 1047).

[13] "I say woman overturns the 'personal,' for if, by means of laws, lies, blackmail, and marriage, her right to herself has been extorted at the same time as her name, she has been able, through the very movement of mortal alienation, to see more closely the inanity of 'propriety,' the reductive stinginess of the masculine-conjugal subjective economy, which she doubly resists" (357).

[14] In a novel by Senegalese author Mariama Bâ (*Une si longue lettre*), a female protagonist reclaims her identity and makes a decisive break with her husband by ridding herself of his name:

"Je me dépouille de ton amour, de ton nom. Vêtue du seul habit valable de la dignité, je poursuis ma route" ["I am shedding your love, and your name. Clothed with the only garment worthy of dignity, I follow my path"] (50). When she leaves her husband, she abandons his name, the sign of her connection to him.

[15] "In giving his name, a name of his choice, in giving all names, the father would be at the origin of language, and that power would belong by right to God the father" (220).

[16] "incontestably for having wanted thus to *make a name for themselves*, to give themselves the name, to construct for and by themselves their own name, to gather themselves there ('that we no longer be scattered'), as in the unity of a place at once a tongue and a tower, the one as well as the other, the one as the other" (221–222). The words in italics are particularly significant in Djebar's situation, since "making a name for herself" is precisely what she has done through writing and filmmaking. It also implies the work of "creating" one's name which exceeds the simple adoption of a new appellation and indicates the commitment to establishing a reputation in that name.

[17] "The proper name should assure a certain passing between language and world, in the sense that it should indicate a concrete individual, without ambiguity, without needing to pass through the circuits of signification. Even if we accept that the system of language is made up of differences and thus of traces, it would seem that the proper name, which is part of language, points directly to the individual it names."

[18] "But there is no proper name. That which we call with the generic common name 'proper name' must also function in a system of differences: a certain proper name rather than another designates a certain individual rather than another."

[19] In "Des Tours de Babel," Derrida addresses the fact that a proper name both necessitates translation and renders it impossible: "Néanmoins celui qui parle la langue de la Genèse pouvait être attentif à l'effet de nom propre en effaçant l'équivalent conceptuel (comme pierre dans Pierre, et ce sont deux valeurs ou deux fonctions absolument hétérogènes); on serait alors tenté de dire *premièrement* qu'un nom propre, au sens propre, n'appartient pas proprement à la langue; il n'y appartient pas, *bien et parce que* son appel la rend possible (que serait une langue sans possibilité d'appeler d'un nom propre?); par conséquent il ne peut s'inscrire proprement dans une langue qu'en s'y laissant traduire, autrement dit *interpréter* dans son équivalent sémantique: dès ce moment il ne peut plus être reçu comme nom propre. Le nom 'pierre' appartient à la langue française, et sa traduction dans une langue étrangère doit en principe transporter son sens. Ce n'est plus le cas pour 'Pierre' dont l'appartenance à la langue française n'est pas assurée et en tout cas pas du même type" (216). ["Nevertheless, someone who speaks the language of Genesis could be attentive to the effect of the proper name in effacing the conceptual equivalent (like *pierre* [rock] in *Pierre* [Peter], and these are two absolutely heterogeneous values or functions); one would then be tempted to say *first* that a proper name, in the proper sense, does not properly belong to the language; it does not belong there, *although and because* its call makes the language possible (what would a language be without the possibility of calling by a proper name?); consequently it can properly inscribe itself in a language only by allowing itself to be translated therein, in other words, *interpreted* by its semantic equivalent: from this moment it can no longer be taken as a proper name. The noun *pierre* belongs to the French language, and its translation into a foreign language should in principle transport its meaning. This is not the case with *Pierre*, whose inclusion in the French language is not assured and is in any case not of the same type" (224–225).]

[20] Christopher Miller addresses the unfortunate misunderstandings resulting from the misreading of Camara Laye's name and the symbolic significance of such oversights. He explains that "Camara is one of the Mande *jamuw*; Laye is an Islamic given name, a shortened form of Abdoulaye. But outside the Mande, the distinction is lost and confusion reigns, a confusion that is symptomatic of the clash between the West and Africa" (116). Lack of awareness on the part of critics has resulted in mistaken attribution of identity: "Critics have ignored the name that ties him to the world he describes in *L'enfant noir*. The family name, identifying the person by ethnic group, clan, and caste, is usurped by the given name, which individuates within the group but is meaningless as a key to identity within the collective as a whole. This is not the result of any conspiracy to rob Camara Laye of his identity; in the context of colonialism and colonial publishing, no conspiracy was necessary. It is a consequence of literacy, of writing and reading an

author's name. There is nothing wrong in the word order 'Camara Laye,' no need for the author to correct it on the page proofs; it is in the usage of the names as French names that things have been altered. It is hard not to think that something has been lost, namely the symbolic power of the name Camara." (117)

[21] In her article on Derrida and postcolonialism, Chantal Zabus laments the (de)construction of the proper name in French, converted from the Arabic, drawing on the work of Abdelkebir Khatibi: "Dans un premier temps, la graphie française est tenue comme réductrice et aggressive. Par example, [Abdelkebir] Khatibi a reconstruit *a posteriori* le nom propre de l'écrivain tunisien Abdelwahab Meddeb, tel qu'il apparaît sur la couverture de son roman, *Talismano* (1979) [. . .]. Par ailleurs, en gageant sur le système oral échoïque de dissémination, Khatibi démontre qu'il y a 'blessure du nom propre' dans la transcription française Meddeb puisqu'elle résulte d'une triple transformation à partir de la koiné littéraire et sacrée [. .] ensuite devenue en arabe dialectal tunisien, Middib [. . .] pour aboutir enfin à la trivialisation scripturale, Meddeb" ["At first, the French writing is seen as reductive and aggressive. For example, Abdelkebir Khatibi reconstructed a posteriori the proper name of the Tunisian writer Abdelwahab Meddeb, such as it appears on the cover of his novel, *Talismano* (1979) . . . By wagering on the oral system of echo and dissemination, Khatibi demonstrates that there is 'wounding of the proper name' in the French transcription of Meddeb because it is the result of a triple transformation beginning with the literary and sacred koiné . . . followed by the Tunisian dialect of Arabic, Middib . . . and ending up finally with the scriptural trivialization, Meddeb"] (263).

[22] For a history of publishing and the importance of the name in this process, see Peggy Kamuf on "literary property" in *Signature Pieces*, pages 59–67.

[23] This emphasis on the legal nature of the name and the notion of responsibility for the text produced takes on special significance in light of the sharp contrast between the written text and the spoken word. Whereas stories in oral tradition are always in a state of flux, changing according to the speaker and the circumstances in which (s)he speaks, the written text is permanent. Putting a story in print freezes it in the form of one particular version. Turning a document over to a publishing house entails the fixation of a text which in oral circulation is always shifting and changing. The "burden" of this act is anything but negligible.

[24] Djebar's four earlier novels were not openly autobiographical in scope. *La soif* (Julliard, 1957), *Les impatients* (Julliard, 1958), *Les enfants du Nouveau Monde* (Julliard, 1962), and *Les alouettes naïves* (Julliard, 1967), were part of a different period in her writing career. *L'amour, la fantasia* (Albin Michel, 1985) marked the first of a projected "quartet" of autobiographical works which presently include *Ombre sultane* (Lattès, 1987) and *Vaste est la prison* (Albin Michel, 1995).

[25] In the 1970s, Djebar did not publish any written material. *L'amour, la fantasia* was the first book to go to print after this hiatus, with the notable exception of a collection of short stories, *Femmes d'Alger dans leur appartement* (des femmes, 1980).

[26] *La nouba des femmes du mont Chenoua* (1978) and *La zerda et les chants de l'oubli* (1982) have been shown at various film festivals; *La nouba* received the International Critics Prize at the 1979 Film Festival in Venice.

[27] "first autobiography written by an Algerian woman in the French language."

[28] Djebar consistently refers to Fadhma Aït Mansour-Amrouche by the autobiographer's first name, perhaps a gesture of intimacy felt toward this female "forebear," perhaps a trace of informality that tends to accompany references to women's work in general.

[29] "Fadhma reclaims possession of her life, by writing it at sixty-four years of age."

[30] "Decidedly, the 'autobiographical pact' dear to Philippe Lejeune is not variable and malleable enough to apply to what we could call a 'coupled' writing: mother and daughter, the first writing, the second following her, the first continuing. . ."

[31] "it is thus in relation to the *proper name* that we are able to situate the problems of autobiography. . . but the place assigned to the name is essential: it is linked, by a social convention, to the pledge of responsibility of a *real person*" (11).

[32] "Literary pseudonyms are in general neither mysteries nor hoaxes. The second name is as authentic as the first; it simply signals this second birth which is the published writing. Writing his autobiography, the author under his pen name will himself explain its origin; thus Raymond Abellio explains that he is calling himself Georges Soulès, and why he has chosen his pseudonym.

The pseudonym is simply a differentiation, a division of the name, which changes nothing in the identity" (12). In "The Autobiographical Pact (bis)," Lejeune embarks on a "rereading" of his earlier text, in which he seems to retract his "'all or nothing' position" on the problem of identity, allowing for a larger definition of the genre. He makes some "confessions" of his own in this essay, and admits the following in reaction to the "anti-Pact par excellence," the book *Roland Barthes by Roland Barthes*: "I believe that my proper name guarantees my autonomy and my singularity [. . .]. But of course it also happens that I believe the contrary" (131).

[33] Lejeune goes on to affirm that it is not the pseudonym "Colette" which prohibits the "Claudines" from being classified as autobiographies, but rather the fact that the character ("Claudine") goes by a different name from the author ("Colette"). It is thus not a breach in identification between the name of the author and the real person, but the lack of equivalence between the author and the protagonist that eliminates this series of books from the category of autobiography.

[34] I would argue that Lejeune's treatment of the pseudonym is far too "easy," as this quotation from Derrida's *Otobiographies* would suggest: "[. . .] le nom de F.N. Ce nom est déjà un faux-nom, un pseudonyme et un homonyme qui viendrait dissimuler, sous l'imposture, l'autre Friedrich Nietzsche. Liée à ces ténébreuses affaires de contrat, de dette et de crédit, la pseudonymie nous induit à nous méfier sans mesure [. . .]" (47). In this reflection on the work of Nietzsche, Derrida indicates that a person who speaks under the authority of a pseudonym always arouses suspicion.

[35] The "author-function" included the understanding that the author is not autonomous, but dependent on circumstances which bring about and/or contribute to the author's work.

[36] I put the word "now" in quotation marks because Foucault focuses on a linear, historical treatment of this phenomenon over time, but I would argue that the distinction is "geographical" and not just "chronological." In some cultures, where the transition to written culture is just now taking place, these conceptions of authorship remain foreign, as Miller's exploration of the phenomenon in *Theories of Africans* indicates.

[37] "The Author, when believed in, is always conceived of as the past of his own book . . . In complete contrast, the modern scriptor is born simultaneously with the text, is in no way equipped with a being preceding or exceeding this writing . . . there is no other time than that of the enunciation and every text is eternally written *here and now*" (145).

[38] "I do not claim here to be either a story-teller or a scribe. On the territory of dispossession, I would that I could sing" (*Fantasia* 142).

[39] "Torch-words which light up my women-companions, my accomplices; these words divide me from these once and for all" (*Fantasia* 142).

[40] Paul de Man accuses Lejeune of committing precisely this error, of interchanging the proper name and the signature without distinguishing between the two terms. See "Autobiography as De-facement."

[41] ["My proper name survives me. After my death, one will still be able to name me and speak of me. Like every sign, 'I' included, the proper name carries the necessary possibility of functioning in my absence, of detaching itself from its bearer."] Derrida explores this in detail in *Otobiographies* where he asserts the following capacity of the name to "live" separately from the person to whom it refers: "Etre mort signifie au moins ceci qu'aucun bénéfice ou maléfice, calculé ou non, *ne revient plus* au porteur du nom mais seulement au nom, en quoi le nom, qui n'est pas le porteur, est toujours et *a priori* un nom de mort. Ce qui revient au nom ne revient jamais à du vivant, rien ne revient à du vivant" ["To be dead means at least this, that no benefit or harm, calculated or not, comes any longer to the bearer of the name but only to the name, in that the name, which is not the bearer, is always and *a priori* the name of the dead. That which comes back to the name never comes back to the living, nothing comes back to the living"] (44).

[42] "One will therefore say that, even while I'm alive, my name marks my death. . . The mark that identifies me, that makes me myself rather than an other, disappropriates me immediately in announcing my death, and in separating itself *a priori* from the same self that it constitutes or assures. . . The signature, and that's precisely that which distinguishes it from the proper name in general, tries to make up for the proper that was disappropriated in the name."

[43] "The act of signing, which cannot be reduced to the simple inscription of its proper name, attempts, by a supplementary turn, to reappropriate the property always already lost in the name

itself. What the signature implies is that to mark a here-now is always *by right* accompanied by the mark of a place and a date."

⁴⁴It is typical for writers of autobiography (even a fictional one) to introduce themselves by name. In Ferdinand Oyono's autobiographical novel *Une vie de boy*, for example, the opening lines of a journal "discovered" by the narrator read like this: "Je m'appelle Toundi Ondoua. Je suis le fils de Toundi et de Zama. Depuis que le Père m'a baptisé, il m'a donné le nom de Joseph." (16) In these three short sentences, we have a full name, the names of the protagonist's parents, and a new name which reflects a change in household, lifestyle, and belief. In these brief lines, we thus find a quick summary of the individual's evolving identity. The change in name is significant, and is therefore highlighted at the beginning of the text; he gives his family names to show where he comes from and provides his new name to show who he now is.

⁴⁵In *Vaste est la prison*, the narrator never reveals the name of the loved one, calling him only "l'Aimé" ["Beloved"] (26). When referring to her daughter, the first name is never used: "Ma fille, à vingt ans, vit à Alger. . . Retrouver ma fille. . ." (319). The same situation usually exists when she evokes her mother, who is simply "Ma mère" (170). As for the dear mother-in-law whom the narrator is surprised to discover has gone blind, the deep bond they share is described, but once again the name of the woman is not uttered: "C'était ma belle-mère, ou plutôt puisque mon divorce datait de deux ou trois ans, c'était mon ex-belle-mère. . . J'allais vraiment dire 'ma mère', tant je l'avais aimée, tant je l'aimais encore malgré cet éloignement" (325).

⁴⁶"my mother would refer to him quite naturally by his first name. . . What a daring innovation!" (*Fantasia* 35).

⁴⁷"These nameless uncles, cousins, relatives by marriage, were for us an unidentifiable collection of individuals to all of whom their spouses alluded impartially in the masculine gender" (*Fantasia* 36).

⁴⁸"The radical change in customs was apparent for all to see: my father had quite brazenly written his wife's name, in his handwriting, on a postcard which was going to travel from one town to another, which was going to be exposed to so many masculine eyes" (*Fantasia* 37).

⁴⁹"Both of them referred to each other by name, which was tantamount to declaring openly their love for each other" (*Fantasia* 38).

⁵⁰Derrida argues that Nietzsche's writing in his autobiographical text *Ecce Homo* is characterized by the use of pseudonyms without proper names, of masks: "Pour l'instant, je lirai Nietzsche depuis la scène d'Ecce Homo. Il y met son corps et son nom en avant, même s'il s'y avance sous des masques ou des pseudonymes sans noms propres, des masques ou des noms pluriels qui peuvent ne se proposer ou produire, comme tout masque et même toute théorie du simulacre, qu'en rapportant toujours un bénéfice de protection, une plus-value où se reconnaît encore la ruse de la vie. Ruse perdante dès lors que la plus-value encore ne revient pas à du vivant mais au nom des noms et à la communauté des masques" ["For the moment, I will read Nietzsche from the scene of Ecce Homo. He puts his body and his name forward there, even if he advances under masks and pseudonyms without proper names, masks or plural names that could only propose or produce—like every mask and even every theory of the simulacrum—by coming back to the benefit of protection, a plus-value where the ruse of life recognizes itself. A losing ruse from the moment that the plus-value still doesn't come back to the living but to the name of names and to the community of masks"] (*Otobiographies* 45).

⁵¹Another interesting parallel between Derrida's interpretation of Nietzsche and Djebar's work involves the name as tied to the mother and consequently "surviving" the death of both the father and the patronym: "[. . .] vous ne pourrez entendre mon nom si vous ne l'entendez pas de cette oreille, comme celui du mort et de la vivante, le nom double et divisé du père mort et de la survivante, de la mère qui survit, me survivra d'ailleurs jusqu'à m'enterrer. Survivante est la mère, survivance est le nom de la mère. Cette survie est ma vie qu'elle déborde, et le nom de ma mort, de ma vie morte, voilà le nom de mon père, ou aussi bien mon patronyme" ["you will not be able to hear my name if you don't hear it with this ear, like that of the dead and that of the living, the double divided name of the dead father and the survivor, of the mother who survives, who will survive me besides to the point of burying me. Survivor is the mother, surviving is the name of the mother. This survival is my life that overflows, and the name of my death, of my dead life, is the name of my father, or rather my patronymic"] (*Otobiographies* 63).

[52] "His own identity, that which he intends to declare and has nothing to do with the disproportionate ones his contemporaries know under this name, under his name or rather his homonym, Friedrich Nietzsche, this identity that he vindicates, he doesn't claim it thanks to a contract with his contemporaries. He receives this identity from an unheard-of contract that he has made with himself."

[53] "At the outset, I had decided to make a film that would take place in the mountains of my childhood, where I had not returned since. . . It was therefore because I had an intimate relationship with many women and not because I was a novelist or because I came with technicians . . . but because of the fact that I was my mother's daughter, because I was from a certain tribe . . . Thus, because I was Bahia's daughter and not at all Assia Djebar or I don't know what, I was able to enter in. . ." Transcription taken from Djebar's comments in Mireille Calle-Gruber's course entitled "Femmes cinéastes" at Université Paris 8 Vincennes. 14 January 2000.

[54] Examples of the word "heritage" in Djebar's work abound. Here are just a few found in two of her autobiographical texts. *L'amour, la fantasia*: "Sous le poids des tabous que je porte en moi comme héritage. . ." (240) ["Burdened by my inherited taboos" (*Fantasia* 214)], "Ma fiction est cette autobiographie qui s'esquisse, alourdie par l'héritage qui m'encombre" (*Fantasia* 244) ["My fiction is this attempt at autobiography, weighed down under the oppressive burden of my heritage" (218)]; *Ombre sultane*: "le lourd héritage" (11) ["the age-old burden of oppression that is our legacy" (*A Sister* 3)].

[55] "And now I too seek out the rich vocabulary of love of my mother tongue—milk of which I had been previously deprived" (*Fantasia* 62).

[56] "for the mother tongue, itself bifide, is the loss of origin (loss of the origin, loss at the origin). . . It is this ancestral legacy . . . that the writer Assia Djebar turns into her veritable heritage, the point of departure for her writing." It is important to note that this *"legs ancestral"* is especially problematic since the mother herself does not really "possess" the language she speaks: "la mère n'est que la gardienne [de cette langue ancienne] dépossédée—doublement" ["the mother is only the guardian, doubly dispossessed"] (Calle-Gruber, 278).

[57] In an interesting move, the narrator Isma of *Vaste est la prison* is addressed by the first person voice that refers to her in the third person. In this "évocation", the difficulty of doing justice to the "polyform voice" is a cause of lamentation: "Mais le reste, le vivant et le mort, le masculin (c'est-à-dire l'orgueil irrédentiste) et le féminin (la lucidité qui durcit ou rend folle) de ce que je crois l'âme de cette terre, le reste donc s'est drapé dans des voiles de poussière, dans des mots français masquant la voix informe—gargouillis, sons berbères et barbares reniés, mélodies et plaintes arabisées et modulées—oui, la voix polyforme de ma généalogie. Comme je m'en dépêtre mal!" (331)

[58] "writing has brought me to the cries of the women silently rebelling in my youth, to my true origins" (*Fantasia* 204).

[59] "Thus my word, which could be double, and maybe even triple, participates in several cultures, but I only have one writing: French."

[60] Derrida also focuses on language in his analysis of inheritance with respect to Hölderlin: "Pour [Hölderlin] nous sommes des héritiers dans notre être même: le langage est donné en quelque sorte à l'existence, au Dasein, à l'homme comme Dasein, afin qu'il témoigne, non pas de ceci ou de cela, mais qu'il témoigne du fait qu'il est héritier dans son être même. Nous héritons du langage pour pouvoir témoigner que nous sommes des héritiers. Autrement dit, nous héritons de la possibilité d'hériter" ["For Hölderlin we are all heirs in our very being: language is given in some way to existence, to Dasein, to man as Dasein, so that he will testify, not about this or that, but so that he will testify to the fact that he is an heir in his very being. We inherit language in order to be able to bear witness to the fact that we are heirs. In other words, we inherit the possibility to inherit"] (*Echographies* 147) The use of the word *"témoigner"* points to the written work of Djebar who takes down the words of "witnesses" and bears "witness" herself to the atrocities committed in her country.

[61] "I am an Algerian woman, but I should make reference rather to the native land, at least to the language of my ancestors, men and women: 'I am an Arab-Berber woman' of 'French writing'. . . Because identity is not only about paper, not only about blood, but also about *language*."

[62] "Yet, thirty years later, I notice that I introduce myself first as a writer, as a novelist, as if the act of writing, when it is daily and solitary to the point of asceticism, has come to modify the weight of belonging."

[63] "Literature aspires to the idiomatic. . . As a writer, I want to write like no other, and thus impose my proper name or rather my signature (for a writing that would be absolutely my own and idiomatic should be considered a signature)."

[64] "To communicate the idiom of my proper name, to impose my law in claiming my name, I must ruse with the language that is precisely not mine (that I receive like the law, Saussure said— but I also received my proper name, I don't baptize myself), I must try to mark this language surreptitiously, make readers who believe they are simply reading literature swallow my name."

[65] The presence of Djebar's name on the cover, on the "title page" is important. Gilmore points out that the presence of the name in this prominent place is not a "given" for a woman: "For women, the title page is frequently the site of a necessary evasion. One reads here not the signature but the pseudonym, not the family name but 'Anon.' The title page of women's writing presents itself not as a fact but as an extension of the fiction of identity, and it is frequently more comprehensible as a corollary to laws regarding women's noninheritance of property" (81). Since I maintain Djebar is more than just a pseudonym, the title page in her case is not an "evasion," but a claim of responsibility for the work that follows. Djebar understands well, nonetheless, that writing extends the "fiction of identity," a point that she elaborates on in her work.

[66] Derrida pays close attention to the inscription of the name in the work of French poet Francis Ponge in *Signéponge*.

[67] "Unlike man, who holds so dearly to his title and his titles, his pouches of value, his cap, crown, and everything connected with his head, woman couldn't care less about the fear of decapitation (or castration), adventuring, without the masculine temerity, into anonymity, which she can merge with, without annihilating herself: because she's a giver" (357).

[68] As Rosello reveals in a text by a different writer, authorship is closely related to a specific writing style: "the strangeness of the formula is a signature. In this case, authorship is a mark of chosen grammatical otherness" (143).

[69] Given this method of writing, Djebar seems to lend herself to a type of authorship Foucault envisions at the close of "What is an Author?," an authorship that slips into anonymity. The discourse that arises from such a conception of authorship revolves around ideas communicated rather than the originator (and the originality) of those ideas: "We can easily imagine a culture where discourse would circulate without any need for an author. Discourses, whatever their status, form, or value, and regardless of our manner of handling them, would unfold in a pervasive anonymity" (138).

[70] "I don't confess myself, rather I confess others for the imponderable and therefore heavy secrets that I inherit without knowing. . ."

[71] "For the literary writing of Assia Djebar is constructed on the title of women: to write, thus, is to conduct a work that gives life, that gives birth. In particular, to all the illiterate sisters of the gyneceum, for whom the writer serves not as the spokesperson but instead, humbly, as the 'voice-carrier.'"

[72] The news of her inability to mother a child is not met with sadness, as the narrator explains: "j'appris le verdict joyeusement: je serais donc merveilleusement stérile, disponible pour des enfants de coeur, doublement de coeur, et jamais de sang!" (313)

[73] "Assia Djebar the artist takes as a model this first artist of the world being born, and—taking advantage of the equivocal form of her Frenchified name—she places herself as a substitute for him and changes him into a woman: Prometheus is no longer Prometheus, but Promethea. Besides—let us say this in passing—the author has long been present in this myth, a truth brought to light paradoxically by the mask of the pseudonym: The woman who loves Prometheus in the ancient texts is called . . . Asia."

[74] "the proper name *belongs without belonging* to the language."

[75] "Derra: the word used in Arabic to denote the new bride of the same man, the first wife's rival; this word means 'wound'—the one who hurts, who cuts open the flesh, or the one who feels hurt, it's the same thing!" (*A Sister* 91).

[76] "it's of the wound, of the cutting at the origin, of the 'cut sound' of the illiterate sequestered ones, that is tied the phrase in truth."

WORKS CITED

Bâ, Mariama. *Une si longue lettre*. Dakar: Les Nouvelles Editions Africaines du Sénégal, 1998; for publication cited.

Barthes, Roland. "La mort de l'Auteur". *Manteia* V (1968): 12–17. "The Death of the Author." *Image-Music-Text*. Trans. and ed. Stephen Heath. New York: Hill and Wang, 1977.

Bennington, Geoffrey and Jacques Derrida. *Jacques Derrida*. Paris: Seuil, 1991.

Calle-Gruber, Mireille. ". . . Et la voix s'écri(e)ra. Assia Djebar ou Le cri architecte". *Le Renouveau de la Parole Identitaire*. Ed. Mireille Calle-Gruber and Jeanne-Marie Clerc. Université Paul-Valéry Montpellier, Centre d'études littéraires françaises du XXe siècle, cahier 2 (1993): 275–291.

———. "Pour une analytique de la globalisation—Littératures de l'altérité: l'exemple d'Assia Djebar." *Literatur im Zeitalter der Globalisierung*. Ed. Manfred Schmeling, Monika Schmitz-Emans, Kerst Walstra. Würzburg: Königshausen & Neumann, 2000. 205–219.

Cixous, Hélène. "Le Rire de la Méduse." *L'Arc* 61 (1975): 39–54. "The Laugh of the Medusa." Trans. Keith Cohen and Paula Cohen. *Signs* 1:4 (1976): 875–894. Reprinted in *Feminisms: An anthology of literary theory and criticism*. Ed. Robyn R. Warhol and Diane Price Herndl. New Brunswick, New Jersey: Rutgers University Press, 1997. 347–362.

Clément, Catherine and Bernard Pingaud. "Une femme pour d'autres". *L'Arc* 61 (1975): 1–2.

Clerc, Jeanne-Marie. *Assia Djebar: Ecrire, transgresser, résister*. Paris: L'Harmattan, 1997.

De Man, Paul. "Autobiography as De-facement." *Modern Language Notes* 94 (1979): 919–930.

Derrida, Jacques. "Des Tours de Babel." *Difference in Translation*. Ed. Joseph E. Graham. Ithaca: Cornell University Press, 1985. 209–248.

———. *Echographies de la télévision: entretiens filmés*. Paris: Galilée, 1996.

———. *Otobiographies: L'enseignement de Nietzsche et la politique du nom propre*. Paris: Galilée, 1984.

———. "Signature Event Context." *Margins of Philosophy*. Trans. Alan Bass. Chicago: University of Chicago Press, 1982.

———. *Signéponge*. Paris: Le Seuil, 1988.

Djebar, Assia. *Femmes d'Alger dans leur appartement*. Paris: des Femmes, 1980. *Women of Algiers in Their Apartment*. Trans. Marjolijn de Jager. Charlottesville: University Press of Virginia, 1992.

———. *L'amour, la fantasia*. Paris: Jean-Claude Lattès, 1985. Albin Michel, 1995. *Fantasia: An Algerian Cavalcade*. Trans. Dorothy S. Blair. Portsmouth, N.H.: Heinemann, 1993.

———. *Ombre sultane*. Paris: J.-C. Lattès, 1987. *A Sister to Scheherazade*. Trans. Dorothy S. Blair. Portsmouth, N.H.: Heinemann, 1993.

———. *Vaste est la prison*. Paris: Albin Michel, 1995. *So Vast the Prison*. Trans. Betsy Wing. New York: Seven Stories Press, 1999.

———. *Ces voix qui m'assiègent. . . en marge de ma francophonie*. Paris: Albin Michel, 1999.

Foucault, Michel. "What is an Author?" *Language, Counter-Memory, Practice*. Ithaca: Cornell University Press, 1977. 113–138.

Gallop, Jane. "'French Feminism.'" *A New History of French Literature*. Ed. Denis Hollier. Cambridge, Massachusetts: Harvard University Press, 1989. 1045–1049.

Gilmore, Leigh. *Autobiographics: A Feminist Theory of Women's Self-Representation*. Ithaca: Cornell University Press, 1994.

Gracki, Katherine. "Writing Violence and the Violence of Writing in Assia Djebar's Algerian Quartet." *World Literature Today* 70.4 (Autumn 1996): 835–843.

Irigaray, Luce. *Ce Sexe qui n'en est pas un*. Paris: Les Editions de Minuit, 1977.

Kamuf, Peggy. *Signature Pieces: On the Institution of Authorship*. Ithaca and London: Cornell University Press, 1988.

Khatibi, Abdelkebir. "Bilinguisme et littérature." *Maghreb Pluriel.* Montpellier: Fata Morgana, 1983. 187–188.

———. *La blessure du nom propre.* Paris: Denoël, 1974.

Lejeune, Philippe. *Le pacte autobiographique.* Paris: Seuil, 1975. Reprinted in *On autobiography.* Ed. Paul John Eakin and trans. Katherine Leary. Minneapolis: University of Minnesota Press, 1989.

Miller, Christopher L. *Theories of Africans: Francophone literature and anthropology in Africa.* Chicago: University of Chicago Press, 1990.

Oyono, Ferdinand. *Une vie de boy.* Paris: René Julliard, 1956.

Rosello, Mireille. *Declining the Stereotype: ethnicity and representation in French cultures.* Hanover, N.H.: University Press of New England, 1998.

Ruhe, Ernstpeter. "Les mots, l'amour, la mort: Les mythomorphoses d'Assia Djebar." *Postcolonialisme & Autobiographie.* Ed. Alfred Hornung and Ernstpeter Ruhe. Amsterdam and Atlanta, GA: Rodopi, 1998. 161–177.

Schimmel, Annemarie. "Die geheime Sprache der algerischen Frauen: Ein Gespräch mit Assia Djebar." *Literaturen: Das Journal für Bücher und Themen* (Oktober 2000): 41–44.

Zabus, Chantal. "Encre blanche et Afrique originelle: Derrida et la postcolonialité." *Passions de la littérature: Avec Jacques Derrida.* Paris: Galilée, 1996. 261–273.

Zimra, Clarisse. Afterword. *Women of Algiers in Their Apartment.* Trans. Marjolijn de Jager. Charlottesville: University Press of Virginia, 1992.

AFTERWORD

Assia Djebar frequently evokes the importance of movement to her work. Not only does the French language provide her with physical mobility, it contributes *élan* to her writing. "The Improper Name: Ownership and Authorship in the Literary Production of Assia Djebar" was written in Djebar's rhythmic wake, so to speak. In the midst of academic activities and travels, I found myself propelled to explore her literary production from a new angle: that of the proper name.

A great advantage afforded scholars who study contemporary writers is the possibility of interaction. I met Assia Djebar in Paris, months before taking an intense interest in her adopted appellation. It wasn't until after the completion of the essay that I had the opportunity to sit down with her in Los Angeles to discuss the topic in detail. I discovered then the thoughts that occupied the novelist on the occasion of her first publication.

Balance was foremost in her mind, according to her story: Striding down rue St. Jacques in the French capital with her fiancé, she listened as recited the ninety-nine attributes of Allah. When he reached *djébbar*, she liked the sound of the word; she was also attracted to its import: "the intransigent one." After some additional searching, she came upon *Assia*, a name signifying "she who consoles." Taking into account both "music" and "meaning," she found this first name to complement the second, phonetically *and* semantically.

I would argue that the two characteristics inherent in her chosen names are representative of Assia Djebar's literary creation: exacting, rigorous, indeed intransigent when it comes to the architecture of short stories, essays, and novels, the author is also comforting, caring, and certainly consoling when she listens to women from her native Algeria and relates their stories in her writing.

Assia Djebar continues to focus on women and their movement, providing historical and geographic context for their battles and tracing their comings and goings. While displacements and migrations have been a part of her texts from the early 1980s, recent publications—from *Oran, langue morte* to *Les nuits de Strasbourg* to *La femme sans sépulture*—are especially attuned to the multifaceted, multilingual situations of persons between France and North Africa. They deal explicitly and profoundly with the challenges and privileges faced by women of Maghrebian origin as they encounter European influences on both sides of the Mediterranean.

It is no accident that Assia Djebar, a woman enamored with movement and metropolises, has of late taken up scholarly residence at New York University. This urban location inevitably inspires, albeit in subtle ways, her current creative production as increasingly open to new experiences of language and loss, of translation and improvisation. At the intersection of languages and cultures, this novelist, theorist, opera librettist, and moviemaker not only reflects (on) innovative possibilities for speaking and writing in her work, she embodies these possibilities in her very name.

Gendered Geographies: Remapping the Space of the Woman Intellectual in Concha Méndez's *Memorias habladas, memorias armadas*[1]

MELISSA DINVERNO

IN THE OPENING pages of her memoir *Memorias habladas, memorias armadas* (1990), the Spanish poet and intellectual Concha Méndez recalls her reaction when she was no longer allowed to attend school as a young girl in Madrid:

> Cuando dejé la escuela a los catorce años, me pasó lo que a las personas que se jubilan; estar acostumbrado a hacer un trabajo que de repente te quitan, te parte por el eje [. . .]. A mí me jubilaron. [. . .] [M]e encontraba en un desierto. Mis padres no me dejaban coger un libro, ni siquiera el periódico; y en las horas de aburrimiento empecé a escribir un viaje imaginario. [. . .] Cuando toda la famila estaba ya acostada y la casa silenciosa, salía de mi cuarto hacia el despacho de mi padre, que tenía un escritorio estilo americano; y ahí, con los mapas del colegio, empecé a escribir. El viaje duraría cinco años y mis metas eran Nueva York y Hollywood; y así, barajando geografías, me transportaba en avión y barco por todo el mundo. Algunas noches no me daba tiempo de escribir porque escuchaba los pasos sigilosos de mi madre que pasaba a revisar el sueño de sus diez hijos. (28–29)[2]

Denied learning at school and reading at home, Méndez depicts herself as having been relegated to an intellectual desert, a space devoid of activity. Banned from the institutional space of the school because she is a girl, "retired" to the domestic sphere, and deprived of news from beyond the walls of the home, Méndez represents her gendered marginalization in geographical terms. Nonetheless, it is precisely in the patriarchal space of her father's office that she stages her defiance of such spatial and intellectual limitation. Slipping into his chair, she uses both the power of writing and the production of space to escape the very patriarchal norms that disallow her both. Populating the scene of writing with her own school maps, she literally reterritorializes patriarchal space, transforming it from a site that is both off-limits and limiting, into one in which she rewrites her own possibilities as a girl and as a future intellectual.

Yet, a fundamental tension underpins this passage: what are we to make of the fact that she writes her resistance from the site of her father's desk, and presumably, with the phallic pen, while she casts her mother as the vigilant, castrating woman that threatens to cut off her intellectual productivity? Is she merely ventriloquizing phallocentrism, representing the feminine as what limits and self-annihilates, since it safeguards and reproduces the very system that oppresses it? Read in this light, her portrayal of this site of resistance indicates a tension between the empowering rewriting of this patriarchal space from the marginalized position of women, and her gendering of power and agency in such a way that women remain on the geographical and social peripheries of power. To what degree does her writing of the past subvert hegemonic gender norms merely to reinstate them? How are we to understand Méndez's conceptualization of agency and the possibility of resistance to imposed gender limitations? As a woman intellectual, what kind of space on the social mappings of power does Méndez articulate for women writers and thinkers?

Significant in its early placement within the memoirs, this brief scene from her childhood frames many of the concerns that surface in Méndez's text: her experience of exclusion, the articulation of complicated notions of gender, the representation of an intellectual space for women, and the staging of resistance through spatial practices.[3] However, little work has been done on Méndez's reflections on women intellectuals or the specifics of her feminist vision *per se*. Working with her poetry, Catherine Bellver and Margaret Persin have perceptively linked Méndez's portrayal of space more broadly to notions of gender.[4] Yet Méndez's conceptualization of gender definitions, the specificity of her use of space in depicting those definitions, and her representation of the experience of being a woman writer remain open fields for critical study. Moreover, with the exception of Roberta Quance's suggestion that Méndez prefers to fashion herself as a rebel in *Memorias habladas* ("Concha Méndez" 142), the text has thus far been approached as a historical document to support readings of her literary work and general assertions of at least a nascent feminism. Her memoir has therefore yet to be considered as a potential site of self-construction, of feminist positioning and resistance.

In the following discussion I explore how Méndez's representations of space in *Memorias habladas, memorias armadas* reveal her articulations of female subjectivity and power. I analyze the recollections within the frame of her situation as a woman intellectual in order to examine her reaction to marginality, her narration of that experience, the dynamics of power that she engages by recreating the past, and the designs she may have on the past in order to make a feminist intervention in the present. Assuming Judith Butler's formulation of gender/sex as regulatory ideals (re)produced through the performance of certain practices (x-xi), I argue that Concha Méndez spatializes gender ideologies as a strategy to construct her own subjectivity as a female writer and intellectual, and as a move that contests her marginalization from social and literary power by dominant patriarchal discourse.

Méndez off (and on) the Map: Cartographic Epistemologies and Rewriting the Past

off the map: out of existence; into (or in) oblivion or an insignificant position; of no account; obsolete . . .

on the map: in an important or prominent position; of some account or importance; in existence . . .

Oxford English Dictionary, *qtd. in King (18)*

The same issues written into her description of her father's office have both confounded and attracted the literary critics who engage Méndez's work, a dynamic that has, unfortunately, played a role in her relative absence from literary mappings of the twentieth century. By now, it has become somewhat of a cliché among the relatively few literary critics that study Méndez's poetry to point out this absence, one that Catherine Bellver and Roberta Quance rightly argue began with the gendered, ambivalent reception she faced from her male colleagues in the 1920s and '30s (Bellver, "Literary Influence," *Absence*; Quance, "Concha Méndez," "Hacia").[5] The vast majority of the relatively scarce critical discourse on Méndez's poetry has been written since 1990, the year the memoir was published. This scholarship, in part, continues the kind of recuperative work critics such as Emilio Miró ("Preliminar") and Margery Resnick began in the 1970s as they attempted to bring Méndez's extraordinary life into focus and her literary corpus into the canon (see Bellver; Ciplijauskaite; Miró, *Antología*; Quance; Sánchez; Valender, "Concha Méndez," Introduction; Wilcox). Critics such as John Wilcox and Catherine Bellver have most insightfully advanced a discussion regarding Méndez's inclusion in the literary canon by exposing the terms of Méndez's gendered exclusion (Wilcox, "Ernestina," *Women*; Bellver, *Absence*, "Literary Influence"). Others have argued that Méndez be incorporated into a feminist history of Spain (Quance; Resnick; Ulacia Altolaguirre; Valender). Inevitably, canonical questions as to what kind of space Méndez should be granted resurface continually in a critical discourse formulated in terms of gender.

Opening a dialogue on cultural cartography in *Mapping Reality*, Geoff King considers the *Oxford English Dictionary*'s definitions of being located "on" and "off the map" as a way to signal the power of spatial representation to create or to negate existence (18). Given the inexistence, or at least the insignificance, of Méndez according to current mappings of literary and feminist canons, the narrative frame that she uses to organize her memoirs is particularly interesting. Indeed, the memoir *is* the map and vice versa, as it reflects an underlying cartographic epistemology that places Méndez at the center and serves both referential (as a framework for remembrance) and anticipatory functions (as a guide to future encounters).[6] Specifically, the memoir structure evokes that of a travel narrative, as Méndez tells her life and configures her subjectivity through spatial referents, with each chapter generally corresponding to a place wherein she moves, and to and from which her past self travels. Her life is thus broadly mapped in terms of the gendered and classed geographies of Madrid, Santander, London, Buenos Aires, Paris, Santiago de Cuba, Mexico City, and Coyoacán, while other chapters (Chapter VIII, for example) stand as multi-layered transitions, focusing on the passage between crucial spaces that she occupies. Within each of these zones on the map of herself, she creates spaces where she formulates her identity as a woman and a writer: cafés, the parks and streets, her homes, literary *tertulias*[7] and clubs, or recital venues, to name a few. The production of space is fundamental to her construction of a gendered subjectivity, as well as to the dual project of legitimation and resistance that the memoirs embody.

Paraphrasing King, mapping as an epistemological tool gives the cartographer power over spaces that threaten to overwhelm the subject (66), security in being able to identify and control one's "place in the world" (40–41), authority to (re)write the organizing principles of (socio-cultural) space and spatial relationships (20), and the ability to reinforce territorial claims (22). Méndez represents her own space of enunciation as marked by gender marginalization, literary-critical exclusion, and geo-political exile; she depicts her positionality as cartographer triply "off the map" and, therefore, on the peripheries of power.[8] In her reading of Méndez's poem, "Mapas," Margaret Persin engages King's conceptualization of social mapping, viewing Méndez's use of maps and cartography in her early poetry as a way of establishing the "possibility of her existence" and offering "a differing positionality" (193). Like Persin, I interpret Méndez's use of cartography as an empowering move, although here in the particular context of her identity as a woman writer. Thus, her engagement of a cartographic structure can be read as embodying a shift in the hierarchy of power, as she uses it to write herself out of cultural oblivion and into a recognizable literary and feminist landscape. Despite her marginalization, in the act of telling Méndez deterritorializes the literary and social map written by patriarchal practices, and locates herself at the center as agent and literary voice, as border-jumper and transgressor of the spatial practices that reinforce hegemonic gender norms. At the same time, she writes her centrality in a way that paradoxically continues to highlight her marginality as a woman, thereby enabling her to critique the very system from which she seeks legitimation. Within this map of herself, the sites she constructs are inevitably marked by a spatial logic that to a greater or lesser degree excludes women, and yet within these spaces, she continues to locate a feminist, critical agency. Méndez thus writes herself "onto the map" in a way that both refuses to ignore her marginalization and celebrates her triumphs of intrusion.

Beyond the Walls: Spatializing the (Ob)Scene of Women's Writing

> [. . .] walls, enclosures and façades serve to define both a scene (where something takes place) and an obscene area to which everything that cannot or may not happen on the scene is relegated: whatever is inadmissible, be it malefic or forbidden, thus has its own hidden space on the near or the far side of the frontier.
>
> Henri Lefebvre, The Production of Space (36)

Throughout the memoirs Méndez is acutely aware that (produced) space, as Henri Lefebvre writes, "serves as a tool of thought and of action; that in addition to being a means of production it is also a means of control, and hence of domination, of power" (26). For Méndez, the form and terms of domination could not be more clear, as she continually depicts space as embodying the gendered power relations of society. Not only does she broadly represent the historic gendering of the public/private spatial division, but, particularly in relation to pre-Republican Spain, she constructs specific institutionalized sites of intellectual activity and the socially appropriate practices which would keep women out of them. Similar to the childhood classroom from which she was exiled (28), the university space is portrayed as a no (wo)man's land when Méndez graphically describes the severe beating she received from her mother after simply auditing one literature class (45). She continues to represent her exclusion from yet another intellectual world through her relationship to Luis Buñuel.[9] Méndez's account of their seven-year relationship includes a list of the traditional spaces of courtship that they occupied (dance halls, the park, the movie theatre, the beach [39–41]), as well as her observation that during all those years, their relationship remained limited to these sites and therefore off-limits to the intellectual space that so profoundly affected Buñuel and his male contemporaries: the Residencia de Estudiantes (40–41). Signaling the production of mutually exclusive spheres, she highlights the dominant social practices that defined that which was artistic/intellectual as male, and frivolous/amorous as female. These concretized norms were reinforced in her household and thus contributed to her arduous self-education (41). Méndez is careful to point out the painful effects of these spatialized gender ideologies, as she juxtaposes the rich cultural and intellectual environment enjoyed by her male peers within the Residencia, to the poverty of her own at home, where "para leer tenía que pedir libros prestados y ocultarlos en la cama" (40).[10] The gender logic set up by Méndez extends as well to the institution of the literary *tertulia*, yet another of the crucial spaces for artistic creativity during the late teens and '20s. In this case, her restricted movement beyond the bounds of the home excluded her from the now-famous late night sessions of the newly forming avant-garde movement in Spain (59). Instead of participating in these literary laboratories and discussions with her male peers, she describes herself as either returning home to a grandmother who would tell stories of parties in a Madrid long-since past (60), or attending a *tertulia* "arcaica"[11] of older men where a woman's presence was always noted, and often sexualized (52–53). Kept out of avant-garde intellectual spaces, she implies that, as a young woman, the door was only open to stepping backward into the past, and despite the interest that it might have held, that past erased the issue of her own intellectual and creative advancement.

Méndez is essentially setting up a series of sites that we see from the outside, locales defined by the barriers she confronts continually and through which she still desires to pass. In each case, there are clear spatial suppositions (assumptions about what one can and cannot do somewhere) in place that function according to traditional gender definitions. The tightly woven coherency of normative social behavior (enforced by parental judgment, physical punishment, dating norms, and curfews) aims to keep women out of these intellectual spaces. Henri Lefebvre

conceptualizes such regulated areas as "scenes," sites which reinforce the hegemonic structuring of society by legitimizing and perpetuating specific practices
(36). Taking up Lefebvre's formulation of the "scene," we can read Méndez's representation of space, then, as a staging of the gendered institutional scene of intellectual practices, a space that by definition (re)produces the traditional patriarchal
male/female binaries. Artistic practices take place within these protected environ-
ments, and women are left outside the door. As an upper-middle-class woman,
Méndez was not allowed into these masculine sites and yet these were ostensibly
among the few social spaces of enunciation which legitimated the intellectual *per
se*, potentially empowering the writer's voice, providing direct feedback on ideas,
making possible professional networking, and assembling an audience. Depicting
herself outside the scene of writing and yet yearning to enter intellectual life, how
does Méndez then represent her response to exclusion?

Michel de Certeau's concept of the "tactic" as a practice of resistance for the
disempowered individual allows us to explore Méndez's construction of a resisting subject throughout the memoirs.[12] Excluded from the legitimized spaces of
(male) intellectual activity, Méndez represents herself as defying normative spatial practices creatively vis-à-vis multiple tactical maneuvers within the system.
Barred from entry into the exclusively male intellectual scene of the Residencia,
she tries to get around those limits and gain access to this space. Although she
and Buñuel had previously broken off their relationship, Méndez sees an opportunity for access when his mother informs her that he is sick in Paris: "se
me ocurrió que, *bajo el pretexto* de informarme de su salud, podría llamar a
la Residencia de Estudiantes" (46, emphasis added).[13] Wanting to meet García
Lorca (someone who became emblematic of the Residencia and was her own first
connection to that group), Méndez calls the Residencia, where Lorca happens to
answer the phone. She piques his curiosity by referring to herself enigmatically
as "la novia desconocida de Buñuel," noting as narrator that "Como era la novia
conocida por referencias, le interesé" (46).[14] Here Méndez portrays a manipulation of the normative gender roles (the worried girlfriend) and a reappropriation
of her own marginalized socio-spatial status (as a woman and girlfriend, she
had not been allowed to enter the space of the Residencia) to capture Lorca's
interest and thereby gain the ear of an up-and-coming writer who participated
in the intellectual environment that she so clearly desired. Inviting him to her
home, Méndez again transforms her father's office, this time reappropriating this
patriarchal space and scene of writing to create an artistic atmosphere that both
highlights her own creativity and stages her entrance into the male intellectual
world of the Residencia:

> Para recibirlo, me puse un batín morado de corte oriental y me pinté la cara
> como en las películas mudas. Llegó. Lo pasé al despacho de mi padre, que era
> una habitación independiente del resto de la casa: tenía los sillones tapizados
> en terciopelo azul y dos grandes balcones que daban a la calle. Encendí en el
> ángulo del cuarto una lucecita, que creaba una atmósfera en claro oscuro. De
> morado, sobre el sillón azul, sofisticada, le conté las cosas que sabía de la Resi-
> dencia; todo lo que viví sin vivir durante años. Fui entonces el mundo secreto

de Buñuel que de golpe se revelaba ante su mundo. Federico y yo nos hicimos amigos. (46)[15]

Proud of her clever use of her environment, she rewrites the designated spatial logic of the office, carefully constructing a seductive theatrical/cinematic space where she performs her own sophisticated, dramatic role of the unknown (but all-knowing) outsider. Turning the disadvantage of socio-spatial marginalization to her advantage, yet still noting her frustration with having been excluded ("todo lo que viví sin vivir durante años" [46]),[16] she depicts herself as finally speaking out from behind a silent façade and connecting with Lorca, who became not only a close friend, but also the key that opened the Residencia to her.

These particular tactics allow her to redistribute social mappings of power and to gain access to the intellectual practices associated with the Residencia, what Catherine Bellver has rightly characterized as her "intrusion" into the Residencia ("Voyages" 112). Nonetheless, her transgressive "intrusion" on the scene is ultimately only partial and momentary, limited to informal gatherings, a few café meetings, and the poetry recitals of male peers. Since intellectual practices are gendered male and take place within exclusionary institutional spaces, women's writing and intellectual activity consequently appear as socially relegated to a geographically marginalized realm akin to Lefebvre's "obscene," that is, the space that lies beyond the scene's walls and enclosures, the space where forbidden acts occur (36). And yet Méndez rewrites these marginalized spaces as potentially productive sites where women can launch their literary careers despite the obstacles. She carefully inscribes her own formative acts of writing and literary development into open, outdoor spaces within the landscape of Madrid: on park benches with Rafael Alberti (47), alone on chairs under the gas lanterns of the city avenues (53), in a pine grove near her house with Alberti and other male literary peers (54), and in the wheat fields behind her home with the peasants that worked the land (61). Méndez imagines herself outside the walls of literary institutions, "on the near or the far side of the frontier" (Lefebvre 36). She sits beyond the legitimized and legitimizing scenes of literary practice and flips this space of abjection on its head, valuing it as an area that institutions cannot regulate or contain, and converting it into a place where female literary activity, although still transgressive, can be made viable. Indeed, both in her construction of her literary development and its juxtaposition with prior gender spatializations, Méndez celebrates the transgressive quality of her stubborn reappropriations of space, of her ability to keep writing at all. Thus we read her occupation of these sites as a subversive practice, since she is an upper-middle-class woman in patriarchy's no-woman's land (sitting on the street alone, at a park with men, with peasants in a field), acting as a woman should not (writing poetry and having intellectual discussions). Her exclusion from the (male) scene of writing is tinged with a sense of empowerment; the hegemonic gender coding that she faces is challenged because she continues to write, and write where she can: in non-literary and off-limits spaces that she refashions tactically for her own needs.

This articulation of a productive (ob)scene of women's writing further crystallizes in her depiction of herself as woman *flâneur*, traversing the city, walking the streets, and exploring different neighborhoods. She frames her gendered journeys through these spaces in daring resistance, as she walks with Alberti and Lorca while reciting poetry on Sevilla Street ("se suponía que por esta calle no podían pasar las muchachas decentes [porque ellas, tan puritanas no se atrevían]" [50]), and explores the *verbenas* and the *barrios bajos* with Maruja Mallo ("Estaba prohibido que las mujeres entraran a las tabernas; y nosotras, para protestar, nos pegábamos a los ventanales a mirar lo que pasaba dentro" [51]).[17] Most importantly, her literary awakening is narrated within this space of the *barrios bajos*, what Rob Shields might call a "zone of Otherness," a geographically marginalized space of the abject Other (4). This area of Madrid is constructed as both deviant and sexual, placed beyond the bounds of respectable society as defined by political, social, and economic hegemony. Méndez's realization of her future vocation and her gendered traverses with her intellectual friends occur within these illicit spaces (44, 50–51). She codes the construction of her literary subjectivity and agency both as a passage into Otherness—a space of illicit behavior—and as a spatial tactic that resists the limiting strategies of hegemonic patriarchal discourse. Méndez at once ridicules the illicit coding and clings to it, reveling in her transgression of the bounds, her ability to occupy that space and snub her nose at those who act out the sedimented practices of the authoritative culture. These tactics culminate in the publication of her first book, an act represented in terms of social and geographic marginality. That is, the final selection of her poems takes place in the outdoor space of the pine grove, and the actual publication coincides with her stepping out onto the suddenly transformed streets (54). As such, she combines these gendered spaces to represent a "making public" that suggests her transgressive literary and social practices. Furthermore, Méndez wraps her publication experience in the female genealogy of Rosalía de Castro (who suffered both social and geo-political marginality), and observes that, in Spain, it is rare for a woman to publish at all (54).[18]

Ultimately, from her awakening to the publication of her work, Méndez's configuration of the (ob)scene creates a series of "counter-spaces": disruptive, resistant sites born of tactical reterritorializations (Shields 53). In these geographically marginalized sites, removed from the literary institutions that reinforce gender difference, Méndez's literary and feminist consciousness is born. She depicts her formative literary work as emerging from these forbidden zones and into the public forum, thereby challenging the patriarchal system that would deny her a scene of writing.

No-Man's Land / Women's Spaces: Making Room on the Scene of Writing

We might ask, then, if Méndez formulates the space of women intellectuals as one that is *always* the (ob)scene, that is, if intellectual survival and resistance to the limits of patriarchal norms can only be staged from outside of the literary establishment. Exploring other models for both resistance and legitimation, we find that Méndez moves beyond the configuration of an in- and outside by constructing intellectual spaces written *by* and *for* women with more complex relationships to the scene of writing: the Women's Lyceum Club of Madrid and the literary circles of Buenos Aires. Instead of being located beyond the scene's walls, these women's spaces are situated within the frame of institutional practices. Here Méndez portrays not one or two women cleverly deploying tactics to rewrite momentarily a space in which intellectual activity can take place, but a community of women who decide to create (however precariously) their own defined spaces of cultural engagement within the larger institutional system. It is precisely this precarious relationship with the gendered norms of the literary scene that distinguishes the representations of the Spanish and Argentine sites, and points to the complexities of the construction of a female identity and intellectual practice within patriarchy.

Méndez describes Madrid's Lyceum Club, of which she was a co-founder, as a formal space for the intellectual, cultural, and social advancement of women. Noting that it was an association founded by women to aid other women of lesser means, she also emphasizes the fact that it was a physical space that allowed for cultural interaction: "sobre todo era un centro cultural; tenía bibliotecas y un salón para espectáculos y conferencias" (49).[19] Unlike her constructions of transgressive outdoor spaces, here Méndez both ascribes stability to the Lyceum's cultural position by noting that these women had rooms of their own, and suggests its legitimacy as an institution by mapping its existence in other major cultural centers—in particular, New York, London, and Paris (49). These women were part of an international organization, not an isolated conversation. And yet, Méndez's representation of this female space points to her conflicted relationship with it as a site for women's intellectual advancement. Although Catherine Bellver may be right in stating that the Lyceum was "designed as a [. . .] place where women could exchange ideas without the interference of men" (*Absence* 35), Méndez's text questions the attainment of that goal and the very possibility of a woman's voice and intellectual independence in that space. That is, she openly criticizes the Lyceum's members either for ventriloquizing male intellectual discourse (calling these women "las maridas de los maridos," since they were the wives of male intellectuals that "venían a la tertulia a contar lo que habían oído en casa" [49]), or for simply lacking a voice (49–50).[20] The Lyceum becomes a permeable and/or mute site where either male conversations seep into the space of the women's *tertulia* and displace their voices, or where women simply fail to participate. Therefore, although the Lyceum generally stands in the memoirs as an advantageous space for women, Méndez nonetheless marks it as a by women and for women effort that is fraught with issues of power, authority, and authenticity. The text thus reflects the complexity of attempts to reterritorialize the legitimated male space of intellectual practices and make room for women on the writing scene. Moreover, despite the institutional context that Méndez creates, she pointedly observes that Spanish male intellectuals' reception of this cultural space for women was mixed at best. While she notes that younger writers such as Alberti and Lorca gave poetry readings at the Lyceum, Méndez remembers that Jacinto Benavente refused to come, "inaugurando como disculpa una frase célebre del lenguaje cotidiano: '¿Cómo quieren que vaya a dar una conferencia a tontas y a locas?' No podía entender que las mujeres nos interesábamos por la cultura" (49).[21] Thus Méndez represents this space as mapped somewhere just beyond the male scene of writing and, therefore, still associated with the (ob)scene.[22]

Her construction of Buenos Aires, however, stands as a fundamentally different model of women's intellectual space and is arguably the only place in the memoirs where she represents a community of women thinkers within the confines of the hegemonic literary system. Indeed, Méndez writes Buenos Aires in a lexicon of women's solidarity that is conspicuously absent from the rest of the memoirs. Framing her arrival within social, economic, and spatial configurations of the marginal, yet noting that the city gives her more room for maneuver (71–72), Méndez begins to narrate her professional and intellectual breakthrough, her path from marginalized outsider to celebrated writer inside the literary walls. More importantly, however, the very possibility of this transformation is narrated through the solidarity offered by other women intellectuals, particularly Consuelo Berges and Alfonsina Storni. Méndez's own occupation of the writing scene is thus predicated on their collective occupation of that space and on her reliance on their intellectual and emotional bonds as women. The close friendship, business relationship, and intellectual exchange that Méndez shared with Consuelo Berges give rise to a repeated use of "nosotras," a series of parallel literary and professional endeavors, and a sense of female companionship reflected in the warmth of their shared office space on Florida Street, where they would comfortably spend "las mañanas ocupadas con el correo y fumando unos cigarrillos turcos de boquilla dorada" (74).[23] Instead of using her father's office momentarily to escape sociospatial marginalization or to stage an incursion into the male intellectual scene, Méndez now occupies her own "despacho elegantísimo"[24] with (and perhaps, in part, because of) a female friend and colleague (74). She depicts these women together, coming and going from their space, working within it, and sharing the act of smoking there (74, 76). Indeed, a woman smoking (which Méndez stages again only pages later in a public site in Buenos Aires) is not socially transgressive here, and she thus articulates a female space that allows for a rewriting of gender norms within its own walls.

Similarly, the act of publication is spatialized differently; it is no longer narrated as a lone woman's emergence into the public space of the street. Méndez now figures her act of publication literally through the published book, opening its legitimizing covers for the reader and displaying contents which point to it as a viable practice where one woman's voice is embraced by those of her female friends and literary peers. That is, Méndez highlights women's presence and participation in the construction of *Canciones de mar y tierra*: in addition to her own poems, it carries a prologue by Consuelo Berges, drawings by Norah Borges, and a poem Méndez dedicated to Berges ("el único [poema] que recuerdo completo entre todos los que he escrito en mi vida" [77]).[25] She immediately thereafter notes that Berges simultaneously published her own book (in turn, with a prologue by Méndez), and both women were celebrated simultaneously by the general public and the literary community (77). Women's voices are thus narrated as wrapped together in the physical space of the book and the literary practice of publishing.

Although men still control print medium (as is the case both here and in her first publication), Méndez's narrative focuses on the representation of her book *per se*, which stands as an embodiment of this supportive intellectual community of women, a space that gestures to the conceptualization of literary creation and publication as events born of female collaboration. This spatial articulation of literary production through the collaborative support of women literally takes center stage in the final scenes of Buenos Aires life that Méndez chooses to narrate. Indeed, the entire chapter seems to lead up to this final representation of her professional success. She places Berges and herself performing a joint poetry reading in support of the new Spanish Republic in one of "los principales teatros de la ciudad" where "entraban multitudes" (81).[26] These two women intellectuals stand together reading not their own, but *each other's* political poetry in the legitimated and legitimizing institution of one of the capital's most important theatres (81). Méndez has moved them together, as two intertwined female voices, within the walls of the literary scene, where they speak the languages of politics and literature to a rain of "vivas" and applause (81–82). Having begun the representation of Buenos Aires from the perspective of the socio-spatial margins, where at first not even the Spanish Ambassador would allow her into his offices (73), Méndez brings us full circle as she occupies the literary scene as the new embodiment of a politicized Spain (81–82). She enters not alone, but inextricably connected to the voice of another woman, as each one breathes life into the words of the other. Unlike the permeable and fragmented space of the Lyceum, the portrayal of intellectual practices in Buenos Aires suggests that this occupation depends on the solidarity between women and the formation of their own supportive intellectual community.

However, her prior concerns regarding women's writing of their own conversations and the possibility of unwanted male intrusions resurface. Describing her life in Buenos Aires with her closest friends, Berges and Storni, she notes that the three often spent time together reading in an elegant bar on Florida Street. No longer staring through the windows as she had done with Mallo, Méndez now places herself with these women together in a locale that was once off-limits to her (the bar), in the urban center of Buenos Aires, and in a neighborhood also associated with the avant-garde literary explorations of the well-known Florida group. Firmly within this masculine, artistic space, Méndez depicts a warm, insulated atmosphere surrounding these literary women: "tenía los artesonados del techo en dorado. Aquella atmósfera cálida nos recogía para pasar la tarde leyendo: a Alfonsina le gustaba Quevedo y a Consuelo, Ortega y Gasset; a mí me venía muy bien cualquier cosa [. . .]" (76).[27] Méndez emphasizes their comfortable, shared practice of literary engagement within this patriarchal space and draws a visual circle of them within the enveloping warmth of the bar. Yet she still notes the potential threat to this circle, as she interrupts this atmosphere with the narration of a male intrusion: "una de las tardes el camarero nos trajo una tarjeta con un aviso impreso: 'Se ruega a las señoras no fumar'. Lo mandaba un hombre de la mesa de enfrente; entonces, para desafiarlos, con la misma cerilla con la que alumbré un cigarillo, incendié la tarjeta. ¿Qué era aquello de que los hombres nos prohibieran fumar?" (76).[28] She interprets this intrusion not as an imposition by one man, but by all men ("desafiar*los*"[29]) that would seek to overwrite the space these women have created, a space where women rewrite the sedimented normative practices that disallow them smoking and, perhaps, synecdochically, reading. Responding defiantly, Méndez's violent image of burning the message with the same match reduces the threat to figurative ashes and, in turn, challenges this attempted male re-reterritorialization. Thus Méndez still notes resistance to women's occupation and rewriting of the male scene, but continues to focus on female staying power and the force of her own conviction that this scene is precisely where women can be.

Despite this narrative construction of a resistant and somewhat insulated community of women thinkers within the institutional walls, Méndez's memoirs gesture toward a more nuanced relationship with patriarchal hegemony. Through the spatialization of gender practices in Buenos Aires, Méndez represents the possibility of a woman's occupation of a space within the literary scene vis-à-vis the creation of a protected community of women, but imagines that viable female space as neither self-sufficient nor autonomous. At the same time that this female community must be wary of patriarchal reterritorializations of its own space, its intellectual existence depends on the very system from which it defends itself.[30] Women may therefore move into the scene of intellectual practices and reap the benefits of institutional legitimation, but, for the most part, Méndez implies that this literary scene remains male-controlled.

Within the Walls: Dwelling in the Male Intellectual Scene in Republican Spain

Now narrating her return to Spain after having achieved professional success outside its borders, how does Méndez construct intellectual spatial practices during the Republic? As opposed to prior articulations of the obscene, is there now room for women intellectuals on the scene of writing? Although Catherine Bellver insightfully suggests that "Méndez' (sic) departure from Spain in 1928 can be seen as a personal response to the exile imposed upon her by the patriarchy" ("Exile" 40), it may be too optimistic, based on Méndez's representation of literary life in Madrid during the 1930s, to assume that her return was characterized by a smooth incorporation into a Spanish "cultural center" ("Exile" 40, "Voyages" 112). Méndez's reconstruction of a Spanish literary center in the 1930s reveals a fundamental shift in gendered spatial distributions and practices vis-à-vis her prior representation of Buenos Aires. This writing of intellectual culture in Republican Spain thus points to both a complex environment for women and a tension in Méndez's own project for legitimation in the memoirs.

Coming on the heels of her depiction of life in Buenos Aires, what jumps to the forefront in her portrayal of the Spanish literary community is the virtual absence of women. Reconstructing the literary *tertulias* at the homes of Vicente Aleixandre and Carlos Morla Lynch, Méndez fills these spaces with so many people that, at times, "no alcanzaban las sillas y teníamos que sentarnos en el suelo" (88).[31] Even so, with the exception of one fleeting reference to the hostess

(89), Méndez seems to invoke a "nosotros"[32] that only refers to literary men and herself. Her own home with Altolaguirre becomes a site defined overwhelmingly by intellectual practices and the constant presence of male writers, as Méndez repeatedly and emphatically describes it as a crucial meeting point for the male-defined Generation of 1927. Through the memoirs, we witness the daily stream of their visits, their *tertulias* (91), and their curious observation of Altolaguirre and Méndez while the couple published the group's work (87, 92). Male bodies both flow through and occupy this intellectualized space, yet Méndez maps herself at the center and represents a seamless association with this group identity. This sense of solidarity between Méndez and these literary men is emblematized in her spatialization of an "hermandad"[33] between herself, Altolaguirre, and Luis Cernuda (91). She depicts the movements of Cernuda's daily life with her and Manuel in their apartment and leaves us with an image of the three around the press, Cernuda now wearing a "mono de mecánico"[34] similar to the outfit Méndez wore while printing (91). The identity-formation mapped by Méndez in the intellectualized scene of their apartment is further spatialized in the actual publications the couple generated in those rooms: "Ya dije que alrededor de nuestro trabajo estaban nuestros amigos, que venían a ver las impresiones todos los días. [. . .] Sin aquellas publicaciones [. . .], no se hubiese podido crear una unidad de grupo" (92).[35] Méndez emphasizes that the pages printed and bound in their home helped create this identity. She ultimately implies that these inextricably connected sites of dwelling and publication were fundamental to the forging of the male-defined Generation. Méndez thus represents a space both written *for* and actually engaged in the production of the literary work of these men.

In her construction of literary life in Madrid, then, Méndez spatializes a group identity in ways quite similar to her depiction of Buenos Aires, though the fundamental difference is that these intellectual and emotional bonds now seem to be between men and include only one woman: herself. From the first moment of Méndez's discursive rendition of the Spanish cultural scene, Consuelo Berges, with whom she had been traveling from Buenos Aires to Madrid, simply disappears (84–85). We no longer see a women's space on the scene of writing as one forged through female solidarity and, in fact, we see no women at all in these intellectual sites. Despite the fact that she was friends with other women intellectuals in Spain during the 1930s, the only women thinkers Méndez mentions in this formative chapter on the Spanish cultural arena are Rosa Chacel and Ernestina de Champourcín, who appear briefly in its last paragraph (93). Although the literary magazine *Héroe* made room for these women within its legitimating covers, Méndez still articulates a gap between them and their male colleagues, separating the women from the "generation" and conceptualizing their space as more similar to that of foreign writers than to that of their own male literary peers in Spain.[36] Unlike the collaborative representation of her publication in Buenos Aires, here women stand both on the borders of publication and, mentioned as they are only at the end of the chapter, on the periphery of Méndez's articulation of a group identity. The cultural center that she reconstructs is clearly a man's world, yet she places herself in those locales physically and psychologically, and avoids an open critique of the absence of other women.

Méndez's portrayal of her own spatial practices within these male sites points to the complicated situation in which she found herself as a woman intellectual. Her participation in an almost entirely male environment is framed by two repetitive references to the clothing she wore while printing, the mechanic's overall that Juan Ramón Jiménez depicted in his now famous 1932 literary portrait of Méndez (157–58). Just prior to narrating the intellectual practices of a male cultural center, Méndez retakes this image and proudly displays herself as wearing the jumpsuit while working on the heavy printing press: "Ya instalada en el cuarto, nadie la pudo mover. Era yo quien la manejaba; la manejaba vestida con un mono azul de mecánico; era difícil y cansado, pero como era deportista, tenía una fuerza increíble. Cuando salía a la calle con aquel mono, la gente se quedaba extrañadísima; no recuerdo haber visto en todo Madrid a otra mujer vestida en pantalones" (87).[37] Similarly, Méndez closes both the representation of the literary scene and the chapter itself with the image of her "vestida de mecánico, la fuerza que hacía girar la imprenta" (93).[38] She directly associates the traditional workman's outfit with force and strength, and thus takes on these characteristics when running the printing press, a site previously represented as controlled by men. Her juxtaposition of these attributes against the public reaction to her pantsuit as a transgression of feminine spatial norms, clearly links the outfit's symbolic strength with masculinity.[39] By dressing in men's clothes, she assumes the masculine power that she feels they embody. We therefore read the spatial terms of Méndez's existence at the heart of this literary scene: she tactically slips into the mechanic's overall, thereby clothing herself in the strength, power and access to the print that she ascribes to masculinity and to this male space of artistic production. Thus materializing her identification with this community, she, in effect, becomes "one of the boys." This masculinization through the tactic of dress is accompanied by what might be interpreted as a narrative ejection of traditional formulations of the "feminine." Specifically, Méndez generally disassociates her wedding, honeymoon, and the birth and death of her first child from the sentimentality that has been constructed conventionally as feminine, representing these events instead through the prism of her intellectual vocation.[40] In this sense, events that could be used to emblematize traditional configurations of femininity are instead articulated in a grammar of intellectual practices, a move that within the context of the memoirs complements the empowering masculinization of the mechanic's overall that Méndez associates with her occupation of the literary scene in Spain.[41]

Our understanding of Méndez's tactical masculinization depends on the balance we strike between the memoirs' two projects: a critique of women intellectuals' socio-spatial marginalization and the legitimation of Méndez as both a writer and woman pioneer. On the one hand, the literary scene in Republican Spain is exposed as one in which women thinkers generally do not find room on the scene. If they do find room, they cannot rewrite that space either as individuals or as a community; instead, they must play by the always already established rules of the game. Indeed, the narrative logic suggests that given the apparent weakness of women's institutional spaces in Spain (the Lyceum) and Méndez's desire to thrive intellectually as she did in Argentina, she steps into the mechanic's overall and constructs a masculinized subjectivity, thereby gaining access to the power of the male literary space. Creating a Spanish cultural center where she is the only embodied, visible woman intellectual, Méndez predicates her existence there on her becoming "one of the boys" in an "all-boys club." Therefore, the memoirs imply that the limits of this liberation in Republican Spain are quite real, as a "shared" space on the intellectual scene means that women must to some degree reproduce the very constructions of masculinity that oppress them. Moreover, by narrating the hostility of the Spanish urban classes toward women who attempted to rearticulate the received patriarchal norms, the text further represents this masculinization as a maneuver that often prompted a backlash.[42] As both Bellver and Quance have argued with respect to female literary production more generally (Bellver, "Literary Influence" 8–10; Quance, "Concha Méndez" 112), Méndez's memoirs suggest the "catch-22" that women intellectuals faced in the 1920s and '30s: to gain professional credibility from her male peers, Méndez distances herself from notions of the "feminine," yet this distancing and concomitant masculinization were seen as socially and biologically aberrant, or at best, an unnatural copy of masculinity. Thus through Méndez's representation of the intellectual environment in Spain of the 1930s, we witness the depiction of her difficult occupation of the literary site.

Nonetheless, although Méndez portrays the lack of acceptance *outside* of the bounds of this male scene, she fails to point to any similar lack *within* this group. While the memoirs support a strong reading of Méndez's tactical masculinization as signaling a complicated occupation of the gendered cultural arena in Spain of the 1930s, the surprising degree to which she represents a shared identity and does not openly question the exclusionary, masculine terrain of this intellectual space (as she so clearly does at other points) should give us pause. For the most part, Méndez departs from a discourse of gender difference and moves toward one of gender sameness. This tension points to the legitimizing project of the memoirs: they strive for her acknowledgement as a writer and as a feminist pioneer. Her apparent acceptance by the members of the Generation of 1927 stands as an example to the reader that she should be incorporated into the literary canon based on her literary vocation, her professional integration within this group, her shared identity, and her publication efforts. By shifting the gender-bias of Spanish male intellectuals to the general space of Spanish patriarchy, Méndez downplays whatever gender difference certainly existed within the Generation of 1927 and subtly advocates her integration into a legitimized (male) literary space and canon. On the other hand, at the same time that she blends into the woodwork of a male-dominated generation, she constructs herself as a woman pioneer. The only woman in "todo Madrid"[43] wearing the mechanic's overall and thereby transgressing societal bounds (87), she alone has gained full access onto the scene with these writers. Indeed, that scene now takes place at her home. Represented as the motor behind the production of their artistic and generational identity ("la fuerza que hacía girar la imprenta" [93]),[44] Méndez is figured as a trailblazer: she now not only has direct access to the print, but mediates the words and identities of male writers. Reading the tension between her spatialization of gender in 1930s Spain, on the one hand, and her simultaneous attempt to downplay gender in particular sites, on the other, we find that Méndez manages to criticize the same patriarchal system from which she seeks legitimation as a writer. Constructing herself as an exemplary woman while ejecting the "feminine" and posing as "one of the boys," she balances the dueling projects of literary and feminist legitimation with the memoir's critique of the socio-spatial marginalization of women.

Dwelling in the "Beyond": Intervening in Contemporary Spaces

> . . .*discourses on space become influential as discourses of space. That is to say that myths become directive images and 'metaphors we live by.'*
> Rob Shields, Places on the Margin *(47)*

We return to the opening frame of her father's office and the tension that Méndez's spatial representation generates as a subversion of imposed gender norms. To what degree does her rewriting of space and spatial practices in the memoirs challenge these norms only to reinstate them? Judith Butler's formulation of the "subversive" as the ability to *reflect* "on the imitative structure by which hegemonic gender is itself produced" and *dispute* "heterosexuality's claim on naturalness and originality" helps us unravel the implications of Méndez's efforts (125). Although Méndez's stagings of opposition certainly show an awareness that gender norms can be imitated and manipulated in order to make room for a level of self-fulfillment, she does not question systematically the underlying notions of gender on which her imitations are built, and she gains access to masculinized spaces through strategies often predicated on traditional idealizations of masculinity and femininity. Méndez crosses over into "men's territory" and thus, in an empowering gesture, shows that women can indeed make this move. However, this *is* ultimately figured as a crossing over, and these gendered boundaries remain in place. Given that Méndez achieves some sense of personal liberation, although she may deploy tactics that reify the very norms against which she struggles, we can read the tension in her representation of oppositional practices as "neither an efficacious insurrection nor a painful resubordination, but an unstable coexistence of both" (Butler 137). Of course, this tension and Méndez's inability to dislodge these notions say less about her own limitations, and more about the strength of patriarchal constructions of gender difference, her cultural context vis-à-vis the political and pseudo-scientific discourses of the day, and the sedimented everyday spaces she inhabited. It is both fascinating and disturbing to read that even as a woman intellectual who fought to write when she was denied either a pen or a space to do so, who participated with men in the literary endeavor, and who valued both oppositional tactics and the joy of evading the limiting gestures of society, Méndez was unable to see the philosophical exit doors just one step beyond where her transgressive actions had taken her. Indeed, the difficulty of questioning and rearticulating gender norms that is played out in the memoirs attests to the fragility of any oppositional, identity-building project.

Nonetheless, the disruptiveness of the *performative* aspect of Méndez's spatial practices, the unconventional physical acts that people witnessed, cannot be underplayed. The cultural constructions of gender/sex in pre-1960s Spain suggest the transgressive impact that Méndez's actions most likely would have had; upon reading the memoirs of contemporaries, literary reviews and, to some degree, contemporary literary criticism, it becomes obvious that Méndez's non-traditional behavior clearly disturbed and challenged people. We cannot ignore that it is precisely the performative side of her acts to which contemporary scholars have related, taking as a feminist "call to arms" the transgressiveness of what she accomplished. In this sense Méndez's act of telling the past becomes a tactic of disruption in the contemporary cultural scene. Sitting beyond the socio-political centers of power and outside the walls of the literary institutions, she spatializes the obstacles women writers have faced and stages ways of getting around those limitations, opening up room for resistance on the level of both everyday and intellectual practices. In so doing, she challenges our constructions of the literary canon, proposes a rewriting of the current feminist mappings of Spain, and charts diverse paths to self-actualization that women living in an oppressive atmosphere could and did take. In the *Location of Culture*, the critic Homi Bhabha writes: "Being in the 'beyond,' then, is to inhabit an intervening space [. . .]. But to dwell 'in the beyond' is also [. . .] to be part of a revisionary time, a return to the present to redescribe our cultural contemporaneity; to reinscribe our human, historic commonality; *to touch the future on its hither side*. In that sense, then, the intervening space 'beyond,' becomes a space of intervention in the here and now" (7; author's emphasis). Dwelling in and speaking from this beyond, Méndez makes her feminist intervention in the present through a discourse on space. By mapping her own experience of gendered bounds, Méndez offers a valuable contribution to the current and future creation of what Rob Shields would call a new discourse *of* space (47), a rewriting of the spatial metaphors we live by and, therefore, of the barriers that women intellectuals continue to face.

NOTES

[1] I would like to thank Alejandro Mejías-López, María Salgado, Akiko Tsuchiya, Melissa Waldman Stem, and my readers at *REH* for their insightful feedback on this article. My thanks to Steven Wagschal for generously helping me prepare the final manuscript for this volume.

[2] All translations in this essay are mine. Transl.: "When I stopped going to school at fourteen, I went through what retired people go through; to be accustomed to doing a job that they suddenly take away from you, it rips you in half [. . .]. They retired me. [. . .] [I] found myself in a desert. My parents didn't let me pick up a book, not even the newspaper; and in the hours of boredom, I began to write an imaginary journey. [. . .] When the whole family was already in bed and the house silent, I would go out of my room towards my father's office, which had an American style desk, and there, with the school maps, I began to write. The journey would last five years and my goals were New York and Hollywood; in this way, shuffling geographies, I would transport myself by plane and ship throughout the entire world. Some nights I wouldn't have time to write because I could hear my mother's muffled footsteps verifying the sleep of her ten children" (28–29).

[3] Henri Lefebvre theorizes spatial practices as acts ranging from the societal designations of a space's purpose, to individuals' actual everyday activities. Thus spatial practices may refer to the designated ways of using spaces and/or the performative act of using them (for example, through dress, movement, or voice). They may either reinforce or undermine the conventional usage and, consequently, the hegemonic structuring of social spaces and society. In this study I engage Lefebvre's triple formulation of space (spatial practices, representations of space, and spaces of representation) to explore Méndez's contestatory practices.

[4] Interventions by scholars such as Bellver, Persin, and Wilcox have contributed greatly to a dialogue on Méndez's gendered textual strategies in her poetry; the first two have studied her engagement of spatial imagery within a feminist discourse of liberation. Although I generally agree with Bellver and Persin, I believe that Méndez's specific gendering of space and agency complicates these interpretations and, consequently, our readings of Méndez's feminism.

[5] The ambivalent reaction of her male colleagues can be found in their own memoirs, interviews, or collected letters, where Méndez is often erased from the literary scene, downplayed in her literary contributions, domesticated as a maternal figure, or criticized as disruptive. See Morla Lynch (243–380) and Salinas (146, 302), as well as texts by Aleixandre (129–31), Gómez de la Serna (146–147), N. Guillén (199–201), and Neruda (148–49) collected in Valender (*Manuel Altolaguirre*).

[6] See Shields regarding the cognitive representation of space and its functions (13–14).

[7] Transl.: "literary gatherings."

[8] Méndez represents her current domestic space as one wherein writing can indeed take place, but which stands far removed from the literary establishment, *tertulias*, or clubs (in effect, a removal reflected in her relative absence from the canon). She also calls attention to the geopolitical exile that disrupted the intensity of her life and work in Spain, and that now threatens to "anchor" her to a space of stasis, nostalgia, and an almost absurd peripheral existence (149).

[9] See Ulacia regarding Buñuel. Bellver rightly observes: "Paradoxically some of the critics, writers, and intellectuals with whom women writers maintained cordial personal and professional relationships made some of the most negative comments on them" ("From Illusion" 213).

[10] Transl.: "in order to read I had to borrow books and hide them in my bed" (40).

[11] Transl.: "archaic" (52–53).

[12] See de Certeau's formulation of the "tactic" as a way for the individual to use the imposed system against itself in order to allow for desires and goals that are not legitimated by the dominant system. Resistance occurs through a reappropriation of normative spatial distributions and/or practices, effectively creating room for maneuver and a shift in power relations (xix–xxiv, 30–40).

[13] Transl.: "it occurred to me that, *under the pretext* of finding out about his health, I might call the Residencia de Estudiantes" (46, emphasis added).

[14] Transl.: "Buñuel's unknown girlfriend"; "Since I was the girlfriend known only through the grapevine, I interested him in me" (46). Though this latter translation might be "he was interested in me," here I choose the literal translation which emphasizes Méndez's implied agency.

[15] Transl.: "To meet with him, I put on a purple smoking jacket with an oriental cut and made up my face like they do in silent films. He arrived. I led him into my father's office, which was independent from the rest of the house. It had armchairs upholstered in blue velvet and two enormous balconies that opened onto the street. I turned on a small light in the corner of the room, which created a chiaroscuro atmosphere. In purple, seated in the blue armchair, sophisticated, I told him the things that I knew about the Residencia; everything that for years I lived without living. I was then the secret world of Buñuel suddenly revealing itself to his world. Federico and I became friends" (46).

[16] Transl.: "everything that for years I lived without living" (46).

[17] Transl.: "supposedly, decent girls couldn't walk down this street (because puritan as they were, they didn't dare to do it)" (50); "street fairs"; "poor neighborhoods"; "Women were prohibited from entering the taverns, and, to protest, we would push ourselves right up against the windows to see what was happening inside" (51).

[18] As in other chapters, men control the mediating power of the press, yet Méndez gives de Castro an important weight here, implying that she too is a mediating force in her publication,

one that has conditioned the male editor (54). The nineteenth-century poet becomes a literary predecessor who opens the door for Méndez and has an identifiable impact on her experience.

[19] Transl.: "above all, it was a cultural center; it had libraries and a large room for performances and lectures" (49).

[20] Transl.: "the wives of the husbands'"; "would come to the *tertulias* to tell what they'd heard at home" (49).

[21] Transl.: "using as an excuse a well-known colloquial expression: 'How can they ask me to give a talk to stupid and crazy women [figuratively: "to give a talk without preparing"]?' He couldn't understand that we women were interested in culture" (49).

[22] The club and its library were also regarded with hostility and as immoral by people beyond the intellectual community, reminding us that these sites were indeed "obscene" spaces in both senses of the word. See Bellver, particularly for the Church's branding of Lyceum members as "eccentric and unbalanced females" ("'féminas excéntricas y desequilibradas'") who should be "hospitalized or confined" (*Absence* 35).

[23] Transl.: "we"; "the mornings occupied with the mail and smoking some golden-tipped Turkish cigarettes" (74).

[24] Transl.: "very elegant office" (74).

[25] Transl.: "the only one [poem] that I remember in its entirety of all the poems that I have written in my life" (77).

[26] Transl.: "the city's main theatres"; "multitudes were entering" (81).

[27] Transl.: "[the cafe] had gold ceiling panel work. That warm atmosphere would gather us in to spend the afternoon reading: Alfonsina liked Quevedo, and Consuelo, Ortega y Gasset; as for me, anything would suit me well [. . .]" (76).

[28] Transl.: "one afternoon, the waiter brought us a card printed with a warning: 'Ladies are asked not to smoke'. It was sent by a man at the table in front. Then, to challenge them, I set the card on fire with the same match I used to light a cigarette. What was that about men prohibiting us from smoking?" (76).

[29] Transl.: "challenge *them.*"

[30] For the most part, access to diplomatic and literary institutions, economic stability (73), and the physical spaces where female identity building takes place (the office, the bar [76]) remain in men's hands. However, an important, though momentary, shift occurs here: women are depicted as somewhat empowered to grant Méndez access to literary spaces (73, 81). This shift speaks to the spatialization of an enabling female connectivity in Buenos Aires.

[31] Transl.: "there weren't enough chairs and we had to sit on the floor" (88).

[32] Transl.: "we."

[33] Transl.: "brotherhood."

[34] Transl.: "mechanic's overall."

[35] Transl.: "I['ve] already said that around our work were our friends, who came to see the print-outs everyday. [. . .] Without those publications [. . .], a group unity couldn't have been created" (92).

[36] One of Méndez and Altolaguirre's most important literary endeavors together was the publication of *Héroe* (1932–33; 1936), the literary magazine and supplements in which many renowned writers of the time appeared. The couple operated the press out of their apartment.

[37] Transl.: "Once installed in the room, no one could move it. I was the one who operated it; I would operate it dressed in a mechanic's overall; it was difficult and tiring, but since I was an athlete, I had an incredible strength. Whenever I would go out on the street with that overall on, people were utterly shocked; in all of Madrid, I don't remember having seen another woman dressed in pants" (87).

[38] Transl.: "dressed like a mechanic, the strength that made the press turn" (93).

[39] Some male peers also donned the "mono de mecánico" in the '30s, conveying both a politicized statement of solidarity with the working class and their own very real involvement in physically "making" the arts. Given her politics, Méndez surely participates in this class solidarity vis-à-vis the mechanic's overall, a double transgression, then, for her as a middle-class woman. Her view of the mechanic's overall also suggests, however, that her male ideal combines conventional, class-biased notions of masculinity and power, as we see in her gender assumptions throughout the text.

[40] Méndez repeatedly links her wedding to literature and the arts, and frames it as a Surrealist event (89–90). Similarly, she depicts a honeymoon spent listening to music and reading literature among male friends (90), and despite the trauma of losing her baby at childbirth, Méndez quickly moves from her first moments of anguish to the literature this loss engendered (92–93).

[41] It is tempting to read Méndez as stepping into the masculinizing mechanic's overall and envisioning herself as feminizing it by (re)producing/creating new texts and the Generation of 1927. However, although there is indeed an articulation of hybridity in the domestic/literary space of the apartment, and Méndez stresses that the identity of this literary generation depended on a press that she physically powered, she avoids more overt tropes of reproduction as well as other traditionally "feminine" roles, making it difficult to determine if she envisions a transfer of a female productivity to a male literary scene.

[42] Once she has returned from Buenos Aires and has begun her publication efforts with Altolaguirre, the feeling of being a "foreigner" ("extranjera") to her past family life and identity as a woman, the physical representation of her ideological distance from the disapproving patriarchal figure of her father, and the disturbed public reaction to her wearing of the mechanic's overall on Madrid's streets, combine to reflect this hostility (87).

[43] Transl.: "all of Madrid" (87).

[44] Transl.: "the strength that made the press turn" (93).

AFTERWORD

Since "Gendered Geographies" is a relatively recent publication, it is difficult to talk about subsequent research that might have informed the essay. However, there are texts that I have come to later that might have enriched the article in interesting ways. In particular, Linda Williams's essay on the performance art of Annie Sprinkle would be interesting with respect to the performative aspect of Méndez's agency and her entanglement in the perpetuation of the same misogynist discourses she was fighting. Elizabeth Grosz's work on space, the body, and the city might add depth to my analysis of Méndez's construction of a gendered subjectivity through the representation of her performance in the city space. Beyond texts that I have come to since writing this essay, there are others I hope will be written. When developing the concept that Méndez's production of space was informed by a gendered logic, I was already working with theories of space, but I had hoped to find a substantial body of work that theorized space from a gendered perspective. However, what seemed to continue to dominate the scene were approaches that assumed abstract bodies, despite allowing the potential for reading specificity into those bodies. Indeed, intellectuals working on performativity and its relation to identity construction most closely approached this problem, but I continue to wonder what a theory of space would look like from perspectives that constantly have gender (among other identities) in mind.

Many issues that underpin this essay inform the direction of my current work. My interest in the production of space and the performative body has grown into a broader project that puts body studies at its center. In particular, I am interested in the body as an imagined space, a multi-layered construction that can be read for cultural, political, economic, and social discourses. Analyzing the ways in which Federico García Lorca's assassinated and previously censored body is inscribed in the public sphere at the start of Spain's transition to democracy (1975–86), I am working on the way that Lorca's body (resurrected, remembered, mourned, repatriated, queered, commodified) provides critical access to the complicated negotiation of national, cultural, social, and economic identities in contemporary Spain. Also, my focus in "Gendered Geographies" on the representation of the past vis-à-vis memoirs has expanded in this project to encompass the processes through which cultural memory is created and the role individual memory, textuality, and life-writing (even Méndez's) play in those processes. I am at work as well on a project that deals with ethics, transnational feminisms, and the editorial production of the Méndez memoirs by her granddaughter. In the context of the Spanish diaspora and political exile, I am interested in what an ethics of both reading and editing women's autobiography might look like and in the way that transnational feminisms may influence the formulation of such an ethics and textual production itself.

Reading Rape in Chaucer; *or* Are Cecily, Lucretia, and Philomela *Good Women?*[1]

RACHEL WARBURTON

I. Proem

Notions of femininity, particularly the evaluative "good women," are intimately linked to conceptions of rapability. Rape is no Aristotelian "accident." Rather, it is deemed essential to our understandings of women and their moral agency. In ways that structure—and limit—social movement and lived possibilities, women learn to understand themselves as rapable. Yet legal codes and other social mechanisms have variously rendered slaves, prostitutes, and lesbians as unrapable at specific historical moments. Under such rubrics, they are already considered unchaste; they are not good women. So, too, when a wife is deemed unrapable by her husband, it is precisely because to "refuse" her husband is to not be a good woman. Rapability is necessary to constructions of femininity, but rape and masculinity exist in no such straightforward relationship. In this essay, I wish to trouble any easy, linear relationship between femininity and rapability, to resist its putative essentialness to gender definition.

This is not to say that rape does not happen. It does. Nor does this mean that if we were just more "liberated," rape would carry no social stigma. That would constitute a complete capitulation to patriarchal absurdity. Rape is historically mutable, socially constructed, "accidental" in the Aristotelian sense but, ironically perhaps, *socially* essential. At every turn, rape is an interpretive act. What counts as rape is often ambiguous, and a legal definition or court ruling might have no relevance for, or might not reach the same conclusion as someone who has been sexually assaulted. In part, the question becomes one of gendered ownership of interpretation. In consequence, the question of my title is one I hope not to answer. That question hinges on the category of feminine goodness that not only subtends both normative masculinity and heterosexuality, but also informs and delimits women's lived possibilities. What I hope to examine instead are the historically specific ways in which "good" women's rapability authorizes a particular model of reading and, by extension, examine how that reading practice underwrites the social and textual legibility of rape.

II. Reading/Writing/Rape

At the risk of occluding the female body, I wish first to examine what is at stake for masculinity in a medieval configuration of reading, writing, and rape. Specifically, I want to explore the various investments in discourses of masculinity articulated through and around both Chaucer's *Legend of Good Women* and the remnants of Cecily Chaumpaigne's complaint filed against the poet. Modern day critical response to both texts, I suggest, re-enacts patriarchal models of literary inheritance. Relations of social and literary exchange of women and feminised sources between men and generations of male authors, including models of reading and writing and inscriptions of literary paternity articulated through and around these texts, are deeply implicated in hegemonic rape narratives. Men writing through/on women's bodies in order to write to or about men is one version of what Gayle Rubin has termed the "traffic in women."[2] Although Rubin's analysis takes kinship structures as its object, her conclusions are also applicable to the structures of literary heritage and descent.

The exchange of women between men in and around Chaucer's *Legend* occurs intra-, inter-, and extra-textually. Female characters are the objects of (usually frustrated) exchange within individual legends. The legends themselves are the penalty paid by their dreamer-narrator to the God of Love as negotiated by Alceste. Caught in his springtime reverie amongst the daisies, the dreamer ("Chaucer") is accosted by the God of Love and his entourage. The god is angry with the dreamer-poet for his rendering of Creseyde and for his translation of *The Romance of the Rose*, which is a "heresye" (F 330, G 256)[3] against Love's laws. Alceste intercedes on the dreamer's behalf. Even if the dreamer angered the God of Love unintentionally, Alceste suggests that the dreamer spend the rest of his life writing about women who were "trewe in lovyng al hire lyves" (F 485, G 475) as penance. The ensuing legends of good women are offered in exchange for the god's forgiveness.

For this project, the poet returns to the same pagan sources that provided material for his offending poetry. As Carolyn Dinshaw argues, "medieval constructions of literary production were figured in terms of gendered traffic between male writer-scribes and readers, between the patriarchal authors, their transcriber-interpreters and the next generation of, presumed male, readers" (57). Read thus, we can position Chaucer's *Legends* within an historical/literary framework of patriarchal literary exchange. In her discussion of medieval theories of reading, however, Dinshaw falls just short of equating medieval constructions of reading with rape. Dinshaw writes, that according to St. Jerome, "the way to read the pagan text properly is to *divest* it of its sinful seductions, its Pauline deadness: to strip it of its garments, shave its hair, and pare its nails." It is this model of reading Dinshaw uses in her analysis of *The Legend of Good Women*. She reads the poem as an exercise in translation into English that claims to render its classical and pagan sources "naked." On Dinshaw's account, Chaucer has "[s]tripped, clipped, and scrubbed his pagan source texts" which "are like female bodies in the narrator's masculine hands" (18, 23, 86).

The passage from Deuteronomy to which Jerome refers, however, involves a captive woman. Here, the ritual purification of the captive female body is followed with a brief period of enforced mourning that concludes with rape. Speaking to the captor about his beautiful hostage, the Deuteronomist (traditionally identified as Moses) offers the following procedure for taking possession of a captive woman: "she shall put the raiment of her captivity from off her, and shall remain in thine house, and bewail her father and mother a full month: and after that thou shalt go in unto her, and be her husband, and she shall be thy wife" (Deut. 21:13). I discuss euphemisms for rape below but will note that here Jerome links the transmitted pagan source text with the raped female body of Deuteronomy by metaphoric association. In order to ensure their continued legibility, their continued circulation from one generation of male readers to the next, or their translation from one language to another, texts must be available to this rapacious reading. Ongoing critical discomfort with both Chaucer's *Legend of Good Women* and with the historical Cecily Chaumpaigne is highly suggestive of the anxious proximity of rape and literary inheritance. I have yoked Cecily together with Lucretia and Philomela not just to remind "us that there are not only *figurative* rapes" in Chaucerian texts but "*real* rapes as well," as Dinshaw does (11), but to insist upon a mutually constitutive relation between fiction and "reality."

In her study of crime in the first half of the fourteenth century, Barbara Hanawalt explains that rape only came to be considered a felony in English law after the 1285 Statute of Westminster II. Furthermore, according to Hanawalt, the statute "also distinguished abduction of women with the intention to sexually assault them and to take their property or their husband's property as a felony that could be tried at the king's suit" (104).[4] In practice, rape was most commonly prosecuted in conjunction with property crimes, rather than as a separate sexual crime: "The prosecution of rape cases was often tied to a charge of accompanying burglary or robbery" (Hanawalt 105).[5] According to Hanawalt's analysis, medieval legal understandings of rape are invested in discourses of interrupted economic exchange. In addition, an individual woman's ability to effectively press charges of rape, even under this new, stricter rubric, is inseparable from her social value. "In practice," Hanawalt cautions, "indictments depended upon the condition in society of the victimized woman. If the woman involved was a young girl, a virgin, or a noble or very high status woman, indictment was likely. But if she was of low status or some slur could be put upon her, the jury would not indict or the case would end in acquittal" (105).

In her analysis of the interrelations between legal and literary representations of rape in medieval France, Kathryn Gravdal finds the denotative meanings of the words available for medieval rape elusive. I rehearse Gravdal's argument at length, as it has many points of intersection with late medieval English representations of rape. The metaphoric associations of words available to describe rape both inform and are informed by legal definitions of those terms. In the absence of the modern day French word for rape, *viol*, medieval French writers took recourse to a variety of elliptical locutions: "The most frequent medieval [French] locution for rape is *fame esforcer*" or "forcing a woman" (Gravdal 3). In order to locate the specifically medieval connotations of this usage, Gravdal examines the "resonances that *esforcer* brings from the vulgar or popular Latin" which include "strong, powerful, mighty" and which bear "distinctly positive connotations of military heroism: courageous, manly, brave, bold, impetuous" (3). As I will discuss, the noun *dede*, the euphemism that is used to denote rape in Chaucer's legends of both Lucretia and Philomela, also carries militaristic associations. "From the notion of strength, manliness, and bravery," Gravdal argues of the twelfth-century range of meaning available to *eforcement*, "we move to the knight's striving after heroism, and then to the idea of forced coitus" (3). This range either evinces an enormous slippage between two mutually exclusive interpretations of the sign or it betrays an anxious proximity between manly bravery and brutality: "The study of medieval law reveals how confusing and tangled the legal notion of the crime of *raptus* can be. Its family of linguistic signifiers contains the marks of this cultural ambiguity" (Gravdal 4). Gravdal continues to explicate the semantic range of words available to describe rape in medieval French:

> Some of the more common meanings of *rapere* are to carry off or seize; or snatch, pluck, or drag off; to hurry, impel, hasten; to rob, plunder; and, finally, to abduct (a virgin). The key semes are those of movement or transportation, appropriation or theft, and speed or haste. (4)

English legal usages of *raptus* bear a similar history as the one Gravdal charts in French legal interpretations: "*Raptus* refers to noncontractual marriage by abduction and/or forced coitus (modern rape). The word is used in different ways at different times, but its standard meaning in medieval law is marriage by abduction" (Gravdal 6). In 1140, the twelfth-century canon law scholar, Johannes Gratian, attempted to restrict the meanings of *raptus*. His *Decretum Gratiani* makes abundantly clear the primacy of the circulation of women to rape narratives. Gravdal summarises Gratian's elaboration of *raptus* as follows:

> The crime consists of four necessary elements: there has been unlawful coitus; the woman has been abducted from the house of her father; the rape was accomplished by violence; and a marriage agreement has not been negotiated previously between the victim and the ravisher. Gratian's new specification that the victim was protected only when abducted from the house of her father underscored the patriarchal nature of this medieval law: it was concerned primarily with the protection of the father's rights, not those of his daughter [. . .] Canon law also disallowed the punishment of forced coitus in marriage, since consent was given at the time of marriage, and further disallowed the prosecution of forced coitus with a prostitute, since a prostitute was not considered to be an honest woman. (Gravdal 8–9)

Here, reading rape depends upon ascriptions of feminine virtue or "honesty," but in medieval terms, these moments of reading are intimately linked to the control of women's circulation between men. The then-recent legal reconfigurations of rape charted by Hanawalt and the gendered social implications of those changes inform both Chaucer's *Legend of Good Women* and the documents concerning Cecily Chaumpaigne's 1380 release of the poet from the charge of *raptus*.

In addition to articulating a reading practice that relies upon the circulation of female heroines between generations of male readers, two of the legends, both from Ovidian sources, narrate rapes of "good" women. Moreover, according to Dinshaw, Chaucer renders his sources naked, stripped, and pared in the process of translation into English. If this model of the translation process holds, the poem is implicated in narratives of both the essential rapability of (good) women and of the necessity of treating pagan sources like captive women. However, the dreamer-narrator articulates his pre-dream relation to literary authority in quite different, although no less patriarchal, terms:

> Thrugh whiche that olde thinges ben in mynde,
> And to the doctrine of these olde wyse,
> Yeve credence, in every skylful wise,
>
> . . .
>
> And yf that olde bokes were aweye,
> Yloren were of remembraunce the keye.
> Wel ought us thanne honouren and beleve
> These bokes, there we han noon other preve.
> And as for me, though that I konne but lyte,
> On bokes for to rede I me delyte,
> And to hem yive I feyth and ful credence,
> And in my herete have hem in reverence. (F17–20, 25–32)

The *Legends'* narrator, who modestly claims to "konne but lyte," offers his "feyth and ful credence" to his literary predecessors. This cultural inheritance is, not incidentally, rendered legitimate by precisely such a performance of both faith in and inadequacy before authority. He offers a model of filial reverence for paternal authorities: "But wherfore that I spak, to yeve credence / To bokes olde and don hem reverence" (F97–98).[6]

The individual legends also rely upon the conventions of hagiography, for the threat of rape is inextricably linked with female saints' *vitae*.[7] The *Legend of Good Women* invokes this hagiographic tradition in a complicated manner.[8] The women catalogued in the *Legend* are, like Christian female saints, cited for their exemplary behavior. Whether the poet invokes hagiography in an ironic or "straight" fashion is, however, an open question. The latter seems unlikely, as all the legends complied are pagan and not the stuff of hagiography proper. But, whether the genre is used for reverence or ridicule, to phrase the question in such terms maintains both an opposition between good women and bad, and the hierarchical divisions by which certain female subjects are legitimated and others denied. This instance, in which good women are separated from bad, is an example of a dividing moment in which, according to Foucault, the "subject is either divided inside himself or divided from others. This process objectivizes him. Examples are the mad and the sane, the sick and the healthy, the criminals and the 'good boys'" (208). Dividing practices, as presented in Chaucer's *Legend*, pretend to allocate but ultimately deny full subjectivity to the female characters. As their stories derive from pagan sources, none of these women can ever be good enough to be securely located in the realm of hagiography. The legends also complicate hagiographical equations between goodness and ruptured chastity or virginity. As Gravdal points out, in "hagiography, no rape is ever completed" (24). The same cannot be said for the rapes of Lucretia and Philomela.

Saints' lives, as models for emulation, constitute one site at which individuals and groups are directed or governed, where fields of possible actions are structured and subjectivity is either granted or denied. Such an architectonic, like a secular hagiography of "good women," structures access to possible subjectivities of others, and works to "govern" actions. Unlike hagiography, in which the content of the saint's life is supposed to inspire emulation, the structure of Chaucer's legendary lends itself to literary emulation and is, therefore, implicated in a nexus of authorization. In this way, the legends offer one ever-productive local center of power-knowledge. This exercise of power is no monolithic imposition from above; rather, it is always relational.[9] Furthermore, a legendary such as Chaucer's, implicated both in discourses of emulation and literary paternity, encourages imitation of the textually inscribed model of reading/raping.

III. Asking for It

The narrator claims to be seduced by the month of May as he temporarily leaves behind his books and gives himself over to the worship of daisies when he promptly falls asleep. An irate God of Love who accuses the dreamer of having maligned love in his waking writings interrupts his dream reveries. The god calls the dreamer his "mortal foo" (F322, G247) and continues enumerating the literary misdemeanours of the textualized poet:

> Thou maist yt nat denye,
> For in pleyn text, withouten nede of glose,
> Thou hast translated the Romaunce of the Rose,
> That is an heresye ayeins my lawe,
> And makest wise folk from me withdrawe;
> And of Creseyde thou hast seyd as the lyste,
> That maketh men to wommen lasse trist,
> That ben as trewe as ever was any steel. (F 327–334)

In one sense, the narrator's crime is to have produced a translation that, in the absence of a gloss, masquerades as a stable text. The discursive assertion of the stability, and by extension the masculinity, of English is part of the ideological apperati of *translatio studii*. A vernacular deemed capable of sustaining Latin texts "withouten nede of glose" begins to approach or to usurp the father tongue.[10] The anxieties that circulate around this proximity are related to the narrative treatment of rape and the exchange of feminine-coded texts between masculine-marked positions.

Fortunately for the dreamer, Alceste intercedes on his behalf and suggests a penance that is acceptable to both the offending and offended parties. She commands the narrator,

> Thou shalt, while that thow lyvest, yer by yere,
> The moste partye of thy tyme spende
> In makyng of a glorious legende
> Of goode wymmen, maydenes and wyves,
> That weren trewe in lovynge al hire lyves;
> And telle of false men that hem bytraien.
> (F 481–486, G 471–476)

Under the elaborate pretence, then, of both rapture by Nature and protestations of authorial inadequacy before paternal sources, Chaucer's dreamer-narrator devises and presents a series of raped, mutilated, and/or abandoned women and assures his audience that these women are good. Alceste does not, however, ask the narrator to alter his "reverence" for his sources. Quite the contrary, she asks him to return to the same body of texts that provided the material for *Troilus and Creseyde* and *The Romance of the Rose*, the precise texts the God of Love found so offensive. He returns to pagan sources and repeats the necessarily rapacious reading. In so doing, he puts stories of *trothful* women circulated between men into literary circulation. The re-citation of sources is cast as redress for the fictionalized poet's rendering of Criseyde, the heroine whose sexual circulation was ultimately controlled by men. Although, as many critics have pointed out, the legends that follow do not follow the criteria set out by Alceste, her demand of the narrator absolves him of responsibility for what follows. After all, she asked for it.[11]

IV.

In two of the nine legends penned by Chaucer's dreamer-narrator, "good women," Lucretia and Philomela, are raped by "false men." Both of these legends begin with the introduction of the assailant. The legend of Lucretia opens with Tarquin and his historical moment, "the exilynge of kynges / Of Rome" (1680–1681), and gestures toward Ovid and Livy as sources. Thus, Lucretia's story, and her chastity, are both commodified and exchanged between groups of men. First, her chastity functions as the grounds for competition between Tarquin and her husband, Collatin, and her rape is offered as implicit justification for exiling the Tarquin kings. Secondly, her story is the legitimate inheritance of the narrator from two ever-paternal sources. This is explicitly the story of "the laste kyng Tarquinius" (1681) and the "horible doinges" (1681) of the Tarquin kings that resulted in their overthrow. Lucretia seems incidental. Indeed, the narrator must backtrack to introduce her: "But for that cause telle I nat this storye, / But for to preyse and draw to memorye / The verray wif, the verray trewe Lucresse" (1684–1686). The ensuing narrative belies this express disavowal and maintains the original narrative interest in Tarquin. After insisting that his purpose is to celebrate Lucretia, the narrator inscribes her within a history of literary inheritance and interpretation that, as discussed earlier, depends upon the traffic in female stories for its intelligibility. "The grete Austyn," the narrator reminds us, "hath gret Compassioun / Of this Lucresse" (1690–1691). Lucretia has St. Augustine's approval as he sympathizes at least partially with her plight, though he could not condone her suicide. While the narrator's invocation of Ovid and Livy establishes his credentials, St. Augustine's sympathy confirms that only because she is understood to be virtuous can Tarquin's assault on her be considered rape.[12]

When Collatin and Tarquin arrive in Rome to test Lucretia's virtue, they spy her in her chamber. Her visibility is unidirectional and she does not, indeed cannot, return their gaze. The two men observe Lucretia chastely discussing her husband with her servants as she awaits Collatin's return. Ostensibly, she is at the centre of the collective male gaze, manifest here as the proprietary eye of Collatin and the lustful stare of Tarquin mediated through the co-ordinating viewpoint of the dreamer-narrator. Lucretia's conversation with her servants, however, shifts the narrative focus away from herself and toward her marital relationship.

> 'What tydyngs heren ye?
> How seyth men of the sege, how shal it be?
> God wolde the walles were falle adoun!
> Myn husbonde is to longe out of this toun,
> For which the drede doth me so to smerte
> That with a swerd it stingeth to myn herte
> God save my lord, I preye hym for his grace!' (1723–1731)

This speech, which concludes with Lucretia weeping, insists on her inscription firmly within heteronormalizing discourses that both require and produce the category of "good" women. Her husband's absence pains Lucretia and proves her virtue: "And eek hire teres, ful of honeste," the narrator insists, "[e]mbelishe hire wifly chastite" (1736, 1737). Lucretia is always already inscribed within hegemonic rape narratives; it is precisely her chastity and her devotion to Collatin— her goodness—that render her desirable to Tarquin:

> Tarquinius, this proude kynges sone,
> Conceyved hath hire beaute and hyre cheere,
> Hire yelwe her, hire shap, and hire manere,
> Hire hew, hire wordes, that she hath compleyned
> (And by no craft hire beaute nas nat feyned),
> And caughte to this lady swich desyr
> That in his herte brende as any fyr,
> So wodly that his wit was al forgeten. (1745–1752)

This passage begins with Tarquin's social status and ends with his loss of "wit" when confronted with Lucretia's "wifly chastite." The intervening lines, far from being about Lucretia, offer the narrator's rendering of Tarquin's obsession with the chaste wife.

The narrator insists upon an inseparable connection between her desirability and the content of her speech. Prior to Tarquin's rhapsodizing on Lucretia's beauty, we are told only that she "sat by hire beddes sides/ Dischevele, for no malyce she ne thoughte" (1719–1720). Her dishevelment and her concomitant absence of malice in her thought demonstrate Lucretia's perhaps futile expectation of temporary withdrawal from a predatory masculine gaze. Tarquin's response to her assumption of even momentary liberty from circulation between men offers a forceful reminder: there is no outside to an interpretive community that interpellates women as objects of sexualized exchange between masculine readers. For it is precisely this absence of malice that allows Tarquin to read her as beautiful, chaste, and rapable. Such are the terms of a good woman's legibility.

As with the opening passages of the legend, the narrator's interest remains squarely with Tarquin throughout.[13] Nearly a quarter of the legend is given over to Tarquin's decision to rape Lucretia. She, on the other hand, is twice silenced by her assailant: once at knifepoint, and once with a threat to malign her name after death by placing the slain body of a slave in her bed. Indeed, Lucretia's longest direct speech in the legend is the lament for her absent husband overheard by Collatin and Tarquin. When Lucretia finally does call her family to tell them of Tarquin's assault, she can hardly speak and cannot look up: "she sit ay wepynge; / A word, for shame, forth ne myght she brynge / Ne upon hem she durste nat beholde" (1834–36). Lucretia's speech is narrated elliptically: "But atte last of Tarquyny she hem tolde / This rewful cas and al thys thing horryble" (1837–1838). As the exemplar of modest and "trewe" wife, she is unable to speak or return the male gaze. As the object of exchange, she is excluded from, but vital to, both verbal and scopic economies. Lucretia does not, indeed cannot, speak the rape, and the rape itself is narrated by apostrophe:

> Tarquinius, that are a kynges eyr,
> And sholdest, as by lynage and by ryght,
> Don as a lord and as a verray knyght,
> Whi hastow don dispit to chivalrye?
> Why hastow don this lady vilanye?
> Allas, of the this was a vileyns dede! (1819–1824)

Rape, intricately intertwined with constructions of feminine goodness, is unspeakable. Instead the narrator invokes the breached codes of chivalry and knighthood, codes which are inscribed at the moment of their transgression. Tarquin and his lost chivalry, Brutus's revenge against Tarquin, and the overthrow of the monarchy— not Lucretia's raped and discarded body—are paramount. If, as Stephanie Jed has argued, the establishment of the lauded Roman Republic is achieved at the expense of Lucretia's violation and suicide, then, in a visceral sense, she is "in no position to realize the benefits of [her] own circulation" (Rubin 163).[14] Furthermore, Chaucer's legend of Lucretia, despite its title and like so many of the story's transmutations before and since, has more to do with the men between whom the story is exchanged than the undermined subjectivity of the raped woman.

V.

Chaucer's rendering of Philomela negotiates and exerts discursive control over literary exchange between generations of male authors. On one level, Ovid's

"Philomela," collected in *The Metamorphoses*, is a story of rape, mutilation, and revenge transformed into song. But this legend is also an allegory of women's frustrated access to public speech, here violently denied. After Tereus lures his sister-in-law, Philomela, to a cave and rapes her, she swears she will tell Procne, his wife and her sister, what he has done. In order to prevent Philomela from communicating with her sister, Tereus cuts out her tongue and locks her in a tower. He returns to Procne and announces that Philomela is dead. Philomela, meanwhile, unable to speak and denied writing material, weaves a tapestry that relates her ordeal. She then arranges for its delivery to her sister, who "reads" and understands her sister's missive. In a night of Bacchic revelry, Procne rescues her sister and the two exact their revenge: making Tereus devour his own son. Procne and Philomela's revenge interrupts paternal descent through sons, giving primogeniture a rather graphic blow. Chaucer's version of the legend, however, erases the Bacchic revelry, the women's revenge and, as with all his interpretations of Ovid's *Metamorphoses*, omits the final transformation. The omission of the women's revenge is a double-edged sword. On the one hand, Chaucer removes that with which readers might find difficult to sympathise. Under erasure in Chaucer's version, the women's revenge is both absent and present simultaneously, and renders them ambiguous victims at best. Consequently, Philomela and Procne do not quite fulfil Alceste's requirements of "good women," as they are not simply the victims of male cruelty. Conversely, the exclusion of their revenge, however repugnant, elides the sisters' agency. As Gravdal suggests for Chrètien de Troyes's version of Philomela, Chaucer "maintains Ovid's aestheticization of the rape in the form of the beautiful tapestry" (62). This reification has the advantage of diminishing the possible implications of Philomela's non-verbal communication with her sister and erasing the threats posed to (literary) genealogy by women's negotiations of speech.

Possessive and violating men again take centre stage in Chaucer's legend of Philomela. The *Legend*'s narrator introduces Philomela's story with a lament to the Creator for having tolerated the birth of Tereus:

> Whi sufferest thow that Tereus was bore,
> That is in love so fals and so forswore,
> That fro this world up to the firste hevene
> Corrumpeth whan that folk his name nevene?
> And, as to me, so grisely was his dede
>
> That, whan that I his foule storye rede,
> Myne eyen wexe foule and sore also.
> Yit last the venym of so longe ago,
> The it enfecteth hym that wol beholde
> The storye of Tereus of which I tolde. (2234–2243)

Just as the so-called "Legend of Lucretia" is really a narrative of Tarquin's demise, so too is Chaucer's version of Philomela avowedly the "storye of Tereus." Furthermore, as the narrator insists, this story is so vile that it corrupts whenever people invoke Tereus's name, and it infects anyone who "beholds" the story.

By extension of this rendering of the putatively material effects of reading, Chaucer's narrator corrupts and infects his audience with the transmission of the legend. But the narrator proceeds to tell the story, albeit with an enormous omission, irrespective of the potential harm to the audience. The actions of Tereus figure here, however, as an assault upon the narrator. More specifically, the *reading* of the rape and mutilation of Philomela (and, presumably, of her and her sister's revenge) pains the narrator's eyes. Philomela's rape and the presumed assault on the reader are of secondary narrative interest. Although the narrator does invoke medieval legal understandings of rape when he insists that Lucretia fainted and felt nothing of Tarquin's assault, his telling of Philomela's story makes no attempt to insert her within contemporary legal standards for rape, and makes no explicit reference to the late medieval legal status of *raptus* as a felony.[15]

As with the legend of Lucretia, Philomela's rape is rendered in an oblique fashion. The elliptical representation of rape continues the narrative deflection away from Philomela and toward the narrator and rapist. The narrator exclaims, "By force hath this traytour don a dede, / That he hath reft hire of hire maydenhede, / Maugre hire hed, by strengthe and by his myght / Lo! here a dede of men, and that a ryght!" (2324–2327). The euphemism *dede*, used at several points in both the legends of Lucretia and Philomela (1824, 2238, 2324, 2327), erases the specificity of sexual violence.

Narrating rape requires either recourse to various euphemisms, military and otherwise, or outright silence. Although reticence in matters of sexuality was the rule and not the exception in courtly literature, that discretion structures speaking relations. Like Lucretia, Philomela cannot speak her rape. In brutal fashion, Philomela is physically denied both speech and writing materials. Bereft of her virginity and her tongue, and confined to a tower, Philomela resorts to weaving: "She could eek rede and wel ynow endyte, / But with a penne coude she nat wryte. / But letters can she weve to and fro" (2356–2358). Upon receipt of her sister's tapestry, Procne is reduced to a similar wordless state: "No word she spak, for sorwe and ek for rage" (2374). The shock of her sister's woven telling renders Procne speechless. The same relations that permit the narrator access to readerly / writerly subjectivity, relations that are subtended by rape, work to reduce and limit the speech of and between Philomela and Procne. While the narrator's physical pain at the inherited ancient text does not disable his own writing, the violated women are rendered passive and silent. In Chaucer's version of the legend of Philomela, the tapestry does not provoke the sisters' revenge; instead it silences and incapacitates Procne. The tapestry has the same effect upon Procne as rape and mutilation had upon her sister. It is perhaps unsurprising that an ideology of reading that requires the hostile exchange of feminized, ravishable texts between generations of men must erase Philomela and Procne's shared literacy and the women's revenge. Chaucer's *Legend of Good Women* sits squarely within the model of literary transmission between generations of men. The *Legend* relies upon an understanding of good women's silence and evasive metaphors for rape that double as models of reading.

VI. Critical Reading/Writing/Rape

In their discussions of Chaucer's *Legend of Good Women*, modern critics—inheritors of the patriarchal text—replicate the inherited models for reading and writing rape: euphemism, ellipsis, and apostrophe. The unstable texts of the legendary offer multiple sites of separation and distinction to the critic determined to naturalize and rationalize power. For example, the existence of two prologues compels some critics to establish primacy or attribute priority to one prologue over the other.[16] Other critics focus on the individual legends in order to determine Chaucer's attitudes toward both his source material and its transmission. Even Robert W. Frank, who examines both the prologue and the legends, treats the prologue and each of the legends individually, dedicating one chapter to each. In so doing, he perpetuates the separation of prologue and tales.[17] The separation of the Prologue from the individual legends permits critics to ignore any relationship between the dreamer-narrator and the raped, mutilated, and abandoned female bodies that follow in the legends, a relationship that I maintain rests upon a shared reading practice. The prologue insists upon, and the legends enact, the circulation of ancient stories about women between generations of male readers and writers. This paper is an attempt to examine two of the legends through that reading practice established in the prologue.

But discursive separation of the sections of Chaucer's legendary is not the only strategy available to modern readers who wish to downplay sexualized power relations between generations of male readers and their female subjects and feminized texts. Even when critics attempt to examine the poem in its entirety, they shy away from some of the more disturbing elements of the narrator's relationship to his material, particularly in relation to the representation of rape.[18] Although he reads prologue(s) and legends alongside one another, Donald Rowe is reluctant (to say the least) to broach the subject of sexual violence upon which, I maintain, the poem depends for its intelligibility and continued circulation.[19] His domestication of sexual violence belongs to the same tradition of reading and writing rape to which Chaucer's poem belongs. In this, however, he is far from alone.[20]

In addition to the literary rapes that circulate through his *Legend of Good Women*, Chaucer's name is also associated with the charge of raping his ward Cecily Chaumpaigne, or more precisely, with the deed that exonerates the poet from all such charges. In this deed, dated May 4, 1380, Chaumpaigne releases Chaucer from "*omnimodas acciones tam de raptu meo tam de aliqua alia re vel causa*" (cited in Cannon 74).[21] The precise meaning of the phrase *de raptu meo* continues to cause Chaucer critics considerable anxiety. Despite his formal pardon, inherent ambiguities in both the wording of the release and in medieval rape law permit continued discussions of Chaucer's presumed guilt or innocence. The absence of specific details of the charge of *raptus* allows critics to debate whether the charge is the equivalent of modern rape or merely kidnapping. Gravdal finds that Chaucer critics confronted with the Chaumpaigne documents resort to the same sort of narrative ellipses and mystifications that she locates in legal transcriptions of medieval French rape cases. "What interests me most," Gravdal writes, "is the language scholars use to mystify rape, whether in the literary or the legal text" (174). John Gardner, notes Gravdal, is a case in point. "It seems possible," he writes, "if not downright likely, that into his busy schedule of 1379 or '80 Chaucer found time for at least one pretty wench" (cited in Gravdal 173). Gardner is not the only one to resort to banal euphemism. Cannon gives the following summary of critical responses:

> these writers have proffered to introduce or discuss the Chaumpaigne release under cover of a wide range of neutral phrases: the euphemisms they have used include 'strange case,' 'escapade,' 'incident,' 'distressing incident,' 'experience,' and, simply, 'case.' Just like the omissions in the memorandum, these more modern omissions of the noun *raptus* studiously avoid the difficult implications with which any mention of rape would be freighted. (92–93)[22]

Various interpretations render Chaumpaigne unrapable and/or textually unchaste. To this end, some critics cast aspersions on her character, insinuating that she pressed charges for the money, or retreating into less-than-neutral philology. The continued currency of the inherited patriarchal text, these contortions suggest, hinges upon the assertion that Chaumpaigne launched a false suit, or relies upon retreat into mystifying euphemisms.

I do not mean to imply that if other documents were found that we might know the truth and be able to make a conclusive judgment of guilt or innocence. For any such documents would, of course, be subject to similarly unstable, (hyper)productive readings and would always be implicated in gendered power-knowledge nexi. Rather, I find hints of the medieval reading practice at work in modern readers who not only emphasize Chaucer's legal innocence, which is a matter of law, but attempt to absolve him either by diminishing the charge or by blaming the plaintiff. If, as I argued earlier, legal understandings of rape are invested in discourses of interrupted economic exchange, the reverse is the case for legitimate literary paternity: uninterrupted inheritance of the patriarchal text requires that the feminized object of exchange between generations of male authors be chaste, free from the taint of rape.

But literary rape, the traffic in stories about violated women between generations of male readers, stands in extremely vexed relation to literal rape. Under the gaze of the dreamer-poet, the good women and the source material are subject to a reading practice that bears more than a passing similarity to contemporary legal discourse on rape. The *Legend's* dreamer-narrator avails himself of elusive and allusive strategies for describing rape, strategies that are full of affect and implicated in a model of literary paternity indebted to rapacious reading. And this literary traffic in stories both informs and is informed by ongoing legal attempts to define literal rape, including recent attempts to read the Chaumpaigne memorandum. To censure Cecily Chaumpaigne or to rationalize rape may ensure the currency of Chaucerian texts in the literary economy, but neither response to the complexities of rape which circulate both within and around the *Legend of Good Women* begins to unpack or challenge the reading strategies that structure the specious category "good women."

NOTES

[1] I would like to thank Glenn Burger, Rob Gray, and Susan Goldberg for reading and commenting on earlier versions of this paper.

[2] In a frequently cited passage, Rubin writes,

> If women are the gifts, then it is men who are the exchange partners. And it is the partners, not the presents, upon whom reciprocal exchange confers its quasi-mystical power of social linkage. The relations of such a system are such that women are in no position to realize the benefits of their own circulation. As long as the relations specify that men exchange women, it is men who are the beneficiaries of the product of such exchanges. (Rubin 163)

[3] This and subsequent Chaucer quotations are from *The Riverside Chaucer*, ed. Larry Benson et al., 3rd ed. (Boston, 1987).

[4] Christopher Cannon offers a somewhat different reading of the same legal texts. "Westminster I lumped rape and abduction together for the first time [. . .] and Westminister II furthered the ensuing confusion by using language that made no distinction at all between these two categories of wrong" (79). Although Cannon and Hanawalt read the letter of the law differently (as medieval interpreters did apparently), they both agree that in practice, rape, abduction, and theft were all combined under the rubric of crimes against male-owned property.

[5] Legal machinations, Hanawalt finds, presume (and discursively construct) the primacy of male ownership: "Even if the property belonged to the wife, the husband was likely to be cited as the victim" (153).

[6] To use Dinshaw's term, Chaucer's dreamer-narrator is an "immasculated" reader. That is, he reads *like* a man. According to Dinshaw, however, Alceste also assumes a masculinized readerly subjectivity: "Alceste and the God of Love [. . .] articulate this immasculated courtly response; wanting to hear only of good women, simply refusing to hear any other kind" (67).

[7] Gravdal finds that often violent trials of chastity are a necessary component of female saints' lives:

> The obvious explanation for the importance of rape in early Christian hagiography is that it corresponds to the new ideal of feminine virginity [. . .] A woman could be saved from her inferior nature only by renouncing sexuality and becoming like a man, *vir*, through virginity. A woman accedes to sanctity by prizing her chastity so highly that she dies for it. Sexual assault is one of the preferred methods of promotion to female martyrdom in early Christian hagiography. (22)

[8] Jocelyn Wogan-Browne compares Chaucer's legends to medieval virgin literature and the Katherine Group in particular. She argues that the *vitae* of virgin martyrs offer a method for women to become masculine, hence "*vir-ago*" (166). Although, as she notes, this model is a decidedly "ambivalent" one for emulation (179), Wogan-Browne finds "the lives do at least open up the possibility of resistant readings, which, in particular contexts, may constitute relative empowerment or recuperation" (180).

[9] Despite Foucault's persistent and insidious exclusion of the (unstable, multifaceted, and chaotic) feminine, his reconfigured notion of power informs my work.

> [Power] is a total structure of actions brought to bear upon possible actions; it incites, it induces, it seduces, it makes easier or more difficult; in the extreme it constrains or forbids absolutely; it is nevertheless always a way of acting upon an acting subject or acting subjects by virtue of their acting or being capable of action. A set of actions upon other actions, [*sic*] [. . .] Basically power is less a confrontation between two adversaries or the linking of one to the other than a question of government [. . .] 'Government' [does] not refer only to political structures or to the management of states; rather it designate[s] the way in which the conduct of individuals or of groups might be directed [. . .] To govern, in this sense, is to structure the possible field of action of others. (220–221)

[10] For a discussion of the relationship between *translatio studii* and Chaucer's *Legend of Good Women*, see Sheila Delany, "The Naked Text: Chaucer's 'Thisbe,' the *Ovide Moralisé*, and the Problem of *Translatio Studii* in the *Legend of Good Women*" in *Mediaevalia* 13 (1987): 275–294.

[11] In Dinshaw's words:

> The narrator himself praises her mercy, praises her generosity in imposing a light penance; but he does in fact have this disturbing female under control. [. . .] He has Alceste ask for simplistic stories of women constantly duped and betrayed. The narrator gets what he wants—a long series of passive women—and adds credibility to it by having a *woman* ask for it. (72)

[12] The narrator is at pains to establish Lucretia's rapability by medieval standards and thus must assert that she does not enjoy being raped. "She feleth no thyng, neyther foul ne fayr" (1818), he assures his audience. But it is precisely her rapability, because of her goodness and chastity, which incites Tarquin's obsession with her.

[13] Elaine Tuttle Hansen begins her analysis of gendered relations in Chaucer's writings with an explicit reference to the narrative investment in the rapists. "The more I looked," Hansen writes, "the more it seemed that the *Legend of Good Women* was best thought of as a poem about men, not women" (3). In his analysis of Chaucer's positioning of Ariadne between Lucretia and Philomela in the legends, Donald Rowe comments that "[f]rom one perspective at least, Ariadne holds the Minotaur to Theseus's throat as surely as Tarquin held a sword to Lucrece's, a perspective that perhaps explains why Chaucer placed her story between those of the ravishers Tarquin and Tereus" (68). Not only does Rowe discursively align Ariadne with Lucretia's assailant, Tarquin, he also refers to the legends of Lucretia and Philomela by the names of their respective rapists. In so doing, of course, he follows the pattern of rendering the rape of women as frustrated exchange between men at work in the poem itself.

[14] Jed's argument is much more nuanced than I suggest here. She examines *quattrocento* Humanists' textual corrections and emendations of documents telling the legend of Lucretia. These "castigations," she argues, epitomise a reading practice that relies upon this foundational rape as it recites it, and this reading practice subtends both republicanism and Renaissance Humanism.

[15] Conversely, Gravdal argues that Chrètien de Troyes differs from Ovid by invoking legal discourse, albeit in the service of protecting male privileges and unimpeded access to women's bodies:

> Chrètien departs from Ovid in framing the sexual relations between Tereus and Philomena as a legal question and then offering a law that might protect Tereus. Chrètien departs even further from Ovid by drawing the reader's attention away from the physical pain and emotional suffering of Philomena. He de-emphasizes the grisly nature of Ovid's tale and focuses on male rights, including the right to pleasure. (63)

To the extent that, as noted above, the dreamer-narrator laments his own pain instead of Philomela's, Chaucer's version of the legend also draws "the reader's attention away from the physical pain and emotional suffering" of Philomela.

[16] John C. French is a case in point. In the absence of external evidence to determine which is the revised (and, therefore, superior) prologue, French attempts an examination of "internal" evidence, which rests upon radically arbitrary value judgements. See his *The Problem of the Two Prologues to Chaucer's* Legend of Good Women.

[17] The final section of Frank's book usefully challenges the "myth of Chaucer's boredom" with the *Legend*. Frank argues that what critics since W. W. Skeat have read as signs of boredom are in fact instances of *abbreviatio* or *occupatio* (189–210). Of course, Chaucer's "refusal to describe or narrate while referring briefly to a subject or scene" (Frank 199) is not simply an indicator of boredom, nor are those moments merely examples of stylistic choices.

[18] In one sense, the text is also fragmentary because it is incomplete and therefore any claims to account for the poem in its "entirety" are also suspect. But to enforce either a complete discontinuity between sections of the poem or to insist upon a simple reconciliation between all the component parts is, I think, to do violence to the productive, and troubling, tensions between prologue and legends, between the narrator and his heroines.

[19] For the assaults upon Lucretia and Philomela, Rowe's book only indexes the euphemism "ravishing" and, most curiously, cross-references it with "constraining." Quite apart from arguments about the semantic range of *raptus, rapere*, and "ravysshe" encompassing both abduction and sexual violence in late medieval English law, Rowe appears to conflate rape/ravishment/constraint in such a way as to domesticate sexual violence. He uses "constrainment," for example, to describe the narrator's relationship to the daisies and Alceste, both of whom entice him to poetry. By extension, then, Rowe likens this constraint to love: "Chaucer pictures his narrator so constrained by love that he arises before day to watch the daisy rise" (43). Rowe also uses "constraint" to describe Philomela's incarceration, thus rendering her plight equivalent to the narrator's "constraint" before the daisy. While I agree that the narrator's apparent (but temporary) subjection to the God of Love and Alceste and the representations of rape that follow are deeply implicated in one another, Rowe makes this connection by an accident of reading, a reading practice inscribed within the text itself.

[20] Christopher Cannon provides the following summary of the various critics' interpretations of "raptus":

> At least one scholar has been sure that in medieval Latin the word *raptus* necessarily meant abduction and contained no connotation of sexual violence at all. A group of other scholars has been equally sure that rape or forced coitus is the only acceptable translation of *raptus* in this period. Yet a third group of scholars has thought that the word *raptus* was so ambiguous in the fourteenth century that it could mean either forced coitus or abduction. (75)

[21] Cannon translates this as releasing the poet from "all manner of actions such as they relate to my rape or any other thing or cause" (74).

[22] Despite his otherwise useful analysis, Cannon lapses into conjecture over possible explanations for discrepancies and omissions in memorandum concerning Chaumpaigne and Chaucer:

> Since Chaucer (as the one released from culpability) is the one connected with *raptus* by the release, it is Chaucer who would have had the most to gain from such an omission. His connections with the courts were clear and broad, and there would have been any number of opportunities for him (or his agents) to make arrangements for the necessary changes to be made. At the same time, if Chaucer did in fact seek this revision, it need not have been part of any sort of subterfuge, since the substitutions that were made did not really change the legal function of the document in any way. For the same reason these changes would not necessarily lay either the clerk who made them or the person or persons who arranged for them open to the serious charge of tampering with official documents. They may well have been made with Cecily Chaumpaigne's full complicity. (Cannon 93)

Although I have not addressed the suggestion of female complicity, it is worth noting that Cannon constructs a narrative in which the documents referring to Chaumpaigne's release of the poet from the charge of *raptus* and the apparent alteration of these documents becomes an exchange between men, specifically, between Chaucer and an imagined clerk. In this vein, see Jed for an analysis of *quattrocento* Italian scribal "castigations," or textual corrections of the Legend of Lucretia. Jed makes explicit connections between editing practices and female chastity. Her analysis informs my suggestion that both medieval alterations of court documents and modern interpretations of those documents are inextricable from a network of gendered power relations.

WORKS CITED

Cannon, Christopher. "*Raptus* in the Chaumpaigne Release and a newly discovered Document Concerning the Life of Geoffrey Chaucer." *Speculum* 68 (1993): 74–94.

Delany, Sheila. "The Naked Text: Chaucer's 'Thisbe,' the *Ovide Moralisé*, and the Problem of *Translatio Studii* in the *Legend of Good Women*." *Mediaevalia* 13 (1987): 275–294.

Dinshaw, Carolyn. *Chaucer's Sexual Poetics*. Madison, WI: U of Wisconsin P, 1989.

Foucault, Michel. "The Subject and Power" in *Michel Foucault: Beyond Structuralism and Herme-neutics*. Herbert Dreyfus and Paul Rabinow, eds. Chicago: U of Chicago P, 1983. 208–22.

Frank, Robert W. *Chaucer and* The Legend of Good Women. Cambridge, Mass.: Harvard UP, 1972.

French, John C. *The Problem of the Two Prologues to Chaucer's* Legend of Good Women. Baltimore: J.G. Furst, 1905.

Gravdal, Kathryn. *Ravishing Maidens: Writing Rape in Medieval French Literature and Law*. Philadelphia: U of Pennsylvania P, 1991.

Hanawalt, Barbara. *Crime and Conflict in English Communities 1300–1348*. Cambridge, Mass.: Harvard UP, 1979.

Hansen, Elaine Tuttle. *Chaucer and the Fictions of Gender*. Berkeley: U of California P, 1992.

Jed, Stephanie. *Chaste Thinking: The Rape of Lucretia and the Birth of Humanism*. Bloomington: Indiana UP, 1989.

Rowe, Donald. *Through Nature to Eternity: Chaucer's* Legend of Good Women. Lincoln and London: U of Nebraska P, 1988.

Rubin, Gayle. "The Traffic in Women: Notes on the 'Political Economy' of Sex." *Toward an Anthropology of Women*. Ed. Rayna Reiter. New York: Monthly Review, 1975. 155–170.

Wogan-Browne, Jocelyn. "The Virgin's Tale," in *Feminist Readings in Middle English Literature: The Wife of Bath and All Her Sect*. London and New York: Routledge, 1994. 165–194.

AFTERWORD

Since I began work on the *Legend of Good Women* several years ago in a graduate course on Chaucer at the University of Alberta, advances in queer theory and sexuality studies have challenged feminist thinking to reimagine female sexuality, and this shift has also been felt in Chaucer studies. Carolyn Dinshaw, for example, followed up her feminist readings of Chaucer in *Chaucer's Sexual Poetics* with readings influenced by the turn toward sexuality in her *Getting Medieval*. Similarly, my thinking has moved away from examining only the ways in which patriarchal discourses limit and contain female sexuality, sometimes by physical force, to considering the possibilities for both female pleasures and intimacy between women. Here, I want to outline briefly some of the recent developments in premodern sexuality studies and suggest the (im)possibilities for female desires, pleasures, and intimacies in the *Legend*.

In addition to Dinshaw's turn toward sexuality, several other recent studies contribute to this vein in medieval studies. Glenn Burger's *Chaucer's Queer Nation*, for example, reads *The Canterbury Tales* through the lens of contemporary queer theory. Burger's emphasis on pleasure is missing from much feminist reading, mine included. His readings of the *Tales'* various perverse pleasures demand a reevaluation of the possible sites of pleasure for the good women of the *Legend*. Philomela and Procne's revenge is so ghastly that Chaucer edits it out. Otherwise, they would not qualify as "good" women. The question remains, however, whether this excision removes a site of pleasure, admittedly a deeply perverse revenge fantasy.

Although Karma Lochrie's primary interest lies in questions of medieval and modern secrecy and its relation to historically mutable subjectivity, her passing comments on the extreme female perversity of Chaucer's legendry and its "gossipyness" are enough to make us wish she had offered a more sustained reading, but they are instructive nonetheless. Following Foucault, Lochrie asserts that secrets only become interesting in the ways they are told. This line of thinking motivates Lochrie to consider sexual conduct, medieval and modern, authorized and forbidden. If, as Lochrie suggests, medieval culture viewed sodomy as "a gender perversion that mimics femininity" and therefore rendered all female sexuality suspect (10), then Chaucer's *Legend* might offer a useful place to consider feminine sodomitical relations. Indeed, the legend of Cleopatra, which opens Chaucer's brief catalog of putatively good women, may provide an excellent place to begin a queer reading of the *Legend*. As numerous commentators have pointed out, Cleopatra is under no rubric a "good woman." Following Lochrie's analysis, Cleopatra's active sexuality renders her sodomitical. Her inclusion in the *Legend*, however, and the placement of her legend at the start of the catalog leads some to conclude that the Dreamer has not learned his lesson or is not performing his penance in earnest. He must be joking. But this familiar dismissal, both of Cleopatra's goodness and the Dreamer's sympathy for women, overlooks the question of Cleopatra's queerness.

Finally, the individual legends present serious obstacles for any analysis of relations between women. The legends themselves are self-contained and discrete. As with saints' lives, the genre to which they are most closely related, the reader is encouraged to see each heroine in isolation. Only occasionally do we glimpse relations between women within the legends—Lucretia and her maids, Philomela and Procne. For the most part the women in the *Legend* are separated from one another in a form of compulsory heterotextuality. This sex/textual separation of women contrasts sharply with Christine de Pizan's *City of Ladies* in which the celebrated women mingle together within the imaginary walls. While we may look for moments of female perversity in resistance to medieval sexual and domestic norms, we must also remember that the structure of the legends hampers too easy a celebration of female pleasures.

WORKS CITED

Burger, Glenn. *Chaucer's Queer Nation*. Minneapolis: U of Minnesota P, 2003.

Burger, Glenn, and Stephen Kruger, eds. *Queering the Middle Ages*. Minneapolis: U of Minnesota P, 2001.

Dinshaw, Carolyn. *Getting Medieval: Sexualities and Communities, Pre- and Post-modern*. Durham: Duke UP, 1999.

———. "Rivalry, Rape, and Manhood: Chaucer and Gower." *Violence against Women in Medieval Texts*. Ed. Anna Roberts. Gainesville: UP of Florida, 1998. 137–60.

Lochrie, Karma. *Covert Operations: The Medieval Uses of Secrecy*. Philadelphia: U of Pennsylvania P, 1999.

Between Complicity and Subversion: Body Politics in Palestinian National Narrative

Amal Amireh

I WOULD LIKE to begin this essay with two nonliterary narratives that exemplify the inextricable interconnection between gender and nationalism in the Palestinian context: The first is an intifada legend,[1] which, with slight variations, told of a stone-throwing incident that purportedly took place in a West Bank town in 1988 at the height of the first intifada/uprising:

> Israeli soldiers chased a group of young Palestinian men and finally caught up with one. As the Israeli soldiers were dragging him towards their jeep to arrest him, a young woman with a baby in her arms rushed up, screaming in anger, at the young Palestinian man. "There you are! I told you not to come here! I told you there would be trouble! Now what do you expect me to do if you are arrested? How will I eat? How will I feed our baby? I'm tired of your irresponsibility! Here, you take the baby and try to feed her!" And shoving the baby into the arms of the dumbfounded young man, she fled. The soldiers, as shocked as the young man, suddenly had a baby to deal with. In a state of bewilderment, the soldiers shoved the young man back into the street, jumped into their jeep and sped away. The man was left holding the baby. Finally, the mother reappeared from behind a nearby building where she had been hiding, went up to the grateful young man, whom she had never seen before, took her baby from his arms, and went home.[2]

The second story was told ten years later, in the spring of 1997, by local newspaper reports in the West Bank. It was about a kind of chewing gum that allegedly was being marketed by the Israelis in the territories of the Palestinian National Authority.[3] According to the Palestinian Ministry of Supply, this was no ordinary gum; it was a "sexual gum" containing hormones. It was said to cause premature sexual activity in young girls, abnormal sexual appetite in teenage girls, and infertility in married women, but it did not affect men. The ministry, the reports assured the public, is doing its best to protect the citizens by cracking down on the local intermediaries who sell such harmful products to the public.[4]

These two stories, which I will return to later, place women at the center of two different nationalist narratives belonging to different periods in the recent history of the Palestinians: in the first women are intifada activists, participating in the national struggle side by side with men. In the second, women are vulnerable to an enemy plot that seeks to harm them and the nation as a whole, but the institutions of their state, currently under construction, are protecting them. These narratives are part of a larger dominant discourse about gender, sexuality, and nationalism that pervades not only the popular media and overtly political propaganda, but also literature.

It is important to remember that these stories are interesting less for what they teach us about actual Palestinian women and men and more for what they reveal about a national discourse that uses women as fictional constructs and ideological signs. In this discourse, sexuality is an essential component that is usually ignored in discussions of Palestinian women and nationalism. Of course it is not surprising, for mainstream scholarship on nationalism has tended to ignore gender altogether. But recent works in feminist and postcolonial studies have shown that constructions of national identity are gendered; that meanings of "nation" are "permeated with notions of masculinity and femininity," and that idealized images and real bodies of women serve as national boundaries. Nira Yuval-Davis sums up the intimate relation between gender and nationalism when she says that women reproduce the nation biologically, culturally, and symbolically.[5] The gendered national narrative is concerned with constructing, using, and disciplining the bodies of both women and men, but feminist scholars, in their efforts to reinscribe women into nationalism, tend for the most part to ignore men and masculinity.[6] My feminist reading of Palestinian nationalism highlights the link between national constructions of femininity and masculinity.

Literature, and culture more generally, occupies a privileged place in nationalism. According to Ernest Gellner, "Nationalism is, essentially, the general imposition of a high culture on society."[7] Literature is the main component of this high, literate culture as Timothy Brennan argues: "The political tasks of modern nationalism directed the course of literature . . . and just as fundamentally, literature participated in the formation of nations through the creation of 'national print media'—the newspaper and the novel."[8] Benedict Anderson's influential argument that nations are "imagined communities" emphasizes the centrality of literature to that imagining; the novel in particular becomes essential to the representation of the nation, communicating "the solidity of a single community, embracing characters, author and readers, moving onward through calendrical time." Moreover, "fictions seep quietly and continuously into reality, creating that remarkable confidence of community in anonymity which is the hallmark of modern nations."[9] Third world nationalisms are no exception, prompting Fredric Jameson to describe the third world novel as a national allegory.[10]

Narrating Palestinian Nationalism

In the Palestinian context, the national demand for recognition and self-determination has been cast as the right to tell the Palestinian story. The Palestinians have been denied not only a homeland, but also "the permission to narrate."[11] As the Palestinian writer Anton Shammas puts it, "The right of return [of the Palestinian refugees displaced in 1948 and 1967] is the right to narrate."[12] And the observation that the anticolonial novelist "was often . . . a nationalist" needs no qualifications when it comes to Palestinian writers.[13] They have been directly involved in the telling of the national story either by holding official positions in the national movement, by being "spokesmen" for it, or by consciously putting their artistic pens in the service of the national cause.[14] Not surprisingly, we find in the work of both male and female writers a reproduction of the dominant gendered national narrative. However, feminist writers like Liana Badr and Sahar Khalifeh have also attempted to clear fictional spaces that allow for a subversive questioning of this dominant narrative. But to avoid the tendency of some postcolonial critics of third world women writers to exaggerate the revolutionary nature of the works and their exceptionalism, especially if they are dealing with women and sexuality, it is imperative that we view such works in the discursive contexts in which they are originally produced and received.[15]

Generally speaking, the Palestinian literary national narrative is erotic and male. In it, as is the case in other nationalist narratives, Palestine is metaphorized as a woman. The dependence of the Palestinian peasant society on the fertility of "Mother Earth" no doubt encourages the use of such a metaphor.[16] The Palestinian is a male lover, a groom, and a defender. Abu Salma, the crowd-pleasing poet of the 1950s, writes in the poem "I Love You More," "Whenever your name sounds in my ears, my words grow more poetic / Planting desire for you on every stoop /. . . Oh Palestine! Nothing more beautiful, more precious, more pure!"[17] Mahmoud Darwish's well-known poem "A Lover from Palestine" unequivocally expresses this relation by presenting the speaker as a Palestinian lover and the woman as Palestine:

> Her eyes and the tattoo on her hands are Palestinian,
> Her name, Palestinian,
> Her dreams and sorrow, Palestinian,
> Her kerchief, her feet and body, Palestinian,
> Her words and her silence, Palestinian,
> Her voice, Palestinian,
> Her birth and her death, Palestinian.[18]

A similar poem by 'Abd al-Latif 'Aql entitled "Love Palestinian Style" begins by invoking Palestinian national symbols to describe the speaker's love for his beloved: "In times of drought you are my figs and olives." The speaker's resistance to his oppressors expresses and strengthens his deep love:

> And when I am led all alone
> To be whipped and humiliated,

And lashed at every police station,
I feel we're lovers, who died from ecstasy,
A dark-skinned man and his woman.
You become me and I become you—
Luscious figs and shelled almonds
And when soldiers smash my head
And force me to sip the cold of prison
To forget you—I love you even more.[19]

According to a poem by Muhammad al As'ad, "Woman alone plays on all the strings / With one stroke / Because she is the entire homeland."[20] This metaphor of the woman as Palestine is employed by women writers as well. The hero of a short story by Samira Azzam tells us that in the dark eyes of his beloved Suad he "saw all of Palestine's goodness."[21] Predictably, the wedding is a central trope in this national narrative;[22] Palestine is a bride and the groom is the Palestinian fighter/martyr: Abu Salma says in "My Country on Partition Day": "We've woven your wedding clothes with red thread dyed from our own blood."[23] For this wedding to be complete the man must possess the woman; he needs to be virile, she must be virginal. In metaphorizing the land as woman, then, the national story becomes the story of the possession of the land/woman by a man.

But one particularity of Palestinian nationalism is that it is a nationalism that consolidated itself in defeat. The major nationalist milestones in the Palestinian national narrative tend to be occasions of military loss. The consensus among Palestinian historians is that *Al-Nakba* (catastrophe) of 1948, which resulted in the establishment of the state of Israel and the displacement of the majority of the Palestinian population, is the most important event in solidifying a Palestinian national identity.[24] The Arab defeat by Israel in 1967 and the resulting loss of the West Bank and Gaza further spurred the coalescing of a Palestinian national consciousness. Paradoxically, for generations of Palestinians, especially the men, Palestinian nationalism was experienced as humiliation. In fact, the tireless efforts of the dominant Palestinian national narrative to cast Palestinian defeats as victories can be understood as an attempt to solve this vexing paradox.[25]

But the Palestinian national narrative of defeat exists, and according to it, the Palestinian male fails to possess the land; the homeland in this narrative is a female body possessed by others. The Palestinian Authority on its Web site laments "the rape of Palestine."[26] This metaphor of the loss of Palestine as rape, which has been a constant in the Palestinian and wider Arab political nationalist discourse, signifies the loss of Palestine as loss of female virginity but also of male virility, since the virile actor now is the rapist/enemy. This male loss of virility is inscribed as Palestinian defeat.[27]

Men in the Sun and the Search for Lost Masculinity

No one has expressed this loss of virility more forcefully than Ghassan Kanafani in his classic novella *Men in the Sun*. Set in 1958, ten years after the catastrophe of 1948, this most canonical of Palestinian narratives represents Palestinian men's degradation and humiliation as refugees through the ideology of male virility. A few lines into the novel, we encounter the following passage describing one of the main characters' relation to the land:

> Every time he breathed the scent of the earth, as he lay on it, he imagined that he was sniffing his wife's hair when she had just walked out of the bathroom, after washing with cold water. The very same smell, the smell of a woman who had washed with cold water and covered his face with her hair while it was still damp.[28]

The erotic relation between the Palestinian peasant, in this case Abu Qais, and the land-as-woman is thwarted. The land Abu Qais is lying on is not Palestine: for he lost his land in 1948 and is now a refugee trying to cross the border illegally from Iraq into Kuwait. So the passage is really about the frustration of desire, a frustration that represents the loss of his very identity as a displaced Palestinian peasant.

The crisis of male virility in the novel is connected to another marker of masculinity in Palestinian culture: the ability to provide. According to Julie Peteet, "Arab masculinity (*rujulah*) is acquired, verified and played out in the brave deed, in risk-taking, and in expressions of fearlessness and assertiveness. . . . Manliness is also closely intertwined with virility and paternity, and with paternity's attendant sacrifices."[29] As a refugee, Abu Qais cannot possess the land, which means he cannot provide for his family. His main motivation in leaving the camp and immigrating to Kuwait is to have a chance to send his son to school, buy "one or two olive trees," and "build a shack somewhere." That his lack of virility is a condition brought about by his loss of his land is established earlier, when his wife gave birth to an emaciated girl, who soon dies, instead of to the son Abu Qais desired.[30]

The masculinity of other men in the narrative is in crisis as a result of their refugee experience. Marwan's father marries the crippled Shafiqa because she owns a house with a concrete roof. In other words, the helpless, undesired woman becomes the provider of shelter for the humiliated man, who loses the respect of his wife and son. Fifteen-year-old Marwan is trying to prove his manhood by becoming a provider for his mother. Assad, too, is on a quest for his shattered manhood. A political activist who has been able to withstand the humiliation of Jordanian jails, he is entrapped by a family tradition that requires him to marry his cousin. His attempt to rebel against this tradition that deprives him of control over his own destiny is blunted by the fact that he is forced to accept the fifty dinar offered by his uncle. His taking the money is an instance of his continued humiliation and "feminization." The three characters' national defeat is experienced as economic disadvantage and a loss of their traditional role as providers for themselves and their families, including their women.

The main representative of Palestinian and Arab degradation in the novella is Abul Khaizuran, the truck driver who promises to take Abu Qais, Assad, and Marwan to the promised land of Kuwait. Before becoming a smuggler and a moneygrubber, Abul Khaizuran, whose name in Arabic signifies machismo, was a fighter in the war. But we learn that his machismo is only skin deep, for during the war he stepped on a land mine, an incident that resulted in the loss of his sexual organs:

> Ten years had passed since they took his manhood from him, and he had lived that humiliation day after day and hour after hour. He had swallowed it with his pride, and examined it every moment of those ten years. And still he hadn't yet got used to it, he hadn't accepted it. For ten long years he had been trying to accept the situation. But what situation? To confess quite simply that he had lost his manhood while fighting for his country? And what good had it done? He had lost his manhood and his country, and damn everything in this bloody world.[31]

There is no ambiguity here; for both Abul Khaizuran and Kanafani national defeat is experienced as castration.

At the end of the novel, the three Palestinian refugees suffocate to death in the inferno of the empty tank when Abul Khaizuran is delayed at the border crossing (significantly, the cause of the delay is the interest of the border officials in his rumored sexual exploits with a prostitute). After robbing the bodies of the three men and then leaving the stiff corpses on the city dump, Abul Khaizuran asks the chilling question, "Why didn't they knock on the sides of the tank?"[32]

Of Men and Guns

Kanafani, who was one of the prominent leaders of the Popular Front for the Liberation of Palestine (PFLP), believed that the Palestinians could regain their manhood and land only through armed struggle. If the Palestinians did not want to end up like his characters on the garbage heap of history, they needed to reverse course, head west instead of east, and give up the illusion of personal advancement and embrace instead the armed revolution. In a speech he gave in 1998 to commemorate the fiftieth anniversary of *Al-Nakba*, Yasser Arafat declared, "We are not mere refugees asking for handouts; we are a deeply rooted people, part of an ancient nation, banging on the walls of the dark tank."[33] His reference to Kanafani's text is no coincidence. Kanafani's vision for redeeming Palestine and its men has been the official line of the Palestinian national movement for more than forty years. The transformation of the humiliated refugees into a people comes about through armed struggle, which, beginning in the early 1960s onward, redeems the emasculated Palestinian man.[34] Although some women received military training and even took part in some operations, their participation was limited and symbolic.[35] It is the *Fida'i*, or the guerrilla fighter, who emerges as the national hero: "For ordinary women and men, the symbols of the [Palestinian nationalist movement] were the leaders of the factions, Arafat and the rest: the guerrillas seen at their posts and driving around in their jeeps proudly displaying their weapons." This iconic role of the *Fida'i* is embodied in the Palestine Authority National Anthem: "I swear under the shade of the flag / to my land and nation and the fire of pain / I will live as a guerrilla [*Fida'i*], I will go on as guerrilla, I will expire as guerrilla until I recover my country."[36]

Indeed, male virility is written into the Palestinian Liberation Organization (PLO) charter of 1964: article 5 defines the Palestinians as "those Arab residents who were living in Palestine until 1947 . . . , and *everyone who is born to an Arab Palestinian father* after this date inside Palestine or outside it." Article 4 states that "the Palestinian character is an essential and undying feature that is passed from *fathers to sons.*"[37] The wedding metaphor reappears and persists: this time the groom is the martyr who "fertilizes the land," in the words of Mahmoud Darwish, speaking for the nation at large.[38] A front-page political ad supportive of Yasser Arafat taken out in the newspaper *Al-Ayyam* on July 27, 2000, by the Palestinian businessman Sabeeh al-Masri', calls Arafat *'asheq* (lover) who "confidently and tirelessly woos Jerusalem, the bride of cities, and the capital of the independent Palestinian state." The Palestinian male is now virile and as a result of his remasculinization, the land of Palestine is fertile again. Poem after poem from the 1960s onward tells the story. Waleed al Halees in "Days in the Life of a Palestinian Boy" writes,

> Hoping for continuance, my father joyfully cast his seed
> into my mother's womb as he lay
> over her, shivering like a stallion. Then he slept,
> dreaming he'd have a boy,
> hoping for life, chanting even in sleep,
> "I'll beget a male child,
> the future ongoing, a boy!"
> Later I surged from my mother
> Toward life.[39]

In another poem he says of his beloved, Mayy: "I pray for the pure fire in her eyes, / Giving her some of my blood to drink; / I lay the child within her and die of desire." The symbolic meaning of this act of "fertilization" is hard to miss, for it engenders a whole nation: "A whole people comes forth from Mayy, / Its hands moistened by wheat and roses. / A homeland comes forth from Mayy."[40]

In the sixties and seventies, fertility became an actual weapon for the Palestinians who remained inside Israel. Golda Meir, the Israeli prime minister, reportedly could not sleep, worrying about how many Palestinians were being conceived or born every night.[41] Believing that "to govern is to populate" the Jewish state saw itself engaged in a "demographic war" with its growing Arab minority. Shimon Peres, another Israeli foreign minister, declared, "Politics is a matter of demography, not geography."[42] Palestinian poets responded to the call to arms with a vengeance. In a poem entitled "Here We Shall Stay," Tawfiq Zayyad threatened that the Palestinians in Israel will "keep on making children / One revolutionary generation / After another." Mahmoud Darwish defied the Jewish state by asserting his identity as a virile Arab in what is probably his most popular poem ever, "Identity Card":

> Write down:
> I am a [sic] Arab
> My I.D. number is 50,000

> My children, eight
> And the ninth is due next summer
> —Does that anger you?[43]

But this pride in virility extends to the West Bank and Gaza, where the Palestinians are the majority, and where they presently have one of the highest fertility rates in the world.[44] It has been noted that even in relation to the occupation "mainstream nationalism contained a stated pronatalist policy using population growth and demographic pressure as an instrument through which to achieve liberation."[45] In Sahar Khalifeh's novel *Wild Thorns*, Zuhdi is a Palestinian from the West Bank who works in an Israeli factory. After physically attacking a Jewish worker who calls him "dirty Arab," Zuhdi is jailed, an experience that politicizes him, causing him to die at the end of the novel in an armed clash with the Israeli army. But his radicalization is first expressed as sexual virility: following his release he sees his wife's body as "a haven of safety in an occupied land . . . this treasure is my fortress that no intruder can violate. The fertile land receives the seed and turns it into a profusion of production and consumption." Even Basil, who is barely out of childhood, is masculinized by his prison experience. He boasts to himself while still in prison, "Well, they said I'd become a man; I'll prove it as soon as I get out of here. The country's full of factory girls."[46] Conversely, those untouched by the spirit of the revolution are almost impotent. The hero of Ghareeb 'Asqalani's short story "Hunger" is so exhausted after a long day of humiliating labor on an Israeli construction site that he cannot respond to his wife's sexual advances: "The woman's body writhes, the smell of sex is in your nostrils, and yet you feign sleep. . . . But sometimes you get fed up and give her the remains of all your manhood."[47]

Feminist Engagements

It is against this hegemonic fertility ideology that Liana Badr's novels and stories should be read. Focusing on the Palestinian experience in exile, Badr seeks to feminize the fertility metaphor by shifting emphasis away from the men to the women. In the short story "A Land of Rock and Thyme," she tells of the massacre of the Palestinians in a refugee camp in Lebanon. The heroine, Yusra, is married to a Palestinian fighter. Their marriage lasts ten days before the husband is killed in an Israeli raid. Yusra, who is pregnant, survives the raids and massacres. Her survival, her memory, and her pregnancy are offered as expressions of hope and continuity of the Palestinian people in exile.

What may seem a celebration of women's traditional roles as mothers is, I would argue, a break with a tradition in Palestinian literature and culture that have always equated nationalism with male virility. Moreover, Badr's stories, set at times of war and told from the perspective of ordinary refugee women, decenters the traditional Palestinian hero: the guerrilla fighter. Finally, in addition to its symbolic meaning, casting the Palestinian woman as a reproducer of the nation, Yusra's pregnancy also has a personal meaning; it is her tangible connection to the husband she loved and lost. Similarly, Aisha's pregnancy in Badr's *The Eye of the Mirror* not only symbolizes the continuity of the Palestinian people in the face of massacres and annihilation, but also restores to Aisha her lost voice. In returning to live with her mother instead of with her dead husband's family, Aisha is claiming the child for herself. She is given the final word in the novel, when she defiantly declares about the unborn child, "'That is my responsibility. . . . I don't want anyone else to take it instead of me.'"[48] Badr's insistence on the personal dimension of her heroine's pregnancy is the precariously thin line that prevents her narratives from being an argument for what one might term "uterine nationalism."[49]

This brand of nationalism, where men bear arms and women bear children, is currently openly advocated by the Islamic movement in Palestine.[50] In a Hamas-sponsored anti-Oslo exhibit entitled "The Intifada Continues" at An-Najah National University in 1997, one crude cartoon shows a woman with a big pregnant belly. Inside is a masked gunman, wielding a Muslim flag. Article 17 of Hamas's charter would be an apt caption for this cartoon: "The Muslim women have a no lesser role than that of men in the war of liberation; they manufacture men and play a great role in guiding and educating the [new] generation."[51] In the Islamic version of the national narrative, a version the secular feminist Badr would not condone, the emphasis on women's fertility and on their roles as mothers is part of a discourse that views secular feminism, in the words of one leading Hamas intellectual in the West Bank, as part of a "clash of civilization" with Islam and "as a Zionist and Western conspiracy to destroy the Palestinian family and to humiliate the Palestinian man."[52] In this context, a feminist celebration of women's fertility and creativity would not have the same subversive potential as when it is used to counter a hegemonic national male ideology that idealizes armed struggle and marginalizes the majority of women in the process.

Gendering the Intifada or Seducing Women

It is no coincidence that this starkly explicit division of labor between women and men advocated by Hamas is articulated in the context of the first intifada.[53] The intifada, which started in 1987 and ended with the Oslo peace agreements in 1994, posed a serious challenge to the dominant Palestinian national narrative. It offered the Palestinian male a chance at redemption, especially after the military defeat in Lebanon and the scattering and neutralizing of the PLO fighters. At the same time, it was a nonmilitaristic form of nationalist activity: fighters were replaced by a largely civil population engaged in peaceful resistance to the occupation. As the story I began with illustrates, women played a visible role in this resistance, in the streets, in neighborhood committees, and in leadership.[54] Their visibility earned them recognition in the Palestinian Declaration of Independence, which extended "a special tribute to the brave Palestinian woman, guardian of sustenance and life, keeper of our people's perennial flame."[55]

This story, and many like it, also shows that women's visibility and participation seriously challenged and threatened to destabilize traditional gender roles.

As one scholar puts it, the intifada "feminized Palestinian society."[56] The young man here is rescued by the young woman who, pretending to be his wife, chastises him in public for not providing for his family. To escape arrest, the Palestinian stands in front of Israeli soldiers holding a baby in his arms instead of a gun or even a stone. This new image clashed with the image of the Palestinian freedom fighter that up to the intifada was the hero of the Palestinian national narrative. The anxiety about the intifada's destabilization of gender roles was expressed in sexual terms as male fear of the female body. One particularly interesting example, which I would like to discuss in some detail, took the form of widespread anxiety about Palestinian women using sex to recruit Palestinian men as collaborators with Israel.

The Palestinian term for this is *Isquat*, which means "causing to fall." Books and pamphlets were written to warn of this Israeli recruiting strategy.[57] Activists from all political groups (Nationalists, Marxists, Islamists) extracted confessions from those who supposedly had fallen; a typical confession goes like this (with variations): after a hard day of stone throwing, the young patriotic man visits with some of his trusted friends in their home. He finds himself alone with a woman, usually the sister of one of the friends, who either seduces him into having sex with her or mixes in some sleep-inducing drug in his tea. The next day, he is called into the Israeli military headquarters and is asked to become a collaborator. When the young man refuses, he is confronted with pictures showing him having sex with the woman. He is threatened with "scandal" and "exposure." Upon hearing this, the man breaks down and becomes a collaborator. He recruits other young men and women either by providing them with women or by having sex with them himself. In his confession, he gives names of people he recruited who, in turn, will be forced to confess their crimes.[58] According to these confessions, men were safer in the street, a place of fraternity and solidarity. Interiors, particularly women's spaces such as homes, seamstresses' shops, and hair salons, are dangerous because they are places of seduction. As the intifada dragged on and the Israeli repression intensified, the collaboration discourse got progressively more perverse, about men confessing to having sex with their sisters and mothers, or about mothers seducing their children. This discourse contributed to an atmosphere of paranoia that made everyone a suspect, especially women. Ironically, then, women's bodies that were shielding the young men in the street from the occupier were in this kind of narrative used inside by that occupier to "penetrate" the nationalist movement.

True men, of course, do not respond to seduction. Masculinity for them means body control. Lila Abu-Lughod argues that "control" is an important element in Arab masculinity: "Real men are able to exact respect and command obedience from others while they themselves resist submitting to others' control." Edward Said notices in his book *After the Last Sky* the "cult of physical strength" among Palestinian men.[59] More than just athletic activities, Karate, boxing, and bodybuilding are part of an ethics of masculinity as body control. This body control is necessary for survival: the nationalist hero in one of Sahar Khalifeh's novels learns that in order to survive torture in prison he had to master "taking his body off." That is "the first lesson." And before he learns *Dhabt el Nafs*, that is, "self-control," he suffers: with every bodily movement the shackle tightens on his wrist. He eventually learns "to hold his breath as long as possible and [to] think of everything except his body."[60] Sexual control is an important part of this masculinity. Julie Peteet notes that "unlike masculinity in the Mediterranean, especially Spain, public displays of lust and sexual bravado are not explicit components of Arab manhood. Indeed self-mastery of lust and romantic emotions is crucial to the construction and maintenance of Arab manhood."[61] But while Peteet translates this sexual control to an absence of sexuality as a component of Palestinian manhood, I would argue for it as a central component of this identity.[62] The collaboration hysteria could be understood only if we recognize this fact. For at some basic level, it was about the loss of sexual control of Palestinian men over their bodies.

But clearly not all men can be heroes. Many who do not have the necessary body control become "victims" of seduction. A one-time collaborator who details his use of Palestinian women to recruit collaborators instructively titles his book *Confessions of a Victim*. To protect these victims who cannot control their bodies two things were necessary: a militarization of the intifada and a redomestication of women. The use of weapons in the latter stages of the intifada, while limited and largely symbolic, sidelined the majority of the civil population but resurrected the traditional Palestinian national male hero who almost disappeared in the early years of the intifada. The use of arms by Palestinian men allows them to assert their manhood in relation to their opponents by putting them on more equal footing with the Israeli soldiers. It also distinguishes the Palestinian men from the Palestinian women by making the former adopt a kind of resistance to the occupation that was always monopolized by men.

The collaboration scare and the ensuing militarization of resistance were accompanied by an aggressive campaign to veil Palestinian women and to remove them from public space.[63] Although the campaign was initiated by Hamas, its success in a very short time and the complicity of the other political groups, who intervened too late and only when their political territory was threatened, shows that the call to veil women and restrict their movement found an echo in the Palestinian hegemonic patriarchal ideology. Supposedly, veiling was necessary to guarantee national security and to preserve the national honor. Actually, it allowed men to assert their power over women by controlling women's bodies at a time they felt their own male bodies were being violated. The collaboration scare coincided with the use of rape and sexual harassment of Palestinian men by their Israeli male prison interrogators in an attempt to "deprive young men of claims to manhood and masculinity." Palestinian national discourse is silent about this violation. As Peteet states, "One cannot return from prison and describe forms of torture that violate the most intimate realm of gendered selfhood."[64] The collaboration hysteria was an attempt to speak the "unspeakable" by articulating male fears of violation and victimization and at the same time by containing these same fears through displacement on women's bodies: in the *Isquat* narrative, women's bodies are dangerous and vulnerable, in need of men's discipline and protection.

The Intifada's Impossible Fictions

Palestinian writers, who for the most part idealize that period in their history, have not critically engaged this dimension of the intifada. One exception is Sahar Khalifeh's novel *Bab el-Saha* [The door of the courtyard]. At the center is Nazha (a name that means "honest, honorable"), a twenty-seven-year-old Palestinian prostitute. Her mother, a prostitute before her and a suspected collaborator, was stabbed to death in the public square probably by her own son, who now is coming after his sister. Although Nazha is alone and vulnerable, she is defiant. She tells a story that is not usually told by the dominant national narrative: a story of a divided, cruel, hypocritical, patriarchal society that exploits poor women like her, then scapegoats them. Palestine, according to Nazha, "is like a monster; she is constantly devouring and is never satisfied."[65] Moreover, while Nazha admits to being a prostitute, she vehemently denies the charge of collaboration and defends her mother. In doing so, she undermines the Intifada ideology that saw women's sexuality as a national threat.[66]

The unwilling audience of this narrative is Husam, a wounded activist, who finds himself trapped in Nazha's ill-reputed house and dependent on her kindness for survival. After much resistance, he begins to see Nazha as a victim and convinces her brother not to kill her. The novel ends with Nazha, of her own free will, lighting up a Molotov cocktail and getting ready to burn the Israeli flag, risking her life in the act. She insists that she is not doing this for the "monster, Palestine" but rather for her brother who has just been shot dead by soldiers.

Regardless of her motives, Nazha redeems herself at the end by joining the intifada, and the intifada is redeemed by embracing Nazha. This is a romance ending to an otherwise brutally realistic novel. For although the intifada forgave some male collaborators who confessed and repented (even saw them as "victims" as I showed earlier), it did not forgive women like Nazha. The fallen bodies of women in a culture that equates female virginity with honor are not redeemable and are always disciplined and punished.[67] Seen in a historical context, this solution to Nazha's predicament is what Mary Layoun calls in another but related context "an impossible fiction." According to Layoun, "impossible fictions" in literary and cultural texts "can suggest to us a story we might not have heard before, a dream we might not have dreamed, a proposition . . . we might not yet have considered."[68] Khalifeh's subversiveness lies in the fact that she dares to imagine an alternative Palestinian community that includes even prostitutes. For this to happen, the society has to radically revise its concepts of male and female sexuality and honor, something the novelist believed the intifada might have the potential to do.

Similarly, Jamal Bannoura's 1998 novel *Intifada* is optimistic about the revolutionary potential of the uprising. As the political coming of age story of the main character Ra'fat, it chronicles this young man's growth and political development from a selfish individualist who is only interested in getting a university degree and a wife into a committed activist and nationalist leader of men. This political development overlaps with his sexual development expressed through his relations to three women.

The first woman in his life is Abeer, his apolitical cousin. Abeer aggressively pursues Ra'fat, tells him she loves him, takes the initiative of kissing him, and even proposes to him. This reversal of gender roles highlights Ra'fat's passivity; with her he is a boyish fop, his sexual desire domesticated and controlled. Ra'fat defies Abeer when he takes part in a demonstration. Being inexperienced, he is rescued from arrest by Rania, a young woman activist, who teaches him different intifada skills. Ra'fat is sexually attracted to Rania and takes the initiative of kissing her, although his is still a timid, hesitant kiss.[69] But Rania chooses to be with another intifada activist. During this phase in his life, Ra'fat becomes more politicized, eventually going to jail and becoming a leader.

After his release from jail, he goes underground. This is when he meets the third woman, Na'eema, who hides him in her house. Na'eema is different from the other women: she is a widow, a mother, and is much older than him. Ra'fat pursues Na'eema and is aggressive sexually with her. He eventually overpowers her and has sex with her, almost against her will. Although this is his first actual sexual intercourse, he succeeds in overwhelming and satisfying the older, more sexually experienced woman. And as if to confirm Ra'fat's maturing virility, the Israeli army attacks the house that night and arrests him. *Intifada* is a male fantasy, where women are subsidiary characters, not interesting in themselves but in the way they relate to the hero's sexual maturity. Ra'fat's successful sexual seduction of Na'eema, who in his words is "the mother, sister, lover" all in one, reinstates proper gender roles: the Palestinian male regains his sexual initiative and is back in control.[70]

But what about Na'eema? The novel ends with her standing outside her home saying farewell to her lover, impervious to the likelihood that her neighbors may condemn her for having a man sleeping in her house. This is the only reference in the novel to the vulnerability of women like Na'eema. If we read Bannoura's novel as a historical narrative documenting the intifada, which is the way the novel was reviewed when it appeared in the West Bank, the silence about the negative practices of the intifada and their implications for women can only be seen as an idealization that falsifies history. But the novel, I would argue, should be read not as a historical record of the recent past as much as another "impossible fiction" about the present and perhaps the future. Along with its remasculinization of the Palestinian man, we also have a celebration of a taboo sexual relation between a man and a woman that would have been condemned not only during the intifada but also in 1998, the novel's year of publication, by a dominant traditional ideology according to which female sexuality is legitimately realized only in marriage, wifehood, and motherhood. When Na'eema objects to their relation on the grounds that it is "treason," Ra'fat answers, "You are not betraying anyone because you are not owned by anyone. You alone own yourself. You have the right to live your life and to enjoy it. What is the value of one's life without love?"[71] Here sex is radically presented as personal agency, as an expression of individual "self-determination."

This gospel of sex/love is subversive of a paranoid national narrative that views women's bodies as threats to national honor and security. Compare it to the view expressed in a statement distributed at Palestinian university campuses by a pro-Islamist student bloc warning the students against the Israeli attempts to infiltrate universities by "spreading damaging concepts and ideas among the students" such as the idea that love between men and women "is a necessity, an academic requirement, even an instinctive need."[72] Against this discourse, Ra'fat's relation to Na'eema, as limited as it is, is dangerously utopian.

Unfortunately, women's participation in the intifada did not translate into gains and their situation did not improve, as Khalifeh and Bannoura would have liked. Khalifeh registers this disappointment in her post-Oslo novel *Al-Mirath* [The inheritance]. Khalifeh here is less optimistic about the redemptive powers of nationalism than she was in *Bab el-Saha*. Set at the end of the intifada and during the early years of the Palestinian National Authority, the novel is crowded with defeated, embittered, and disillusioned men and women. Prominent among them is Mazen, the one-time revolutionary fighter and leader in Lebanon. Here he is a pathetically narcissistic figure, full of self-pity, living on his memories of the glorious past in Beirut, and crying over his lost love for Salma, the woman-as-revolution. Along with these psychological scars, he is physically scarred: a bomb exploded and left him with a limp. The best this defeated warrior can do is to organize a cultural celebration, which, in the face of checkpoints, settlements, and oppressed crowds, begins as a farce and ends up with death and tragedy.

Fitna is the much younger second wife of a dying patriarch. Since her husband has only one daughter and no sons, and since she could not get pregnant during their marriage, she devises a plan to have a male son who will inherit his father's property and money. Fitna gets pregnant through artificial insemination done at Hadasa, an Israeli hospital in Jerusalem. The Jewish doctor assures her that she will have a boy. Fitna announces her pregnancy after her husband's death, claiming that she is carrying his child. Although her husband's family does not believe her, there is nothing they can do. During the cultural revival celebration Mazen organizes, Fitna gives birth to a sickly boy and then dies from postpartum bleeding at an Israeli checkpoint. The novel ends with Fitna's mother, her daughter dead next to her, thrusting the new born in front of the Israeli soldiers and saying, "Thank you very much, this is your share."[73]

While Fitna is not a particularly sympathetic character, we understand her predicament. She, too, Khalifeh shows, is a victim of a patriarchal society that values women for their abilities to reproduce men. The novel offers a sharp feminist critique of the patriarchal Palestinian society that idealizes hollow men like Mazen and pushes women like Fitna to extreme measures to get a male child. But this critique, I would argue, is contained by a nationalist ideology that views victory and defeat in terms of men's and women's bodies. What Khalifeh does in *Al-Mirath* in 1998, is what Kanafani did in *Men in the Sun* in 1962—that is, figuring Palestinian defeat through sexuality. Khalifeh's men in the novel are either sexually impotent, physically repulsive, or, like Mazen, symbolically castrated. The women's bodies are sexually frustrated, exploited, or, in the case of Fitna, penetrated by the enemy.[74]

It is tempting to read this episode as an example of Khalifeh's confounding of boundaries, where the lines separating Palestinians and Israelis are blurred and made fluid through women's bodies. But this reading, I believe, is not possible if we consider the novel in the historical and cultural context of the post-Oslo period. This is the period of confused boundaries, where the borders of Palestine are dangerously blurred. Instead of the borders of sea and river written in the PLO charter, or even the river and the imaginary Green Line of the post-1967 war, now we have a potential Palestine that will be constructed, puzzle-like, from areas with no names, marked only by the letters A, B, and C. The chewing-gum scare I mentioned at the beginning of this essay found an echo among the people because it expressed their anxiety about fluid, porous borders that were constantly shifting and left them confused and vulnerable.[75] Not surprisingly, women's bodies, or in Cynthia Enloe's words, women as "nationalist wombs," are "the most *vulnerable* to defilement and exploitation by oppressive alien rulers; and most susceptible to *assimilation* and cooption by insidious outsiders."[76] And since vulnerability is a constitutive element of sovereignty, the Palestinian Authority, which claimed that through the Oslo agreements it was liberating land and building a state, found in this scare a chance to shore up its faltering legitimacy by assuming the role of guarding sovereign national borders against enemy infiltration. Seen in this context, Khalifeh's novel employs a traditional national discourse about men's and women's sexuality that ends up containing and blunting its otherwise subversive feminist critique of Palestinian society.

Khalifeh's reproduction of some of the fundamental patriarchal metaphors of the hegemonic national narrative is symptomatic of the limitation of the current Palestinian feminist discourse that continues to recycle a nationalist patriarchal ideology regarding women's bodies and sexuality. An example was the slogan inscribed on a banner hanging in several major West Bank cities on the occasion of International Women's Day in 1999. It read: "Woman makes up half of society and gives birth to the other half." Two Palestinian feminists have argued just before the breakout of the Al-Aqsa Intifada that the currently stagnant Palestinian women's movement needs to exploit the moral symbolism of motherhood to better mobilize Palestinian women against the occupation.[77] These slogans are informed by an understandable pragmatism that wants to adapt feminist ideas to a Palestinian context and wants to avoid artificially imposing so-called Western ideas on a culture that has long borne the burden of colonization. But they do so at the cost of leaving unquestioned a conceptual framework that is patriarchal and that plays a constitutive role in shaping both the nation and gender relations within it. Palestinian feminists need to shape a new theoretical discourse that questions these structures. This discourse in turn could help clear the ground for a new literary discourse, one that breaks away from tropes, metaphors, and ideologies that continue to circumscribe women's lives and to prevent them from being full citizens of the nation.

NOTES

[1] According to Sharif Kanaana, legends are "narratives, tales, or stories set in familiar locations in the recent or historical past. They are circulated by word of mouth in contemporary

society and focus on a single episode related to a socially important and controversial theme. The episode is usually presented as true but miraculous, bizarre or otherwise improbable. It exists in multiple forms and is usually recreated with every new telling" (Kanaana, "The Role of Women in Intifada Legends," in Annelies Moors, Toine Van Teeffelen, Sharif Kanaana, and Ilham Abu Ghazaleh, eds., *Discourse and Palestine: Power, Text, and Context* [Amsterdam: Het Sphinsus, 1994], 153–61; quotation from 153). This particular legend appeared in printed form, which gave it a factual dimension. I would like to thank Margaret Yocom for drawing my attention to the "legend" as a narrative genre relevant to this essay.

[2] Virginia Quirke, "Politics—Middle East: Women Look at Their Contribution to the Palestinian Uprising," November 8, 2000, online at www.oneworld.net (June 17, 2002).

[3] A year earlier a similar scare was reported in Egyptian newspapers. For a discussion of that episode see Mai Ghoussoub, "Chewing Gum, Insatiable Women and Foreign Enemies: Male Fears and the Arab Media," in Mai Ghoussoub and Emma Sinclair-Webb, eds., *Imagined Masculinities: Male Identity and Culture in the Modern Middle East* (London: Saqui Books, 2000), 227–35.

[4] See *Al-Ayyam* and *Al-Quds* newspapers in May, June 1997.

[5] Nira Yuval-Davis, *Gender and Nation* (London: Sage, 1998), 26–67. There is now a growing body of literature on gender and nationalism. One interesting question concerns the relation between feminism and nationalism in colonial and postcolonial societies. There are two schools: One argues for the compatibility of the two, showing how in many third world countries, feminism and nationalism were linked in the nineteenth and twentieth centuries and that nationalism and feminism fed each other (see Kumari Jayawardena, *Feminism and Nationalism in the Third World* [London: Zed Books, 1986]). The other argues that things have changed since, and now there is tension between the two, with nationalism trying to subsume feminism and thus no longer playing a progressive role vis-à-vis women's liberation (see Valentine M. Moghadam, ed., *Democratic Reform and the Position of Women in Transitional Economies* [Oxford: Clarendon Press, 1993] and *Gender and National Identity: Women and Politics in Muslim Societies* [London: Zed Books, 1994]). This dichotomy between good nationalism versus bad nationalism, I believe, is in need of serious interrogation.

[6] For feminist scholarship on gender and nationalism see Nira Yuval-Davis, "Gender and Nation," in Rick Wilford and Robert L. Miller, eds., *Women, Ethnicity, and Nationalism: The Politics of Transition* (London: Routledge, 1998), 23–35; Caren Kaplan, Norma Alarcón, and Minoo Moallem, eds., *Between Woman and Nation: Nationalism, Transnational Feminism, and the State* (Durham: Duke University Press, 1999); Wilford and Miller, *Women, Ethnicity, and Nationalism*. For a collection that includes significant discussion of masculinity in relation to gender and nationalism, see Andrew Parker, Mary Russo, Doris Sommer, and Patricia Yaeger, eds., *Nationalisms and Sexualities* (New York: Routledge, 1992).

[7] Ernest Gellner, *Nations and Nationalism* (Ithaca: Cornell University Press, 1983), 57.

[8] Timothy Brennan, "The National Longing for Form," in Homi Bhabha, ed., *Nation and Narration* (New York: Routledge, 1990), 44–70; quotation from 48.

[9] Benedict Anderson, *Imagined Communities: Reflections on the Origin and Spread of Nationalism* (New York: Verso, 1991 [1983]), 27, 36. Mary Layoun argues that nationalism is constructed as a narrative (Mary N. Layoun, "Telling Spaces: Palestinian Women and the Engendering of National Narratives," in Parker, Russo, Sommer, and Yaeger, *Nationalisms and Sexualities*, 407–23; argument on 411). For other discussions of the connection between nationalism and narrative, see Bhabha, *Nation and Narration*.

[10] Aijaz Ahmad contested this claim because it homogenizes third world literature and denies issues of class, race, and gender that are strongly present in this literature. While Ahmad makes a compelling argument, Jameson's emphasis on the centrality of nationalism to third world literature is valid because often in this literature issues of race, gender, and class are entangled with the nationalist question. See "Jameson's Rhetoric of Otherness and the 'National Allegory,'" in Ahmad, *In Theory: Classes, Nations, Literature* (London: Verso, 1992), 95–122.

[11] Edward Said, "Permission to Narrate," in *The Edward Said Reader*, ed. Moustafa Bayoumi and Andrew Rubin (New York: Vintage, 2000), 243–66.

[12] Anton Shammas quoted in Ammiel Alcalay, "1001 Palestinian Nights," *Village Voice*, March 18, 2002.

[13] Leela Gandhi, *Theory: A Critical Introduction* (New York: Columbia University Press, 1998), 152.

[14] Examples of the first category are Yehya Yakhlaf and Liana Badr, both of whom hold official positions in the Palestinian Ministry of Culture; Ghassan Kanafani and Hanan Ashrawi are the most prominent examples of the second category. All Palestinian writers would include themselves in the third group.

[15] I have written about this tendency in Amireh, "Framing Nawal El-Saadawi: Arab Feminism in a Transnational World," *Signs: Journal of Women in Culture and Society* 26.1: 315–428.

[16] Yuval-Davis, "Gender and Nation," 29. She writes, "A figure of a woman, often a mother, symbolizes in many cultures the spirit of collectivity, whether it is Mother Ireland, Mother Russia or Mother India. In the French Revolution its symbol was 'La Patrie,' a figure of a woman giving birth to a baby; and in Cyprus, a weeping woman refugee on roadside posters was the embodiment of the pain and anger of the Greek Cypriot collectivity after the Turkish invasion" (29).

[17] Abu Salma, "I Love You More," in Salma Khadra Jayyusi, ed., *Anthology of Modern Palestinian Literature* (New York: Columbia University Press, 1992), 97.

[18] Mahmoud Darwish, "A Lover from Palestine," in *The Palestinian Wedding: A Bilingual Anthology of Contemporary Palestinian Resistance Poetry*, comp. and trans. A. M. Elmessiri (Washington, DC: Three Continents Press, 1982), 127.

[19] 'Abd al-Latif 'Aql, "Love Palestinian Style," in Elmessiri, *The Palestinian Wedding*, 117–19. This poem has become one of the popular songs by the Palestinian group Sabreen.

[20] Muhammad al As'ad, "A Song," in Jayyusi, *Anthology of Modern Palestinian Literature*, 121.

[21] Samira 'Azzam, "Bread of Sacrifice," in Jayyusi, *Anthology of Modern Palestinian Literature*, 389–99.

[22] For a similar discussion of the wedding as a familiar trope in Palestinian culture, see Mary N. Layoun, *Wedded to the Land? Gender, Boundaries, and Nationalism in Crisis* (Durham: Duke University Press, 2001), 147–48.

[23] Abu Salma, "My Country on Partition Day," in Jayyusi, *Anthology of Modern Palestinian Literature*, 95. Because of the idea that the martyr is a groom whose funeral is his wedding procession a Palestinian mother is urged to ululate in celebration upon hearing the news of the martyrdom of her son.

[24] Rashid Khalidi, *Palestinian Identity: The Construction of Modern National Consciousness* (New York: Columbia University Press, 1997); Issam Nassar, "Khamsoun 'aman 'ala a-Nakba: I'adet al tafkeer fee kitabat tareekh al hadath" [Fifty years since the catastrophe: Rethinking the writing of history], online at the Palestinian Ministry of Information Web site, www.pna .org (January 12, 2003). According to the "Brief History of Palestine: Al Nakba wal Sumud," *Al-Nakba* is the central event. It is the beginning of the narrative; online at www.pna.org (March 18, 2002). This is not to say that Palestinian nationalism was created by 1948 or by the conflict with Zionism in general. As Muhammad Y. Muslih explains, "What Zionism did was provide the Palestinians with a focus for their national struggle. . . . The origins and growth of Palestinian nationalism as a distinctive force . . . can be found in the inter-Arab processes" (delineated in Muslih, *Origins of Palestinian Nationalism* [New York: Columbia University Press, 1988], 217).

[25] Khalidi, *Palestinian Identity*, 195.

[26] Palestine Ministry of Information, "Brief History of Palestine."

[27] The Palestinian groom in Michele Khleife's film *Wedding in Galilee* is impotent. The bride takes her own virginity to avoid scandal. Mary Layoun, in her otherwise insightful discussion of the film, does not recognize the lack of male virility as a trope in Palestinian culture (Layoun, "A Guest at the Wedding: Honor, Memory, and (National) Desire in Michel Khleife's *Wedding in Galilee*," in Kaplan, Alarcón, and Moallem, *Between Woman and Nation*, 92–107).

[28] Ghassan Kanafani, *Men in the Sun and Other Palestinian Stories* (Boulder, CO: Three Continents Press, 1997), 21.

[29] Julie Peteet, "Male Gender and Rituals of Resistance in the Palestinian Intifada: A Cultural Politics of Violence," in Ghoussoub and Sinclair-Webb, *Imagined Masculinities*, 103–26.

[30] Kanafani, *Men in the Sun*, 27, 24–25.

[31] Ibid., 53.

[32] Ibid., 74.

[33] Yasser Arafat, "President Arafat's Speech on the 50th Anniversary of the Palestinian Catastrophe *Al Nakba*," online at the Palestine Ministry of Information Web site, www.pna.com (January 12, 2003).

[34] For the centrality of armed struggle to Palestinian national identity, see Yezid Sayigh, *Armed Struggle and the Search for State: The Palestinian National Movement, 1949–1993* (Washington, DC: Institute for Palestine Studies, 1997).

[35] The majority of politically active Palestinian women worked in popular mobilization. Of the thirty-four Palestinian women interviewed by Amal Kawar for her study *Daughters of Palestine: Leading Women of the Palestinian National Movement*, only four (Laila Khaled, Fatima Bernawi, Eisheh Odeh, and Rasmiyeh Odeh) started as guerrillas, but their fighting careers were brief ([Albany: SUNY Press, 1996], 24).

[36] Kawar, *Daughters of Palestine*, 47. See also the chapter "Feday: Rebirth and Resistance" in Baruch Kimmerling and Joel S. Migdal, *Palestinians: The Making of a People* (Cambridge: Harvard University Press, 1993), 209–39. The full text of the Palestine National Anthem can be found at www.national-anthems.net (April 12, 2003).

[37] Palestine Liberation Organization Charter (in Arabic); online at www.palestineaffairs council.org (March 15, 2002). For a discussion of the concerns the Palestinian women's movement has with the male definition of Palestinian identity as articulated by the PLO charter, see Islah Jad, Penny Johnson, and Rita Giacaman, "Transit Citizens: Gender and Citizenship under the Palestinian Authority," in *Gender and Citizenship in the Middle East*, ed. Suad Joseph (Syracuse: Syracuse University Press, 2000), 143–44.

[38] Mahmoud Darwish, "Mahmoud Darwish's Speech at the Occasion of the *Nakba*" (1998), online at the Palestine Ministry of Information Web site, www.pna.com (January 11, 2003).

[39] Waleed al Halees, "Days in the Life of a Palestinian Boy," in Jayyusi, *Anthology of Modern Palestinian Literature*, 163.

[40] Ibid., 133.

[41] Nira Yuval-Davis, "The Jewish Collectivity and National Reproduction in Israel," in Khamsin Collective, *Women in the Middle East* (London: Zed Books, 1987), 61.

[42] Quoted in Yuval-Davis, *Gender and Nation*, 30.

[43] Tawfiq Zayyad, "Here We Shall Stay," in Jayyusi, *Anthology of Modern Palestinian Literature*, 227–28. Darwish, "Identity Card," in John Mikhail Asfour, ed. and trans., *When the Words Burn: An Anthology of Modern Arabic Poetry, 1945–1987* (Ontario: Cormorant Books, 1988), 199.

[44] According to the Palestinian Central Bureau of Statistics, the fertility rate in the West Bank and Gaza (excluding East Jerusalem) in 1996 was 6.24. It is 5.61 for the West Bank and 7.44 for Gaza (Palestine Central Bureau of Statistics, *The Demographic Survey in the West Bank and Gaza: Preliminary Report* [Ramallah: Palestinian Central Bureau of Statistics, 1996]).

[45] Jad, Johnson, and Giacaman, "Transient Citizens," 153. Yuval-Davis notes, "A common Palestinian saying a few years ago, for instance, was: 'The Israelis beat us at the borders but we beat them in the bedrooms'" (Yuval-Davis, "Gender and Nation," 31). The most recent version of this "procreation machismo" goes like this: "Sharon is losing the demographic war with the Palestinians. What do you expect people locked-up in their homes to do, especially when the power is out and no TV?" (Ghassan Abdallah, "Palestinian Humor: Daily Life under Israeli Occupation," online at www.miftah.org [January 16, 2003]).

[46] Sahar Khalifeh, *Wild Thorns* (London: Al Saqui Books, 1985), 174, 126.

[47] Ghareeb 'Asqalani, "Hunger," in Jayyusi, *Anthology of Modern Palestinian Literature*, 381–88.

[48] Liana Badr, *The Eye of the Mirror*, trans. Samira Kawar (London: Garnet Publishing, 1994), 264.

[49] Geraldine Heng and Janadus Devan, "State Fatherhood: The Politics of Nationalism, Sexuality, and Race in Singapore," in Parker, Russo, Sommer, and Yaeger, *Nationalisms and Sexualities*, 349.

[50] This emphasis on women as producers of the nation or the collectivity is not restricted to Islamic ideology. See Yuval-Davis, *Gender and Nation*. Also it has been a bone of contention

between feminists and Marxists in Nicaragua under the Sandinistas (Moghadam, *Gender and National Identity*, 5).

[51] "The Covenant of the Islamic Resistance Movement (Hamas)," (August 18, 1988), online at MidEast Web Historical Documents, www.mideastweb.org/history.htm (January 14, 2003).

[52] Bassam Jarrar, "Women's Rights or a Clash of Civilization?" *Al-Ayyam*, March 3, 1998.

[53] This first intifada is not to be confused with the ongoing one, which started in September 2000 and is usually referred to by Palestinians as Al-Aqsa Intifada.

[54] Much has been written about the Palestinian women's role in the first intifada. See Islah Abdul Jawwad, "The Evolution of the Political Role of the Palestinian Women's Movement in the Uprising," in *The Palestinians: New Directions*, ed. Michael C. Hudson (Washington, DC: Center for Contemporary Arab Studies, Georgetown University, 1990), 63–76; Rita Giacaman, "Palestinian Women in the Uprising: From Followers to Leaders?" *Journal of Refugees Studies* 2.1 (1989): 1–10; Joost R. Hiltermann, *Behind the Intifada: Labor and Women's Movements in the Occupied Territories* (Princeton: Princeton University Press, 1991); Suha Sabbagh, ed., *Palestinian Women of Gaza and the West Bank* (Bloomington: Indiana University Press, 1998).

[55] Palestinian Ministry of Information, "The Palestinian Declaration of Independence" (1988; in Arabic), online at the Palestinian Ministry of Information Web site, www.pna.org (January 14, 2003).

[56] For examples of other stories or legends about the role of women in the intifada, see Kanaana, "The Role of Women in Intifada Legends." Even when celebrating the heroism of the woman, these legends contain an embarassing if not humiliating moment for the young man. Suha Sabbagh, "Palestinian Women Writers and the Intifada," *Social Text* 22 (1989): 62–78; quotation from 62.

[57] See, for example, the pamphlet issued by Fateh entitled *Nathareyat al Dawa'er al Handaseya* [The theory of geometric circles] and *Abdulla Issa's Al-Masyada* [The trap] and 'Adil 'Amir's novel *Al-Zafirun bi-l-'Ar* [The shamed]. Sexual (and other forms of moral) blackmail to pressure young men and women into collaboration probably was always one of the strategies used by the Israeli occupation. See Salim Tamari, "Eyeless in Judea: Israel's Strategy of Collaborators and Forgeries," *Middle East Report* 164–65 (1990): 39–45. But what concerns me here is the hysteria regarding this phenomenon during the intifada and its cultural meanings and ramifications for gender relations.

[58] This summary is based on several hand-written confessions that I collected through personal contacts while researching this issue in the West Bank in 1997–1998. I would like to thank Al-Najah University students who gave me access to this material.

[59] Lila Abu-Lughod, *Veiled Sentiments: Honor and Poetry in a Bedouin Society* (Berkeley: University of California Press, 1986), 88–90; Edward Said, *After the Last Sky* (Boston: Faber and Faber, 1986), 271.

[60] Sahar Khalifeh, *Bab el-Saha* [The door of the courtyard] (Beirut: Dar al-Adaab, 1990), 63.

[61] Peteet, "Male Gender and Rituals of Resistance," 122 n II. Peteet mentions this aspect of Arab manhood as a way to dismiss or underplay sexuality as a marker of Arab masculinity. Sexuality is largely absent from her discussion of Palestinian masculinity and is only mentioned in the concluding paragraph in her brief discussion of "rape" as a new strategy used by Israeli interrogators "to thwart the meaning and agency of physical violence as rites of passage to masculinity and manhood" (121).

[62] In her novel *The Map of Love*, Ahdaf Soueif presents an Arab hero who is in total control of his sexuality. Sharif Pasha, the Egyptian hero, declares his love to Anna, the English woman, in a letter. During the first meeting between the lovers after that confession, Anna wonders why he didn't show his passion openly before since there were many opportunities for him to do so. He answers, "It took every atom of strength that I had not to pull you into my arms." He adds that he had to keep his hands behind his back because if he "had let them they would have reached out for [you]" ([New York: Anchor Books, 1999], 285). The first sexual contact between the two lovers occurs after the man proves his control over his body on previous occasions.

[63] Rema Hammami, "Women, the Hijab and the Intifada," *Middle East Report* 20.3–4 (1990): 24–31.

[64] Peteet, "Male Gender and Rituals of Resistance," 121.

[65] Khalifeh, *Bab el-Saha*, 219.

[66] One of the "common sense" anthems for activists during the intifada was "Suquot akhlaqi ya'ni suqout amni; i.e., morally questionable = security risk." Ussama Mohammad, personal communication, An Najah University, 1998.

[67] For a rare critical discussion of the Palestinian unforgiving attitude toward "fallen women collaborators," see Muhammad Bayyoumi, *Thaherat Tasfeyat al 'Umala': at-Tareekh wa Juthour al-Azma* [The phenomenon of liquidating collaborators: The history and roots of the crisis] (Palestine: al-Hay'a al-Khayreya, 1994), 157–59. The author criticizes Palestinian culture from a nationalist-Muslim perspective, not a feminist one.

[68] Layoun, "A Guest at the Wedding," 94–95.

[69] Jamal Bannoura, *Intifada* (Ramallah: Dar Al-Shorouq, 1998), 143.

[70] Ibid., 417.

[71] Ibid., 418.

[72] "Al-'Adou Yastahdefu Jame 'atana . . . fal-Nahmeeha" [The enemy targets our universities: Let us protect them]. Statement distributed at An-Najah University and signed by Lajnat al-Taw 'eya wat-Tawjeeh.

[73] Sahar Khalifeh, *Al-Mirath* [The inheritance] (Beirut: Dar al-Adaab, 1997), 316.

[74] The name *Fitna* means beauty but has another meaning that is impossible to ignore in this context. *Fitna* in Muslim discourse also means political and social chaos, the latter often produced by unregulated female sexuality.

[75] Mai Ghoussoub understands the chewing-gum scare in the Egyptian context as an expression of men's fear of women. I obviously believe that in the Palestinian context it is enmeshed with issues of nationalism and sovereignty as well as gender.

[76] Cynthia Enloe, *Bananas, Beaches, and Bases: Making Feminist Sense of International Politics* (Berkeley: University of California Press, 1989), 54.

[77] Rima Hamami and Eileen Kuttab, "The Palestinian Women's Movement: Strategies Towards Freedom and Democracy," *News from Within* 15.4 (1999): 1–7.

AFTERWORD

I became interested in writing this essay during the first Palestinian intifada, which broke out in 1987 while I was a graduate student in Boston. With the rest of the world, I watched with fascination as my countrywomen participated in a civil disobedience movement to protest twenty years of Israeli occupation of the West Bank and Gaza. They took to the streets as stone throwers and demonstrators, and they participated in neighborhood committees whose responsibilities included offering alternative schooling to children, planting victory gardens, distributing food supplies, and collecting trash. However, the most dominant female figure to emerge during this period was that of the women using their bodies in public space to shield and rescue young stone throwers, most of whom were male. In doing so, these bodies were disobedient, posing a challenge to armed Israeli soldiers and to the traditional gender dynamics of Palestinian society. Much feminist literature was written about the new role these women were assuming and how they were altering gender relations in Palestinian society itself.

That intifada slowed its pace and eventually came to a halt in 1993, with the signing of the American-brokered Oslo Peace Agreements between Israel and the Palestinians. Soon afterward, I moved back to the West Bank and could observe firsthand the gender dynamics in the society in which I grew up. The dominant discourse, now disseminated by a Palestinian National Authority that was the nucleus of a future Palestinian state, did not seem to deviate from the traditional national narrative when it came to women and men, particularly the uses of their bodies: men were the fighters and liberators and women were the providers of sons. In fact, if there was a change, it was signaling a more conservative attitude now that the Palestinian state seemed within reach. This is when I started doing some fieldwork about the intifada, looking mainly at the way cultural texts engage issues of gender, nationalism, and sexuality. I was particularly interested in the collaboration hysteria that played a crucial role in moving women out of the streets back to the home, thus minimizing their visible role in the uprising. This shift for the women coincided with the tendency to militarize the intifada, which became increasingly dominated by groups of armed youth. The essay that resulted from that work, which is included here, showed that sexuality and ideas of femininity and masculinity were crucial to the Palestinian national narrative. It also showed that attempts to subvert that dominant discourse meant subverting views of male and female bodies and their relation to the homeland. I concluded by showing that while feminist national discourse had the potential to challenge the dominant male national narrative, it also was complicit with it.

While I was writing that essay, another intifada broke out. Unlike the first one, which took the form of civil disobedience with the participation of many segments of Palestinian society, the al-Aqsa intifada became quickly militarized and involved mostly young men. Suicide bombings were used, and the suicide bomber, not the stone thrower, emerged as the representative action figure of this intifada, especially in the eyes of the world. Although women's participation was much more curtailed, there were about nine women suicide bombers. The figure of the female suicide bomber attracted much attention both in the West and the Arab world. She seemed to force new questions about women's relation to nationalism and violence. My most recent work, which is a continuation of this essay, has focused on this figure and the impact it has had on gender relations in Palestinian society. Does this figure challenge in any way the national conception of women's bodies? How does this explosive body differ in its cultural and political impact from that of the male body engaged in the same violent act? I have recently argued that as a consequence of the militarization of Palestinian society, women's participation in suicide bombings in fact reinforces some of the most traditional categories of femininity and masculinity.

~ 2004 ~

Good Sex, Bad Sex: Women and Intimacy in Early Modern Spain

LISA VOLLENDORF

NEARLY THREE DECADES have passed since Foucault assumed the onerous writing of a history of sexuality, and sex continues to intrigue us at the scholarly, popular, and, indeed, personal levels. In *The History of Sexuality* Foucault spoke of frank attitudes toward sexuality and a relatively fluid model of intimacy, making few distinctions between public and private before the eighteenth century. Georges Duby, Philippe Ariès, Chartier, and their collaborators further delved into intimate matters in their five-volume series, *A History of Private Life*, building their collection around the basic assertion that, as societies changed and modern nation-states solidified, private thought, action, and emotion emerged as the bedrock of social interaction and personal identity. *A History of Private Life* employs varied textual, material, and artistic artifacts, providing passage into the intimacies of interaction and identity. Thus we read about memoirs, furnishings, plastic arts, and boudoirs in volume three, *The Passions of the Renaissance*. These glimpses into individuals' private worlds set the stage for understanding the histories of sexuality and intimacy yet provided little direct evidence of women and others whose lives differed from those of men of the dominant classes.

Recent research has extended the work of Foucault, Duby, and Ariès. As Thomas Laqueur's *Solitary Sex: A Cultural History of Masturbation* demonstrates, issues that used to be considered inaccessible have been revisited in the past decade. In terms of gender analysis, scholars have turned their attention to topics as diverse as friendship, desire, motherhood, and breastfeeding.[1] Scholars of early modern Spain have found that women's texts contain rich information about friendship, sexuality, and other intimate matters. María de Zayas, Mariana de Carvajal, Ana Caro, and their seventeenth-century cohort unapologetically built plots around female friendship and desire. Biographies of women religious frequently construct narratives that reject sexuality and express distaste for sex. Inquisition trials contain more lurid information and accusations about defendants' sexual practices, including masturbation, pollution (i.e., orgasm), and illicit affairs. The variety and frequency with which eroticism and desire appear in women's texts obligate us to include multitudinous attitudes and behaviors in our considerations of sexuality.

An example of the layered information found in texts from the period appears in the statements of Maria del Caño, wife of the Moorish hermaphrodite Eleno/a de Céspedes. In the 1580s, the Inquisition put Céspedes on trial for bigamy and sorcery. The trial hinged on determining the sex of the defendant. When Céspedes's wife testified, she was asked numerous questions about the couple's sexual practices. When asked whether she had touched her husband's shameful parts, Caño responded that "[ella] había oído decir que [él] tenía dos sexos ansí por esto como por haber oído a otras mujeres que se gozaban con sus maridos alguna libertad tenía ésta gana y lo procuraba con cuidado de tentarle sus partes de hombre por ver qué cosa era [. . .]."[2] In mentioning her unsuccessful attempt to touch her husband, she revealed that women did indeed discuss sexuality openly. Caño simultaneously let inquisitors know that she felt similar desire and tried to act on that desire. Her simple answer to one question reveals much about sexuality and intimacy in Spain, providing glimpses into the thoughts, actions, and everyday lives of women.

As these examples suggest, texts by and about women from the sixteenth and seventeenth centuries have opened up the most intimate matters for our consideration. One surprising aspect of Spanish women's texts from the period is the frequent mention of sexuality. The dearth of women's writing before the sixteenth century makes it difficult to know how early modern women's views on sex differed from previous eras. Possibly women in western Europe traditionally had liberal views toward sexual matters. Preceding the advent of the printing press and the Renaissance emphasis on the individual, few documents or social circumstances would have allowed for the expression or recording of such views. The mid-sixteenth century Council of Trent impacted discourses surrounding sexuality enormously: Post-Tridentine insistence on full confession, the extension of the Inquisition's power to try clergy for solicitation, and heightened regulation of marriage rituals brought sexual details to public and Inquisitorial attention. Without religious biographies, fiction, letters, and Inquisition or legal documents to guide us, we lack direct access to people's experiences of these intimate matters.

While a single explanation for frequent discussions of sex in early modern women's texts might be hard to pinpoint, Foucault's assertion about open treatment of sexuality in the early modern period certainly applies in the Spanish context to women as well as to men. Indeed, what surprises readers today is not merely the inclusion of sexual details, but their explicit nature in prose fiction, trial records, spiritual biographies, and other texts. Detailed treatments of sex and the body provide opportunities to determine which topics women deemed appropriate for public and private consumption.

By drawing on varied sources, we can compare the views expressed by those of various class, ethnic, and religious backgrounds. Context of production must also be considered when deciphering issues of intimacy and sexuality. Women answering inquisitors' or confessors' questions about sex produced different discourses from those writing fiction or memoirs. Statements made by defendants, autobiographers, and even literary characters cannot be taken at face value: properly deciphering these discourses requires theoretical engagement with each text and its context. Scholars have yet to articulate a fully developed methodology of sexual history that attends to these questions of difference.

By identifying women's strategies for discussing matters of sexuality and intimacy, this essay provides a starting point for that methodology. Women across class and ethnic lines used similar strategies for self-authorization. Notably, early modern women relied on cultural ideologies related to motherhood, menstruation, and sexuality to gain legitimacy in numerous contexts. The repetition of such legitimizing strategies in fictional texts, spiritual biographies, and Inquisition cases confirms the link between sexuality and authority, showing that women appropriated dominant beliefs about their sex and used them for personal and political advantage. The evidence of such strategies among women of varying backgrounds suggests that gender was a sufficiently decisive category of identity that women, notwithstanding class and ethnic lines, often experienced early modern Spanish culture in similar ways. Consideration of gender experienced through the lens of sexuality facilitates laying the foundations for a more complete history of women and intimacy in the Hispanic world.

I. Attitudes toward Sex

Legal and other historical sources provide basic information about sexuality and gender relations. As James Casey summarizes in *Early Modern Spain: A Social History*, studies of parish records demonstrate that Spaniards in the sixteenth and seventeenth centuries often married earlier than some European counterparts: the average age of marriage was approximately twenty-two, with men marrying slightly later than women. Spanish women enjoyed property rights that others in Europe did not. Dowry rights surpassed those of women in other nations, for example (27–28; 201–02). Moreover, women participated in the public sphere more than previously believed. In *Gender and Disorder in Early Modern Seville*, Mary Elizabeth Perry shows that women's participation in Seville's labor force included working in all-female businesses. Widows of guild members in that port city inherited shops, tools, and even the guild membership of their deceased husbands (15–17).

This position of relative privilege had its limits. Women had to rely on men to represent them in the legal realm. If widows in Seville remarried, they lost their shops and guild memberships. Throughout Spain, women could sign contracts, but their signatures often were discounted. Early modern law stated that daughters could not be forced to marry against their will, but in practice parents often dictated the choice of partner for their daughters. Perhaps more than any other single factor, Fernando and Isabel's push for religious and ethnic homogeneity had negative repercussions for women, eventually leading to implementation in the mid-sixteenth century of the *limpieza de sangre* statutes.

Of course, anxiety over female sexuality preceded the rise of the Spanish nation. David Nirenberg shows that concern about interfaith sexuality had been building since the massacres and mass conversions of Jews in 1391. Subsequent intensification of sexual control was articulated in the fourteenth century, when Christian leaders began to segregate Jews from Christians and, by the 1440s, to speak of descendants of converts as different from "natural" Christians (Nirenberg 1088–92). Rife with anti-semitism, these attitudes maintained their hold on certain thinkers and politicians over the next 150 years, culminating with the codification of sexual and racial anxieties in the *limpieza* statutes, which restricted those of purportedly impure genetic make-up, prohibiting so-called *nuevos cristianos* from holding political office or enjoying other privileges of the old Christians.

By tying ethnicity to blood lines, the statutes provided further justification for regulating female sexuality. Family honor now rested on female chastity more than ever before. Indeed, a family's very survival and status depended upon the ability to prove untainted Catholic heritage. Laws regulating prostitution and edicts prohibiting use of the veil speak to anxieties about female sexuality that resulted from increasing emphasis on ethnic (i.e., Catholic) purity in the sixteenth century. The combination of *limpieza* with the tightening of restrictions on spiritual expression in Counter-Reformation Spain adversely affected women. Marriage, sexuality, and spirituality were governed tightly, provoking increased vigilance of daughters, wives, widows, and nuns.[3]

As suggested, the connection between women and their bodies emerges as one key to understanding intimacy in Counter-Reformation Spain. Again, the phenomenon was not entirely new. Nirenberg terms the role assigned to prostitutes in medieval times the "incarnation of the sexual boundary between religions" (1076). In late medieval and early modern periods, this role was extended to women in general. The *limpieza de sangre* statutes profoundly impacted gender relations, reinforcing the dominant view of women as vessels of man's seed and renewing pressure on women to present themselves as honorable and chaste.

Rigid definitions of femininity appeared in many well-known texts, including Luis Vives's *Instrucción de la mujer cristiana* and Luis de León's *La perfecta casada*. Women, associated with the home's domestic space, were expected to be obedient and silent. The only acceptable alternative to the life path of an obedient daughter becoming an obedient wife was religious life, where women—safely enclosed in convents—were protected and guided by male clerics and a paternalistic church. Dominant models of femininity within and outside the church viewed women as requiring protection to keep them from the dangers of a predatory world and from their own proclivity to disobedience.

Canonical Golden Age literature teems with examples of the dangers of female sexuality. Alternately critical and supportive of the policing of sexuality, many literary texts paint an overly anxious society. Male authors highlight and even criticize the extent to which masculinity and honor were imbricated in female chastity and containment. Playwrights including Lope and Calderón depicted female characters as victims of suspicious, hypocritical husbands in the wife-murder plays. Picaresque tales, chivalric novels, and *Don Quijote* depict the importance of legitimacy and lineage.

Until recently, little was known about women's perspectives on issues related to sexuality and social control. Repeated regulations concerning female clothing suggest that women frequently disobeyed rules governing their attire. Perry's research on gender in Seville expands a growing body of scholarship on women's active roles in the public sphere. Recent attention to convents has yielded abundant information about active, engaged women who thrived in religious houses.

Nonetheless, limitations still exist in our understanding of this formative period. Until the feminist writings of Santa Teresa, María de Zayas, and Sor Juana Inés de la Cruz were incorporated into the canon, scholars of early modern Spain and colonial Latin America relied on male-authored texts almost exclusively for their understanding of contemporaneous sexual politics. We now know that Zayas's direct engagement with physical and psychological domestic abuse offers a unique perspective on gender relations. Likewise, Sor Juana's forthright accusation of male hypocrisy in such texts as "Hombres necios" and *La respuesta* provides a counterpoint to an otherwise all-male canon. Unprecedented access to more nuns' texts than ever before opens up a world wherein nuns acted as spiritual and moral advisors to their sisters and to women beyond convent walls.[4]

Notwithstanding the incorporation of a handful of early modern women's texts, our knowledge of sexuality and anxiety in Inquisitional Spain remains extremely limited. That women disobeyed prohibitions on certain kinds of clothing does not tell us fully what they thought about such prohibitions. That women acted on their own behalf as guild members and seamstresses does not tell us how they managed to survive in the public sphere in a society that mandated their silence and enclosure. There are limits to what can be known about women's history without returning to the archives to rescue the hundreds, if not thousands, of women's voices recorded in texts as far-ranging as Inquisition depositions, spiritual auto/biographies, letters, poetry, and fiction.

Documents representing different arenas of textual production—the convent, the book market, and Inquisition tribunals—capture the revelatory potential of early modern women's words. From the religious context came *Idea de perfección*, a mixed-genre text recounting the life story of Sor Catalina de Jesús y San Francisco (1639–77).[5] Written in 1693 by Sor Catalina's son, Padre Juan Bernique, *Idea de perfección* blends spiritual biography and autobiography. The son, himself a priest, constructs a narrative that initially appears to coincide with standard hagiography. As an author controlling the representation of his mother's biography, he tries to present a seamless story of sanctity and piety for instructing others and glorifying his mother's memory. The imperatives of hagiography clash with the complex psychological challenges confronted by this priest-turned-author as he takes readers on a journey through his mother's life.

The psychological complexity of both mother and son in *Idea de perfección* directly relates to issues of sexuality and intimacy. The narration of Catalina Bernique's journey to becoming Sor Catalina develops these issues with varying degrees of self-consciousness. As *Idea de perfección* tells it, the young Catalina's family forced her to marry against her will while she was in her teens. Catalina disliked marriage and sex so intensely that she prayed for her husband's death. One month later, he died. Rejecting familial pressure to re-marry, Catalina Bernique abandoned her role as mother of three and entered a third-order Franciscan convent, where she lived the rest of her life as a religious leader.

Like many religious women, Catalina de Jesús wrote at least two versions of her life story (her *vida*), which she later burned. She also wrote many letters to her son, whom she asked to write her biography. Accordingly, Bernique tells us that he reconstructed his mother's life story based on the letters and *vidas*. The biography allegedly quotes the subject's own documents, with her words set in italics to distinguish them from the son/narrator's. The combined auto/biography does not avoid uncomfortable issues centering upon Catalina's dislike of marriage and motherhood. Indeed, Bernique includes many quotes revealing Sor Catalina's supreme dislike of the sexual aspects of her secular life.

The narrative of the Berniques' marriage exemplifies the prominent role of sexuality in religious hagiography. For instance, Sor Catalina wrote about her teen years, bluntly assessing her displeasure at the prospect of marriage:

> *Conjuráronse contra mí todas las criaturas y todos los medios que se pueden pensar para que esto [el matrimonio] se consiguiese. Entraba con tal disgusto en el matrimonio y con tanto aborrecimiento, que no puedo decir con verdad de adónde me venía porque los deseos y propósitos que antes tuve de guardar castidad y ser religiosa los tenía muy olvidados. Diéronme unas calenturas no sé si certifiqué fueron de pena.* (Bernique 19)

Such lamentations about married life resonate with other biographies of women religious. Indeed, negative attitudes toward secular marriage constitute one of the many formulas of female hagiographical writing. This formulaic aspect makes it impossible for modern readers to decipher the extent to which the rejection of secular marriage resulted from Sor Catalina's desire, in her words, to "guardar castidad y ser religiosa." The possibility exists, for example, that such details were included to convince readers and the Catholic community of Sor Catalina's destiny for religious life.

Regardless of the motivations of biographer and autobiographer, Sor Catalina's numerous articulations of her disdain for sex and marriage serve the purpose of reconstructing a history of intimacy. Sor Catalina offers various tidbits about the difficulties of life with Bernique, which she describes as pain, suffering, and hatred (i.e., "ahogos," "trabajos," and "aborrecimiento al marido" [26]). She states outright her revulsion to sex: "*Valióme para todas estas ocasiones el natural, que su Magestad me había dado, que aborrecía todo lo que era contrario a la virtud de la castidad*" (26). These emphatic rejections of sexuality contribute to a portrait of chastity and piety and reveal connections between physical and psychological health, as evidenced by the fevers suffered by the young Catalina upon her marriage to Bernique. Besides evincing the young woman's piety, her strong emotions and physical illness reveal high levels of sexual anxiety.

Many religious biographies include similarly anxious attitudes toward sexuality. *Vidas* constitute a large number of the texts by and about historical women in the early modern period. This largely-unstudied corpus provides many opportunities for examining strategies used by women religious and their male biographers to deal with the challenges of the sexual self. The dangerous physical repercussions of sexuality, such as the fevers mentioned by Sor Catalina, echo many depictions of female literary characters punished for their perceived promiscuity. In literature as in life, female chastity was rewarded by the dominant Catholic culture. Not all representations of female sexuality were negative. As Teresa Soufas's *Dramas of Distinction: A Study of Plays by Golden Age Women* suggests, many women from seventeenth-century Spain wrote literature that depicted strong female characters wholly capable of articulating and achieving their desire. Admittedly the most famous author of the period, María de Zayas (1590—?), filled her *Novelas amorosas y ejemplares* (1637) and her *Desengaños amorosos* (1647) with numerous warnings about the dangers of male/female relationships. Yet she also included poignant examples of women who defined their own desire and strove to avenge sexual wrongs against them.

Moreover, Zayas portrayed intimate female friendship as a counterpoint to the violence and *desengaño* often experienced in courtship and marriage. Notably, Zayas's ailing protagonist Lisis finds such solace in the companionship of her slave, Zelima, that she eventually recovers from her illness. The revelation of Zelima's identity (as the noblewoman Isabel) and story (of rape and subsequent slavery) strengthens the bond between the women. At the end of the *Desengaños*, Lisis announces her intention to follow Isabel's example and enter the convent. The scene in which Lisis rejects marriage and takes the hands of her two friends, Isabel and Estefanía, reinforces the message that alliances among (upper-class) women and retreat to the convent represent the best self-defense against a misogynist culture.

The ending of the *Desengaños* ranks among the most remarkable examples of female friendship in Golden Age literature. Zayas's endorsement of female homoerotic desire constitutes an equally striking representation of women's intimacy. In "Amar sólo por vencer," Esteban disguises himself as a handmaid (Estefanía) in order to gain entry into a young woman's house. Esteban uses his disguise to become part of the young woman's private circle. Expressing love toward Laurela at every chance, Esteban/Estefanía openly defends female same-sex love: "(S)upuesto que el alma es toda una en varón y en la hembra, no se me da más ser hombre que mujer; que las almas no son hombres ni mujeres, y el verdadero amor en el alma está, que no en el cuerpo; y el que amare el cuerpo con el cuerpo, no puede decir que es amor, sino apetito [. . .]" (317). This statement has received much critical attention, given its forthright endorsement of women's homoeroticism. It figures among the few examples in prose fiction of theatrical homoerotic encounters frequent between cross-dressed characters on stage.

Unlike the stage, where audience reaction remains an unknown factor, Zayas's prose provides a built-in response to the homoerotic encounter, as other characters witness the flirtatious behavior and hear the statement spoken in Esteban/Estefanía's defense of same-sex love, yet make no condemnation: family members and their servants convey little more than curiosity and mild mockery at the new handmaid's desire for Laurela. Eroticism only turns dangerous when Esteban reveals his true sex. As the Spanish state confirmed with the *limpieza de sangre* statutes, the risks of heteroeroticism related to familial honor, status, and even survival. Zayas's fictional Laurela suffers the consequences of these risks when, after having sex with Esteban, she is killed by vengeful family members.

By contrasting bucolic homoerotic exchanges with the dangers of male-female desire, María de Zayas suggests fascinating possibilities of female-female intimacy. Had Laurela been punished for expressing same-sex desire, the moral of the story would be very different. Unlike the vilification of male sodomy depicted in Zayas's "Mal presagio casar lejos," the endorsement of female homoeroticism communicates an accepting attitude toward women's desire for each other. Reflecting views that male sodomy mis-used semen for non-reproductive practices, Zayas's condemnation of male homosexuality nonetheless stands in stark contrast to her positive valoration of women's love for each other.[6]

Plays written by Zayas and her cohort also validate women's expressions of desire. Ana Caro's *Valor, agravio y mujer* depicts a female protagonist's struggle to win back the man who wronged her. Zayas's only known play, *La traición en la amistad*, also portrays women who seek to satisfy their own desire and right the wrongs done to them. All of the plays in Soufas's *Women's Acts*, comprising five women playwrights' texts, focus on female desire. The woman-centered worlds of these and other authors exhibit common concern with voicing women's experiences vis-à-vis sexuality and gender relations in early modern Spain. These authors portray relationships with men as variously problematic and rewarding. Female friendship, too, provides solace as well as competition. Taken as a corpus, female-authored prose and drama of the seventeenth century offer many opportunities for analysis of representations of women's issues.[7]

Just as women playwrights depicted various attitudes toward intimacy, Sor Catalina de Jesús and María de Zayas expressed differing attitudes toward female sexuality. Juan Bernique's inclusion of his mother's expressions of disgust toward marriage and sex responds to his desire to represent an idealized religious figure untainted by a sexual past. Seeking to justify his mother's sexual past but also her rejection of marriage, Juan Bernique walked a fine line in *Idea de perfección*. This balancing act includes unusually explicit information about one woman's rejection of sexuality. In a very different balancing act between orthodoxy and heterodoxy, María de Zayas wrote into her texts an endorsement of female-female desire. Remaining within the realm of the acceptable, Zayas stripped that desire of its physical components, presenting it as different from bodily love, or pure *apetito*, in Esteban/Estefanía's words. The extraordinarily different depictions of sexuality in *Idea de perfección* and "Amar sólo por vencer" reflect widely varying attitudes and strategies of representation in women's texts.

II. Women and Intimacy

The texts of Sor Catalina and María de Zayas reveal attitudes toward sexuality in the realms of courtship and marriage. An overt defense of intimacy in a specifically religious context appears in the Inquisition case of Teresa Valle de la Cerda. Born in the late 1500s, Valle founded a convent in 1623 and subsequently became its abbess. Soon afterward, members of the Benedictine monastery of San Plácido came under Inquisitorial fire for their unusual spiritual practices.[8] Isabel Barbeito Carneiro's edition of excerpts from Valle's trial record, letters, and autobiographical *memoriales* portrays a woman struggling to maintain her dignity and uphold her beliefs while attempting to avoid further inquisitorial persecution. Valle's ordeal with the Inquisition lasted several years, during which other nuns in her convent were tried by the Holy Office. Despite the difficult circumstances and high stakes that Valle and others faced for charges of prophesy and demonic possession, the abbess repeatedly defended physical intimacy between nuns and priests.

In several autobiographical statements (*memoriales*) written for the tribunal between Valle's arrest in 1629 and her exoneration in 1637, she justified and explained several spiritual practices that had come under inquisitorial suspicion. Over time, the *memoriales* shifted the blame from the nuns to the convent advisor, Padre Francisco García Calderón, a shift compatible with the Inquisition's casting of blame on García, who eventually bore the blame for the convent's "charismatic" Catholicism. Valle's transition from defending to blaming García indicates a politically astute mind at work. Moreover, her defense of nun-confessor physical intimacy remains a fascinating example of one woman's approach to intimate matters.

As abbess and founder of the convent, Valle occupied a different position from other nuns who, during their audiences with the tribunal, spoke ill of the abbess and her faulty leadership. During much of the trial, Valle adopted protective, rather than accusatory, attitudes toward her charges. In an early *memorial* (from 11 June 1629), Valle defended the entire convent, noting that nobody thought the hugs and kisses between priests and nuns dangerous, "Y ansí, los consentí con el Padre fray Francisco, teniéndole en lugar de padre y estando tan segura de su santidad como tengo dicho" (177). Here Valle used the Church's familial language to describe relationships between confessors and nuns. Her terminology was misleading, given the accusations' sexual implications.

Navigating the difficult territory of sex, Valle emphatically denied ever receiving kisses on the mouth from priests or anybody else, "por el grande peligro que tienen [los besos] de deshonestidad" (177). She repeatedly defended touching and described as unfounded and ill-motivated any testimony from nuns who claimed they were sexually harassed. She alluded particularly to others' jealousy, stemming from the confessor's predilection for Valle: "En muchas, muy grandes sentimientos de que no les hiciera muchas caricias, y parecerles que las hacía a las demás y a ellas no" (176).

Alleged demonic possession and unorthodox sexual practices occupied center stage in this case, and Valle responded to all such accusations in her *memoriales*. Describing the hand-holding, caressing, and kissing in the convent, she defended these practices along with her own habit of requesting that the confessor give his chewed food to her during meal times (248). Valle ultimately deemed all such physical intimacies diabolical, suggesting that after many attempts at justification, she eventually complied with the Inquisition's desire for renunciation and penitence. Interestingly, in the final *memorial* Valle did not renounce the food-chewing behavior completely. In this document from 1637, which Barbeito Carneiro calls the *memorial decisivo* because it precipitated Valle's exoneration, the nun described the curative powers of food-sharing. Yet, in an apparently conciliatory gesture, she added that the devil, attempting to win her over, could have been responsible for the cures (248).

On the local level, Valle's numerous descriptions of intimate behaviors between nuns and priests help us glean insight into the behaviors and customs of one religious house. As with many Illuminist and other non-dominant Christian groups then in Spain, the San Plácido Inquisition trial records evoke a highly-charged environment in which sexual expression informed spiritual practice. Unlike the sublimation of sexuality in mainstream Counter-Reformation Catholicism, convents often created opportunities for a comparatively expressive, open role for sex and intimacy. Indeed, monastic women frequently expressed awareness of the dangers of special friendships in convents, as exemplified by nuns' repeated references to this issue.[9]

Explicit discussions of intimacy in the trial record of Valle de la Cerda open up the question of authority and power between priests and nuns and, more generally, between men and women. As the trials progressed, Valle increasingly positioned herself as a nun duped by a confessor, a woman duped by a man. Yet the authority she enjoyed as a well-connected upper-class woman, founder and abbess of the convent, clearly put her in a position of power. Teresa Valle de la Cerda facilitated with the male clergy a different kind of Catholicism in which men and women had more access to knowledge and to each other than the church hierarchy usually would permit. The liberal views toward intimacy found in this convent and among other religious groups throughout the era point to women's role in forging models for interpersonal relationships that bypassed restrictions of the dominant culture.

III. Authority and Femininity

Texts by Sor Catalina, María de Zayas, and Teresa Valle de la Cerda advocated distinct models of femininity that shared an emphasis on female autonomy. The narrative about Sor Catalina, for example, attempted to justify the nun's unpopular decision to leave several children behind and seek fulfillment in religious life. Similarly, Zayas and Valle de la Cerda challenged traditional norms of femininity by writing texts that endorsed practices condemned by the dominant culture.

All three women questioned and even rejected the dominant model of femininity that demanded female silence, enclosure, and containment. But with what authority did they make such a move? The roles played by each individual in her respective community—as mother, nun, writer, for example—accorded women a certain authority. The challenges each put to the dominant culture related specifically to autonomy and, more particularly, sexual autonomy, thus leading us to consider the strategies used by women to seek authorization in a society that accorded them little authority.

The link between the sexual self and the independent self is undeniable among early modern Spanish women for whom we have written records and texts. Expanding textual research enhances access to women's thoughts, behaviors, and words, revealing how women adapted dominant views toward femininity to their own purposes. Female defendants in Inquisition trials frequently drew attention to their femininity to justify their ignorance, as did Teresa Valle de la Cerda or the prophet Lucrecia de León, the subject of Richard Kagan's *Lucrecia's Dreams*. Like Santa Teresa de Jesús, whose brilliantly simple writing style allowed her to write complex theological texts, women of all social classes and ethnic backgrounds often used non-threatening, subordinate postures to their advantage.

The prominent role given to female bodily experience by writers as diverse as María de Zayas, Sor Catalina de Jesús, and Teresa Valle de la Cerda suggests that women often had an acute awareness of their being seen first and foremost as bodily vessels. This awareness provided a point of departure for legitimization in a climate that denigrated women. Zayas used this awareness to her advantage when writing for a public inexperienced in reading women's texts: she foregrounded her gender, announcing it in her preface. Her novellas frequently portrayed the physical consequences of women's subordination, illuminating a hypocritical cultural system that left her sisters exposed to exploitation and abuse.

Sor Catalina and her son collaborated in a life narrative that also responded to dominant ideologies about women's physical selves. The narrative of Sor Catalina's life aimed to sanitize sexual experience by detailing the physical and psychological illnesses that sexuality caused the young wife. Contrarily, when facing inquisitional disapproval, Teresa Valle de la Cerda continued to defend physical intimacies between nuns and priests. The nun's emphasis on the calming, curative effects of such intimacies flew in the face of church orthodoxy precisely because Valle de la Cerda embraced, rather than rejected, the sexuality of the women who had entered her convent.

Valle's trial record thus captures a fundamental paradox of early modern Spanish society. Women were viewed as inherently sexual beings, yet were not supposed to act on that sexuality. Valle de la Cerda and many other religious women subverted this paradoxical outlook by embracing the physical in the name of spiritual fulfillment. Close ties between femininity and sexuality clarify women's reliance on the physical self as a source of authority.

The connection between femininity and sexuality helps us understand why one merchant-class defendant, tried for Judaizing in 1650, attempted to avoid torture by telling inquisitors that she had her period ("el mal de las mujeres"). Invoking taboos about menstruation and women's bodily difference, the defendant attempted (unsuccessfully) to convince the men not to touch her bleeding body. Like many other women whose words come down to us through archival sources, the defendant called on the authority—and the attendant mystery and idealization—accorded the female body in early modern Spanish society. Other female witnesses and defendants similarly tried to use their difference—as women—to convince male inquisitors of their innocence. Some mentioned both their sexual inexperience and their desire for sexual knowledge, reflecting again the conflicting impulses facing women, who had to be knowledgeable but always seem innocent.[10]

Catalina de Jesús y San Francisco, María de Zayas y Sotomayor, and Teresa Valle de la Cerda lived at almost precisely the same time. As members of the privileged class, they had access to literacy, which few in their society enjoyed.

While we cannot speak to the similarities between their experiences beyond these commonalities, textual records suggest that these women were highly concerned with questions of female sexuality. Sor Catalina expressed rejection of her role as wife and mother in letters and other autobiographical texts. Zayas used fiction to explore the repressive consequences of women's secondary status. Her texts also examined the potential for positive relationships between women as friends and, in one brief instance in "Amar sólo por vencer," as lovers. Teresa Valle helped create a convent culture that encouraged intimacies between nuns and confessors. Insofar as these women used the written word to defend unorthodox beliefs about femininity and sexuality, all figure among those whose stories belong to the still unwritten history of intimacy.

As more historical records are studied, we better understand the powerful influence of gender on women of all class and ethnic backgrounds. Allyson Poska's research on Galician peasants who defied prohibitions on extramarital affairs and bigamy, for instance, recalls that certain cultural practices considered legitimate at the local level conflicted with dominant cultural proscriptions. Another powerful example of the role played by class in the early modern period arises from research on female mystics and demonic possession that underscores a class distinction whereby upper-class women were more often considered legitimate mystics or visionaries than their lower-class counterparts.[11] Similarly, lower-class female defendants in sorcery trials often discussed their work as legitimate and beneficial to the women who hired them. Accused sorceresses invoked their attempts to repair broken relationships, improve sexual performance, or stop violent behavior without apology or a sense of wrongdoing.[12] The attitudes of witchcraft defendants and Galician peasants augment our understanding of sexual practices among different groups in Spanish society. Likewise, Perry's latest book, *The Handless Maiden: Moriscos and the Politics of Religion in Early Modern Spain*, traces the intersections of gender and class with religion and minority status. Such scholarship highlights the crucial fact that class, ethnicity, religion, and other markers of identity influenced women's interactions with early modern Spanish society.

The textual record suggests powerful connections among women's experiences while also reminding us of the need to consider regional, class, and other variations on the experience of gender in early modern Spain. Literature, Inquisition records, and convent documents help fill the gaps of a history still dominated by the voices of male politicians, authors, and clerics. The examples of Sor Catalina de Jesús, María de Zayas, and Teresa Valle de la Cerda confirm that women had strong opinions about sexuality that, at times, differed significantly from the cultural norm. Inquisition records of women from the merchant and lower classes suggest, too, that women shared information about sexual practices among themselves and relied on each other for advice and guidance in intimate matters. Women of different backgrounds frequently used their femininity as a source of authority when seeking to legitimize their voices in a variety of contexts. Deciphering the particularities of the imbrication of sexuality with femininity and authority requires examining such differences.

Fiction, biographies, and Inquisition records confirm that women in early modern Spain recorded their views on good sex, bad sex, and everything in between.

María del Caño's reference to her friends' discussions of sex finds its complement in Zayas's fictional representations of female same-sex love. Catalina de Jesús's rejection of sex in marriage finds a counterpoint in Valle's embrace of sexuality in the convent. Such texts reveal that women spoke to confessors and inquisitors about intimate matters and also discussed similar topics with the public and with each other. A complete history of female intimacy will consider the complex stories of these and other women who weighed in on the interworkings of gender and sexuality in early modern Spain.

NOTES

This article is an outgrowth of a book project on *The Lives of Women: A New History of Inquisitional Spain*. Generous research support has been provided by The Monticello College Foundation Fellowship; The Newberry Library; an Ahmanson-Getty Postdoctoral Fellowship from UCLA's Clark Library and Center for 17th and 18th Century Studies; and numerous grants from Wayne State University's research funds and Humanities Center. I thank Barbara Simerka and Alison Weber for their generous criticism of earlier drafts.

[1] One example of such revisionism appears in recent studies on female same-sex desire. See Bernadette Brooten, *Love Between Women: Early Christian Responses to Female Homoeroticism*; and Sherry Velasco, *The Lieutenant Nun. Transgenderism, Lesbian Desire, and Catalina de Erauso*. For an overview, see Traub, "The Rewards of Lesbian History," or her book, *The Renaissance of Lesbianism in Early Modern England*.

[2] The Céspedes record lacks regular folio numbers, but this quote appears in the third section on folio 41v. Israel Burshatin has written extensively on Céspedes and should be credited with bringing the case to the attention of a large scholarly audience (e.g., "Interrogating Hermaphroditism in Sixteenth-Century Spain"). Chapter 1 of Vollendorf's *Women and Culture in Spain: (1580–1700)* analyzes the Céspedes trial at length. On the understudied topic of masturbation, Inquisition records provide good documentation, as per Jacqueline Holler's citation of a defendant before the New Spain tribunal who admitted that she touched her "shameful parts" and used a mirror to look at her genitalia (225).

[3] General information about early modern women's legal status appears in Casey, *Early Modern Spain: A Social History* (192–221); Anne J. Cruz and Mary Elizabeth Perry's introduction to *Culture and Control in Counter-Reformation Spain* (i–xxiii); Perry's *Gender and Disorder in Early Modern Seville* (14–32); and Mariló Vigil's *La vida de las mujeres en los siglos XVI y XVII* (1–17). Georgina Dopico-Black's *Perfect Wives, Other Women: Adultery and Inquisition in Early Modern Spain* discusses views toward femininity. Nirenberg discusses sexual anxiety in "Conversion, Sex, and Segregation."

[4] Madre Hipólita de Jesús y Rocaberti wrote an entire volume of advice for widows in book two of her *Tratade de los estados*, for example, instructing women whose husbands had died not to remarry but, instead, to seek out other widows with whom to live (192).

[5] Citations from Bernique and Sor Catalina are taken from *Idea de perfección*, with Sor Catalina's citations in italics as per the original text. Punctuation and spelling have been modernized for ease of reading. Analyses of Catalina de Jesús appear in Vollendorf, *The Lives of Women*, chapter 6; and Isabel Barbeito Carneiro, *Mujeres del Madrid Barroco. Voces testimoniales* (86–94). Isabelle Poutrin's *Le voile et la plume, Autobiographie et sainteté féminine dans l'Espagne moderne* analyzes women's vidas.

[6] So as to avoid over-simplifying implications of early modern representations of homoeroticism, I refer readers to Mary Gossy, "Skirting the Question: Lesbians and María de Zayas"; Amy Katz Kaminsky, "María de Zayas and the Invention of a Women's Writing Community" (409–10); Sherry Velasco (13–24); and Vollendorf, "The Future of Early Modern Women's Studies: The Case of Same-Sex Friendship and Desire in Zayas and Carvajal."

[7] Soufas's *Dramas of Distinction* analyzes the plays in *Women's Acts* in terms of gender.

[8] Teresa Valle de la Cerda's writing and related materials appear in Barbeito Carneiro. *Cárceles y mujeres en el siglo XVII* (125–265). Carlos Puyol Buil discusses the case in *Inquisición y política en el reinado de Felipe IV*.

[9] Writing in the tradition of Santa Teresa, who warned against intimate female friendships in her constitutions. Madre María de San José, in *Instrucción de novicias*, proscribed limitations on nuns' interaction with each other (419–20). As to Santa Teresa, Alison Weber's *Teresa of Avila and the Rhetoric of Femininity* remains the classic study of the saint's sophisticated writing style. Cruz provides an overview of religion and sexuality in "Juana and Her Sisters: Female Sexuality and Spirituality in Early Modern Spain and the New World."

[10] The Inquisition case of the defendant accused of Judaizing is the subject of chapter 2 of Vollendorf's *The Lives of Women* and is discussed in Barbeito Carneiro's *Mujeres del Madrid Barroco* (51–56). Zayas's reliance on bodily discourse is the subject of Kaminsky's superb article, "Dress and Redress: Clothing in the *Desengaños amorosos* of María de Zayas y Sotomayor."

[11] Moshe Sluhovsky concludes that "possessed upper-class nuns were more likely to be labeled 'visionaries' than diabolically possessed" (1369), while Haliczer, in *Between Exaltation and Infamy: Female Mystics in the Golden Age of Spain*, provides evidence for the lower-class status of women deemed "false mystics" (105–24).

[12] Sexuality was the focus of Inquisition and legal cases throughout the period. See Juan Antonio Alejandre, *El veneno de Dios: La Inquisición de Sevilla ante el delito de solicitación en confesión*; Stephen Haliczer, *Sexuality in the Confessional. A Sacrament Profaned*; Allyson M. Poska, *Regulating the People: The Catholic Reformation in Seventeeth-Century Spain* (particularly 101–26); and María Helena Sánchez Ortega. "Sorcery and Eroticism in Love Magic."

WORKS CITED

Alejandre, Juan Antonio. *El veneno de Dios: La Inquisición de Sevilla ante el delito de solicitación en confesión*. México: Siglo Veintiuno, 1994.

Barbeito Carneiro, Isabel. *Cárceles y mujeres en el siglo XVII*. Madrid: Castalia, Instituto de la mujer 1991.

———. *Mujeres del Madrid Barroco. Voces testimoniales*. Madrid: HORAS y horas, 1992.

Bernique, Juan de. *Idea de perfección y virtudes. Vida de la V. M. y sierva de Dios Catalina de Jesús y San Francisco. Hija de su tercera orden y fundadora del Colegio de las doncellas pobres de Santa Clara de la Ciudad de Alcalá de Henares*. Alcalá: Con licencia de Francisco García Fernández, Impresor de la Universidad, 1693.

Brooten, Bernadette. *Love Between Women: Early Christian Responses to Female Homoeroticism*. Chicago: U of Chicago P, 1996.

Burshatin, Israel. "Interrogating Hermaphroditism in Sixteenth-Century Spain." *Hispanisms and Homosexualities*. Ed. Sylvia Molloy and Robert McKee Irwin. Durham and London: Duke UP, 1998. 3–18.

Caro Mallén de Soto. Ana. *Valor, agravio y mujer*. Soufas, *Women's Acts*, 163–94.

Casey, James. *Early Modern Spain: A Social History*. NY and London: Routledge, 1999.

Catalina de Jesús y san Francisco, (Sor). *See* Bernique, Juan de.

Céspedes, Elena/Eleno de. Inquisition Trial, Archivo Histórico Nacional, Madrid. Sección Inquisición. Leg. 234, Exp. 24.

Chartier, Roger, ed. *A History of Private Life. Vol. 3: Passions of the Renaissance*. Cambridge, MA, and London: Belknap Press, Harvard UP, 1989.

Cruz, Anne J. "Juana and Her Sisters: Female Sexuality and Spirituality in Early Modern Spain and the New World." *Recovering Spain's Feminist Tradition*. Ed. Lisa Vollendorf. NY: The Modern Language Association of America, 2001. 88–120.

Cruz, Anne J., and Mary Elizabeth Perry, eds. "Introduction." *Culture and Control in Counter-Reformation Spain*. Minneapolis: U of Minnesota P, 1992. i–xxiii.

Dopico-Black, Georgina. *Perfect Wives, Other Women: Adultery and Inquisition in Early Modern Spain.* Durham, NC: Duke UP, 2001.

Duby, Georges, and Philippe Ariès, eds. *A History of Private Life.* Vols. 1–5. Cambridge, MA, and London: Belknap Press, Harvard UP, 1986–1990.

Foucault Michel. *The History of Sexuality.* Vol. I. 1976. Trans. Robert Hurley. NY: Random House, 1990.

Gossy, Mary. "Skirting the Question: Lesbians and María de Zayas." *Hispanisms and Homosexualities.* Ed. Sylvia Molloy and Robert McKee Irwin. Durham: Duke UP, 1998. 19–28.

Haliczer, Stephen. *Between Exaltation and Infamy: Female Mystics in the Golden Age of Spain.* Oxford: Oxford UP, 2002.

———. *Sexuality in the Confessional. A Sacrament Profaned.* NY: Oxford UP, 1996.

Hipólita, de Jesús Rocaberti (Madre). *Tratado de los estados. Dividido en cinco libros.* Valencia: Vicente Cabrera, 1682.

Holler, Jacqueline. "'More Sins Than the Queen of England': Marina de San Miguel before the Mexican Inquisition." *Women in the Inquisition. Spain and the New World.* Ed. Mary E. Giles. Baltimore and London: The Johns Hopkins UP, 1999. 209–28.

Kagan, Richard. *Lucrecia's Dreams. Politics and Prophecy in Sixteenth-Century Spain.* Berkeley: U of California P, 1989.

Kaminsky Amy Katz. "Dress and Redress: Clothing in the *Desengaños amorosos* of María de Zayas y Sotomayor." *Romanic Review* 79.2 (1988): 377–91.

———. "María de Zayas and the Invention of a Women's Writing Community." *Revista de Estudios Hispánicos* 35 (2001): 487–509.

Laqueur, Thomas W. *Solitary Sex: A Cultural History of Masturbation.* NY: Zone Books, 2003.

María de San José (Salazar), (Madre). *Instrucción de novicias. Jesús Maria. Diálogo entre dos religiosas que Gracia y Justa se llaman sobre la oración y mortificación con que se deben criar las novicias.* 1602. In *Escritos espirituales.* Ed. Simeón de la Sagrada Familia. Roma: Postulación General, 1979. 407–90.

Nirenberg, David. "Conversion, Sex, and Segregation: Jews and Christians in Medieval Spain." *Amercian Historical Review* 107.4 (October 2002): 1065–93.

Perry, Mary Elizabeth. *Gender and Disorder in Early Modern Seville.* Princeton: Princeton UP, 1990.

———. *The Handless Maiden: Moriscos and the Politics of Religion in Early Modern Spain.* Princeton: Princeton UP, 2004.

Poska, Allyson M. *Regulating the People: The Catholic Reformation in Seventeenth-Century Spain.* Boston and Leiden: Brill, 1998.

Poutrin, Isabelle. *Le voile et la plume. Autobiographie et sainteté fémenine dans l'Espagne moderne.* Madrid: Casa de Velàzquez, 1995.

Puyol Buil, Carlos. *Inquisición y politica en el reinado de Felipe IV: Los procesos de Jerónimo de Villanueva y las monjas de San Plácido, 1628–1660.* Madrid: Consejo Superior de Investigaciones Científicas, 1993.

Sánchez Ortega, Maria Helena. "Sorcery and Eroticism in Love Magic." *Cultural Encounters: The Impact of the Inquisition in Spain and the New World.* Ed. Mary Elizabeth Perry and Anne J. Cruz. Berkeley: U of California P, 1991. 58–92.

Sluhovsky, Moshe. "The Devil in the Convent." *American Historical Review* 107.5 (December 2002): 1379–1411.

Soufas, Teresa. *Dramas of Distinction: A Study of Plays by Golden Age Women.* Lexington: U of Kentucky P, 1997.

———, ed. *Women's Acts. Plays by Women Dramatists of Spain's Golden Age.* Lexington: U of Kentucky P, 1997.

Traub, Valerie. *The Renaissance of Lesbianism in Early Modern England.* London: Cambridge UP, 2002.

———. "The Rewards of Lesbian History." *Feminist Studies* 25.2 (Summer 1999): 363–94.

Valle de la Cerda, Teresa. Inquisition proceedings and autobiographical writings. See Barbeito Carneiro, *Cárceles y mujeres.* 125–265.

Velasco, Sherry. *The Lieutenant Nun. Transgenderism, Lesbian Desire, and Catalina de Erauso.* Austin: U of Texas P, 2000.

Vigil, Mariló. *La vida de las mujeres en los siglos XVI y XVII*. Madrid: Siglo Veintiuno, 1986.

Vollendorf, Lisa. "The Future of Early Modern Women's Studies: The Case of Same-Sex Friendship and Desire in Zayas and Carvajal." *Arizona Journal of Cultural Studies* 4 (2000): 265–84.

———. *The Lives of Women: A New History of Inquisitional Spain*. Nashville: Vanderbilt UP, 2005.

Weber, Alison. *Teresa of Avila and the Rhetoric of Femininity*. Princeton: Princeton UP, 1989.

Zayas y Sotomayor, María de. *Desengaños amorosos*. 2nd ed. Ed. Alicia Yllera. Madrid: Cátedra, 1993.

———. *Traición en la amistad. Friendship Betrayed*. Ed. Valerie Hegstrom. Trans. Catherine Larson. Lewisburg, PA: Bucknell UP, 1999.

AFTERWORD

Spain and the rest of the Hispanic world suffer from a pervasive stereotyping that casts Hispanic men as *machista* and women as meek subordinates. For centuries, scholarship on Spain's Golden Age (1500–1700) has reinforced this misconception by refusing to incorporate the concerns of everyday people, particularly women and minorities. As a result, Spanish history of the age of empire still has a capital H: it tells of important men who solidified state power, expanded an empire, and consolidated a Catholic nation. This is History without women.

Given this focus on kings and conquistadors, it is no wonder that students in the United States—including Latino students—dismiss the Spanish as hopelessly backward and barbaric. When teaching courses on the Golden Age in Spanish letters, a feminist instructor can almost see the educational opportunity wilt as students read about honor-obsessed men killing their wives and then fail to make any connection between today's culture and a violent, sexist past. By excluding all but the most influential members of society and claiming that records of women's words do not exist, scholars have clouded our understanding of life as it was experienced in a tumultuous, nation-building time that, in many ways, resembles our present age of expansion and globalization.

My work is motivated by the desire to make connections with the past and is animated by a simple set of questions: What were women up to during Spain's age of empire? What did they have to say about honor and colonialism? Most specifically for the purposes of the essay, what did they think about the cultural obsession with controlling their sexuality?

The answers were easier to find than I ever could have guessed. Indeed, the archives are teeming with intimate stories of Hispanic women's lives. Jews, Christians, and Muslims. Rich and poor; titled and illegitimate; wives and singlewomen. All these women's stories can be found if one cares to look. Letters, legal depositions, Inquisition records, convent documents, and texts written for the book market contain women's representations of their daily lives and concerns. Some fifty women appear as subjects in my book on the topic, *The Lives of Women: A New History of Inquisitional Spain*. Of those fifty, only a handful had ever before been studied.

A disproportionate number of those women discussed issues of intimacy in their texts. Of course, women were seen as fundamentally libidinous and therefore open to demonic influence. Furthermore, they were prohibited from expressing their desire in any positive way. Yet positive expressions of desire and intimacy abound in records of women's words. When Inquisition cases did not relate to sexual practice, women often mentioned desire. When literary genres did not traditionally revolve around friendship or desire, female authors built their plots specifically around those topics. And nuns, mistakenly viewed as asexual by many, frequently invoked sexuality, eroticism, and intimate friendship as important components of their lives.

"Good Sex, Bad Sex" is about learning to reread archival documents, to seek out and interpret the excess rhetoric that can be found in otherwise formulaic legal, hagiographic, and literary texts. It is about capturing the experiences of women. In the end, the entire project is feminist and ongoing: it is about creating a bridge to the past by which we might understand the lives of women and others whose experiences have not yet been integrated into history.

~ AFTERWORD ~

How the Florence Howe Award Helped Change Literary Studies

ANNETTE KOLODNY

IT IS IMPOSSIBLE to overstate the impact and continuing importance of the Florence Howe Award for Feminist Scholarship since its inception in 1974. For recent generations of scholars who grew up with feminist inquiry as part of their college curriculum, a brief look backward may be in order. Graduating from high school in 1958 and from college in 1962, as I did, I don't think I even realized how invisible women were in the education I had just received. To be sure, we knew that George Eliot was a woman. Jane Austen and Emily Dickinson were usually introduced to us in high school. We were told that Harriet Beecher Stowe had written an antislavery best-seller that helped foment support in the North for civil war, but no teacher actually assigned *Uncle Tom's Cabin*. In high school civics courses or college history surveys, names like Margaret Fuller, Elizabeth Cady Stanton, and Susan B. Anthony were mentioned as women ahead of their time who had agitated for female suffrage. But while we read *about* them, we never read anything written *by* them. Although Lorraine Hansberry's *A Raisin in the Sun* was *the* Broadway hit of 1959, the year I was a sophomore English major at Brooklyn College in New York, no women of color were on any reading list. And only because one of my sisters began to explore her sexuality, tapped into a closeted lesbian grapevine, and brought home a much-worn copy of Radclyffe Hall's 1928 novel *The Well of Loneliness* did I divine there might be anything like a tradition of lesbian literature. With precious few exceptions, then, for my generation, women were either absent from the arts and public life, or they were the invisible helpmates of significant males.

Then, as the 1960s progressed, personal and political discontents exploded—and came together: the civil rights movement, the anti–Vietnam War movement, the United Farm Workers' movement, the early gay and lesbian rights movement, the beginnings of the environmental movement, and the general questioning of unjust authority and inequitable treatment between and among different groups in the United States. What we then called the women's liberation movement was a part of it all, and many of us came to it through our prior involvement in one or more of the other great catalysts of the decade.

To be honest, literature was a small part of the mix. Nonetheless, the heady days of consciousness-raising groups and the women's liberation movement of the late 1960s and early 1970s revealed the slight presence of women in almost every textbook or reading assignment from grade school through college. Whether we studied literary texts in graduate school or in small independent reading groups, anything we could find written by women fed our desires to recover a sense of our past, our prior accomplishments, and our shared sisterhood across lines of race, religion, ethnicity, class, region, and sexual preference. Those of us who studied literature in graduate programs in the late 1960s and early 1970s were determined to rediscover our literary foremothers, even when our male professors told us there weren't any. And we were determined to examine all the ways in which literature— by men and by women both—had constructed and deconstructed femininity and gender roles. Our first triumphs were archival: we discovered a wealth of women writers dating back to Sappho. Our second triumph was to teach ourselves and our students how to read the codes and nuances, the subterranean resistances, and the acts of outright courage inscribed in women's texts. Our third triumph was the renewal of theory: we grappled with the inadequacies of available modes of liter- ary analysis and, when necessary, invented our own.

By 1974, there was a wealth of new feminist scholarship on the general subject of gender and literature. But the women who produced that scholarship were dismissed as faddish, or they were said to be working on second-rate writers. Too many of those women (myself among them) were denied promotion and tenure. At least part of the reason women were failing to make it through the promotion and tenure process was that, in addition to a general hostility toward our feminist work, we had too few venues in which to place our essays, and most university presses were still hesitant about developing lists in the new feminist scholarship. Since we couldn't publish, we were perishing.

In my area of American literature, for example, the major and oldest estab- lished journal in the field—the journal of the American Literature Section of the MLA—is *American Literature*. But in the years before 1974, the vast majority of the articles and book reviews in that journal were written by male scholars, and the few women authors who received attention (mainly from male scholars, of course) included Anne Bradstreet and Emily Dickinson or, less frequently, Flan- nery O'Connor, Eudora Welty, Ellen Glasgow, Edith Wharton, and Willa Cather. The first article to appear in *American Literature* with even a modestly feminist point of view was Blanche H. Gelfant's fine study of Willa Cather, "The Forgot- ten Reaping-Hook: Sex in *My Ántonia*," which appeared in the March 1971 issue. Even so, feminist critics continued to submit their work to that journal, as to many others, albeit with little success. Several feminist friends of mine papered their bathroom walls with their rejection slips.

Then, in 1974, the Women's Caucus of the Modern Language Association named a prize for Florence Howe, one of the caucus's founders, a previous MLA president, a visionary pioneer in the field of women's studies, and a cofounder of the Feminist Press. The caucus thereby effectively announced that the new feminist scholarship was important and here to stay. That scholarship could be weighed, it could be judged, and it could be held to the highest standards of excellence. Feminist scholarship also now carried the imprimatur of approval from a group within the prestigious Modern Language Association. With the initiation of the award, nonfeminist and mainstream journals that had previously been closed to feminist scholarship gradually became more receptive.

Even a journal like *American Literature* began to change under the rising pressure of the profession's grudging acceptance of feminist approaches. Beginning with the March 1974 issue, *American Literature* carried two decidedly feminist articles, both written by feminist critics about women writers: Cynthia Griffin Wolff's "Lily Bart and the Beautiful Death" and Claire Katz's "Flannery O'Connor's Rage of Vision." From then on, feminist critics and feminist approaches were no longer invisible in the pages of this esteemed journal. Additionally, an entirely new pantheon of women writers soon began to appear in the articles and in the book reviews alike—everyone from Djuna Barnes and Adrienne Rich to Zora Neale Hurston and Phillis Wheatley. Aiding that process of acceptance was the fact that mainstream journals like *American Literature* sought out at least one token feminist to add to their editorial boards. Thus feminist submissions could be assured of at least one potentially sympathetic reader. With more and more articles by and about women appearing in journals, moreover, the same university presses that published the journals increasingly recognized the growing demand for scholarly and critical books by feminists. By 1980, several prestigious university presses could point to impressive lists in the general areas of feminist theory and gender and literary history. Winners of the Florence Howe Award (along with the honorable mention recipients), especially, had little trouble getting their book manuscripts vetted by university presses. A great deal had changed.

While the advent of the Florence Howe Award cannot, by itself, account for all this, that award was certainly a major player in the pressure for acceptance because it gave our enterprise a new legitimacy. Indeed, had they had the opportunity, many of the long-established journals would have carried even more feminist materials. But another factor had now entered the equation: the new journals that women themselves were establishing.

The early and mid-1970s saw the introduction of several feminist journals that provided even more welcoming venues for the publication of the new feminist scholarship. *Off Our Backs* had been publishing since 1970; *Quest: A Feminist Quarterly* began publishing in 1974; and from 1972 on, several distinguished and slightly more mainstream feminist journals began appearing. In 1972, Wendy Martin founded *Women's Studies: An Interdisciplinary Journal*; that same year *Women's Studies Quarterly* began publication (enlarged from what had formerly been the *Women's Studies Newsletter*); and *Feminist Studies*, under the editorship of Claire Moses, made its first appearance. In 1973, Janet Todd was the founding editor of *Women and Literature*. Two years later, *Signs: A Journal of Women in Culture and Society* appeared under the editorship of Catharine R. Stimpson, and *Frontiers: A Journal of Women's Studies* published its first issue. In 1976, *Camera Obscura: A Journal of Feminism and Film Theory* began publication, and in 1978, *Women's Studies International Quarterly* made its first appearance. Simultaneously, nonfeminist mainstream journals began to devote special issues to the subject of women and feminism. In the winter of 1975, for example, the journal *Diacritics* published the special issue *Textual Politics and French Feminism*.

I retell this well-known history only to emphasize the fact that as the 1970s progressed, mainstream journals found themselves competing with the new feminist journals for articles that used feminist critical approaches. And everyone wanted to publish a Florence Howe Award winner. Yet all this publishing activity did not immediately translate into significantly increased success for feminist critics in the promotion and tenure process. Annette Niemtzow, who in 1975 published one of the best feminist studies of Henry James in *American Literature*, was later denied promotion and tenure at Bryn Mawr. Despite the recent appearance of my first book, *The Lay of the Land: Metaphor as Experience and History in American Life and Letters*, in 1975, I was denied promotion and tenure in the English department at the University of New Hampshire. Subsequently, I initiated one of the earliest Title VII discrimination suits and sued the university for sex discrimination and anti-Semitism. That lawsuit resulted in many important case law precedents and was finally settled out of court in October 1980. But during those long five years, even though I continued to do research and publish, I was never sure I would really have a career. In fact, my essay "Dancing through the Minefield: Some Observations on the Theory, Practice, and Politics of a Feminist Literary Criticism" was written during a bleak period when I was contemplating the end of what was then my brief career in academe. But in 1979 the as yet unpublished essay won the Florence Howe Award, which by itself gave me the courage to fight on. For that, I am forever grateful for what this award meant to me personally.

Now, as a seasoned veteran of the culture wars, I have come to understand what the Florence Howe Award meant to the academy in general. It validates the worth of every critic and scholar who engages in feminist practice. Beyond that, the award has continued to signify the fact that feminist scholarship forever transformed the shape and the subject matter of literary inquiry in the United States and around the world. After all, we continue to discover new women writers, both past and present, and we continue to experiment with both theory and critical methodology. As this latest collection of Florence Howe Award winners makes clear, we are no longer constrained by language or by geography. Our reach is increasingly global—and will continue to be so. As a result, feminist scholarship continues to widen the discourse of and about literary matters. At its inception, the Florence Howe Award helped to give our enterprise, in all its diversity, both legitimacy and visibility. It does that still, even today. That is the award's gift to us all.

WORKS CITED

Gelfant, Blanche H. "The Forgotten Reaping-Hook: Sex in *My Ántonia.*" *American Literature* 43 (1971): 60–82.

Hall, Radclyffe. *The Well of Loneliness.* 1928. New York: Anchor, 1990.

Hansberry, Lorraine. *A Raisin in the Sun.* 1959. New York: Vintage, 1994.

Katz, Claire. "Flannery O'Connor's Rage of Vision." *American Literature* 46 (1974): 54–67.

Kolodny, Annette. "Dancing through the Minefield: Some Observations on the Theory, Practice, and Politics of a Feminist Literary Criticism." *Feminist Studies* 6.1 (1980): 1–25. Rpt. in *Feminisms: Gender and Literary Studies.* Ed. Robyn Warhol and Diane Price Herndl. New Brunswick: Rutgers UP, 1991. 97–116.

Niemtzow, Annette. "Marriage and the New Woman in *The Portrait of a Lady*." *American Literature* 47 (1975): 377–95.

Stowe, Harriet Beecher. *Uncle Tom's Cabin; or, Life among the Lowly*. 1852. New York: Norton, 1994.

Wolff, Cynthia Griffin. "Lily Bart and the Beautiful Death." *American Literature* 46 (1974): 16–40.

NOTES ON CONTRIBUTORS

Amal Amireh was born and raised in El Bireh in Palestine. She received her BA in English literature from Birzeit University and an MA and PhD in English and American literature from Boston University. She is now associate professor of postcolonial literature at George Mason University, Fairfax. She is author of *The Factory Girl and the Seamstress: Imagining Gender and Class in Nineteenth-Century American Fiction* (2000) and coeditor of *Going Global: The Transnational Reception of Third World Women Writers* (2000) and *Etel Adnan: Critical Essays on the Arab-American Writer and Artist* (2002). Her essays and reviews have appeared in many publications. Her current research focuses on gender, nationalism, and Islam in postcolonial literature.

Linda S. Bergmann, associate professor of English at Purdue University and director of the Purdue Writing Lab, has started writing-across-the-curriculum programs and writing centers at the University of Missouri, Rolla; the Illinois Institute of Technology; and Hiram College. Her teaching includes first-year composition; undergraduate courses in literature, pedagogy, and literacy; and graduate seminars in writing program administration. She has published articles in *Language and Learning across the Disciplines, Feminist Teacher, A/B: Auto/Biography Studies, American Studies,* and *Works and Days*. She recently coedited *Composition and/or Literature: The End(s) of Education* (2006), and she is currently completing a textbook on research writing.

Mary Paniccia Carden is assistant professor of English at Edinboro University of Pennsylvania, where she teaches American and ethnic literatures. She is coeditor of *Doubled Plots: Romance and History* (2003), and her articles on the work of Zitkala-Ša, Jane Smiley, Willa Cather, Ann Petry, Toni Morrison, and John Edgar Wideman have appeared in *Prose Studies, Frontiers: A Journal of Women Studies, Modern Fiction Studies, Journal of Contemporary Thought, Twentieth Century Literature,* and *Contemporary Literature*. She is currently at work on a manuscript entitled "Sons and Daughters of Self-Made Men," which examines intertwined dynamics of nation building and gender construction in America.

Jean Ferguson Carr is associate professor of English and women's studies at the University of Pittsburgh, where she was director of composition and codirector of the Faculty Diversity Seminar. She coauthored *Archives of Instruction: Nineteenth-Century Rhetorics, Readers, and Composition Books in the United States* (2005); edited two volumes of the works of R. W. Emerson (1979, 1983); and coedits the Pittsburgh Series in Composition, Literacy, and Culture. She has written on Dickens ("Writing as a Woman: Dickens, *Hard Times*, and Feminine Discourses," 1989, and "Dickens and Autobiography," 1985) and on women's writing ("Collaboration," 1995, and "Nineteenth-Century Girls and Literacy," 2003).

Abby Lynn Coykendall is assistant professor of English literature at Eastern Michigan University, specializing in postcolonialism, the novel, and eighteenth-century literature.

She is currently working on two book projects, "The Femme Fatale and Empires at Sea: The Rhetoric of Conquest and Rape in Reverse" and "Conjuring Inherited Empire: Gothic Real Estate and the Eighteenth-Century Novel." The first is a study of the carnivorous fashion consumer in eighteenth-century poetry, especially that of Swift, Pope, and Gray; the second is a study of the intertwined discourses of nationality, historicism, and gothicism in the late-eighteenth-century novel.

Carolyn Dever is professor of English and women's and gender studies and associate dean of the College of Arts and Science at Vanderbilt University. She is the author of *Skeptical Feminism: Activist Theory, Activist Practice* (2004) and *Death and the Mother from Dickens to Freud: Victorian Fiction and the Anxiety of Origins* (1998). With Margaret Cohen, she edited the collection *The Literary Channel: The International Invention of the Novel* (2002). She is working on two books, "Queer Domesticities: Fiction, Form, and Eros in Victorian England" and a memoir titled "Crazy Things."

Melissa Dinverno is assistant professor of Spanish and affiliate of West European studies at Indiana University. She has written on gender identity and feminism in twentieth-century Spain, theory and politics of editing, and the work of Federico García Lorca. Her critical edition of Lorca's poetic collection *Suites* is forthcoming from Cátedra (Madrid). She is currently writing a book on editorial theory and alternative practices that enable the editing of texts for gender and sexuality and preparing another on the cultural construction of García Lorca and its link to Spain's contemporary political, cultural, and social identities.

Roseanna Dufault is professor of French and chair of modern languages at Ohio Northern University. She is the author of *Metaphors of Identity: The Treatment of Childhood in Selected Québécois Novels*, editor of *Women by Women: The Treatment of Female Characters by Women Writers of Fiction in Québec since 1980*, and coeditor of two volumes of critical essays on Franco-Canadian women writers. She has published articles on Anne Hébert, Marie-Claire Blais, Gabrielle Roy, Louise Maheux-Forcier, Ying Chen, and Anne-Marie Alonzo in various journals and anthologies. She is past president of the American Council for Québec Studies, past president of the Women's Caucus for the Modern Languages, and a member of the executive committee of the MLA Francophone Literatures and Cultures Division.

Susan Fraiman is professor of English at the University of Virginia, where she teaches courses in feminist theory, cultural studies, and the novel. She is the author of *Cool Men and the Second Sex* (2003) and *Unbecoming Women: British Women Writers and the Novel of Development* (1993) and editor of the Norton Critical Edition of *Northanger Abbey* (2004). Her articles on topics ranging from George Eliot to affirmative action have appeared in *PMLA*, *Critical Inquiry*, *Feminist Studies*, *NWSA Journal*, *American Literary History*, the *Minnesota Review*, and *Callaloo*. Forthcoming in *New Literary History* is her essay "Shelter Writing: Desperate Housekeeping from *Crusoe* to *Queer Eye*."

Molly Hite is professor of English at Cornell University, where she teaches twentieth-century literature and theory. She is the author of *Ideas of Order in the Novels of Thomas Pynchon* (1983), *The Other Side of the Story: Structures and Strategies of Contemporary Feminist Narrative* (1989), and two novels, *Class Porn* (1987) and *Breach of Immunity* (1992). She has written articles on postmodernist and modernist fiction, feminist theory and practice, and academic culture. "Virginia Woolf's Two Bodies" is part of her new book, "Weird Woolf."

Florence Howe is emerita professor of English at the Graduate Center, City University of New York, and emerita director-publisher of the Feminist Press at the City University of New York, founded in 1970 and responsible for the rediscovery of scores of "lost" women writers in the United States and in many other countries. Since 1994, she has been at work on Women Writing Africa, an archival retrieval undertaking of the Feminist Press, projected to appear in four regional anthologies of African women's oral and written literature. She has written or edited more than a dozen books and more than a hundred essays. She is the editor of *No More Masks! An Anthology of Twentieth-Century Poetry by American Women* (1973 and 1993) and *The Politics of Women's Studies: Testimony from Thirty Founding Mothers* (2000) and the author of *Myths of Coeducation: Selected Essays, 1964–1983* (1984). Since early 2005, she has been working again as Feminist Press publisher.

Stacy Carson Hubbard is associate professor of English and adjunct associate professor of comparative literature at the State University of New York, Buffalo, where she teaches courses in nineteenth- and twentieth-century American literature, women's writing, visual culture, and poetry and poetics. She has published essays on Thomas De Quincey, Gwendolyn Brooks, Edna St. Vincent Millay, Marianne Moore, Marilynne Robinson, poetry and photography, and Jane Addams and Frank Lloyd Wright. She is currently at work on a study of feminism and the Emersonian tradition in America.

Kristine Ibsen is professor of Spanish American literature at the University of Notre Dame. A specialist in Mexican studies, she is the author of *Women's Spiritual Autobiography in Colonial Spanish America* (1999) and *Memoria y deseo: Carlos Fuentes y el pacto de la lectura* (2003). An expanded version of her essay in this volume was published in *The Other Mirror: Women's Narrative in Mexico, 1980–1995* (1997), which she edited. She is currently working on a cross-disciplinary study that examines literary and artistic representations of the second empire of Mexico.

Annette Kolodny is the College of Humanities Professor of American Literature and Culture at the University of Arizona, where she previously served as dean of the College of Humanities. Her experiences as a feminist in academic administration are recounted in *Failing the Future: A Dean Looks at Higher Education in the Twenty-First Century* (1998). Her earlier books examined the developing mythology of the western frontiers: *The Lay of the Land: Metaphor as Experience and History in American Life and Letters* (1975) and *The Land before Her: Fantasy and Experience of the American Frontiers, 1630–1860* (1984). Awarded the Florence Howe Essay Prize for Feminist Criticism in 1979 for her essay "Dancing through the Minefield: Some Observations on the Theory, Practice, and Politics of a Feminist Literary Criticism," Kolodny has continued to publish in the field of feminist criticism and critical theory.

Alison Rice teaches French and francophone literature in the Department of Romance Languages and Literature at the University of Notre Dame. Her book *Time Signatures: Contextualizing Contemporary Francophone Autobiographical Writing from the Maghreb* (2006) focuses on the work of Hélène Cixous, Assia Djebar, and Abdelkébir Khatibi. She has published articles on francophone women writers, including Andrée Chedid, Maryse Condé, Leïla Sebbar, and Brina Svit, as well as interviews with Julia Kristeva and Germaine Tillion. She is currently working on a project titled "Metronomes: Women Writers in Paris. A Series of Filmed Interviews."

Roberta Rubenstein is professor of literature at American University, Washington, where she teaches courses in modernist fiction, women's fiction, and feminist literary theory. She has published more than thirty articles and book chapters on modern and contemporary women writers and three books: *The Novelistic Vision of Doris Lessing: Breaking the Forms of Consciousness* (1979); *Boundaries of the Self: Gender, Culture, Fiction* (1987); and *Home Matters: Longing and Belonging, Nostalgia and Mourning in Women's Fiction* (2001). The recipient of several awards for scholarship and teaching, she was selected as American University's Scholar/Teacher of the Year in 1994.

Mihoko Suzuki is professor of English at the University of Miami. She is the author of *Metamorphoses of Helen: Authority, Difference, and the Epic* (1989) and *Subordinate Subjects: Gender, the Political Nation, and Literary Form in England, 1588–1688* (2003) and coeditor of *Debating Gender in Early Modern England, 1500–1700* (2002). She has served on the MLA's Delegate Assembly representing women in the profession and on the Committee on the Status of Women in the Profession and was president of the Women's Caucus for the Modern Languages. She currently serves on the selection committee for the William Riley Parker Prize and as review editor of *CLIO: A Journal of Literature, History, and the Philosophy of History*.

Lisa Vollendorf is associate professor of Spanish at California State University, Long Beach. She is author of *The Lives of Women: A New History of Inquisitional Spain* (2005), *Reclaiming the Body: María de Zayas's Early Modern Feminism* (2001), and editor of *Recovering Spain's Feminist Tradition* (2001) and *Literatura y feminismo en España* (2006). She is currently writing a book, "Sex, Women, and the Law in the Hispanic World: One Thousand Years of Violence."

Rachel Warburton is assistant professor of English at Lakehead University, where she teaches seventeenth-century literature, women's writing, and literary theory. Her areas of research include histories of sexuality, early modern cultural studies, and the radical writing of the English Civil War years. She has written articles on seventeenth-century Quaker women's friendships, early modern pornography, and the gendered semiotics of cross-dressing.

Sandra A. Zagarell is Donald R. Longman Professor of English at Oberlin College. A senior editor of *The Heath Anthology of American Literature*, she has also edited volumes of writing by Mary E. Wilkins Freeman, Caroline Kirkland, and, with Lawrence Buell, Elizabeth Stoddard. She is editor, with Paul Lauter, of the literature section of the *Encyclopedia of New England Culture*. Her numerous articles on nineteenth-century American literature include several on Sarah Orne Jewett and Elizabeth Stoddard. Her work in progress includes "Modeling the Nation through Narratives of Community."

Joyce Zonana was associate professor of English at the University of New Orleans, where she has served as director of women's studies. Her articles have appeared in *Signs, Tulsa Studies in Women's Literature, Journal of Narrative Technique*, and *Victorian Poetry*. She has published personal essays in the *Hudson Review* and *Meridians* and has recently completed a memoir entitled "Aroosa: Dreams of Arrival." In the aftermath of Hurricane Katrina, she has relocated to New York City, where she has accepted a position at Borough of Manhattan Community College.

~ INDEX ~